Our Aging Population: The Social Security Crisis

Our Aging Population: The Social Security Crisis

Edited by Carol Chambers

Facts On File

460 Park Avenue South, New York, N.Y. 10016

Our Aging Population: The Social Security Crisis

Published by Facts On File, Inc.
460 Park Avenue South, New York, N.Y. 10016
© Copyright 1983 by Facts On File, Inc.

Library of Congress Cataloging in Publication Data

Main entry under title:
Our aging population—The Social Security Crisis.

Includes index.
  1. Aged—United States—Addresses, essays, lectures.
I. Chambers, Carol.
HQ1064.U5093   1983   305.2'6'0973   83-1413
ISBN 0-87196-875-4

International Standard Book Number: 0-87196-875-4
Library of Congress Catalog Card Number: 83-1413
9 8 7 6 5 4 3 2 1
PRINTED IN THE UNITED STATES OF AMERICA

Contents

Preface

Age 65 is no longer a dividing line between young and old, working and retired, active and quiescent members of society. It is not unusual today for Americans to live 20 to 25 years after the traditional retirement age, and the over-65 population is as diverse a group as any other. They are rich and poor, healthy and ill, busy and idle in much the same proportions as any other age group. Yet even with the elderly portion of the U.S. population approaching one-quarter of the total, misconceptions about the elderly abound. In particular, the perception that they are as a group impaired and poverty-stricken has proven a stumbling block to understanding problems in federal policy.

The myths that most of the elderly are victims of poverty, living in nursing homes, disabled by disease or isolated from family and friends have not been dispelled, despite ample evidence to the contrary. Much of federal policy for the aged, which is in fact a patchwork of programs ungrounded in any coherent plan, reflects these popular misconceptions. The vast majority of the elderly, however, own their own homes, do not suffer from serious financial problems, and are fully able to take care of themselves and to be productive. Today's elderly are the most self-reliant older population in our history.

At the heart of current national interest in the elderly is the major government program for their assistance, Social Security, which was enacted in 1935. This program and Medicare, enacted in 1965, continue to have a greater impact on the 25 million aged in the United States than all other federal programs combined. The widely publicized funding problems of the Social Security system elicit an emotional response because they touch directly on a primary fear of most Americans—that they will be left destitute in their own old age. Few would argue with the need to provide compassionate care for the elderly in need. As the tidal wave of the postwar "baby boom" generation moves toward retirement, leaving only a relative ripple of its own progeny to provide for its welfare, this need will become more pronounced. But it is far from clear that an age-entitlement program is the best way to meet it. The proposals for reforming the Social Security system are legion, and the arguments between proponents of different approaches form an impassioned national debate. Few controversies so directly concern the future of every disputant.

In the editorials that follow, a picture emerges of the Social Security crisis as it is perceived by the nation's major newspapers. The editorials were chosen not to favor any one point of view, but to represent the wide diversity of views from across the nation on nearly every facet of this complex problem. The issues raised are of interest not only to the elderly and to those who are paying for their Social Security benefits, but to every one of us who hopes to live to a 'ripe old age.'

May, 1983   Carol Chambers

The Graying of America

Reports by the United States Bureau of the Census released in 1980 through 1982 have brought the rapid growth of the elderly population to the attention of the American public. The 1980 census revealed that the median age in the U.S. had risen to 30 from 28 during the decade beginning in 1970, and that the number of persons over 65 years old had increased by 28%, as compared to an 11% increase in the nation's total population over the same period. The over-75 segment of the nation's elderly had grown in the last decade by a startling 37%. The Census Bureau forecast that the median age of Americans, which reached 30.3 years in 1981, would rise to 36.3 years in 2000 and to 41.6 years in 2050. Life expectancy for women, it was estimated, would increase from an average 78.3 years in 1981 to 83.6 years by 2050: for men, a rise in life expectancy from 70.7 years in 1981 to 75.1 years in 2050 was anticipated.

The increase in the number of the elderly has been accompanied by a concomitant increase in their political power. The growing participation of senior citizens in the political arena is reflected in the burgeoning of lobbies for the elderly; the American Association of Retired Persons (AARP), National Council of Senior Citizens and Gray Panthers are only a few of the groups that have formed to protect the interests of those who are 65 and older. Senior citizens are also better-represented at the polls than any other age group. Their swelling ranks are truly changing the face of America.

Boston Sunday Globe
Boston, Mass., February 3, 1980
The national forecast
— a new crystal ball

The ultimate political question, it is said, is: "Who gets what?" Virtually all political events are viewed in those terms including that most political of all: the preparation of the annual federal budget that allocates about one-fifth of the gross national product. In recent years, however, the federal budgeteers have gingerly undertaken a new exercise, a tentative forecast of the domestic needs 10 or 20 or 30 years into the future.

Amidst all the numbers and detailed policy discussion in the Carter Administration's proposed budget for fiscal 1981, the relatively brief foray into crystal ball gazing reads like a light romance. How does it end? Happily for some, it would seem, and uncertainly for others. Some issues that are the focus of much current domestic debate — productivity, youth unemployment, the housing crunch — could virtually vanish only to be supplanted by a whole new agenda.

The principal ingredient in any social forecast is population data. The postwar baby boom has been the major determinant of domestic needs subsequently. The young put enormous pressures on local school systems and local taxes; they fueled a major expansion of higher education as they aged; now the fortunate among them are pressing into the housing market and crowding the workplace while the less fortunate are unemployed in troubling numbers.

As analyzed in the new Carter budget for fiscal year 1981, this means that passage of the population bubble through locally supported schools has reduced local budgets as a percentage of the GNP; as college enrollments decline in turn, there are new pressures on colleges to consolidate, as we in Massachusetts know well; the entry of inexperienced young workers into the labor force is blamed for some proportion of the nation's decline in productivity; the demand for housing has sopped up capital that could otherwise be invested in the machinery that could propel productivity.

Based on this pattern, Administration forecasters expect the future demand for new housing to decline sharply, from 1.5 million units a year in the next five years to 950,000 units a year in the 1990s. The housing squeeze, a chronic problem today, should loosen substantially. The rate of growth in the labor force in the 1990s is projected to be but one-third of the present rate. Rather than chronic unemployment, "it is possible that labor shortages will develop," the budget suggests. That, in turn, should increase the pressure on businesses to invest in improved production techniques to spur productivity. Further, it is argued, because the children of the baby boom will have reached their peak earning power, the savings should be available to finance the needed investments.

Speculation about the impact of these changes is, of course, risky. But it well may be that the infants of today and tomorrow will, as they mature, find the work-a-day world a little less imposing. Whether they take to swallowing goldfish or writing great poetry or inventing their own 21st century distractions will be interesting to contemplate in our dotage.

But, of course, the circumstances in which the rest of us will dote is perhaps the biggest puzzle for the future. The Carter forecasters gave more than passing consideration to the issue — maybe, in part, out of their own self-interest. Right now, for every person of retirement age there are five people of working age. By the year 2035, the Carter forecasters estimate that ratio is expected to narrow to two workers for each retiree.

From that striking prediction a whole series of questions arise. How will pensions, and especially social security, be financed? What will be the impact on working life? Will people work longer, reducing pressure on Social Security? Will part-time work become more commonplace? What are the implications for the health-care system, for the demand for doctors, for the development of extended-care facilities for the aged?

The Carter forecasters report that, if current trends continue, the number of people over age 85 will triple by 2035. Will their strong political influence reverse the much-lamented decline in respect for the elderly? Might the sheer demographics strengthen family ties? Or will more and more Americans be shoved aside, effectively warehoused? Finally, the budget suggests that the aging of the population, if it results in increased pressure for government programs to meet the needs of the elderly, may have profound effects on taxes.

How will those who are opposed to increased intervention in the economy by the federal government react? The Carter forecasters suggest that the fact that the population of Europeon countries is older than ours may account for the greater government involvement in life there. Will that be the consequence here? If not, what private institutions will meet the needs of the elderly? If so, how will government be made efficient and sensitive to individual needs? The preliminary rounds of that debate are well under way in this country and could dominate national politics for decades to come.

Of course, social and economic forecasts have rarely proven entirely accurate. Four little letters — OPEC — symbolize dramatically the risks of gazing into the crystal ball. The projections in the President's budget for fiscal 1981 may seem laughably wrong-headed by fiscal year 2001. But surely it is more sensible to ponder and plan for an uncertain future than to face the uncertainties that are assured if we ponder the future not at all.

The Virginian-Pilot
Norfolk, Va., January 3, 1978
Workers and Dependents

America's grandparents and great-grandparents expect extra years to enjoy the growing number of babies. And while no one can be anything but delighted with the prospect of greater life expectancy or the receipt of a birth announcement, the burden of a large dependent population on those in the middle—the work force—has given many cause for concern.

They may relax, at least until the year 2005, and no one is ready to predict how things will be then. The dependency rate has been dropping precipitously, and should continue to do so for the next few decades. That means the number of people working in relation to those who don't will continue to rise.

A decrease among the young and healthy supporting the old and frail is a specter, not a reality. Because the birth rate from 1915 to 1940 was particularly low, there aren't that many people about to retire. And the proportion of the population under 20 is expected to decline to 30 percent in 2000 from 38 percent in 1970. In addition, the size of the work force has risen dramatically. Young people seem to be going to work earlier; the period of schooling has peaked and is on the decline. But the big change is in the number of women at work. They now total 46 percent of all workers.

In 1965, for every 151 nonworkers, 100 worked. Ten years later, it was 123 to 100. The trend is expected to continue toward parity.

Given these figures, why is Social Security in trouble? Primarily because of its expanded scope. In 1950, 3.5 million people received benefits; in 1975 the number was 32.1 million, and the amounts of those benefits were far higher.

What happens after 2005 when baby-boom children become retirees? It could be that reading demographics then won't be much fun—unless a smaller work force is so efficient that old folks on the dole will have no worries.

San Francisco Chronicle
San Francisco, Calif., July 11, 1979

The Middle Age Of America

A DEMOGRAPHIC MILESTONE of some import to all of us in this country was passed with hardly a ripple of public attention the other day. On July 1, 1979, when most minds were focused ahead to the observance of Independence Day, the median age of all Americans lit precisely at 30.

While the citing of figures (medians in particular) can lead to portentous or misleading comment, this simple statistic is worth pondering. In short, more people are living longer. And the baby boom has abated. Those forces bring the median up.

This median was only 23 in 1900 (it edged above 30 in 1955 before the spate of new babies brought it down), and the census bureau projects that the national age will rise to 35 by the year 2000, and up to 37.8 by 2040. That's an age that not so many centuries ago was considered elderly — even if the scriptures did put man's term at threescore and ten.

THESE PROJECTIONS POINT to a future with a growing senior population that will be retired on Social Security pensions provided, in part, at least, by a younger element already finding it difficult to get jobs. Somewhere in between will be the middleaged, trying to cope with the competing demands of both youth culture and elderly.

Still, 30 is not the menacing age it was back in the 20s, when some considered it the end of the road. A little grey hair becomes Uncle Sam. Maturity, indeed, may help these disparate age groups to find a common ground.

THE INDIANAPOLIS NEWS
Indianapolis, Ind., June 2, 1981

The elderly American majority

Americans are getting older, living longer and having fewer children, but the nation has no plan to cope with this top-heavy population.

The numbers tell the story. During the decade of the '70s the median age of the nation rose to 30 years from 28, because the number of elderly people increased and because the number of children under 15 dropped. The Census Bureau reported recently that there were 25.5 million people over 65 years old, 28 percent more than in 1970.

With much wringing of hands, government agencies publish head counts and predict the need for drastic national changes in policy, in use of the work force and in allocation of resources. However, very little concrete planning is taking place. Instead, existing programs are being cut — leaving a void — while the population shift relentlessly advances.

Programs to provide meals and other assistance to keep older people out of hospitals and nursing homes is threatened by the Reagan administration's proposed budget cuts. Social Security is in serious trouble as are Federal medical programs.

Also, fewer people in the money-earning work force means fewer people who must pay for the support of the elderly. Already burdened with heavy tax tolls, their future financial obligation will undoubtedly increase.

The large increase in people over 65, which exceeded by far the 11 percent growth rate for the nation's population as a whole, was caused by advances in medical science, nutrition and economic security. Because of these advances, the person who has already reached age 65 may expect to live until age 80.

For much of America's history, age groupings have measured out to an almost perfect pyramid, with each succeeding age showing uniformly fewer people until there were only a few at the pinnacle. However, in recent years that has changed.

A major part of that change is because of a decline in fertility. In 1960, when the total population was 180 million, there were 20 million children under age 5. By 1970, that age group had dropped to 17 million. From 1970 to 1980 even greater declines occurred. Meanwhile, the number of persons over 65 doubled from 1950 to 1980.

Still, institutions, government agencies and Congress have failed to cope with the problem. They have neither provided for the health and security of the elderly population nor protected the working, younger taxpayer from an impossible financial burden.

With all the reports and statistics available, there is no question of advanced warning; the population is shifting and rapidly. (The national median age is projected to be 36 by 2000 and 38.4 by 2010.) Time is short, the information known, but where is the imagination, the creative legislation which should come from American leadership?

President Reagan, his Cabinet and the legislators should make this one of their highest domestic priorities.

Oregon *Journal*
Portland, Ore., June 3, 1981

The politics of aging

The two news stories appeared only days apart. The U. S. Senate rejected, 96-0, President Reagan's proposal to cut Social Security benefits for people retiring before age 65. And the Census Bureau issued a report saying the U. S. median age has risen to 30 years, up from 28.

The bureau says 25.5 million people are age 65 or older, 28 percent more than in 1970. Once before, in 1950, the nation's median age climbed to 30.2 (meaning half were over that age and half under).

But the 1950 figure was because the birth rate dropped during the Depression, when families faced economic conditions not conducive to feeding more hungry mouths. That Depression-decade generation now is in its 40s, an age group which is smaller than the one in its 50s.

After World War II came the baby boom, which continued until 1957 when a decline in births began.

Not all groups have such a relatively high median age. Whites had the highest, 31.3. Asians clock in at age 28.6; blacks at 24.9. American Indians, Eskimos and Aleutian Islanders at 23, and people of Spanish origin (not a racial designation) at 23.2. Blacks and Hispanics have a higher birth rate and lower longevity than whites.

The main trend found in the report is that the number of people over age 65 doubled from 1950 to 1980 because people are living longer.

The implications for national, state and local policy could be almost revolutionary. For the president and Congress, the job of changing Social Security — which some actuaries say could go broke in a year if changes aren't made — will be harder. The Census Bureau projects a median age of 36 in year 2000 and 38.4 by 2010, and that means a larger group of senior citizens. The push for bigger private pensions will be stronger.

State and local governments will be urged to put more taxpayer money into programs for the elderly, maybe property tax relief, nutrition and nursing homes.

The aging of the American population will be more pronounced. Fewer Americans will be working in productive jobs. More will rely on Social Security, and tinkering with those benefits will be more difficult.

TULSA WORLD
Tulsa, Okla., May 26, 1981

An Aging America

THE U. S. Census Bureau has confirmed what previous studies have clearly indicated: The fastest growing segment of the population is the elderly.

One in 10 Americans in 1980 was over 65, pushing the median age of the country past 30 for the first time since 1950 before the baby boom lowered the median age.

The problems that come with this development already are showing up in the nation's politics.

President Reagan and the Congress are facing what perhaps is the major dilemma as they consider ways to make the Social Security program financially sound.

One one hand, the rising number of oldsters are pushing for more liberal Social Security benefits. Yet the changing makeup of the population makes that impossible.

Currently, there are three workers making payments to provide benefits for one retiree, but if the pay-as-you-go approach continues, there will be only two workers for every retiree in 30 years.

An obvious solution is one taken by Reagan; encourage people to work longer. But Reagan's first suggestion in that direction met with a storm of opposition from workers contemplating retirement at age 62.

Congress of course is promising not to cut benefits, but the facts of the 1980 census demand otherwise. It is time for everyone to start reconsidering the "right" of retirement at ages 62 or 65.

St. Louis ♞ Review

St. Louis, Mo., October 23, 1981

Grey Power

The past few years have seen the beginning of a decided change in the demographic make-up of American society. We have begun to experience the switch from a child-dominated, child-oriented society to an older society with more stress on the needs of older adults and less on the needs of the young.

We can hail or bewail that tendency, but it is real. The overwhelming number of young people is getting older and its replacement in new children is considerably less numerous. The demographic guarantee is that this phenomenon is not a passing thing, but one which will mark society for the rest of this century.

The Church adapted itself admirably to the baby boom. As a matter of fact, even in the pre-World War II years of relatively stable age proportions in the population, the Church had a special concern for the young because of the necessity it felt to make Catholic education a high priority for Church activity. After the Second World War

the Church was almost predominantly a Catholic school-PSR-CYC dominated community.

We hope that the Church will be as quick to make the necessary adjustments so as to serve a growing older population as effectively as it has served youth.

Parishes and other Church organizations are gearing up to do just that, but we feel that the vision of service to the elderly has been unnecessarily limited. We seem too content to take the organizational practices used with the young and apply them to seniors. So we pack older parishioners into buses to look at the fall foliage and taste the Hermann wine. We try to provide bingo and card parties to "keep grandma off the streets." Basketball courts are re-striped so the old folks can play shuffleboard too.

All of that is great. The old have earned a bit of leisure and fun time, similar to what they had as teenagers. But our older parishioners want and

deserve more than that.

Older parishioners possess a wealth of experience and competence and often have the free time to devote those talents to the Church. A bookkeeper does not forget how to add when he reaches 65. A manager does not forget how to manage. A nurse, a retired medical technician, a former teacher — all have skills valuable to a parish community and all too often not used by that community.

Parishes must overcome the feeling that the parish is an extension of the school. Parish councils should represent all the parishioners, not just school parents and their contemporaries. Flexible schedules should be developed to let older parishioners contribute their services to the extent of their ability. And most of all, older people must know that the Church welcomes their continued participation and that their contributions of time and talent are as valuable as they have ever been.

The Washington Star

Washington, D.C., May 31, 1981

Only Yesterday

It seems only yesterday that America was a kid in blue jeans, living with 14 other kids in blue jeans, all of them convinced that, far from beginning at 40, life ended at 30. If the Census Bureau didn't have so many numbers to prove the point, it would be hard to believe what has happened to that kid.

But there it is. Gathering the variety of rosebuds that was in vogue a decade or two ago has aged more than the individuals who were young then. It has turned the statistical prototype into a not-so-young person living in a very small household.

For the first time since 1950, there are as many Americans over 30 as under. And where, 10 years ago, an average of 3.11 people shared living quarters — already a bit down from the legendary American family of four, let alone the still more legendary extended family that included Grandma and Grandpa and Auntie who never married — today's figure is a mere 2.75.

As for our part of the country, it's more so. Virginia and Maryland average out on a median age of 30 but the median District resident is 31 plus. In household size, too, the District figure, which, at 2.39 people, is the lowest in the nation, pulls down the slightly higher than average Virginia and Maryland figures for an area composite of a bare two and a half

people per household.

It's hard to say whether this numerical vision worries economists or social psychologists more. While that median 30-year-old with the one plus roommates is no strain on either the economy or the social fabric, the existence of such a person implies a lot of variation up and down the generational lines.

The economists seem to feel rather like the man in the old joke who subtracted all the over-age, under-age, jailed, insane and otherwise incapacitated people from the labor force and found that he was the only one in the country who was working. The people due for government support keep getting more numerous. The ones whose taxes pay the bill are ever fewer.

Meanwhile, social psychologists direct their anxieties toward the solitary old age that awaits more and more people thanks to concepts of self-realization that stress personal success and pleasure above commitments to partners or children. Early retirement and employers' reluctance to risk involvement with the medical and other problems of the elderly already make it an idle old age as well as a lonely one for many Americans.

There are, however, signs that at least some of what's wrong with this picture may be cor-

rected by pressures from other troubled areas. Because nursing homes are so expensive and hard to regulate, there is growing interest in alternatives for the infirm old who have families — subsidized home care, for example.

Also, as the middle-aged and elderly population swells, the impossibility of sustaining the social security system with so many more on the receiving end than the contributing side will undoubtedly keep more people working longer. Good for the financial health of the system and for the emotional health of many who, as things stand now, are pushed out of the mainstream of economic and social life while they are still vigorous.

Similarly, public knowledge of the system's insecurities has influenced a certain number of people to change their long-range money strategies. A recent opinion survey discloses that 85 per cent of young adults are not counting on social security to take care of all their eventual retirement needs but plan to make other arrangements; they think of their social security taxes as merely another contribution to government revenues.

There are still warnings in those census figures. So long as they're noticed, though, we can regard them with the optimism of will rather than the pessimism of logic.

THE SACRAMENTO BEE

Sacramento, Calif., September 1, 1982

As The Nation Grows Older

Dr. Robert N. Butler, who has just left the post of director of the National Institute on Aging, warns that the nation is ill-prepared for the problems that loom when "the baby boom grows gray." That's the generation born between 1946 and 1964. It forms a huge blip on the population curve and by the year 2020 will comprise more than a fifth of all Americans.

Yet despite that coming demographic tilt, Butler sees no concerted national effort to assure that older citizens remain healthy and productive as long as possible. Medical education in this country all but ignores geriatrics. Butler, in fact, is leaving the institute he has headed since its inception in 1977 to head the first department of geriatrics at an American medical school — Mount Sinai School of Medicine in New York. He points out that medical research on the problems of aging has been virtually non-existent and that, until his agency intervened, various government-funded disease studies largely failed to include the over-65 population. This, despite the fact that this group suffers the most illness.

Butler also cites instances of conflicting and ill-conceived policies everywhere pertaining to the economics and sociology of aging. For example, the idea of raising the Social Security retirement age to 68 overlooks the fact that because of life-prolonging measures there are more disabled people in that and other older age groups. Government proposals to raise the health insurance premiums of older workers conflict with other policies seeking to keep older people on the job longer — the higher premiums will cause companies to hire or retain fewer older workers.

Butler is a psychiatrist widely regarded as one of the nation's most distinguished experts on aging, in both psychological and physical disciplines. His departure from the National Institute on Aging is a distinct loss to the nation, but his advice will continue and is clearly worth heeding. The administration should give the matter of the appointment of a successor to this able man the most serious attention.

The Evening Gazette

Worcester, Mass., July 11, 1981

Baby Booms and Echoes

The effect of the end of the postwar baby boom is obvious in education. Schools are closing, enrollments are down, teachers are being laid off and colleges are worrying about getting enough students. The bulge in the U.S. population caused by the baby boom is causing many other effects, some subtle and long-lasting.

A recent publication by Congressional Quarterly outlines some of the social conditions that may be linked to demographics — the numbers of people and their distribution in the United States. Included in the list are: the student activism of the 1960s and self-centeredness of the 1970s. High unemployment, inflation, pessimism about the future and the slackening of productivity growth may also be tied to the unusual burst in the postwar birth rate, according to the report.

The baby boom, which peaked in 1957, was more a 1950s phenomenon than an immediate response to the war; the birth rate actually fell from 1947 to 1950. Unexpected by social scientists, the baby boom was a temporary reversal of decades of falling birth rates. During the 16 years after World War II, 64 million babies were born. During the 16 years preceding the war, only 41.5 million were born. The boom as seen on demographic charts looks "like a python that swallowed a pig," the research report said.

Born to parents who were becoming more affluent during the 50s and reared under generally permissive guidelines, these children were taught to expect much of life and themselves. When they entered college, this huge group found it had social cohesiveness and political power. Colleges became centers of political and social unrest when the boom babies enrolled.

During the 1970s, though, the "boomers" entered the job market, inexperienced, by the millions, finding competition stronger than they ever expected. Industrial investment couldn't keep up with the expanding labor market, so productivity growth slowed. Unemployment, under-employment, and salaries lagged behind the record of the previous generation.

In their late 20s and 30s, the "boomers" entered the period of biggest expenditures and lowest savings. They bought houses and cars, appliances and furniture. Prices soared, credit expanded, savings dropped.

An "echo" in the birth rate seems to be occurring now, as postwar boomers have children. The current growth of conservatism may be related to the boomers settling down.

"Now, as it washes up in the 1980s, the baby-boom generation is experiencing a shift in the way it thinks about itself and its future. Optimism is yielding to pessimism. Altruism is yielding to narcissism. The generation that grew up convinced of its special place in society is not finding it," the report states.

Problems of the future — increased demands on social services, health care and retirement funds — are inevitable consequences of this population bulge getting older. By 2030, more than twice as many Americans will be over age 65 as today.

The "baby boom" theory is only a partial explanation of these political, economic and social phemonena. But society — its ideas, successes and problems — is a compilation of its people. The baby boom of the fifties was a dramatic event in America's population history. Its effects certainly have been, and will be, profound.

The Kansas City Times
Kansas City, Mo., August 17, 1982
The Aging of America

Thoughtful Americans did not have to await the updated results of the 1980 census to realize that substantial shifts are occurring in the age structure of the national population. The young are declining in numbers as those in their later years increase. Those trends have had a profound effect on the nation and they will continue to do so perhaps into the next century.

The signs have been visible for some time. The large number of elementary school closings is one tipoff. So are the financial problems plaguing the Social Security system at the other end. The statistics, released last Friday by the Bureau of the Census, cover the period from April 1, 1970, until July 1, 1981. They add substance to the conclusions many had reached on their own.

The three age groups at the bottom of the scales all declined — under 5 years, down 1.3 percent; 5 to 13 years, down 16.4 percent, and 14 to 17 years, down 1.8 percent. At the other end, those Americans 65 and over increased by 31.4 percent. The most conspicuous change in between reflected the aging of the Baby Boom that followed the Second World War. As a result, the age group between 25 and 34 years old went up a whopping 55 percent over 1970 when most of them were still in the school and college brackets.

The impact on government has been tremendous and it will continue to grow, affecting programs across the spectrum of American life — education, social services (particularly in health and medicine), the tax structure and so forth. Some attention is already being focused on those problems, but not nearly enough. Unless more thought and planning, coupled with effective long-range action, follow, America's current population problems will seem like child's play compared to what lies ahead.

THE KANSAS CITY STAR
Kansas City, Mo., December 30, 1982
Can posterity count on Social Security?

If anything should convince the country and its leaders that the Social Security system must be put in order, it's the latest statistics on longevity in America.

A baby born last year can expect to live 74.1 years. That is not such a great old age. What is noteworthy is that it's more than three months longer than the average life expectancy of a baby born in 1980. Furthermore, more people who reach the later years can expect to live longer than ever: nearly to 82 for those in the 65-to-70 age group.

What these and similar demographic statistics like the birth rate surge have to do with Social Security is rather simple. In coming decades and in the next century, there will be more retired persons and more very old retired persons drawing out of the fund. It is scary enough to realize it is critical for the well-being of today's elders to get the system into shape. But certain forces which cannot be changed are pressing us into the next century. So it is the secure old age of ourselves—blue-collar workers, managers and national policy-makers—that is also being debated. And the old age of our children.

Cursory attention to rising life-expectancy figures often interprets them as signs of a longer life but misses the most important point of such figures: They are averages. The trend indicates that more people are living beyond their 70s, more a result of lower infant mortality rates along with eradication of childhood diseases and young adult killers than of massive numbers living to extreme old age. The normal life span has not been greatly lengthened. But more people are reaching it.

Before the year ends, we will witness again some consequences of unforeseen forces beyond the control of Social Security administrators. Too little money is coming in to pay benefits. So $13 billion will be borrowed from health and disability funds. This could be just a taste of what is to come, if political timidity and economic and demographic fairy tales obscure the necessity for solid changes.

Old age should not be fraught with financial trapdoors. A decently comfortable and stable life is the least we want for our elders. But unless Congress and the administration perform with courage and wisdom, most can forget it.

The Birmingham News
Birmingham, Ala., January 1, 1983
Dimensions

One of the first items deserving action by the new 98th Congress is of course the Social Security problem. Indeed, "desperately demanding" might be a better term than "deserving," for the dimensions of the problem are greater than the majority of the public perhaps realizes.

How bad off is Social Security? The big numbers have been bandied about for months, but perhaps a quick review of the overall situation would give a better feel for the problem.

Consider this: In the mid-1950s, only 20 percent of the people 65 and older received Social Security benefits. Today, more than 90 percent receive checks. Average monthly benefits have increased since 1950 by 250 percent — *after* taking inflation into account. At the same time, the proportion of the population over 65 has increased, while Americans have begun retiring somewhat earlier and the average life expectancy has gone from 62 in 1935 to about 74 today.

Because of such trends, the country's retired people have been drawing much more out of Social Security than they put in. According to one estimate, the average 1982 retiree will receive total benefits that are almost three times the value of his or her total lifetime contributions to the system.

And that's not the end of it. Under current projections, Social Security's problems will become overwhelming when members of the baby-boom generation start retiring around the year 2010. In order to cover their benefits, the system would have to accumulate a reserve of $1.5 trillion — or half again more than the current national debt.

This, of a system which, if it continues operating under present law and policies, is expected to ring up $200 billion in debt during the next seven years.

This, quite obviously, is a situation which cannot be allowed to continue. It is very much to be hoped that both the administration and the Congress can agree on a workable approach to the problem which will neither unduly harm recipients nor cripple wage earners whose contributions are the heartblood of the program. Certainly, in the face of such a crisis, the time for partisanship has passed.

Part I: Problems

The major problem facing the Social Security system is very simple: it is running out of money with which to pay its beneficiaries. Once this funding difficulty is analyzed further, however, it becomes apparent that it is compounded by many other problems. The fact that 'elderly' is no longer synonymous with 'needy' has long been established, yet the very suggestion of altering the program to decrease benefits paid to even those recipients with substantial incomes causes an outcry. Social Security has become sacrosanct. Workers, meanwhile, are chafing under the increasingly burdensome taxes imposed on them to support current beneficiaries of the system. The easiest way to shore up the finances of the system, by raising the payroll tax even further, could cause a 'generation gap' far greater than that caused by differences in attitude; the young may revolt against supporting their elders if it is accomplished at the cost of their own financial devastation. In such a climate, it is not surprising that a growing proportion of workers express little confidence that the Social Security system will be of significant benefit to them when they retire.

Funding Problems Grow Severe

For its first forty years the Social Security system experienced little difficulty in financing promised benefits to retirees and other recipients. As recently as 1971 the system was still running such a healthy surplus, forecast to reach nearly $1 trillion by the year 2025, that Congress decided to index benefits to the inflation rate. By the mid-1970s, however, high rates of unemployment and inflation combined to cause short-term deficits that have persisted ever since, despite the huge payroll tax increases passed by Congress in 1977.

In their 1982 annual report, the system's trustees predicted that without legislative changes the retirement fund would be too depleted to pay benefits on time by July, 1983. Even with continued interfund borrowing, they reported, all three trust funds combined (OASI, HI and DI) would be unable to cover the necessary expenditures by sometime in 1984. Skeptics have charged, however, that the Administration has exaggerated the threat of Social Security's impending bankruptcy in order to be able to reduce the overall budget deficit. Small adjustments in payroll taxes or benefits, they say, would tide the system over until the retirement of the "baby boom" generation.

Sentinel Star

Orlando, Fla., February 17, 1981

WHEN Social Security was enacted in 1935 it was not intended as a retirement program. It was to be an additional nut the average worker could add to plans for retirement with dignity.

And, for a time, the plan worked. Insurance companies and others in the investment business sold thousands of retirement programs to people who, until then, couldn't put aside enough money to make such plans worthwhile.

Softened by time and egged on by a beneficent Congress, perceptions shifted toward thinking of Social Security as THE retirement program. As expectations rose, Congress rose to the challenge.

Today, the awful fact is that without immediate changes, the program will face serious cash flow problems by late next year and be bankrupt in 1983. With that jolting news, the only question left is, in what form shall those changes be?

Higher contributions won't work. In four years the maximum levy has jumped from $965 to $1,975, and half the nation's workers now pay more Social Security tax than income tax.

The most serious problem with Social Security is what has been called the "grandpa bulge." Too few workers are supporting too many retirees.

In 1935 there were 11 adult workers in the labor force for every one 65 or older. Today the ratio is less than 3-to-1; by 2020 the figure will be 2-to-1. Consider also that the worker reaching 65 in 1935 typically started working before he was 15 and physical demands of labor in those days were far greater. A corresponding retirement age today would be at least 75.

One of many Social Security proposals is one by Florida Democratic Sen. Lawton Chiles. His bill includes eliminating mandatory retirement at 70, raising normal retirement from 65 to 68, dropping earnings restrictions for retirees and halting student benefits.

Like others attempting to fix the ailing program, Sen. Chiles is silent on the matter of including the 6 million federal, state and local employees in the program. Of course, that would be a potent lobby to buck, but it would also fatten the income in a realistic and fair way.

Nonetheless, Sen. Chiles' bill is a good start. It reflects the societal changes since 1935 and would flatten the "grandpa bulge," which is essential. However, the bill is no more than a fix. It is not a cure.

The cure would come in returning Social Security to the kind of program it was intended to be, a retirement supplement. Even that demands a major restructuring of the program's scope and possibly a rethinking of how it is to be financed.

Detroit Free Press

Detroit, Mich., June 10, 1979

CONGRESS PULLED the Social Security system back from bankruptcy last year by passing hefty payroll tax increases. It had no alternative at the time, but the taxpayers are howling, and the system's long-range problems are still far from solved.

The retirement and survivors' trust fund is due to run dry in 2028, while the Medicare fund could go broke as soon as 1994. The whole system may collapse even quicker if Congress bends to the pressure to roll back the tax increases scheduled for the next four years without enacting some sort of comprehensive financing to replace them.

President Carter's plan to save money by cutting benefits is expected to go nowhere, and not without reason, as he literally proposed to reduce the widow's mite and the orphans' due. Some in Congress are kicking around a European-style value-added tax, or VAT; but since VAT is tacked onto goods at every stage of production, it is hugely inflationary, the wrong medicine for now.

The House Ways and Means committee has reported out a reasonable bill to reform the disability portion of Social Security, adjusting benefits so that recipients don't make more on the dole than they do by working, and removing the barriers to rehabilitation and return to employment. The changes would save $1 billion a year of the program's $14 billion annual cost.

We seem to be moving inexorably, however, to the point where income taxes will have to pick up part of the Social Security deficit. Political reality dictates it: What Congress is ever going to tell 38 million or more Social Security recipients that their envelopes will be empty next month?

Objectors say drawing from the general fund will break the historic tie between what a wage earner puts into Social Security and what he takes out, reducing it from an insurance-pension program to another form of welfare. But as Rep. William Brodhead, D-Detroit, keeps pointing out, one-third of the system's funds are eaten up by Medicare, which was not part of the original Social Security design; financing Medicare and disability payments from general revenues would not only rescue the system but permit a cut in the regressive payroll tax.

The system's ills are also woven into the larger troubles of inflation and hospital costs. Cost-of-living increases will push up Social Security benefits by nearly 10 percent on July 1; Medicare costs continue to soar in the wake of uncontrolled hospital bills like the tail on a kite. If inflation seems to have slipped the leash, beyond anyone's power to call back for the moment, hospital cost containment is still within reach—if only Congress would grasp it. If Congress can't deal straightforwardly and rationally with that first step, who will trust it ever to deal honestly with the complexities of the Social Security issue?

The Birmingham News

Birmingham, Ala., May 19, 1981

The debate in Congress and in the administration over what to do to rescue Social Security may wax hotter then either budget or tax debates. It is also likely to become more acrimonious as members attempt to be numbered among the good guys; that is, opposed both to cutting benefits and raising Social Security taxes.

While much may be wrong with the Social Security system, the big problem causing consternation is money — the system is about to run out of the wherewithal to pay those benefits so many rely upon as their only income.

For instance, in 1980, 114 million persons in the work force paid $99 billion into the system, but Social Security paid out $101 billion to 35 million persons, leaving a deficit of $2 billion. Even with higher Social Security taxes this year for both employees and employers the balance between income and out-go is too close for comfort. The problem is further weighted by an additional number of retirees getting higher checks due to inflation.

The problem was not unforeseen. Actuaries and economists for years have been warning that the hand-to-mouth manner in which Social Security was financed was certain to result in bankruptcy. From the beginning, Social Security benefits have been paid out of current income and not out of a mythical self-perpetuating trust fund invested like most pension funds that realize income from investments.

Congress and Congress alone is responsible for the plight of the system today. Over the years, motivated by party politics, Congress has increased benefits and loaded the system with strangling appendages for political gain but with little thought given to how the bills would be paid over the long run. The problem is now so critical the question is not whether reforms shall be made but what shape those reforms will take.

Basically, only three moves can be made to put the system on a sounder financial footing:

● Increase the Social Security tax;

● Reduce benefits;

● Or shift a major portion to financing benefits to general tax revenues.

The first is unattractive since Social Security taxes are already high with some parying far more in Social Security taxes than in income taxes. It is becoming too big a load for workers and too big a burden for employers who pay half.

Great opposition also exists to using general revenues for Social Security, since to do so would turn it into a welfare system. And when reducing benefits, even such as Medicare, is mentioned, congress men's eyes tend to glaze over.

When Social Security was started in the '30s, about 11 workers were taxed to support one beneficiary. Today that ratio is down to slightly more than three workers per retiree. Some predict the ratio will fall to as low as two to one after the turn of the century.

The best solution seems to be a mix of the three alternatives: Cut benefits some and gradually increase the age of eligibility for retirement benefits.

There is nothing magic about age 65. That age was chosen in the beginning simply because it was the age Bismark chose for Germany's retirement system. If the retirement age was moved back one month each year until the 21st century, it would yield billions more in available revenues for the trust fund.

Whatever is done, Congress cannot neglect a solution much longer. If the system should run out of money, chaos would result, a far worse fate for Congress than the criticism that will come from a workable remedy, however severe it might be.

THE MILWAUKEE JOURNAL

Milwaukee, Wisc., July 12, 1981

Senate Democrats have a point when they say President Reagan exaggerates Social Security's financial problem. They are right, to a degree, in criticizing his remedies. And they are correct in asserting that there would be less need to squeeze Social Security if Reagan were not trying to lavish so much money on the military.

However, we hope the Democrats in Congress aren't planning to sweep Social Security's troubles under the rug, as they and their Republican colleagues have done so often over the years. Social Security does have difficulties — both long-run and short-run — and correction will cause some pain.

The problem has been building for decades. In the early years of Social Security, many people paid taxes into the system but relatively few received benefits. The ratio in 1950, for example, was 14 taxpayers for each recipient. Congress could keep the tax rate low and greatly liberalize benefits without any immediate worry about bankrupting the fund. But the easy ride didn't last. By 1970, the ratio of taxpayers to recipients was only 4 to 1. (It's expected to be 2 to 1 in the year 2025.)

In the last decade, the problem has been aggravated by (1) inflation, which rapidly boosted the cost of benefits because they were pegged to the Consumer Price Index, and (2) unemployment, which held down the number of persons paying taxes into the retirement fund. Despite steep payroll tax increases, the retirement fund faces the prospect of running somewhat short of money by the end of next year and seriously short in future decades. Obviously, something has to give.

Although a noninflationary boom could ease the short-run problem, such a development is anything but a sure bet. Reagan administration officials promise noninflationary prosperity when pushing for income tax cuts, but they project economic woe when arguing for scaled down Social Security. To

be on the safe side, Congress should take at least some modest steps to cope with the short-run difficulty. And for the long-run, more extensive changes are clearly needed.

As a beginning, lawmakers should start basing retirees' benefit increases on something more realistic than the Consumer Price Index. It tends to overstate the inflation rate. One solution would be to peg the Social Security raises to either the CPI or the average wage increase, whichever is lower.

As another useful step, Congress should tighten various fringe benefits of Social Security. Among these are payments to college students who are the children of deceased or retired workers, burial benefits that are paid to beneficiaries' estates regardless of need, "double dip" benefits that many retired federal and state employes receive after a minimum stint in private employment.

For the long term, Congress should consider gradual increases in the age requirements for both normal and early retirement. Reagan was wrong to propose an abrupt slashing of early-retirement benefits. That would unacceptably break faith with people who have worked for many years in expectation of retiring under certain conditions. However, it would be acceptable to start phasing out the early retirement option at some point in the future, except perhaps for strenuous jobs that take a heavy physical toll. An increase in the normal retirement age would be consistent with increased longevity. In 1950, a 65-year-old could expect to live to age 79. Today, the figure is 81.

And why not tax at least a portion of Social Security benefits as regular income? Most recipients would not be affected because their total income would not be high enough, but billions of dollars would be collected from well-to-do recipients.

In short, it's not enough for members of Congress to yell about the flaws in Reagan's proposals. Flaws aside, he has identified a problem and Congress should be developing responsible solutions.

THE RICHMOND NEWS LEADER

Richmond, Va., June 18, 1981

Those who think that the talk about the Social Security system's financial problems is just chit-chat haven't been listening to Robert J. Myers.

Myers, the deputy commissioner for programs at the Social Security Administration, says flatly that the trust fund for Old-Age and Suvivors Insurance will run out of money next year. If that occurs, pensioners would not receive reduced checks pro-rated on the basis of available funds. Instead, no checks would go out until enough money came in from payroll taxes to mail the checks in full.

Democrats contend that Social Security's short-range problems can be solved by a transfer of funds from the healthier trust funds for disability and Medicare. Myers does not agree. He repeats the three options that Republicans know to be available: Reduce benefits, increase payroll taxes, or find money somewhere else. That "somewhere else" usually is interpreted to mean an infusion from general treasury funds, but there is no surplus in general funds to transfer. Any new revenues for Social Security would have to be borrowed, adding to the projected deficit.

Democrats keep hoping the Social Security problem will resolve itself. They criticize the Reagan administration's ideas for restoring the system to solvency, but they offer no ideas of their own to stave off disaster. If Myers' worst fears are realized and millions who rely on Social Security checks have to wait for their money, will the Democrats be prepared to take the rap?

The Dallas Morning News

Dallas, Texas, June 20, 1981

THE political game, apparently, has to be played out on Social Security. But we are already very deep into the fourth quarter, and time is wasting.

It seemed inevitable that the politicians would dodge and evade the hard choices needed to save a system that has been headed for disaster for years. Since the Goldwater fiasco of 1964, incumbent politicians and those who hoped to become incumbent have avoided the subject as though their political lives depended on it — as perhaps they did.

But the Reagan administration, early on, grasped this prickly nettle and presented a plan to get the system back in balance. And then came the deluge. All those timid souls who had for so long danced away from the subject suddenly became lions of demagoguery, denouncing Reagan's supposed callousness toward the elderly.

The media chorus came in on cue, with columns and cartoons accusing Reagan of trying to curry favor with the rich at the expense of starving pensioners, of spending money on gold-plated military gadgets while reducing the old folks' diet of dog food and day-old bread. And then many of the elderly, desperately aware of their dependence on Social Security — but unaware of the fact that Reagan's cuts affect primarily those who retire in the future rather than present retirees — responded as expected.

They cried out in understandable fear. They wrote their congressmen. They called their newspapers and wrote letters decrying the supposed cruelty of Reagan and anyone else who would touch the Social Security system, who would change it in any way.

Given the willingness of politicians to play to the pensioners' fears with Social Security, this distressing state of alarm and confusion was probably inevitable. But it is also inevitable that somewhere, some time, Americans are going to have to turn from all this noise and listen to the people who know the facts.

Such as, for example, the commissioner of the Social Security Administration, who was in Dallas Wednesday. He didn't get the ink or the foot-age given to a Tip O'Neill speech about how Reagan hates the poor. But what he said was extremely relevant:

"After the rhetoric is over, we still are facing insufficient funds," said John Svahn. "Unless we do something, we can't pay benefits in September, 1982."

No doubt the games-players will discount this warning as propaganda from a man allied with Ronald Reagan, that well-known hater of the poor.

Let those who believe that listen to Milton Gwirtzman, who headed the Social Security Commission, named during Jimmy Carter's administration to study the financial base of the system. He told congressmen earlier this year that we are "coming very close to the margin of safety."

Then, to make sure no one misunderstood that ominous warning, he added: "When we talk about Social Security having 'cash flow' problems, it is a gentle way of saying that if nothing is done, some time next year Social Security checks will just not go out."

Meanwhile in Washington and in the national media, the oratorical and ideological game goes on. And the clock of reality keeps ticking away.

St. Louis Globe-Democrat

St. Louis, Mo., June 4, 1981

If Social Security is to survive and be restored to good fiscal health, Americans are going to have to bite the bullet hard.

The tragedy is that so few people in the country appear aware of the true severity of the situation. With childlike confidence they seem to think that keeping one's fingers crossed will assure an unending continuation of Social Security benefit payments.

President Ronald Reagan attempted to lay the facts on the line in a valiant effort to alert the public of the danger that lies ahead in the not-too-distant future unless effective action is taken. The response was loud and clear: Anguished howls of protest from coast-to-coast and from one border to the other.

Perhaps expecting Social Security recipients to comprehend the actual plight may be asking too much. After all they have been conned and confused for decades by members of Congress who kicked around the supplemental program for retirees as a vote-getting political football.

This is the 46th year since the inception of Social Security. Even to this late date, many members of Congress continue to wander about not knowing which way to turn to put the program on its feet again. Some are looking for sleight of hand trickery to provide a miracle.

That's the game Capitol Hill has played through the years. This approach finally has pushed Social Security to the brink of disaster. It's hard to believe that some senators and representatives still want to play the same old precarious game.

One congressional body that should know better is the House Social Security subcommittee, which favors borrowing billions of dollars from income tax revenues in a scheme it hopes would solve the system's short-range problems. It is this sort of irresponsiblity that has led to the problems that have put the program on the endangered list. All this proposal would do, in effect, is create more long-range problems further undermining the program's stability.

The federal government has been operating in the red for 22 consecutive years. How does one borrow from an entity that hasn't been able to pay its own bills since 1959?

This type of fiscally insane borrowing accelerates inflation that has become a major threat menacing retirees in what was to have been their golden years. It appears as if some congressional big spenders are determined to see that the federal budget is never balanced and that inflation is pushed higher.

With the federal debt almost at the $1 trillion mark, the Reagan administration is in no mood for more costly fiscal tomfoolery on Capitol Hill. It is adamantly opposed to borrowing from general revenues.

There are some instances where a case can be made for removing certain benefits from funding through Social Security. Medicare is an example. This program is not funded by taxes based on a worker's earnings.

The House Ways and Means Committee has approved cuts totaling $560 million in addition to reductions of $2.6 billion that had been recommended last month.

One of the problems is that the federal government didn't level with people regarding the program. Social Security never was intended to be a full retirement pension. Political windbags made it look that way when they tacked on more benefits without providing for adequate funding.

Now people are being told the bitter truth but it's too late for retirees to make other provisions. Those still working should heed the plight of the current crop of suffering retirees and take action to faithfully store away a nestegg to make their own retirement more secure.

"SOMEDAY, SON, ALL THIS WILL BE YOURS....."

The Knickerbocker News

Albany, N.Y., March 10, 1981

One facet of federal government reality that affects most of us sooner or later is Social Security. Almost all wage earners pay into the fund; almost all of us expect something back when our road runs out of pavement and we retire into the slow lane.

The doomsayers and gloom purveyors would have us believe Social Security is teetering on the brink of a financial abyss just before beginning the long stumble into dark night. Scary stuff, that, since Social Security supports millions of elderly now, and millions upon millions more will come to depend on its monthly check in the next few decades.

It's almost impossible to decide which prognosticator to believe; each has his or her own personal timetable for disaster. Bankruptcy is one year away. Or 10. Or 20. Or something in between. A few lone voices in this particularly nasty patch of wilderness say that no, everything's shaky but basically sound and, with a few changes, nobody will go hungry, nobody will go broke.

We're with the rest of you — we don't know which to believe, either. But we are certain that changes in the Social Security system as it now operates are necessary, vital. And the sooner the better.

For one thing, it is senseless for the federal government to run one Social Security system for the country and another, separate one for its own employees. To exempt federal employees from the Social Security system may have made sense, common or political, when it was done, but that is no longer the case.

Herding federal employees into the fold will not save Social Security — they retire, too — but adding hundreds of thousands of solid wage-earners to the national plan will help Social Security stave off immediate problems. It would give the government a few years' breathing space to think about longer-term solutions.

Federal employees obviously don't want to join the crowd; they have their own plan, better in some ways than Social Security and getting even better with time because of collective bargaining. But in this case, the good of the many must overshadow the good of the few. Let federal employees take their retirement straight, like everyone else, if it will help get Social Security on solid ground, to everyone's benefit.

Another problem is retirement age. Squawk we might, but 65 is growing younger every year and the age at which most of us retire must be raised.

Part of Social Security's problem has its roots in the better lives we've been living for the past few decades. More people are living longer, so more money is being paid out for a longer period of time. With more people in retirement, there are proportionally fewer workers paying into the system to take care of those drawing out.

So, sometime in the next few years we simply must ease up the the age for receiving Social Security. . . to 68, possibly even to 70. It must be done gradually; those already retired mustn't be hurt. But we have to do it.

We also have to reconsider our national policy of automatic Social Security raises in response to increases in the cost of living. The inflation rate is calculated by using many factors, many of the most important not pertinent to the elderly and retired — mortgage rates, for instance, which are very heavily weighted. It's likely a special cost of living figure for the elderly would result in fewer and smaller increases at no real cost to their quality of life.

And we as a nation must consider all of the add-ons we have pinned onto Social Security since it was initiated almost 50 years ago: Medicare, disability, survivors' benefits, the lot. Social Security was designed to supplement — *supplement* — the pensions of the retired. It is only when it began to expand beyond this purpose that financial troubles came to call. Is Social Security the proper vehicle for taking care of widowed spouses and their children? Until the children are 22? Isn't there a better way, one that will burden the worker less heavily, to handle these social problems?

The Philadelphia Inquirer

Philadelphia, Pa., July 31, 1982

President Reagan has accused Speaker of the House Thomas P. O'Neill of "sheer political demagoguery" for having asserted that the administration wants to cut Social Security benefits. Well, demagoguery is in the eye of the beholder. As it happens, the administration did propose a slew of benefit cuts last year, but Mr. Reagan quickly backed off when the flack started flying. Earlier this year, Senate Republicans had plans for $40 billion worth of savings in Social Security over the next three years, but they dropped them from their budget when they and the White House looked at the calendar and saw November.

What would Mr. Reagan say about the remarks of his Social Security commissioner, John A. Svahn, the other day? Speaking to the American Society of Hospital Personnel Administrators, Mr. Svahn said that the Social Security Administration will have to borrow $7 billion to meet its obligations and viewed this development with alarm. This is, he noted, the first time the system has ever had to borrow money and went on to say that after November, when the bulk of the borrowing will occur, "it goes downhill from there."

How to arrest the downhill slide? "Either you're going to have to start paying an awful lot more . . . up to 25 percent . . . or we're going to have to expect less," said Mr. Svahn.

In reality, the borrowing is no big deal. The Social Security disability fund happens to have a surplus on hand, and last year Congress enacted temporary legislation to tap it. If the economy continues to deteriorate, the system could — technically — run out of money by the end of next year. Let it be emphasized that one reason the system is having problems now is the deteriorated economy. When Congress raised the payroll tax during the Carter administration, it could not anticipate the oil-fueled rate of inflation and the subsequent deep recession that has so reduced collections.

Let it also be emphasized that while the Social Security System has problems, these are not as monstrous as Mr. Svahn asserted. Starting around 1990, contributions to the system will expand considerably, as the post-World War II baby boom population matures. About the year 2025, as those people begin retiring, a new problem will arise, but that problem too is manageable if some sensible changes are begun now.

What changes? The first and most obvious one is a gradual raising, perhaps one month a year, in the retirement age, from 65 to 68. People are living longer than they lived in the 1930s. They're healthier. Those who still want to retire at 65 ought to be allowed to do so, at lower retirement income, but those who want to continue working should be encouraged.

Second, the cost-of-living adjustment ought to be modified slightly downward. Just about everyone agrees that the increased benefits, set several years ago to reflect inflation, do not accurately reflect actual increases in the cost-of-living of retired people. According to the National Commission on Social Security, if the cost-of-living increase had been linked either to the Consumer Price Index or a wage index, whichever is lowest, the system would not now be facing its current short-term financing problems.

Third, bringing all government employees into the system would inject about $14 billion into Social Security — a sum that would in itself be enough to take care of the system's short-term financial problems. Fourth, double-dipping by those who receive both Social Security and government retirement benefits ought to be limited.

The Social Security System isn't broke, but it does need timely fixing. There's no use expecting anything to happen before November, but after November, when a bipartisan national commission is supposed to turn in its report, the administration and Congress should get cracking on the job before another even-year November begins to loom.

Houston Chronicle

Houston, Texas, July 30, 1982

Social Security Commissioner John Svahn's announcement this week that the Social Security system would have to borrow $7 billion to keep the system in operation is a very clear answer to those who thought the talk in Washington and elsewhere about the precarious financial condition of Social Security was mostly exaggerated political falderal.

Americans have been reading and hearing about Social Security's financial problems for months now, but there has been a tendency to disregard most of the warnings because they have been so tinged with political overtones. If there was so much urgency, then why was Congress moving so slowly? But when the system actually has to borrow money to meet its obligations, it is irrefutable evidence of just how real the problem is.

Svahn said the old-age program for the first time would have to borrow up to $1 billion in October and $6 billion in November from its disability insurance trust fund to maintain present benefits. Svahn said that was but the beginning, unless changes are made: "It goes downhill from there." Americans, he said, are going to have to "start paying an awful lot more now or we're going to have to expect a lot less."

Social Security press spokesman Jim Brown said the system could borrow enough to get through July 1983 but "after that there will not be enough to make payments on time." He was backing up a similar statement made in May by Treasury Secretary Donald T. Regan, who added: "This is not a scare tactic — this is fact."

Social Security touches so many people in so many different ways, those who pay and those who benefit, and involves such staggering figures that proposed changes are approached warily, both from a fiscal and a political standpoint. But the announcement about having to borrow to stay afloat underscores the fact that changes must come.

While the debate about Social Security's unsound fiscal footing has aroused skepticism about the system, it has solid support among Americans of all income categories. They want Social Security to survive, but they will have to be convinced that any changes are reasonable, necessary and fair.

That will not be an easy job for Congress.

ST. LOUIS POST-DISPATCH

St. Louis, Mo., January 5, 1983

The Social Security buck stops with the 98th Congress, and if it has any sense it will dispose of the issue this year rather than next, when it would be certain to get caught up once again in electoral politics. At the same time, though, Congress shouldn't let itself by taken in by those who insist that it solve the problem once and for all. To expect Congress, or any other institution for that matter, to see more than 10 years down the road is asking too much.

In a nutshell, Social Security's problem is that outlays have been running ahead of tax collections, mainly because inflation has pushed expenditures up while recession has held revenues down. A sustained period of vigorous, inflation-free economic growth would go a long way toward solving the problem, but few analysts foresee such a happy development. Instead, they expect growth to be anemic for the rest of the decade and for Social Security to face a $150 billion deficit as a result. This distressing prospect is being used as a pretext for demanding extensive, fundamental changes, but they are neither desirable nor necessary.

What Congress will have to do is fashion a combination of tax increases and benefit changes that will keep the system whole without altering the basic structure. The former could be achieved by advancing the tax increases scheduled for later in the decade, the latter through a less generous cost-of-living formula and perhaps even a one-time postponement in the effective date of the increase. Finally, Congress could provide for automatic transfer of funds from general revenue to Social Security whenever unemployment rose above a certain level.

There are many combinations available, and it is essential that Congress settle on one of them this year. And it is equally essential that it distinguish between the need for corrective action and the campaign to discredit Social Security that its right-wing enemies are mounting in the name of reform.

The Wichita Eagle-Beacon

Wichita, Kans., January 9, 1983

When Miss Ida Fuller, of Ludlow, Vt., the nation's first Social Security beneficiary, died early in 1975, at the age of 100, news reports estimated she had received more than $20,000 in benefits over the 35 years since her 1939 retirement. Her brief pre-retirement investment in the system had equaled her first benefit check for $22.54. The 417th check she received just prior to her 100th birthday in 1974 was for $109.20 — a tiny amount compared to the $800 or more many retirees receive now.

Because Social Security never was set up on a sound actuarial basis as insurance and private retirement funds are supposed to be, the system now is in very big trouble. It is even now preparing to use $13 billion in borrowed funds to keep the benefit checks flowing because the system's income in the form of Social Security payroll tax revenues no longer are adequate, especially in an economic period when, due to widespread unemployment, there are far fewer paychecks to be taxed.

Although taxing earnings to build up a retirement funds trust seemed perfectly logical in the years when the system's revenues safely outpaced its expenditures, the situation has now deteriorated into, in effect, a case of taxing Peter to pay Paul. When pyramid-scheme entrepreneurs do this, luring investors with generous "dividends" paid not out of earnings but out of others' investments, it is properly denounced and prosecuted as fraud. In the case of the Social Security system, it has to be excused, apparently, as the result of good intentions carried out with bad, or perhaps insufficient, judgment.

But because millions of older Americans depend on their benefits as a means of survival — in many cases their principal means of paying for the food they eat, the utilities that heat and light their homes, what clothes they wear — the Social Security system somehow must be kept viable. It isn't their fault that what they paid in during their working years didn't equal what they now must draw to cope minimally with inflated living costs.

But it's obvious some very tough decisions must be made by Congress and by the Reagan administration to keep the system solvent.

It's obvious, in fact, that things must be done on at least two levels: First, there must be stop-gap actions, taken on an emergency basis, to help the system weather its current financial crisis. Second, there must be, as soon thereafter as possible, a complete evaluation and recognition of Social Security's organizational shortcomings, and a reshaping — or, perhaps, even replacement — of the system. This would be in order to reconstruct on a sounder financial base all government programs intended to help working Americans prepare for their post-retirement years.

What must be done must be done.

The bipartisan National Commission on Social Security Reform seems about to agree that another increase in payroll taxes probably will be necessary. It's obvious that one will be. But it's equally obvious that can be only a first-aid approach, and better solutions must be found in the near future.

Another idea under consideration is taxing half the Social Security benefits of recipients with incomes in excess of $12,000 a year. Actually, many retirees with large incomes from investments and inheritances willingly would forgo those benefits and probably should.

The Social Security base also should be broadened — at least until a better way of financing the system and better alternatives can be created — by bringing employees of the government and of non-profit organizations under it.

Those are a few ideas that make sense.

But what is done, must be done quickly. The survival of millions of Americans is at stake, as well as that of the Social Security system itself.

CHARLESTON EVENING POST
Charleston, S.C., December 8, 1982

Peter G. Peterson, investment banker and former commerce secretary, is one of a growing number of expert witnesses who have testified recently to the unhealthy state of the Social Security system. In articles in the New York Review of Books, Mr. Peterson made an important point in blunt language. The financial problems of the Social Security program, he wrote, "are not minor and temporary, as most politicians, at least in election years, feel compelled to insist. Unless the system is reorganized...Social Security is headed for a crash."

Many, if not most, politicians have minimized the serious condition of the Social Security retirement fund because they believed it expedient to do so. Politicians have no qualms about getting political mileage out of Social Security, but they avoid taking — or even talking about — remedial action for fear they will offend some constituents. The last thing a pol wants to do is to give the impression he is even considering reducing benefits, current or future.

Mr. Peterson is not subject to such constrictions. He has advocated as corrective measures a one-year freeze on cost-of-living increases, limited increases in the future and a tax on all benefits in excess of the amounts retirees paid into the system. His suggestions for curing Social Security ills are among several offered lately by people and organizations outside of government. A solution proposed by the National Taxpayers Legal Fund, for example, was described on this page Tuesday in a column by James J. Kilpatrick. Some of these propositions might be flawed, but the point is that Congress is getting the benefit of others' thinking on the matter — and some of the thinkers carry right impressive credentials.

The need to rescue Social Security becomes more obvious daily. Unemployment is creating a greater imbalance between the pay-in and the pay-out. The retirement fund is facing a shortfall of at least $150 billion by 1990. You would think U.S. senators and representatives would be leaping at the opportunity to be — in constituents' eyes — the saviors of the Social Security, instead of just sitting around jawing about keeping promises to long-time contributors.

The Virginian-Pilot
Norfolk, Va., December 9, 1982

In the hotel whose name Richard Nixon will always remember, a group of more than 30 journalists spent Tuesday listening to seven authorities address the matter of Social Security. "Solving the Social Security Crisis" was the name of the conference put on by the Washington Journalism Center, and the speakers in the Watergate Hotel included three members of the National Commission on Social Security Reform; Rep. J.J. Pickle, chairman of the House subcommittee on Social Security; and Paul Simmons, the deputy commissioner of Social Security.

The conference covered the basics of the budgetary crisis, so much so, in fact, that "Solving the Social Security Crisis" should perhaps have been styled, "Basics About Social Security."

One basic fact that has obviously intensified interest in Social Security was explained by Alexander Trowbridge, president of the National Association of Manufacturers and a member of the president's commission on Social Security. Last year, as he laid it out, Congress authorized borrowing among Social Security funds, of which there are three — Old Age and Survivors Insurance, disability and hospital. OASI is running low on money and has been borrowing from the hospital and disability funds, which are doing relatively better. But this interfund borrowing must end by law on Dec. 31. OASI unquestionably will borrow as much as it can, but its total borrowings will enable it to keep the checks in the mail until only June.

As Trowbridge said, the urgency is to keep the checks coming, not only through 1983 but also through the rest of the Eighties. OASI will need $150 billion to $200 billion to make do through 1990, when the baby boom generation should be paying enough taxes to support the retired population. Another problem exists later — sometime after 2020, when the baby boomers themselves have taken to rocking chairs, and when there may not be enough workers to support them. Thus, as all the speakers agreed, the long and short of the Social Security problem are veritable long- and short-term problems.

What to do about them, however, got no more answer Tuesday than it had got before. The speakers were content with the basic structure of Social Security, and were agreed that the chief questions, as formulated by Larry Smedley of the AFL-CIO, are whether the growth in benefits will be cut and if so by how much, and whether the growth in taxes will accelerate and if so, again, by how much.

The speakers reiterated suggestions previously made about benefit cuts (such as tying the cost-of-living increases to wage increases, not the consumer price index) and tax increases (such as moving up the already scheduled payroll tax increases). No speaker was so intellectually bold as to suggest a separation of the insurance and welfare functions of Social Security, with the latter being paid for out of the general fund. Neither was anyone interested in entertaining the idea that Social Security be made voluntary for folks under, say, age 45. The speakers were cautious and politic, trying to say nothing that would become a front-page headline. The speakers were this way, even though the forum seemed designed to encourage inquiry. Social Security apparently has become one of those issues upon which people are afraid to exercise even the weeist bit of freedom of speech.

Even so, let me note that none of the speakers indulged in Social Security myths and indeed several of them tried to dispel some of them, including such favorites as "The system isn't going broke — they're just playing politics with it" and "I earned my benefits by paying into the system" and "The government's using my Social Security money to buy guns." Folks, they're not playing politics with Social Security — the OASI fund is going dry. And you don't "earn" benefits from the money you pay into the system. Social Security taxes aren't interest-earning deposits for the individual paying them; the taxes support the currently retired. The system thus is pay-as-you-go or, as Deputy Commissioner Simmons more accurately put it, "pay-as-you-went." Finally, Social Security taxes go to nothing else than Social Security benefits (there is, of course, a little administrative overhead). They don't buy guns. Neither, for that matter, do they buy butter.

When Congress finally does "solve" the Social Security crisis, it should simultaneously ask the Social Security Commission to undertake an advertising campaign to help wipe out such myths, some of which are as old as the system itself. Social Security has dollar problems, all right, but it also is widely misunderstood.

THE ARIZONA REPUBLIC
Phoenix, Ariz., July 29, 1982

CONGRESS can't dawdle much longer on reforming Social Security.

The system is sinking into the red.

Come October, the retirement program will have to borrow $1 billion from the disability insurance trust fund to keep checks going to beneficiaries.

Come November, it will have to borrow $6 billion more.

As time goes by, the situation will get worse, not better.

The basic problem is that Americans are having fewer children and living longer.

In addition, an ever-increasing number of state and local governments and non-profit organizations are quitting the system, in part because they're afraid it might go bust.

Thus, every year, workers paying Social Security taxes have more and more beneficiaries to support.

Congress has aggravated this problem by mandating annual cost-of-living increases for beneficiaries.

Social Security Commissioner John Svahn predicts that, unless Congress does something about it, by 2010 it will take 25 percent of the U.S. payroll to keep the system solvent.

Nearly 4 million workers for state and local governments and non-profit organizations no longer are covered by the system, and 149,000 others are preparing to leave.

Several congressmen have urged a change in the law to prevent this.

They also want the law amended to force the 2.8 million federal civil servants to join.

There are many other possible reforms that should be considered.

A bipartisan presidential commission is now doing so, with a mandate to report by the end of the year.

Once it does, Congress should act, and act swiftly.

It would be a national calamity if the system went bankrupt.

THE DENVER POST

Denver, Colo., January 12, 1983

FOR SHEER political courage, Colorado Sen. Bill Armstrong has few peers in Congress. Despite facing re-election next year, he's willing to "bite the bullet" on Social Security reform. Most politicians would probably compare Armstrong's actions to "biting the cynanide capsule." It has long been considered political suicide to advocate anything except open-ended increases in benefits. But the fact is that Social Security is threatening to break down without basic reforms.

Forget the specific causes of the cash crunch due to hit the system this summer. The underlying problem is in the changing makeup of the U.S. population. For every person now drawing benefits, 3.3 persons are working and paying taxes into the system. Under present law, when the postwar "baby boom" generation becomes eligible to draw benefits, there will be only two workers supporting each beneficiary.

Coupled with automatic benefit hikes in the present law, that means the Social Security tax burden must double by about 2015, according to Milton Gwirtzman, chairman of the National Commission on Social Security appointed by President Carter. That isn't politically or economically supportable.

Don't confuse Carter's forthright commission with the latest Social Security commission appointed by President Reagan. Reagan's politically divided panel has agreed on little except that the system is about $200 billion short of the cash to pay projected benefits through 1989.

It has virtually ignored Social Security's long-range demographic problem. Even in the short run, the commission has split along ideological lines. Liberals basically have held out for tax increases that would total about $170 billion by 1989. Conservatives, led by Armstrong, have sought to reduce the future growth of benefits.

That latter point deserves underscoring. No one seriously proposes cutting the existing level of Social Security benefits to present recipients. The question is whether to slow future growth. One reform with broad support is to stop linking Social Security benefits to the Consumer Price Index, tying them instead to increases in average wages.

Actually, in 28 of the 36 years since World War II, wages rose faster than prices — that's what economic growth is all about. If the economy returns to health, Social Security benefits would rise faster with a wage index than a price index. That's fine: A growing pie allows everyone a bigger slice.

A more basic reform would be to raise the retirement age to 68. The present age of 65 was set by Bismarck in Germany a century ago when few lived to see it. Today, most Americans are vigorous and alert at 68. Raising the retirement age gradually by 1995 would cut the program's cost without cutting benefits to those actually retired and dependent upon it.

Beyond that, liberals will probably demand some tax increases as the price of any basic reform. But Armstrong is quite right to hold the line against further increases in the regressive payroll tax which now supports the system. Many Americans already pay more in Social Security taxes than income taxes, particularly when the employer match is considered. That tax is in effect a tax on jobs, and as it rises, it creates more unemployment.

A better alternative has been discussed by some Democrats: taxing half of Social Security benefits for single retirees with incomes above $20,000 and married couples with incomes above $23,000. The poor, who depend on Social Security the most, would pay nothing under that proposal. The affluent could afford to pay taxes on the portion of their benefits which reflect employers' contributions.

Conventional wisdom aside, we doubt that Armstrong will suffer politically for his candor. As the system heads Titanic-like to its midsummer rendezvous with disaster, we think the public will admire those leaders who forthrightly urge a change in its course — not those demagogues who cry "full-speed ahead" and can't see the iceberg.

The Miami Herald

Miami, Fla., January 11, 1983

NEARLY everyone who studies the subject knows why the fiscal basis of Social Security is threatened:

• Earlier retirement and greater longevity have lengthened the average retirement period by nearly 35 per cent since 1935.

• Insurance became welfare as every recipient was guaranteed permanent support. Most recipients today will receive five times as much as they paid in.

• The ratio of workers to retirees dropped to 3-1 today from 16-1 in 1950.

• Automatic cost-of-living increases tied to the Consumer Price Index (CPI) wrecked the budget. The CPI has risen 136 per cent during the past decade. Wages, on which the system's income is based, rose 122 per cent. Yet benefits rose 205 per cent.

The system now faces a deficit of $150 billion to $200 billion by 1990, when contributions from the post-World War II baby boom should stabilize it. When today's 35-year olds start to retire in 2010, an even greater crisis looms.

The issue is volatile — thanks, in part, to the intransigence of Miami Rep. Claude Pepper. He has ridden the emotions of his frightened age-mates to a kind of populist-hero status. Any suggestion to correct the system's imbalances is met by a shrill, orchestrated chorus of opposition from the elderly.

President Reagan got burned in an earlier foray into the thicket. He now stubbornly refuses even to meet with the House Speaker or offer guidance to his own National Commission on Social Security Reform. That group thus seems unlikely to produce recommendations before its new deadline of Jan. 15.

If the President will lead, and if Democrats want to lessen their party's reputation for fiscal irresponsibility, the solutions can be reached. They lie in a combination that includes:

• Delaying new cost-of-living increases two months per year for three years to restore the balance between wage gains and pension increases. Fifty billion dollars would be regained.

• Tying future pension raises to wage gains instead of to the inflated CPI, thus maintaining equity between workers and retirees. This should save more than $50 billion by 1990.

• Removing both the income-tax exemption on Social Security benefits for recipients with income above $25,000 and the regressive penalty on retirees who continue to earn wages. Wealthy pensioners thus could share with low-income workers in supporting the elderly poor. An estimated $55 billion would be raised by 1990.

• Including employes of the Federal Government and of nonprofit organizations in Social Security. This would bring in about $115 billion by 1990, but also would increase the long-range liability when those workers retire.

Today's workers rightly resent the fact that half of all Americans now pay more in Social Security taxes than they do in Federal income taxes. Nevertheless, those workers know that they are tomorrow's retirees. It therefore is in the best interests of everyone except the demagogs and political opportunists to adopt the solutions that are so obvious to so many.

President Reagan is understandably gun-shy on the issue. If he wants an even more-worrisome thought to ponder, however, he should consider what fodder his own abdication of leadership would offer to the many who want his job in 1984.

The Kansas City Times

Kansas City, Mo., January 18, 1983

The Social Security convulsions in America continue apace, increasing in frequency and intensity as if following a Karl Marx formula for the recurring crises of capitalism. A large row over the plan by the National Reform Commission can be predicted. But as in the case of the inevitability of capitalist collapse, Social Security doesn't have to die either. Nor does Social Security have to destroy the nation financially.

In the past, Congress has set up these horrendous crises, scaring the elderly out of any possible serenity and then riding to the rescue. But there can be little doubt that the United States is approaching a point of no return on whether Social Security can be handled rationally. A plan for the foreseeable future should be settled now. The power of the elderly as a political lobby is formidable. If reasonable limits are to be placed on Social Security, it needs to be done soon.

The elderly hardly can be blamed for exerting pressure in this atmosphere of panic and fear engendered by congressional timidity and political doubt. What must be done is what always has needed to be done:

First, the United States must try to determine exactly what old age is going to mean in this country and what the country will do about it. Should the government be expected to finance entirely the retirement of the elderly? Should it be a subsistence minimum, a comfortable minimum or a higher minimum? How much should be determined by need? How will inflation and deflation be handled?

Second, the nation then must decide how retirement will be paid for. What is fair and practicable? What is possible without a taxpayer rebellion?

One way or another, the elderly will be cared for in this civilized society. The decisions are to what extent and by whom.

THE DAILY OKLAHOMAN

Oklahoma City, Okla., December 20, 1982

PROSPECTS for a lasting solution to Social Security's mounting problems aren't improved by governmental figures reflecting a continuing decline in industrial production.

The Federal Reserve Board reports a November drop of .4 percent in factory output to the lowest production level in five years. Most categories of industrial production continued to slump, including autos, metals and the heavy machinery that factories would need to support any new upturn in output.

With factory operators steadily reducing production, more layoffs of workers are considered inevitable, and unemployment seems certain to rise above the November level of 10.8 percent, already the highest in 42 years.

Rising unemployment will reduce the number of workers paying into Social Security and worsen its near-term problem of onrushing insolvency. But more than a near-term problem is involved in the figures reflecting a continuing decline in the nation's rate of productivity.

Declining productivity of recent years roughly coincides with the massive growth of deficits in the retirement fund. Increased productivity is largely a function of rising investment in modernized plant and equipment.

But the savings needed to support such investment are woefully inadequate, partly because Social Security retirement benefits far exceed the average worker's contributions to the system, thus largely relieving him of the necessity to save for his old age.

Savings by individuals and families in the United States have long fallen short of average savings elsewhere in the world. One explanation is that taxing policies elsewhere often encourage savings, whereas the laws of this country reward borrowing and consumption spending.

The spendthrift trend in this country has extended even to the business community, where heavy borrowing for purposes of corporate takeovers has become conspicuous of late.

But, of course, the federal government is the greatest spendthrift of all, financing its enormous deficits by gobbling up the savings generated by its citizens and corporations. The federal deficits have become so huge and are projected so far into the future that they bring into question the economy's ability to sustain a recovery if and when one develops.

So-called optimistic Social Security projections for the near and medium terms assume an improbable rate of sustained growth in productivity of about 3.1 percent to 3.3 percent per year from 1985 to 2005. This assumption far surpasses the actual rate in any comparable period in this country's history.

Under Social Security's "pessimistic" scenario, the annual deficits of the retirement and disability funds would exceed $100 billion by 2005. Even under this projection, the growth of productivity is assumed to be 1.9 percent, a rate higher than the 1.2 percent actually realized during the decade of the 1970s.

If the future of Social Security is linked inevitably to that of the nation's lagging economy, the continuing decline in industrial production must be viewed as a chilling development by those searching for a way to rescue the failing system.

Oklahoma City, Okla., January 31, 1983

EVEN before Congress has acted on a national commission's proposals for salvaging Social Security, fears are expressed that the troubled system may be headed for a new crisis before the end of the decade.

Robert J. Myers, deputy commissioner of the Social Security Administration, says the system could be in trouble again by the mid-1980s "if we have what happened in 1980 all over again."

Roaring inflation in 1980 gave Social Security recipients a 14.3 percent increase in benefits, although average wages and payroll tax receipts rose less than 9 percent. The result was a heavy outflow of reserves from the retirement trust fund.

To prevent this from occurring again, the National Commission on Social Security reform recommended that cost-of-living payments be the lower of the average increase in wages or the government's Consumer Price Index if the old-age and disability funds fell below a level equal to 20 percent of one year's benefit payments.

The commission saw this provision as an automatic stabilizer to protect the system "against the possibility of exceptionally poor economic performance," but didn't make it effective until 1988. Myers said he thought it would be needed sooner.

But regardless of whether Congress accepts all the recommended "reforms," the chronically flawed Social Security system isn't likely to stay above water as long as it maintains the pretense of being an insurance system. It isn't, of course, and never was anything more than a mechanism for transferring income from a steadily diminishing taxpaying base to a constantly growing army of retirees.

Revenues collected in the name of Social Security are spent like other tax collections for the government's general current purposes, and are acknowledged by IOUs deposited in the system's various trust funds. The so-called trust funds are nothing more than cash-flow accounts. Social Security is confiscating a large and growing part of the nation's pool of savings and is diverting it into immediate consumption.

Retired Americans have been receiving far more than they and their employers paid into Social Security through taxes. This was possible as long as the working population was growing much faster than the roster of recipients.

But the system started springing leaks when the ratio of recipients to taxpayers reached 1 in 3, as it does now. Shortly after the turn of the next century, the ratio is expected to narrow to 1 in 2, and like any other Ponzi scheme, Social Security then will fold unless changes more fundamental than now being proposed are made.

Entitlement Concept Faces Challenge

The Social Security Act, passed by Congress under the Roosevelt Administration in 1935, was intended to insure that Americans would not suffer extreme privation in retirement. Its structure reflected a compromise between considerations of need and of a return on contributions. (Lower-income retirees received a higher percentage of their past contributions, while higher-income retirees received larger payments but a lower proportionate return.) This hybrid system, a compromise between insurance and welfare, helped to perpetuate the long-held illusion that each recipient was getting back his or her own contribution. In fact, due to demographic factors and coverage growth in the early years of the system, the typical participant has received far more than he or she contributed.

An understanding of the transfer payment system, under which present generations of taxpayers pay the benefits of current retirees, has become more widespread in the past decade. National attention has focused on the funding problems of Social Security and other programs, and on the Reagan Administration's attempt to curtail these so-called "entitlement" programs. So entrenched have the greatly expanded benefits become in the retirement expectations of Americans, however, that lawmakers have become extremely reluctant to attempt Social Security reform.

The Salt Lake Tribune

Salt Lake City, Utah, September 16, 1981

In the plaintive budget-balancing song the second verse is not the same as the first but it is hauntingly similar.

Once again the country is being worked up to accept the absolute need for reduced federal spending if inflation and high interest rates are ever to be brought under control.

This time the script apparently calls for Congress rather than the White House to take the lead. in trimming the military budget while hanging tough but eventually crumbling before the hard realities where domestic spending trims are indicated.

President Reagan's announcement over the weekend that military spending would be reduced $13 billion over the next several years with only $2 billion of the cut coming in 1982, was not the kind of carving that critics of his economic program had in mind.

Congress, which went merrily along with the administration's generous defense spending early in the summer, reportedly is willing to make much deeper slashes now rather than whittle away again at domestic programs.

All the talk of dire need for additional spending curbs only weeks after Congress and the White House thought they had finished squeezing for a spell, is leading to public confusion on a spectacular scale.

Consider the figures. The three-year tax cut President Reagan pushed through Congress early this summer will deprive the treasury of some $280 billion. But budget trims so far projected for the same period total only about $135 billion. Against this background, the $13 billion the president agreed to cut from defense spending is hardly reason for elation.

It is beginning to appear that the stage is being set for a long-delayed assault on a whole herd of holy cows on the domestic side of the fence, to wit, the so-called "entitlement" programs. These include Medicare and Medicaid, federal pensions, Social Security benefits and others.

Long before Reaganomics became a popular term, the entitlement stranglehold on federal budgeting was coming under intense scrutiny. These programs, which account for a sizable portion of federal spending, are virtually untouchable without special legislation. But always in the past the political support for tampering with the entitlement programs simply couldn't be mustered.

Even if Congress were to impose additional cutbacks on military spending, the gap between revenue loss and reduced federal outlays would remain impressively wide. But even modest inroads into entitlement spending could produce sizable budget-balancing savings because the sum of the entitlement programs is so big.

There is still one hope that is given little credence by critics and isn't even referred to much anymore by the Reagan people. It is the original premise that the tax cuts will so spur the economy that the revenue void will be quickly closed. But, unless it begins to happen, and soon, the budget wolf is going to be huffing and puffing around the entitlement programs' heretofore invincible doors.

Oregon Journal

Portland, Ore., August 24, 1981

As it is presently operated, it is no secret that the Social Security fund is going broke.

Will it? Not very likely. Maybe nothing governmental is guaranteed, but keeping Social Security afloat is one of the better bets.

Obviously some changes will have to be made to head off bankruptcy. But Rep. Ron Wyden, D-Ore., saying he senses a commitment through all philosophical persuasions in Congress to save Social Security, contends the reductions proposed by President Reagan will not have to be made.

If it is true that Congress and the administration plan to save Social Security, some argue that the program's date with bankruptcy should not even be reported because of the effect on the elderly who are dependent on it for their livelihood.

But it is that very reporting that is the best assurance that it will be saved, because the governmental system comes under pressure from the people to save it.

Over the long haul, the Social Security system ought to be purged of all services using its funds except its basic pension program.

Not that such services as health, education and disability are not important. It is just that they should be moved to other agencies with other funding, which would free Social Security to do that which it was intended to do — help with retirement income.

Wyden believes that is the direction Congress will take. Over the long run, such a system should be self-supporting. For the short run, Social Security may have to be shored up until it can be put on a sound fiscal basis.

Senior citizens relying on Social Security need not be unduly concerned that their support will disappear, due in part to the fact that their voices have been heard.

Another group also deserves some reassurance. They are at the other end of the age spectrum, the young workers.

Many of them are disturbed by the withholding from their wages for Social Security, believing they are contributing to a bankrupt system from which they will receive no benefits.

But there is every indication that Social Security will be around when they reach retirement age, again, in part, because their voices have been heard.

The issue is not so much whether the country can afford Social Security. The more pertinent question is whether the country can afford not to have it.

The Courier-Journal
Louisville, Ky., January 6, 1981

WHEN CONGRESS in 1965 extended Social Security survivors' benefits to college students beyond the normal cutoff for children at age 18, the step was regarded as merely a sensible expansion of financial aid to needy families. Fulltime students, so long as they were unmarried, continued to be eligible for survivor's checks until age 22.

But as the last two presidents have acknowledged, this form of student aid has become a costly, redundant instance of budgetary "fat" and should be ended. It appears to be high on president-elect Reagan's list of government "entitlement" programs to be trimmed or, as in this case, eliminated.

President Carter's proposal

Originally, the extension of survivors' benefits was designed to help 295,000 children of Social Security beneficiaries at an annual cost of $195 million. But by 1978, there were almost 800,000 eligible college students and yearly benefit costs were totaling more than $1.5 billion. So the following year President Carter, in his ill-fated "austerity" budget cuts, proposed to phase out the program over four years while keeping it in force for current recipients.

Mr. Carter's proposal was similar to the approach taken by Gerald Ford, in his last budget, of proposing to trim marginal Social Security programs to ease financing difficulties. But Congress killed the Carter measure, along with a plan to end the Social Security lump-sum death benefit of $255.

Since then, spending for college-age Social Security survivors has continued to escalate, reaching $2 billion this year. But the primary reason for abandoning this benefit is that it's a wasteful duplication of the extensive student grants, loans and scholarships created since 1965. The federal government now has student loans in effect of at least $5.3 billion.

The cutback proposed by President Carter in 1979 was instantly attacked by interest groups that always have regarded the Social Security system as sacrosanct. Each proposal for a new look at the effectiveness of various Social Security programs has raised the anger of a coalition of labor, racial, religious and senior-citizen groups. This coalition argues that *any* change in benefits would upset public confidence in the basic New Deal program of old-age retirement.

In response to this pressure, politicians were in no mood to carefully consider President Carter's complaints of excess cost or duplication in student benefits and other programs. Instead of hailing his effort to ease the ever-mounting Social Security payroll tax burden on wage-earners, Congress went on to adopt the biggest Social Security revenue bill in history — reflected anew this month in sharply higher payroll deductions.

After Mr. Carter's defeat on the student benefit issue, he dropped the proposal. It did not appear in the budget he sent Congress in 1980 — an election year. It would be a favor to Mr. Reagan if Mr. Carter were to revive it in his lame-duck budget this month.

Mr. Reagan's turnabout

As Mr. Reagan discovered during his campaign, the pressures against changing government benefit programs can be fierce. Thus, he first opposed the present twice-yearly cost-of-living adjustments in federal pensions. But he quickly switched signals when organizations of government employees rose in collective wrath. And any reductions in social spending proposed by Mr. Reagan are bound to receive the automatic criticism of those who believe him a heartless reactionary indifferent to the needs of the disadvantaged.

But the Social Security student benefit is not one of the "safety net" features needed by poor people. It goes to rich and poor alike. Congress created the program in 1965 to help the college-bound; it has done much more, since then, to help this group. Those Americans who are serious about wanting more fiscal realism in Washington will agree that it's past time to drop the extra benefit.

THE INDIANAPOLIS STAR
Indianapolis, Ind., June 1, 1981

President Reagan's proposals to slash tens of millions of dollars from Social Security benefits is causing plenty of heat but not much light.

Some facts about the S.S. system are forgotten in the general uproar. First, the system was sold to the public as an alternative for people in their senior years having to depend upon charity or their children.

The truth was something else. The only reason S.S. is not considered a handout is because most people don't like to think of it that way. Unpleasant truths are often blocked from the human mind. But S.S. payroll taxes *never* paid for more than a fraction of the benefits that were promised. The only way the system keeps going is to tax today's workers to pay for today's retirees.

Through the years a powerful coalition of organized labor, social planners and older citizens' groups ignored the necessity of controlling the ever-rising costs of the system. That determined lobby convinced the public that generous benefits were a "right." It was always considered crass to discuss who would pay the bill.

Actually, the late Sen. Robert Taft of Ohio did ask the question. He said that there was no way S.S. could avoid going bust unless the funds were earmarked for that purpose alone. They weren't so earmarked. He was called an "obstructionist" and his objections brushed off.

So the party went on. Today, the fiddler who played at this dance macabre is presenting his bill — and it is a whopper!

What to do? Well, the government could print the trillions of dollars needed but that would throw the country into an inflation that would make Germany's in the early 1930s look like fun and games.

So there are only two alternatives. The money either must be raised from younger workers, thus reducing their purchasing power, or denied to prospective beneficiaries.

There's no other way and either way a lot of people are going to be pretty irate. It's unfair to blame Mr. Reagan for the bill. He didn't run it up. He's just the guy we appointed to settle with the fiddler.

THE DAILY OKLAHOMAN
Oklahoma City, Okla.,
September 26, 1981

UNTIL and unless it induces Congress to do something about the so-called entitlements, the Reagan administration won't have much hope of balancing the huge federal budget.

Many of these programs, which call for fixed-formula outlays to qualifying individuals, contain built-in increases that are controllable only if Congress chooses to rewrite the laws authorizing them.

But proposed changes encounter heavy opposition, principally because nearly 70 million people get money from one or more of the entitlement programs.

Social Security payments go to 36.5 million people at a cost of $154.4 billion annually. Medicare goes to 28.4 million at an annual cost of $47.2 billion. Medicaid goes to 23 million at a cost of $17.2 billion. Food stamps go to 21.5 million at an annual cost of $9.3 billion.

Others receiving entitlements include 1.9 million federal civilian retirees, 1.4 million getting military pensions, about 4.2 million receiving aid for the indigent, the elderly poor and the disabled, and 10.9 million receiving aid for families with dependent children.

Such spending accounts for the biggest single item in the ever-growing federal budget, but the Reagan administration has its work cut out if it hopes to make much of a dent in it.

The Oregonian
Portland, Ore., November 11, 1982

Nearly half of the federal budget is going to pay off Americans with automatic benefits, entitlements if you will, that range from Social Security and government pension programs to farm supports and food stamps. That Social Security is in serious trouble, both in the short and the long hauls, is now officially evident in the National Commission on Social Security proposals for major changes to meet predicted huge deficits.

But unless the entire entitlements program is reformed, picking only on Social Security will not be fair nor will it free up the national budget in the long term to provide for adequate defenses, better education and vital social programs, all of which are suffering because entitlements are growing out of control.

Consider that in 1970, entitlements — Social Security, the largest expenditure, followed by Medicare, civil service, military retirement and on down to the smallest, food stamps — represented only a third of the U.S. budget. By 1980, entitlements had soared to nearly half of a much larger budget. In fiscal 1983, budget resolutions indicate an expenditure of $770 billion, of which $362 billion will go to entitlements, or automatic payoffs to Americans, over which Congress cannot appropriate a fixed amount as it does with other budget items. Only a tiny amount, or one-sixth of the entitlement budget, goes for welfare, or means-tested programs. Half of all entitlements, or a quarter of all federal spending, are in Social Security and Medicare.

Neither the Congress nor the Reagan administration has had the gumption to push hard for short-term and long-term Social Security reforms. That these can be done without doing political violence to Social Security is evident. Putting newly hired U.S. employees under Social Security, for example, would save $35 billion, cutting future cost-of-living increases and speeding up scheduled tax increases are among the recommendations aimed at producing nearly $200 billion in extra funds.

A proposal to dip into the general fund, which is what is being done to finance military and civil service retirements, must be resisted for Social Security at all costs. If Congress gets hooked on general fund money to meet Social Security shortcomings, it will never find the political courage to reform the system. Not only is Social Security in big trouble, but so is Medicare, which is increasing at a faster rate than Social Security, and has obvious needs of greater economies in the use of and payment for services.

It is not fair to continue to squeeze dollars out of the means-test programs, such as Aid to Families with Dependent Children, food stamps and Medicaid, the lowest spenders in the entitlement pantheon, while the big engines race ahead virtually out of control. The big entitlement programs, along with the defense budget, must not continue to be exempted by the Reagan administration from top-to-bottom pruners, lest talk of balanced budgets becomes no more than stale campaign rhetoric.

RAPID CITY JOURNAL—
Rapid City, S.D., October 13, 1981

Private sector analysts have been saying for years that federal spending can't be brought under control until entitlement programs are restrained. In light of that assessment, an upcoming review of federal entitlement programs is in order.

These programs are open-ended: Individuals meeting the qualifications specified by law are entitled to draw benefits, and in most cases no overall spending limits are imposed.

The largest of all the entitlement programs is Social Security. Others are federal civilian and military retirement, welfare, food stamps and veteran's programs.

Total federal outlays for entitlement programs have increased from $88.7 billion in 1972 to an estimated $350 billion in the fiscal year which has just begun.

In that period, Social Security outlays have gone from $41 billion to $165 billion; federal pensions from $11.4 billion to $46 billion; welfare from $9 billion to $21 billion; food benefits from $1.9 billion to $17 billion.

Part of the problem with entitlement programs is that benefit levels are geared to the Consumer Price Index to insure they are not eroded by inflation. Use of the CPI, however, exaggerates the actual impact of inflation by over-stating the home ownership component. High real estate prices and mortgage interest rates affect home buyers directly but push up the CPI as a measure of inflation also affecting those not buying homes.

Also, the CPI has been going up faster than the average industrial wage. As a result, the income of people receiving federal benefits has been going up faster than that of individuals paying those benefits through their taxes.

Fiscal realities are forcing the Reagan administration to deal with the thorny problem of entitlement programs sooner than it had planned.

In searching for targets for new budget cuts, the president and his economic advisors realized their options were limited. In order to hold the budget deficit as close as possible to the target of $42.5 billion, they determined it would be necessary to review the entire concept of entitlements which constitute the major portion of non-defense spending and recommend reforms sooner than planned.

Reagan has already come under attack for seeking relatively modest adjustments in some of the entitlement programs. But there is no alternative to dealing head-on with this complex area of federal finances.

The entitlement concept assumes that areas of substantial and increasing federal spending are immune from fiscal discipline and that the U.S. Treasury is bottomless.

It was that kind of thinking that put the American economy in the sorry state it is in today. A reversal of that thinking is necessary if the recovery process is to succeed.

Erosion of Public Confidence

Social Security, from the perspective of the 1980's, appears to be a chain-letter or pyramid scheme, in which those who participated at the beginning realized a far greater profit than will those who follow. Future retirees, according to most estimates, are likely to do less well under the Social Security system than they could using the same funds in a private investment program. The days of expanding benefits and programs would appear to be over. Frequent warnings by the system's trustees and other government officials about impending bankruptcy have taken their toll; public opinion polls have shown a marked increase during the eighties in the proportion of workers who feel they will receive greatly decreased benefits, if any at all, when they retire.

the Charleston Gazette

Charleston, W. Va., June 3, 1981

AMERICANS are well aware that their Social Security system is in grave financial difficulty.

A nationwide poll — 1,500 interviews — sponsored by the National Federation of Independent Business and conducted prior to the Reagan administration's announcement that it intended to revamp the system produced these findings:

▲ Almost two-thirds (60 percent) of the sample believe that the retirement income program should be "changed in basic ways," while 32 percent want it "left as is."

▲ Only 17 percent consider the Social Security program "financially sound," while 14 percent are undecided and 68 percent perceive the program to be in financial trouble.

▲ A large majority of Americans (81 percent) are looking to Social Security to provide a part of their retirement income. Confidence in the program, however, diminishes the younger the individual. Thus, 46 percent of older Americans are depending upon Social Security for the main source of their retirement income; only 15 percent of young adults are.

▲ Two-thirds of Americans worry about their retirement income. Only 28 percent express confidence in the future and say they are "unconcerned."

▲ A majority (58 percent) think that they would get a better return on their personal and their employer's Social Security contributions were all payments into the fund to go into a bank. Only 22 percent say that Social Security provides a better deal.

▲ Far and away the most important finding of the poll is the 2-to-1 margin (55 percent vs. 27 percent) by which respondents say that they would rather see taxes raised than benefits reduced. Given the choice, respondents even favor the sales tax to cutting benefits.

This sentiment emboldens us to suggest, as a way of bailing out Social Security, a 1 percent national sales tax on all services and goods, save health care and food, until the Social Security fund is in good financial condition. Services of a doctor and of a hospital and clinic would be exempted along with medical drugs and food. Restaurant and fast order meals would be taxed.

Unless action is taken promptly, the fund will be bankrupt in 1982. Social Security is the nation's lifeline to its citizens in retirement. It is every American's responsibility to make this lifeline strong and secure. A national sales tax would involve every American and would in time raise the sum needed to rescue Social Security.

FORT WORTH STAR-TELEGRAM

Fort Worth, Texas, November 24, 1981

With the press of other economic difficulties getting so much attention in Washington these days, the Social Security problem has been put on the back burner. But it won't go away.

A new Louis Harris poll indicates that while the government has been relatively quiet about Social Security's financial situation lately, the American people have been quite vocal.

The new poll, commissioned by the National Council on Aging, found that most Americans are willing to accept higher taxes to keep the retirement fund healthy and to prevent any reduction in benefits.

"The Social Security system is inviolate and is viewed as a bedrock financial institution that must be preserved at all costs," pollster Harris told a recent news conference in Washington.

Nevertheless, the latest poll showed, few Americans expressed confidence that the program will survive. In fact, among people between 18 and 54, a 68-29 majority say they have "hardly any confidence" that the system will have any money to pay them when they reach retirement age.

It should be clear from the intense feelings Americans share about Social Security that the government must act quickly to shore up the program and restore public confidence.

A number of very sound recommendations have been made during the past year toward that end. Among them are a gradual phasing-in of a higher minimum retirement age (from 65 to 68), a significant reduction in benefits for workers who take early retirement, inclusion in the system of federal employees and others now exempt from Social Security taxes and the reduction of automatic cost-of-living increases by linking them with a more reliable gauge than the Consumer Price Index.

The entire matter is a delicate political issue, but it certainly won't become less delicate as the 1982 congressional elections approach.

In his economic message to the country on Sept. 24, President Reagan offered to name a bipartisan task force to study the Social Security situation and to make recommendations for immediate action. Congressional Democrats have balked at the suggestion on the ground that the formula for staffing the task force favors the Republicans.

This is far too important a matter to get bogged down in petty partisan bickering. The task force idea is a sound one. At least, it's a starting place. And we need to get started soon.

Herald News
Fall River, Mass., November 21, 1981

A poll commissioned by the National Council on Aging indicates that most people would agree to pay higher taxes to preserve Social Security benefits more or less as they are.

The poll was conducted by Louis Harris, who is one of the most highly respected of all the professional samplers of public opinion.

Its results seem to prove that the American people would be willing to increase the amounts withheld from their pay to fund the Social Security system.

There was more confusion about whether they would support automatic cost of living increases in the benefits, but an evident willingness to have the system funded from the federal government's general revenues if need be.

As might have been anticipated, the National Council commissioned the Harris organization to take the poll while Congress gingerly prepared to tackle the problem of how to keep the system solvent.

Public outcry prevented the President and Congress from cutting back on Social Security benefits a few months ago, but left the problem of the system's solvency unanswered.

The importance of the poll is therefore not that it means that the system's financial difficulties no longer exist, but that the public believes the system is so important that it will agree to pay more to preserve it.

It will serve as ammunition for the National Council when that organization tries to stave off any future cutbacks in benefits or services.

It also suggests that tampering with Social Security will be very risky, even for the President or the solons on Capitol Hill.

The Birmingham News

Birmingham. Ala., December 7, 1982

Actuaries for the federal government predict that by 1990 some 40,566,000 Americans will receive Social Security benefits amounting to an estimated $305.1 billion yearly — if the system is not broke.

Social Security is already almost bankrupt, with benefits paid out each month exceeding the amount of money coming into the trust fund. But don't count on Congress moving with any degree of haste to correct the disparity.

While Republicans have been sounding alarms for some time, for the most part Democrats in control of the House are dragging their feet even on proposing a solution. They are full of bluster and righteous rhetoric about the rights of the elderly and try to blame Ronald Reagan for the fix the retirement system is in. But thus far they have lacked the courage to define the problem, to take any responsibility for it or to propose methods for making the system financially viable.

But Americans have not yet given up on the system. They say they want to keep it solvent. According to a survey conducted for The Merit Report, over half — 54 percent — says they are willing to see their own taxes increased to keep the system solvent.

At the same time, a substantial minority — 35 percent — says it is unwilling and 11 percent expressed no opinion.

According to the survey, opinion is not evenly distributed across the nation. Respondents in the Northeast and South most favor increasing taxes, with 60 percent in both regions approving higher taxes. But those in the North Central states approve higher taxes by 48 percent and those in the West by only 41 percent.

While 61 percent of persons 50 and over are willing to pay higher taxes, those 18 to 34 who are willing to pay more drop to 50 percent and approval is only 49 percent for ages 35 to 49.

Although 61 percent of those with incomes under $15,000 are willing to pay more, only 50 percent of those earning over $25,000 are willing to pay higher taxes.

As one would expect, those closer to retirement age and those with lesser incomes seem to feel they have a higher stake in Social Security than those with better incomes or some years away from retirement. Even so, approval for higher taxes is surprisingly high.

ALBUQUERQUE JOURNAL

Albuquerque, N.M., December 15, 1982

Procrastination is nothing new regarding Social Security. Putting off hard decisions has contributed to declining public confidence that the system will be solvent over the long term.

Now the nation's leaders, workers and retirees must put aside personal and political preferences to hammer out a solution to the system's problems.

Confidence in the system is ebbing at a time when the government is borrowing from other funds just to make the monthly payments to retirees. Americans' confidence was further eroded when the presidential panel established to consider solutions postponed a final public meeting to make recommendations.

The debate about specific solutions has become more sophisticated, partly due to the work of the presidential commission, and partly because of the interest and expertise of private economists and organizations.

The system should provide a "floor" for eligible beneficiaries and not attempt to replace the income of the worker who died, retired or was disabled.

To remain solvent, the system must receive in payroll taxes as much money as it expends. The rebuilding job thus must consider ways to replenish expenditures without unfairly taxing current workers.

At the same time, current beneficiaries count on payments to provide essential income. It would be unfair, not to mention inhumane, to unfairly reduce benefits for those whose incomes are marginal.

The most hotly debated changes likely to be recommended include reduction in the rate of growth of benefits, acceleration of already-legislated payroll tax increases, placement of welfare responsibilities of Social Security (like Medicaid) into the general revenue fund, requiring employees of the federal government and non-profit groups to join, and to raise the retirement age.

We believe the system can achieve long-term solvency only if hard decisions are made. The retirement age must be raised gradually. Reduction in the rate of growth of benefits can be achieved by tying benefits to the rise in wages rather than prices.

The public should be better educated about Social Security. Many regard it as an insurance program when it really is a welfare program funded by a contract between generations. Today's workers are supplying funds to today's beneficiaries. Today's workers thus have little idea how much they've paid into the system, nor how much to expect in payments upon retirement.

The Social Security system depends on public faith that it is and will be a solvent supplementary income system. The sooner Congress restores that faith, the better.

THE COMMERCIAL APPEAL

Memphis, Tenn., November 21, 1981

PRESIDENT REAGAN'S proposals last summer for cuts in Social Security increases met so much congressional criticism that the administration beat a hasty retreat. But there was more to the opposition than partisan politics. A recent Louis Harris poll indicates that most Americans support at least the current level of benefits and would even favor tax increases to keep the system solvent.

The finding would seem to rebut those who have argued that younger workers would strongly resist higher pay-roll taxes to protect retirees and that "generational warfare" could break out between young and old over the Social Security issue.

The poll, however, also showed mixed feelings about the system. While two-thirds of the respondents favored use of federal funds, including income taxes, to pay for benefits and all age groups approved higher taxes, if necessary, more than half — 54 per cent — said they had "hardly any" confidence in the Social Security system.

Would the results have been different if the workers had been asked whether they favored a tax schedule that will divert up to $3,950 this year from their potential income to the Social Security trust funds? Next year the maximum tax, shared by employers and employes, may be $4,200 or more, depending on the average annual increase in wages.

The troubles in the system usually are described in terms of such huge amounts of money that the layman can do little more than blink in bewilderment. In their 1980 report, for instance, the Social Security trustees said that the retirement and disability trust funds could run $71 billion short of benefits through 1990. What does $71 billion in new taxes mean? Can't the government just shift funds from some other source?

In terms of paycheck dollars, the amounts are infinitesimal by comparison, but perhaps much more meaningful. Last year the tax rate was 6.13 per cent on income up to $25,900, for a maximum withdrawal of $1,378 each for employes and employers and a combined maximum of $2,756. The cost to employers comes out of wages that employes might otherwise earn, is added to the price of products or limits the number of new jobs.

This year, the rate went up to 6.65 per cent on a maximum income of $29,700, for a combined maximum tax of $3,950. Next year, the rate will rise to 6.70 per cent, with the maximum income indexed to average wage increases. And the bite will continue to get larger. In 1985, the rate will be 7.05 per cent.

How many thousands of dollars are American workers really willing to forego to finance benefits? What other services would they agree to have cut if general funds are used? Health care? Education? Defense? Or would they prefer that benefits be adjusted in one of various ways that have been proposed to reduce the shortfall in the trust funds and to keep pay-roll taxes from climbing?

TO REALLY GET a fair assessment of what workers think and to give them a clearer set of choices, it would seem to be necessary for the government to make more accessible the effects that different reform plans would have on costs, benefits and wages.

The protection offered by Social Security is a powerful attraction. Its attractiveness may even increase relative to the vagueness and generality with which it's defined. Public opinion polls, by their nature, are vague. Who wants to deny help to the elderly? But there's bound to be considerable confusion behind responses that indicate both a lack of confidence in the system and a willingness to pump it up with more taxes.

Growing Taxpayer Burden Causing Generational Conflict

Each year, the number of people receiving Social Security checks increases in proportion to the number of people paying Social Security taxes. As a result of this simple demographic fact and economic factors, the number of workers required to supply the benefits to one retiree, if each contributed the maximum annual amount, has shrunk from 42 workers in 1945 to 3.2 workers in 1983. Just since 1970, the maximum annual tax has risen from $374 to $2,392. Persistent inflation and unemployment are partly to blame for the greatly increased burden on taxpayers; another contributing factor since 1975 has been the indexing of Social Security benefits to the cost of living, which has risen faster than the salaries of taxpaying workers. When the "baby boom" generation, or those taxpayers now between 30 and 50 years old, reach retirement age, the strain on those remaining in the work force will greatly increase. As this demographic bulge swells the ranks of the retired, the number of taxpayers supporting one beneficiary will drop even further. According to projections made in 1982 by the trustees of the system, there will be only two covered workers for every beneficiary by 2030.

If those now paying taxes could be assured that they would receive the same generous benefits in retirement as their predecessors, the system might be tolerable. The National Commission on Social Security Reform has estimated, however, that to maintain currently mandated benefit levels would cost the Social Security Administration an insupportable $1.5 trillion over the next three-quarters of a century. The growing realization that workers who are now taxed heavily to finance the retirement of the elderly will not themselves reap the same rewards is one that threatens to pit young against old.

THE ATLANTA CONSTITUTION
Atlanta, Ga., February 11, 1978

Who says the taxpayers aren't being heard?

Last December, just before recessing for the holiday season, Congress passed a huge increase in Social Security taxes, as much as three times in some cases. It seemed a rather safe thing to do; Social Security is sacred, you know. With its benefits increasing so tremendously, Social Security was running into financial difficulties. The obvious answer, of course, was to raise taxes. That had always been the answer, had it not? Soak it to the taxpayers again.

Now, they're back in session and — you know what? — there are moves underway to reconsider that big Social Security tax increase. Congress isn't the only one who got the message. Speaking earlier this week to a joint economic committee, Treasury Secretary W. Michael Blumenthal said, "The entire issue of Social Security and financing requires another look."

And most of all, Social Security costs — the taxes it costs — must be kept reasonable and fair. Those taxes have gotten unreasonable and unfair. And our senators and representatives have gotten the message.

THE INDIANAPOLIS STAR
Indianapolis, Ind., January 9, 1978

American paychecks have now begun suffering the biggest bite yet taken by the item labeled "FICA" — standing for, if your sense of humor can abide it, Federal Insurance Contributions Act, alias Social Security.

FICA last year took 5.85 per cent of the first $16,500 earned. This year it will take 6.05 per cent of the first $17,700.

Under new legislation enacted late in 1977 by Congress, FICA will grow even more in 1979 and then steadily throughout the coming decade until it takes a bigger share of many incomes than the Federal income tax. The employer pays a matching tax.

By 1988 FICA will have separated the taxpayers from $227 billion more than it would have under previous law.

As the year begins it is not encouraging to ponder the chronic fiscal cross that the average American taxpayer must bear. The cross is this: the taxpayer must work the first four months of the year for government. Identifiable taxes now consume one-third of his income.

Not until May 1, if the entire tax burden were to be extracted from his pay on a priority basis, would he be working for himself.

Of course taxation is not all that government is bleeding from the American breadwinner's income. Through its addictive practice of deficit spending and inflation, government is also leeching away his income through an expanded money supply and cheaper currency, which help pay for vote-buying handout programs.

That goes on all year long. So in actuality the breadwinner is getting more than one cross to bear. He is getting a double cross. In more ways than one.

The Evening Gazette
Worcester, Mass., March 28, 1978

Critics of the Social Security system say it's a poor investment for young middle-income and upper-income workers.

Because of changes voted by Congress last year, workers with middle and upper incomes will pay more in Social Security taxes in years to come than they can hope to get in benefits. Young, low-income families will still be getting a good investment. Those who will benefit the most are workers nearing retirement age.

Social Security is not supposed to be a system of welfare. It is supposed to be a retirement system to help older people live in comfort and security. But resentment is bound to build up if some segments of the population have to pay more than what they consider their fair share. Perhaps upper income workers do not have to receive every dollar they put into the system. But trouble is brewing if they are gouged too heavily to keep the system afloat. Congress is now struggling with this problem, which is both economic and political.

No one wants old people to go hungry or to be in need. But many middle income wage earners now feel that they just cannot take the increases called for by the new Social Security legislation.

For workers who can afford it, a separate system of retirement benefits would probably be the best buy. But only federal employees and employees of state and local governments are permitted this option. This should be changed, both to broaden the Social Security payroll tax base and to make Congress and other federal workers more responsive to the problems of the system.

Joining the Social Security system would give legislators and bureaucrats valuable insight. They would be able to analyze bills to increase the payroll taxes, as well as benefits, with an eye to the effect on their own pocketbooks.

It has been predicted, repeatedly in past years, that the Social Security system will go bankrupt. This need not be the case. A national pension plan need not be financed by crippling payroll taxes. Benefits can be kept in line with what the system can pay for.

All working persons are asking for is some financial security for the retirement years. A well-managed Social Security system along with government policies to control inflation can provide that.

BUFFALO EVENING NEWS

Buffalo, N.Y., February 13, 1978

The Carter administration and many members of Congress are having sober second thoughts — as well they should — about the whopping Social Security tax hikes approved only last December. You may recall that those added taxes over the next decade, equally shared between workers and their employers, will total a staggering $227 billion.

When President Carter signed the bill into law, he passed out the pens as if it were a great achievement. The administration's general position was that the increases were painful but necessary and that, in any event, they could be offset by planned cuts in personal income taxes.

But now a somewhat red-faced shift of position seems to be under way. Testifying before a congressional committee, Treasury Secretary Michael Blumenthal remarked that the "entire issue of Social Security financing requires another look. The increases voted by Congress are a heavy burden for a certain group of taxpayers and need to be reviewed."

He can say that again. And the "certain group of taxpayers" most burdened by the mistaken action of last December is the group of salaried people broadly known as the American middle class. The Social Security tax explosion that awaits millions upon millions of such families can be easily identified.

This year, the first $17,700 of a person's earnings are subject to a 6.05 percent payroll tax. Only three years from now, the income base will have soared to $30,000 and the rate on all of that to 6.65 percent for the employee *and* for the employer. By 1987 — nine years from now — the taxed wage-base will be $42,000 and the rate 7.15 percent.

To illustrate this tax bombshell another way, here is what workers and families with certain annual earned incomes will contribute in total Social Security payments this year and in 1981:

Annual Income	1978 Payment	1981 Payment	Percent Increase
$15,000	$908	$998	9.9%
$20,000	$1071	$1330	24%
$25,000	$1071	$1663	65%
$30,000	$1071	$1975	84%

When you consider how inflation pushes workers both into higher payroll-tax brackets and into higher personal income tax brackets, even as it whittles away at their real buying power, you can see why such a tremendous jump in Social Security taxes has begun to produce an angry cry of protest from middle-class citizens all across the country. Federal taxes of every kind, not to mention state and local taxes, are squeezing the hard-earned incomes of these families.

Social Security financing did need to be shored up. But Congress blandly rejected all the proposed options which, together, could have greatly reduced the punishing rate of increase in payroll taxes. These included bringing now exempt federal employees into the system; slowing down the rise in some questionable Social Security benefits; gradually raising, late in this century, the age at which full benefits would be received, and financing medicare out of general revenues.

But Congress chose this other route of socking it to the middle class with this painful boost in payroll taxes. Ironically, just before the House finally approved the increases last Dec. 15, Rep. Barber Conable of Alexander, the ranking Republican on the Ways and Means Committee, argued that a "vote against this bill will not end Social Security. It will give us a chance to reconsider a major mistake." Two months later a growing number who rejected his advice then seem, belatedly, to be agreeing with him.

The Dallas Morning News

Dallas, Texas, January 19, 1978

UNPLEASANT THINGS, so Adam Clymer of the New York Times reports, fell on the ears of congressmen who, as good congressmen should, have been listening to their constituents during the holiday break.

It was not just that many voters expressed a low opinion of the President, or apathy about his energy program. It was that yells of anger were heard concerning the $227 billion Social Security tax increase that Congress had just voted.

That should be no surprise. To be sure, Congress tried to disguise its handiwork. Girding for the '78 elections, our representatives postponed the new increases until 1979.

Taxpayers are getting rather hard to fool these days, however. They seemingly have taken to reading newspapers and watching news programs. When the perpetrators of the tax boost turned up back home, they were treated to a show of indignation. Colorado Sen. Floyd Haskell told Clymer his constituents were "appalled" by the vast increases.

Appalled they might well be. In its broadest sense, the tax boost is a drag on the economy; it will force taxpayers to hand over to the government money they otherwise would have spent or saved. Business expenses will increase, obliging price increases, deferring hiring, smaller wage increases or a combination of all three.

Congress would have it believed that the tax increase socks it mainly to "the fat cats." Fat chance. The bite begins at about $20,000, a good middle-class income these days.

The middle class and the poor have always disproportionately borne the burden of Social Security taxes, which are the most regressive taxes presently going in this country. Now the middle class' burden is to increase still more.

Not that congressmen will themselves notice. They are after all exempt—under a law passed by other congressmen—from paying Social Security tax. Other people's take-home pay may dwindle, but not that of our congressmen. They are safe, immune from the consequences of their own action. It must be nice.

But didn't taxes have to be raised to keep the Social Security system afloat financially? The answer is yes; the taxes just didn't have to be raised the way or the amount Congress raised them.

The system's problems being deep and numerous, basic reform is called for. The age at which benefits begin needs to be raised gradually to 68, and the benefits themselves need to be scaled down on the good old theory that porterhouse is nice but sometimes all you can afford is ground meat.

All government employees—including congressmen—need to be brought into the system; this would increase the system's long-term liabilities, but these would be lessened by the above reforms. Meanwhile these newly recruited members would bring with them a lot of needed cash.

None of these things did Congress choose even to think about. All in fact that Congress can think of now is extricating itself from hot water by a general tax cut next year. We'll take it. But we also want reform of the Social Security system thought about long and hard. It seems the least that Congress owes us.

UNCLE SAM WANTS YOU

MEDICARE SOCIAL SECURITY DISABILITY

CONRAD
©THE LOS ANGELES TIMES 1981.

THE RICHMOND NEWS LEADER
Richmond, Va., January 16, 1978

Congressman Floyd Spence of South Carolina came across an early copy of a booklet, *Security in Your Age*, issued in 1936 by the Social Security Board. This is how the booklet described the financial structure of the then-fledgling Social Security system:

> The taxes called for in this law will be paid both by your employer and by you. For the next three years you will pay maybe 15 cents a week, maybe 25 cents a week, maybe 30 cents a week or more, according to what you earn.
>
> That is to say, during the next three years, beginning January 1, 1937, you will pay one cent for every dollar you earn, and at the same time your employer will pay one cent for every dollar you earn, up to $3,000 a year. Twenty-six million other workers and their employers will be paying at the same time.
>
> … Beginning in 1940, you will pay, and your employer will pay 1.5 cents for each dollar you earn, up to $3,000 a year. This will be the tax for three years, and then, beginning in 1943, you will pay 2 cents, and so will your employer, for every dollar you earn for the next three years. After that, you and your employer will each pay half a cent more for three years, and finally, beginning in 1949, 12 years from now, you and your employer will each pay 3 cents on each dollar you earn, up to $3,000 a year. *That is the most you will ever pay.* [Italics added.]

Congressman Spence likens this explanation to the title of an old country song called, "How Can I Believe You When You Tell Me What You Tell Me When I Know You've Been a Liar All Your Life?" In 1958 the maximum payroll tax paid by an employee (matched by his employer) exceeded $100 for the first time. In 1966, the maximum passed the $200-a-year mark; the maximum went over the $600-a-year level in 1973. This year, the maximum paid per employee/employer will exceed $1,000 each. Within a decade, the maximum payroll tax will increase to more than $3,000 a year, paid each by worker and employer.

That is quite a leap from the $90 maximum a year, to be paid each by worker and employer, that the Social Security Board solemnly promised would be "the most you will ever pay" for Social Security benefits.

The Salt Lake Tribune
Salt Lake City, Utah, January 3, 1978

Like a preliminary fight before the main boxing event, this year's relatively modest Social Security tax increase is a mere warm-up for things to come during the next decade.

Social Security financing amendments approved by Congress last month to take effect in 1979, were enacted in response to clear and present dangers to the system's fiscal soundness. But the remedy, in the form of drastically increased tax payments, especially by upper income workers, could prove as great a threat to the system as it now exists as did underfinancing.

Emphasis here should be on "could."

It is highly uncertain how workers will react to the added taxes. The tax base has been increased seven times and tax rates hiked 12 times since the program began in 1935. Each increase was accepted with a minimum of grumbling.

There is reason to think the tax bite that begins to take effect a year hence will induce vocal, perhaps politically organized opposition on a scale unknown in the system's 40 year history. But creation of organized opposition and effecting relief are not one and the same.

Against any army of Social Security tax protesters that might emerge next year, there will stand a better organized though possibly smaller force of Social Security beneficiaries.

William C. Mitchell, a professor of political science at the University of Oregon, describes such a confrontation as a "classic collective-choice situation in which a relatively small number of highly motivated voter-beneficiaries (33 million) each of whom receive a substantial benefit, confronts a much larger number (104 million) of relatively apathetic voter-taxpayers, each of whom bears a relatively small tax burden.

"Such conflicts are invariably won by the highly motivated," Prof. Miller concludes in an American Enterprises Institute pamphlet "The Popularity of Social Security."

The Mitchell premise is good only so long as the unorganized voter-taxpayers perceive their new Social Security tax burden as "relatively small" and remain "apathetic." What if the latest amendments so enrage most workers they shake the apathy and demand relief?

"I think you are going to see a tax rebellion on this in about a year," says Jerry J. Jasinowski, assistant Secretary of Commerce for policy. "Congress is going to reverse itself and we are going to come back to some form of general fund financing."

There, folks, is your answer.

Going to outright, if only partial, reliance on general fund money represents a shocking departure from Social Security mythology as well as hallowed fundamentals. But the general fund option is becoming ever more politically appealing in the current financial crunch.

Dipping into the treasury to shore up Social Security means Congress would not have to cut benefits. At the same time it could placate taxpayers by camouflaging increases in Social Security contributions. Workers and their employers would still foot the huge Social Security bill but the relationship would be blurred.

What happens once the Social Security camel's nose is inside the general fund tent is anyone's guess. Predictions range from dire to the sublime. One thing seems certain: for better or worse Social Security will never be the same again.

ARKANSAS DEMOCRAT
Little Rock, Ark., March 29, 1978

Sen. Dale Bumpers says he hasn't heard many complaints from Arkansans about the huge rise in Social Security taxes Congress voted last year. He adds that he doesn't have an opinion right now on whether the tax should be rolled back. Of course, Bumpers isn't up for election, so he doesn't share in the House panic to undo what was done last year.

The House already has rollback legislation in the hopper— basically, a proposal to switch health and disability taxes off payroll witholding to the income tax— the Treasury, that is. After all, the House originated this "biggest tax increase" in history—$227 billion by 1987.

Meanwhile, though, the acting head of the Social Security Administration, Don. I. Wortman, says that he doesn't understand the negative public reaction to the SS increases—that they don't come to all that much. It's the press, Wortman says, that stirred everybody up by writing that the taxes amount to a "tripling" of withholding in nine years. Why, a man making $10,000 this year will be paying only $130 more a year in SS taxes by 1987, Wortman says. And a $15,000-a-year earner will see his withholding rise by only $165 at the end of those 9 years.

Well, it's true that only the $40,000-a-year man will see his taxes triple by 1987, as Wortman says. But what he doesn't say is that $10,000 and $15,000 salaries won't be standing still in those nine years. Neither will inflation— which is expected to push a $10,000 salary to $18,000 by 1987. So those who experience that salary rise won't see their SS witholding rise by a mere $130 in 1987; it will jump to $682—five times the 1977 figure.

And if the jump in salary from $10,000 to $18,000 is a product of inflation and nothing else, today's $10,000-a-year earner won't be any better off in 1987 than he is today, and his SS tax bill will have quintupled.

It's this that taxpayers are complaining about, and it's why the House is in such a sweat to lighten the load. Senator Bumper's lack of opinion on the subject notwithstanding, we expect that the Senate, too, will start to feel the rollback fire before the year is out. Only a third of the senators are up for reelection, but we expect that they're enough to infect the rest of the 100 with some of the urgency the House feels.

THE MILWAUKEE JOURNAL
Milwaukee, Wisc., January 16, 1981

The stiff increase in Social Security taxes is sharply diminishing your latest pay raise. Congress should put the zip back in inflation-ravaged paychecks by enacting some offsetting tax relief.

For people paying the maximum Social Security tax this year, the jump will be a whopping 24%. Not only is the tax rate increasing, from 6.13% to 6.65%, but the maximum amount of taxable salary will rise from $25,900 to $29,700. Roughly 15% of those paying into Social Security will be taxed the maximum.

There is justification for the increase. Social Security is a pay-as-you-go retirement benefit system with today's workers paying for today's retirees. The boosts in the tax and the taxable base-income are necessary to keep the program from going broke.

But with the tax at almost the 7% level and destined to hit 7.15% by the middle of this decade, many people — particularly those at low income levels — will be paying more Social Security than income taxes. That was not envisaged when the retirement system was created almost 50 years ago. Moreover, a form of double taxation is taking place: In taxing your income, the government takes no notice that it has already taken a sizable bite through Social Security taxes.

What kind of relief would be equitable? Short of radically changing the concept of Social Security and the level of benefits paid, there will continue to be a need for the employer-employe tax at its present high levels. That is necessary to keep Social Security solvent and to fulfill the promises made to retirees when they were the contributors.

But at least the government should acknowledge that it is taxing salaries twice, and make some accommodation. An income tax credit for all or part of the money taxed away by Social Security would be a good solution, and more equitable than a deduction, since a tax credit would favor lower income persons. Those who paid no income tax at all could get their Social Security tax credit as a cash refund.

The incoming Reagan administration is on record favoring tax relief in 1981. Some of its proposals are too sweeping, but this is one that it and Congress should consider seriously.

The Miami Herald
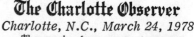
Miami, Fla., January 2, 1981

NO, THAT'S not a mistake you'll find on your first paycheck of 1981. It'll merely be Uncle Sam taking a bigger bite for Social Security. You shouldn't be surprised; it happens every year.

This year the percentage withheld increases to 6.65 from 6.13 on earnings up to $29,700. The maximum to be withheld for the year rises by $387 to $1,975.

While wage earners will notice the change right away, pensioners will have to wait until July for their annual cost-of-living boost in benefits.

This fiscal year, Social Security benefits are expected to rise to $135 billion from $115 billion last fiscal year. Monthly retirement checks now range from $135 to $660.

Raising the payroll deductions and the monthly benefits is about the only noticeable change Congress accomplished with Social Security during the Carter Administration. Studies indicate that the Social Security trust fund remains in as precarious a condition as when Mr. Carter took office, pledging reform.

Moreover, Congress seems no closer to basic reforms such as placing Federal employes under Social Security or removing from the program those non-pension types of benefits that are essentially welfare or social-insurance programs.

Eventually, though, something's got to give. The actuarial tables tell the story: As the population ages and the work force shrinks, the regressive Social Security tax will verge on the confiscatory for the average wage earner.

Reversing the Social Security trust fund's long-range trend toward insolvency should be a high priority for the Reagan Administration. Any progress at all will be an improvement over Mr. Carter's four years of good intentions and stopgap remedies.

The Charlotte Observer
Charlotte, N.C., March 24, 1978

The smoke from angry taxpayers has blown through Congress so fiercely it seems likely the new Social Security tax, which hasn't even taken effect yet, will be repealed. That would hardly be the answer to the system's problems, but the public's anger is a sign people are catching on. They see pay raises made meaningless by inflation and increased taxes and they are, we believe, beginning to understand that some basic choices must be made.

Social Security may be at the top of the list only because the headlines over the new tax make it so visible. What Social Security needs is, first, clear definition of its purpose. Social Security began in the '30s as a basic insurance system to cover the essentials of life for the elderly. It has been evolving over the years into a national pension system that attempts to provide not basic social insurance but comfortable pensions for an ever larger segment of America.

Fewer people each year are paying Social Security taxes, relative to those receiving Social Security checks. The inevitable result is that money either flows out faster than it flows in or taxes must go up. Only now that taxes are scheduled to go up — tripling, in some instances, over the next 10 years — Congress is finding it has a growing tax revolt on its hands.

Rep. James Martin's office reports little mail on the subject, but elsewhere in Congress the blitz is on. House Speaker Tip O'Neill of Massachusetts has already advised the White House to come up with a way to limit the tax increase: "I told them they better move, because if they don't, Congress will."

There is no way to tinker with the taxes to make them painless. Paying some of the costs out of general revenue, for instance, tends to conceal Social Security's real cost, but it doesn't bring down the number of dollars required. Nor does rolling back the latest tax increase, as a number of Democrats want to do. That just returns to government financing its obligations by borrowing, risking even more ruinous inflation than that which the country is now suffering.

The best hope is that the Carter Administration and Congress will use the public's anxiety over the tax increase to take a top-to-bottom look at Social Security. Everything needs to be reexamined, including the idea of delaying Social Security benefits until age 68. If that basic examination happens, then the poorly conceived tax bill that is causing such a fuss will have done the country a service after all.

Post-Tribune
Guarding Your Interests Daily

Gary, Ind., January 2, 1981

It really is hard to keep a stiff upper lip when you come right off celebrating the new year's birth, bleary-eyed from watching bowl games — and are confronted by a bigger Social Security bite.

It's no surprise, but it's unpleasant anyway. The higher tax bite is bad enough, but the cold fact that the Social Security program is precarious makes it worse.

Congress has pledged to keep it going, with some new kinds of financing. The new Reagan administration is considering some changes, despite promises it would not tamper with the program. Clearly, it deserves a high priority.

tion. The number of workers supporting the program in proportion to the number of people receiving benefits has severely decreased. There is a loosening of the rules on how much recipents can earn on their own, which helps. Those 65-71 can earn $5,500 this year without losing benefits, up from $5,000. People under 65 have a ceiling of $4,080, up from $3,720.

Columnist Andrew Tully cited an unfairness in the system that our lawmakers ought to take seriously — but they probably won't. The new Republican House leader, Rep. Bob Michel of Illinois, says Congress should think about scaling down Social Security's au-

SOCIAL SECURITY

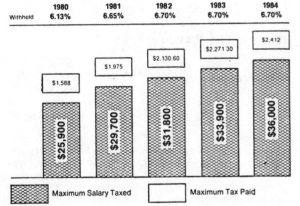

Withheld	1980 6.13%	1981 6.65%	1982 6.70%	1983 6.70%	1984 6.70%

$1,588 — $25,900
$1,975 — $29,700
$2,130.60 — $31,800
$2,271.30 — $33,900
$2,412 — $36,000

Maximum Salary Taxed   Maximum Tax Paid

The spiraling cost to worker and employer is almost cruel, as the chart shows. In 1979, the maximum wage on which Social Security taxes were based was $22,900, with worker and employer paying a 6.13 percent tax each. Last year the percentage was the same, but the base wage jumped to $25,00. The chart tells the rest.

So for some, the deduction will be continous as the new year starts, only higher than last year. For others, in higher pay brackets, the deduction will start anew and drag on much longer. Whether these increased taxes will keep the program solvent is a ques-

tomatic annual cost-of-living increases which are tied to the Consumer Price Index.

People over 65, he said profoundly, don't buy houses and can avoid high mortgage interest rates. True. But the federal pension system is funded by everyone, and that includes those who will have to depend on Social Secutiry when they retire. The pension system is safe. And federal retirees get two cost-of-living adjustments a year, not one, like Social Security recipients.

That second adjustment costs the taxpayers an estimated $1 billion a year. Tully calls it a pension racket. At least it is unfair.

The Des Moines Register

Des Moines, Iowa, January 5, 1981

On New Year's Day, the Social Security tax rate went up from 6.13 percent on the first $25,900 of wages to 6.65 percent on the first $29,700 — meaning smaller paychecks for tens of millions of Americans.

The increase is just one more chapter in a continuing saga. In 1970, the Social Security tax rate was 4.8 percent on the first $7,800; the most that anyone had to pay was $374. After annual increases in the amount of earnings subject to tax and five increases in the tax rate, the 1981 maximum tax is $1,975.

More increases are scheduled. By 1990, the rate is scheduled to be 7.65 percent on the first $66,900, for a maximum payment of $5,118. Not even these increases will keep the Social Security system afloat more than a few years into the 21st century.

One big problem is that the number of retired people is growing faster than the number of workers who pay Social Security taxes. Another is that benefits have been increased faster than the rise in the cost of living.

Until now, Congress has chosen tax increases to postpone the day of reckoning, but as the rates become punitive, there will be more resistance. General revenues could be tapped,

although this has been resisted because of belief in the myth that Social Security is insurance, that everyone pays for her own annuity. This is not so: Today's workers pay a tax that is barely enough to provide benefits for today's retirees.

Benefits could be reduced. If done carefully, this would not be too painful. The reduction most often suggested is gradually raising the retirement age from 65 to 68. Today's young workers are expected to live longer than their parents, so three more years of work should not deprive them of a retirement as long as their parents are enjoying.

Many politicians prefer to postpone dealing with the coming crisis, because it isn't expected before the year 2010. This is a shortsighted attitude. It is far easier to make adjustments now while the big baby-boom generation still is relatively young than 20 years hence when it is on the verge of retirement.

The future of Social Security is an issue that touches the life of almost every American. The choices are not easy, but pretending a problem does not exist only makes it harder to solve. The Reagan administration can make a constructive start on confronting the coming crisis in Social Security by initiating a national dialogue on the issue.

FORT WORTH STAR-TELEGRAM

Fort Worth, Texas, January 3, 1981

There'll be a surprise in those first paychecks in 1981.

The Social Security tax has increased from 6.13 percent to 6.65 percent, and the amount of income subject to the tax increases from $25,900 to $29,700.

That represents a 24 percent tax increase for those who pay the maximum.

The $10,000-a-year wage earner will pay $52 a year more, and the $20,000-a-year wage earner will kick in an additional $104.

Even that won't be enough. Social Security collections in 1980 are expected to total $120.9 billion, but the system will pay out $121.2 billion. For 1980-81, the system is diverting part of its disability account income to the retirement account.

Congress thus must wrestle again with the system's problems.

Even so, the rate of taxation through 1986 is fixed by law, topping out at 7.15 percent in 1986. The recurring financial jolts will be a forceful reminder to Congress that the Social Security system is in trouble.

Some analysts trace the system's big trouble to an action by Congress in 1972 that tied Social Security to the cost of living index, based on a conviction that rising wages

and a healthy economy would cover the increases.

Recession, inflation and other factors put the system in a tailspin and forced Congress in 1977 to boost payroll taxes by $227 billion, the largest peacetime tax hike in the nation's history.

The tax increase, which will pinch this year, was intended to put the system back on an even keel for 50 years.

However, a new round of double-digit inflation is playing havoc with the finances. A new fix won't be easy from any standpoint.

The Congressional Budget Office last year presented a number of possibilities for reducing the federal budget, including a couple of ideas for Social Security.

A cumulative five-year savings of $39.6 billion could be realized by the paying of Social Security cost-of-living increases at 85 percent instead of 100 percent.

A cumulative five-year savings of $36 billion would result in taxing one half of Social Security benefits.

Either course is not likely to be acceptable politically, and the same can be said for further tax increases.

That is a measure of the difficulty faced by a new Congress.

Herald News

Fall River, Mass.,
January 16, 1981

Everyone is noticing the extra deduction from his or her pay for Social Security. Nobody likes it, but almost everyone is willing to put up with it for the sake of the system which gives the nation's senior citizens, as well as many who are not so senior, whatever financial security they have.

The trouble is not so much that Social Security costs the working man or woman more than it did. The trouble is that, even so, it is less secure than it should be.

As with almost everything else relating to the economy, the unremitting inflation is largely to blame. Inflation has outrun the capacity of Social Security to meet its obligations and still have a more or less constant reserve of funds.

Over and above the ill effects of inflation, however, is the fact that the number of persons eligible for Social Security benefits is steadily increasing.

The combination of these two principal factors has called into question the capacity of the Social Security system to pay for itself, as it has ever since its inception during the Great Depression well over 40 years ago.

That is why, even with the funds automatically produced by the increased deductions we have all become directly aware of, the future solvency of Social Security is in doubt.

The Social Security system is far too important to millions of people for its future to be in question for any reason. Now, well in advance of any real crisis, the new administration and Congress should proceed to a thorough reorganization of the way the system is financed.

A recent congressional study of the problem suggests funding the system through income taxes, which would have to be increased for this purpose by 2.5 percent.

This may not be the best solution, but at least it is a solution, and as such, deserves serious consideration.

THE INDIANAPOLIS STAR

Indianapolis, Ind., February 24, 1983

The traditional rift between generations is being exacerbated by the growing controversy over Social Security. This unfortunate development was evident in Indianapolis Saturday during a Southside legislative forum sponsored by Rep. Philip R. Sharp (D-Ind.).

Retirees among the 300 persons in attendance said they had paid into Social Security all or most of their working lives and they deserved the promised benefits, including cost of living raises. Some even cited service in World War II to buttress their claim.

Young working adults argued that they don't get automatic wage increases and expressed resentment for having to pay increasingly more into a nearly bankrupt system from which they may get nothing in return.

Both sides pleaded for understanding and sympathy. Yet those qualities are likely to be scarce as Congress in coming weeks debates recommendations of the bipartisan study commission amid the competing demands of organized lobbies.

The strident militancy that marked the local forum echoes the tone of national discussion in recent years. Demagoguery reached fever pitch in the 1982 campaign with the slogan "Save Social Security. Vote Democratic." Frightening the old folks became a national pastime.

In response, groups lobbying for the elderly grew more vocal. In reaction, there were new arrivals on the political scene, groups formed to represent the shrinking pool of wage earners who saw no relief and scant future benefits.

Today there are at least two fast-growing national groups dedicated to protecting the Social Security interests of younger workers. The war between the old and the young is heating up. The seeds of discord sown by irresponsible partisanship is yielding a sorry, if predictable, harvest.

The Boston Herald American

Boston, Mass., January 5, 1981

Those who did their Christmas shopping on credit cards have two reasons for dreading January. Not only do the bills start coming in, but for many Americans the government has arranged to accompany this with a cut in take-home pay. The Social Security payroll tax goes up effective Jan. 1.

The increase is the stiffest one so far among those voted by Congress in 1977 to keep the Social Security program afloat. The tax will rise from 6.13 percent to 6.65 percent, and the maximum earnings on which it will be applied will rise from $25,900 to $29,700.

For someone earning $10,000 a year, this means a Social Security tax of $665 in 1981, or a $52 increase. On up through the brackets, it raises the tax to a maximum of $1,975.05 for those earning $29,700 or more, for an increase of $387.38. And for employers, the same increases apply to the duplicate tax they pay on the wages or salary of each employee.

Typically, anyone who wants to complain will be swinging at shadows. The tax increase is "automatic" under legislation passed by the 95th Congress three years ago. The costs which make it necessary are among the "uncontrollables" in the federal budget. Somehow, there is never anyone around to accept responsibility when the stark reality of Social Security financing confronts us.

It now falls to a new administration to tackle both the short-term and long-range dilemmas posed by the Social Security system. For one thing, President-elect Reagan's economic program must deal with the fact that the increase in Social Security taxes in the coming year will take $15.4 billion out of the pockets of the same people who are supposed to benefit from the cut in personal and corporate income taxes which Mr. Reagan is advocating. This could make his tax cut a "wash" where economic stimulus is concerned.

Increased Social Security taxes will continue to hobble tax reform on into the future. With the schedule of increases scheduled for the next five years, the tax will rise to 7.15 percent on a maximum of $44,100 by 1986, for a top of $3,153 each for the employee and employer.

The only way to ameliorate this drag on personal incomes and the economy as a whole — one which will grow even worse as we near the end of the century — is to make structural reforms in the Social Security program.

The pain of January's surge in payroll deductions will serve a purpose if it helps break down political resistance to those reforms. Ideas for solving the perennial Social Security "crisis" are amply available from one study group or another, including Mr. Reagan's transition task force on Social Security and a President's Commission on Pension Policy soon to make its report.

What has been missing is the political will to make significant steps backward from what Social Security has been promising to those who support it. While it would not be fair to break faith with those now relying on a Social Security benefit, or planning to retire within the next few years, changes can and must be made in commitments to those who will become beneficiaries further down the line.

During his campaign Mr. Reagan had to defend critical statements about Social Security he had made in the past. "No one dependent on Social Security today is going to have the rug pulled out from under him," he declared. True, but the problem for the new administration and Congress is that the floor is so slippery the rug could fly out whether anyone pulls it or not.

Withdrawals Reflect Growing Problems, Lack of Confidence

Under the terms of the original Social Security legislation, state and local government employees as well as employees of non-profit organizations were not required to participate. Once they opted to withdraw, however, they could not return to the fold. For most of its existence, participation in Social Security was so attractive that coverage was constantly expanded to include new lists of occupations; most governments and non-profit agencies elected to join. Since the mid-1970's, the crisis in public confidence has been reflected in the rush of applications by local governments and non-profit organizations to withdraw. Two of the most visible desertions in recent years have been by Alaska, in 1979—the first state ever to withdraw—and by Los Angeles County, Calif., in 1982. During 1982 the drop-out movement accelerated rapidly as lawmakers discussed the possibility of barring withdrawal from the financially troubled Social Security system in the future.

The Virginian-Pilot
Norfolk, Va., January 5, 1978

Norfolk is in fashion in pondering whether to maintain its membership in the Social Security system. By legislating sharp increases in the payroll tax to finance benefits expanded years ago, Washington all but invited cities and counties—most of which are strained to balance their budgets and to curb property-tax increases—to reconsider their Social Security involvement.

Norfolk City Hall is proceeding cautiously toward reevaluation of Social Security arrangements for municipal workers in light of the latest payroll-tax hikes decreed by Congress and accepted by President Carter. That is well. While participation of public employes in the Social Security plan is not mandatory (Norfolk's policemen and firemen are not enrolled), the City could not rejoin the system should it withdraw. Moreover, what Congress has done to assure Social Security's solvency for the next five decades it could undo, and perhaps will undo in some measure.

For Social Security's growing burden on employers, employes, and the self-employed alike is stirring discontent. Some lawmakers foresee a massive grass-roots protest after the first of the most recently legislated tax boosts takes effect in 1979. Grousing about this year's bigger tax, prescribed by a prior law, meanwhile is likely. On New Year's Day, the payroll-tax rate applicable to employes and employers went to 6.05 percent on the first $17,700 of wages from 5.85 percent on the first $16,500. The rate applicable to the self-employed went to 8.1 percent from 7.9 percent. Thus the burden on all workers covered by Social Security became heavier, and on employes earning $17,700 or more it increased from $965.25 to $1,070.85.

That is the sort of jump people notice. Norfolk City Hall has long contemplated this year's increase and the increases in prospect. Its cash pinch sharpened its concern. Fairfax County,

dismayed by the trend, has filed with the Social Security Administration formal notice of intention to withdraw from the system in two years. Alexandria is thinking about following suit.

Some 30 percent of public employes, including Federal employes, spurn Social Security for other plans. Bellevue, Washington, as Norfolk Finance Department official Franklin Rosen told City Council this week, withdrew from the system in 1972 to improve employes' retirement benefits. That would be Norfolk's goal also, should it pull out. Financially troubled New York City bade farewell to the Social Security system a while back to ease stress on the municipal purse and also to gain benefits for employes.

What has been a slow drift of localities to the Social Security exit could become a rush as implications of Congress' "solution" to the system's woes become apparent. In any event, reconsideration of Social Security's merits by Norfolk and others adds to pressures on Washington to modify its handiwork. Raising beyond 65 the age at which persons become eligible for full benefits, reducing benefits, financing Medicare with general Treasury funds instead of payroll-tax revenue, and bringing the 6 million Federal public workers not now covered by Social Security into the system are among proposed changes being discussed. Congress bought time with its Social Security financing overhaul last year. It also bought a peck of trouble.

Roanoke Times & World-News
Roanoke, Va., January 15, 1978

The city of Norfolk is pondering withdrawing its employees from the Social Security system, an idea which has come to mind in other local governments. It's a case of every man for himself and the devil take the hindpart. Unfortunately, the hindpart is reserved for those forbidden the privilege of opting in or out.

Many, if not most, of Norfolk's city employees have already established eligibility for Social Security. As everybody ought to know by now, the system depends on people working to support those retired. If Norfolk decides to withdraw, its city government will steadily retire people eligible for Social Security; but it will be producing nobody to put money in the pot to support that retirement.

So the federal government will just have to tax other people a little bit more to make up the difference.

Norfolk officials may decide not to go through with the withdrawal. New York City, which once made noises for opting out, at last report had decided to stay with it. But the new Social Security law, with its spectacular rates and bases, could suggest a reconsideration of the first consideration.

Telling the truth about Social Security is a guaranteed way not to make friends but one of these days the grand illusion will have to pop. If every local government that wants out gets out, the system is in deep trouble. If every person that wants out could get out, the system would promptly become, in capital letters, DEFUNCT.

There is only one classification of people who are permitted a choice and a profitable option: federal employees. At one stage in the development of the new law, a committee was considering making it impossible for state and local governments to withdraw. The news from Norfolk suggests the need, posthaste, for such a prohibition; and soon one bringing in also the federal employees. If anybody is required to be on the SS Social Security, everybody should be required; and there should be rotation among the galley slaves.

THE DAILY OKLAHOMAN
Oklahoma City, Okla., September 23, 1979

INFLATION-harried Alaska is a special case, and the decision of its workers to withdraw from Social Security doesn't necessarily portend a wholesale exodus on the part of other state and local governmental employees.

Nationwide, 98 governmental bodies in 16 states have indicated they want out of the federal program at the end of the year, and 147 others have said they plan to withdraw in 1981.

Recurring increases in Social Security payroll taxes and deficits threatening the sprawling federal system are causing some states and localities to think about dropping out and establishing their own pension programs.

Workers in Alaska who pressed for the vote said higher wages there meant higher SSA payroll taxes, even though retirement benefits were the same as those in states where living costs were lower.

But the difficulties attributable to inflation are shared by other retirement programs as well, and the systems of the states and localities have problems of underfinancing distinctly their own. Many state and local governments have known for years that they weren't putting aside enough money to redeem their future pension liabilities.

The problem of underfinancing of retirement systems for public employees is national in scope and is present at all governmental levels. With continuing inflation, the presumption is strong that the unfunded liabilities of those programs will rise in response to future pay boosts, more aggressive bargaining by unionized public employees, and the trend toward earlier retirement.

Withdrawal from Social Security might have near-term attractions, but employees of the states and localities should undertake it only after long and serious reflection on possible future hazards.

The Cincinnati Post

Cincinnati, Ohio, September 25, 1979

The vote by state workers in Alaska to withdraw from the Social Security system ought to be a warning that the program is in serious trouble.

The state employees have said, in effect, that they don't believe that what they will get out of the program is worth what they're paying to stay in it —a vote of no confidence in Social Security.

Although it is the first time employees of a state government have voted to withdraw, it is not an entirely isolated case. A total of 98 governmental bodies of various types in 16 states have decided to withdraw at the end of this year, and another 147 have said they will pull out by the end of 1981. Some 100,000 workers are involved altogether. Several state governments didn't join Social Security in the first place.

That ought to tell Congress two things: that payroll taxes to finance Social Security programs are too high; and that the loophole that allows government workers to opt out of the system needs to be closed.

The high, and growing, cost to workers and the general financial shakiness of the Social Security system are matters that need prompt attention in Washington. Congress must devise a plan that puts less drain on paychecks and assures workers that benefits will be there when they reach retirement age.

Congress also ought to make Social Security "universal"—that is, every worker should be covered. As it now stands, federal employees have their own retirement plan and are exempt from Social Security taxes. State and local government employees have a choice of being in or out of the system.

Logically, if Social Security benefits are good enough for the people who pay the salaries of government workers—we refer to taxpayers—they ought to be good enough for the public's so-called civil servants.

Members of Congress are among the several millions of federal, state and local government workers who don't share the burden of financing Social Security. If they did they probably would be more responsible in dealing with it.

The Bulletin

Philadelphia, Pa., September 18, 1979

Is the defection of Alaska's 14,450 state employes from the Social Security system — the first group of state workers to do so — the start of a deluge of governmental employes, or just an unusual situation?

Alaska's higher wages did mean higher Social Security payroll taxes while retirement benefits were, of course, the same as for the rest of the country. Also, many of Alaska's employes are young or are past retirment age and drawing other pensions.

To those extents, Alaska's situation is exceptional. But their move is hardly unique among public employes. So far, 98 local government bodies in 16 states have said they want out by the end of the year anu 147 more have announced plans to leave the program.

Social Security officials are probably right in predicting that some of these will change plans and hang in after they test the water elsewhere. Alaska officials, for instance, warn that the state can't match federal benefits.

The main point, however, is that Social Security has problems, not the least of which is the increasing payroll tax rate. The maximum tax will almost double in the next five years to $2,412 a year. And despite the increases, the system expects a deficit of $2.3 billion this year and another one in 1980. The current recession and inflation add further burdens.

President Carter has proposed some reforms that would save some $4.2 a year by 1984. They include limiting disability benefits to four-fifths of earnings before disablement; phasing out student benefits in favor of federal education grants and loans only; reducing parents' benefits by lowering the maximum age of children from 18 to 16, and closing minimum-benefit loopholes. The proposals seem justifiable and would cause little dislocation in proportion to the savings gained.

But beyond that, we would encourage Congress to think broadly about Social Security. It was founded in 1935 as a sort of universal pension program. And it has been a great success, so successful in fact that other programs — the health trust fund linked to Medicare and some welfare schemes — have been heaped onto it.

There are valid arguments for financing the old-age benefits out of payroll taxes, but funding these add-ons the same way may topple the entire structure.

Buffalo Evening News

Buffalo, N.Y., September 16, 1979

The decision of Alaska's state employees to withdraw from the Social Security system next Jan. 1 probably does not foreshadow any such trend among thousands of other public employees, whose participation in the national pension program is optional.

Not only did fewer than half of Alaska's 14,000 state employees participate in the vote, but the decision to withdraw, while a solid majority, wasn't overwhelming. Moreover, oil rich Alaska, where prices have risen even faster than in most other states, is not typical of the nation as a whole.

Yet none of this should persuade Congress to dismiss the Alaska decision as irrelevant. It may well be a symptom of growing strains in the Social Security system, and some sentiments felt by state workers there do echo similar reservations elsewhere. Apparently the prime cause of disenchantment among Alaska public employees was the rising cost of contributing to the program. "I guess people felt the cost of Social Security was more than they were willing to pay, or that they wouldn't get the return they wanted," said the director of the state's retirement and pension system. Even more surprising: the decision to withdraw came in spite of warnings from state officials that Alaska would be unable to duplicate Social Security benefits.

The point, then, is not that these employees dropped Social Security because of some alternative plan with superior benefits, but that they were willing to sacrifice some benefits in order to cut their own current contributions.

Hence, part of the Alaskan message to Congress, echoing similar sentiments among many tax-pressed workers elsewhere, may be for it to do what was once thought politically unthinkable: To cut back some marginal benefits in order to preserve essential ones, within a financial structure which American worker-voters are realistically willing and able to support.

THE ATLANTA CONSTITUTION
Atlanta, Ga., November 15, 1981

THE FULTON County Commission has until the end of this year to decide whether county employees will remain in or pull out of the Social Security system. They are currently unsure: Employees split evenly in a vote last year and a consulting firm has recommended the county stay in.

Our recommendation is the same as the consultant's: Stay in. The first reason is that lower-paid employees — and that should be the bulk of the county's work force — will fare better under Social Security than alternatives. Social Security is set up so that lower-income workers pay a greater percentage of their incomes into the system as taxes than do workers in upper income ranges. But, the system is weighted to compensate them more generously upon retirement.

Another reason is psychological. The Social Security system is in trouble. For the first time in its history workers are beginning to question its benefits and cost and to doubt its long-term solvency.

It is important as a matter of faith that government employees — who are among the few who are permitted by law to withdraw — remain in as a signal to those in the private sector that the system is worthy of trust.

We don't believe Congress is going to permit Social Security to go broke. But it is galling to those in the private sector that at the first sign of trouble, government workers jump ship. They have as much an obligation as do workers in the private sector to support the nation's elderly poor and it is offensive that they would seek to shirk that burden.

Eventually, Social Security's problems will be solved. Fulton should be reminded that once it withdraws, it will never be permitted back.

We urge them, therefore, to consider not only the well-being of its blue-collar work force but the message it will send to others — and to remain in with the rest of us to solve Social Security's troubles and to enjoy its protection.

THE DAILY OKLAHOMAN
Oklahoma City, Okla., July 26, 1982

AT a time when the financially ailing Social Security system desperately needs more rather than fewer "contributors," it is confronted with a growing trend toward dropouts by state and local governments and by non-profit organizations.

Social Security is optional for an estimated 13.3 million state and local governmental workers and about 4 million employees of non-profit organizations. About 2.8 million federal civil servants also are excluded from the system.

The payroll tax, which provides old age, survivors, disability and Medicare coverage for more than 100 million workers and their employers in the private sector, is compulsory for them.

A report released the other day by the Social Security Research Office discloses that about 149,000 employees of 308 state and local governments are ready to pull out of the troubled system. About 543 non-profit organizations, including 271 hospitals with 192,000 workers, also have filed withdrawal notices.

Earlier, it was mostly the states and cities that were giving the required notice of two years before withdrawal became effective. But Social Security's trustees said in their latest annual report that "in late 1980, a sharp upward trend began in the number of non-profit employers, especially hospitals, filing advance notices of termination."

Health and Human Services Secretary Richard S. Schweiker says many non-profit hospitals "are being swayed by . . . private insurance organizations that promise protections similar to Social Security but at less cost." He says it alarms him that hospitals should be deserting a program that provides a major source of their revenues through Medicare.

Since 1959, the state of Alaska and 880 other governmental employers have withdrawn from Social Security, pulling a total of 172,000 workers out of the program. Alaska deserted the system with its 14,500 state employees in 1979.

However, most employers withdraw their termination notices before the two years have expired. A total of 206 state and local employers with 538,000 workers rescinded termination notices between 1959 and 1981.

The trend toward withdrawal is explained in part by the shocking increases in Social Security taxation that began in 1979 and will continue into the lengthening future. These increases are attributable largely to the 1972 escalator provision linking benefits to the government's ever-rising consumer price index.

But the onerous effects of inflation fall on everyone. There is no equity in a system that requires most workers in the private sector to participate through forced tax "contributions" but allows public employees and employees of non-profit organizations to pick and choose.

Some members of Congress are seeking to prohibit any more dropouts, and several study panels have called for mandatory coverage of federal civil servants. Both measures should be included in the recommendations expected after the first of the year from the commission now studying proposed changes in the system.

RAPID CITY JOURNAL—
Rapid City, S.D., July 16, 1982

As if the Social Security System didn't already have enough problems, the number of state and local governments and non-profit groups filing applications to withdraw from the system has surged in recent months.

Social Security officials say they have received 1,151 such notices this year from groups which plan to withdraw by 1984. There were only 1,085 withdrawals between 1959 and 1981. Six hundred dropped out between 1975 and early this year.

Among the non-profit groups are hospitals. Sixty-three of them plan to withdraw in 1982 and 302 in 1983.

Although Social Security participation is mandatory for all private employers and employees, including the self-employed, governments and non-profit organizations were given the option to withdraw from — or never to join — the retirement system when the original Social Security legislation was written in the 1930s. The reason was to avoid perceived constitutional barriers of mandatory coverage of employees of such groups. Maine, Massachusetts and Ohio have never joined the system.

Organizations that plan to withdraw must give the federal government two years notice. They do not have to notify workers of a withdrawal decision. Once a group has left the system, the employer cannot again seek Social Security coverage for his employees.

Proposed federal legislation to discontinue the withdrawal option may be the reason for the increase in withdrawal notices.

A congressional subcommittee study found that governments and non-profit groups choose to leave the system mainly because of what it costs them in taxes. Most of the groups believe they can offer a similar pension plan at a much lower cost. The number of governments filing notices of withdrawal rose after 1977 amendments in the law raised taxes substantially and concern increased about the system's financial condition.

Withdrawal of all the groups that have filed notices to leave the system before 1981 could cost the trust funds $800 million in lost taxes. A loss of that magnitude could cause a tremendous loss in confidence for others remaining in the system, according to a Social Security spokesman.

It's possible that not all of the groups will go through with withdrawal. However, the more than 1,500 governmental units and non-profit groups that have filed applications, under the option they have, is an indication of widespread lack of confidence in the system. Were the same option available to employers in the private sector, it's almost certain the numbers of those wanting out would be much higher.

All this suggests that Congress must bite the bullet and make the changes necessary to insure solvency of the Social Security system.

THE BLADE

Toledo, Ohio, January 21, 1983

EFFECTIVE Jan. 1 the Social Security system lost 75,955 contributors who work for counties, school systems, and other public agencies which have the option of dropping out of the system provided they give two years' notice.

When short-term and long-range financial problems plague the Social Security system, it ill behooves such lesser agencies of government to exercise a choice that is denied individuals working for private firms. The actions were taken by local governments at a time, too, when the recent bipartisan Social Security financing compromise makes it at long last a possibility that new federal employees and those who have served less than five years in the Government will be required to participate in the Social Security system.

The largest defector last year was Los Angeles County, with 55,000 employees. Unions representing them objected to the move on grounds that the county's pension plan is not equal to the protection provided by Social Security.

The erosion of public-employee membership in the federal system is disturbing. It is expected that more than 100,000 workers will be pulled out of Social Security next January and another 63,000 or more in January, 1985.

Some question has been raised as to whether mandatory Social Security coverage of lesser governmental units is constitutional because of the pension obligation such governments would incur. Congress should invite a test of this question if necessary by passing legislation forbidding Social Security dropouts and extending coverage to all new employees of governmental bodies.

The aim should be universal coverage of working Americans. There may have been a rationale for a dual pension system when civil servants were paid substantially less than employees doing the same work in private enterprise. This has long since ceased to be the case, and it is only fair that government workers share both the burden and the benefits of Social Security.

St. Petersburg Times

St. Petersburg, Fla., January 22, 1983

One of the little-noticed but vital parts of the Social Security commission's package for balancing that program would close the door for organizations and governments seeking to leave it. This new abuse makes a strong case for keeping Social Security mandatory and universal.

FOR MOST of the Social Security program's life, the rush has been into the program. Many groups of workers and dependents seemed to want coverage.

In the mid-1970s, as the payroll tax increased, that changed. Congress allowed nonprofit organizations and state and local governments to withdraw.

So many short-sighted groups have been withdrawing that the exit door became a serious problem. The Los Angeles County Commission dropped its 55,000 workers out of the program last month. Alaska dropped out earlier. In all, 487 local and state governments and 995 nonprofit organizations plan to leave in the next two years. The trust funds lost $250-million from the 100,000 workers who were withdrawn last month.

A selfish attitude lies behind some of these withdrawals. The employer saves 6.7 percent of total wages. Workers no longer pay their 6.7 percent share of the tax. Yet workers who have been covered for long enough to qualify for a Social Security pension, which must be most current workers, remain qualified. The persons hurt most are new workers, who don't have a voice in the decision. Since many state and local government workers qualify for other pensions after 20 years, many of them undoubtedly plan to become double dippers.

THE PRESIDENTIAL commission wants to put an end to such withdrawals by requiring coverage for all employees of nonprofit organizations in 1984 and by banning any more governmental withdrawals once Congress puts its recommendations into law. Congress should do exactly that.

Despite some poorly disguised attempts to use the program's problems to make drastic changes in it, most Americans have learned that voluntary Social Security won't work. It would convert the program to private pensions for the rich and welfare for the poor, with much self-interest-driven manipulation in between. A necessary part of a balanced Social Security program is universal coverage.

Los Angeles Times

Los Angeles, Calif., December 10, 1982

If you think Social Security reform will come easily, consider the plan of the Los Angeles County Board of Supervisors to drag 55,000 county employees, some of them kicking and screaming, out of the federal retirement system this year.

If the board moves ahead, county employees will be taken out of Social Security on Dec. 31—the largest single withdrawal in the history of the troubled national pension program.

That is the very day that the special commission on Social Security reform is scheduled to hand its final report to President Reagan and Congress.

Between now and 1990, Social Security expenditures will exceed income by $150 billion to $200 billion unless Congress raises taxes, cuts benefits and makes other changes in the system.

The commission has worked for a year analyzing the system's problems and preparing a list of options for solving them.

One change that the commission is almost certain to endorse is that federal workers be folded into the system to broaden the program's revenue base. Federal workers have never been covered by Social Security, preferring their own quite-generous pension plan.

We had assumed that the commission would also recommend inclusion of state and local workers as well as employees of hospitals and other tax-exempt institutions who can now choose to be in or out.

But the commission is concerned about the constitutional implications of the federal government's taxing state governments for the employer's share of contributions to the system, even though the practice has never been challenged in court. Its report may well be silent on the question.

Congress can make up its own mind about the constitutionality of taxing state and local governments. If common sense rules, Congress will vote to include everybody in the system.

Exemptions for government workers were perhaps understandable in the 1930s, when relatively few Americans worked for government. They make no sense at all today, when one employee in seven is on a government payroll and when the Social Security system is starving for income.

Debate over whether to go ahead with the plan to cut Los Angeles County employees loose from the system reads like a profit-and-loss statement, as though the debaters were tycoons and entrepreneurs rather than politicians and bureaucrats.

The political tycoons figure that the county can save $36 billion a year in Social Security contributions if it cuts itself free from the program. The entrepreneurial bureaucrats, at least those in the upper brackets, talk about the bigger annuities and smaller tax bills that they could enjoy if they were not forced to contribute to Social Security as most taxpayers who do not have government jobs.

But the breaks would not be spread evenly. Some county workers would be better off without Social Security, but most apparently would not.

In these times of money funds and tax-exempt savings and similar self-improvement plans, it may sound old-fashioned to talk of Social Security as a program under which Americans pool their resources to help one another cope with a common, and inevitable, condition—old age. But, old-fashioned or not, that is the essence of the system.

When you have money to spare and a long time to go before retirement, it is easy to find better deals than Social Security. But good deals are hard to come by for the elderly who depend on the system for food and housing and who must constantly worry about how many better deals it will take to grind Social Security down to nothing.

Given the special commission's hesitation in the matter of coverage of state and local government workers, pulling the largest local government out of Social Security could grind the system down substantially. It could start a stampede of other local governments out of the system.

As a matter of equity, if not of conscience, government workers belong in Social Security. The pressures on Congress to take them out or leave them out of the system when it starts rewriting the law next year will be severe, and Congress may not have the will to resist. But the Los Angeles County Board of Supervisors should at least postpone its final decision on removing county workers from the system until Congress has completed its review.

AKRON BEACON JOURNAL
Akron, Ohio, January 9, 1983

SOCIAL SECURITY, it seems, doesn't have enough trouble. At a time when it needs as many taxpaying contributors as it can get, it is losing them in record numbers.

Effective this Jan. 1, 75,955 employees of 100 counties, school systems and other public agencies who had been in the system were taken out. That tops by more than 41,000 1979's worst previous drop-out record for non-federal public employees, whose participation in the system is at the option of their employers.

And worse is apparently still to come. About 275 public agencies have given notice that they plan to pull 104,506 more employees out at the end of 1983, and 112 more with 63,149 workers have signaled their intention to drop out at the end of 1984.

The biggest single group in this year's "desertions" was the 55,000 employes of Los Angeles County. It came over vigorous objections by their unions, which say the local pension plan's protection is not equal to Social Security's.

The departure of those 55,000 will mean a $143 million loss in revenue for Social Security.

This trend is regrettable, coming at a time when for the good of the system Social Security coverage should be broadening, not narrowing.

One step under consideration is to start folding into the system new federal employees, both to increase the number of contributors and to lessen the inequity between federal pensions and the benefits for millions of other Americans who have no choice about Social Security coverage.

Congress has the power to do that. It is less certain that Congress has the power to "draft" non-federal public workers into the system; there is an unresolved constitutional question.

But Social Security would be sounder, and fairer, if it could somehow be made universal for all working Americans.

THE PLAIN DEALER
Cleveland, Ohio, January 9, 1983

It made headlines, but Los Angeles County's withdrawal from the Social Security system was no surprise. By law, such defectors must give two years' notice. But the loss of so many contributors — 55,000 — is partly offset by the propaganda value to the system of such a blow. At one time, critics would have used the Los Angeles move to prove that, given a choice, many workers and employers will opt out of Social Security. Now the same phenomenon can be exploited by those out to rescue the system from the financial doldrums. Social Security simply must be put on a sounder footing to discourage such defections.

Pressure is growing on President Reagan's bipartisan commission on Social Security reform to mend its current split along party lines and come up with a series of worthwhile recommendations by Jan. 15, the new deadline. Then with the president and House Speaker Thomas P. O'Neill Jr. presumably satisfied that his own party is effectively insulated from the inevitable heat that is generated by Social Security, Congress can get on with essential changes.

One proposal both factions agree on is that all new federal employees should be forced into Social Security. At present, civil servants are excluded. They have their own pension plan, which calls for higher individual contributions than currently demanded by Social Security.

Of course, the latter was never intended to be a full pension. It made no sense for federal employes to join Social Security when it was set up in 1937. But times have changed and, willing or not, they will be called on to help bail out the system. Their cash contributions will be valuable, of course, but the psychological effect of having them in the system will be even more important.

Government workers have promised to fight a bitter battle against any move to force them into Social Security. They are right to insist that their existing pension benefits and opposition to Social Security are often misunderstood by the public. But that is a matter of education. They, too, have an obligation to understand that basic flaws in Social Security threaten the confidence of millions of Americans in the government and its promises. We believe a sound case can be made for bringing new government workers into the system.

For most Americans, Social Security is mandatory. Many local and state governments, which have a choice, have pulled out of the system. Ideally, they should be brought back in but that would probably bring a long court battle over the constitutional question. For now, we endorse the reform commission's proposal to enlist federal workers. The sooner the better.

THE SACRAMENTO BEE
Sacramento, Calif., January 13, 1983

The most obvious reason urgent action is needed in Congress to salvage the Social Security system is that the trust funds from which recipients are paid are nearly broke, kept afloat only by interfund borrowing. Less obvious, but a growing problem, is that state and local governments are bailing out of the system in increasing numbers. The latest defection, allowed by law for public or quasi-public institutions, was Los Angeles County, which removed its 55,000 employees from the system at a cost to the federal treasury of $130 million a year.

What hurts even more is that many workers no longer contributing to Social Security still will benefit from it because they have worked long enough to be vested. Thus they can look forward to two pensions upon retirement without having to pay the escalating Social Security payroll tax in the meantime.

Los Angeles' departure was the largest ever, bringing the cumulative total of dropouts since 1975 among state, county and city governments as well as school systems, hospitals and other non-profit organizations to at least 750,000, representing more than 300 institutions. Another 400 or so public employers have served the two-year notice required by law that they intend to quit.

The most common reason given for bailing out of Social Security is the mounting cost, both to employers and employees. Los Angeles County Supervisor Peter Schabarum estimates the county will save $35 million a year in employer contributions, and that workers can invest the money they save in Social Security contributions for a better return. The immediate saving is obvious, but to make such assumptions about alternative investments is conjecture at best.

What is most unsettling about the rising number of defections is not the financial impact alone, great as that could be if the trend continues. The greater danger is a deterioration of the already shaky public confidence in the Social Security system. In the absence of early and significant action by Congress, proposals to make the entire system voluntary for everyone, far-fetched as they may seem now, may begin to appeal to a wider public. Privately employed workers and self-employed persons, none of whom have the option of leaving the system, can scarcely view with satisfaction the opting-out by public employees.

One thing on which the largely divided Social Security Advisory Commission agrees is that federal employees now outside the system should be brought into it. That would be a step in the right direction, as would a study of the feasibility, and constitutionality, of bringing in state and local public workers. If Social Security is to survive in anything like its present form, the concept of universality should be broadened. That still leaves the broader question of how the system will be financed, a problem that can scarcely be resolved in the face of a continuing clamor to bail out.

THE MILWAUKEE JOURNAL

Milwaukee, Wisc., January 11, 1983

The Social Security system needs to be repaired for a variety of reasons, not the least of which is preservation of public confidence in the retirement program.

According to recent news accounts, defections from the system are running at an all-time high among two broad groups for which Social Security participation is optional — state and local government units and private, nonprofit organizations. So far, 400 such groups, with a total of 160,000 employes, have announced their intention to withdraw from the program.

Although the withdrawals deprive the federal government of Social Security payroll revenue, they do not necessarily produce a commensurate reduction in the government's pension liability. The reason: Workers have already earned Social Security pension rights.

The trend is distressing, even if it remains confined to the groups that are now voluntary participants in Social Security. However, the most frightening aspect is that a wholesale defection of those groups could erode support for Social Security in the larger population.

Even though most of the working population is now legally required to participate in Social Security, pressure for conversion to a voluntary plan could develop rapidly if public support for Social Security began to unravel. Once it was made optional, Social Security could not hope to have tax revenue sufficient for its needs.

Actually, the program should be moving toward universal coverage. That means all presently exempt groups, including federal employes, should be compelled to enroll. Commendably, the National Commission on Social Security reform seems ready to urge movement toward universal coverage.

It is also heartening to see the commission leaning toward a proposal to require that affluent retirees pay income tax on a portion of Social Security benefits. We cannot think of a fairer way to generate revenue needed to help close the gap between Social Security's income and outlays.

However, the commission also should recommend restraints on the growth of benefits. Without some hold-down on the benefit side, the Social Security payroll tax burden can become too heavy for working taxpayers. Again, public support for the program is at stake.

Lincoln Journal

Lincoln, Neb., January 8, 1983

Los Angeles, Calif., County's withdrawal of its 55,000 employees from the Social Security system draws attention to yet another defect which needs congressional attention — the dangerous escape clause.

Ever since Congress a decade ago directed the automatic indexing of Social Security benefits, the system ceased being what millions still regard it to be, a retirement program. That it's not. Not any more.

Annual indexing converted Social Security into a national income maintenance program. Current benefits have an insufficient linkage to length or financial depth of prior participation. They cannot be so linked, either, not when the overwhelming majority obtain much more than they as individuals, plus their employers, originally deposited during working years.

But because we still cling to the pension image of Social Security, the law also continues to allow state and local governments — once voluntarily in the system — to drop out after two years' notice. One supposes the theory is that state and local governments, if they wish, can provide retired workers with benefits just as good, if not better.

On Jan. 1, 1983, some 100 local governments — including Los Angeles County — withdrew from Social Security. Those 100 units had a total of 75,955 contributors. Another 167,000 public employees would be lost as participants by the end of 1984 if expressed intentions are carried through.

Compared to the 9.4 million state and local government workers now in Social Security, the above losses aren't critical. But the trend is very worrisome. Social Security, in dreadful financial shape at best, can't afford the defections.

If Congress acknowledges Social Security to be what we've described here, a modified federal income maintenance program, one of the constructive actions it must take is to sweep in everybody as a financial participant. And then it should simultaneously bolt the back door.

Lincoln, Neb., January 24, 1983

If the bipartisan Social Security compromise is enacted by Congress in coming months, a little number introduced into the 1983 Nebraska Legislature by the old partnership of John DeCamp and Loran Schmit presumably would be a nullity. But rather than take any chances, DeCamp and Schmit's LB349 should be derailed regardless.

The bill is direct and simple. It would move to take all public employees in Nebraska out of the Social Security system.

Existing law grants states and nonprofit institutions the right to withdraw from Social Security two years after giving official notice of such an intent. That escape hatch would be permanently sealed under one of the provisions of the compromise winning approval of President Reagan, Speaker of the House Thomas O'Neill Jr. and 12 members of the 15-member national Social Security Commission.

The Journal is resolutely in favor of closing the escape route, as well as ordering into the Social Security system all new federal workers.

But even if Congress didn't decide to plug the loophole, it still would be a desperately bad bargain for Nebraska to end its agreement with the feds, providing Social Security coverage for state and local government workers.

Is there anyone out there who thinks the State of Nebraska and its subdivisions, from their own resources, would have provided the current degree of Social Security protection if Nebraska had never consented to be part of the national system? Anyone who does so think is smoking a funny kind of cigarette.

The day of risking the weakening of Social Security through alternative programs which might have individual advantages for certain people, or even a better investment record, has passed. For better or worse, Social Security is a basic program of income maintenance in this country.

It can be supplemented — and should be supplemented — by Individual Retirement Accounts and other tax-shelters for those capable of doing so. But it must remain a fundamental bulwark of social protection and social justice, and allowing an erosion through unit withdrawals is to be resisted, without qualification.

Rocky Mountain News

Denver, Colo., January 11, 1983

THE withdrawal of Los Angeles County from Social Security points up the need to start moving toward a day when every U.S. worker is part of the nation's basic retirement system.

Some 2.8 million federal civilian workers are outside the system, along with about 4 million local and state employees and nearly 1 million persons who work for non-profit organizations such as hospitals. Most of these never were included and some have pulled out under a special escape provision of the law.

This means that about 8 million workers and their employers are not sharing the cost of Social Security. That represents a huge loss to the Social Security fund which must be picked up by workers and employers who are forced to contribute.

The withdrawal of Los Angeles County's 55,000 local government workers will cost the Social Security system an estimated $143 million this year. And Los Angeles County wasn't alone in defecting Jan. 1; about 20,000 workers in 100 other local governments also pulled out.

The government of Alaska took its 14,500 workers out of the system three years ago. Unless this withdrawal loophole is plugged, it can be expected that other state and local governments and non-profit units will be tempted to withdraw because of Social Security's shaky financial footing and the prospects of ever-larger payroll taxes to shore it up.

A first order of business when Congress tackles the many facets of the Social Security problem should be to ensure the eventual universality of the system by requiring that all new government workers join the system.

It simply is not fair to let several million workers, including members of Congress, escape sharing the burden.

The Virginian-Pilot

Norfolk, Va., February 14, 1983

The national commission on Social Security recommended, among other things, that "state and local governments which have elected coverage for their employees under the [Social Security] program should not be permitted to terminate such coverage in the future." The commission made this recommendation to Congress, of course, but don't think it hasn't been noticed outside of Washington. The city of Suffolk, for example, is now trying to withdraw from Social Security before the escape route is cut off.

Recently City Council adopted a resolution of intent to withdraw from the system. The action was taken on economic grounds: The city believes it can do better for its employees on the private market. Suffolk would like to take the money a municipal employee now pays into Social Security, together with the contribution for that worker the city makes, and plough it into a variety of programs that would protect workers in the same ways Social Security does, but to a greater extent.

Accordingly, some money would become "deferred compensation," available (and taxable at lower rates) upon retirement. Some money would go into disability insurance, some into term life insurance, some into medical insurance.

There is little reason to doubt that Suffolk should be able to get a more attractive old-age insurance and welfare package. In recent years more and more state and local government employees have been dropping out of Social Security — a record 76,000 pulled out last year, and another 104,500, including now the municipal employees of Suffolk, have filed for withdrawal. This great exodus wouldn't be occurring if market alternatives didn't seem to offer more than Social Security does.

Some question exists, of course, as to whether Suffolk can complete its exit from Social Security. The reform commission also recommended that any governments that haven't completed the termination process by the time Congress enacts legislation on this point should be forced to remain in the system. Inasmuch as this process takes two years, and assuming that Congress acts this spring, Suffolk might find itself almost two years too late. Suffolk and other governments trying to drop out of Social Security undoubtedly will be lobbying Congress for time to complete their withdrawals.

Congress ought to grant such a request, on the grounds of fairness. But it would also be well-advised to ask what it is about Social Security that makes so many government employees think so little of it, and to try to change that, even if it means going beyond the commission's recommendations and embracing more comprehensive reforms. It may be time, for example, to consider splitting apart the insurance and welfare functions of Social Security, in order to make the insurance part more economically attractive. In any event, Social Security cannot have a very bright future if more and more Americans continue to lose confidence in it.

THE WALL STREET JOURNAL

New York, N.Y., January 7, 1983

President Reagan's Social Security advisory commission reportedly will recommend that federal workers be brought into Social Security, though Congress has been loath to drag all those unwilling federal employees into the program it prescribes for nearly everyone else. It now also seems that the urge by state and local governments to take their employees out of Social Security is nearly as strong as the desire of federal employees to stay out.

According to an AP dispatch from Washington, defections from the system among those employer and employee groups who have the option of withdrawing are running at an all-time high. The system lost 75,955 state and local government employees last year and governments employing a further 104,506 have announced their intention of dropping out at the end of this year.

In addition, 177 non-profit agencies, which also have the option of being in or out, were scheduled to withdraw last year and a further 900 are threatening to leave over the next two years. Social Security doesn't have an exact count of the number of employees involved but it is said to be several hundred thousand people who work in colleges, hospitals and other non-profit institutions.

The exercise of this option of course further worsens the plight of the Social Security system, which is skating toward depletion of its funds by the middle of this year—despite the interfund borrowing resorted to late last year. The defections are not a large percentage of a system that encompasses 116 million workers, but small fractions can look like big fractions when you're nearly busted.

More significant is the reason for the defections. Those state, local and non-profit agencies that have opted out have obviously concluded that Social Security simply is no longer worth the candle. Older employees who have already qualified for benefits are protected. Younger employees face the prospect of paying more into the system and having more paid in on their behalf than they can expect to recover in retirement benefits. Their employers conclude that there is little point in continuing to pay the Social Security tax when less money applied to a funded retirement plan will provide their employees with better retirement protection.

This arithmetic has occurred to federal employees as well. They already have a generous retirement plan paid for by federal taxpayers. Why should they get involved in the burdens of Social Security? Especially so since many of them manage to work elsewhere just long enough to qualify for the minimum benefit, the level at which the Social Security remains the best bargain in terms of pay-in and pay-out.

The option of staying out is of course not available to employees and employers in the private sector. Their role is to stay in, whether they like it or not, and continue to transfer an increasing part of their income to retirees, disability insurance beneficiaries and survivors. Congress, lacking the political courage to curb the growth in benefits, will try to squeeze private sector employees until their yells become too loud to ignore. That may not be long considering the speed with which those who can get out are voting with their feet.

The Seattle Times

Seattle, Wash., January 10, 1983

THE battered Social Security system suffered a fresh setback the other day when 100 local governments exercised their option to pull out of the program.

Federal, state and local governments and nonprofit organizations such as colleges and hospitals are not required to belong to Social Security, although most do.

The agency lost a record 75,955 individual contributors through withdrawals at the end of 1982. By law, withdrawals take place, after two-year notices, at the end of the calendar year. The increasing number of pullouts is carrying the troubled system in the wrong direction.

The National Commission on Social Security Reform — the group charged by President Reagan with making some hard recommendations to pull the system out of the red — is expected to urge that more workers and employers be required to join.

An effort to include federal workers, in particular, would touch off a fierce political battle in Congress, with powerful government unions leading the charge against it.

But perhaps the year-end shock just given the system — particularly the withdrawal of 55,000 Los Angeles County workers — will help nudge the administration and Congress into taking the politically tough decisions that are necessary to move Social Security onto a sound financial footing.

St. Louis Globe-Democrat

St. Louis, Mo., January 7, 1983

Most state and local governments, along with non-profit agencies such as colleges and hospitals, joined the Social Security system although they weren't required to do so.

Many of them seem to be acknowledging that it wasn't the wisest of moves and are deserting the program in record numbers. They say they can provide their employees with comparable benefits at lower cost.

The dropout movement is snowballing. Nearly 76,000 individuals were withdrawn from the ailing system on Jan. 1. About 275 governmental units are threatening to pull out 105,000 workers at the end of the year and 112 other agencies with 63,000 more are planning to do the same at the end of 1984. About 900 non-profit agencies, with hundreds of thousands of employees, also are threatening to pull out in the next two years.

The mounting defections are an indictment of the manner in which members of Congress have mishandled the program. Capitol Hill has gone out of its way time and again to avoid coming to grips with the system's mounting fiscal problems.

The mounting dropout trend comes at an inopportune time. As participants pull out, their Social Security tax payments stop, making matters more precarious for the program.

Most of the 116 million workers who are covered by Social Security cannot leave the program. Congress has an obligation to do right by the 116 million contributors and the 36 million recipients who count on their monthly benefit checks. Time is running out but the program can be rescued. The decision, for better or for worse, is in the hands of Congress.

Internal Problems Plague Administration

The major problems that have beset the Social Security system involve external factors such as unforeseen demographic changes and economic developments. Occasionally, however, a problem within the administration of the system itself will come to light, drawing censure for the waste incurred in a system already plagued by financial difficulties. Some of these smaller problems include overpayments due to fraud or computer error, fraudulent use of Social Security cards, unwise investment of payroll tax dollars and delays in payments caused by the system's outmoded, inefficient computer system. One particularly attention-catching problem was uncovered in a 1981 inquiry by the Health and Human Services Department. Investigators discovered that upwards of 8,000 recipients within a 15-year period were listed as deceased in Medicare records. The loss in payments to the dead was estimated at up to $60 million.

The Dispatch

Columbus, Ohio, June 10, 1981

WHEN YOU'RE sure that everything that can go wrong has gone wrong, that is the time to prepare for — well, prepare for something else to go wrong.

That seems to be the predicament of the Social Security system.

Everyone who can count in big figures seems to agree the system is rapidly approaching bankruptcy. Everybody has a plan to turn things around and put the system back on a financially-sound course, but every other expert dislikes that plan and has another one he thinks is better.

Even those without a plan are quick to say something must be done and done soon.

All this adds up to some sort of chaos

and surely things cannot get worse. But they can.

The Social Security computers could go on the blink and add an extra zero or two to each of the 36 million monthly checks, or they could just stop writing checks.

Social Security Commissioner John A. Svahn reported the federal agency's main computer hardware consists of 18 large computers which are so ancient that none such is still being made. Two of these are being used to furnish spare parts to keep the other 16 running.

That, however, is becoming more and more difficult, according to Svahn. He wants to redesign the agency's computer system. That, he figures, will take five years and $500 million.

As we said, things can get worse.

The Kansas City Times

Kansas City, Mo., November 15, 1978

Occasionally, reports originate in Washington pinpointing abuses in federal programs. An annual refrain from lawmakers, both new and used, wafts across the country signaling a need to crack down. Somewhere between the idea and the action, though, the fervor seems to wane until we hear the same tune again the following year. Now the song plays again, with promises that lassos, guns and other heavy artillery will be used to eliminate waste, fraud and other abuses, particularly in entitlement programs, those historical disbursements that are large and set by law, like Social Security.

Now the report, documenting abuse, and the call for straightening crooked ways coincide. The matter won't come up again in six months or a year from now — if officials get busy and if the legislative leadership resolves to pursue corrections until the gaps are plugged that allowed it to happen in the first place.

The cheating has to do with the fraudulent use of Social Security numbers. The General Accounting Office, which has urged Congress to pass a law to end it, estimates it costs taxpayers more than $15 billion a year. That would be a nice chunk to drop into the struggling Old-Age and Survivors Insurance Trust Fund. It would amount to more than all the

savings projected by cutting selected benefits in the program.

The GAO wants Congress to enact a law making it a felony to fraudulently obtain or use one or more Social Security numbers or to alter, reproduce, counterfeit, buy or sell a Social Security number or card. It is now a misdemeanor to furnish false information to obtain a number but it is not a crime to counterfeit a card, alter a valid card or lend or sell a card to another person. The proposal to replace old Social Security cards with new tamper-proof ones will help little: Dishonest people can still get multiple Social Security numbers by using false birth certificates, driver's licenses, baptismal or immigration records.

Shocking as it is to see the cost of allowing such rampant fraud to occur, it is even more disturbing to realize that these thieves are taking funds that rightfully should flow to the large majority of honest retirees and disabled workers. The crooks surely don't care. The question is, does anyone else?

Congress should put attention to this crime high on the list when it takes a look at rehabilitating the Social Security system, as it has promised. It makes little sense to tamper with benefits when such fraud continues unchecked.

THE RICHMOND NEWS LEADER

Richmond, Va., May 17, 1979

There are numerous protected interests in Washington, but perhaps no agency enjoys more immunity from public accountability than the Social Security Administration. Congress may cast a suspicious eye on the spending or accounting practices of almost any other arm of the bureaucracy, but it seldom gives Social Security more than a passing glance.

Occasional reports, however, suggest that the Social Security Administration is far from perfect in its stewardship of the nation's largest income transfer program. A $500 million mistake in the Pentagon's figures may put numerous top-level military brass on the spot with Congress, but errors by the SSA that run into the billions go unremarked on Capitol Hill. In an agency that dispenses $130 billion a year in benefit checks, the river of waste simply goes undammed — and Congress apparently prefers it that way.

Not long ago, for instance, the SSA reported that it has on hand about $69 *billion* that it cannot credit to anyone's earnings. The SSA blames the problem on incorrect names or Social Security numbers reported by employers, mostly for transient workers. Some the money will be correctly credited when a few retiring workers present proof that they have earned additional credits. About half the money was collected before 1955, however, and the SSA believes that most of the workers owed credit for those taxes are dead.

The SSA also rounds out the totals of its benefits checks to the nearest dime, at a cost of an additional $64 million a year. Ineligible students and disabled workers drawing benefits under the Supplemental Security Income program receive some $750 million a year in overpayments. At least 10 per cent of the 2.6 million workers drawing $15 billion a year in disability payments are ineligible for their checks. The SSA also loses about $200 million a year in interest income it would earn if state and local governments paid their employee payroll taxes weekly or bi-weekly (as private employers do) instead of quarterly.

Those billions in losses add up to a wholesale pattern of waste unlamented by Congress or other national leaders. Meanwhile, Social Security payroll taxes have become confiscatory, and future increases will expropriate even larger portions of workers' pay. Despite these huge infusions of money into the system, at least 80 per cent of those polled in a public survey last fall expressed little or no confidence that Social Security ever will pay off in their retirement years. Maybe some small part of that lost confidence would be restored if Congress called the SSA to account for its waste. By ignoring the problem, Congress only insures that it will grow worse.

The Houston Post

Houston, Texas, October 10, 1981

The Social Security system paid out about $3.3 billion more than was collected last year. Two-thirds of that deficit could have been avoided by better money management. The Social Security fund trustees invested $40 billion in federal securities, as required by law, but put the money in low-yielding debt instruments when other government securities offering a much higher return were available. That $40 billion was put in Treasury securities yielding only 8.3 percent when it could have earned 13.5 percent if placed in other eligible federal or federally guaranteed securities. The difference would have been more than $2 billion.

The practice of investing Social Security funds in special Treasury securities issued at below-market interest rates is defended by the argument that the lower interest rates save the government money by reducing the interest costs of the federal debt. The practice should be discouraged. To use the struggling Social Security system to help reduce the overall federal deficit is unfair and impractical. The Social Security deficits must be made up by various means now under study, all of which will be supported by taxpayers anyway.

The Evening Gazette

Worcester, Mass., October 15, 1981

Critics and congressmen have been telling anyone who will listen for a long time that Social Security is heading for bankruptcy.

If it does, the system will grind to a halt. Checks will not be mailed.

But the problem-beset system of paying retirement benefits to 63 million Americans might just stop any minute and the failure won't have anything at all to do with the money running out.

Social Security checks are handled by a computer system, a large, lumpy computer system. That system operates on 76 different sets of operating instructions and contains 20 years of computer technology all rolled up into one cranky, finicky system that no one seems able to repair, replace or comprehend.

Just to update cost-of-living increases took 20,000 hours of hand work on the Social Security computer. On a modern machine, the work could have been done in two or three days, the new Social Security commissioner says.

Figuring out how to take certain names out of the system, as ordered by Congress, would take 18 months so the work will be done by hand. The computer has so large a backlog that it can and often does take months or even years before the machinery discovers that a client has moved or died or gotten married — all of which would require some alteration of the benefit check. And the system has fallen as much as three years behind in recording the retirement contributions of millions of Americans.

John A. Svahn, the new commissioner at SSA, says 20 years ago the computer that runs social security was among the best in the business. But as computer technology got better, more machines were plugged in to handle an increasing workload. The basic procedures the machines use, though, were never thoroughly modernized. It is, he says, like building a log cabin, adding a wing made of 2 by 4s, another made of brick and a fourth made of glass. "After a while it gets kind of hard to find your way around," he says. Worse, the people who figured out how to get the system to perform parts of its job often neglected to tell anybody just how the machines were told to run.

It isn't that no one knew the problem was developing. The General Accounting Office has issued 32 separate reports since 1974. Plans to solve the problem have been written, then junked with the changing times.

Now the agency is moving its computer operations — lock, stock and barrel — into a new building about a mile away from the old. The biggest benefit of the move will apparently be that the computer will get a brand new device designed to make sure that the power never fails and the checks always get printed on time.

That they are being sent to the right people is more of a problem.

What's hard to understand is how such a major move could even be contemplated without some effort to modernize and rationalize the computer systems that crank out bought-and-paid-for benefits.

If the machine finally conks out for good some day and can't be fixed, you can bank on it that someone will blame the computer.

THE INDIANAPOLIS STAR

Indianapolis, Ind., October 15, 1981

While retired individuals are concerned about how much they earn on their own savings accounts, the government does not seem very interested in how much interest can be earned on their Social Security investment.

Sixth District Congressman Dave Evans (D-Ind.) made a good point this week when he suggested that even while they are being paid out about as fast as they are coming in, Social Security dollars might still be earning a lot more interest. Evans contends that almost $47 million in the three Social Security trust funds at the end of the fiscal year earned only 8.3 percent interest in 1980 but could have earned as much as 13.5 percent had they been invested in government securities at market rates.

The extra interest, according to Evans, could have provided up to $2 billion additional for the trust funds or approximately 60 percent of the $3.3 billion deficit the funds suffered in 1980. He blames the situation on poor management, outmoded regulations and laws and what he says is a conflict of interest for the secretary of the treasury, who must seek the lowest rate possible to finance the government's general fund debt but get the highest rate possible for Social Security trust fund money.

Evans suggests that it may be false economy to look to general revenues to help finance Social Security when "the harsh fact is right now the general revenues are being subsidized by money from Social Security.

"At a time when significant Social Security benefit cuts are being enacted, we should settle for nothing less than the maximum return on trust fund monies," Evans said.

That principle is a sound one but we hope that popular political argument on this element of the Social Security problem and a bill Evans has introduced to correct it, are not considered outside the context of the overall Social Security problem. The entire issue deserves calm, bipartisan consideration, not merely quick political fixes of the sort Congress unwittingly used to create the problems in the first place.

The Idaho STATESMAN

Boise, Idaho, October 4, 1981

The bungle through which as much as $60 million in Social Security payments were made to deceased recipients shouldn't have happened. It besmirches a good program.

The mistake won't break the Social Security budget. Sixty million dollars is 0.0004 percent of the estimated $141.4 billion budget for payments to recipients in 1981 and the 8,500 cases uncovered to date in which the payments were made represents 0.0002 percent of the program's 35.8 million recipients. Still, if the error hadn't been made there would have been a little bit more money in the Social Security kitty.

At least the source of the problem — a failure to compare Medicare death records with Social Security death and retirement rolls — has been eliminated. Also, cases in which the payments were kept illegally by relatives of deceased recipients are being referred to the Justice Department for prosecution.

It's too bad the financial troubles facing the system can't be solved as easily.

OKLAHOMA CITY TIMES

Oklahoma City, Okla., October 3, 1981

IT MAY not have much overall impact on Social Security's financial problems, but the Reagan administration finally has discovered one possible source of savings that should be acceptable politically.

Social Security Commissioner John A. Svahn says investigators have uncovered 8,518 cases in which benefits still were being paid to persons listed as dead on Medicare records. Nobody should complain if these benefits are terminated.

The 8,518 cases reviewed so far involved Medicare's records through March 1981. Svahn says a total of 10,000 cases involving improper payments of up to $60 million may be turned up by bringing the investigation up to date.

Until a few months ago, no one had bothered to compare the Medicare death records against Social Security's disability and retirement rolls, Svahn said, but "they will be routinely matched in the future."

That such a rudimentary precaution should have been overlooked all these years is indeed "absolutely amazing," as Svahn describes it. A correction is long overdue, although it is a "reform" that won't go far toward solving the financial woes of the sprawling Social Security program.

CHARLESTON EVENING POST

Charleston, S.C., October 8, 1981

Tales of fraud and waste in the federal bureaucracy have become routine. But just when you think you've heard it all, along comes a report about a computer system crisis within the Social Security Administration that, all other problems aside, makes one wonder if the agency can survive.

While the massive computer system may be on the verge of a nervous breakdown, the shocker is that employees within the agency apparently have been intent on bringing it down. The General Accounting Office currently is investigating 45 acts of vandalism by employees including computer memory discs being intentionally scratched, tapes containing beneficiary information thrown in the trash and machinery being damaged. Someone even urinated on one large computer disc-drive unit.

There are more than 8,000 cases where Social Security benefits are being sent to people who have been dead for at least two years and officials now say that some of those cases indicate "employee involvement." In addition to outright fraud, some employees reportedly attempted to intimidate the outside experts brought in to try to fix the system. There were constant threats of sabotage, including the destruction of the computer program tapes. While no one went that far, there were instances where plugs of operating computer equipment were kicked out of the wall sockets and air conditioning systems unplugged, causing valuable machinery to overheat.

As if that's not enough, the system itself, which gives the orders to print checks that total 23 percent of all federal spending, may be terminally ill. Reports are that the 1,200 computer programs that run the system have been amended so many times that no one understands them anymore. When the system had to be re-programmed last June because of cost-of-living increases, the effort required 20,000 man-hours of programmers' work and 2,500 hours of computer processing time. Then the system nearly collapsed before the checks could be sent out. While honest taxpayers have been responsible for uncovering some whopping mistakes from that effort, at this point no one knows the extent of the errors.

The talk now is that the Social Security computer system needs might have to be contracted out to a private company that can understand and support large computer operations. That should have happened yesterday. Congress should be up in arms.

We'd been told the Social Security crisis was monetary — that the retirement fund could run out of money before the end of 1982 unless something is done. Now we learn that a crisis within could be even more threatening.

RAPID CITY JOURNAL—

Rapid City, S.D., October 8, 1981

The woes and abuses of the Social Security system have been well documented lately, and various recommendations have been tossed around by Congress and the Reagan administration about how to cure its ills.

U.S. Rep. J.J. Pickle, D-Texas, who's in charge of the House subcommittee which oversees the system, has said "there is no more important issue" than restoring financial stability to Social Security. But he admits, "The prospects are not very pleasant."

Now, from the Wall Street Journal, comes the chilling report that a fair share of the system's problems are internal, specifically meaning within its huge computer complex at Woodlawn, Md. The newspaper reported the problem is compounded by "fraud, sabotage, human error and confusion.

"The 1,200 computer programs that run the system have been amended and amended to the point where no one really understands them anymore. That, coupled with a chronic lack of trained computer technicians at the Social Security agency, is making even simple changes dictated by Congress difficult to put into effect."

It's no small problem. That computer system next year will authorize the writing of some $170 billion in checks to 50 million people, including recipients of Social Security retirement and disability insurance benefits, Medicare and supplemental benefits for the blind, disabled and aged.

But, the newspaper reported, the computer center's ability to perform its large task is hampered internally by low morale and acts of vandalism by employees, several documented cases of employee fraud (one person drew a 10-year prison sentence upon conviction), records complicated by misspelled names and other misinformation, and a general lack of trained personnel. Many good employees have left for better paying jobs in the private sector. The computer system that was considered the best available when it was installed during the 1960s has become much less efficient, adding, in no small part, to the overall problems Social Security faces.

Social Security officials say new hardware and a new computer building are needed. Congress authorized the building but not the new computers. Now officials say computer system work may have to be contracted out to a private company to become more efficient.

Meanwhile, illegal payments totaling millions and other abuses of the system continue. It's kind of like wondering why the mechanic didn't fix your car and finding out he doesn't know how to use a wrench.

So, perhaps before coming up with new legislation to financially cure the system (which likely would mean payroll deduction increases), the mechanics of the system should be overhauled. That's easier said than done, but so are the other — the chicken before the egg — proposals Congress and the administration are discussing.

AKRON BEACON JOURNAL

Akron, Ohio, October 4, 1981

ALL DURING his election campaign, President Reagan criticized the waste and fraud in federal government — as candidates for high office are wont to do. He promised, as candidates usually do, that if elected he would weed out such waste and fraud.

Apparently he meant what he said.

Among the early indications:

● In a federal review of Social Security disability claims, government officials found that 17 percent of the working-age population claim they are unable to work because of some sort of disability. But when examiners started their review, they disallowed 38 percent of the first 1,300 claims examined in New York, and 28 percent in New Jersey — even more than federal officials anticipated. The review is not yet finished.

● An inquiry involving the Health and Human Services Department, the Social Security Administration, postal inspectors and the FBI has revealed that up to $60 million has been improperly paid out to recipients of Social Security *after* their death. Some of the payments continued for 10 to 15 years, with the biggest payout to date of $63,000 to someone who died in 1967.

● Efforts will be intensified to recover $25 billion in overdue debts owed to the U. S. government. The administration may ask the Congress to turn these debts over to private agencies and to authorize garnishment of wages for federal employees with overdue loans.

It's too bad that people cheat and neglect to pay their debts, but it's good that President Reagan is keeping his promise. These three inquiries alone are a good beginning — one that would go a long way toward finding another few billion to apply against that trillion-dollar deficit.

The Boston Herald American

Boston, Mass., October 23, 1981

It's hard to believe in these days of precise computerization that the Social Security Administration has been sending out monthly checks to persons who have been deceased for as long as 15 years.

Such checks in the mail must have proved too much of a temptation to relatives of the dead. They signed them and cashed them with no one being the wiser.

Recent evidence shows some 8,000 dead people have been sent checks over the years — a federal bungle that has cost $60 million. No wonder Social Security is in bad straits.

SSA Commissioner John Svahn says he finds such payments astounding. "The thing that amazes me," he says, "is that no one ever thought about it, no one ever did anything about it."

Now the Department of Health and Human Services is busy fixing the glitch. It believes a sizable part of the illegal payments can be recovered. By removing the dead from the rolls $26 million can be saved the first year alone.

Svahn said computer tapes of the Social Security Administration and of Medicare will be matched from now on so that a death will be immediately known by both. County coroner and funeral home reports also will be checked to find any others that are deceased and still receiving Social Security funds.

It's about time.

BUFFALO EVENING NEWS

Buffalo, N.Y., October 8, 1981

Social Security is a vital federal program that has generally remained untainted by scandal. It has a fine reputation. And that is the best reason we know for vigorous investigation of evidence suggesting that Social Security checks continued to be paid to perhaps 8,000 recipients after they had died.

These overpayments may tally more than $60 million, federal officials indicate, and they would result from friends or relatives of former recipients cashing their Social Security checks after they had died.

It is possible, too, that the scandal is broader than is now known. The 8,000 cases under investigation all involve former Medicare patients. But this category includes only 20 million of the 36 million pension recipients.

Social Security Commissioner John Svahn remarked that the "thing that amazes me is that no one ever thought about it, no one ever did anything about it." Now, fortunately, the problem has been detected and something is being done to correct it.

The objective should be to reclaim the lost funds and, equally important, to tighten procedures in ways that can protect Social Security from any future scandal. The present investigation must be pressed, its dimensions fully explored and exposed. Whatever steps are necessary should be taken to prosecute offenders and assure that those responsible repay the program for benefits fraudulently received from it. That is the best way to preserve Social Security's reputation as an effective, cheat-free program.

The Cincinnati Post

Cincinnati, Ohio, October 7, 1981

The Social Security Administration may have paid more than $60 million to 8518 dead people. In one instance, Social Security checks were sent out to a deceased person every month for 15 years.

The "slip-up" came to light when the SSA discovered that in 8518 cases its employees had not matched death reports of Medicare patients with Social Security rolls to make sure that benefits were cut off.

Most of the checks, which averaged $242 a month, were presumably cashed by relatives or friends of the deceased, and officials are confident that "a sizeable part" of the overpayment will be recovered, with or without legal action.

They are also looking into the possibility that some dishonest Social Security employees who monitor death notices may have diverted payments to themselves.

With public confidence in the integrity of the Social Security system as low as it is, SSA officials had better take a long, hard and thorough look.

The Seattle Times

Seattle, Wash., October 5, 1981

THERE'S no excuse for the large number of persons recently revealed to have illegally cashed Social Security checks sent to dead relatives, but the crime certainly has been aided and abetted by an inept Social Security Administration.

The revelation that government investigators have uncovered at least 8,500 cases in which Social Security benefits are still being paid to people listed as dead on Medicare records is a sad commentary on bureaucratic efficiency. The investigation may uncover as many as 10,000 dead people whose accounts are still drawing monthly Social Security checks involving up to $60 million in overpayments.

The most troublesome aspect is that while Medicare is run by Social Security's sister agency, the Health Care Financing Administration, Social Security handles its computer records. And, until a few months ago, no one had ever checked the Medicare death records against the Social Security disability and retirement rolls.

In this computerized age, it must not have been that difficult a task, because Social Security says it will cross-check the records from now on.

Several of the payments to dead people stretch back to 1966, the year Medicare started. A total of $63,000 was paid to someone who died in 1967.

The relatives who received the checks should have notified Social Security of the deaths. Many will be prosecuted for illegally cashing the checks, and the government says it expects to recover most of the known overpayments.

That hardly excuses an oversight dating back 15 years. Social Security faces enough problems without $60 million foul-ups.

THE BISMARCK TRIBUNE

Bismarck, N.D., October 14, 1981

The woes of the Social Security program continue to mount.

And not all of those woes can be attributed to a changing work force, inflation or past congressional desires to provide too many benefits for too many people.

Some of the woes have their beginning much closer to home, like in how the program is administered in the most basic sense.

As if the program didn't have enough problems just keeping its financial head above water meeting its legitimate obligations, now word comes that it may have made more than $60 million in overpayments to, of all things, dead people.

There's nothing very complicated about what has happened. Government investigators have uncovered at least 8,500 cases in which Social Security benefits are still being paid to people who are listed as dead on Medicare records. The number of dead people still receiving benefits may reach 10,000 before the investigation is completed.

And if things go as they normally do in such bureaucratic foulups, the 10,000 and $60 million figures may be grossly understated when all the returns are in.

And although a great effort is being expended within the Social Security administration to blame an "archaic" computer system for the continued payment of benefits to dead people, the fact is that the technology and methodology to prevent the problem did exist within the program.

All that had to be done — and what was done, in fact, to uncover the problem — was to check the Medicare death records against the Social Security disability and retirement rolls. That is not a simple task, of course, but it certainly would appear to be reasonable, particularly in light of the fact that of the first 2,850 such cases initially checked, 1,100 were found to show dead people getting undeserved benefits.

And, it is a step that the administration is now taking as a matter of regular procedure. A case of closing the barndoor after a $60 million horse has gotten away.

For some reason, we don't share the administration's optimism that it will be able to recoup the overpayment as easily as it says. And if it does, it probably will cost $70 million to get back the $60 million.

At a time when great debates are going on in Congress and across the country about cutting minimum Social Security benefits and making other severe adjustments in the program to keep it solvent for the next generation, it is totally disturbing to see such poor management.

It is obvious that more needs to be done to clean up the Social Security act within its own administration before the public can be expected to approve more far-reaching changes in the program.

THE DAILY HERALD

Biloxi, Miss., December 1, 1981

Everyone who cares at all about the fiscal integrity of the Social Security System experienced some degree of shock several weeks ago upon learning that the government is paying benefit checks to people listed as dead on Medicare records.

Investigators initially reported 8,500 cases, but at the same time Social Security Commissioner John A. Svahn said the continuing investigation may uncover as many as 10,000 dead people still receiving Social Security checks. As much as $60 million in overpayments may be involved. In one case, $63,000 has been paid out on the account of someone who died in 1967.

A system already in trouble because it has too few workers paying into it and too many taking too much out of it, doesn't need sloppy and incompetent office procedures to add to its woes. There is a move in Congress to mandate administrative reforms.

Not long after the payments to the graveyard residents were revealed, columnist Jack Anderson advises us that because the benefit checks are actually dispersed by the Treasury Department, not by the Social Security administration, Social Security is charged as if the money had been spent but is deprived of the use of undisbursed funds whenever benefit checks go uncashed. There are some $203 million in uncashed Social Security checks, a sum which, if invested at current interest rates, could generate substantial revenues for the Social Security trust fund.

Concerned about payments to dead people, Louisiana Rep. Robert L. Livingston proposed a system to let the government know when a beneficiary's payments should be stopped. His bill has 31 co-sponsors, an optimistic indication of its chance of passage.

His plan would require states to file with the Social Security Administration the name, SS number and death date of every individual who died within a six-month period. That's so simple it's difficult to believe that someone in the vast Social Security System hadn't thought about it years ago. Each state requires a death certificate be filed in every death; passing that information along to Social Security should be simple.

It should also be simple for Congress to adjust the bookkeeping procedures so that the Social Security System would receive whatever benefits are possible because of uncashed checks it has caused to be issued.

Both actions would be relatively minor adjustments to the vast Social Security System and certainly won't be sufficient to cure that system's major problems. But they would help some and the system needs all the help it can get.

ALBUQUERQUE JOURNAL

Albuquerque, N.M., October 5, 1981

It looks like the Reagan administration may have found a place to cut Social Security expenditures in a manner that will go unchallenged in Congress.

A check between Social Security and Medicare computer data revealed that as may as 10,000 dead persons may be receiving monthly Social Security checks. The total could be up to $60 million in overpayments.

Reasons for the benefit checks continuing to flow to deceased recipients ranged from fraud on the part of heirs, to failure of the Social Security Administration to purge their records when notified of the late recipients' death.

It's disheartening to learn that such a discrepancy would be allowed to grow to such a volume before being discovered. In recent years, the deteriorating condition of the system's financial reserves have been widely known.

But it tracks with a widely-held perception of government, the perception that significant cuts could be made in federal budgets through the elimination of waste and fraud.

The Book of the Dead is kept by vital statistics bureaus in every state in the union. The Social Security Administration maintains fulltime offices in most major cities in the country.

With upwards of $60 million or more to be saved, it seems like somebody from those offices could routinely check the public records on death certificates and purge the names of the expired from Social Security rolls in every state.

County clerks sometimes have problems with dead persons "voting," the Social Security Administration has a problem with the dead collecting benefits. If we could just figure a way to keep the dearly departed on the tax rolls, their immortality would be complete.

Lincoln Journal

Lincoln, Neb., August 9, 1982

Even if the Social Security Administration solves its prime problem — locating enough cash to pay citizens what's due them — it still faces another major headache. That's figuring out exactly who is eligible for benefits, and how much.

To begin with, the system is running two to three years behind in recording earnings on which Social Security taxes were paid. On top of that, it is making errors at an astounding rate.

For 1978, corrections are being made in about 3 million accounts, including some 575,000, or 90 percent, of those drawing U.S. Air Force pay. For 1979, corrections will probably total around 2 million, and the same for 1980. Who knows what that tally will be on 1981, since Social Security workers are just getting around to doing the record keeping for that year?

In an effort to cope with the situation, the Social Security Administration itself is recommending that citizens check every two to three years to see what's been credited to their account. You mail in a postal card available at Social Security offices.

The system then, in a few months, sends you back a record of what shows up under your number. If it seems out of line, you should make inquiries. This is what one CBS technician did, and it led to the discovery that Social Security had failed to list any 1979 earnings for 8,000 CBS employes

Such monitoring is sensible, but as more and more citizens ask for an accounting, the burden on the system can only increase, putting it further behind in its work.

The villain in all this — or at least one villain — is the system's computers. They were modern in the mid-1960s but no longer. So much fooling around has been done with them over the years that virtually no one knows exactly how they work.

Social Security Commissioner John A. Svahn has a $478 million plan to install new computers and programs and avert what he calls "a disaster." You don't do that kind of project overnight, of course, so the sooner it gets started the better.

Congress has yet to resolve basic long-range questions confronting Social Security. That, too, will take time. What it should do quickly is insure that the system has the resources to bring its record keeping up to date.

Benefits may, in years to come, be less than what citizens had hoped for. But at least recipients should have the assurance that they will be paid accurately and promptly.

The Tennessean

Nashville, Tenn., July 23, 1982

THE age of the computer has brought its own brand of headache to the Social Security Administration.

Early last March, 539 retired workers received checks averaging $4,400. Many were puzzled. So were Social Security offices when some of the people began bringing the checks to Social Security's attention.

The problem began when the computers used to code the tapes that trigger benefit checks with the wages earned by retirees in 1981 hit a snag. The amount would be compared with the amount the agency withheld on the basis of advanced estimates of earnings. Previous benefits paid and legislative changes would be factored in and a payment or a notice of an overpayment would be sent to retirees.

Unfortunately for the Social Security Administration, improper validation of the tapes before they left the computer caused them to refund the entire amount withheld.

Computer headache number two for the agency has been a system simply known as UPS (uninterruptible power source). UPS, a $2 million complex of storage batteries and jet-powered turbine generators, is supposed to keep the power running to the computers at all times. Except, the agency discovered, during thunderstorms. Twice this year — during thunderstorms — UPS went down, leaving the computer center powerless.

So now, according to Social Security's Mr. John R. Wicklein, the agency will seek an additional $650,000 for electronic diagnostic equipment that will show whose fault it is when the power goes down.

The third headache comes from a computerized access-control system designed to discourage fraud, theft and damage to equipment by permitting only persons who work in a given area to enter that area.

The system has not stopped computer fraud. Inspectors learned in March that a claims representative embezzled $104,500 through a variety of ruses, including the creation of six fictitious beneficiaries.

Federal inspectors who interviewed the claims representative discovered that his computer manipulations had triggered electronic "alerts" — the only catch was the alerts were always handled by the claims representative, who was allowed to audit his own cases.

Mr. Wicklein says his agency has added controls to reduce vulnerability and is busy installing new "intelligent terminals" to keep a record of the author of each computer entry and provide an audit trail that will make it easier and faster to trace the perpetrator.

Unless there's a thunderstorm.

The Star-Ledger

Newark, N.J., August 11, 1982

As though there weren't already enough doubts and questions about the future of Social Security payments, along comes word from Washington that the people who administer the program are, to put it nicely, somewhat error-prone.

For 1980, Social Security Administration personnel have already detected and corrected 2 million mistakes in entering individuals' earnings, and the search for errors is still under way. Before the records closed on 1978, the error correction total was 3 million — including 14,000 employes of one company, Western Union.

What makes this staggering accumulation of annual mistakes especially worrisome is that each employe or self-employed person is supposed to make certain that his or her own record at Social Security is correct. This is a responsibility most people don't know they have.

Pension and other Social Security benefits are based largely on earnings that have been subject to the Social Security tax. Errors could easily translate into reduced benefits.

Acknowledging its propensity for error, the Social Security Administration now advises everyone paying into the system to check every two or three years on the accuracy of his account. A postal-card form is available from Social Security for this purpose.

It's a shame that government can't be depended on to do a more accurate job than it is doing. But under the circumstances, persons subject to the Social Security tax would be foolish not to make the suggested check on the bookkeeping every two or three years.

Portland Press Herald

Portland, Maine, September 23, 1982

The Social Security Administration says it has made more than $2 billion in overpayments to recipients who fail to report income that would have reduced their benefit checks.

Certainly there's something to be said for the federal government making a vigorous effort to collect those outstanding debts. But there's no defense for the scare tactics which apparently have been employed to hound elderly recipients, sometimes just to collect a few pennies.

According to testimony before the House Select Committee on Aging, Social Security officials have used repeated dunning notices, intimidation and misinformation in an effort to get recipients to return overpayments. A 93-year-old man was told his benefits would be cut off unless he made good on a $2.88 debt. One Social Security office held a "Debt Collector of the Month" contest, rewarding the agency employee able to extract the greatest amount of cash from overpaid recipients.

In its defense, the agency also cited horror stories, including that of bank vice president who cheated the government out of extra payments. At the same time officials admitted that as many as half of its overpayments were the fault of the agency itself.

Cheating, of course, should not be tolerated. But in view of the large number of overpayments to the elderly and the poor resulting from mistakes by the government, gentle persuasion—not collection-agency threats and harassment—would seem to be the better course.

DAYTON DAILY NEWS
Dayton, Ohio, February 9, 1983

You can't take it with you, not that Social Security didn't try to add to the eternal reward of many.

Now Social Security is trying to update its records, hooray.

Thousands of checks have been cranked out to people who died years ago. Most of the cases involved relatives who have failed to get Social Security to turn off the check-writing machine. Rather than fight the computer any longer, they simply stored the checks until a human being became interested enough to intercede. In one case, the daughter of a woman who died in 1975 turned over 90 unopened checks totaling more than $23,000.

With the new direct deposit system, some people are not aware that they're getting money to which they're no longer entitled. They're being asked to repay. And for those folks out and out defrauding the system, the administration promises prosecutions.

When Social Security paid out a lump sum death benefit, funeral homes would notify the system in order to collect the money directly. That benefit no longer exists and no notification system has replaced it.

The long-term answer is obvious. Each state should take the Social Security numbers from recorded death certificates and send them to Washington. Sure, it adds another layer of bureaucracy to government, but it is a layer that will save the faltering Social Security system millions of dollars annually.

The News American
Baltimore, Md., February 10, 1983

In these days when everyone is a number and government is supposed to know all about our lives, it's amazing to learn that the Social Security Administration has trouble finding out when someone dies. A pilot program under way in 11 states already has revealed that out of 6.7 million death records studied, in 6,757 cases one file showed the individual dead and another showed the person alive. And this is costing Social Security millions of dollars a year as checks continue to be sent to someone who died.

One death under investigation dates back to January 1960. Since that time Social Security has sent out checks totaling more than $50,000 in the individual's name. More than half the cases studied date back more than a year, and the average erroneous payments amount to $5,600 a person. Social Security officials are estimating that by the time the pilot program is completed more than $100 million will be saved. Starting April 1, the program will be extended to other states.

Of course, people found cashing those checks are subject to prosecution, but the records have been kept so poorly that prosecutions haven't put a dent in the racket. The puzzling thing is the admission by Social Security officials that the administration does not regularly check state death records. It seems such a simple and quick way to correct the problem.

Social Security is estimating that once the records are brought up to date nationally hundreds of millions of dollars will be saved. After that they ought to pipe the death records into their own computers on a daily basis.

The Arizona Republic
Phoenix, Ariz., February 11, 1983

DEAD men tell no tales, and therein may lie the appeal of cashing checks written to them.

Social Security checks — $100 million worth, maybe more — have been cashed by live people forging dead people's signatures in at least 11 states during the past couple of decades.

Officials of the Social Security Administration are using computers to track down the ghouls gouging fellow taxpayers.

What they've uncovered so far is only "the tip of the iceberg," they admit.

Some of the amounts are small. They may be only the work of widows and widowers who figured they had their spouse's last check coming to them.

From forgers, banks and merchants, the government has collected only $87,000, although the feds did intercept $418,000 worth of uncashed checks.

So far, no one's been arrested during the pilot effort against the grateful undead — but officials say the Secret Service will be asked to go after some of the offenders.

Such fraud is a blow to anyone defending Social Security. One of its staunchest defenders, Rep. Claude Pepper, D-Fla., pronounces himself surprised at the magnitude of American cheating on fellow Americans.

Pepper wants heavier penalties for fraudulent use of Social Security benefits.

It could come to that, if enough citizens show their anger over such abuse.

More effective would be clearer language on the checks themselves that it's a federal crime to convert the checks, and that even the banker or the merchant who fails to check the endorser's identification may be penalized.

The Pittsburgh Press
Pittsburgh, Pa., February 11, 1983

The government is slashing some Social Security benefits by 100 percent and nobody is complaining, not even Claude Pepper.

The ax is aimed at checks which are sent to people after they're dead — sometimes long after.

In a pilot computer project, the Social Security Administration is matching its rolls with death records from 11 states, New York City and the Veterans Administration. So far it has come up with 1,411 cases in which the government kept grinding out checks to deceased beneficiaries to the tune of $6 million.

One case went clear back to 1960.

"When we get everything completed," says a Social Security spokesman, "we think it could yield close to $100 million just as a result of the pilot."

And when the computer search is expanded to other states beginning in April, it could reach "several hundreds of millions of dollars" in erroneous payments.

★ ★ ★

Even if only half that much money were saved — plus the recovery of funds from those who fraudulently cash checks made out to deceased persons — it would wipe out Social Security's short-term financing problem.

Officials should move with more than deliberate speed to bring all 50 states into a records-matching system on a routine and permanent basis.

The Birmingham News
Birmingham, Ala., February 13, 1983

The Social Security snafu which has resulted in perhaps hundreds of millions going to persons who have departed this vale of tears has inspired the expected landslide of jokes.

Perhaps we have come to expect such shocks from a government which can't seem to deliver properly on even the simplest of tasks without waste, fraud, negligence and abuse.

But is the snafu really a laughing matter? Don't Americans who look to Social Security as a safety net in old age deserve better? Don't those who willingly pony up their taxes each year deserve better than to have 10 to 25 percent of their money ripped off through fraud, abuse or carlessness?

Surely, the Social Security system has people capable of setting up procedures which will eliminate most of the fraud, if not all of it. But even its bookkeeping and auditing processes must be suspect.

During the current probe, an investigator came upon one case where the survivors had tossed checks totalling about $10,000 into a drawer, waiting to hear from someone in government as to what to do with them.

Would any business ignore the fact that it had $10,000 in uncashed checks on its books without an investigation? Shouldn't Social Security auditors have questioned the checks months if not years ago?

And Congress must share the blame. Has its oversight committees ever re-examined the Social Security Act and its amendments to determine if they need tightening?

Congress is not the most careful bunch when it comes to writing legislation. Many of the bills it approves with gusto are full of legal potholes and snares which are exploited by both power-hungry bureaucrats and the persons they are supposed to serve.

One trusts the administration will push the current investigation until death rolls in every state have been checked for mis-payments and those guilty of deliberate fraud are prosecuted to the limit of the law, and required as part of any sentence to repay every penny they have obtained illegally.

Part II: Solutions

All proposed remedies for the financial predicament of the Social
Security system must rely either on raising taxes or cutting benefits, or on a
combination of these two equally unpopular alternatives. The only reform
that would involve neither is an expansion of coverage to include federal
employees and other workers not currently covered by Social Security, thus
increasing the income of the system without increasing the payroll tax for
those already paying it. This proposal is a popular one, but would not solve
the long-term problems of Social Security since the newly covered workers
would eventually have to be paid benefits; most of the advantage to the
system would accrue in the short term, beginning an estimated three to
four years after new employees began contributing. Those proposals that
attempt to compensate for the anticipated revenue shortfall when the
"baby boom" generation retires—such as raising the eligibility age for
retirement benefits, changing the formula for benefit increases or taxing
benefits—would entail a decrease in benefits for recipients, either now or in
the future. Even the seemingly innocuous suggestion that some part of
Social Security benefits be paid from general revenues carries the hidden
threat of a hike in income taxes to cover the costs of the system.

This dilemma, whose resolution would appear almost certain to enrage
either the taxpayers or the elderly population, has caught politicians in a
vise. Some lawmakers have argued that structural changes in the system
are unnecessary, and that the problems of Social Security funding have
been magnified by Administrations anxious to lower the national deficit. In
this view, solvency could be achieved by small measures enacted as they
became necessary. (The system has been running at a deficit since the
mid-1970's, but only recently has the retirement fund been faced with
complete depletion. Solvency is usually defined as the presence of at least
three months' outlays in the three trust funds.) The debate over these
issues in the following pages is fierce, since the interests of most of the
population are directly involved.

Mandating Coverage for All Workers

Universal coverage is one of the measures most often proposed as a means of bringing additional income into the Social Security system. Those not now covered comprise about 10% of the work force, including all federal government employees, about one-fourth of the employees of state and local governments, and about one-tenth of the employees of non-profit organizations. Proponents of mandatory coverage for all workers argue that it is unfair for federal workers in particular to be able to opt out of the system, since workers in the private sector have no such choice. Many federal workers earn so-called "windfall" Social Security benefits by spending a short time in covered employment after becoming eligible for generous civil service pensions. Adherents of universal coverage also favor prohibiting the future withdrawal of state and local government employees and non-profit agency employees from the system. Most proposals have recommended bringing all new federal workers into the system.

Opponents of universal coverage argue that the federal retirement system would collapse from the resulting shortage of funds normally supplied by new workers, and that the pensions of retiring workers who had paid into the federal plan would have to be paid with Treasury funds—or in other words, by taxpayers.

the Charleston Gazette

Charleston, W. Va., August 28, 1981

SOCIAL SECURITY may be good enough for the common folk of America, but it isn't good enough for Congress.

Congress has its own retirement plan, thank you.

This is an outrage: one plan for the governed, another — better plan — for the governors.

Not all governors agree that they and other federal employees should have a retirement program superior to the one the people they represent have.

Rep. Cleve Benedict of West Virginia's 2nd District, we're happy to report, is co-sponsoring legislation to provide social security coverage for congressional members.

The legislation, however, won't be knocking anybody down in the rush to get to the Oval Office for the president's signature. It's buried deep in the confines of the subcommittee on Social Security of the House Ways and Means Committee.

Benedict supports the legislation because as he says: "I believe that members of Congress should not be exempt from a program created by Congress. If we are a part of the system, we will move quickly to resolve the financial problems of the program."

How many other West Virginia congressmen support the bill Benedict backs? How about it Rep. Nick Rahall? Rep. Mick Staton? Rep. Bob Mollohan? Sens. Jennings Randolph and Bob Byrd? Do you think it fair that the people have one retirement program and you another?

THE RICHMOND NEWS LEADER

Richmond, Va., April 14, 1980

Columnist Sylvia Porter recently has been telling her readers that the inordinately high Social Security payroll tax buys them a bargain package of benefits. If Social Security is such a bargain, why are public employees gearing up for a massive lobbying effort to resist being forced to participate in the program?

Under current law, public employees may choose not to be included in Social Security, and about 7 million of them have made that choice. Public employees also may withdraw from the program once they have participated in it, and Alaska's state workers have been the most recent to pull out. Meanwhile, Congress is desperately seeking ways to expand Social Security revenues, and a special commission is scheduled to recommend universal coverage in a report to Congress soon.

So public employee groups have raised more than $3 million to finance opposition to such a proposal. Federal employees specifically want to be spared Social Security coverage, and for good reason: They now pay 7 per cent of their income into the federal retirement system, and many of them can expect generous pensions. They are eligible to retire at 55, in comparison with minimum retirement age of 62 under Social Security. Federal retirees also receive semi-annual cost-of-living increases; Social Security beneficiaries receive but one. Although federal pensions in excess of worker contributions are taxable and Social Security benefits are not, federal workers still think they have a better program.

As economist Martin Anderson has noted: "I think that one of the most extraordinary things about the Social Security program is that the people who passed the program and the people who are administering the program have seen fit to exempt themselves from it, and they have set up their own retirement pension funds. Maybe they know something the rest of us don't." They know something, all right — that the individual can get much better returns from his money invested elsewhere. Public employees have a good thing going, and they can't be faulted if they refuse to exchange it for a bad bargain.

The Boston Herald American

Boston, Mass., April 8, 1980

An independent study shows it is feasible to make Social Security coverage universal — bringing in some 7 million government workers and non-profit group employees.

Their exclusion is costing the system nearly $2 billion a year. Federal employees' unions have bitterly opposed any moves to bring their members under Social Security. And it is easy to see why.

Government workers pay 7 percent of their salaries toward their own retirement plan. They can retire at age 55 after 30 years of work. They also can qualify for Social Security benefits through part-time or other work in the private sector.

And in the end they wind up with overgenerous payments intended for the poor because Social Security records make it appear they earned no money during their government service.

The report, issued recently by the Social Security Coverage Study Group, made no recommendation about universal coverage. But the group leader, Boston lawyer Joseph W. Bartlett, says he personally endorses universal coverage. He said at the very least the way such benefits are figured for government retirees should be changed.

Congress had such a universal measure before it three years ago but the House voted to commerce a two-year study instead.

Now the study has been completed and it's time to move ahead.

ALBUQUERQUE JOURNAL

Albuquerque, N.M., May 1, 1981

It would be a satisfying symbolic gesture for the well-taxed American worker if a bill to force President Reagan, Vice President Bush and every congressman to pay social security taxes were to pass.

The taxes from the nation's top two executives and 535 lawmakers would hardly wipe out the Social Security Administration's cash flow problems overnight, but the symbolism of charging the taxes to those who raise them would help the program's image with America's workers.

Most congressmen, however, are probably eligible for Social Security retirement benefits from activities prior to their election to Congress, so support for the proposal may be thin.

But should it by some quirk pass, we would suggest that Congress look beyond its own house to the 1.8 million federal civil servants currently exempt from Social Security taxes. The addition of that group to the taxing net of Social Security would make a most meaningful contribution to the program's solvency.

The Cincinnati Post

Cincinnati, Ohio, July 17, 1981

Amid all the loud talk in Washington about the danger of the Social Security System's running out of money, there is a strange silence on a move that would nudge the trust funds toward solvency.

The move is to make Social Security universal, that is, to require all employed persons to pay into the system for their future retirement benefits.

About 90 percent of the work force is covered by Social Security. There are some 7 million workers outside the system, most of them federal, state and local government employees.

However, about 70 percent of these so-called uncovered employees end up qualifying for Social Security benefits because they work at some time in jobs covered by the system.

Here is the unfairness: On average, the uncovered employees qualify for two-thirds of the benefits that they could draw if they had paid into the system for their entire working careers. But they pay less than one-third of what covered employees pay in Social Security taxes during their careers.

It won't be easy to correct this overpayment of government workers. First, they form a potent political class. Second, they and the politicians who employ them both enjoy pensions better than the ordinary Social Security recipient, and nobody wants to blow the whistle.

Also, the change would have to be made by Congress and, by no coincidence, Congress has bestowed on itself a remarkably generous pension plan and is unlikely to want to open discussion of public-employee benefits.

But if Social Security is to survive without levying backbreaking taxes on workers, universality is the way to go. If every employee were covered, the system would gain an additional $101 billion through 1986, thus solving most of its problems.

And if congressmen could be made to pay Social Security taxes, a vast improvement in their behavior would result. Seeing the chunk withheld from their pay checks would give them a better understanding of the burden borne by the non-privileged class (private workers) and would deter them from voting for ever-higher benefits.

The Evening Gazette

Worcester, Mass., January 26, 1983

One proposal made by the National Commission on Social Security Reform is to require Social Security coverage for all new federal workers.

That makes sense in a lot of ways. But it doesn't explain just what should be done with the present Civil Service Retirement System, which covers about 2.7 million government workers and pays out benefits to about 1.7 million who have retired.

That retirement system has been the envy of many employees in the private sector. Although federal employees contribute a bit more of their pay than do people who come under Social Security (7 percent compared to 6.7), the average retirement benefit under Civil Service is about $1,050 a month, compared to about $406 a month for Social Security. (However, Civil Service pensions are taxable, whereas Social Security benefits have not been. Under the new plan, some Social Security benefits will be taxed.)

Those generous government pensions are made possible by substantial grants — about $15 billion a year — from the Treasury, that is, the rest of the taxpayers. Small wonder that the Social Security segment of American workers regards the Civil Service Retirement System as a very fat perk, and unfair to boot.

But the federal workers have a case. For many of them, the government retirement system is the only pension they have to look forward to. If no more government workers are added to it, how long can the system continue to pay benefits? Who will pick up the estimated $170 billion in obligations? Without a huge subsidy, the Civil Service Retirement System will run out of cash in 20 years or less.

Furthermore, they argue, if all new government workers are put under Social Security, the government will have to create new pension plans to supplement Social Security benefits, just as many private employers do now. Given all those considerations, they ask whether the shift to Social Security would really save the government money.

Sen. Majority Whip Ted Stevens, trying to answer those points, has proposed a three-tier pension system for government employees, starting with the regular Social Security System, building on it with an extra contribution plan something like a private pension system, and topping it off with a voluntary thrift plan that would permit workers to put in extra money, matched by the federal government up to 3 percent of the worker's salary.

The federal workers' unions oppose the Stevens plan on the ground that it would be less generous than the current system, which probably is true.

Nonetheless, the feeling is growing that federal employees should be put on a par with their fellow Americans as far as government pensions are concerned. Phasing out the Civil Service Retirement System and putting all future government jobholders under Social Security is going to be complex and costly. But the arguments for doing it are stronger than those for not doing it. What's more, the reasons for making the change get more compelling all the time.

THE CHRISTIAN SCIENCE MONITOR

Boston, Mass., February 4, 1983

In urging that new US government workers join the social security retirement program — rather than be allowed to stay in their own federal retirement plans — the National Commission on Social Security has taken a stand that makes sense financially and politically. Such a change would add an additional $30 billion in revenue to hard-pressed social security coffers by the end of the decade. It would enable the government to begin to prune back on the enormous expenses involved in funding liberal federal pension plans — money that would be better spent on improving current salaries.

Perhaps as important, such a reform would lead to greater comparability between federal and private retirement plans. There is certainly an aspect of unfairness when the federal government sets up a national retirement program that excludes the employees who work for the federal government itself.

Congress should move on the plan to integrate new and future employees into social security as expeditiously as possible.

The issue is not one of penalizing government workers, or making federal service less attractive than employment in the private sector. Given the need for first-rate people in government, that ultimately would be self-defeating. In fact federal salaries should be comparable to and, in some essential cases, higher than those offered by the private sector. Rather the issue, as many critics have noted for years, is one of bringing fairness to a federal retirement system that in many respects has provided benefits to civil servants far more generous than those enjoyed by workers in similar positions in the private sector.

To cite just some of the disparities:

● According to the Employee Benefits Research Institute; median benefits for retired federal employees in 1979 were $6,728 a year. That compares to $2,199 for pensioners in private plans.

● Federal employees with 30 years of service can retire with regular benefits at age 55. Future annual benefits are linked to increases in the cost of living. In most cases, persons in private pension plans cannot retire with full benefits before entering their 60s. Future benefits are not always linked to annual cost-of-living increases.

● Many federal employees actually parlay two US government pensions by retiring early (say at age 55), and then taking a private job that qualifies for social security benefits.

● Few private retirement plans come near equalling the benefits of the Civil Service Retirement System, which bases retirement income on the three highest consecutive years of pay, with a minimum pension pegged at 80 percent of actual salary.

Federal employees are already mounting intensive public relations and lobbying campaigns to scuttle the commission's proposals as well as several new changes in the current federal pension plan just proposed by President Reagan in his fiscal 1984 budget requests. Among other things, Mr. Reagan would require that contributions from federal employees rise to 11 percent of pay by 1985, up from the current 7 percent. Mr. Reagan would also eventually hike the retirement year for full benefits to age 65, rather than 55.

Congress should not be reluctant to consider making these changes, as well as go ahead with the integration of federal employees into the social security system. At a time when the government's primary retirement plan is threatened with insolvency, it is unfair for the government to maintain a separate and singularly generous pension program for its own employees.

The San Diego Union

San Diego, Calif., January 6, 1983

Republicans and Democrats on the Social Security Reform Commission are said to have agreed that federal employees should be brought into the system. Inasmuch as the two sides on the commission have been unable to agree on any of the various other options for reform, there is some hope that the final report will not be devoid entirely of recommendations.

But the commission will have to agree on a lot more if its report, due Jan. 15, is to have more than academic significance. Drawing federal workers into Social Security has been one of the least controversial of the proposals for shoring up the system, and it promises a minimum of help. Indeed, if the step were taken without other major reforms, it could add to the long-term problems of Social Security.

The way it is now, federal employees are part of a retirement system with benefits 2½ to 3 times more generous than those paid under the average private pension plan. More than 70 percent of current federal pensioners have worked in the private sector long enough to become eligible for an additional benefit from Social Security. This is patently unfair to workers in private jobs who are required by law to pay Social Security taxes throughout their working lives.

Changes in the federal retirement system to deal with the inequities of double-dipping would be in order whether Social Security was in trouble or not. The proposed reform emerging from the commission would treat the problem in a way that would have only a slight impact on the Social Security deficit looming for the balance of the 1980s.

If *all* government employees — federal, state and local — were required to pay into Social Security, the new revenue would cover at least one-third of the $150 billion to $200 billion deficit foreseen between now and 1990. But there appear to be constitutional barriers against requiring employees of state and local governments to participate. And there is no enthusiasm, on the commission or in Congress, for taking promised retirement benefits away from federal workers who have been paying into their separate pension system for many years.

So what is left is a proposal that new federal employees and those who have been working for the government for less than five years be added to the Social Security rolls. This would produce only $13.5 billion in additional revenue during the next five years — no more than a start at overcoming the deficit.

President Reagan and Congress should be wary of reforms which would bring new workers into the Social Security system without enacting reforms that would control benefits promised to the same workers. Additional workers are an asset to the system only while they are working. They become an additional liability later on.

Extending the coverage of Social Security is a quick way of relieving the short-term cash problem, but to do so without making changes in the benefit structure for future retirees will only aggravate the longer range problems of the system. That drives home the importance of coupling any revenue-raising measures with changes in the benefit structure which will assure the long-term financial future of Social Security.

It is timely and fair to require government employees to participate in Social Security — but not if it forces them to become passengers aboard a ship that isn't seaworthy.

Fort Worth Star-Telegram

Fort Worth, Texas, February 7, 1983

It is noteworthy that when House Majority Leader Jim Wright proposed that congressmen be sure to include themselves under Social Security, the only objections raised were about the possibility that self-employed congressmen might be seen as trying to reduce the amount of tax they already pay.

Wright offered the proposal, admittedly, as a symbolic move.

It is obvious that whatever additional Social Security would be paid into the system by 535 representatives and senators (assuming all were now excluded, which they are not) would be no more than a tiny droplet in the bucket and would do nothing, by itself, to repair Social Security's financial flaws.

But as many readers who replied to a recent *Star-Telegram* Peoplegram indicated in their comments, the rest of the tax-paying public would derive considerable satisfaction from the knowledge that their elected representatives were feeling the same tax bite.

Congress must be included, one way or another. Even if it is merely a symbolic step.

And Congress seems to realize this.

Politicians, though, are sensitive to anyone's charges that they are actually reducing their participation in the taxing process. Especially when they have only recently allowed their own salaries to be increased.

A way can be found, surely, to put Congress under the Social Security umbrella, in the same boat with the rest of us, without allowing congressmen any exceptional and unusual benefit.

Symbolic? Yes. But also about time.

The Orlando Sentinel

Orlando, Fla., January 22, 1983

Federal workers may pose the biggest obstacle to Social Security reform. The president's reform commission recommends bringing new federal employees under the Social Security umbrella, but government workers don't want any part of it.

By any measure of fairness, there is little support for their argument. If for no other reason, most federal retirees — 73 percent — already dip into the Social Security fund. And they pay less in proportion to what they get out of it than do recipients who have spent their entire careers in the private sector.

The reason? Most federal employees work in a private-sector job at some time, thus paying something into the system and qualifying for the benefits. Many take advantage of their plush federal pension system, which allows a full pension at age 55, and retire to work at a job covered by Social Security. They lose nothing from their civil service pension.

The reform commission recommends bringing all new federal employees — including members of Congress — under Social Security as of January 1984. Nonprofit organizations, which now have the option of being in or out, also would be forced into the system. State and local governments, which have been bailing out of the system in huge numbers, could no longer leave.

The solvency of Social Security would be better served if some of the present federal workers could be included, say at the 10-year service level. Certainly there is sound argument to bring all local government workers back into the system, but that, too, has been sacrificed for the sake of a workable compromise.

Federal workers argue that they have their own pension system and shouldn't be forced to pay into Social Security. Two of their union leaders are fanning the protest with hints that those pensions are to be replaced by Social Security.

The reform commission proposal does not touch the present retirement program. It merely places the federal worker in the same position as a private-sector worker with a pension plan. And that's only fair.

Raising Eligibility Age for Retirement Benefits

Since the Social Security program began in 1935, the age at which a retiree could draw full benefits has remained 65. In 1956 the program was amended to allow women to retire at 62 with actuarially reduced benefits; men were given the same choice in 1961. The average life expectancy of Americans at birth has risen by more than a decade in the intervening years, from 62.9 years in 1940 to 73.6 years in 1980. One of the most frequently recommended legislative changes to ease the financial strain on Social Security has been to raise the eligibility age, usually to age 68 or 70, to reflect this increased longevity.

Proponents of raising the retirement age argue that it would help counteract the drain on the system that will occur when the "baby boom" generation begins to retire, leaving a relatively sparse "baby bust" working generation to pay their retirement benefits. Paying benefits sooner rather than later to most beneficiaries would of course also save the system money in the short term. In addition, many proponents contend that older people are in much better health than they were 40 years ago, and that continued work is actually beneficial for those who are able to manage it. The overwhelming majority of such proposals specify that the change should be gradually phased-in so as not to unfairly penalize those who are currently approaching retirement.

Those who oppose raising the eligibility age raise several objections. One of them is the fact that a majority of workers who claim early retirement benefits attribute their decision to poor health; such retirees might not be covered at all unless the requirements of the disability and Supplemental Security Income programs were liberalized to include them. Another is that the longevity of most minority groups is less than that of the white population, and minorities might thus bear the burden of such a change disproportionately. Some opponents also contend that raising the retirement age is a benefit cutback that would be unfair to those under 40 in the current working force who are paying higher payroll taxes than ever before over a working lifetime.

Discussions of the eligibility age often involve the pros and cons of early retirement, since most proposals to raise the age for full benefits would raise the age for actuarially reduced benefits by the same number of years. Opinions differ widely on several subjects: whether early retirement is an unaffordable luxury or a necessity imposed by health considerations; whether increased longevity indicates that the over-65 population is actually healthier today, or whether the elderly simply survive longer because of medical advances that allow life to continue with chronic disabilities and handicaps; whether working past the age of 65 is beneficial for the majority of the elderly; and what the cumulative effect of a growing number of early retirees would be on the working force as a whole. Whatever its merits, the option of retiring early has become a popular one; between 1955 and 1975, the proportion of men between 60 and 64 who were no longer in the work force doubled to 34%.

THE ARIZONA REPUBLIC
Phoenix, Ariz., May 23, 1981

IN a recent editorial, *The Republic* declared that Congress must not simply reject President Reagan's proposals for Social Security reform, that it must come up with alternatives.

Unless it does, the editorial warned, the system will go bankrupt in another year or two.

The editorial suggested one possible alternative: changing the method for determining how much benefits should be raised to compensate for the rise in the cost of living of the beneficiaries.

The present method, based on the Consumer Price Index, greatly exaggerates the increase.

Here is another possible alternative:

Raising the age at which workers become eligible for benefits.

At present, a worker can receive full benefits at 65 and partial benefits at 62.

This made perfect sense in 1935, when Social Security came into being.

A child in those days had a life expectancy of 61 years.

Today's child, however, has a life expectancy of 74 years.

Between 1968 and 1977, life expectancy at 65 rose from 12.8 years to 13.9 years for men, and from 16.3 years to 18.3 years for women.

Given these statistics, many students of Social Security believe the retirement ages should be raised gradually, at the rate of two months a year starting in 1983, until they reach 65 for partial benefits and 68 for full benefits in the year 2000.

Congress should explore every idea for keeping the Social Security system solvent.

The Kansas City Times
Kansas City, Mo., May 23, 1979

Mentioned as one possible long-range major change in the Social Security system is raising the minimum age at which retired workers could draw benefits. Before any middle-aged or older workers panic and start a protest march to Washington in angry and unequivocal opposition, it should be stressed that the idea assumes a very gradual phase-in, slowly raising the retirement age until the year 2010 or later, when the drawing of maximum benefits would begin at 70 instead of the present 65.

Although Hale Champion, undersecretary of the Department of Health, Education and Welfare, this week referred broadly to that kind of alteration, intensive study and public discussion must ensue before any decision is made to consider such a change. Assuring protection for the seniors of the 21st century at the cost of breaking faith with either this generation of retirees or workers would be reprehensible.

Certain demographic and social realities justify a hard look at the idea. A series of employee-employer tax increases have been legislated through 1981 to pay the mounting cost of Social Security; others are planned between then and 1990. However, experts predict rates will have to be boosted again to meet the needs of the "baby boom" generation that will reach retirement age in the year 2015. A basic long-range problem in Social Security financing is the ratio of workers paying into the system to retirees drawing out. Today there are 193 aged for every 1,000 persons of working age; by 2055 there will be 556 for every 1,000, precluding a dramatic change in the birthrate or a major scientific breakthrough arresting a killer disease or aging itself.

The maximum number of persons who can be 65 up to the year 2043 is now written in stone because their births have been recorded. One way of changing that ratio is for potential beneficiaries to continue longer as workers before they draw retirement benefits.

Further, life expectancy has increased since the creation of the U.S. Social Security system; it is nearly 10 years longer now than the 63.5 years when the first benefits were paid in 1940. The abolition of mandatory retirement at 65 recognized the vigor and productivity of older persons and the fallacy of the notion that a dependent old age begins at the chronological year of 65.

In view of changed attitudes and projected needs of future generations, it is not irresponsible to consider modifications along age lines in the Social Security structure. Action certainly must not be taken hastily. Fortunately, there is time to investigate, study, discuss and argue the issue if that work begins now.

THE DENVER POST

Denver, Colo., May 17, 1981

THE U.S. SOCIAL Security system, already confronting a short-term cash crunch, faces long-run bankruptcy unless major reforms can alter the demographic forces which drive it.

Social Security's problem stems from the fact that, despite political pretensions that it parallels private pension plans, it is simply an income transfer program taxing active workers to pay retirees and other beneficiaries.

Private pension plans invest contributions from workers and employers and earmark the principal and interest to provide benefits for workers when they ultimately retire. But current Social Security taxes simply pay for current benefits. A private employer who attempted to copy that system would be in violation of federal pension laws.

Such a scheme was workable when it began in 1935 because there were many workers paying for each of the few beneficiaries. But the average life expectancy has grown by nine years since the program's origin. That otherwise happy fact has swelled the ranks of those drawing benefits at the very time the trend toward smaller families is reducing the relative size of the work force. When the "baby boom" hits the normal retirement age of 65, experts predict there will be only three active workers for every beneficiary — imposing a crushing burden on workers and threatening the system's solvency.

The only realistic answer is to provide incentives for older workers to remain productively employed. After all, Americans not only live longer now than in 1935, they are also healthier. Federal law recently recognized that fact by banning mandatory retirement before age 70.

Paradoxically, it also continues to encourage *early* retirement by offering only slightly reduced Social Security benefits for those leaving the work force at 62. Worse, people who work past age 65 lose $1 in benefits for every $2 earned above a certain limit — practically forcing them into retirement that many don't want or cannot afford.

President Reagan has proposed reducing future (not present) benefit levels by about 10 percent. But the cornerstone of his plan is a reduction of benefits for early retirement coupled with elimination of the earnings limitation. Instead of encouraging early retirement, he wants older workers to leave their skills and experience in the work force. At age 70, Reagan certainly realizes that older workers aren't "washed up" as existing law implies.

Colorado Sen. Bill Armstrong, who heads the Senate Social Security subcommittee which will review the Reagan plan, has already praised it. We hope Armstrong will use his influence to broaden the scope of the hearings and encourage American firms to begin to copy retirement plans in other nations that more realistically adapt to the human life cycle.

In the United States, for instance, the United Auto Workers and United Steelworkers unions have successfully negotiated plans encouraging workers to retire after 30 years on the job — even though many of them are still younger than 50.

Well, after 30 years in a steel mill, a worker might indeed want less-demanding tasks, but he is hardly ready for the slag heap. In Japan, older production workers are encouraged to quit their jobs at, say, Datsun to work for a supplier closely tied to that company. Such work may be less demanding, but the worker's earlier experience is invaluable to his new employer. Somewhat reduced salaries at the new job are augmented by payments from the old employer.

There's a similar difference between white-collar workers in Japan and the United States. In this country, a worker usually retires from the highest position of responsibility he has ever held into complete idleness, an emotional shock which often triggers a physical decline.

In Japan, older white-collar workers often step down a notch to jobs slightly less-demanding in daily effort. In turn, they form a sort of industrial "privy council" to advise and consult with company management on policy issues where their seasoned perspective is priceless.

Such a gradual adjustment of job responsibilities which reduces physical demands on older workers while making maximum use of their experience and judgment makes far more sense than the American "up or out" system. President Reagan's reform proposals are sound but need to be followed through with reform in the private sector to achieve their full objective of staving off "social insecurity" for older and younger workers alike.

ST. LOUIS POST-DISPATCH

St. Louis, Mo., October 14, 1981

Though a firestorm of opposition forced President Reagan to withdraw virtually all his proposals for cuts in Social Security benefits, most of them remain under consideration, albeit in altered form, both at the White House and on Capitol Hill. For that reason a recent study of early retirement by a sociologist at the University of Maryland is pertinent.

It will be recalled that the Reagan package of Social Security revisions included a plan to make early retirement less attractive. Under existing law, those who retire at age 62 receive about 80 percent of the benefit they would have received at age 65. Mr. Reagan wanted to reduce the early retirement benefit to 55 percent of the full benefit, which would save about $17 billion in the first four years.

The proposal was predicated on the belief that people took advantage of the early retirement option because they didn't want to work any more, but the study by the Maryland sociologist, Eric R. Kingson, found otherwise. By far the major reason for early retirement, Mr. Kingson reported, was poor health. Fifty-one percent of the white males who took early retirement and 55 percent of the black males who did so had previously received disability payments. Poor health was also given as a reason for taking early retirement by an additional 34 percent of whites and 36 percent of blacks, though they had never collected disability. Their assertions were verified, however; they died in disproportionately large numbers within a few years.

That left 15 percent of the whites and 9 percent of the blacks who might be presumed to have retired early because they wanted to whittle, but in fact the percentage is smaller, because some of that group was forced into early retirement by the inability to find a job after being laid off.

What these findings tell us is that reducing the early retirement benefit would not really discourage early retirement, for almost all those who leave the work force at age 62 do so involuntarily. Hence, to reduce the early retirement benefit would be to penalize people for bad health or for being unable to find work.

the Charleston Gazette

Charleston, W.Va., October 21, 1981

WITH regard to Social Security's early retirement rules, findings of the American Association of Retired Persons, which can hardly be considered a disinterested party, are supported by a University of Maryland researcher, Dr. Eric R. Kingson.

As the AARP researchers also found, Kingson's study shows that early retirements are not motivated by a desire of people in the 62-64 age bracket simply to take it easy. Writing in the Autumn edition of *The Journal of the Institute for Socioeconomic Studies*, Kingson said Americans seek early retirement "for reasons of health or because of inadequate skills, these workers cannot any longer hold jobs." His analysis of early retirement claims shows:

▲ Fifty-one percent of the white males and 55 percent of the black males had previously received disability insurance.

▲ Thirty-four percent of the whites and 36 percent of the blacks reported work-limiting health problems as they withdrew from the labor force but had not previously collected disability.

▲ Fifteen percent of the whites and 9 percent of the blacks reported no health problems.

Kingson compared the mortality rates of the unhealthy group to those of the healthy and disabled groups. He reported, in rather macabre language, that the self-professed unhealthy group validated their claim of ill health "by dying." He found that 42 percent of the unhealthy group choosing early retirement between 1966 and 1975 died by the year 1975, as compared to 33 percent of the disabled group and 15 percent of the healthy group.

It may be necessary to reduce benefits to early retirees. We think a phased-in reduction would be fairer — and obviously far less shocking to those preparing to retire — than an abrupt reduction. In any event, it appears from Kingson's findings that no reduction should be accompanied by allusions to laziness.

The Congressional Budget Office suggests that making 68 instead of 65 the normal retirement age — the age at which one can start collecting Social Security — would reduce federal spending $17 billion a year. It also could reduce the national boredom quotient by keeping gainfully occupied a few years longer a lot of experienced workers who are still close to their productive primes.

Certainly something is going to have to be done to keep the Social Security system solvent. It's been slipping deeper and deeper into the red since about 1974, and last year what the system paid out to retirees exceeded workers' and employers' contributions to the old-age fund by nearly $2 billion. The situation is going to get increasingly out of balance as time goes on unless major changes are made.

Because the system is making monthly benefit payments to about 31.4 million retirees and survivors, the payout rate is enormous. There were predictions last spring that the government could have trouble meeting the old-age benefits payroll by this time next year.

It may be in their own self-interest that many 65-and-over workers will want to keep working as long as possible (the present federally blessed mandatory retirement age is 70) in order not to add to the drain on the system and in order to continue payments into it through payroll deductions. Thus, they may help ensure, at least slightly, the likelihood there still will be money in the old-age benefits fund when they are ready to start drawing on it.

Besides, some older workers reason, staying on the job helps keep them fit and alert, a theory with which at least some psychologists agree.

If each year's Social Security tax receipts are going to have to be put to work immediately helping fund that year's benefit payments, then there may be real practicality in such additional Congress Budget Office suggestions as:

● Eliminating the mandatory retirement age of 70, which might have the effect of increasing the work force by 195,000 by the year 2000.

● Changing private pension plan regulations that limit the amount of work a retiree could do.

● Lowering from 72 to 64 the age at which a person could earn an unlimited amount and still collect Social Security benefits. That, it estimated, would add at least 150,000 people to the work force.

It isn't likely such reasoning, or such possible law changes, will persuade any present retirees to reenter the work force. But older workers able to produce may find them logical, and it may be easier to sell such system changes than those that would imperil what present beneficiaries already have gotten used to.

Chicago Defender
Chicago, Ill., May 26, 1981

The battle is on in Washington over how Social Security should be administered. The new tough regime wasn't long waiting before it threatened a cutback in help to the aged, the infirm and thousands of others.

One of the proposals was that nobody gets any Social Security until the age of 68, a new retirement age. By that time hundreds of thousands between 65 and 68 would be gone. They have it it all figured out.

There is no doubt that there is a great problem in financing old age help for 35,000,000 people — but these people helped build the country for the past half century; when they were young, they fought for Social Security, and at a time when inflation is making everybody a bit poorer, there is nothing to be gained by getting rid of the older folks by means of starvation.

Chicago, Ill., May 18, 1982

Something is doing and has been doing for some time about the retirement age of 65 for workers in most lines of labor. It has to do with the strain that the Social Security system is under and the threats of its deteriorating in coming years.

The issues aren't yet all that clear. Many people are simply ill or tired out by the time they reach 65 and welcome retirement, provided they can secure Social Security help. Others want to keep working and earning and don't need to leave their jobs.

Employers are grappling with how to best use aging workers. Government people are coming up with various proposals. John Rother, staff director and chief counsel for the Senate Special Committee on Aging, told about 50 representatives of academia, business and government: "It is time to break down the stereotype of a person over 65 as a dependent person."

We don't yet know where all this will go, who it will help and who it will hurt, but the citizenry and the labor force and minorities need to watch what the government says it is going to do or what the Congress is trying to put over.

Tulsa World
Tulsa, Okla., May 15, 1981

OFFICIALLY, the Reagan Administrtion's Social Security reform package leaves the conventional retirement age at 65. The President rejected suggestions for gradually raising it to 68 or 70. But unofficially, retirement at 65 can no longer be taken for granted by the average American worker.

Officials say the Reagan package does not penalize Americans for retiring at 65, but it does offer "incentives" for those who work one, two or three years past that age. So the effect is the same. To get maximum available Social Security benefits, a worker would have to stay on the job for the extra three years. Industry will no doubt follow the Government's lead in encouraging or forcing later retirement.

But don't blame Reagan for the delayed retirement trend. It has been in the wind for several years and for various reasons. Improved health and life expectancy have encouraged many people to voluntarily work past the conventional retirement age. The term "elderly" has simply been redefined. The average American is no longer frail or sick at age 65.

Older people themselves have fueled the trend toward late retirement by demanding the right to stay on the job past 65.

Indeed, Federal law now prohibits a company from forcing a worker to retire solely on account of age until his 70th year.

Rep. Claude Pepper, D-Fla., an octogenarian, was the author of that law. Today, he is one of the most bitter critics of the Reagan plan which takes away benefits for persons who retire before 65 and offers incentives for those staying on until 68.

But Pepper should have seen it coming. His own 70-year retirement law will surely be cited many times in the coming debate as evidence of the willingness of Americans to accept later retirement — and fewer benefits if they choose to retire at 65.

For better or worse, the so-called "Golden Years" of retirement for the average American are almost certainly going to be shortened.

ARKANSAS DEMOCRAT
Little Rock, Ark., June 6, 1981

Now that the Democrats have got all the political mileage they can out of denouncing President Reagan's Social Security reform proposals, they've joined Republicans in what Senate Majority Leader Howard Baker says is a genuinely bipartisan conference on the problem. Translation: Both parties know something must be done to save Social Security.

Having vetoed 96-0 Mr. Reagan's proposal to penalize people who retire early, senators on both sides are facing the fact that something equally drastic must be substituted to keep pension checks safe. They've already agreed that drawing on the Treasury for pension-check money would be too heavy a drain.

The only remaining option is to push full-benefit retirement age past age 65, perhaps to 68. That won't be popular either, but the political side of Social Security has been mined out. It's time to get down to reality.

THE MILWAUKEE JOURNAL
Milwaukee, Wisc., June 26, 1982

President Reagan chose the right target but the wrong arrows when he took aim recently at the high cost of Social Security. Rep. J. J. Pickle (D-Tex.), chairman of the House Social Security Committee, has a proposal that comes much closer to the mark.

Reagan was correct in his conviction that something had to be done to save Social Security from bankruptcy, or to protect workers from ever-more-burdensome payroll taxes. But his solution was seriously flawed.

He proposed to jerk the rug from under persons nearing early retirement, leaving them with pensions much smaller than they had been led to expect under existing law. At the same time, for reasons that don't add up, he suggested letting other workers draw full benefits without penalty at age 65 while remaining fully employed.

Pickle's proposal, which is said to have growing support among both Democratic and Republican congressmen, seeks to keep the pension system solvent by (1) using a more realistic method of computing retirees' cost-of-living raises and (2) gradually raising the normal retirement age.

At present, cost-of-living raises are tied to the Consumer Price Index, a measure that tends to overstate the cost of living in periods of high inflation. One answer would be to revise the CPI itself. Another would be to peg the raises to the increase in prices or wages, whichever was lower. Such a change, in addition to easing Social Security's financial problem, would restore an element of fairness to the system. As it is now, retired persons get raises equal to the full Consumer Price Index while most of the workers who are paying for the system have to settle for smaller raises.

As for raising the retirement age, it could be accomplished in small increments over a long period of time, so the government would not have to break faith with people already well along in their working years. However, even that gradual change would help greatly in reducing the system's long-range financial problems.

While Congress is considering the subject, we think it should give thought to taxing currently exempt Social Security benefits as regular income. Most recipients would not be affected because their income would not be high enough to be taxable. However, the tax yield from those in the taxable range would amount to billions of dollars.

For much too long, Congress has shied away from enacting the reforms that a sound, affordable Social Security system requires. It is good to see signs that some members finally are coming to grips with the task.

Milwaukee, Wisc., January 19, 1983

The bad news about Social Security is that the fund is suffering grave financial strains. The good news is that moderate reforms — if undertaken promptly — can avert the need for drastic action down the road.

A gradual increase in the age for retirement — and for early retirement — is a prime example of a relatively modest step that eventually can do a lot to repel the insolvency threat. The president's Social Security commission reportedly is likely to endorse the idea of raising the 65-year retirement age by one month a year, beginning in the year 2003, until it reached 66 in 2015. That means that Americans born in 1938 would have to wait an extra month to retire; those born after 1949 would wait a full year. Similarly, the early retirement age would be raised from 62 to 63 on the same gradual basis.

Some experts believe that the proposed changes are too limited. Perhaps. However, two points seem clear: First, some tinkering with retirement-age rules, while regrettable, is necessary to bring income and outgo into ultimate balance. Second, if the changes are adopted now and later phased in, they would not unfairly disrupt the retirement plans of today's older workers.

It is worth noting, too, that the "normal" retirement age of 65 is rather outdated when one considers how the average life span has increased. When Social Security began, most persons could not expect to live to 65. In 1980, 68% of the men and 82% of the women could expect to reach that age. The average person retiring at 65 today can look forward to 16 years of Social Security benefits.

The presidential commission already has made some reasonable recommendations for closing much of the financial gap confronting Social Security in the years ahead. It has called for some $169 billion of increased revenues and cost reductions between now and 1989 — by accelerating scheduled tax hikes, taxing some Social Security benefits, imposing a six-month delay on the cost of living adjustment, providing incentives for workers to retire later. But more needs to be done. Gradual changes in the retirement age would help greatly to round out the remedy.

DESERET NEWS
Salt Lake City, Utah, January 19-20, 1983

The President's Commission on Social Security Reform needs to drop the other shoe.

When the commission outlined its recommendations the other day for raising $169 billion to keep Social Security solvent, its suggestions still fell about a third short of the amount of cash needed to do the job.

Now the 15-member blue-ribbon study group is toying with an idea for closing the gap in a way that seems sensible and relatively painless — namely, by gradually increasing the age of retirement.

Under a tentative plan still under consideration by the panel, the present retirement age of 65 would be raised one month a year, starting in the year 2000, until it reached 66 in 2015. At the same time, the early retirement age of 62 would gradually be raised to 63. After the year 2020, further increases in the retirement age would be linked to increases in the average life-span.

It's easy to argue for such a change. Americans are living longer today than they did 40 years ago when Social Security retirement benefits first became available. On the average, people at age 68 today have at least as many remaining years of life as their counterparts had at age 65 four decades ago. Older people also are in better health than they used to be. Older people who continue to work are generally reported to be happier and stay healthy longer than those who retire. Moreover, the demand for older workers is expected to pick up later in this decade as the growth in the labor force tapers off, reflecting the low birth rates since the mid-1960's.

Even so, some fundamental questions need to be answered before the government starts mandating a higher age for retirement.

How would industry react? Would it alter private pension plans in response? Would benefits accrue between ages 65 and 66, or would they be frozen at age 65?

What would be the effect on the payroll outlays that companies make for Social Security? Would corporate pension plans retain attractive provisions for early retirement, as some do now? Would they tend to impose penalties for early retirement? Or would they provide attractive incentives to remain on the job beyond age 65?

Maybe some of these questions can't be completely answered until after the Social Security law is actually changed. But to the extent that it's possible, let's test the water before plunging head-first into a mandatory higher age for retirement.

INDUSTRIAL WASTE

Richmond Times-Dispatch

Richmond, Va., January 12, 1983

A study by the Social Security Administration has confirmed what many observers of life's vicissitudes may have suspected already: Persons who keep working beyond age 62 tend to outlive those who take early retirement.

Reviewing the case histories of 64,382 workers eligible for Social Security, the administration found that among men who had filed 20 years ago at age 62 for early retirement benefits, 81 percent were still alive six years later, while 86 percent of those who kept working were still alive. Twelve years later, only 42 percent of the male early retirees were still alive, compared with 51 percent of the men who retired later. (The pattern was similar for women, but the gap was much smaller.)

This finding may lend added force to the argument that the retirement age ought to be raised gradually to 67 or 68 as one way to ease Social Security's increasingly grave financial condition. A trend within recent years toward early retirement — now favored by nearly 70 percent of eligible workers — has been intensifying pressures on the fund. By the year 2012, when it is projected that there will be only two workers' taxes to support each retiree (compared with 16 workers per recipient when Social Security was created in the 1930s), early retirement may be among those luxuries the nation will no longer be able to afford.

Regardless of any possible implications for public policy, the statistics suggest that ending a 40-year routine of daily work is a jolting transition for many persons — one that cuts short the leisurely, nonworking years of many Americans who worked hard to get there. Finding ways to continue productive work into what now is considered to be the age of retirement may add years to life, much as fascinating hobbies add life to the years of graying Americans.

THE KANSAS CITY STAR

Kansas City, Mo., January 14, 1983

Work is not hazardous to your health.

In fact, research indicates that staying on the job may contribute to a longer life. A new study looks at more than 64,000 non-disabled men who became eligible for Social Security between 1962 and 1972. Of those who took retirement benefits at age 62 in 1962, 81 percent were still alive six years later. But among their peers who did not retire early, 86 percent were still alive. The difference in survival increased with passing years. For example, 42 percent of the early retirees lived 16 years after retirement to age 78, the last year checked, but 51 percent of the non-retirees lived to 78.

Women showed a similar pattern, but the difference in survival rates was much smaller, according to Social Security analysts who did the study. Poor health played a part in the early retirement decisions, hence was a factor in poorer survival rates. That factor was not as great as in earlier surveys.

At the same time, a substantial body of research and conclusions by medical and psychological clinicians stresses that many negatives associated with retirement, including loss of power, esteem and income, produce emotional stresses and physical effects that may be life-threatening.

More and more in recent decades earlier retirement has been seen as desirable, a fringe benefit of a good employee contract. At the same time, the principle of allowing, even encouraging people to work longer has gathered support. It's half of an ideal condition: when able people have the option of retiring young or working until they're ready to quit. It is unfortunate that financial gains from private pensions and public benefits reduce incentives to continue productive activity on the job.

CHARLESTON EVENING POST

Charleston, S.C., February 3, 1983

Gradually extending the retirement age is advocated by the reform commission as one procedure for reinforcing the financially insecure Social Security retirement fund. A majority of commission members is said to favor implementation of a plan whereby anyone born in 1949 or later would have to wait until age 66 — rather than 65 — before drawing full benefits. Given the unhealthy state of the retirement fund, such a change should get the attention of Congress, but only because grave situations demand drastic remedies.

The retirement fund situation can accurately be labeled grave when administrators pay out thousands more dollars every hour than are being paid in by employers and employees. The fund got out of balance when the worker-retiree ratio changed, and Congress got so overly generous with benefit payments. Faced with the task of undoing what past Congresses have done, the current Congress must consider all options for corrective action. Pushing up the retirement age is one option.

Even in the grave situation, however, Congress should guard against overreacting. Any changes in retirement age for those now participating in the system should be held to the absolute minimum. Running up the age of those not yet in the workforce — and not yet paying into the retirement fund — might be justified on actuarial grounds. Changing the rules for those already playing the game is patently unfair. It is a remedy that should be considered among the last resorts.

The Virginian-Pilot

Norfolk, Va., January 28, 1983

One of the proposals considered — but ultimately abandoned — by the National Commission on Social Security Reform was raising the age limits for eligibility to a level more in keeping with today's life-expectancy rates. It is a problem that must be dealt with soon, because the gap between retirement age and life expectancy continues to increase.

The potential for the gap existed from the moment the system began. Frank Bane, the first executive director of the Federal Social Security Board, looked back at those first years of Social Security in a recent interview and announced: "I made a mistake. . . . I believed old man Solomon. He didn't know what he was talking about. Threescore years and 10? He was way off base."

In 1930, American life expectancy was 59.7 years. In 1980, it was 73.8 years.

If Mr. Bane had his way, he would revise the system, moving the eligibility age from 65 to 68 and the early-retirement age from 62 to 65. But he would make the changes gradually, and "I would emphasize that no one under conceivable circumstances is going to lose a dime of what they are now — underscore 'now' — getting."

Mr. Bane, now 90 and living in a nursing home in Alexandria, helped establish the actuarial tables for Social Security and says he knew at the time that they might have to be changed. But he also knew, in 1935, that any changes would be way down the road. He was more concerned with helping Americans weather the storms of the Great Depression. The future would have to be taken care of in, well, the future.

Today Mr. Bane criticizes himself for being myopic. But, if this is an example of shortsightedness in preparing for the long-term effects of Social Security, he is not alone. Current forecasts indicate that life expectancy in the year 2020 will be 74 for men and 82 for women. This means that, by 2020, life expectancy will have increased by *one-third* more than anticipated in the original Social Security actuarial tables. The retirement figures must be adjusted to that reality.

THE RICHMOND NEWS LEADER

Richmond, Va., January 31, 1983

Frank Bane died at the age of 90 a few days ago. Perhaps he is not well remembered for his role in Franklin Roosevelt's New Deal administration during the 1930s. Yet Bane's name may be familiar to Virginians who recall him as a Randolph-Macon graduate who became the Commonwealth's first commissioner of welfare.

After passage of the Social Security Act in 1935, Bane was named executive director of the Federal Social Security Board. He served in that post for three years and helped draft the actuarial basis on which Social Security would operate for decades to come. And what happened? He told a *Washington Post* reporter, "I made a mistake."

The "mistake," of course, lay in not anticipating the huge jumps in longevity rates that would occur as better health care improved life expectancies. In 1900, the average American could expect to live 47.3 years; by 1930, the longevity rate had increased to 59.7. Not many Americans during the 1930s expected to live much longer than 60 years, and thus Social Security's retirement supplement was geared to kick in at age 65. Today the average American can expect to live more than 73 years, and there are growing numbers of retired workers in their 80s and 90s.

If he could have gone back to the 1930s and redrafted the actuarial tables to reflect the realities of the 1980s, Bane said, he would have raised the retirement age from 65 to 68 and the early retirement age from 62 to 65. He thought that change would be possible today, if the increases were phased in gradually, and if retirees were reassured they would not lose a penny of their current benefits.

Bane's "mistake" is one that successive special commissions on Social Security have been reluctant to rectify. The only concession to the problem made by the most recent blue ribbon commission was to consider an increase of only one year in retirement age, from 65 to 66. Yet the increase Bane thought advisable would wipe out, in a single stroke, most of Social Security's long-term financial shortfalls.

Perhaps some future commission will risk the rage of a growing number of current and prospective retirees to propose a higher retirement age. Granted, 65 may be a logical retirement age for workers in some occupations, while workers in other jobs may still be going strong at 70 or 75. Workers in high-stress occupations who want to retire at 65 could be treated the way early retirees at 62 are treated now.

The Social Security dilemma cannot be viewed in a vacuum of a retirement system's red ink alone. In coming decades — despite the baby boom and the current high jobless rate — economists believe the nation will face a labor shortage. That shortage would occur when the labor market experiences a diminished pool of workers resulting from recent low birth rates. Unless the gap is to be filled mostly through immigration, Americans may have to work longer before retirement. So it may be that an increase in the retirement age will be needed as a solution to not just one problem, but two.

At any rate, Bane's hindsight may prove enlightening to today's experts who always promise to be tough about Social Security and then settle for a quick fix. Unfortunately, the latest commission opted for the quick fix of more taxes, and thus the basic flaws in the system remain.

Raising Payroll Taxes or Accelerating Tax Hikes

One method of restoring temporary fiscal soundness to the Social Security system, that of raising the payroll tax, has been frequently mandated by Congress. The wage base, or the amount of a person's annual earnings subject to the payroll tax, has risen from $3,000 in 1935 to $6,600 in 1965 to $35,700 in 1983. The tax rate, or the percentage of a person's earnings under the wage base that is withheld, has risen from 1% in 1935 to 4.8% in 1970 to 5.4% in 1983. The obvious argument against further increases in payroll taxes, or acceleration of already scheduled increases, is that they are already so high; the Social Security tax exceeds all other taxes that about a quarter of Americans pay. Yet a surprising number of taxpayers, according to public opinion polls, would be willing to support higher payroll taxes in order to prevent the collapse of a system to which they have already contributed so much of their earnings. Surveys have indicated that the majority of workers would prefer higher taxes to reduced benefits or a higher eligibility age.

The Birmingham News

Birmingham, Ala., September 29, 1982

The National Commission on Social Security Reform recently floated a trial balloon by releasing a staff paper indicating that a 14 percent increase in taxes is needed to avert a crisis. It's a trial balloon which needs to be punctured immediately.

A 14 percent increase in taxes is no solution at all. Unlike those now receiving benefits, young workers will never get back benefits equaling taxes paid. Such a solution is unfair and it is terribly short-sighted to burden young people — not to mention employers – with additional taxes amounting to $125 billion over seven years.

The benefit structure is where the crisis needs to be addressed, not at the tax end. Unless that structure is changed to halt the system's financial hemorrhage, no tax level workers can afford will be enough to put Social Security on a sound basis. Even if the punitive 14 percent tax proposal on active workers were adopted, the system could be in trouble again within five years.

If Congress considers this proposal seriously, it will not be because members believe it is fair to workers, but because most congressmen lack the courage to tackle the real cause of the system's trouble: A benefit program that far exceeds contributions present beneficiaries have made.

In view of the political cowardice which characterizes Congress, however, another attempt at a temporary solution is almost certain. It is still far easier to push back the day of reckoning than to say no to well-organized voter blocs.

THE ATLANTA CONSTITUTION

Atlanta, Ga., September 24, 1982

Don't panic. No one has suggested boosting the Social Security payroll tax to 14 percent, although that's the impression that is getting around.

The Social Security retirement program is facing severe financial problems that must be solved by Congress. The trust fund that finances retirement checks has dipped so low that, for the first time in history, it will probably have to borrow next month from the system's other funds — Disability Insurance and Hospital Insurance (Medicare). Current law permits such borrowing only through the end of this year, however.

For longer-range answers, recent news stories have indicated that one option being considered is raising the payroll tax "14 percent in January." Some quick-draw politicians have misunderstood this to mean "*to* 14 percent."

Boosting Social Security taxes to 14 percent would be political suicide for Congress. That is not going to happen.

The current payroll tax is 6.7 percent on earnings up to $32,400 annually, for a maximum of $2,170.80. A boost of 14 percent would be approximately .94 percent, increasing the rate to just over 7.6 percent. Even that relatively small boost has not been officially recommended by any authority.

In any event, quick fixes in the tax rate cannot much longer keep Congress from facing the major changes that are needed to ensure the long-range financial stability of Social Security. A bipartisan National Commission on Social Security Reform, appointed by the president, is scheduled to report in November.

Congress, when the commission reports, will have to find the political gumption to make basic and long-lasting changes. It is not yet certain what those will be, but by one means or another, they surely will have to include slowing the rate of growth of Social Security benefits and increasing, over a period of years, the eligibility age to 67 or 68.

RAPID CITY JOURNAL—

Rapid City, S.D., December 7, 1982

Increasing Social Security tax rates quickly over the next several years, one of several proposals being advanced to solve the system's financing problems, would severely depress the growth rate of the economy according to a new study by the U.S. Chamber of Commerce's Forecast Center.

Speeding up the three Social Security tax increases now scheduled for 1985, 1986 and 1990 are among the options being considered by the National Commission on Social Security Reform to bring in nearly $200 billion the retirement system will need to remain solvent over the next six years. Between now and 1990, the tax is scheduled to increase from 6.7 percent each on employers and employees to 7.65 percent each.

Speeding up the tax increase would mean smaller paychecks for workers which in turn would mean less consumer spending. With less consumer spending, the gross national product, a chief indicator of economic activity, would also grow at a slower annual rate.

Under the Chamber's worst-case scenario in which the 1990 tax rate of 7.65 percent would be advanced to 1984, 2.2 million jobs would be lost because businesses would be paying higher taxes — funds they would otherwise use to expand and hire new workers.

Under that scenario, gross national product would be $120 billion lower, and total business investment $48 billion lower over six years.

The second option, moving the 1986 tax rate of 7.15 percent ahead to 1984, would cost 300,000 jobs and slow the GNP by $20 billion. Total business investment would drop by $9.2 billion.

And phasing in the 1990 tax rate of 7.65 percent in 1987 would cost 2 million jobs, the GNP would decline by $105 billion and total business investment would be $41 billion lower.

In any case, none of the three options would raise the necessary $200 billion the Social Security system needs by 1990 because the increase in the tax rate would cause a reduction in economic activity and result in a lesser amount of revenue being generated for Social Security than expected.

With the U.S. unemployment rate already in double digits, the commission should look elsewhere for the $200 billion Social Security needs.

THE WALL STREET JOURNAL
New York, N.Y., October 7, 1982

One sure sign that the National Commission on Social Security Reform is heading down the home stretch: The noise level of leaks has gotten louder and more informed. The loudest leak to date is that the commission will recommend a hike in the payroll tax.

This leak is not a drip either. It comes with a lot of firm numbers. For instance, the leak runs, if already scheduled tax increases were moved forward, the $46 billion increase in collections by 1985 could be used to cover the short-term deficit. Currently the individual tax rate is 6.7%; but the 1977 law bumps this up, in four steps, to 7.65% by 1990. Well, then, the leak rushes on, instead of drawing out the agony over seven years, let's kick up the rate immediately.

The leak also comes with supporting double talk. Claude Pepper, a member of the commission and the ranking Savonarola of the Seniors, denounces any talk of raising the payroll tax. The proposed tax increase he says, is not a tax increase—certainly not—it's merely an acceleration.

Well, as taxpayers who pay for the deliberations of the commission, we'd like to point out that the commission's last name is Reform and that raising our taxes is not a reform. Quite the contrary. Given the history of Social Security financing, a reform would be *not* raising taxes.

Consider the average Americans entering the work force in 1950. By 1980, they saw wages go up 490% and Social Security taxes skyrocket by over 2,000%. Yep: Social Security taxes have climbed even faster than federal income taxes. And they're still zooming. There's that legislated increase to 7.65% by 1990 and an estimated rate of 8.6% by 2010 just to keep the system in place.

But these average Americans, along with all those over the age of 40, are lucky. They will get more out of the Social Security system in benefits than they will have put in through taxes. The unlucky ones are the generation somewhat under 40 years of age, who will get less out than they will have put in. Stanford economist Michael Boskin figures that the return for their investment in old age income security will be negative—and will grow substantially more negative the younger they are.

Moreover, raising taxes is not only not a reform, it ignores the long-term crisis which should be addressed now: the coming demographic crunch. In 30 years or so, the baby boom bulge will start trading in its Perrier for Geritol. This swelling number of retirees will have to look to a labor force diminished both by its absence and by the baby bust generation which followed it to finance its Social Security benefits.

The crunch promises to be a wicked one: Each retiree will depend on the tax money thrown off by as few as two workers. (This is in contrast to

a ratio of one to three-and-a-half today, or of one to over 16 in 1950.) Tax rates necessary to maintain current benefits in such a situation could easily touch 10%.

Of course, this crisis is down the road. When it comes, most of our elected representatives and members of the commission will be, to put it delicately, beyond worrying. Why not then, the leak pours on, raise taxes now? The resulting inequities in the intergenerational transfers can be

remedied later (after I've retired from office on my federal pension) and more tax money now will tide Social Security over its temporary present embarrassment.

Funny, but some of the same people were saying the same sorts of things back in 1977. They said that by passing a gigantic increase in Social Security taxes, the system—which had been running in the red—would be restored. Forever flush.

Well, they passed their tax package. And we've already been hit with

four of the scheduled increases from that package. Yet the Social Security system is still in the red. Bright red.

Raising taxes is neither a short-term nor a long-term answer. Indeed, raising taxes will only impede healthy economic growth, making Social Security revenues even more anemic and the current and coming crisis even more severe. If raising taxes is the kind of reform that the commission has taken a year to come up with, then we want our money back.

The Orlando Sentinel
Orlando, Fla., January 20, 1983

In 1977 Social Security was on the brink of collapse, so Congress did what it usually does in such cases. It raised taxes — the largest peacetime tax increase in American history.

Americans were told that the system would be safe through 2050. Yet four years later, Social Security was again at the brink, hanging by its fingernails. The drain was too much for the system's limited resources.

Asking workers again to shoulder all the burden in saving Social Security would invite rebellion. For 25 percent of the work force, Social Security is the largest tax they pay. Nevertheless, a tax increase is part of the compromise package worked out by the Social Security reform commission. This time, though, it is only part of the answer. The burden of saving the system will be shared with those getting the benefits.

The compromise accelerates some tax increases already set for later this decade. That adjustment will raise $40 billion in six years and is one of the two biggest

items on the commission's list of cures. The other involves changes in automatic cost-of-living increases to save $40 billion.

Ideally, there would be no increase in taxes. That would mean cutting benefits, possibly by discouraging early retirement or delaying normal retirement. But compromise is part of governing, and the cost this time is worth the result.

Nevertheless, the taxing crowd should heed the protests of younger workers. For years it has been the retirees who have had time to lobby and who have flocked to the polls. Their influence produced greater benefits and higher taxes to pay for them. That tax will top $4,000 a year for some workers by the end of the decade, and the generation that must pay it doubts that the system can survive. Those doubters are making themselves heard.

This increase proposed by the reform commission is part of an equitable compromise and Congress should accept it. But Congress should also note the cry of those who caution: "Enough is enough."

The Washington Post
Washington, D.C., October 19, 1982

THE NATIONAL Commission on Social Security Reform set up last year by President Reagan is still a month away from deciding on recommendations to shore up the Social Security trust funds. Top White House aides, however, are already ruling out one major option being considered by the commission. President Reagan, it is said, is adamantly opposed to further increases in the payroll tax.

There are good reasons to treat a payroll tax as a last resort. The payroll tax is already scheduled to rise in steps from 13.4 percent, split between workers and employers, to 15.3 percent in 1990. With unemployment over 10 percent—and likely to remain high for some time to come—increasing labor costs is a bad idea. In recent years, the non-wage parts of labor compensation—payroll taxes, health insurance and other fringe benefits—have been rising faster than wages. This makes employers reluctant to hire more workers, especially lower-paid workers for whom payroll taxes and other benefit costs are high relative to wages.

Ruling out a payroll tax step-up, however, would leave the commission with few ways to cover Social Security's imminent shortfall. Looking to the next century—when a rapidly rising aged population spells continuing difficulty for the trust funds—options, such as deferring the retirement age, can be

considered. But uproar over the administration's earlier Social Security proposals made it clear that the public will not tolerate major benefit changes for those already at or near retirement.

Immediate action, however, is needed. Next month, Social Security's retirement fund will have to borrow money from the disability and Medicare funds to cover payments. If Congress allowed borrowing to continue, all three funds would run short in 1984, even if the economy improved considerably. To keep the system on a sound footing over the next five years, a gap of $50 to $60 billion must be closed. Raising that kind of money requires a sharing of burdens between those who get the benefits and those who pay for them.

Some remedies have merit. These include making retirees pay income tax on half of their benefits. Extending Social Security coverage to new government employees is also a needed reform. But a major part of the savings would still have to come from limiting cost-of-living increases for all retirees. Even with inflation down, this last alternative would not be popular. But Social Security beneficiaries have been better protected against inflation than the average worker and taxpayer in recent years. Now, with so many workers facing unemployment, limiting benefit increases would be fairer than adding greatly to the payroll burden.

Changing the Formula for Benefit Increases

In 1972, Congress mandated automatic annual cost-of-living adjustments (COLAs) for all recipients of Social Security benefits, to begin in 1975. (Before 1975, benefits were not formally indexed, and increases were made on an ad hoc basis by Congress.) The 1972 legislation based computation of the annual benefit increases on the Consumer Price Index (CPI). For most of the twentieth century, annual gains in wages had exceeded rises in prices. Since 1974, however, when inflation and unemployment began to rise rapidly, the opposite has been true; increases in the CPI have outpaced average annual wage increases. The COLA is the only part of Social Security tied to the CPI; contributions by taxpayers before entitlement remain tied to wages. Thus, Social Security outlays have increased at a faster rate than payroll revenues, draining the system's reserves. (In 1980, for example, wages rose about 8%, but Social Security beneficiaries received an increase in benefits of more than 14% because of high inflation.)

Most recommendations for changing the indexing standard for benefit increases seek to make the system less sensitive to changes in the economy. These include: indexing benefits to average wages in years when price increases outstrip increases in average earnings; raising the benefits by some specified percentage of the CPI rather than its full extent; placing a cap on the COLA so that benefit increases would not exceed a specified percent, even should the CPI rise beyond that percent; and delaying COLAs by some months or increasing the intervals between them.

Another frquently mentioned possibility is developing a special consumer price index for the elderly to reflect their consumption needs. Proponents of this idea reason that the CPI is a poor indicator for the elderly because it reflects the price of new homes and home mortgage rates, while approximately 70% of the elderly own their own homes. One problem with such a special index is that a substantial portion of Social Security beneficiaries are not elderly.

THE ARIZONA REPUBLIC
Phoenix, Ariz., March, 28, 1978

HAVING acted in haste on Social Security, Congress now is repenting in haste, too.

Last December, faced with the approaching bankruptcy of the system, Congress voted to hike Social Security taxes by $227 billion over the next 10 years.

House Speaker Thomas P. O'Neill Jr. was very proud of what Congress had done, and so was President Carter, who called it "a courageous act."

Then, the complaints started roaring in from the folks back home. Two weeks ago, in a complete about-face, O'Neill asked the president to come up with a proposal to scale down the projected tax increases.

Other members of the House aren't waiting to hear from the president.

✔ Rep. Abner Mikva, D-Ill., has introduced a bill to cut about $38 billion from the projected tax increase by removing disability and Medicare benefits from the Social Security system and funding them instead from general tax revenues.

✔ Rep. Al Ullman, D-Ore., chairman of the Ways and Means Committee, wants to use part of the crude-oil tax, proposed by Carter in his energy package, to help finance Social Security.

✔ Rep. James Burke, D-Mass., believes the Treasury should foot one-third of the bill for the system.

None of the proposals would lessen the burden of taxes on individuals and employers. They would merely shift part of the burden from Social Security taxes to income and corporation taxes.

In a paper prepared for the American Enterprise Institute for Public Policy Research, a resident scholar, Rudolph G. Penner, has come up with what we think is a better idea.

Until last year, Social Security benefits were raised on the basis of both average price and wage increases. They rose more quickly than either, enabling some beneficiaries to receive more money than they had earned before retirement.

Last year, Congress voted to index future benefits to wages only.

Penner believes they should be indexed to prices only.

Over the long run, prices rise more slowly than wages, not by very much, but by enough, says Penner, so that in 75 years the savings for the Social Security system would amount to about $500 billion.

This would not remove the immediate need for a tax increase, but, by the end of century, when the relatively few people born during the Depression retire, the savings would be enough to cover the retirement of those born during the post-World War II baby boom without any further increases.

Social Security beneficiaries won't like Penner's plan, of course, but they cannot legitimately complain about it. For it does protect them against inflation. And those still working will appreciate the decreased burden.

The Chattanooga Times
Chattanooga, Tenn., February 28, 1981

Stories about the Social Security system's precarious financial conditions recur like bad dreams, and this year is no exception. Despite sweeping changes in the funding schedules enacted by Congress in 1977, recently released studies warn the system, especially the retirement trust fund, is speeding toward bankruptcy. That puts a crucial responsibility on Congress and President Reagan to do the necessary thing to maintain the system's financial integrity.

Like nearly everything else, the Social Security system is adversely affected by the economy's woes; high unemployment, for instance, has drastically reduced its revenue collections. But inflation's effects are worse, primarily because, in 1974, Congress linked benefits to increases in the Consumer Price Index. Such generosity was welcomed, naturally, by the nation's retirees. But it has done much to cause the system's current problems: the income/benefit ratio is out of whack. Unless Congress either abandons or revises downward that indexing arrangement, Social Security could be permanently crippled.

Prior to delivering his economic message to Congress, President Reagan exempted Social Security benefits from his budget axe, hardly surprising when you consider the politics of the issue. But he needs to match that with pressure on Congress to reform the system. There are several reasons why that reform is needed: to protect the benefits of nearly 40 million retired or disabled persons, to ensure against the loss of benefits for future retirees now paying into the system, and to restore the system's credibility among young workers.

Obviously when Congress set up the index system, it couldn't have foreseen the sustained double-digit inflation that would force Social Security benefits upward. But it doesn't take a mathematical genius to know that when the rate of increase in the CPI consistently exceeds the rate of increase in wages, nothing but trouble lies ahead. Last summer, for instance, Social Security retirees received a 14.3 percent increase — against a national average wage increase of less than 10 percent. Even with the hefty increase in the payroll tax rate and wage base imposed in January, the system is still paying out more than it is taking in. The problem is made worse when you consider that the worker/retiree ratio is worsening. Currently, there are about three workers to one Social Security beneficiary; some experts estimate that in another 35 years, the ratio will about two to one.

In reforming the system, Congress has several options. It can reduce the index figure, in effect removing the built-in housing and interest rate factors. Or it could limit benefit increases to less than the actual increase in the CPI. The best choice, it seems to us, would be to junk the index and adjust benefits on the basis of current economic conditions, taking into account the fiscal soundness of the retirement and disability trust funds.

Both the Democrats and the Republicans share much of the blame for the system's problems. The former have unhesitatingly voted for increases in benefits in the past usually during election years. But the Republicans introduced and helped pass the indexing legislation. Unless both groups join in taking responsibility for restoring the system to fiscal soundness, they will have another cross to bear: the imminent collapse of that system.

The Detroit News
Detroit, Mich., August 11, 1982

President Reagan's National Commission on Social Security Reform will soon recommend a change in the system's benefit structure linking future cost-of-living increases to wage rates rather than to the Consumer Price Index (CPI).

Specifically, the proposal suggests that benefits be adjusted annually to reflect the percentage increase of wages as measured by the hourly earnings index for all private nonfarm employes. The formula would also factor in a percentage reflecting estimated productivity gains beginning in 1990.

The proposed reform has already caused considerable controversy, but, if enacted into law, it could save Social Security from financial ruin. Commission Chairman Alan Greenspan believes that linking the benefit formula to unit labor costs can't help but strengthen the system because it frees the Social Security Trust Fund from fluctuations in the national economy.

In the long run, he says, you would have essentially the same benefit levels. The crucial difference is that the revenues and expenditures would be brought into balance.

Mr. Greenspan contends the new formula "would give beneficiaries a larger increase than present law allows under good economic conditions and a smaller increase under bad economic conditions."

Robert Myers, chief actuary of the Social Security system for 23 years, predicts the change would also clear up the uncertainty in the program's financing because the adjustment avoids the disparity between wages and prices.

The present practice of indexing Social Security benefits to the CPI has produced benefit increases of 40 percent for the past three years while average wages have increased by only 30 percent during the same time period.

Moreover, full indexing of Social Security benefits to the CPI only adds fuel to the inflationary fire that destroys everyone's purchasing power.

There have been four Social Security tax increases since 1977, with more to come. The maximum Social Security tax paid this year by workers and employers is $2,171, and this represents a 7,000 percent increase over the rate paid in 1935 when the system was started.

Since 1949, average wages have increased by 470 percent while income taxes have risen 570 percent. During the same period, Social Security taxes have jumped an average 5,100 percent!

It doesn't take a psychic to predict that the system will eventually collapse if the cycle continues unchecked.

Small wonder, then, that 75 percent of those between the ages of 25 and 44 have little or no confidence that there will be a Social Security system when it's time for them to retire.

The question now is whether Congress has the courage to change a system that is clearly out of control. The evidence to date is not encouraging.

St. Louis Globe-Democrat
St. Louis, Mo., June 17, 1981

The concept of increasing the benefits paid to citizens on Social Security, military pensions and other federal programs to reflect rapidly rising inflation makes sense.

But "indexing," as it is called, apparently has become too much of a good thing as far as the federal budget is concerned.

An analysis by the Center for the Study of American Business concludes that efforts to balance the federal budget are being "severely handicapped" by the widespread practice of indexing federal programs. The study found that nearly $417 billion, or 43.4 percent, of the 1981 budget is considered "uncontrollable" because it is indexed to the spiraling Consumer Price Index. If interest on the national debt is added, the proportion reaches 53 percent. Aggravating the problem is the fact that the CPI actually overstates price increases.

Clearly, the White House and Congress should address this practice of indexing so many federal programs. While it started out as a means of ameliorating the effects of inflation it now also apppears to be contributing to higher prices.

Another bad aspect of indexing is that, in making so many people immune to the effects of inflation, it tends to lessen public opposition to deficit spending and excessive money creation which fuel the price spiral.

The time has come for the White House and Congress to take a long, careful look at what indexing has done to the federal budget and inflation. It may well be that indexing will have to be scaled back in order to get the galloping federal budget, rising interest rates and inflation under control.

THE PLAIN DEALER
Cleveland, Ohio, March 8, 1982

Social Security was one of the "Sacred Seven" federal programs President Reagan specifically spared from his budget-chopping ax. But Social Security is in danger.

Tides of population are producing more oldsters eligible to collect their retirement benefits — and creating fewer young workers to pay into the shaky Old Age and Survivors Insurance fund.

Today's bad times are making the trouble acute. The economy is stagnant. Nearly eight million are out of work. Jobs are scarce. That is forcing more people into retirement — onto the Social Security rolls.

And inflation keeps stepping up Social Security benefits. Those benefits are tied to the Consumer Price Index (CPI) to keep retirees' incomes from losing the race with soaring prices.

The CPI is under attack. Critics say the index is raising Social Security benefits too high too fast, though it does not lift retiree benefits faster than inflation. But a price index should not be used as a cost-of-living index. This year there may be an all-out effort to trim the cost of this adjustment to Social Security.

According to the CPI, inflation added 12.5% to consumer prices in 1980. Giving retirees a similar increase would keep them even with inflation, but possibly it would give them more than their living costs went up.

The CPI keeps accurate track of the price of its carefully selected market basket of meat, milk, bus fare, shirts, rent, vegetables, fuels and whatever else people buy.

But it does not keep track of the actual cost of living. Its market basket is around 10 years old. Meanwhile consumers have shifted from expensive beef to cheaper pork and chicken. They do not eat out so often. They don't burn so much gasoline.

That kind of change is better reflected by the Personal Consumption Expenditure (PCE) measure of the Commerce Department. Its weightings change with the patterns of consumption. And it measures homeownership in terms of rental equivalent.

Homeownership is a massive 25% or more of the CPI's components. And the CPI reflects sky-high home prices and sky-high mortgage rates as they are today. Those prices are not fair in showing what old persons' housing costs them.

Eighty percent of older people on Social Security own their own homes, and 80% of those own them free and clear. If they are still paying on a mortgage, the interest rate is less than today's prohibitive 13% or 14%.

Of course Social Security is only one federal program in which the CPI figures. Many of those other programs need the CPI as it is, containing the high-ticket homeownership data. Today's rates and prices are important in union contract cost-of-living clauses, which affect people of all ages.

But for Social Security and other pensioner classes, the CPI is probably faulty. Bureau of Labor Statistics economists are working on alternatives to it. The five they are watching now all would alter the homeownership component, using rental equivalent or some other modification.

Some other version of the CPI should be chosen soon by the wisest governing minds. Meanwhile, a genuine cost-of-living measure should replace the CPI for Social Security indexing. And the changeover to a new, fairer CPI should be done as promptly as its elaborate and complex system allows.

The Morning News

Wilmington, Del., August 11, 1982

SOCIAL SECURITY STANDS out as the untouchable in the current budget cutting, tax hiking tug of war. But that immunity from manipulation will end abruptly once the November elections are over and the president's commission on Social Security comes in with its recommendations.

As everyone knows, adjustments in Social Security will have to be made, and made promptly, if the trust fund is to be kept out of the red. The need for change has been made clear; what is still not certain is how these changes are to be made.

While the presidential commission is far from having finished its task and has agreed on no specific recommendations, periodically it sends up trial balloons about possible changes. One such balloon was sent skyward this week.

The commission, we are told, is considering tying the benefit increases in Social Security to a nationwide wage index rather than keeping the present link to the Consumer Price Index. This change would have merit.

● Wages reflect the health of the economy better than prices. So tying the Social Security benefits to them would be more realistic.

● In a healthy economy, as wages rise, the Social Security taxes paid rise with them, and so the trust fund can also pay out proportionately higher benefits.

● There are numerous items on the CPI that have less effect on the lives of the retired than on those still employed; among these are houses and cars, and even the outlay for clothes diminishes with retirement from the work force.

● Recently, Americans have experienced the curious phenomenon that those on Social Security were getting substantially higher percentage increases in their "paychecks" than those still in the work force whose raises fell substantially below the rapidly climbing cost of living. Over the last three years, average wages increased 30 percent, while the CPI went up 40 percent.

A chart prepared by the Social Security reform commission shows that since 1975, when automatic benefit increases tied to the CPI began, lower benefits would have been paid out under the wage-link except for 1977, when the wage-tied formula would have brought about a bigger increase. In economically stable times, the differences between the two formulas are minor. For instance, in 1978, the present formula yielded a 6.5 percent boost, while the proposed formula would have resulted in a 6.3 percent increase. In 1980, however, the increases to beneficiaries were at 14.3 percent, while under the wage-linked formula they would have amounted to only 6.8 percent.

It is discrepancies such as the one in 1980 that have contributed to putting Social Security into its present troubled situation. To assure that they do not occur again, tying Social Security benefits to nationwide wage rates makes good sense. This is a trial balloon that should fly.

THE DAILY OKLAHOMAN

Oklahoma City, Okla., August 16, 1982

PROPOSALS for shoring up the ailing Social Security system have long included a recommendation that cost-of-living adjustments be linked to changes in nationwide wage rates rather than fluctuations in the Consumer Price Index.

Critics of the index contend it exaggerates the living costs of many Social Security recipients because it includes interest costs for home mortgages which in their case were mostly paid off years ago. Defenders of the existing formula say older people have medical expenses and other financial burdens that exceed the general run of living costs as reflected by the CPI.

Whatever the merits of these arguments, the proposed change is expected to be included in the recommendations of a 15-member presidential commission which is scheduled to report before the end of the year.

Under the proposal, Social Security benefits would be adjusted annually to reflect the percentage increase in nationwide wage rates, minus a certain percentage to account for assumed gains in productivity. If the revised formula had been in effect this year, recipients would have received a cost-of-living increase of 6.2 percent instead of 7.4 percent.

Alan Greenspan, chairman of the bipartisan National Commission on Social Security Reform, says he favors the proposed new formula because it would help stabilize the system, reducing the sensitivity of the trust funds to fluctuations in economic activity.

"Over the longer run," says Greenspan, "you are tying benefits to the price level. Unit labor costs will move with the price level over the long run." But Social Security recipients may not be impressed greatly by conjecture over what to expect in the "long run." In the long run, as the saying goes, they'll all be dead.

Fully aware of the explosive nature of the subject, the commission hasn't yet voted on any substantive proposals, and is trying first to build a consensus. But a consensus will be hard to find, even on a suggestion as relatively bland as the one changing the cost-of-living formula

That change is opposed by Lane Kirkland, president of the AFL-CIO, who is a member of the commission, and by the American Association of Retired Persons.

It has long been apparent that something was going to have to be done about capping the ever-rising cost-of-living adjustments if the long-term solvency of Social Security and all other federal pension programs was to be assured. The proposed change in the method of computing the COLAs further complicates the problem without really solving anything basically.

Past reports by Social Security study groups have agreed that the current retirement age of 65 should be raised gradually to 68 in light of the fact that people are living longer productive lives. This matter is almost certain to be addressed in the forthcoming report of the Greenspan commission.

But the details of any proposed changes will be surrounded by controversy that could make the latest study just another of many already accumulating dust in the archives.

Arkansas Gazette.
Little Rock, Ark.,
September 7, 1981

A "bipartisan" solution to the problem of financing Social Security is the expressed goal of Richard Schweiker, the secretary for Health and Human Services. It is a nice thought to entertain, in advance of the reassembling of Congress after the August recess. The probable bipartisan solution will be legislation to allow the Social Security retirement fund to borrow from the Medicare and Disability funds, thus postponing a reckoning.

Even in his honeymoon period, which is probably over now, President Reagan could not do much with cutting the cost of Social Security retirement benefits. He got through a phased elimination of student benefits, and the early elimination of the minimum benefit, measures that saved maybe $2 billion or $3 billion a year, which isn't much on the Brobdingnagian scale of the Social Security disbursement. There was heavy opposition to dropping the minimum benefit, and the word is that the administration will reestablish that benefit under welfare, at least in part. The budget savings will thus be diminished.

Back in the spring, the President sallied forth with much bolder propositions for cutting the costs of Social Security but beat a quick retreat before the might of the grand army of Social Security beneficiaries. Politically, the consequences of Social Security reform are hazardous if not brutal.

The melancholy part of the whole controversy is that there is one place — the COLA, Cost-of-Living Adjustment — where several billion dollars a year could be reasonably saved by using the average wage index, rather than the Consumer Price Index, in measuring the annual increment for Social Security recipients. At one point last spring the Senate, controlled by the Republicans, passed a resolution making the substitution on the COLA but the proposition was later lost in the shuffle. We rather doubt that the Republican leadership in the Senate or the Democratic leadership in the House or the administration will propose to reform the COLA this fall. There will be a splendid bipartisan agreement, we suspect, to leave Social Security retirement benefits alone and borrow money from the other components to tide the fund over through the next election.

The Orlando Sentinel
Orlando, Fla., January 19, 1983

When Rep. Wilbur Mills made his brief bid for the Democratic presidential nomination in 1972, he succeeded in passing legislation that set automatic cost-of-living increases in Social Security benefits. It made the Ways and Means Committee chairman many friends among retirees. But those COLAs — cost of living adjustments — are a burden that have almost killed the Social Security system.

A limit on COLAs was one of the first agreements out of the Social Security reform commission, though members knew it would be a lightning-rod issue. Many retirees say they are being forced to give up something they are entitled to receive.

The commission's recommendation is to postpone July's automatic increase for six months. It also calls for automatic reductions in future raises when the Social Security trust fund begins to run short. Those changes would save an estimated $40 billion during the next seven years.

Such an adjustment is modest enough, considering the damage COLAs have caused. The worst feature was to tie those increases to the same index used to determine living costs for young families. Their needs are much different from those of retirees. The result was that Social Security benefits, adjusted for inflation, increased 37 percent during the 1970s while real wages remained level. As the economy staggered, the trust fund was paying more from a dwindling pool of money.

It is understandable that many retirees get nervous at the mere hint of curtailing future benefits. Though Social Security was not meant to be a primary source of retirement income, two-thirds of the nation's elderly get at least half of their cash from the system. It is the sole income for 60 percent of unmarried women over 65. Social Security was intended to provide only part of retirement's needs.

A collapse of Social Security is much worse than a restraint on future benefits. If the system is to be healthy again, trimming the COLAs is part of the cure.

St. Petersburg Times
St. Petersburg, Fla., January 7, 1983

"Those people presently on Social Security are going to get their checks and their checks are not going to be reduced below what they're presently getting."

President Reagan intended those words as reassurance to the 36-million retirees on Social Security that their checks will keep coming. Unfortunately, he left so much unsaid that few persons are likely to be reassured.

All Americans should be concerned about this most successful and vital of federal domestic programs, but two groups are intensely interested in Social Security's current difficulty: Those already retired and receiving checks and those persons in middle age who, along with their employers, have contributed to the trust funds during all their working lives and are counting on retiring in the years ahead.

WHEN THE President promises that "checks are not going to be reduced below what they are presently getting," he raises the issue of the continuation of the cost of living adjustments (COLAs). Before 1975, Social Security benefits were raised to compensate for inflation at the whim of Congress. The process was thoroughly politicized, with increases often coming in election years followed by charges that the party in power sought political gains.

Both the Republican and Democratic platforms in 1968 called for adjusting benefits automatically to inflation. The GOP platform promised: "We will strengthen the Social Security system and provide automatic cost of living adjustments under Social Security." When COLAs became law in 1972 and were implemented in 1975, the program was vastly improved. That significant reform ought not to be abandoned because of the program's present problems.

Of course, no one could anticipate the effects of rising energy costs on the economy. The consumer price index soared while wages (and Social Security taxes) lagged. That is one reason for the present shortages in the trust funds. COLAs now are sometimes criticized, but few people note that without them the nation's senior citizens would have fallen far behind in the struggle against inflation. If COLAs must be changed as a part of a balanced program including more revenues, a fair approach would be to link them to wages rather than consumer prices. We have supported that in the past and we believe many retirees would support it as part of a way to bring the program back into balance.

AT HIS PRESS conference Wednesday, President Reagan again refused to offer any leadership to the commission studying Social Security. That is what is badly needed if people are to be reassured about the program. Instead of complaining about the 1977 tax increases for Social Security, the President should be explaining why they were necessary. Instead of dodging responsibility, the President should be working out a compromise with Congress that will carry the program over this temporary shortage.

No one in Congress can offer that leadership. The commission cannot do it alone. Our nation functions on a presidential system. Only the president has the standing to pull conflicting interests into a workable compromise.

Doubts raised by the President himself with previous criticism of Social Security taxes, suggestions for making the program voluntary and cuts in benefits cause much of the present uncertainty.

If the President wants to quiet all the fears raised about Social Security, he will have to persuade people that he fully supports Social Security's goal of a public program guaranteeing all older Americans a basic pension that will allow them to live out their lives with dignity.

Using General Revenues; Imposing a New Tax

One of the most popular proposals to bail out the Social Security system, recommended by several study groups, would be to pay some part of benefits from general revenues. Most frequently, it has been suggested that all or part of Medicare be financed this way. Funding through general revenues could be accomplished either by increasing personal income taxes and corporate profits taxes, or imposing a new tax such as an alcohol, energy or value-added tax. Both ideas have received recurrent attention in Congress.

The substitution of income taxes for payroll taxes is especially attractive regarding Medicare because the benefits received under that program are not linked to the level of prior earnings, as are the retirement and disability benefits. They are calculated on a cost-reimbursement basis irrespective of the financial need of the recipient. Hence, a major rationale for using the payroll tax—to link benefits to taxes paid, weighting them in favor of the poor—does not apply. From this viewpoint, Medicare should never have been placed under the payroll tax, and a more logical alternative to the present system would be a national health insurance program.

One argument made against general revenue financing is that workers not covered by Social Security and thus not eligible for Medicare benefits would be contributing to the program. Some opponents also fear that the major cause of Medicare's growing financial problems—the escalating costs of medical care and hospitalization—would be exacerbated through the use of a less visible tax. The result, they warn, might be less concern with the urgent necessity of hospital cost containment.

The Miami Herald
Miami, Fla., February 9, 1978

TAXES don't hurt as much if you don't know you're paying them. That seems to be the rationale behind the latest search for new ways of supporting the perennially imperiled Social Security System.

Congress may have expected a pat on the back when it put the system on more solid financial ground by raising the ante both wage earners and employers will pay in coming years. To soften the blow, the increases were scheduled to start a full year away, in January 1979, and then escalate gradually. At last, the crisis was over.

This mild euphoria apparently ended as soon as the public started reading newspaper projections that showed an individual's payroll tax for Social Security could more than triple by 1987. Even in the lower-income ranks, the bite is scheduled to roughly double. Employers had read the forecasts early and were already voicing their anguish.

So now comes a bill introduced by five congressmen and two senators that would cut the planned payroll tax rate by almost a third. It would do so by using general revenues — ergo, income-tax money — to support the ever-costlier Medicare and disability-insurance programs.

Actually, the move makes some fiscal sense. When the system was designed, it was meant as a retirement supplement.

Medical care and disability can very logically be listed as welfare functions that ought to be supported by the income tax.

But the bill's supporters made their real purpose clear, by saying they wanted to ease the bite of "an intolerably burdensome payroll tax for middle-income taxpayers and for many businesses." Softening the blow, they contended, would spur hiring and curb inflation.

Trouble is, there are only two realistic ways of raising the money for Medicare and disability, expected to be about $37 billion next year and $93 billion annually by 1987. Those ways are higher income taxes or more deficit spending.

Although it may take some of the pressure off low-income families, the proposed change would leave middle-income workers and businesses just about where they started under the present plan. It's hard to see how the tradeoff could spark fresh investment if other taxes rose, or curb inflation if the Government had to borrow more.

Only one thing is certain about the plan, if it ever manages to be written into law: The paycheck stub item marked "FICA," for Social Security deductions, will be smaller. Perhaps the sponsors figure that's popular enough. Most people have resigned themselves to fat increases in the withholding tax, and besides, there's always a chance Congress will pass an election-year tax cut.

THE INDIANAPOLIS STAR
Indianapolis, Ind., February 13, 1978

A loud, prolonged howling throughout the nation, heard with blood-chilling clarity in Washington, is being interpreted on Capitol Hill as the first battle-yell in a ready-to-explode tax rebellion.

After piling that heavy new Social Security tax on top of the other income tribute exacted with painful regularity by our lawmakers, what did they expect?

One way or another, government consumes in the neighborhood of 40 percent of the substance of middle-income families. And so, from one end of the country to the other, middle-income Americans are howling.

"The public will not stand for the rate of taxes that has been imposed," Rep. William Brodhead (D-Mich.) told a news conference.

So what does Congress intend to do about it? One right thing would be to curtail some of the welfare features that have so increased the drain on Social Security of late. Another right thing would be to cut unhealthily bloated spending programs throughout the government correspondingly to lower income taxes, producing a lesser overall individual tax load.

But some leaders propose to do the wrong thing. Their plan is to dip into general tax revenues to help finance Social Security. This would eliminate one sound feature of the existing system, which is bookkeeping that now lets taxpayers know how much of their money is going into Social Security. The individual taxpayer feels it. It is painfully high, hence his screaming.

It would be a backward step to end the clear-cut accounting and begin shifting Social Security financing out of the daylight and into the murky, treacherous jungle of the deficit-ridden general budget. There even economic experts are led astray, amid fiscal mirages and sinkholes, by the chanting of fiduciary witch-doctors and the beating of the willful spendthrifts' tribal drums.

If Congress should make this change, the opportunities for further corruption of the Social Security program — for its conversion into a lucky-dollars giveaway to millions who have contributed little or nothing to the funding — would multiply.

The proposal is both dangerous and deceitful and, if carried out, would lead to a bleeding much worse than the one that is making middle-income taxpayers howl.

THE SACRAMENTO BEE
Sacramento, Calif., February 21, 1978

Ever since Congress voted for a heavy increase in the Social Security tax last November, Rep. Al Ullman, chairman of the House Ways and Means Committee, and Sen. Russell Long, chairman of the Senate Finance Committee, have been worried about the effect on the voters.

They're afraid that when Social Security levies are combined with income taxes the result will generate more political heat than any legislator can stand

They may be right, but the alternative they suggest for collecting the taxes is even worse.

The idea (it has not been formally proposed or submitted) is to levy a tax on every stage of production of manufactured goods until it reaches the consumer.

Ullman is advocating what he calls a "transaction-type tax on the wholesale level." He says it wouldn't be a value-added tax, which is a favorite among European nations, but of course that is exactly what it would be. Painless, perhaps; hidden, yes; but still pernicious.

The suggestion, in essence, is to levy a national sales tax. Since it would be included in the retail price of the product, the consumer wouldn't realize he or she was paying it.

Ullman says food and other essential consumer products might be exempted, but that's beside the point.

The idea is to substitute one sneaky, regressive tax for a highly visible one. No thanks, Al, we'd rather know what we are paying when we pay it.

Lincoln Journal
Lincoln, Neb., April 4, 1978

Rep. Al Ullman, chairman of the House Ways and Means Committee, has a terrible idea:

Pass President Carter's proposed tax on crude oil at the wellhead and temporarily use the billions of new dollars as substitute for higher Social Security taxes directed by Congress last year.

What a way to make a mess worse!

If Congress does go along with a wellhead tax, that revenue rightly should be channeled into energy-related sectors, or taxpayer rebates.

If what Ullman tosses out as a trial idea were accepted, the so-called "temporary" earmarking would be attached with buckets of Elmer's Glue, not light adhesive tape. It would become a fixed part of financing Social Security benefits.

Better that Congress do what it didn't have enough sense to accomplish in Lyndon Johnson's era — shift the costs of underwriting a health care system for Social Security beneficiaries from the trust fund to national general revenues.

The Salt Lake Tribune
Salt Lake City, Utah,
April 7, 1978

Would the marriage of an energy tax and the financially troubled Social Security system be a happy one?

The possible romance is still mostly a gleam in some congressmen's eyes. It is by no means certain of vigorous support on Capitol Hill or in the White House. Still, the proposal is being talked up as an acceptable way to cut recently imposed new Social Security taxes and discourage energy consumption in the process.

At first glance diverting energy tax funds to an ailing social program seems almost an inspired concept. This presumes that an energy tax will somehow emerge from a House-Senate Conference Committee still wrangling over a controversial energy bill. The House approved such a measure but it has reportedly been dropped in conference. The tax could, however be revived.

A fundamental danger in any such mating is that it probably would lock an energy tax into the picture forever. Raising or lowering the energy tax might then become the main vehicle for determining the level of Social Security benefits rather than the present payroll tax.

That may or may not be good but it would sure be different. And, like proposals for financing Social Security from the general fund, it opens the door to irresponsible benefits expansion far beyond that which occurred under payroll tax financing.

"Splicing" an energy tax and Social Security cannot be called a union made in heaven. But considering the manifold problems facing both parties, the affair deserves consideration.

Los Angeles Times
Los Angeles, Calif., March 17, 1978

Under growing pressure from the voters, members of Congress are looking for ways to scale down the massive payroll-tax increase that they imposed on the American worker in December. A badly needed new Social Security financing plan was enacted then to keep the system from going broke.

The new taxes will take $75 billion more out of the private economy over the next five years, half of it from workers and half from their employers.

The added taxes are a big chunk out of family budgets. A household earning $20,000 a year paid $965 to Social Security last year, but would see $1,330 go to the system in 1981.

The tax increases tend to curb the job market, because higher payroll levies increase the already-high cost of hiring people.

Next year will be the first year of the new tax system, and some $6.4 billion more will be collected than under the old law. How to moderate this heavy blow is the goal of current discussions in Congress.

Aides to Chairman Russell B. Long of the Senate Finance Committee, among others, are studying whether President Carter's proposed new tax on domestic crude oil could be used to finance part of Social Security's needs.

Rep. James A. Burke (D-Mass.) has another idea: a bill that would raise about $35 billion a year for Social Security—roughly one-third of the system's needs—from the general revenue brought in by individual and corporate income taxes.

We don't like either approach, because keeping Social Security tied to the payroll tax acts as a needed brake on pension benefits.

A better solution is being pushed by Rep. Abner J Mikva (D-Ill.) and Sen. Gaylord Nelson (D-Wis.). Resurrecting an idea introduced by an advisory council in 1975, Mikva and Nelson propose to take the costs of disability insurance and Medicare hospital coverage out of Social Security's budgets.

We've always thought that this shift should be part of a refinancing package. Hospital insurance consumed 15% of the combined Social Security tax collections in 1977, and is expected to take 22% by 1985. Its costs are estimated at $19 billion this year, but are expected to approach $35 billion by 1980. That is roughly $350 in payroll-tax contributions from each of the estimated 100 million workers in the country today.

Phasing Medicare and disability insurance gradually off the payroll tax and onto the income tax would distribute their burdens more nearly in relation to ability to pay. The expected normal growth in income-tax revenues would make the transfer possible, although not easy.

Carter's plan to cut personal and corporate income taxes by about $25 billion a year would have to be adjusted for the impact of the Mikva-Nelson proposal. That should not be difficult or complicated.

As to Social Security's basic pension system itself, we think it should stay firmly planted in the payroll tax for at least the next 20 years. After the year 2010, circumstances could begin to change dramatically. That is when the big bulge in population will have passed age 65, and the people born after World War II will have begun collecting pension benefits and thus taking money out of the system.

New answers will be needed then to keep the system going, and they may have to include the abandonment of the payroll tax as Social Security's bedrock. Maybe then. But not now.

St. Petersburg Times

St. Petersburg, Fla., January 17, 1981

It's a fluke of our system that a defeated president is required to prepare and submit a budget almost on the eve of his successor's inauguration. This time, especially, the president-elect wants to alter as much as he can, and the profound changes that have occurred in Congress tempt him to try.

Not for long will Citizen Carter be able to recognize the budget he leaves behind him. Ronald Reagan wants tax cuts. Instead, Carter proposed a 10-cents-a-gallon gasoline tax increase. There is no chance, not even a far-fetched one, that Congress will agree.

THE BUDGET, however, is more than just a spending plan. It is also a political statement. And it would be tragic if the winds of change that are sweeping down on Washington were allowed to obliterate the constructive recommendations that Carter was attempting to leave upon the capital's fickle political landscape.

The most important was his suggestion that Congress discard tradition and use general revenue funds to help out the Social Security system, whose retirement account faces a cash-flow crunch within two years. When Carter speaks about Social Security, even his enemies owe him the respect of listening. He recommended and signed into law a massive increase in Social Security taxes. Those were courageous acts that were cited against him in last year's campaign, but had he not taken them his successor would be facing a Social Security crisis right now.

WHAT CARTER proposed in his budget message is that Congress select from all or some of these options:

✔ Allow the retirement fund to borrow from the smaller trust funds that finance Medicare and payments to the disabled.

✔ Allow the retirement fund to borrow from general tax revenues as necessary.

✔ Finance Medicare from income taxes, so as to divert to the retirement fund the portion of the Social Security payroll tax that now supports Medicare.

✔ Raise payroll taxes yet again.

SWITCHING Medicare to a general revenue base would release $32.5-billion this year, and $39-billion in fiscal 1982, for assistance to the hard-pressed retirement fund. It would add $24.3-billion

this year, and $27.3-billion next year, to general revenue expenses supported primarily by income taxes. Why the difference? It's simply that the Medicare program is taking in more money from its pledged revenues than it is paying out.

Medicare should not depend on Social Security payroll taxes. The only relationship it bears to Social Security is that one must be eligible for Social Security to enroll in Medicare. (Even so, those who aren't eligible — mostly retired government and military personnel — can buy in to Medicare at a special, high monthly fee.) The benefits available to a Medicare recipient depend solely on the state of that person's health and the ceilings set by law. They have nothing to do with that person's previous income level or the number of years he or she paid Social Security taxes. Social Security retirement checks, on the other hand, are based on previous earnings.

IN EFFECT, Medicare is a general medical entitlement program for almost *all* persons over 65, which is financed out of Social Security taxes simply because Congress seized upon a separate, pre-existing source of financing. This was supposed to protect Medicare from politics. But the reverse proved true. Because Medicare depends on the highly visible payroll tax, Congress is not only afraid to increase Medicare benefits; it is unwilling even to sustain them. Medicare now pays for only 40 percent of the average enrollee's medical bills. The benefits, however meager, bear no relationship to lifetime earnings, which exacerbates the regressive nature of the Social Security payroll taxes.

There's nothing radical to the idea of using general revenue for Medicare. It's already being done. General revenue, not the Social Security tax, pays the federal government's share, more than $9-billion a year, of Medicare Part B, the optional supplemental coverage for physicians' bills. General revenue should pay for the basic hospitalization coverage, too.

That would counteract the regressive aspect of the Social Security tax, make it politically feasible for the Congress to expand Medicare coverage and put the retirement fund on a sound footing. Workers and retirees have a common interest in these objectives and should be urging the Congress to comply.

Albuquerque, N.M., February 12, 1978

Congress, worried about its political neck this year, goofed last year when it approved sharp increases in Social Security taxes. Obviously, many people have been stung by the new rates, and their outcry has stirred new thinking in Washington.

The massive tax increases reflected in the 1978 payroll checks were a simple solution to a complex problem that has the program paying out more than it is taking in.

It had been the subject of debate for many months, and Congress wanted to avoid tax action in an election year. However, during the discussions, various ills were identified, indicating several treatments were needed for a cure.

Among them was one which is the focus of new legislation recently introduced in both houses. The proposal would reduce the payroll taxes by financing some of the benefits from general revenue — the income tax system.

Specific benefits proposed for removal are the disability insurance program and Medicare hospital insurance. That would leave benefits only for retired workers and their dependents or survivors.

Such treatment was strongly advocated prior to the rash increases in December. But, many members of Congress saw such a move as a "foot in the door that could lead to a great Treasury raid."

Now, financing the cost of disability and Medicare out of income tax revenues, just like any other government program, seems to make sense. And now, Congress might be pursuing the right approach to a solution.

THE DAILY OKLAHOMAN

Oklahoma City, Okla., May 31, 1981

MEDICARE'S rapidly rising costs are seen as a fatal drawback to President Reagan's proposals to keep the Social Security system solvent while still limiting future increases in the payroll tax.

A. Haeworth Robertson, a former chief actuary for the system (and a graduate of the University of Oklahoma), says the payroll tax will have to be increased to 10 percent or more, even if all of Reagan's proposed benefit cuts are approved. He says this is the prospect because the administration ignored the rising costs of Medicare in its long-range projections.

The present congressional mood is to reject or modify some or all of the administration's key proposals. Confronted with a hostile congressional reaction, the administration appeared to be backing down when Health and Human Services Secretary Richard S. Schweiker told the House Select Committee on Aging that "we are willing to entertain other ideas."

One such idea is a proposal by Chairman J.J. Pickle, D-Texas, of the House Social Security subcommittee to transfer half the money in the still-flourishing

Medicare trust to the ailing retirement fund that is threatened by bankruptcy as early as next year if nothing is done to salvage it. The Medicare trust would be reimbursed out of general revenues.

The proposal is part of legislation submitted by Pickle which contemplates a reduction in early retirement benefits but would postpone these cuts for at least 10 years. In order to find money to meet the immediate threat, Pickle was forced to resort to general revenues.

It's said there are no politically easy solutions to the accumulating difficulties of the vast Social Security system. But because it wouldn't directly damage any particular class of recipients, the proposed transfer of funds from Medicare would entail none of the political hazards associated with such explosive proposals as sharply reduced benefits or still higher payroll taxes.

Thus the eventual financing of Medicare out of general revenues is by no means inconceivable, despite the present opposition of conservatives in both branches of Congress as well as the White House.

The Courier-Journal

Louisville, Ky., February 16, 1978

CONGRESSMAN REÚSS of Wisconsin calls President Carter's plan to reduce income taxes as compensation for the stiff increases in Social Security levies a new kind of Gresham's law. He's right.

This time, it isn't bad money driving out good, but a regressive payroll tax forcing cuts in the more progressive income tax. If a bad tax really is replacing a good one, as millions of angry Americans have been telling their congressmen, why not look for fairer ways of keeping the Social Security system sound?

One alternative being seriously pushed on Capitol Hill would use general taxes to pay for two newer Social Security programs — disability insurance, enacted in 1957, and Medicare hospital coverage, adopted in 1964. This would leave the largest Social Security benefits — old-age and survivors insurance — reliant on payroll taxes. But it would permit a cut of about one-third in the sharply higher rates now projected from 1979 on.

Support from general revenues is not a new idea. The authors of Social Security seem to have anticipated that, when the system reached maturity, the half-employer, half-employe contributions would be changed to one-third from each and the remaining one-third from general taxes.

More recently, Social Security advisory committees have proposed dipping into general revenues. President Carter last year proposed temporary infusions of income-tax funds whenever unemployment topped 6 percent and thus sharply reduced payments. But the conservative Senate Finance Committee defeated the idea.

Though Social Security taxes rose January 1, that was provided by previous law. The new rates approved in 1977 were delayed until 1979 because of congressional worry about the effect of a steep new payroll tax on the economy at this time — and on this year's congressional elections.

The tax is regressive

The cumulative effect of the scheduled rates is a $185 billion bite in the eight years following 1979, or the equivalent in lost spending money of 3 percent additional unemployment. Computer simulations show that use of an income tax to raise the same revenue would have a much less depressing impact on the economy.

But it's not only immediate economic effects that bother critics of the Social Security payroll tax. It's unfair. Like a sales tax, which is not based on ability to pay but hits low-income people harder because they must spend a greater percentage of their money on goods, it's regressive. And it has the additional inequity of taxing everyone on the same wage base. This is now $17,700, and it's scheduled to rise to $42,600 by 1987. Thus the assembly-line worker may pay the tax on his entire income, while the movie producer pays only up to the same wage ceiling and may have several year-end months in which he pays no tax.

Keeping the payroll tax for Social Security sometimes is defended on the ground that both employer and employe share the bite: 6.05 percent of earnings this year. But that's misleading, too, since the employer's share actually is money that otherwise might provide raises or more jobs, and since what he pays also is chargeable on corporate returns as a cost of doing business.

Yet it's obvious that shifting to general revenues for the disability and health segments of Social Security should not be sold as a miracle cure for what ails the system. Paying for these two costly insurance plans out of the general budget clearly would require such compensating adjustments as higher income tax rates or cuts in federal spending. Neither could be called easy. But the point is that either would be fairer than the payroll bite.

(There's an additional argument for switching to general revenues for disability and Medicare. It's that those who don't pay into Social Security — such as members of Congress and other federal employes, who have their own retirement system — would begin to provide through income taxes a share of the social cost of aiding the disabled and the needy elderly.)

The proposed law will get a hearing only when its chief sponsor, Wisconsin's Senator Nelson (Senator Huddleston is a co-sponsor), believes he has enough public support to clear the Finance Committee hurdle. Because Congress just finished an extensive Social Security debate, that could be next year, but Mr. Nelson has promised hearings this year in his subcommittee on Social Security financing.

To many, the plan will seem so sensible that they'll wonder why it can't be given priority over the administration's proposed reduction in income-tax rates. Why let a new Gresham's law operate, when a more progressive means of paying the heavy Social Security bills of the future appears to be available?

The trouble is that Congress already is cynical about its habit of raising retirement benefits in election years. It resists funneling general tax funds into Social Security, mainly from fear that having two sources of funds would double the temptation. But this risk could be lessened by using general revenues only for Medicare and disability payments, rather than the more politically potent retirement benefits for all.

The combined impacts of an aging population, inflation and recession convinced Congress last year to bite the bullet for future stability in the Social Security trust funds. This was commendable, but in its wake the long-predicted taxpayer revolt against the payroll method seems to be coming true.

Mr. Carter's income-tax cut would transfer funds from a progressive tax to make up for a regressive payroll bite. Why not do it the other way, by converting two more recently enacted parts of the entire Social Security system to the fairer general-revenue tax?

The Virginian-Pilot

Norfolk, Va., November 10, 1982

Over the weekend House Majority Leader Jim Wright offered his suggestions on rescuing Social Security. They were the first major ideas put forward since last Tuesday's election. They should also be the first to be tossed aside.

Mr. Wright says that $25 billion could be saved in the next three years if one-third of the nation's older workers were enticed to keep their jobs by the "carrot" of tax credits ranging up to $2,000. He also says that a 50-cent-per-gallon excise tax increase on liquor could help finance the system. So, he continues, could switching the government's offshore oil-lease revenues from the Treasury to Social Security.

The problem with each of these suggestions is the same. Each would enable Social Security to drink — for the first time ever — from the general fund. The tax credits — whose ability to cause later retirement has been disputed by Social Security actuaries — would deplete the general fund by like amounts. And it is the general fund that contains revenues from the alcohol excise tax and the offshore oil leases. The latter, not incidentally, would be an unreliable source of revenues for Social Security, given the volatility of the oil business.

Mr. Wright's proposals reflect the mind of a man who evidently believes that the Social Security deficit — expected to be $150 billion over the next seven years — can simply be absorbed elsewhere in the federal budget. Mirrors beyond the imagination of man would have to be invented, however, to keep a Social Security bailout by the general fund from adding to the huge budget deficits already expected through the end of this decade. Inevitably, other taxes beside the excise tax on liquor would have to be raised. The great question Mr. Wright fails to address is whether the American economy, already underproducing and in recession, can afford to be loaded down with another staggering load of taxes.

Midterm Democratic gains in the House of Representatives resulted in part from the party's ability to use and manipulate the Social Security issue. It is now incumbent on Democrats to face up to the hard choices, not avoid them by irresponsibly loading the system's problems onto the general budget. At some point Democrats are going to have to talk about the very measures Mr. Wright opposes but which appear to be the only realistic options — increasing payroll taxes and cutting benefits. It would help if Mr. Wright, a key leader in the House, would change his mind and give these options serious attention.

Eliminating the Minimum Benefit

The minimum benefit is received by Social Security beneficiaries whose average monthly earnings would, under the usual formula for determination of benefit levels, qualify them for less than that amount. Instituted to provide a cushion against poverty for those recipients who relied almost entirely on their benefits for income, the amount of the monthly minimum benefit has risen from $10 in 1935 to $122 in 1981. The minimum benefit was frozen by Congress at the $122-a-month level as of 1979, and eliminated entirely in 1981 for anyone who became eligible after Jan. 1, 1982.

The minimum benefit came under criticism in the late 1970s when a number of studies revealed that those who received it were often people with other sources of income. For many recipients, their other income far surpassed that provided by the benefit. A substantial portion of these recipients were federal workers who had also worked long enough in covered employment to qualify for "windfall" Social Security benefits. The primary objection to the elimination of the minimum benefit is that there are some elderly recipients who are ineligible for coverage under the Supplementary Security Income (SSI) program, are not covered by private pension plans, and have worked only sporadically in employment covered by Social Security; they would receive a negligible monthly benefit as their sole income.

The Dallas Morning News
Dallas, Texas, July 23, 1981

IT'S easy to understand why some people are confused about efforts to cut the minimum Social Security benefit.

That's because most people don't understand what the minimum benefit is. They're afraid it means losing part of their Social Security benefits. And unfortunately, the Democratic leadership is attempting to use that uncertainty to put the Reagan administration behind the eight ball. The result is the cruelest kind of political hypocrisy, with Democratic leaders playing on the fears of senior citizens for a short-lived political gain.

Rep. Donald Riegle, D-Mich., has cried that the effort to cut the minimum benefit is "about as heartless a thing as you could do." Sen. Russell Long, D-La., has criticized the harm that would be done to "those dear little people." House Majority Leader Jim Wright has claimed in pious pronouncements that the cutback would hurt old women who are counting on Congress to defend them.

Crocodile tears. The truth is, dropping the minimum benefit of $122 a month for 3 million questionable recipients would have a negligible impact. And by saving $7 billion in the next five years, the cutback could go a long way in saving the system for the 35 million deserving recipients — ironically these are the ones who are most frightened.

An analysis of the numbers involved shows that 800,000 of the 3 million current recipients have a total income of $20,000 a year or more and actually do not need the minimum benefit, which was intended as a welfare floor for the truly needy. Another 1.7 million are either "double-dippers" who receive dual benefits or persons who are classified as minimum beneficiaries only through accounting technicality and who also do not really need the small stipend. Another 200,000 are college students or minor dependents.

The remaining 300,000 are those whose precise income or need is not known. But according to Social Security estimates, those remaining few would most likely qualify for Supplemental Security Income, which is intended to help retirees in need who do not qualify for other Social Security income. All told, those needy could qualify for $9,600 a year in SSI, state supplemental security income, food stamps and Medicaid, much more than the $122 a month minimum benefit would provide.

So much for the political scare tactics that attempt to portray the plan as a heartless administration throwing helpless senior citizens out on the streets. As conservative Rep. Phil Gramm, D-Texas, pointed out, the Democratic leadership is calling for the continuation of unearned benefits for non-needy citizens while cloaking themselves in the mantle of "protecting" the system. In doing so, they are allowing the system to be drained of $7 billion, jeopardizing the system and people they claim to be protecting.

That's politics as usual for the liberal leaders. But as the facts become known, voters who come to understand exactly what the minimum benefit is all about, may not be fooled, or forgiving.

THE KANSAS CITY STAR
Kansas City, Mo.,
March 30, 1981

It's all very well to talk about cutting persons enjoying a "windfall" from the Social Security program. But that's a false description of many receiving minimum Social Security benefits, therefore a phony frugality proposed for the federal budget.

One change in Social Security proposed by the Reagan administration is elimination of minimum benefits. They go to persons who are insured—that is, who have earned enough quarters to qualify for the program but whose earnings have been so low that if benefits were computed normally, the checks would be quite small, perhaps $50 a month. The minimum benefit provision ensures that no one eligible for Social Security receives less than $122, far from a princely sum for anyone without other income. Administration apologists claim that the needy losing the minimum benefits could apply for Supplemental Security Income (SSI), a welfare program, and therefore would not be materially hurt.

The so-called windfall applies to some federal employees retiring before the age of 65 who find another job, working just long enough to qualify for Social Security. Their collection of checks is contrary to the intent of the provision: to help those with a very small lifetime income. Little justifiable outcry could be made against eliminating benefits in the case of government employees who retire early and collect minimum benefit checks. According to a spokesman for the Department of Health and Human Services, however, a large share of the estimated 200,000 persons who stand to lose the $122 monthly would be women aged 62 to 65. It would be a devastating blow to these women after a lifetime of discrimination in low-income jobs, women without private pensions or spouses upon whose earnings they could draw Social Security benefits. They could not qualify for SSI until the age of 65. It would be interesting to hear arguments about why they aren't "truly deserving."

If a distinction could be made between older persons whose only source of income is the minimum Social Security program (and certainly no one would be living very extravagantly on $122 a month) and those for whom it is frosting on the cake, fine. Otherwise this budget cut would be a cruelty rather than an economy. The idea should be revamped or dropped.

Chicago Tribune

Chicago, Ill., July 21, 1981

It doesn't take a lot of brains to figure out how to save Social Security from the bankruptcy scheduled for next year — only a little courage. President Reagan demonstrated his when he proposed to reduce or eliminate an array of benefits. But Congress has refused to match Mr. Reagan's bravery, preferring instead to preserve unneeded payments at the peril of the system.

In their latest act of timidity, House Speaker Tip O'Neill and majority leader Jim Wright have begun to mobilize to salvage the minimum benefit — which the House had voted to abolish in its budget reconciliation bill. This $153-per-month payment goes to people who have contributed only negligible sums to the trust fund during their working lives. It was established in 1939 to protect poor workers who were frequently unemployed, and is defended as a provision essential to those most in need.

But over the years it has become instead a windfall for many affluent retirees. The pressure to reverse the vote comes from people who are well off — particularly retired federal employes, who make up 15 per cent of all minimum beneficiaries. The average federal retiree now getting the minimum benefit has a federal pension of more than $900 per month. In all likelihood he took a part-time job just long enough to qualify for Social Security on top of his civil service pension. Another 12 per cent of minimum beneficiaries have working spouses with incomes averaging more than $20,000 per year.

The elderly poor would lose nothing from this change. For every dollar they would lose from their minimum benefit, they would gain a dollar from Supplemental Security Income, Social Security's welfare program. More than half of minimum beneficiaries would suffer no reduction in income.

In the case of people who get offsetting payments from SSI, the government would save Social Security funds but lose an equal amount in general revenues. This is because SSI is not funded by the payroll tax. Since the immediate danger is to the retirement fund, the savings is worthwhile, even though one part of it is cancelled out.

Mr. O'Neill and Mr. Wright, posing as paragons of moderation, say they'll agree to eliminate the minimum benefit for future retirees if current ones are spared. But they know this change would save only a trivial sum, while the President's would save $1.3 billion next year. Scrapping the minimum benefit is only the beginning of efforts to save Social Security. But if these House leaders have their way, it may be the end.

The Houston Post

Houston, Texas, September 24, 1981

Testimony before a congressional panel the other day helps explain why it is often hard to make substantive cuts in the cost of government. On President Reagan's recommendation, Congress voted to eliminate the minimum Social Security benefit. That will save the financially strapped pension program an estimated $6.4 billion over the next five years. But Alice Rivlin, director of the Congressional Budget Office, warned the House Social Security Subcommittee that it will increase federal and state welfare costs.

The minimum benefit of $122 a month is paid to about 3 million people. The administration estimates that nearly a third of the recipients are also drawing pensions as retired federal employees who had worked in private industry long enough to qualify for Social Security benefits. With the elimination of the minimum Social Security benefit next March, however, many of the remainder could become eligible for such federal assistance programs as Supplemental Security Income and Medicaid to which most of the states contribute.

Rivlin told the House panel that, while repeal of the minimum benefit would save the Social Security System $1.4 billion in fiscal 1983, federal SSI expenditures would increase by $400 million to $650 million and federal Medicaid costs may go up an additional $100 million for that fiscal period. There is no way to estimate the additional costs to state governments, partly because the amounts contributed to these programs by individual states vary, as do their welfare programs.

The beleaguered Social Security program needs all the financial relief it can get, even if it must be obtained by shifting some responsibilities to other federal and state programs. But the taxpayers, who foot the bill for government at all levels, should be aware of the bottom line.

The Philadelphia Inquirer

Philadelphia, Pa., August 13, 1981

Last October, presidential candidate Ronald Reagan pledged he would protect benefits of "those now receiving — or looking forward to receiving — Social Security." That sounds clear. No ifs, ands or buts.

In his television speech a couple of weeks ago, President Reagan made another pledge: "I will not stand by and see those of you who are dependent on Social Security deprived of the benefits you've worked so hard to earn," he declared.

"You will continue to receive your checks in the full amount due you. In any plan to restore fiscal integrity of Social Security, I personally will see that no part of the plan will be at the expense of you who are now dependent on your monthly Social Security checks."

That sounds clear, too, but it is replete with ifs, ands and buts. A White House spokesman later admitted the language had been "carefully chosen." Take the word *dependent*. Does that mean fully dependent? If so, it means that people partially dependent on Social Security might lose benefits. Take the word *due*. Who decides what is due and what is not, and on what basis?

Take that little word *earn*, in the phrase, *"benefits you've worked so hard to earn."* What about the people who receive the $122-a-month minimum benefit, which Mr. Reagan wants to abolish as "an unearned benefit"? The italicized phrase, it turns out, had been added to Mr. Reagan's original language, because the Reagan administration is determined, as part of the cuts in Social Security benefits it has proposed, to kill the minimum benefit, at a supposed saving of $7 billion over the next five years.

Now who are these people receiving that "unearned benefit"? Consider, first, a special case. In 1972, the Congress made eligible for the $122-a-month minimum benefit several thousand elderly nuns and male clerics who, having taken vows of poverty and receiving no cash income, had not been eligible for Social Security before. In an amendment, Congress allowed their religious orders to make payments in their behalf, calculated on the basis of an income equivalent of around $100 a month.

It is true, of course, that these people have not contributed much to the system. To become eligible for minimum payments, a worker must have worked 40 quarters in jobs on which Social Security payments are made. The members of the cloistered orders have not even had time to do that.

Is it just to deprive them of their minimum benefits? Some might argue that it is: They swore vows of poverty, didn't they? Let them go on welfare, or charity. Others of a more compassionate nature would argue, however, that they have indeed worked hard, all their lives, to earn a decent retirement, and that depriving them of $122 a month is a poor way to save money.

Most people receiving minimum benefits have worked the necessary 40 quarters, or more, but usually in very low-paid jobs, like domestic service or migrant farming. There are about three million of them, mostly women in their 70s. About half a million are 80 years old or older. About 80,000 are over 90.

The Reagan administration insists that most of them are not "dependent" on Social Security. That depends on how you define "dependent." One thing is certain, and that is that not many of them will get a dime's worth of benefit from the tax cuts the administration and Congress have bestowed.

What about those former government employees, civilian and military, who, having retired at, say, 55, have worked 10 years in other jobs (or moonlighted along the way) and have made themselves eligible for a "double-dip"? There are some of them, but they are in small minority. The problem can easily be handled by passing a law saying that anybody drawing an annual government pension of perhaps $15,000 or $20,000 is not eligible for Social Security payments, or perhaps by taxing pension income over a certain level.

In the budget-slashing bill, Congress went along with the administration and eliminated the $122-a-month minimum benefit, but in separate action the House voted, 404 to 20, to preserve it. The Senate will have the legislation on its agenda when it returns from recess. It should pass the bill.

There are sensible ways of improving the Social Security system, the most sensible being to tap the general revenues for the noncontributory Medicare and disability funds, but it is neither sensible nor compassionate to eliminate benefits for those whom Texas Democratic Rep. Jim Wright accurately described as "among the poorest and the oldest and the most politically defenseless in our society."

The Washington Post
Times Herald

Washington, D.C., July 14, 1981

TAKE A WOMAN in her 80s who has very little money. One day soon she will open an official-looking envelope containing a machine-typed letter that informs her that the Social Security check she's been receiving for over 15 years will henceforth be reduced by about $100 a month, more than a fourth of her poverty-level income. There's some fine print she can't make out. It says that, if she'll dispose of her modest savings, she might be able to go on welfare to make up some of her loss.

Tear-jerker? Of course—but it's also a live possibility for many recipients of the Social Security minimum benefit who, under the provisions of the two budget bills now headed for conference, will share an income loss of about $1 billion starting next year. We don't know how many such cases there are among the total, but neither does Congress or David Stockman. Perhaps this is why they found it easy to make this cut while shying away from others affecting more vocal segments of the Social Security population.

The Social Security Administration estimates that there are about 3 million people receiving benefits close to the minimum, 2 million of whom will be likely to face a significant income loss. These are people who, as a result of low wages or relatively few years of employment covered by Social Security, would qualify at retirement for benefits smaller than $122 a month. Some may have worked for many years as domestics, farm workers or in low-wage self-employment not covered by Social Se-

curity at the time. Others may have entered the labor force late in life after the death of a supporting relative or desertion by a spouse.

On the other hand, some with substantial property income or a working spouse may be relatively well off. A small percent are retired federal workers, some with ample pensions, who earned a Social Security benefit in a few years of private sector employment. The only estimates people have on how many fall into what category of need come from a 1977 survey, but since it only covered people then entering the rolls it didn't give a good picture of minimum beneficiaries, most of whom are known to be quite old—over half a million are said to be in their 80s—and almost all of whom are women. A third of the group might recoup some or all of their loss from welfare, if they're willing to apply. Welfare grants, however, are typically less than a poverty level income and are offset by income from savings or pensions while Social Security is not.

Federal retirees are cited as the main target of the cut, although they make up only six percent of the group and the better-off federal pensioners who get more than the minimum won't be affected. If others in the group are similarly well-situated, as the administration claims, then surely nothing can be lost by adding a little safety net. How about exempting from the cut anyone with an income of less than, say, $5,000 a year? If no one is that poor, it won't cost anything. If, on the other hand, it turns out that many of the people at risk are both old and far from well-off, these are savings the society should reject.

Washington, D.C., July 21, 1981

MOST OF the people now receiving the Social Security minimum benefit are not the sort who can launch massive letter-writing campaigns or work the halls of Congress. Perhaps as a result, an administration proposal eliminating the minimum benefit for people with low earnings records moved with little notice into both the budget bills being reconciled in a Senate-House conference.

Now one group among the 3 million people potentially affected has been heard from—about 14,500 nuns and male clerics belonging to religious orders. Last week, spokesmen for the nuns caused a good deal of squirming among members of Congress on both sides of the aisle, lending strength to efforts by House Majority Leader James Wright and others who are sponsoring a resolution—scheduled for a House vote today—calling for retention of the minimum.

The appearance of the nuns and male clerics came as a surprise to almost everyone. Under the normal conventions of Social Security and other social insurance programs, members of cloistered religious orders wouldn't be eligible. Since they have taken a vow of poverty, they receive no wages and pay no payroll taxes, relying instead on the orders they have joined to provide them with room, board and other necessities. Amendments to the Social Security law in 1972, however, allowed the orders to make contributions on behalf of their members on the assumption that the benefits they receive have an income value of about $100 a month. The Social Security benefit formula is weighted to give a very high rate of return on low earnings, but in this case the taxes paid are so low that the nuns' benefits would be very small without the minimum floor.

They would, however, retain full eligibility for Medicare.

Spokesmen for the religious orders pressed for a special exemption from the minimum-benefit termination. They argue that their members do not have available the welfare alternative suggested by David Stockman as the proper recourse for the needy, since they have taken a vow of poverty. Since welfare and Social Security are, as far as we know, paid in the same currency—and since welfare benefits are typically set so as to make sure that recipients stay in poverty whether they want to or not—this seems a curious argument. Moreover, since other minimum beneficiaries actually *sacrificed income* to gain coverage while the nuns and clerics did not, special treatment is hard to justify.

Putting a spotlight on the religious orders has, however, drawn useful attention to the plight of all the elderly for whom adjustment to a sudden reduction in circumstances will be even more difficult. While ending the Social Security minimum for future beneficiaries can be justified—under current law, the benefit is already scheduled for a gradual phase-out—abruptly changing the rules for people already relying on the benefit does not. Of the group at risk, 1.5 million are over the age of 70, close to 100,000 are over 90. Two million stand to lose an average of 40 percent of their current benefits and, according to the Congressional Research Service, 800,000 are potentially without alternative sources of income. Gradual disclosure of one sad case after another caused by an almost unexamined budget decision is not a happy prospect for Congress or this country.

THE WALL STREET JOURNAL
New York, N.Y.,
August 5, 1981

If reforming Social Security is a hot potato, then dropping the minimum benefit law is nothing less than a nuclear warhead. And Republican outrage with the Democrats for playing touch football with it is surely justified.

Neither Republicans in Congress nor in the administration advocate dropping the minimum benefit as, for instance, a-way-of-balancing-the-budget-off-the-backs-of-the-poor. Clearly, people who need those payments but who would not be picked up through other aid programs should be taken care of. Just as clearly, Congress expects to do so when it continues consideration of the Social Security bill.

Historically, minimum benefits were meant to protect those people whose wages were too low or whose employment too infrequent to qualify them for regular OASDI benefits. But nowadays the elderly poor can and do get much better federal aid from SSI, food stamps and Medicare. There are, however, some 300,000 who will fall through the federal aid net if minimum benefits are scrapped. But acknowledging and remedying that problem doesn't change the fact that minimum benefits, though originally targeted for the very needy, have become icing on the retirement *gateaux* for government pensioners and some others who are not poor.

Among the three million people pocketing the minimum benefit of $122 a month are a solid chunk of retired government employes. Federal (plus some state and local) workers are not covered by Social Security. Instead, they have their own pension plan which allows retirement as early as age 55. Thus, government workers can retire from serving the public weal at 55, enter the Social Security system and retire at age 65 with two pension checks. For farsighted workers, the procedure is to moonlight in a covered job while serving the public weal. Estimates put the number of retired federal civil servants who are "double recipients"—as it's politely called—at almost half of all federal retirees. Nobody knows how many state and local servants are doubly receiving.

Another chunk of beneficiaries are the retired rich who qualify under the low earnings, limited employment category because they've spent a great deal of their working life in Palm Beach. It's easy for these people to slip in and out of covered employment. And smart, too. The payroll deductions necessary to qualify for minimum benefits are so small, the expected return on temporary jobs can be better than buying Teledyne at three times earnings.

Cutting out the double-dippers and coupon-clippers would save around one billion dollars in 1982 alone. As budget cuts go, this one is a beauty: It's not only a sitting duck, but it ought to be too embarrassed to squawk. That should go double for the Democrats.

Taxing Social Security Benefits

One of the least popular measures suggested to ease the deficits of the Social Security system has been to tax some portion of recipients' benefits. Many advocates have proposed taxing one-half of the old-age benefits; the rationale for this is that the half of employees' contributions paid by the employer is not subject to the corporate income tax. (The other half of the contributions, paid by the employee, is withheld from income that is also subject to the income tax.) The major objection to this proposal is that it might significantly reduce the retirement income of many elderly people who were already living on subsistence incomes.

Another proposal has been to tax the benefits of only those whose annual incomes exceeded a certain amount. Some opponents of this idea say that it would turn Social Security entirely into a welfare system; those who had contributed the most would receive the least in return. Those beneficiaries who had planned for their retirement by partaking in private pension plans and accumulating savings, opponents say, would be penalized for their foresight. Legislation has been repeatedly introduced, in fact, to remove the existing limitation on the amount a retiree can earn without this income resulting in decreased Social Security benefits. Under legislation passed in 1977, the ceiling on the amount a person between 65 and 72 could earn without affecting his benefits was hiked to $4,000, rising gradually to $6,000 in 1982. Persons 72 or over could receive benefits without regard to earnings. The Social Security reform bill passed in 1983 both imposed a tax on benefits received by higher-income recipients and decreased the penalty for those retirees who continued to earn incomes after age 65. (See p. 178.)

Minneapolis Star and Tribune

Minneapolis, Minn., November 7, 1981

For fear of getting mugged by old folks, the Senate likes to cringe and pledge its allegiance to everyone near or past retirement age. It crosses its heart and hopes to die rather than even think about changes in Social Security. The latest expression of this unattractive fawning was a vote this week, 72 to 0, abhorring the very notion of an income tax on Social Security benefits. A similar unanimous vote made the same point only last July. And in May the pious senators rapped President Reagan's knuckles, 96 to 0, for daring to suggest that people retiring early take a smaller percentage than now allowed of the pensions they could claim at age 65.

The sanctimony about seniors has obvious aims: To placate a powerful lobby and fend off punishment by people who insist that what the government gives it may never take away. Unfortunately, the Senate's bad habit has harmful results as well: It paints the legislators into a corner that will have to be escaped when, inevitably, Social Security benefits are changed; and it hoodwinks wishful voters with promises that most senators know cannot be kept.

Most citizens probably know that the promises are phony, too. Social Security is a money transfer from employed people to their retired elders. Young and old alike strongly approve that transfer, consider it a matter of justice and want it to be generous. But you haven't been reading the papers if you don't yet realize that the present transfer system is genuinely in trouble. Part of the trouble comes from demographic changes: The number of income-earners to pay each pensioner's monthly check has dropped dramatically and will drop still further. Another part comes from Social Security's greatly broadened benefits: Health care and disability must be paid for, and pensions go up in lockstep with inflation, regardless of what happens to wage-earners' pay.

The upshot of these factors, aggravated by recession, is a looming cash shortage. Even at close to 7 percent and rising, the money taken from each paycheck today (plus an equal amount taken from employers) is not enough to cover what is promptly paid out to Social Security recipients. So reserves are dropping low, and whether the crunch will come this winter or sometime later, few analysts disagree that it is going to come. Despite what senators seem to wish, the question is how to solve that problem, not how to deny its existence.

There are many good-faith proposals to consider. Some seek to increase income for the Social Security trust funds; others would reduce the benefits those funds must cover. Elements of both approaches combine equitably in suggestions to tax one half the old-age benefits received by Social Security pensioners. The money is income, after all, and the half originally paid by employers now escapes taxation altogether. Making that half taxable when received as pensions would not penalize the poor, since the poor do not pay income taxes anyway. Nor would it tax the better-off elderly at rates as high as younger people pay, since everyone 65 or older already gets an extra income-tax exemption. And the revenue raised could be dedicated in support of the Social Security system, to help solve its solvency problem.

Making benefits taxable is not the only way to save Social Security, and probably not sufficient by itself. But it is a constructive proposal that deserves consideration along with many others. It does not deserve the fright reaction and cheap rejection so piously voted by the Senate this week. That sort of response not only ignores the real Social Security challenge, but insults the intelligence of voters both old and young.

THE INDIANAPOLIS NEWS
Indianapolis, Ind., June 11, 1979

What is it that brings Democratic Sen. Birch Bayh and Republican Sen. Barry Goldwater together?

It is a bill just re-introduced before Congress that would enable Social Security beneficiaries to earn as much income as they want, without being in danger of losing benefits.

Although Social Security is a means of income redistribution, it is not welfare. Its benefits are paid to those who have worked in the past and have, in fact, been forced to contribute to the system. No need must be established before benefits are paid.

Yet, under the retirement test applied to Social Security recipients, if a beneficiary earns more than a stipulated amount, he must forfeit all or some of the benefits which come from his forced contributions.

Prior to the 1977 amendments to the Social Security Act, a retiree was denied $1 of benefits for every $2 he earned over a $2,500 exempt amount. Eventually benefits were cut off entirely. This limit on earnings continued until the retiree was 72.

The 1977 amendments made the limits on penalty-free earnings more generous. The earnings limit is now increased yearly. It stands at $3,480 for a beneficiary under age 65, and at $4,500 for someone age 65 to 71. For those age 65 to 71, the limit will rise each year until it reaches $6,000 in 1982. After 1982, no earnings limit will apply to people age 70 or older.

Bayh and Goldwater, both of whom have championed this cause in previous sessions, would remove the ceiling in 1983 — after the 1977 amendments have taken full effect.

We can't imagine why Congress would purposefully want to deny working to those with no other way to supplement their Social Security, but it has. Retirees able to acquire a portfolio of stocks and bonds to provide extra income are not penalized by the earnings ceilings.

We also can't imagine why Congress purposefully wants to deprive the economy of the productivity and income from those who can still work, but it has.

Frequently cited as the reason for retaining the earnings test is the extra cost of Social Security payments without it. Eliminating the retirement test at age 65 would increase payments anywhere from $2 billion to $4 billion per year.

But the benefits of eliminating the earnings test would be greater both psychologically and economically.

There were 11.3 million citizens age 65 to 72 who were eligible for benefits in 1976 and subject to the earnings test. Of this group, 1.4 million deliberately worked less to keep their incomes below the ceiling. There is no logic or dignity to forcing capable people to stop working.

Further, balanced against the added benefits paid, must be the benefits contributed by those who work. There is the value of the productivity of their work, the revenue from taxes they would pay (estimated at $500 million a year in Federal taxes alone) and, ironically, the Social Security taxes that would be deducted from their bigger paychecks. One study has concluded there would be no true cost to removing the Social Security earnings test altogether.

Social Security benefits are benefits individuals have earned. They are a matter of right, not of welfare. It is time Congress permitted those rights to be claimed in full.

The Cincinnati Post

Cincinnati, Ohio, May 2, 1980

Consumer price index increases for the first three months of 1980 have triggered an automatic increase of 14 percent in Social Security benefits, beginning in July. That is good news for 36 million Americans who get Social Security checks. It is bad news for those considering the higher payroll taxes needed to support the program.

The summer increase in benefits will bring the cost of Social Security to about $135 billion in 1981, a figure already anticipated in the budget now before Congress. It is one of the items neither the administration nor a majority of Congress is inclined to challenge in an effort to balance the budget.

While the maximum monthly benefits will rise to $653 in July, the average benefit will come to about $330 — a sum that doesn't go very far for anyone totally dependent on Social Security for support. By choice or necessity, many elderly persons supplement their retirement income by working. Recognizing that fact, Sen. Barry Gold-water and a score of colleagues are proposing that Congress eliminate the $5,000 annual limit on the amount a person retiring at 65 can earn without sacrificing a part of his Social Security income. They base their argument on economic facts of life, and on fairness.

Whether older persons earn extra money should have nothing to do with their Social Security benefit, say the senators. The money that working people pay into Social Security is theirs. The government's only responsibility is to pay it back.

The point is well taken. So far, Social Security reform has been pursued primarily in hopes of curbing rising costs of the system. Structural changes might be necessary in that effort. Principles of fairness also can underlie reform, however. The Goldwater proposal merits congressional consideration, even if it would lead to a $6-billion increase in outlays.

Chicago Tribune

Chicago, Ill., December 13, 1982

The National Commission on Social Security Reform apparently is considering what politicians regard as unthinkable: taxing Social Security benefits. That proposal, if it is made, would be a big step forward, signalling a new understanding the system's problems and the political courage to deal with them honestly.

The exemption of Social Security benefits from taxation is one of the system's many anomalies, often defended but never justified. It doesn't square with the system's character as a purported insurance program, nor with those elements that resemble welfare. If Social Security is merely insurance, why shouldn't it be taxed like any other pension? If it is intended to redistribute income from the wealthy to the poor, what sense does it make to let well-to-do retirees escape taxation on their benefits? Channeled back into the trust fund, such revenues would make the system's financial prospects much brighter.

Social Security's diehard apologists will raise the specter of poverty-stricken widows being robbed of what little they have. But old people who are also poor won't owe any taxes anyway.

Only those beneficiaries who enjoy other substantial sources of income will be affected.

Of course the employee's "contributions" to the trust fund are already taxed. But the other half of Social Security payments, those from the employer, are not. So by all rights at least half of the money paid out to retirees should be treated as ordinary income.

It might even be a good idea to tax all benefits, since they are mostly a windfall, representing a return wildly out of proportion to the original payment. The average retiree gets back his entire investment in less than a year—and then continues to draw benefits (paid to either him or his widow) for another quarter of a century.

It's too early to know if the advisory commission will risk the wrath of the nation's 36 million Social Security beneficiaries, or if Congress will be brave enough to follow its example. The history of Social Security debates offers no reason for optimism. But the fact that this proposal is being considered may mean that the coming debate will be different.

Houston Chronicle

Houston, Texas, August 15, 1982

The general assumption is that when the country faces up to the changes that are going to have to be made in Social Security, there will be only two real options: raise taxes or cut benefits, or more likely a combination of both, and the struggle will be fought out along those lines.

It is entirely possible, however, that the biggest battle over Social Security could involve a third approach: changing the fundamental principle of the system from an insurance-type to a welfare-type.

Aside from its minimum-benefit provision, Social Security has generally been kept firmly to the principle of benefits received for payments made, and kept outside the realm of welfare. There are no "means" or "need" tests. Regardless of their income or assets, people receive what they paid for. Rich, poor or in-between makes no difference.

Changing this insurance-principle to one in which people receive benefits according to their "need" could have a certain built-in constituency on the left because of its income-redistribution aspect. It could attract some non-ideological support from the middle and right because it could be viewed as less politically painful than across-the-board tax increases and benefit cuts.

Such an approach would also generate fierce opposition, ranging similarly across the ideological spectrum. The change would be considered fatal to the Social Security system and to public support of the system.

Whatever else could be said of all this — and much can and will be — it is a measure of the difficulties Social Security finds itself in that such a drastic change would even be considered.

THE MILWAUKEE JOURNAL

Milwaukee, Wisc., December 14, 1982

The idea of taxing Social Security benefits appears to be gaining support among members of President Reagan's Social Security study commission.

Although no one is suggesting a tax on benefits paid to persons of modest means, it makes sense to tax a portion of benefits that well-to-do pensioners receive. The proceeds could be used to shore up the overdrawn Social Security fund. Regrettably, the idea is very hard to sell to segments of the public.

A lot of people tend to think of such a levy as double taxation. They are only fractionally correct. It is true that employes' contributions to the Social Security system come from income that is also subject to income tax. However, the equal amount of Social Security that the employer pays is not subject to the corporate income tax. It is subtracted as a business expense.

Thus, it certainly would be fair to require retired persons to report half of their Social Security benefits as ordinary income, paying taxes on it if their total income was sufficient to put them in a taxable bracket. The less affluent still would not have to pay an income tax, and the more affluent could afford it.

Although we are not now prepared to suggest taxing more than half of the benefit, a case can be made for doing so. Consider some pertinent facts:

— The average wage earner who paid Social Security taxes from 1937 through 1981 contributed a grand total of $7,209 to the retirement fund, according to a recent report in the New York Federal Reserve Bank's Quarterly Review.

— The maximum Social Security tax any wage earner could have paid into the fund in that period was $11,346.16.

Those figures may surprise many people whose impression of Social Security taxes has been strongly influenced by the steep rates paid in recent years. It should be remembered, however, that the maximum individual Social Security tax was only $30 a year from 1937 through 1949 and did not exceed $100 until 1959.

Even when adjusted for inflation, the contributions cover much less than half of the average person's total pension costs.

People who honestly ponder the figures will be hard put to argue that it is wrong to tax even half of the benefit of those retirees who are clearly able to pay.

The Des Moines Register

Des Moines, Iowa,
January 21, 1983

Social Security is so important to so many people that drastic changes are difficult. The recommendations of the commission could be precedents, however, for evolutionary change.

One precedent sure to face congressional opposition is the proposal to tax certain old-age benefits. Retirees whose income from, sources other than Social Security exceeded $20,000 (or $25,000 per couple) would pay income tax on half of their Social Security benefits. All benefits are now tax-free. (The rationale for taxing only 50 percent is that half of each worker's contribution into the system was paid by the employer, so income taxes never were paid on that portion.)

On the other end of the spectrum, there is a proposal to grant workers an income-tax credit for a portion of their Social Security taxes. Workers never get to take the money home, yet it's counted as taxable income. In theory, this is fair; retirement benefits are tax-free, so contributions into the system should be subject to income tax. The recommended income-tax credit would last for only one year. But it would be a precedent.

Social Security taxes are regressive. They have risen faster than the federal income tax. Many low-income workers pay more in Social Security than in income taxes. Over the years, Congress may give more attention to attempting to ease the burden through income-tax credits for Social Security contributions.

Such an evolution, if it happens, would reverse the existing system. Instead of taxable contributions and tax-free benefits, there would be tax-deductible contributions and taxable retirement benefits in the same manner as with private pensions and Individual Retirement Accounts.

CHARLESTON EVENING POST

Charleston, S.C., March 10, 1981

Not long ago, a presidential study commission revived an old issue: Should Social Security benefits be subject to federal income tax? President Reagan, after thinking about it for "40 seconds," said "No, they paid taxes on that money when they sent it in." Good for him.

It is one of our pet peeves that Social Security "contributions" are not considered deductions by federal and state tax authorities. If, on top of that, the federal government were to begin collecting income tax on the benefits it eventually pays out, an injustice would have been compounded for workers who live long enough to get back from Social Security at least some of what they have paid in. (Social Security has expanded far beyond its original charter for providing a financial floor under elderly, retired workers, and is now a principal vehicle for federal income redistribution.)

Various plans have been presented to keep the Social Security trust funds from going broke. We believe the most sensible proposals thus far are those which gradually would raise the Social Security retirement age and change the present formula for determining cost-of-living increases.

A third proposal frequently put forward is simply to continue raising Social Security "contributions" from employers and employees. With the number of retired Americans growing so rapidly, and the number of those who pay the freight about to decline dramatically, it is simply unrealistic to fund deficits of the system in this way.

The Orlando Sentinel

Orlando, Fla., January 23, 1983

How can you justify taxing Social Security benefits? How can you take money from those the system is supposed to help?

Hold on. The Social Security reform commission's proposal is to tax only half the benefits of retirees whose incomes are well above the national median. Those are people who can get by without the help. Furthermore, the money would go back into the fund to help those really in need. It is no more than fair.

But, you say, one of the nice things about Social Security is that it isn't welfare. There is no "needs" test. People can accept the checks without embarrassment because they paid for it. Won't this make it welfare?

The truth is that a great part of Social Security today is welfare, and that portion grows each year. Consider just one of those parts: In 1980, the total employer and employee taxes, including interest, of the average worker retiring at age 65 was $24,206. Yet that average worker will draw $125,125 from the fund.

Social Security was never intended to be a major portion of a retirement program. It was to supplement, to ward off destitution. It was one of the three legs on the so-called milking stool of retirement: pension, savings and Social Security. For a time it worked well. It was the nut that encouraged savings and pension programs.

At present, Social Security benefits are not taxable. By taxing half the benefits paid to people who have substantial retirement income, the program will be shifted back toward that original concept. The tax would apply to single people with income from other sources of $20,000 or more. For couples, the cutoff would be $25,000. Those people are not about to be snapped up by the jaws of poverty.

That change will produce an estimated $18 billion during the next six years. It can help salvage the program and, as part of a compromise package, it adds a measure of fairness.

RAPID CITY JOURNAL—

Rapid City, S.D., February 22, 1981

A proposal to tax some Social Security benefits should be given short shrift.

A former head of the Social Security Administration has suggested that Congress consider phasing in a plan to tax Social Security benefits when the benefits and other income of retirees are over a certain amount, such as $20,000 a year.

It is one of several suggestions for changes in the system to rescue the main Social Security trust fund which pays retirement benefits.

While Social Security has always been sort of a transfer system in which workers are taxed to pay benefits to retirees, the proposal to tax benefits of retirees whose income exceeds a certain amount would be an exercise in social engineering that would make the system a real income transfer program.

Social Security was not designed as a total retirement plan. Benefits were to supplement private retirement plans and other assets accumulated by individuals during their working years.

Taxing the benefits of Social Security recipients who, by dint of their own efforts, have been able to build up financial resources perhaps beyond those of others would be nothing more than penalizing success.

Everyone who contributes to Social Security does so on the basis of their salary or wages. When a person retires he or she is entitled to the benefits earned on the basis of what they paid in. There is no justification for taxing some because they have been able to build up their nest egg.

The San Diego Union

San Diego, Calif., January 12, 1983

The Social Security Reform Commission is said to be considering a proposal to require retired persons to pay tax on their Social Security benefits if their retirement income is above a certain level — perhaps $15,000 a year for a couple. Sen. Robert Dole, a member of the commission, regards this as "one of the less painful options" for Social Security to cut its losses.

The proposal assumes that retirees with private pensions or investment income in addition to Social Security would suffer little pain by having their Social Security benefits diminished by a tax. No doubt that is true for many Americans with a more or less comfortable retirement income, but what should concern us here is not the pain or lack of it for any individuals but the blow this idea strikes at the very essence of the Social Security program.

Those who support an income-related tax on Social Security benefits are saying that those who need the benefits the least should give some of the money back to the government. To put it another way, those who are the neediest should get the most from Social Security.

Or better yet — "From each according to his abilities, to each according to his needs," as Karl Marx put it when he formulated such concepts of redistribution of wealth and income-leveling in the 19th century.

Social Security needs reforms which will carry it back toward fiscal soundness as an insurance program. It does not need reforms which would only propel it into the abyss of an out and out welfare program. A tax on benefits to be paid only by those who can "afford" it would be a subtle but significant acceptance of a means test to determine eligibility for benefits or their amount — a test alien to Social Security as we have known it until now.

Social began in 1935 as a means for workers to finance an insurance program promising them a pension benefit in retirement. Both the payroll tax and the benefits were so modest at the beginning that the program could be considered only a supplement to provisions for old age that workers would make for themselves. Its benefits were never intended to be the sole support of a retired person or couple.

Forty years of expansionary tinkering with the program have confused its purpose, undermined the principles on which it was founded, and left it on the brink of financial collapse. It is ironic that one of the proposals for saving Social Security would wipe out the logic and fairness of its tax-free benefits.

A worker's payments into Social Security are taxed when they are earned. Unlike the employer's share of Social Security taxes, and contributions to private pension plans, they are not deductible on federal income tax returns. To tax the benefits coming back to the worker in retirement would be a form of double taxation.

Reformers desperate for a new source of money to bail out Social Security will argue that the employer's contribution, or the amount of benefits that exceeds what a worker paid into the system, ought to be taxed at the time benefits are paid. Even if tax theory supports that argument, it hardly supports the premise that the benefits of well-off retirees should be taxable while others are not.

A program that bases pension benefits upon need rather than an earned entitlement that is uniform for all participants is not what Social Security started out to be. If the reformers want to move in the direction of such a program, they should acknowledge that they are abandoning Social Security as retirement insurance and creating a welfare system for the elderly based on a test of need.

THE ATLANTA CONSTITUTION

Atlanta, Ga., January 16, 1983

Demagogic nonsense reigns on the subject of Social Security, the myths of which are perpetually argued as fact. The fact, plain and simple, is that the system is running out of money and either taxes will have to be raised or benefits cut, or both.

That is the issue at hand. What the system was or was meant to be is irrelevant. What Congress, the administration and the blue-ribbon commission appointed by both to study the system have to confront is the system as it is now and will be in the future, unless changed.

Rep. Bill Archer (R-Tex.), a commission member, announces his opposition to any plan that would tax a portion of Social Security's benefits to affluent retirees. That, he insists, would be "a serious threat to the basic character and credibility of the system."

That's about like wandering into the war-ravaged South after the Civil War and insisting that the basic character and credibility of the magnolias-and-mint-juleps lifestyle is threatened. What "basic character and credibility?" we ask. The BC&C has already been destroyed. The issue now is reconstruction.

Besides, even granting the existence of a BC&C, any alternative proposal that would solve Social Security's central problem would go just as far. The system was intended to be self-sufficient, that is, with its own taxes providing benefits. Unless changes are made in the tax-load or benefits, that money will perforce come from general revenues, hence tax revenue from all sources. That most assuredly would destroy the system's BC&C.

Another simple fact is that half of the benefits paid, even if one argues that benefits are earned in full, have never been taxed. The employee's portion was taxed; the employer's was not.

Taxing the untaxed half would be fair. But that is not even the proposal. The proposal is to tax the untaxed half for high-income taxpayers, not the poor.

That most assuredly is proper.

Substituting Mandatory Private Pensions

Because demographic and economic changes over the last forty years have made the future of the Social Security system so uncertain, many people have suggested abandoning it altogether in favor of private retirement programs. Two developments in 1981 sparked increased interest in this alternative. One was the recommendation by the President's Commission on Pension Policy that a minimum universal pension system be required of all employers as a supplement to Social Security coverage. The other was the passage of President Reagan's tax reform bill, with its provision for liberalized individual retirement accounts (IRAs) allowing an individual to deduct up to $2,000 annually in contributions from their taxes. More importantly, IRAs were made available for the first time to those already covered by company pension plans.

Proponents of a mandatory private pension system to replace Social Security usually stipulate that immediate vesting in the private plans would have to be required, to end loss of coverage for workers who change jobs or who work intermittently. In addition, they acknowledge that such a plan would have to be gradually implemented, allowing those workers over a certain age to continue in the Social Security system rather than lose their past contributions to it. Advocates argue, however, that the benefits of switching to a private retirement system are manifold: it would eliminate the demographic difficulties in having one generation pay for the retirement of another, ease the administrative costs of determining the eligibility and benefit levels of retirees, and stimulate the economy by channeling large amounts of capital into investment rather than consumption.

The Burlington Free Press
Burlington, Vt., October 5, 1981

Abolishing the Social Security system may appear to be a preposterous idea because it is the only means of subsistence for millions of the nation's elderly.

But the system is sagging under the weight of multiple problems that have developed in recent years and it appears to be only a matter of time before drastic revisions must be made in the program to save it. Just what form they will take is a matter for speculation but it is possible that Social Security taxes may have to be increased to provide additional funds. Workers, who will have little to say about such increases, even then will not receive any assurances that money will be available to support them when they retire.

Suggestions are being made that a new private mandatory retirement system be developed in which contributions of employers and employees would be deposited in individual retirement accounts and would be handled without government intervention.

Under the proposals, the same amount of money as is now being collected under Social Security would be contributed by employees and employers. Those who are now receiving Social Security payments would continue to collect until they died. The program could be handled by a truncated bureaucracy as a result of the elimination of the task of administering the contributions of millions of workers who would fall under the new system. Some of the money to meet the program's obligations would come from workers who did not qualify for the revised retirement plan and general funds during the phaseout period. Proponents of the plan have suggested that the new program be installed for workers 40 years old and under.

A compelling case can be made for the proposal. A person who entered the work force at 25 and worked for 40 years at $20,000 a year would accumulate over $1 million in an individual retirement account at 10 percent interest compounded annually. Annual contributions would be $2,660 over that period. Under Social Security, a worker who earned $20,000 a year for 40 years would be entitled to $6,660 in annual benefits. If a retiree lived to be 75, total Social Security payments would be $66,600.

Adoption of such a system would mean that other Social Security programs, including Medicare, aid to dependent children of workers who died before retirement and supplemental security income, would have to be supported by general revenues. That method might lead to greater accountability on the part of those selected to run the programs and might curb some existing abuses.

Abolishing the Social Security system as it now exists would not be as preposterous an idea as it first appears, since it would provide more security for younger workers while at the same time guaranteeing that those who are now receiving benefits would be protected for the remainder of their lives.

Such a revision of the system should be given serious consideration by officials who will be asked to cure the ailments of the Social Security program.

The Detroit News
Detroit, Mich., October 9, 1981

A recent survey conducted by Sindlinger and Co. of Media, Pa., reveals that a substantial number of Americans doubt the soundness of the Social Security system.

The random sample found that 59.5 percent of the public believes that participation in the program should be voluntary. The study also showed that two-thirds of those surveyed think private pension alternatives are a more efficient method of providing retirement benefits.

Nearly 85 percent of the respondents have little or no confidence in the system's financial stability. Yet the majority of Americans favor the continuation of Social Security.

One suspects that people are caught in a double bind. They know that something is fundamentally wrong with a retirement system that is on the verge of insolvency. But, like passengers on a runaway train, they see little choice but to sit tight and hope for the best.

So, while the Sindlinger survey found that nearly half of those questioned favor increasing Social Security benefits, 82 percent *oppose* raising taxes to pay the bill.

During the coming months there will be numerous studies and analyses of America's Social Security dilemma. But one thing is already clear — the current system is in shambles. Unless Congress has the courage to make some hard decisions on benefits and eligibility, we doubt that Social Security will ever be more than the misnomer it is today.

The Knickerbocker News
Albany, N.Y., May 19, 1981

Mr. Reagan would have us all save more and spend less; he would also have us rely less on Social Security. Why not combine the two?

At the moment, only those Americans who are self-employed or whose employers have no pension plans can open IRA or Keogh savings accounts, with their attendant tax advantages. These accounts bank income against the future; no income tax is charged on the money put into such retirement accounts, up to a maximum amount per year. After retirement, when one's income is lower, the deferred income savings are taxed, but typically at a much lower rate.

Why not allow all Americans to open IRA-type accounts? The federal government could set a limit to yearly savings, and regulate the accounts as is now done.

The benefits would be resounding. Individuals would find themselves with savings accounts to draw upon for their retirement years; the banks would have more money to invest and loan out. Interest rates might fall. This could stimulate construction and business investment, cutting unemployment. Inflation moderates when individuals begin saving instead of spending. We could be showered with good results, and we can't think of a single bad thing that would happen as a result of extending this advantage to us all.

Oh, there is a minor consideration: The government would have to sacrifice a bit of income; considering Mr. Reagan's tax-cutting proclivities, that is surely a small burden for him to bear.

We think expanding the IRA savings program is an idea well worth exploring.

Oregon Journal

Portland, Ore., October 3, 1981

A presidential decision to forget about cutting Social Security benefits may be prudent politically, but it only delays the day of reckoning. A group of national business and education leaders says it's not only Social Security but the nation's entire retirement system that needs attention.

The Research and Policy Committee of the Committee for Economic Development (CED) warns that "a retirement disaster is on the way."

A few statistics bring the bad news. In 1900, only 4 percent of the U.S. population was over age 65. Today it's 11 percent and in 50 years it could double. By the year 2050, combined Social Security taxes could be 25 percent of the nation's covered payroll or, if economic growth is slow and demographics are unfavorable, as high as 45 percent of payroll.

CED's recommendations for changing Social Security are relatively modest. The retirement age should be raised from 65 to 68, and early retirement from 62 to 65. The method of relating benefits to inflation — using a Consumer Price Index that overstates inflation — should be revised.

CED wants private companies to keep maximum flexibility in establishing pension plans. But the study also urged Congress to increase incentives for personal savings for retirement and to encourage expanded coverage by employer pension plans.

The amount that individuals can place in individual retirement accounts or Keogh plans should be raised even higher. Employee contributions to pension plans should be tax deductible, says the report.

And although the report argues that each company should be able to choose the retirement plan that best meets its needs, the report notes that many plans contain "defined benefits" instead of "defined contribution." Those with defined benefits promise a fixed set of benefits which fail to keep up with inflation. The report suggests that employers should improve private pension plans voluntarily, such as trying earlier vesting (the time required for employees to acquire rights to all or part of a pension).

Considerable growth in Social Security and private pension plans has occurred in the last two decades. With the number of senior citizens increasing, the issue looms as one of the most controversial of the decades ahead.

BUFFALO EVENING NEWS

Buffalo, N.Y., December 31, 1981

Americans are beginning to read and hear a good deal about the IRA — not the Irish Republican Army, but the Individual Retirement Account program approved by Congress last summer as part of President Reagan's Economic Recovery Tax Act.

The new program, an expansion of a concept originally authorized by Congress in much more limited form in the mid-1970s, is a welcome tax reform that broadens the choices available for an estimated 50 million American workers in enlarging their income after retirement.

Since the retirement-savings plan applies only to workers who earn income, full-time or part-time, it is an incentive for work. And federal income taxes on IRA savings of up to $2,000 annually are deferred until the retirement years, when the tax bite will normally be much less than during the working years.

Thus, the IRA is one device through which the federal income tax system is used to encourage thrift and savings rather than consumption.

That should benefit both workers and the nation as a whole.

Previously, IRAs were open only to workers not covered by pension plans at their place of employment. Now they have been made available for all workers. This is especially justified when it is considered that most private pension plans are not keyed to inflation; prices rise but retirement benefits don't. The IRAs will also help those workers who enroll to supplement Social Security benefits, which were never intended to provide total retirement income.

For the economy as a whole, the IRA program should expand the pool of savings that supplies investment for new homes, apartments, plants and equipment. As a nation, Americans currently save a lesser portion of disposable personal income than people of most other industrial nations. In 1980, for example, Americans saved 5.6 percent of that income. The Japanese saved 21 percent, the British 15 percent, the Canadians 10.3 percent. So incentives for savings, including IRAs and other devices, will help to spur savings and investment, which have lagged in this country in recent years. These benefits should outweigh the loss of tax revenues resulting from the IRAs.

With so many workers becoming eligible for IRA plans, competition by financial institutions (banks, mutual funds, brokerage houses, insurance companies, etc.) for this new business is sure to become increasingly intense.

One question every worker must answer is whether he or she wants to participate at all. Age and other factors could make a difference. And for those who answer in the affirmative, there remain differences among specific IRA plans to evaluate. The best plan for one worker may not be the best for another.

Whatever the answer in an individual case, the IRA program is now available to all workers and remains an option for building retirement income that each might profitably explore.

The Register

Santa Ana, Calif., September 4, 1981

One little-publicized feature of the tax package just signed into law should be of interest to most workers. Individual Retirement Accounts (IRAs) will be permitted for all workers, even those now enrolled in company pension plans, as of Jan. 1, 1982.

IRAs are not new, but they haven't been available for everyone. Perhaps it would be interesting to review their provisions.

Under the new law, workers may deposit up to $2,000 per year ($2,250 for taxpayers with nonworking spouses) in a special savings account with a bank, savings institution, mutual fund, insurance company or even a stock brokerage firm. The deposits and interest are excused from taxes until retirement age. Withdrawals may begin at age 59½. Withdrawals made before that age are subject to tax and a penalty.

That may not sound exciting or new, but it does put a self-sufficient retirement within the reach of most working Americans. A 35-year-old person with a family of four and an income of $24,000 per year (the national median) could build a $300-per-week nest-egg by retirement at 65. Here's how.

A contribution of $1,000 per year — a little less than $20 per week — will yield a tax saving of $220 per year, which is some help. If such a contribution is maintained for 30 years at 8 percent interest, the retirement fund will total $133,770 at age 65. That's enough to set up a 15-year annuity program paying $300 per week. Those amounts would be greater, of course, for people able to save more than $1,000 per year or earn a higher rate of interest than 8 percent. $300 a week may not be much in 30 years if inflation continues, but it couldn't hurt.

It's worth noting that this kind of return compares rather favorably with what people retiring on Social Security can expect. There's no sleight-of-hand here, just saving and compound interest. But it does make you wonder why we tolerate a program like Social Security.

What if . . . what if we had the option of putting our social Security "contribution" into an IRA rather than into the SS system. People earning $24,000 a year pay a good deal more than $20 a week into Social Security. The nest-egg that could be accumulated by putting the money into an IRA instead would be quite impressive.

We were just thinking. Hmmmm. . . .

THE RICHMOND NEWS LEADER

Richmond, Va., June 17, 1981

The Reagan administration has devised an ingenuous way of accomplishing two worthy goals: Increasing personal savings and decreasing reliance on the Social Security system as the primary source of retirement income.

Both goals could be achieved if Congress approves the administration proposal that favored tax treatment now accorded to some workers for Individual Retirement Accounts be extended to all workers. Under the current system, IRAs are open only to workers whose employers do not offer private pension plans. Those who set up IRAs may contribute $1,500 a year to their accounts and deduct those contributions from their gross incomes. Taxes on the IRAs are deferred until the workers begin withdrawals from their accounts at a later date, when contributors would be in lower tax brackets.

The administration would increase the maximum contributions from workers with no private pension plans to $2,000 a year. Workers with private pension plans could contribute $1,000 a year taxfree to an IRA. The tax deferment would cost the treasury no more than $300 million a year. If these projections are sound, the economy would gain billions of dollars for capital investment that probably would generate more in new taxes than the treasury would lose. An IRA is not a deposit-and-withdrawal form of savings; its contributions are made on a long-term basis. Thus the new investment funds would become available on a reliable basis.

Many workers are covered by private pension plans they consider inadequate, but under current law they are not permitted to supplement those private pensions with IRAs. Some workers change jobs too frequently to become vested in private pensions, but the law does not allow them to open an IRA to protect themselves. The changes proposed by the administration would remedy these deficiencies.

Moreover, with the Social Security program in danger of perilous shortfalls between revenues and promised benefits, it is sound public policy to encourage workers to use more initiative in providing for their retirement needs. As inflation has plundered the resources of many retired persons, Congress has surrendered to the temptation to keep expanding Social Security until many now regard the program as the sole source of retirement money. But Social Security never was meant as more than a retirement supplement.

By encouraging workers to rely more on IRAs and private pension plans, the administration hopes to relieve some of the pressures that are threatening to bankrupt Social Security. Meanwhile, a source of badly needed capital investment funds would be expanded, thereby helping the overall economy. Any proposal that offers two such salutary results has to have a lot going for it.

Richmond, Va., December 28, 1981

The current round of advertisements by banks to attract new Individual Retirement Accounts exposes the fraud that the Social Security System is perpetrating on millions of young workers. These ads present figures that show what a poor investment Social Security actually is.

Beginning January 1, any worker will be able to invest a maximum of $2,000 a year in an IRA (up to $2,250 for a worker with a non-working spouse) and deduct his IRA contributions from his income taxes. Taxes on the IRAs will be deferred until the investor begins withdrawals at age 59½ or older. These IRAs could provide a lucrative source of new investment funds for banks, and a comfortable retirement income for those who take advantage of the new program, as the banking ads illustrate:

● A worker who opened an IRA account at age 25 and contributed the maximum $2,000 a year at 10 per cent interest would have more than $1,175,900 from his $80,000 investment at age 65. His IRA would furnish him a monthly income of some $12,600 until age 80.

● A worker who contributed the maximum allowed, beginning at age 30, at 12 per cent interest, would have an IRA worth $1.2 million from his investment of $70,000 at age 65.

● A worker who opened an IRA at age 20, at 13 per cent interest, would have more than $5.2 million at age 65 on his maximum work-life contributions of $90,000 to the IRA.

By coincidence, the maximum Social Security payroll tax levied on a worker's pay will exceed $2,000 for the first time when Social Security taxes increase on January 1. The wage base on which the maximum tax is imposed will rise from $29,700 to $32,400, and the tax rate will increase from 6.65 per cent to 6.7 per cent. The maximum tax thus will increase from $1,975 this year to $2,170 in 1982. With inflation and cost-of-living increases, the new maximum wage base will not be unknown among 30-year-old blue-collar workers. Because an employer must match the worker's payroll tax, the Social Security program will reap millions of maximum $4,340 payroll tax collections in 1982.

If Social Security taxes remained at the 1982 level — and they are scheduled to continue their inexorable rise both in wage base and tax rate — a 30-year-old worker and his employer would contribute a maximum of $151,900 over a 35-year working life. Invested in a 13 per cent IRA, only $70,000 of that sum would be worth almost $1.5 million in 35 years. Does anyone imagine that the Social Security program offers such a pay-off to young workers 35 years down the road? Of course not. And the public is not fooled, either: A recent opinion survey reported that 68 per cent of respondents between the ages of 18 and 54 gave Social Security a vote of no-confidence.

The IRAs are voluntary, of course, and the figures now available are based on projections that may fluctuate with varying interest rates. The rate of inflation compounded over several future decades may erode the value of an IRA balance — $12,000 a month may not be much if bread costs $20 a loaf. But at least an IRA is a constant; the investor knows at any given time what he can expect from his retirement account, and he selects the means of investment. If he dies before retirement or before using all of his account, his beneficiary will receive the account. Meanwhile, a working wife can set up her own IRA and provide for her own retirement. (An IRA is not intended as an estate investment, however; penalties are imposed if an IRA investor does not begin to draw down his account at age 70½ by amounts calculated actuarially by the Internal Revenue Service.)

By contrast, Social Security is mandatory for all but a handful of workers. Benefits have few ties to contributions, because the system is geared to provide low-income workers a higher ratio of benefits to taxes paid than higher-income workers receive. If a worker dies without dependent children and with a wife not at retirement age, Social Security swallows all of his contributions except for a token death payment. A working wife may pay Social Security taxes for a lifetime, only to find at her retirement that her benefits will be higher if she draws on her husband's work record as his dependent, and the program merely devours all of her — and her employer's — payroll taxes. And, of course, Social Security taxes keep rising without a proportionate increase in promised benefits.

In short, Congress unintentionally laid bare the dismal returns from Social Security when it expanded the availability of tax-deferred IRAs to all workers. As long as IRAs were open only to workers without employer-provided pension plans, the truth about the sorry prospects Social Security offers young workers could be speculative. That truth is that only those already retired or retiring within the next few years will get their money's worth from Social Security. At the end of this year, any worker who has paid the maximum in payroll taxes since the program began 41 years ago will have remitted a total of $14,765 to Social Security, a sum doubled by his employer's payroll tax. According to the local Social Security office, a worker retiring now at age 65 who is eligible for the maximum benefit will receive $752 a month, with his 65-year-old spouse eligible for 50 per cent of that benefit, for a total of $1,129 a month. In only a little over two years (and the maximum benefit will rise next year with the cost of living), the worker will receive a total payback of all of his and his employer's payroll taxes. Younger workers will not be so fortunate — and they know it, thanks to the wave of publicity about the IRAs.

AKRON BEACON JOURNAL
Akron, Ohio, August 31, 1981

PRESIDENT REAGAN and Congressional Democrats and Republicans will need to cooperate in a legislative high-wire act when they return to Washington after Labor Day to keep the Social Security system intact.

That won't be easy, especially since Democrats have found the President to be vulnerable with voters on Social Security issues. On other key concerns such as budget and tax matters, the President has marched over his political opponents with ease. With Social Security, Democrats saw the frigid public reaction to the President's proposed reforms earlier this year and now see an opportunity to get even.

"It is without a doubt our big issue today, and there's no close second," said Rep. Tony Coelho, D-California, chairman of the Democratic Congressional Campaign Committee.

The Democrats may think they have found an issue, but reform of the Social Security program is too urgent and vital to get tangled up in partisan politics.

Without cooperation and some enlightened action on the part of the President and the Congress, there can be no balancing of interests and needs. With Social Security actuaries predicting that the old-age and survivors fund could run out of money by the fall of 1982 unless corrective steps are taken, the Congress and the President owe the nation a concerted effort to work together on this matter.

In some ways the climate for reform should be better now than in several years. Passage of the President's tax-cut program has helped offset some of the recent growth in Social Security taxes. Moreover, sections of the same new law make it more attractive for any worker to set up an Individual Retirement Account (IRA).

IRAs are tax-deferred savings and investment plans that allow workers to put away cash for their retirement. Taxes on the contributions and accumulated earnings do not have to be paid until the money is withdrawn in later years.

Under existing rules, only employees not covered by a retirement plan at work can open an IRA. But starting next Jan. 1, any worker can set up an IRA, regardless of whether he or she is covered by an employer's plan.

In the long run, this should encourage many workers to become less dependent upon Social Security; it may also make cuts in benefits easier to accept, especially for those who don't face retirement choices in the near future.

Not that Americans are about to swallow without complaint any benefit slashes the President and lawmakers in Washington can agree on. Among many Americans, there is still a feeling that the government owes them a monthly Social Security check at maximum levels upon retirement, regardless of need. But that attitude must change if the Social Security is to be preserved and not break the backs of American workers by laying on them heavier and heavier payroll taxes.

Of the numerous options open to the President and the Congress, selective benefit reductions remain preferable to higher payroll taxes.

What is important is that Republicans and Democrats alike on Capitol Hill join hands and cooperate in getting across that high wire safely. The feat will take courage and statesmanship.

The Boston Globe
Boston, Mass., December 30, 1981

Probably the hottest tax reduction gimmick to come along in years is the new Individual Retirement Account that allows taxpayers to deduct up to $2000 apiece ($4000 for married couples when both work) from taxable income in connection with setting up retirement funds.

Newspapers, magazines, brokerage houses, insurance companies, banks, credit unions are all publishing reams of material on the new tax break. Businesses that offer ways to invest money in such accounts are scrambling to attract clients. Individuals are beginning to look around for the most attractive investment or combination of investments.

Apart from being desirable as a way to help individuals prepare for retirement, IRAs are also viewed as an encouragement to savings and an investment, both sorely needed by our economy. There is doubt that money invested in IRAs will really be new savings or investment since there is no way to prevent anyone from diverting money from an ordinary savings account, money market fund, common stocks or other assets and into an IRA account.

One unnoticed and still unmeasurable shortcoming of the IRA system is the political impact it may have on the nation's Social Security system. Principal participation in IRA programs is expected to come from middle- and upper-income households – essentially the 25 million households that now itemize deductions when filing their federal income tax returns.

The danger is that their commitment to the new IRA accounts may sap some of the political support for necessary changes in the Social Security system to make it financially sounder. Some pressure may build to increase the current $2000 maximum deduction rather than strengthening the tax-supported Social Security system.

Given the existence of the IRA accounts, future increases might be justified on the basis of inflation. Congress should guard carefully against making any tradeoffs in which IRA rules are liberalized while uncertainties remain about Social Security.

The Social Security system's real problems should not be forgotten in the political climate of more generous IRA rules. Such liberalization could further undercut vital support for the relatively minor but important changes the Social Security system needs to ensure its smooth operation over the next decade.

DAYTON DAILY NEWS
Dayton, Ohio, January 22, 1983

So far, some Republican senators and others opposing the Social Security rescue plan have one thing in common: They have not proposed anything better.

Of course a lot of people dislike the notion of having to pay higher taxes to keep the system solvent. But where else is the money supposed to come from? Santa Claus?

And some retirees' organizations dislike restraints on benefits. But unless Santa Claus *does* appear, that restraint has to be part of the deal. Retirees ought not get benefits that accelerate faster than the wages of those paying the taxes.

Others are saying that Social Security needs *real* reform because it is carrying on contradictory functions — redistributing income and providing pensions. Social Security does indeed have inherent tensions; it has been built for different purposes. But those who say they want reform should say exactly what reform they want so the consequences of *their* agendas can be considered, too.

Do they want to dismantle the system, using the private pension alternative? Well, variations of that have been proposed by conservatives, and though the concept has been worth discussing, the basic concept of Social Security, as it is, has widespread support in this country. It is that basic system that this Republican administration, in cooperation with the Democratic leadership, is trying to repair.

It is a lot easier to crab about the system when one doesn't have to put forward lucid ideas for straightening it out — ideas that would be acceptable to people on both ends of the philosophical spectrum.

Part III: Developments

In December of 1977, Congress passed legislation mandating massive increases in Social Security payroll taxes. President Carter declared that although the Social Security system had been "on the road toward bankruptcy," the tax hikes would ensure "that it will be there permanently and in sound condition." That optimism has long since evaporated, in the face of demographic and economic changes that have once more threatened the system with bankruptcy. Members of Congress, always unwilling to alienate large portions of their constituencies, have been caught between appearing insouciant or pressing for changes that would adversely affect either taxpayers or the growing elderly population.

The agonizing nature of the decisions that had to be made is reflected in the waverings of Congress over nearly all aspects of the issue between 1978 and the present. Between the congressional battles can be heard the tolling bell of disaster, in the form of trustees' reports and commission studies warning that the system was or would soon be on the verge of collapse. As Congress tried to fashion a compromise that would rescue the system from insolvency, observers charged that the lawmakers were more concerned with "politicizing" the issue than with resolving it. Indeed, the charges and countercharges hurled by Democrats and Republicans alike often turned the issue of how to solve the system's problems into a political squabble. In the end, a delicate compromise was woven not by Congress but by a bipartisan commission appointed for that purpose. It remains to be seen whether the Social Security reforms recommended by the commission and passed by Congress in 1983 will be successful, or whether the optimism they have engendered will be as short-lived as that felt in 1977.

Mandatory Retirement Age Raised to 70

Until 1978, age 65 marked the onset of old age and the time for mandatory retirement for most workers in the United States. Under a bill signed in April by President Carter, however, the mandatory retirement age for most employees was raised to age 70, in recognition of the growing body of healthy older workers in the labor force. The legislation, passed overwhelmingly by both houses of Congress in March, would cover all employees of private businesses staffed by more than 19 workers—or some 70% of the nation's labor force—effective Jan. 1, 1979.

The bill also completely abolished mandatory retirement—then set at age 70—for most employees of the federal government. That provision would become effective Sept. 30, 1978. Nearly all state and local government employees, like private sector employees, would have their mandatory retirement age lifted to 70. Exceptions included those in certain occupations, such as police officers and firefighters, who could still be forced to retire earlier. Others given special consideration in the bill included college professors and corporate executives. Until July 1, 1982, colleges could still force tenured professors to retire at 65, and corporations providing pension benefits of $27,000 a year or more (exclusive of Social Security) could force high-level executives to retire at age 65.

The bill was conceived by Rep. Claude Pepper, a 77-year-old Florida Democrat and adamant defender of the interests of the elderly. Pepper stated that the elimination of the retirement rule in the federal government would "demonstrate the desirability of a complete ban on mandatory retirement in the private sector." The measure, whose easy passage was widely seen as a reflection of the increased political power of senior citizens, could also significantly reduce the financial drain on the Social Security system if enough people continued to work past age 65.

The Salt Lake Tribune

Salt Lake City, Utah, March 25, 1978

Almost a century after Otto von Bismarck decided that 65 was a proper retirement age for Germans in the 1880s. Congress has overruled him.

Both House and Senate passed an amendment to the Age Discrimination in Employment Act raising the mandatory retirement age to 70 in private business and eliminating it altogether for federal employment. President Carter's signature is expected to follow swiftly.

Bismarck settled on 65 when Germany established the first social retirement system years before the United States instituted Social Security in the 1930s. It was an arbitrary figure then and medical advances since have made forced retirement at 65 even more difficult to defend.

Will expected economic and personal benefits to the elderly balance out the predicted decrease in jobs for the young? That is a major worry attending the new retirement age. The answer at this point is pure speculation.

Rep. Claude Pepper, the 77-year-old Florida Democrat and moving force behind the amendment, says the Department of Labor estimates only about 200,000 workers between ages 65 and 70 would choose to remain on the job the first year and somewhat fewer in subsequent years. If that proves to be the case there should be minimal effect on job openings. But there is another factor that is beginning to surface and the new retirement law could bring it quickly to the fore.

That factor is the proposal to raise the age at which Social Security benefits become available from 65 and 62 to 68 and 65 (the lower ages are for early benefits at reduced rates). The new age levels are being proposed as one means of easing financial stresses on the Social Security system.

If the Social Security age requirement is increased then those 200,000 or so people Rep. Pepper mentioned would number in the millions. And job opportunities at the other end would shrivel accordingly.

All that is future talk, however. Perhaps the single greatest and most immediate plus factor in a higher retirement age is the boost it will give to the self-image of older Americans.

They may, as Rep. Pepper and the Labor Department say, choose not to work after 65. But at least the choice will be theirs. And that can mean the difference between seeing oneself as a useful human or a human discard.

The Saginaw News

Saginaw, Mich., March 23, 1978

The most obvious thing about the new mandatory-retirement-at-70 bill sweeping its way through Congress is that Congress wants it out of the way in a hurry.

As we've said, Congress knows a motherhood and apple pie issue when it sees one in an election year.

And with a growing bloc of older Americans flexing ever greater political muscle, it's doing what comes naturally on this one. The House has given the age-retirement reform bill its final blessing with hardly a voice raised against, and sent it on to the Senate for final pro-forma action.

The least obvious thing about it is just how well it's going to fit down over a socio-economic system that has been fine-tuned to retirement — across a broad spectrum of human activity — at age 65.

The answer is it can't be made to fit instantly.

That's why it has been written with delayed effective dates for industries and colleges and universities.

There are just too many labor-management pension systems and tenure agreements now in force to wipe them out overnight.

But it's inevitable that we're going to have this new law, so it makes sense for everybody to start getting used to the idea.

We have been generally opposed to a law that imposes blanket federal judgment on corporate management as to when is a right time to retire. Many companies have never enforced retirement at 65.

Up to now, that has been a matter of decision for businesses based on their own best judgment.

All the previous law ever said (the Age Discrimination in Employment Act of 1967) was that employers were barred from retiring, firing or otherwise discriminating against workers between ages 40 and 65 solely on the basis of age.

Well and good. But the new law shouldn't be advertised as ending discrimination based on age. It just raises the age of discrimination to 70 and applies it to virtually all private industry.

There's no lack of appreciation for what the new law will mean to those who are fit and want to work beyond 65.

But in truth, Congress has written a very complex law that discriminates in other ways. Corporate executives could still be forced to retire at 65 — but the way has been cleared for thousands of federal employees to work to 70 and beyond.

We just hope the law will not result in large numbers of great personnel problems — or dashed expectations as it becomes enforceable.

Chicago Tribune
Chicago, Ill., March 28, 1978

Last week first the House and then the Senate passed a bill raising the compulsory retirement age for most workers in the private sector to 70, and removing any age ceiling for employes of the federal government. The principal sponsor, Rep. Claude Pepper [D., Fla.], says that after expected presidential approval of this measure he will introduce another outlawing all mandatory retirement at any age.

Present practice varies from one employer to another, though the compulsory retirement age of 65 has long been accepted by many large employers. Among the principal arguments for Rep. Pepper's bill is that it will gratify the increasingly influential "senior citizen" lobby and that it will provide some financial relief for the Social Security System, by deferring payments to people enabled to keep their jobs after 65.

But the measure constitutes another conquest for the federal government of a decision-making power formerly in private hands and formerly exercised in a variety of ways. Under totalitarianism, nearly everything that is not required is prohibited. As these columns have said before, we would rather see retirement ages neither mandated nor forbidden by federal law.

Rep. Pepper observes that employers will still be able to discharge workers of any age for incompetence. But nearly everyone knows how red tape and other obstacles and inhibitions can keep on the payroll employes rightly judged incompetent, employes grudgingly tolerated until their 65th birthdays. In effect, the new legislation enables vast numbers of people to decide unilaterally when they will exchange a salary for a pension.

In much of the economy, the long-term trend has been towards retiring earlier rather than later. Many, if not most, employes will decide not to accept prolonged tenure on their jobs. But many will accept, with mixed results for their employers and for the public interest. Economic forces might well have been left to fine tune the boundary between working years and retirement.

WORCESTER TELEGRAM.
Worcester, Mass., March 29, 1978

The full impact of the legislation that will raise mandatory retirement age from 65 to 70 is not known. But the consequences will be far-reaching.

On the positive side, raising the retirement age will help end the myth that one's productive life is over at age 65. Many senior citizens have valuable skills and expertise to contribute to their employers. Many resented being shown the door at the arbitrary age of 65. Of course, 70 is also an arbitrary age line, but it does give people five more years if they want it.

Keeping older persons in the work force will also ease the Social Security burden on younger workers. When people stay on the job past their 65th birthdays, they add to the Social Security tax revenues and reduce the amount of benefits paid out.

How many workers will choose to keep working beyond 65 is not known. Some now are choosing early retirement at 62. Not everyone wants to go to his or her grave carrying a lunchpail.

However, Sears, Roebuck & Co., which suspended its mandatory retirement age of 65 in anticipation of the bill, reported that 45 percent of its employes who were approaching retirement indicated they wanted to stay on the job. At Connecticut General Life Insurance Co. in Bloomfield, Conn., an estimated 20 percent of those scheduled to retire this year will continue working.

There are some potential disadvantages to the change. Keeping people on the job after 65 will reduce the opportunities for jobs and promotions for younger people. It may mean less imagination and vitality in the middle and top echelons of some companies.

To be sure, workers can still be fired for cause, such as incompetency. The legislation states this explicitly. But such actions can make for awkward personnel problems. Incompetency is not always a simple matter to prove.

For many people in this country, work is a source of deep satisfaction. Though raising the retirement age will cause some headaches for companies that have to adjust their pension funding and medical insurance premium payments, the legislation will also provide important benefits.

As time goes on, we suspect that the benefits will become somewhat clearer and the drawbacks less formidable than they may seem now. With people living longer and staying more vigorous, a longer working life for more and more is in the cards.

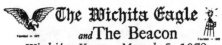

The Wichita Eagle and The Beacon
Wichita, Kans., March 5, 1978

Congress is on the right track in its efforts to strike down discrimination against senior citizens.

A House-Senate conference committee has agreed on a bill that would raise the mandatory retirement age from 65 to 70 and ban forced retirement of federal employees. The conference committee report must be approved by both houses and the president must sign the bill before it is law.

If it passes, as it probably will, perhaps the ban on forced retirement will be an example to employers in private industry.

Efforts have been made to end discrimination against minority races, women and others, but too little has been done to erase prejudice against older people in the work force.

Yet for every three employed persons, there is a retiree who probably still would like to be working but was forced to retire, according to a recent study. Twenty years ago nearly half of all men over 65 were still in the work force, either employed or actively seeking employment. Now only a fourth are working and this percentage is declining.

The philosophy of the market place has brainwashed many Americans into the belief that a person is over the hill at age 70. But in a brief presented to the U.S. Supreme Court, the American Medical Association asserted that while some persons lose judgment, ability and physical dexterity at 40, others retain these qualities past 80.

An individual's mental and physical health can be impaired by forced retirement through loss of status, lack of meaningful activity, fear of becoming dependent and isolation, the AMA said.

At the same time society is burdened with the support of many older persons who could be productive.

Working men and women should retire for two reasons only: if they want to or if they are unable to function. These conditions may occur at age 42, 26, 38 or 87.

Author and playwright Garson Kanin said once that a man "who is told that on his 65th birthday he will no longer be useful, lives through the same sort of agonizing countdown as a man condemned to death — and finally allows a silly system to transform him overnight into a superfluous non-entity."

Hastings College of Law, Stanford, Calif., will not hire anyone younger than 65 as a full-time professor. Some of the world's most famous and most accomplished people are far older than 65: Marshal Tito, 85; Adm. Hyman Rickover, 78; Sen. S.I. Hayakawa, 71, for example.

The granting and continuance of employment opportunities ought to be based on competence and ability — not on age.

THE CHRISTIAN SCIENCE MONITOR
Boston, Mass., January 10, 1978

The growing "senior liberation movement" means more than "helping older people to find jobs," to quote the title of this week's Monitor series by Richard J. Cattani. It must be seen in the perspective of America's on-again, off-again history of regard for the elderly. And, as the series points out, the myths to be dispelled go well beyond such job-related notions as that ability, energy, and creativity normally flag with time.

For example, the public misconception is that some 40 percent of the elderly are in nursing homes. The fact is that only five percent are.

More than half the public sees the elderly as "not feeling needed." Fact: only seven percent of those over 65 complain of this feeling.

Half the public sees ill health as a serious problem for the elderly. Fact: only a fifth of the elderly cite this problem.

We could go on. In short, aging is not the debilitating process it is cracked up to be. This finding underlies the current legislative effort to outlaw mandatory retirement in the federal government and extend the permissible mandatory retirement age from 65 to 70 in private business.

Is the nation as ready for this as it should be? Apart from all the pros and cons based upon statistics, a fundamental need is for a relationship between the ages based on the kind of fellow feeling necessary in other human relations. This "fraternity of age and youth, a brotherhood of the generations" is put into historical context by David Hackett Fischer of Brandeis University in his recent book, "Growing Old in America." He rightly sees this sense of brotherhood as the appropriate contemporary alternative to the nation's early exaltation of age and oppression of youth (1607-1820), glorification of youth and victimization of age (to about 1970), and the present concern for dealing with age as a social welfare problem.

A far-ranging debate would be needed before launching such a departure as Mr. Fischer's "national inheritance" plan. But the country's thought must be open to considering various options as, under social security, more and more elderly Americans become dependent on fewer and fewer working Americans. His plan would deposit a check ($1,400) for each American at birth in a federal insured bank or in government securities. At 8 percent this would grow to $225,000 in 65 years, when the income could provide a pension of more than $15,000. Mr. Fischer recognizes the vulnerability of such a plan to inflation. But he argues it could be a brake on inflation. The effect would be the opposite of deficit spending because the program would be funded before the money was spent. Federal bureaucracy would be reduced through use of the private banking system. Each person's capital would eventually return to the government and could be used for such purposes as reducing the national debt.

The point is not that this is necessarily the way to go but that a sense of brotherhood between generations would be enhanced by some way of ensuring that neither youth nor age is economically dependent on the other. Thus it would become easier to consider all members of every generation as individuals. Their constitutional right of free choice would be made practical instead of being thwarted by discrimination based on age.

Already many of the elderly themselves are breaking out of the categories of age and asserting their individuality. Some retire early, some late. Many prudently look ahead and make the best use of available means for bolstering independence in later years. Enough are seeking further education to make educators take account of the increasing average age of students.

Future unlimited — defined by free choice. That is what senior liberation is all about. It is everybody's movement.

The Kansas City Times
Kansas City, Mo., April 8, 1978

The new law on mandatory retirement, signed Thursday by President Carter, has a most ironic provision. Two major studies will be required to determine the statute's effects on individuals, businesses and the economy. It is a textbook example of government getting the cart before the horse.

This is one of the most drastic, profound changes to be imposed on Americans in many years. Everyone is affected, whether they are in the latter part of their work years or nearing the time they will enter the labor market.

The unknowns are underscored by conflicting views on the issue. Warnings have been sounded that the law, which raises forced retirement from 65 to 70 in the private sector and eliminates it entirely for federal workers, will disrupt employment practices. This could have an adverse impact on minorities, especially youths with a chronic unemployment

problem, and in general dampen upward mobility of younger employees.

Somehow the Labor Department has concluded that the effect will be limited. A department report indicates that employees will hold to a long-range pattern of retiring early — before 65. There also could be economic benefits, supporters contend, particularly savings on Social Security payments.

The unfortunate aspect of this legislative exercise was the haste and lack of study. Perhaps after thorough consideration, and a review of the legalities involved in mandatory retirement, this action would have been appropriate. There is no way to know, of course. Americans now will be subjected to government by trial and error rather than by a considered, reasoned approach that should have been taken on this most important decision.

The Star-Ledger
Newark, N.J., February 10, 1978

The nation's older citizens are fast becoming a political force to reckon with in Washington and state capitals these days.

The influence of growing "gray power" represents a positive dimension for this previously quiescent group, reflecting its increased numbers and a more cohesive, highly visible posture.

Evidence of the legislative impact senior citizens is having could be seen in the House and Senate passage of measures raising the retirement age to 70.

Surprisingly, the strong opposition to the higher retirement from such influential groups as the Chamber of Commerce and the National Association of Manufacturers was able to elicit an insignificantly small number of negative votes in both houses.

A Chamber lobbyist complained after the lop-sided Senate vote that it's "very difficult for any congressmen to vote against the elderly." It hasn't always been that way, but there has been a marked trend in favorable legislative responses to the problems of aging in the last decade.

* * *

It began with the adoption of Medicare legislation in 1965, a wide-ranging piece of social legislation that served as a catalyst for the old people's lobby. There have been a string of legislative successes since that breakthrough.

A strong lobbying effort was responsible for the Older Americans Act, which finances service programs for the elderly, a law that protects private pension plans and more recently, the passage of an amendment by the Senate that would lower utility rates for senior citizens.

The basic strength of gray power is numerical. There are 23 million over-65 citizens, one of every 10 Americans. By the turn of the century, the longevity factor will increase even more dramatically than it has in the last 77 years.

The legislative emphasis on the elderly represents an essential government response to a social condition that will require an even more expansive commitment of resources in the future. But it is imperative that it is done on a carefully planned, well-ordered basis . . . not an emotional over-reaction by vote-conscious legislators.

Payroll Tax Rollback Considered, Rejected

Early in 1978, there was considerable support in Congress for the idea of rolling back a series of tax increases just voted in December, 1977. These increases had not yet taken effect, but a previously scheduled increase had hiked payroll taxes at the start of 1978. The resultant clamor from angry taxpayers caused many lawmakers to have second thoughts about the wisdom of the additional tax hikes, to take effect in 1979, that were mandated by the 1977 law.

The House Ways and Means Committee May 17 voted, 21–16, against legislation to reduce the payroll taxes. This action reversed a 19–18 vote taken a week earlier, when the committee tentatively approved the tax cut. House Speaker Tip O'Neill told the committee before the May 17 vote that President Carter had said he would veto a rollback if it cleared Congress.

Meanwhile, the trustees of the system reported that the tax hikes enacted in late 1977 had restored financial health to the system, at least through 2011 or 2012. The May 16 annual report stated that the new taxes ensured that the system by 1981 would be taking in more revenue than it would be paying out in benefits.

St. Louis Globe-Democrat
St. Louis, Mo., March 30, 1978

Sen. William Proxmire, D-Wis., has made an important point that seems to have escaped most of his Democratic colleagues in Congress.

It is this: It would be unwise to cut Social Security taxes without making a corresponding cut in federal spending.

"Congress and the president must take out their red pencils and get to work to prevent the proposed cuts from forcing up prices and interest rates," said Proxmire.

Coming from a Democrat with a liberal voting record, this is rather refreshing. He is right, of course. For if Congress follows through with its plan to roll back the big Social Security tax increase it voted last December, it will increase the deficit by the amount of the tax cuts if it fails to make corresponding spending reductions. That, in turn, would force more borrowing by the Treasury and more money creation by the Federal Reserve, and prices would go up even faster than they are going up now.

President Carter should be the first to agree with Proxmire because he repeatedly promised to balance the federal budget during the campaign. But instead he is continually increasing federal spending and proposing big boosts for education, cities and many other favorite programs.

In view of the president's virtual abandonment of his pledge to bring spending in line with revenues, it is up to Congress to make the reductions proposed by Senator Proxmire to match planned Social Security tax cutbacks.

There is so much fat in the federal budget that it could be cut substantially without hurting essential programs. The effort is not made, so the budget grows out of control and the deficits soar past $60 billion a year. This may continue to be the case until citizens elect senators and representatives who will concentrate on saving the taxpayers' money rather than use so much of their time trying to find new ways to spend it.

THE MILWAUKEE JOURNAL
Milwaukee, Wisc., March 29, 1978

Congressmen are scurrying around frantically in search of a short term, politically palatable alternative to the steep Social Security tax increases they voted last fall. Such second thoughts probably are inevitable in an election year, and indeed something is needed to ease the Social Security tax bite. President Carter's proposed income tax cut is an acceptable form of offsetting relief.

However, the lawmakers' larger task is to find long range solutions to the formidable problem of financing future retirement benefits. Wisconsin's Sen. Gaylord Nelson has made some sound suggestions for such an inquiry. Recognizing that last year's Social Security tax measure was an ill-considered reaction to crisis, Nelson proposes that the Senate establish a special committee to examine Social Security and related programs over the next three years.

For example, he wants the committee to consider broadening Social Security's base of support by including federal employes, who are now covered under separate retirement programs. Indeed, the whole subject of public employe pensions needs review, especially in view of the fact that relatively few taxpayers can ever expect to enjoy benefits on a par with those of the civil service and the military.

Nelson also calls for a close look at the Social Security benefit structure, to determine what levels of retirement income the program should hope to maintain. It's a painful question that cannot be safely ignored in the coming years as retired persons represent an ever larger share of the total population. For example, should maximum benefits be available to high income people? Put another way, should benefits, at least to some extent, be scaled according to need?

Especially welcome is Nelson's suggestion that the committee explore the relationship between Social Security and private pension plans. If Social Security taxes pre-empt too much of the national income, many employers and employes may be hard put to keep private plans intact. Yet about one-third of American workers have no retirement coverage other than Social Security, and their needs cannot be overlooked. So there's a question of striking a proper balance between Social Security and competing retirement programs.

A study committee also should take a look at reducing or eliminating the regressive, flat-rate payroll tax that now finances Social Security. The major alternative source of money would be general revenue raised by the progressive income tax — a tax better reflecting ability to pay.

The next time Congress undertakes major Social Security legislation it should not be an exercise in ineptitude. Appointment of a study committee, as Nelson suggests, could result in guidelines for intelligent, enduring reforms. It should be created forthwith.

The Salt Lake Tribune
Salt Lake City, Utah, April 10, 1978

Although there is good reason to have another look at Social Security tax increases passed last year there is no urgency for doing the job right away.

A number of factors argue for postponing the reappraisal. They include:

Despite a 3-to-1 margin in favor of rolling back taxes, members of the Democratic Caucus indicated no agreement on how this could be accomplished. In fact, the resolution calling for the reduction was couched in vague terms because of the diversity of opinion on how to implement a tax cut. Plainly, the majority party doesn't have a plan to accomplish what its members seem to want.

The tax increase contained in the 1977 Social Security amendments do not begin to take effect until 1979 and project into the 1980s. That means there will be plenty of time to conduct a thorough review of Social Security and various options for keeping it solvent long before the full burden of the new tax schedule is felt.

This being an election year, any changes voter-conscious congressmen might favor are certain to be overly influenced by re-election ardor. Social Security is too immense and too complicated to be tinkered with under the influence of an impending election.

Although the new payroll tax schedule is weighted against higher income earners it is not yet clear that the predicted taxpayer revolt against the new rates has materialized. Testimony by former Social Security officials last week suggested that once taxpayers realize the benefits that await them upon retirement they will accept the new schedule.

A comprehensive examination of the Social Security system is in order, partly because of the 1977 amendments and partly because the discussions that preceded them did not range far enough. But the job should be assigned to the new Congress which takes its seats the same month the new, higher taxes go into effect.

Newsday

Long Island, N.Y., March 27, 1978

There are almost as many ideas for reducing Social Security taxes in this election year as there are members of Congress. Representative James Burke (D-Mass.) wants to finance Social Security with general Treasury funds for the first time. Representative Abner Mikva (D-Ill.) would trim $38 billion from the Social Security tax by removing Medicare and disability benefits from the system. House Ways and Means Committee Chairman Al Ullman (D-Ore.) would tap the crude-oil tax—should Congress pass it. The Joint Economic Committee would junk President Carter's income tax cut and instead reduce Social Security payroll taxes.

There's considerable merit to some of the ideas now making the rounds on Capitol Hill. But where were their sponsors only last December, when Congress passed a massive tax increase that was supposed to put Social Security on a sound fiscal footing for the rest of the century?

President Carter proposed then that general Treasury funds be used to help finance Social Security, but that idea was quickly hooted down by Republican and conservative Democratic members of Congress who insisted it would turn Social Security into a welfare program.

Now many who opposed Treasury funding have suddenly decided it's probably the only way to reduce the impact of the massive $227-billion tax boost Congress voted last December. And they're probably right.

But nobody knows for sure. That's why we think the brightest idea now making the rounds is Wisconsin Senator Gaylord Nelson's. Nelson, chairman of the Senate Social Security subcommittee, would impose a three-year moratorium on the increases voted last December, and make up the difference from general revenues.

A moratorium would give the several commissions now studying Social Security the time to make a careful evaluation of viable long-range alternatives for funding the system—and there are many. And it would allow a limited test of the effects of financing part of Social Security—probably Medicare and disability benefits—out of general revenues.

The idea of Congress ramming through an "emergency" Social Security bill to help the hapless taxpayer in an election year has to be the worst of all those now circulating in Washington.

St. Petersburg Times

St. Petersburg, Fla., March 20, 1978

Just before Christmas Congress bravely marched up the hill to rescue the Social Security System. Now a lot of its members are trying quietly to sneak back down, leaving it once again crying for help.

The lawmakers in December were proud to assure the old folks their retirement checks had been made as secure as Fort Knox. What they would like to do now is tell everybody still at work this extra protection for the Social Security Fund won't cost them anything much.

WE THINK the public, old and young, is smarter than that. But for those who forget, the problem was this: Social Security taxes, after 40 years, no longer were staying ahead of Social Security checks. The Fund was being depleted. Drastic steps were required to start raising more money.

Congress approached the problem with what appeared to be considerable courage. It knew benefits couldn't and shouldn't be cut. So it passed a bill to raise taxes, gradually but substantially, bringing income and outgo steadily back into balance.

However, after a couple of months the applause from retirees now has died down. And some lawmakers claim to be receiving complaints from those still at work. The complaints of course are about the awesome new taxes. And Speaker Thomas P. (Tip) O'Neill says members are stampeding to cut them.

THE FUNNY THING about those reported complaints is that none of the new taxes has even gone into effect. They begin to take hold, on payrolls and pay checks, only next year, and even then will barely be noticed except by those making more than $18,000 a year.

However, that group happens to include a lot of the influential folks who not only write letters to congressmen but who usually get a reply. They also vote. And all 435 House members of course are gearing up now to run for election.

That helps explain why a bunch of House Democrats huddled Wednesday in support of a bill to cancel those unpleasant tax boosts. Instead, under their plan, extra funds required to keep Social Security stable would be appropriated from "general funds." Republicans denounce this plan but offer one of their own that has the same effect.

THAT SOUNDS fine, until you consider that the government's general funds, supported mostly by the income tax, are those that already are running $60-billion yearly into the red. And Congress even now is considering enlarging that deficit by cutting those taxes.

So the general fund plan, for now anyway, is *Alice in Wonderland* stuff. Considering the present state of the government budget, it means that the billions of dollars in new money needed will simply have to be borrowed.

That means bigger deficits. Higher interest costs. More inflation. It means ducking out on the basic Social Security problem, which is that if American workers are to continue to be able to count on retiring in some kind of comfort, they have to start paying more while they work.

IT IS TRUE that in its rush to bail out the Social Security System, Congress may have gone a little too far in raising the taxes. Eventually, under the law passed in December, both the tax rate and the base pay against which it is levied will rise to almost prohibitive levels.

But that increase will take place gradually and over a number of years. Congress will have plenty of time before the pinch starts to consider alternative plans. The income tax, and the general fund, undoubtedly will figure in the final solution.

And once President Carter gets a grip on the budget, and the government quits spending so many billions it doesn't have, they undoubtedly should. The income tax, unpopular as it is this time of year, is about the fairest tax so far devised.

Except for the illegal evaders and the relatively few legal avoiders, it hits hardest at those best able to pay. The Social Security tax on payrolls, on the other hand, nicks the poor at the same rate as the rich, although under the new law for much smaller total amounts.

BUT CLEARLY this isn't the time to tackle that problem. This is the time to stand firm for keeping Social Security on its traditional basis. Pay-as-we-go is a concept all but forgotten elsewhere in government. But for four decades it is what has kept Social security sound. Congress should not be allowed to abandon it lightly.

The Des Moines Register

Des Moines, Iowa, March 10, 1978

A partial rollback of the Social Security tax increase approved by Congress late last year came a step closer to reality when the House Ways and Means Committee approved reducing the payroll tax and the wage base on which the tax is levied.

Congress voted to hike Social Security taxes because the system had been paying out more than it was taking in for several years, and the deficits were going to get larger. The tax hike was not ideal, but it had the advantage of making the payroll tax more equitable by raising the taxable wage base from $17,700 in 1978 to $42,600 in 1987.

Congress is now feeling the heat from taxpayers earning more than $17,700. The scheme approved by the Ways and Means Committee directs most of its tax benefits to these higher paid individuals by lowering the taxable wage base. The reduction also in the payroll tax rate would give some aid to individuals earning less than the newly proposed wage base.

Such "reform" does not improve the equity of the payroll tax. Nor does tinkering with the Social Security system only months after a major overhaul increase public understanding and support for the system.

Several studies of the financing of Social Security are in progress. Congress would be smart to wait until the studies are completed before further modifying the system.

Herald News

Fall River, Mass., May 16, 1978

The House Ways and Means Committee has voted to roll back about the scheduled increases in Social Security taxes. The vote could not have been closer, 19 to 18, and the fact that it was so close suggests that it is impossible to predict how Congress will finally act in relation to it.

The administration wants to preserve the scheduled increases as they stand in spite of their unpopularity, but the House is much more concerned about widespread public resistance. The committee's vote reflected that concern, and since the public attitude is unlikely to change, the House as a whole will be reluctant to leave the scheduled increases unchanged.

This is especially the case in an election year. The White House which does not face endorsement by the electorate this fall, can afford to disregard public dislike of the Social Security tax increases. Congress cannot.

These political considerations are probably confusing the real issue, which is how Social Security is to be maintained in the face of growing deficits. No one can ignore the deficits; no one thinks that Social Security can be discarded. The problem is how to pay for it.

If the House, for instance, wishes to roll back the scheduled increases, in the face of White House disapproval, then it should make plain how it thinks the deficits can be made good. It cannot simply discard an unpopular tax without reference to making up the lost revenue.

The battle over Social Security's fiscal future will be with us long after next November's elections have come and gone.

Sentinel Star

Orlando, Fla., May 16, 1978

THE WAYS and Means (and Expediency) Committee of the U.S. House of Representatives has voted to halve the 1979 and 1980 Social Security tax increase and make up the deficit from general revenue.

The vote was, to be sure, a tight 19-18, but by coming down on the side of political expediency the committee has tossed the Social Security grenade onto the House floor.

The increased tax, which proved to be an election-year albatross, was to underwrite the looming insolvency of the Social Security trust funds. Last year $98.2 billion was collected from employee payroll deductions and employer matching funds and from Medicare premiums, but more than $103.8 billion was paid out. The difference came from Social Security reserves.

Elementary arithmetic confirms the peril of that practice but the proposal made by Rep. Sam Gibbons, D-Tampa, to simply divert general revenue into the trust is as irresponsible as dipping into reserves. It simply transfers financial responsibility from the employee's payroll deduction to his income tax obligation. In the process it perverts the old-age retirement plan by making it an outright welfare measure.

Social Security was conceived as a supplement to retirement income. Had Congress honored that concept the system would have remained self-supporting. Instead, it has been burdened with disability and Medicare benefits and is in serious trouble.

The financially honest remedy is the logical one: relieve the retirement funds of the extraneous health and disability expenses. Those obligations are a welfare responsibility. Shifting them to the Health, Education and Welfare budget will provide a more accurate accounting of their cost, lighten the drain on workers' salaries and restore the integrity of the Social Security Act.

The Virginian-Pilot

Norfolk, Va., March 15, 1978

Indecision over the proper form of remedial funding of the Social Security system was apparent in the House Ways and Means Committee's narrow recommendation for rolling back higher payroll taxes scheduled to begin next January. The Committee rejected eight options before settling uncomfortably on a transfusion from general funds to make up the difference. Swallowing his convictions, Chairman Al Ullman, D-Ore., broke an 18-18 tie and sent the proposal to the House floor for a vote.

Whatever its fate, the proposed revision represents a capitulation in the sporadic fight, going back more than 40 years to the origins of the Social Security system, over tapping general revenues. The change reluctantly endorsed is a stopgap two-year plan that would take $14.5 billion from other taxes to meet Medicare hospitalization costs. The offset would be a return to the 1977 taxation level on a higher salary base, sparing workers at maximum deduction levels and their employers $123 next year and $190 the year after.

Details may prove irrelevant since the plan, assuming House approval, has slight chance in the Senate. Like Mr. Ullman, Senate Finance Chairman Russell B. Long, D-La., considers using general funds for Social Security irresponsible and would be in a position to spike the notion. Mr. Ullman, who has been around Capitol Hill long enough to know the minds of Congressmen, fears that opening up general revenues could lead to higher benefits paid for through deficit spending. His vote sending the bill to the floor was not as contradictory as it appears: the House Democratic caucus agreed, by a 3-1 ratio, to support the rollback, and he was bound to honor its wishes.

Mr. Ullman has accused his caucus fellows of yielding to constituent pressure, principally from middle- and upper-income taxpayers who would bear much of the burden of the 1977 changes. However, even if popular discontent has been exaggerated there is an inflationary booby trap in the higher Social Security taxes voted last year. Workers would want more pay to cover deductions and employers would seek to pass on higher matching taxes to customers.

Rollback opponents agree with the Administration that interim changes should be avoided pending completion of the study Congress authorized last year on short-term and long-term solutions to deficits facing Social Security. The system's problems are considerable. Costs have escalated rapidly, threatening to exhaust trust funds soon, while a smaller work force must support more longer-lived retirees a few decades hence. Meanwhile, Medicare expenses have been increasing at a gallop.

Alternatives to insolvency of the system are few and uninviting. Reducing benefits would be politically unthinkable. Making Social Security self-supporting again through higher taxation may be impractical as well as unpopular. Spreading the burden over other tax sources could be the choice, however lamented. Mr. Ullman and his Committee appear to sense the drift of events.

DAYTON DAILY NEWS
Dayton, Ohio, March 20, 1978

Yes. No. Maybe. No, the Social Security tax increase scheduled for next year won't be passed. At least for now. Probably.

The House Ways and Means Committee, which recently voted to reduce the payroll tax increase next year, making up the difference with money from the treasury, has changed its mind back again and will let the increases stand.

Though the public mood is unpredictable, Congress could hear more clamor next year as the higher rate grabs on. But the committee was wise to remain dubious about tapping the treasury since that would make it much easier to raise benefits than to raise the means of paying for them other than printing more money.

But Social Security recipients do need the benefits and what modest increases are in the works. And Congress should take a look at the whole system — a review that has been promised for years but never fulfilled.

Some small reforms could help — possibly by increasing the number of years one must pay into the system before getting full benefits, for example. But a more significant improvement would be to lower the rate of taxation — to 5 percent, say, — while removing the cut-off point for the taxes.

That would be better than the proposed tax increases scheduled because it would be easier on lower-income and middle-class workers who now carry a disproportionate share of the burden.

ARGUS-LEADER
Sioux Falls, S.D., May 19, 1978

The House Ways and Means Committee has acted responsibly in voting 21-16 against any reduction in Social Security taxes. The vote turns back an effort to use $14.5 billion of income taxes to make up a cut of the same size in Social Security taxes.

Congress took a courageous step last year when it voted to increase Social Security tax rates and the upper limits of salaries to which it applies, effective in 1979. The step effectively assured the fiscal soundness of the Social Security system into the first decade of the 21st century.

Pressure from the public this year resulted in an election year attempt to roll back the increases. The pressure for the rollback was in the House, where all the members are up for re-election this year. The rollback faced an uncertain fate in the Senate, and the promise of a veto by President Carter if it had gotten through Congress.

We empathize with citizens who see their deduction for Social Security exceeding their federal income-tax withholding. But we believe that this step to maintain the Social Security system's fiscal basis is the better way to go. It represents fiscal propriety.

What is needed now in Washington is more of the same: there should be no cut in income taxes until Congress trims deficit spending.

President Carter has agreed to trim his proposal for an income tax cut of about $25 billion to approximately the $19.4 billion recommended by the House Ways & Means Committee for the 1979 fiscal year. This is still out of harmony with sound fiscal policy when the spending plan calls for a deficit of nearly $51 billion in a $498.8 billion budget starting Oct. 1.

Balancing outgo with income would be the best way Congress and Carter could fight inflation.

THE PLAIN DEALER
Cleveland, Ohio, May 18, 1978

For at least the last year, Congress has wrestled with a Hobson's choice over Social Security. Faced with the undeniable evidence of benefit payments rising faster than revenues, Congress had either to increase taxes substantially or enact commensurate reductions in benefits, or some combination of both.

Last December, Congress approved a whopping $85.7 billion Social Security payroll tax increase stretched over the next six years, the largest single tax hike in American history.

And how the taxpayers howled!

This year, an election year, the Democratic caucus in the House voted overwhelmingly for a resolution requesting the House Ways and Means Committee to roll back part of the payroll tax increase.

There was no mandate for reducing benefits, mind you, just for a reduction in new payroll taxes.

The committee agonized over, and then systematically rejected, each proposed new source of revenue until it arrive at the shopworn proposal to dip into the Treasury for funds to pay Social Security benefits.

It then voted 19-18 to replace the $15.5 billion in Social Security payroll tax increases over the next two years with funds from the Treasury's general revenue.

Yesterday, in a fit of good sense, the committee reversed itself, voting 21-16 to restore the $15.5 billion in added Social Security payroll taxes.

A spokesman for committee chairman Al Ullman, D-Ore., explained it this way: "Right now we have a discipline between taxes and benefits. If you want higher benefits, fine, but you'll have to pay higher taxes. If you remove that discipline (by dipping into the Treasury), the discipline is gone."

Exactly.

Increasing Social Security benefits is a popular act for a member of Congress. Raising the necessary taxes is not.

Removing the necessity for keeping Social Security revenues abreast of benefit payments is simply another inducement for the kind of buy-now, pay-later deficit financing that has already helped give the economy an intractable case of inflation.

When it was enacted during the 1930s, Social Security was billed as an actuarially sound old-age pension insurance program. It wasn't. It is not that today.

But at least current law requires Congress and the taxpayers to weigh the desire for higher benefits with the pain of added taxes.

That pressure is what stands between a reasonably responsible Social Security program and one that could quickly get completely out of control.

FORT WORTH STAR-TELEGRAM
Fort Worth, Texas, May 23, 1978

A confused and frustrated House Ways and Means Committee has reversed itself to now oppose a roll back in Social Security taxes.

The rollback was politically appealing to many lawmakers in this election year, and it would have been welcomed by most taxpayers.

Yet the unpopular turnabout was the only sensible way for the committee to go.

Without the increase in taxes due to take effect next year, Social Security would be in serious trouble.

Whether the funds come from the present contributory system or from general revenues, the taxpayer still must bear the burden. But a general revenue-financed system changes the concept of benefits as a right to one of benefits according to need. Social Security becomes only another welfare program.

Yielding to demands for increased benefits without compensating tax rate increases, the Congress has created the present strain on the system, but cutting benefits now is unthinkable.

The hefty tax increases voted last year should keep the system solvent well into the next century, the system's trustees have informed Congress.

Just how inflationary those tax increases will be when both the rate and the taxable base go up next January remains to be seen. But Social Security is not a free ride. Taxpayers must pay the bill.

To roll back the program-saving tax increase would only delay and magnify the distress.

Congress would do well to leave it be.

And to resolve to never, never again take credit for increasing benefits without at the same time accepting the unpopular responsibility of raising taxes to pay for a politically popular beneficence.

BUFFALO EVENING NEWS
Buffalo, N.Y., May 19, 1978

The House Ways and Means Committee is suffering from schizophrenic leadership among its Democratic majority. Last week it correctly voted to recommend a lowering of Social Security taxes scheduled to hit workers hard next year. But now, uncertain and opposed by the Carter administration, it has reversed itself, preferring to keep the higher taxes on the books.

And they are higher. The maximum Social Security tax paid this year is $1071 for an individual worker, plus an equal amount paid by his or her employer. Unless Congress modifies the law, this maximum will rise by $333—or a painful 31 percent—in one single, steep jump next Jan. 1.

By pushing up employers' labor costs, that will of course push up prices. And by shrinking a worker's take-home pay, it will both generate pressures for higher wages and reduce spendable income just when the business upturn could be flattening out and turning sluggish. So there are several advantages to a modest cutback in the Social Security taxes due next year.

Since members of Congress and other civilian federal workers pay no Social Security taxes, they don't personally feel the pinch. If they did, perhaps there would be more interest in a rollback. But we hope this issue isn't dead yet. At the very least it should be acted upon, even without Ways and Means Committee support, by the full Congress this year.

THE DAILY HERALD
Biloxi, Miss., May 19, 1978

"After that, you and your employer will each pay half a cent more for three years, and finally, beginning in 1949,...you and your employer will each pay three cents on each dollar you earn, up to $3,000 a year. That ($90) is the most you will ever pay."

That promise appeared in a bulletin entitled *"Security in Your Old Age"*, issued by the Government Printing Office in 1936. The promise has long since been broken, of course, as Congress discovered the simple truth that before it can give money away, it must first take money from the taxpayers.

Relearning that lesson, Congress heeded actuarial warnings that the Social Security System was slip-sliding into bankruptcy and recently raised the rate of contributions into the system.

Some Congressmen had second thoughts about the increases and began a movement to roll back the hikes to a more modest level. Their effort failed day before yesterday when the House Ways and Means Committee reversed itself and voted to kill a rollback bill it had approved a week earlier.

If you are a worker contributing to the Social Security System with the expectation of one day receiving benefits, or if you are now a beneficiary, you are undoubtedly thankful that Congress reconsidered and withstood the rollback temptation.

The reason is found in the report that the trustees of the system released on the same day the Ways and Means Committee defeated the rollback. The trustees said that increased contributions "restored the financial soundness" of the system, at least until 2010. Generally, the system's life has been extended for another generation.

The trustees also recommended no action be taken to change the financing arrangements of the system "at this time," holding out an indefinite hope that if the system continues to remain healthy, some rollback might be possible at some future date.

But for now, workers and employers this year will continue paying 6.05%, up to a maximum payment of $1,070.85. Next year, payments will be at a 6.13% rate, up to $1,403.77 on the first $22,900 of earnings. Contributions will continue rising until 1987 when maximum payments will exceed $3,000.

In return, employers and employees can be assured that the system is temporarily secure, until the early years of the next century.

Currently, there are three active workers paying into the system for every beneficiary drawing out of it; projections are that by 2030, the ratio will be only 2-1.

Generations yet unborn and youngsters not yet in the work force are destined, it seems, to even higher payments that today's rates.

Contrary to the 1936 government promise, the most a worker will ever have to pay hasn't yet been envisioned.

THE CHRISTIAN SCIENCE MONITOR
Boston, Mass., May 19, 1978

Social security reform once again has been pushed to the back burner in Congress. And once again American workers are the losers. Not only will they be hit with substantially larger payroll tax bites beginning in January, but the long overdue start toward a comprehensive overhaul of the system has been put off at least until next year.

What had been some glimmers of hope that Congress would finally come to grips with the long-term funding problems of the social security system quickly faded when House Speaker O'Neill and the Ways and Means Committee both did some quick backpedaling under pressure from the Carter administration.

Only two months ago Speaker O'Neill was prodding the administration to submit a new social security financing bill. And only a week ago, the Ways and Means Committee approved a plan for rolling back some of the payroll tax hikes Congress legislated last December. It would also have shifted some of the funding for Medicare from social security to general revenues, a move toward shoring up social security against projected long-term losses. Population shifts in years to come will put more older Americans in retirement with fewer younger workers contributing to social security.

Hence some method of funding other than the payroll tax must be found. There has been growing support in Congress for relying on general revenues to provide for Medicare's increasing expenditures. Medicare benefits are not tied to earnings and, in our view, do not logically belong under social security.

The payroll tax hikes enacted in December will have the desirable effect of restoring financial soundness to the near bankrupt social security system through the year 2030. That does give the United States Congress ample time to tackle the still unresolved long-term financing problem. But Medicare funding is still in trouble. And in the meantime, the regressive payroll tax, coupled with inflation, will make it even harder for U.S. workers to balance their family budgets.

Now Congressional leaders are saying "next year" they will tackle comprehensive social security reform. We hope they mean it.

The Hartford Courant
Hartford, Conn., May 20, 1978

President Carter's call last year for sharp increases in the Social Security taxes was coherent and clear, while congressional response was timid and disjointed.

The massive hikes eventually approved in Congress represented the largest peacetime tax hike in history, and congressmen began to back off almost immediately. Last week, the powerful House Ways and Means Committee tentatively voted to send a rollback bill to the floor, but this week, the legislation was killed, virtually assuring that the tax increases will go into effect.

As the political flip-flopping indicated, Congress was simply not prepared to deal with the issue. That does not mean that legitimate reform of the Social Security system is not justified. Ways and Means Chairman Al Ullman of Oregon has promised a major review of the program next year, and we hope he makes it stick.

Social Security is not a retirement insurance program in the true sense of insurance, and the changing demographics of America will not allow the luxury of that misconception to continue indefinitely, without putting a frightening burden on wage earners.

Medical benefits and disability payments in particular have little relationship to the recipient's work experience or contributions into the system. Those programs should be funded by general tax revenue.

Social Security is increasingly a broad-based income-transfer system — a welfare program, perhaps the best such program in the nation. The financial and political liabilities of the program can best be resolved by expanding its funding base beyond the artificial limits of particular workers and private companies.

The Topeka Daily Capital
Topeka, Kans., September 19, 1978

Before the Senate Finance Committee the other day, G. William Miller recommended a one-year deferral of higher Social Security taxes.

Miller is the chairman of the Federal Reserve Board. The Fed, in its controls over currency, may have more leverage over the economy than the president of the United States. So when the chairman of the Federal Reserve Board speaks, people listen.

We hope Congress is listening closely and acts accordingly by including the temporary rollback in this year's income-tax-cut bill now being drawn up by Congress.

Miller pointed out to the senators that deferral of the Social Security hike could reduce inflation by one-half of 1 percentage point. This is because the tax-payer only pays half the Social Security tab each year. Your employer coughs up the other half. Under the Social Security hike, now envisioned to take effect on Jan. 1, American business as a whole would have to throw about $4 billion more into the social Security till.

Miller's hypothesis — and he is undoubtedly correct — is that businesses will finance this cost by raising prices. A total price increase of this magnitude would be clearly inflationary.

Miller's advice is quite sound — and timely. It should also prove politically potent. The head of the Fed does not always (and certainly should not always) take positions on economic policy that flatter the short-term interests of the taxpayer. But on the issue of Social Security tax increases, his position neatly meshes with the desire of every wage-earner not to have yet a bigger F.I.C.A. chunk taken out of the paycheck.

Congress doesn't usually listen to the wage-earner, but it often listens to the chairman of the Federal Reserve Board. That's why there's now hope on this one.

The Miami Herald
Miami, Fla., September 11, 1978

HAVING listened to advice from almost everyone who wanted to say a few words on the subject, the Senate Finance Committee is now working on its own version of a tax bill. There is little evidence that it will take any of the advice, especially that of Federal Reserve Board Chairman G. William Miller, who shared his thoughts with the committee last week.

Mr. Miller, concerned as he should be with the stability of the dollar, likes the House-passed bill that would cut taxes by $16.3 billion. But he would prefer something closer to $15 billion. Along with that, he suggests postponing the scheduled Social Security increase in payroll taxes from Jan. 1, 1979, to the same date in 1980.

We can agree that postponing the tax would let employers keep $4 billion rather than match the $4 billion taken from wage-earners, and thus the pass-along effect of inflation would be delayed. But it would only be delayed — to return with a price-raising vengeance a year later.

What Social Security needs, and must have, is a sound basis. There must be reliable income to fund the retirement of Americans who pay all their working lives but face the prospect of a bankrupt retirement system.

The solution, as we have pointed out before, is not to tinker with the system, or delay it, but to return it to its original purpose of providing retirement benefits.

The system faces bankruptcy, and the workers face escalating pay-ins for the next quarter-century, because Social Security has been raided by tacked-on welfare programs. Medicare and disability payments come out of the fund.

Medical care must, of course, be provided for those who have to have it and can't afford it on their own. But this money should come from general revenues — income taxes, mostly — rather than retirement funds.

Perhaps the shock value of seeing the takeout from next year's first paycheck will generate the outrage that will get the attention of Congress and result in a sensible restructuring of the Social Security system. Unless this is done, $37 billion in non-retirement benefits will go to Medicare and disability payments. By 1987, the cost will be $93 billion.

A tax cut next year might enable some workers to break even on the Social Security increase, but only for one year. But taxes can't be cut every year, and if the Social Security tax goes up every year, nobody will be able to afford to retire.

The system simply isn't fair. It must be changed.

The Seattle Times
Seattle, Wash., September 8, 1978

THE House of Representatives last month passed a tax-cut bill that holds considerable promise for encouraging job-producing investment by private industry.

The Senate Finance Committee is now considering how to make its own version of the bill even more conducive to a stronger economy. One way might be to heed some advice given the committee this week by G. William Miller, chairman of the Federal Reserve Board.

In a marked split with the Carter administration, Miller urged a one-year deferral of the heavy Social Security tax increase due to take effect January 1.

The deferral would save employes and employers each $4 billion next year.

Miller rightly noted that the Social Security tax is "both inflationary and regressive," and recommended that a deferral be enacted "only with an explicit and urgent commitment" to deal next year with the Social Security system's long-range funding problems.

Last spring it had appeared certain that Congress would respond to the sounds of distress being heard on every hand over the outsized Social Security tax increases, which will cut take-home pay by as much as $334 next year and considerably more in the following years, while increasing employers' costs by equal amounts.

But the momentum for a rollback vanished as soon as public shock over the size of the scheduled increases appeared to have worn off. The House Ways and Means Committee, under pressure from the administration, backfed away from thoughts of financing health-insurance and disability parts of the Social Security system out of general Treasury revenues.

Under Miller's deferral proposal, Congress would have another year to take a look at that plan before outsized Social Security payroll take-outs are imposed.

And $8 billion additional for Social Security would not be taken out of the economy in a year when, according to most forecasters, economic growth is due to slow down.

The Finance Committee should take note, too, of Miller's estimate that a $4 billion increase in employer contributions to Social Security next year would add roughly one-half per cent to the inflation rate.

Minneapolis Star and Tribune
Minneapolis, Minn., September 9, 1978

Next Jan. 1 a Social Security tax increase begins that over the year will cost $8 billion. It's bound to have an impact on both inflation and politics. Half the amount will be paid by employers, directly raising their costs of doing business, and inevitably adding to the prices of their products. That will boost the rate of inflation by about half a percentage point. The other half of the higher tax will come straight off the top of people's paychecks. Last winter a much smaller increase provoked cries of pain that made many in Congress seriously consider rescinding or reducing it. Next winter's feelings are not apt to be much different.

That makes it tempting to raise hopes again that Social Security taxes can somehow be rolled back. Some candidates for Congress have already talked about repealing the increase. And this week Federal Reserve Chairman William Miller lent that idea respectability. He proposed to the Senate that the new withholding be deferred for a year.

Miller is mistaken, both politically and economically. An election-year danger is that legislators will like the headlines but ignore the fine print. It might prove dangerously easy to "defer" a higher tax. It would be much harder to balance that deferral — as Miller rightly insists should be done — by rejecting income-tax reductions already near approval. And it would be harder still to follow up — as Miller also urges — with a hard-nosed study of Social Security financing that would have to lead to even higher withholding in 1980 or to a later trimming back on old-age benefits.

The economic mistake stems from the political, and has two parts. First, postponing the tax increase for Social Security would not reduce the government's obligations. It would, however — unless clearly matched by other taxes not now in the works — add several billions to the federal deficit. That deficit is fundamentally more inflationary than the payroll tax itself. Making it larger is no way to bring down the cost-of-living index.

Second, going light on payroll taxes would again call in question the financial soundness of the Social Security system. It is not yet a year since Congress summoned the courage to require the payments that will cover promised benefits into the 1990s. Even with the increases, Social Security remains underfinanced and will need new revenues by the turn of the century. Now is no time to start compounding that future problem.

The fight against inflation demands sterner measures than a tempting cut in payroll withholding. At its unlikely best, Miller's proposal to the Senate would shave a temporary fraction off cost-of-living increases. At worst, it would make later inflation more severe and aggravate problems that already loom large in the Social Security system.

Shortage of Funds Forecast: 1979–1981

Succeeding annual trustees' reports were not as sanguine as that of 1978 about the future of the Social Security system. In 1979 the trustees warned that despite the scheduled tax increases enacted in 1977, the trust fund for retirees' and survivors' benefits, in the event of a recession, could be depleted by 1983. Other reports—in 1979, 1980 and early 1981—by the Congressional Budget Office, congressional committees and federal panels confirmed the trustees' warnings: the system was rapidly running short of money. In addition, it was estimated in 1980 that at the current rate of population growth, there would be only two taxpayers for every person receiving Social Security by 2020, creating an intolerable tax burden on working people.

Numerous suggestions were made for shoring up the system. Among them were taxing retirees' benefits, eliminating or reducing automatic cost-of-living increases, making the system universal and raising the retirement age to 68 or 70 from 65. The President's Commission on Pension Policy recommended in its interim report in 1980 that Congress consider requiring all private employers to offer pension plans for their employees.

Increasingly, as the reports of the financial future of the Social Security system grew more pessimistic, there were calls for structural changes in the way it was administered, rather than a continued reliance on tax increases, to avert a crisis.

THE CHRISTIAN SCIENCE MONITOR
Boston, Mass., April 20, 1979

Congress has yet to find a way to ensure the long-term solvency of America's social security system. In 1977 it enacted a stopgap measure that provides for drastic hikes in payroll taxes over a 10-year period in an attempt to keep up with the demand for benefits from retired people. With the increase in the retired population expected to accelerate as the post World War II "baby boom" reaches retirement age around the year 2015, however, even the steep tax hikes already enacted will not be sufficient.

Congress needs to return to the drawing board and this time, instead of merely tinkering with the present inadequate financing system, it must tackle the difficult but necessary structural reforms. The warning this week from the trustees of the social security system that a recession could threaten the government's ability to pay retirement benefits on time starting in 1983 underscores the precarious nature of the current system.

The trustees in essence were warning Congress — which has been leaning toward pulling back on the 1977-enacted tax hike — that it would endanger the system to reduce the social security tax without either lowering benefits or tapping some other source of revenue.

Lowering benefits not only is politically distasteful but it also raises legitimate questions about the government's obligation to meet its commitment to people who have contributed to the system over many working years in anticipation of receiving ·retirement benefits. For that reason proposals to reduce benefits generally do not get far in Congress. But the key House Ways and Means Committee has approved a measure that would, at least, make a slight dent in outlays. It would cut back on disability payments to the tune of about $1 billion a year. And this appears to be the one proposed reform likely to be enacted this year.

The problem with current disability benefits is that they are so high — $11,000 a year in nontaxable income for a worker formerly making $16,000 — that recipients have little incentive to return to work, even when they become physically able to do so. Too many never go back to work once they are on disability. Moreover, any disabled person who earns more than $280 a month loses all benefits, including Medicare health insurance. Thus many disabled people take jobs as volunteers or work for reduced salaries in order not to lose Medicare.

The proposed legislation would lower benefits enough to make work attractive; it would also allow those who return to work to continue to get medical care.

This same approach – i.e. improving the incentive to work – is embodied in another long-term measure for shoring up the social security system; it, too, should be studied carefully. Gradually raising the retirement age from 65 to 70 over a period of years would save billions. It would provide older workers with a strong incentive to stay in the labor force, thus increasing the time in which they pay taxes and reducing the period in which they receive benefits.

Although many Americans have been opting for early retirement – between 62 and 64 years of age – some economists point out that this, too, is partly the result of the "retirement incentive" built into the current system. They note that for low-income workers, for instance, tax-free social security benefits are worth almost as much as their taxable wages. Another possibility would be to allow retirees to work part-time without losing all of their social security income.

Various proposals have been put forward for revising the method of financing social security. Shifting certain benefits programs, such as Medicare and disability insurance, to general revenues is an idea that has merit. Using income taxes to support such so-called "welfare" aspects of social security would be less burdensome on taxpayers and more progressive than the current payroll tax. Some argue that use of general revenues would destroy the insurance concept on which the social security system was built. But social security has never been an insurance program in the usual sense; benefits are weighted heavily in favor of low-income contributors. About 40 percent of all social security taxes now go for programs in which the beneficiaries need not have contributed. Congress and the public ought to recognize this as one form of "social insurance" — the type of assistance all other industrial nations use some general revenues to pay for.

Bringing federal employees into the social security system would greatly strengthen it in the short run. And other proposals, such as those to introduce a value-added or national "sales" tax, or to tax certain benefits, ought to be studied closely. Regardless of which approach is chosen, the basic question Congress must answer is: How much can Americans afford?

It is obvious the current system of financing must be replaced. Even with the stiff tax increases already scheduled, the system will be underfunded by an estimated $800 billion over the next 75 years. A basic restructuring is called for, and further delay will not make the choices any less difficult.

Des Moines Tribune
Des Moines, Iowa, May 1, 1979

The trustees of the Social Security system told Congress the other day that it would be unwise to cut Social Security taxes for at least several years unless Congress is willing to cut benefits or find other sources of revenue for the system. This is good advice.

In late 1977, Congress approved a bill that will raise Social Security taxes by more than $200 billion in the coming decade. Many members of Congress recognize that such tax increases won't be popular with their constituents.

The trustees warned that, even with the scheduled tax increases, the system could have cash-flow problems beginning in 1983 if the U.S. economy continues to suffer high inflation and unemployment.

The trustees' projections do not reflect revenues that would be gained if Congress were to bring federal workers and other non-covered public employees into the system. The U.S. Chamber of Commerce has suggested that doing so would permit deferment of some of the scheduled tax increases. But a postponement only delays the inevitable facing of the issue.

We hope that the pain of the scheduled tax increases will encourage Congress to take a hard look at the long-term future of Social Security. For if benefits are maintained at the levels set under current law, workers will have to bear an increasing tax burden in the years ahead to support the growing number of elderly Americans.

President Carter's 1980 budget message projected that 50 years from now the United States might have to devote as much as 28 percent of its gross national product to retirement and health benefits for the elderly, up from only 11 percent at present.

Has Congress been too generous with the elderly? Will young workers 50 years from now be willing to sacrifice so much of their income to support the retired? These are the questions that must be answered before Congress toys with major cuts in Social Security taxes.

The burden might be spread more equitably by putting general revenues into Social Security benefits, but over the long run there will be no free lunch for Social Security. Benefits will have to be paid for.

RAPID CITY _JOURNAL_

Rapid City, S.D., May 2, 1979

The precarious position of the Social Security system indicates the necessity for Congress to tackle difficult, but necessary, structural reforms to ensure long-term solvency of the program.

Despite higher taxes, reserves in the Old Age and Survivors Trust Fund dipped by $4.3 billion during the past year. That prompted trustees of the fund to warn that a recession in the next year or two could create severe cash-flow problems and jeopardize the system's short-range actuarial soundness.

The crunch could come as early as 1983 when there might not be enough cash on hand to make ordinary monthly payments to the nation's retired recipients, who currently total 34.4 million persons.

In 1977, after a bitter battle, Congress enacted huge payroll tax increases in an attempt to make the system more solvent. This was only a stop-gap measure and basic reforms in the system still are needed.

One such reform would be a reduction in disability benefits. Current benefits are so high — $11,000 a year in non-taxable income for a worker formerly making $16,000 — that recipients have little incentive to return to work even when they become physically able to do so. Moreover, any disabled person who earns more than $280 a month loses all benefits, including Medicare health insurance. Lowering disability benefits and allowing those who return to work to continue to get medical care would make returning to work more attractive.

Improving the incentive to work could also be achieved by gradually raising the retirement age from 65 to 70 over a period of years. It would provide older workers with a strong incentive to stay in the labor force where our lagging productivity could benefit from their experience. That reform would increase the time in which older workers pay taxes and reduce the time in which they receive benefits.

Shifting certain benefit programs such as disability and medical programs to general revenues would lift the burden on payroll taxes. About 40 percent of all social security taxes now go for programs in which the beneficiaries need not have contributed. These programs ought to be recognized as social insurance programs and paid for by general revenues.

The current system of financing Social Security must be overhauled. Congress should quit tinkering and face up to the task. Delays will not make the choices any less difficult.

The Cincinnati Post

Cincinnati, Ohio, May 3, 1979

The annual report by the trustees of the Social Security system is an argument against the occasional clamor in Congress to slash Social Security taxes.

Social Security Commissioner Stanford G. Ross says the report shows that the system is sound and in "good financial shape for the next 50 years." But the reason it's in good shape is that Congress showed unaccustomed courage in voting to raise Social Security taxes to keep the system solvent.

Even with the new contributions flowing in, the system is not entirely free of potential cash-flow problems if the U.S. economy goes into a severe recession. In a worst-case projection, high inflation and high unemployment, the old age benefit fund could dip dangerously low by 1983, righting itself a few years later. A similar 1983 problem with the Medicare fund could be eased by transferring to it money from the newly invigorated disability fund.

No one, particularly the higher income worker upon whom the new tax increases fall heavily, is enthusiastic about paying higher Social Security taxes. Employers feel the bite, too; they must match, dollar for dollar, the taxes paid by their employees.

But Social Security has become a bedrock of American social policy. It has been well administered—so well, in fact, that Congress felt free over the years to load it down with obligations without seeing that it was properly funded. The recent tax increase was the result.

Now, to roll back those taxes, or to suspend further tax increases, without trimming back benefits would be irresponsible.

Perhaps the day may come when the Medicare program or the disability program could be transferred out of the Social Security system and financed by other federal taxes, if the federal budget is balanced. This would ease the burden on the Social Security payroll tax.

But until Congress musters the gumption to restructure the basic framework of the Social Security system, any talk about cutting taxes while maintaining benefits is absurd. It can't be done.

The San Diego Union

San Diego, Calif., April 28, 1979

Whether the news about Social Security is good or bad depends on where one stands in the labor force — on the active rolls, or retired.

Pensioners who have been watching inflation shrink the buying power of their Social Security checks have the good news that help is on the way. Benefits will rise by nearly 10 percent in July, reflecting an automatic semi-annual cost of living adjustment.

But that same news is not so good for the employees and employers paying a Social Security tax that took one jump this year and is scheduled to rise even more sharply in 1980. Trustees of the system are now questioning whether these tax increases, voted by Congress in 1977 with a promise that they would solve the Social Security financing problem, may turn out to be not enough.

The trustees recently issued a report saying the system will be "financially sound for well past the turn of the century," but with an ominous qualifier. A recession serious enough to raise unemployment to 8 percent while inflation remains at 6 percent or more could put a "severe" strain

on Social Security trust funds as early as 1983.

That's what happened during the recession of 1975, creating the crisis which Congress purportedly solved in 1977 by increasing the tax and by revising the formula for applying cost-of-living benefit increases. The trustees — Social Security Commissioner Stanford Ross and cabinet secretaries Michael Blumenthal, Ray Marshall and Joseph Califano — now seem to be saying that the problem isn't solved after all.

Economists are predicting a business slowdown of some degree this year. It would not have to be very severe — given the current inflation rate and its impact on benefits — to produce another serious imbalance between the amount of money going into the Social Security pipeline and the amount going out.

Obviously the 96th Congress must grit its teeth and face the truth about Social Security. First, it must reject the tantalizing notion that the tax increases voted in 1977 can somehow be rolled back as a pre-election gift to voters in 1980. Even the quali-

fied optimism of the trustees would be insupportable if this new infusion of trust fund income were cut back.

More important, the House and Senate must act on the Social Security reforms proposed by President Carter earlier this year as a further means of bringing future demands on the system under better control. It must also proceed with the overhaul of the disability side of Social Security to overcome its demonstrated flaws — benefit levels and other provisions which create a disincentive for the disabled worker to seek retraining and another job.

The burden which the new Social Security tax schedules will place on American workers and their employers in the 1980s is as heavy as they can be expected to shoulder. If there are new cracks appearing in the facade, the repair work must be done in the area of the promises the system is making to future beneficiaries and not in higher taxes.

That's a tough order for Congress, which is only comfortable adding new promises to federal programs, not retracting old ones. But the truth is knocking insistently at the door.

'I'll move on this matter when the mood hits me, sir, and not before!'

The Washington Star
Washington, D.C., August 10, 1979

There were mingled sighs of relief and groans two years ago as Congress undertook to buttress the fragile finances of the Social Security system. The timbers for the shoring up were steeply increased payroll tax rates and expanding the deductible base. That ought to do it, they said on Capitol Hill, for the next 40 years.

Congress was off the mark, it now appears, by something more than three decades.

The blame for this stunning miscalculation apparently must be laid to that all-purpose villain, circumstances. And circumstances in this instance, according to the Congressional Budget Office, are the combined ravages of inflation and recession.

In a letter to Rep. Robert Giamo, chairman of the Budget Committee, CBO director Alice Rivlin warned the other day of a "significant deterioration" in the Social Security system's financial soundness over the next five years. "Outlays will rise rapidly because benefits will rise automatically with inflation, and the rising benefits and weak labor market conditions will induce more people to retire," she said. "At the same time, revenues will lag as employment and wage rates fall or grow less rapidly."

The most serious threat is to Old Age and Survivors Insurance, the largest of the three funds that make up the Social Security system. (The Disability Insurance programs and the Hospital Insurance fund, from which Medicare payments are made, are in somewhat better shape.) Under the Congressional Budget Office's new projections, the OASI trust fund is projected to decline from 34 per cent of annual outlays in fiscal 1979 to 8 per cent in fiscal 1983 and 5.4 per cent the following year. "These levels would be insufficient to maintain the cash flow of the program," the Rivlin letter said.

There is greater likelihood, of course, of the Senate chamber being turned into a disco-roller rink than that the 35 million Americans receiving Social Security payments will be left adrift. What Mrs. Rivlin's letter makes clear is that legislative remedy is required and with some urgency.

She outlines six possible courses of action, one of which would be to again raise the Social Security payroll tax. But this would have the effect of "increasing unemployment and adding inflationary pressure during a period when we will be trying to reduce both." It would also be enor-

mously — and justifiably — unpopular and, thus, an unlikely option for Congress. Indeed, the Carter administration, though insisting that a tax cut to alleviate the recession would be premature now, has indicated that if there is one down the road, it should be in the form of payroll-tax reductions.

Another option would be to shift revenues to the old age fund from the disability or the health funds, though this would still leave the system vulnerable should the economy dive deeper into recession.

One of the quickest methods by which Congress could address the five-year projected shortfall, Mrs. Rivlin said, would be to limit the increase in Social Security benefits to that allowed for wages under President Carter's guidelines — the June Social Security increase, for example, was 9.9 per cent while the administration's wage guidelines called for 7 per cent; the Congressional Budget Office projects a 10.3 per cent benefit increase for next June under the automatic indexing system. There is merit to this possibility but, again, the political dust it would kick up will severely inhibit Congress.

Another option would be to transfer general tax revenues into the old age trust fund to compensate for the reduction in revenues due to economic conditions. Mr. Carter proposed and Congress rejected that method in 1977, a decision which hindsight no doubt causes some members to regret, with reason.

The last point suggested by Mrs. Rivlin has a much to recommend it. This would involve financing the health/Medicare fund from general revenues, while transferring that program's trust balances and tax receipts to the old age fund. "Because the HI (Health Insurance) receipts would be more than sufficient to maintain a reasonable OASI fund balance relative to outlays, the total payroll tax rate could be cut if it was determined that a non-inflationary form of fiscal stimulus was called for," the CBO letter said.

That is sensible. Congressional action, or reaction, when the Social Security system's finances get wobbly has not been particularly imaginative or foresighted. But we hope that, provided with a reasonable menu by Mrs. Rivlin, the House and Senate will take a bit more thoughtful look at the problems this time.

The Dallas Morning News
Dallas, Texas, August 6, 1979

A COUPLE OF weeks ago Social Security Commissioner Stanford G. Ross pronounced the end of an era. Gone, said Ross, are the days of ever-expanding benefits. Ahead lies "a decade of reform" and "painful adjustments," brought on by Social Security's increasingly unmanageable costs.

More recently, Alice Rivlin, director of the Congressional Budget Office, warned that Social Security's plight grows direr all the time. She raised the likelihood of a "significant deterioriation" in the system's soundness over the next five years.

Meanwhile, economic recession has prompted the White House to mull the possibility of rolling back some of the enormous Social Security tax increase enacted two years ago and implemented last January.

Singly or collectively, these are developments of consequence. The need for Social Security reform — a need widely bruited throughout the '70s — no longer is seen approaching us from afar. We are eyeball to eyeball.

The system, to be sure, is nowhere near collapse. It is time, even so, for hard decisions as to what it will be like in the future.

The problem is money — and where to get it. The stupendous tax increase of 1977 was supposed to fix things for elderly and disabled recipients over the next 40 years. Yet the tax is a serious drag on the economy.

Even if the tax is not rolled back, inflation and rising unemployment will play havoc with Social Security's finances. Unemployment, of course, reduces payments into the system; inflation raises the benefit levels. The biggest loser, according to Mrs. Rivlin, is the system's biggest trust fund, that which aids the elderly.

Than Social Security there is no hotter political potato; which is why real reform will doubtless wait until after the 1980 elections. The solutions are painful. General revenue financing? But this consummates Social Security's conversion into a welfare system. A scaling back of future benefits, as indicated by Ross? But this penalizes present workers.

Notwithstanding, these things must be thought on. And so must lesser reforms, such as cutting off college students who draw benefits.

One way or another, Social Security must get back to its original purpose — the provision of *supplemental* benefits to the retired and hard-up elderly. Here, as always, private enterprise has a role to play. We need to encourage increased reliance on private retirement plans, less reliance on Social Security. If there is, in the end, another way, someone please point it out. We haven't noticed it.

THE INDIANAPOLIS STAR
Indianapolis, Ind., December 31, 1980

With the first paychecks of the new year, American workers will again be painfully aware of the state of the nation's Social Security program. Some people will feel a pinch of up to 25 percent more in such deductions. Both Social Security tax rates and the size of the wage base upon which they are calculated will be going up Jan. 1.

A most discouraging aspect of the increase is that younger people who will be paying into the fund will not be "investing" in retirement themselves. The Social Security taxes they pay now will immediately have to be passed out to current beneficiaries of the program. And the need for ever larger current amounts is growing, chiefly for two reasons.

Older Americans may indeed be fortunate to have their benefits automatically increasing to keep abreast with increases in the cost of living.

But the problems with Social Security have gained significant momentum, not only because those benefits are indexed to the rate of inflation but because the numbers of retired people receiving them have also grown dramatically.

So the challenge is how to keep older people with an adequate retirement income yet get the Social Security fund on a solid financial footing and not dependent on hand-to-mouth feeding.

As one measure of how the current Social Security system is sapping the vitality of the country, such retirement payments in 1979 consumed 8 percent of the Gross National Product compared with 2 percent in 1950.

There is no doubt that Social Security will become one of the most important issues of the new Congress. A solution is not likely to come from a single approach, such as merely reducing benefits or expanding the minimum eligibility age.

While some adjustments may be necessary just to keep the system viable in the next few years, the best long-range alternative may be to work out new funding for Social Security in the larger context of general tax reform.

CHARLESTON EVENING POST
Charleston, S.C., December 4, 1980

The Social Security system in this country has been in trouble since the 1960s. The present problem is based on the fact that there are less people working, therefore fewer contributing to the fund while, at the same time, inflation is driving up the amount of benefits. Another factor was Congress incorporating the disability and Medicare programs under the Social Security umbrella. An obvious third contributing factor is the growing percentage of the population over 65 years old — 11 percent now and expected to increase to 23 percent by the year 2020.

The Social Security fund will begin to run out of money in 1982 and will be $3 billion in the red by 1983. The deficit could run as high as $27 billion by 1985. Regrettably, there are no politically acceptable or popular remedies to the problem — either the benefits have to be cut or the taxes have to be raised to support them. And Congress has raised the amount that workers and employers contribute to the fund seven times since 1967. The next increase comes on January 1 when many Americans will be nicked for another one-half percent of their pay for Social Security.

Last month a Federal panel suggested that the retirement age for full benefits be gradually increased to 68, beginning in 2000. If adopted, it would mean those born after 1935 would have to work longer to qualify for benefits.

We hope the Congress faces the reality of the problem and approves the panel's recommendation. We'd even urge that consideration be given to raising the age qualification for Social Security earlier than the year 2000. Americans are living longer now, and older Americans should be encouraged to work as long as they can be productive.

THE PLAIN DEALER
Cleveland, Ohio, November 11, 1980

Congress is discovering slowly and painfully that the crisis of the Social Security system is a reflection of what ails America's economy.

High unemployment, inflation and retarded economic growth in real terms are combining to rob the Social Security system. For example, one million Americans unemployed for a month equals $100 million in lost Social Security taxes. Social Security's trust fund for retirees and survivors' benefits could be depleted by the end of 1981, despite the higher Social Security tax rates enacted by Congress.

This likely drain on this particular trust fund can be eased considerably. Social Security can shift revenues from other health and disability trust funds. But over a long term this amounts to robbing from one account to pay another. It is a practice that cannot be tolerated for long without dire consequences.

Three years ago Congress grasped at a rescue operation. It enacted a series of amendments imposing higher Social Security taxes through 1982 on employers and workers — 90% of whom contribute to the system. Now, the Joint Economic Committee of Congress, in a bipartisan study, has found that the higher taxes have contributed to further stagflation. They are obstacles to genuine economic expansion. And the Social Security system is still in deep trouble.

Any further increases in mandatory contributions from employers and workers would be counterproductive. Labor costs would rise — again. Disposable income of workers, already eroded by inflation, would be drained — again. Capital for investment so critical to creating new jobs and revitalizing America's industrial base would be lost — again.

The Joint Economic Committee rightly concludes that the key ingredient to salvaging Social Security for this generation rests with proper tax measures to stimulate investment by business and industry. Increased investment will eventually provide a more healthy economy, increase employment and achieve the desired goal of adding revenues to the system.

We urge members of the 97th Congress to consider the Joint Economic Committee's sound advice for an "investment-based economic growth policy."

As painful as it may be, Congress also needs to consider changes in how Social Security benefits are distributed. Perhaps the retirement age for benefits should be raised. Social Security adjustments for cost-of-living increases are said by some experts to go beyond the actual effects of inflation on the elderly. This adds to the system's financial burdens.

Lincoln Journal
Lincoln, Neb., December 29, 1980

Oh, wouldn't it be pleasant if the warming glow of Christmas, reinforced by the Sun Bowl results, could extend for weeks and weeks? After Jan. 1, we're going to need vat-sized servings of good cheer.

Locally, new and higher natural gas and electri rates confront us. About them you presumably already know much, although there always are some who never get the word until bills arrive. Outraged, they then write letters to the Public Mind, charging a conspiracy of silence.

More to the point of this commentary, Social Security taxes also increase on Jan. 1 by decree of a Congress past.

Be alert; in this area, rates aren't the only thing rising. So is the amount of earned income subject to the payroll tax. A kind of double whammy.

The rate bounces upward from 6.13 percent of taxable earnings to 6.65 percent. Beyond that, the maximum amount of taxable earnings against which the Social Security payments apply has been boosted from $25,900 to $29,700.

For an individual paying the maximum tax in 1980 and again in 1981, the composite increase is 24.3 percent.

[Once again we think it important to stress that an employer must match every employee's Social Security tax contribution, dollar for dollar. When it goes up, so does the company's pay-in responsibility. Substantially higher Social Security taxes scheduled in a matter of days may especially hit firms already weakened by a slow economy.]

What is duck soup to predict is that the reaction of American workers and businesses to the Social Security tax changes will be even greater support for the income tax reduction promised by Ronald Reagan as quickly as possible after his inauguration.

The wave of national endorsement for an income tax cut — even though it will increase the national government's deficit and just possibly prolong or even invigorate inflation — will be very difficult for any political figure to oppose.

But let us be clear about what happens. Neither a personal income tax reduction nor changes in the tax code for businesses will cure what ails the Social Security system. An aspirin which temporarily blots out the pain of a toothache doesn't fill a cavity.

This newspaper renews its editorial call for at least one fundamental change in the $149 billion Social Security system: pay for Medicare programs out of the national general revenue, not Social Security accounts.

That has been the plea here since the mid-1960s. No one has provided a documented, compelling case why the two programs should be fiscally merged. On the contrary, the hard evidence of the 1970s points to the opposite conclusion.

THE SAGINAW NEWS

Saginaw, Mich., November 20, 1980

Through no fault of its own, the Social Security system is getting closer to failure faster than anyone had thought. The fund could run out of cash in two years, perhaps sooner.

Social Security will not fail, of course. We cannot afford to let it fail. It provides financial peace of mind for millions of retired Americans. They have earned their benefits, and they have been encouraged through a lifetime of work to have faith in the system.

But to ensure that the faith was not tragically misplaced, the system will have to be changed, and quickly. Both a congressional study and advisers to President-elect Ronald Reagan agree on that.

Both reports pinned down the basic problem. The number of workers paying in is not keeping up with the growing numbers of retirees taking money out.

About 35 million persons now draw benefits. The number is expected to grow to 47 million within 20 years. Meanwhile, the birth rate is stagnant. America is graying, and its younger population can't keep up with benefit bills that are rising along with the inflation rate.

Many kinds of reforms have been suggested, and the answer undoubtedly is in some combination of those.

But in our view, the solution should include two essential points.

First, no person already covered by Social Security should suffer; our senior citizens deserve that clear reassurance.

Second, the Social Security tax rate should be held down as much as possible. Ideally, there should be no further tax increases. Our working persons already are due for a shock Jan. 1 when the rate goes from 6.13 percent to 6.65 percent, and taxable income rises $4,000, to $29,700.

What's left to change is the internal system — not its existence, but its future definition of who gets how much, and when.

Several proposals especially deserve a close look to see whether they can save money without unduly undercutting benefits.

One is bringing *new* federal employees under Social Security, yielding a net gain of $2 billion a year.

Another, much bigger money-saver is raising the normal retirement age from 65 to 68. More people are living longer, and many are working longer, now that retirement at 65 no longer can be forced.

A third is changing the basis for figuring benefit increases. The change wouldn't be in the basic benefits, but in slowing down their growth. In the past year, Social Security recipients were among only three groups in the entire economy which actually enjoyed an increase in "wages." Even retired federal workers lost ground.

But it would be grossly unfair to break the promise of possible retirement at 65 without some compensation. One way to encourage personal investment for retirement would be letting workers set up a tax-deferred retirement account, the so-called IRA, even if they're covered by a pension plan. Another is tying retirement benefits more directly to how much workers are now paying in.

When you look back on it, those wild-eyed schemes to make Social Security partly voluntary weren't so crazy after all. If we keep compulsory taxes down while encouraging individual self-insurance, we'll be heading in that direction. And it may be the only way to preserve the system itself.

The Hartford Courant

Hartford, Conn., December 16, 1980

The misconceptions and guesses that riddle the current Social Security system are difficult to overcome, but the bottom line — the hard facts — for 1981 are depressingly clear.

On Jan. 1, the level of income subject to Social Security tax will increase from the present $25,900 to $29,700, and the percentage of tax taken will rise from the current 6.13 to 6.65. Even with those increases, the system will once again face financial crisis in a year or two, according to a congressional study released in November.

The nation's policy generators have flooded the market with remedies, but the only alternative that Congress has been comfortable with up to now has been a steady increase in taxes to support the existing plan.

There are few programs in the national welfare apparatus that so defy rational analysis as Social Security, for it affects most Americans, and it is wrapped in the protective clothing of a pension system, or an insurance plan — which implies a funding stability and an obligation to provide benefits, far out of proportion to the reality of the system as it is.

The November report from the Joint Economic Committee of Congress suggests a variety of possible remedies, from raising the eligibility age for retirement benefits, to lowering certain benefits, to requiring exempted federal employes to participate in the program. Similar ideas have been expressed for years, and they inevitably drown in a flood of emotional criticism.

Ronald Reagan and his new team are also exploring some changes in the system — and perhaps it will take a man who has pledged to govern as if he would only serve one term, to deal with the problem in a sufficient manner.

While Social Security has been marketed and advertised in a manner similar to an insurance or pension program, in fact it has become a massive welfare system — a worthy, valuable and effective welfare program to be sure, but a welfare program nonetheless. The money taken from worker paychecks each week is not squirreled away for the future retirement of those workers, as in a traditional pension program, but is quickly paid out to persons already eligible for a hodgepodge of payments — many of which have no connection to old age and retirement, and to how much the recipient has paid into the system.

For an income transfer system as widespread and massive as the Social Security system has become (in Connecticut, for instance, 15 percent of the total population is receiving Social Security payments), the funding base must be broadened beyond the paychecks of workers who are making less than $30,000 per year. Congress has been afraid to fund the system from general tax revenue, for fear that Congressional lack of discipline would tap the treasury irresponsibly.

The rationalization that workers could pay for their own benefits worked well when an increasing work force and increased productivity could provide enough funds to keep the system afloat, but a declining birth rate and increased longevity have begun to take their toll.

Assuming that Congress could muster the courage to raise the retirement age from 65 to 68, or reduce the relatively generous cost-of-living increases, the system might struggle through the next 20 years without major new tax increases. But the politics of Social Security probably dooms such changes, and even if they were made, the crisis would emerge again in time.

Eventually, the stigma that hangs over the term "welfare" must be dealt with, and much of what is now called Social Security should be paid with general funds. Massive welfare programs should be funded through progressive corporate and personal income taxes, not narrow payroll taxes of a work force struggling to support a growing number of elderly recipients.

St. Louis Globe-Democrat

St. Louis, Mo., February 23, 1981

Frantic SOS signals are being sent out to rescue a foundering Social Security system.

What happened? Congress had adopted a 10-year schedule of annual tax increases totaling $227 billion that was to have assured the system's good economic health through 1987. President Carter was considerably more optimistic. In December 1977 he predicted — inaccurately — the system would be "on a sound financial basis . . . throughout the rest of the century."

This is not the case. Social Security is considered to be in such dire straits that the trust fund which provides money to pay supplemental income benefits to retirees could be penniless in early 1983 and more than $63 billion in the hole by 1986.

The situation isn't likely to improve until Congress distinguishes between benefits earned and paid for with the payroll tax during a retiree's working years and other social obligations that properly should not be funded with Social Security taxes.

Services that should be removed from Social Security and funded by general revenue include Medicare and disability benefits. Benefits for college students of a disabled parent or a retiree over age 65 should be shifted into some educational program not connected with Social Security. The $255 burial payment probably should cease. As a one-time payment, this small sum involves extensive processing that makes its cost effectiveness dubious.

In 1972 Congress seriously undermined Social Security by automatically increasing future payments in current (not inflated) dollars. As an example, a worker whose salary averages $1,000 a month will receive $433 monthly upon retirement now. In 1995 the comparable benefit will be $471 and by 2025 it will climb to $570 in current dollars.

Inflation will further intensify this heavy burden facing the diminishing number of workers in the future supporting a growing total of retirees. Now is the time to correct the error of 1972, long before the higher benefits are scheduled to become effective.

One suggestion, made by the Congressional Budget Office, to increase Social Security revenues is to foist a second payroll tax of one-half percent atop the increase that became effective Jan. 1. Actually, it would be a 1 percent boost since both the worker and employer contribute equal amounts.

It's time for Congress to get off the tax-and-tax-some-more binge. That's an easy route for Capitol Hill to follow. But it's extremely hard on workers and employers, who already pay a combined payroll tax of 13.3 percent on incomes up to $29,700.

Rep. J.J. Pickle, D-Texas, chairman of the House Ways and Means Subcommittee on Social Security, reflects the dangerous pollyannaish attitude prevailing on Capitol Hill. Although admitting that a major supplemental income fund "will run short of reserves to pay a month's benefits sometime in 1982," he still contends, "This is not an emergency."

Such a fate could spell calamity for many of the 35 million Americans who receive the monthly checks. That development also would shake up the 114 million workers who pay taxes into the program.

To correct the long-range problems that Congress built into the system will take major surgery. In the past, Capitol Hill has proved itself to be a quack by prescribing questionable remedies.

That practice won't work any longer. This time around it will have to be the real thing. Young workers already are justifiably wary of Social Security. Retirees should recognize the situation. Restoring the program to good health will require give and take from both the young and old for the common good.

Rockford Register Star

Rockford, Ill., February 24, 1981

The Social Security system is in trouble and the trouble is getting worse. That's been no secret for a long time, even if our congressmen would like to believe otherwise.

And there is no secret about what is causing the problems:

Increased longevity and lagging birth rates — exaggerated right now by increasing unemployment — has changed the ratio between workers paying into the system and retirees drawing from it.

But now the Congressional Budget Office has spelled out just how much trouble the system faces.

The budget office's deputy director, Raymond Scheppach, has told the House Social Security Subcommittee the Social Security retirement fund will run out early in 1983 and could be $63.5 billion in the red by 1986 — a deficit which at the present rate would reach $128.9 billion by 1990.

In short, the congressmen were told, the retirement benefit program is in danger of going bankrupt in a big way.

"That is not going to happen," Scheppach was told by Rep. J.J. Pickle, D-Texas, who is chairman of the House Social Security Subcommittee. "The committee will find some way to fix Social Security without raising taxes," Pickle added.

Just how Congress will get that job done is the problem.

There are several proposals:

—We could allow the system to go bankrupt, but that has to be almost unthinkable.

—There are suggestions to decrease benefits or mandate even greater increases in Social Security taxes. Those are proposals which would create terrible burdens on either the retirees or the wage earners.

—There are proposals worth-considering that would phase in an increase in retirement age and restrict some benefit eligibility.

—There is a proposal to borrow heavily from the federal Treasury to keep the plan solvent and there is another plan to attach a 2.5 percent surtax on income taxes for Social Security purposes. Both suggestions would mean subsidizing the program from general revenue sources and would force either greater budget deficits or major tax increases.

—Finally, there is a plan to tap surpluses which now exist in the Medicare and disability Social Security programs to help finance retirement benefits. This solution would be the least painful and would be a step toward keeping the Social Security program self-sufficient — but also probably would be a short-term solution.

Most important of all, however, is that Congress take heed of Scheppach's warning and stop ignoring the growing problems. Any solution which keeps the Social Security system self-sufficient for an extended length of time will serve better than the recent congressional record of simply hoping the problem will go away.

The Dallas Morning News

Dallas, Texas, February 23, 1981

WITH HIS proposals to retard the growth of government, President Reagan's getting down to economic fundamentals. You say, so what? The obvious reply is that fundamentals are what you get down to when you want permanent solutions.

If you don't want such solutions, get out the cosmetics kit — as did Congress in 1977 when it voted the biggest tax bill in American history, $227 billion, to rescue the Social Security system. It was proclaimed in the White House and the halls of Congress that Social Security was safe for the next decade.

How ironic, then, to mull the Congressional Budget Office's recent report that money for retirement checks is running out already — that, indeed, by 1986 the trust fund on which these checks are written could be $63.5 billion in the red. May stunned taxpayers ask of their representatives: What happened?

They may and should. What happened was that Congress and the President failed in 1977 to address the reasons Social Security was running out of cash. They assumed the answer was just to come up with more cash.

Various things are wrong with various of the fundamental assumptions on which Social Security presently stands. One assumption is that you can cope with the effects of inflation just by indexing benefits to the cost of living. In fact, you can't. Benefits presently are rising faster than average income in the working economy — 14.3 percent vs. 9 percent last year.

Another false assumption is that you have only to increase taxes whenever the system gets into deep financial waters. The trouble is that Social Security taxes already are so high as to be a drag on the economy. They preempt money that, profitably invested, would create jobs and new growth.

As these taxes increase, the willingness to pay them diminishes. The present generation of workers is not comforted by predictions that in the next century it will take two active workers to support each Social Security beneficiary.

Fundamental reform is plainly what Social Security needs. What reform is more basic than bringing inflation under control? This alone would virtually solve the cost-of-living payment problem.

Additionally, many congressmen want — without imposing on the truly needy, for whom Social Security was designed — to tighten eligibility requirements. One way to do this is to phase in a new, higher retirement age.

Whatever the case, it is to fundamentals that the friends of Social Security now must look. We can't just raise taxes, world without end. Or, rather, we can — if, some fine day, we want a vital social program to fall down around our ears.

THE DENVER POST

Denver, Colo., February 15, 1981

NOW THAT President Reagan has announced Social Security programs will not be cut back in his search for federal budget economies. it is time to take a careful look at the system's basic problems.

Social Security somehow has managed to stay barely a step ahead of fiscal disaster. but disaster is gaining steadily. The system is expected to have serious cash-flow problems within less than two years, and the problem will get worse as the population grows older. Clearly. the system must be reformed before its failure destroys the retirement plans of a generation of Americans.

U.S. Sen William Armstrong. R-Colo.. is the latest to add his voice to the clamor for reform. Now that the Republicans have taken control of the Senate. Armstrong is in a position to have special influence. He is chairman of the Senate Finance subcommittee responsible for trying to rescue the program. And he says he wants a cure that won't require increasing taxes or borrowing from the nation's general revenues.

That's an ambitious aspiration. Armstrong wants to perform surgery on the system's structure. not just revive it briefly with a fresh injection of money. He says he isn't ready to endorse any specific solutions. but he's looking at changes in eligibility or benefit levels — not for people now receiving benefits. but for those who will become eligible down the road.

Armstrong thinks one short-term answer might be to borrow from two funds fed by the same payroll taxes that support Social Security — elderly health insurance and disability payments. But he definitely doesn't want to raise those payroll taxes any more. As it is. annual increases already are programmed into the system through 1985. Nor does he want to raise income taxes so general-fund money can be transferred to Social Security.

A longer-term solution might be to raise the retirement eligibility age — gradually — from the present 65. People not only are living longer these days. they're also getting healthier and able to work longer. But the change should be. as Armstrong suggests. gradual.

"I wouldn't in any sense want to give anyone the impression we are going to move quickly or tinker carelessly or in haste with the Social Security system." Armstrong told an interviewer last week. "We didn't get into this problem in four years or three years or 24 years. We got into it in 35 years. and we're going to have to get out of it in the same way."

Colorado's junior senator makes sense. It would be unfair to reduce the benefits of people now relying on the system. or to change the timetables for workers only a few years away from retirement.

But it is possible. and probably necessary. to trim future benefits for the younger generation whose taxes now support the system. Without some change. that same generation will be forced to assume. before long. an impossibly burdensome tax load.

THE ATLANTA CONSTITUTION

Atlanta, Ga., February 2, 1981

If you don't contribute — please do not take anything out.

That may be one approach the Senate finance subcommittee could use in finding a cure for the ailing Social Security system. Asking taxpayers to ante up more money from their paychecks cannot continue to be a method to fund the system.

It's understandable why taxpayers are already upset over increased Social Security deductions. Workers keep putting in more and more, while at the same time they are told that the money may run out before the time comes for them to reap the benefits of the system.

Sen. William Armstrong, R-Colo., heads the finance subcommittee that must decide how to relieve Social Security from its financial headaches. He feels that increasing deductions is wrong. He also is looking at restrictions on who can be a recipient, and at decreased benefits, to make the system work.

It will be hard to ask people who have paid into the system for years to take a cut in retirement benefits, but eliminating recipients who do not put dollars into the system could save a lot of money.

Those who do not put money into the system cover a broad range of people, including spouses caring for children of retired, disabled or deceased workers. That is a sensitive area, and it is sometimes difficult to determine whether in fact some spouses actually need the income. However, there are Cuban refugees and immigrants from other countries who have never put a dime in, but draw some form of Social Security funded by the same money from the paychecks of workers in private industry and business. Although refugees drawing from the Social Security pool may be a small part of the mammoth budget, there could be some savings. The government must find some better way to take care of these people.

Social Security is the largest single entitlement program in the federal budget at $138 billion. And it is in trouble. Experts expect to have a cash-flow problem with the retirement fund by late 1982. The system will face a more serious financial crunch during the next century because the ratio of workers paying into the system to retirees collecting benefits is shrinking rapidly.

There is a tendency on the part of some, including Armstrong, to borrow from other funds in the Social Security system — namely the health insurance and disability payments. The funds are in good shape but are financed by the same payroll taxes that finance the retirement program. So why use the "Borrow from Peter to pay Paul" theory and put both of those funds in the same shambles that the retirement fund is now in?

It is possible to save Social Security, but lawmakers must use sound reasoning and good business judgment to return the system to former health. If money is borrowed, there must be some way to put it back. And what about the millions of federal and state government employees who don't take part in the program? Would the system be strengthened by adding them? There must be other unexplored ways of putting the system on sound financial ground. Any businessman will tell you that it's hard to borrow your way out of debt.

The Topeka Capital Journal

Topeka, Kans., February 22, 1981

The House subcommittee on Social Security received testimony this week which underscored a well-documented problem — the Social Security trust fund which pays old age and survivors insurance is being stretched to the limit.

The Congressional Budget Office estimates that unless Congress changes the program, the trust fund will be depleted in two years and could be $129 billion in the red by the beginning of the 1990 fiscal year.

As recently as four years ago, Americans were assured Social Security had been "taken care of" with a series of tax increases. Now we're back to square one. The tax increases were not the answer, and the reason should have been obvious.

It will be impossible to keep Social Security solvent by relying only on a higher percentage tax and by raising the wage ceiling to which the tax applies. It will be impossible because the most elementary principle of demographics is working against it: Today, it takes three workers to support one Social Security pension. By the time the generation of the post-World War II baby boom retires (only about 30 years from now), that ratio will be two workers for one pensioner.

Fertility rates now are about half what they were in 1957, meaning that early in the 21st century we will have a much smaller labor force attempting to provide pensions for a much larger retirement class.

These people are already born; there is nothing hypothetical about the squeeze that will come in about 25 years. It will happen. Unless, of course, Congress can find a way to prevent it.

Various remedies have been suggested, but most fall into two categories — a reduction in benefit commitments or adding new sources of revenue.

Reducing benefit commitments includes such proposals as raising the retirement age (curiously, the trend nationally has been toward earlier retirements), or reducing benefit payments.

For a while it appeared that new sources of revenue, specifically, a Value-Added Tax. would be found. But, as it should be, VAT is on the back burner now.

Subcommittee chairman J.J. Pickle, D-Texas, assessed the situation as "not an emergency," a description subject to question. The fact is, the situation is tenuous now and will get worse unless Congress enacts major changes; the sooner the better.

Wisconsin ▲ State Journal
Madison, Wisc., March 4, 1981

A presidential commission appointed long before President Reagan took office has made several recommendations on how to save money on Social Security. Most of the ideas are bad.

For example, the commission suggests taxing Social Security benefits. That is, tax the benefits after recipients (along with employers) have been taxed to finance the Social Security system for the 30, 40 or 50 years of their productive careers. That's a double whammy.

Another recommendation is that retirement age for regular Social Security benefits be raised from 65 to 68 for those 53 years of age of younger. This is an idea that may have some merit in the long run, but the federal government has an obligation to fulfill promised benefeits to people now approaching retirement age. They have paid into the Social Security system on the assumption they can retire at 65 with regular benefits.

If a higher retirement age is decreed, it should be done only for persons at the beginning of their careers who can plan for a later retirement.

There is justification for fears that unless something is done to scale back Social Security benefits, the program may be bankrupt when the World War II baby boom hits retirement age between 1995 and 2010. Higher Social Security taxes already are being imposed because of the drain on the system.

Much of that drain is due to congressional fiddling with Social Security. Additional benefits have been added with little concern for how they would be financed. Social Security's annual cost-of-living adjustment is pegged to the Consumer Price Index despite the fact the index is based one-fourth on the cost of buying a home — something retired people do seldom, if ever.

Social Security began during the Great Depression as a "floor." It was not intended then to be a freestanding retirement system. Unfortunately, it is the only retirement resource that about half the retired people have.

We cannot return to the days when Social Security was truly a supplemental retirement system, but some of the extra features can be eliminate to improve Social Security's financial situation and more attention given to general-fund financing now that the program has been elevated in importance by Congress.

The Houston Post
Houston, Texas, January 23, 1981

Another study of the financially troubled Social Security system has just been completed, this one by a congressional advisory commission. And what measures does the panel recommend that Congress consider to cure Social Security's money ills? Raise the age of eligibility for full retirement benefits from 65 to 68. Let benefits lag behind inflation. Use general revenue funds to help pay the cost of Social Security. Require government workers hired after 1985 to join the system. If these proposals sound familiar, they should. In one form or another, they have all been made before by various bodies studying the giant pension system's fiscal problems.

The results of the two-year study are a reminder that we don't have many options for shoring up Social Security's financial foundations, and most of them are politically unpopular. The recommendations of the National Commission on Social Security should, nonetheless, be given close scrutiny by Congress. From these proposals and others similar to them, the lawmakers must eventually prepare legislation to protect the long-term health of the program that provides retirement, disability and medical benefits for millions of Americans.

The panel says its proposal to raise the retirement age should not begin to take effect until 2001 and be phased in over the next 11 years. It recommends a 2½ percent increase in the income tax to help pay for the rising cost of Medicare. That would cover about half the basic costs of the program that provides hospitalization insurance for those 65 and older. Though similar recommendations have been made several times previously, they have encountered strong opposition from those in Congress who contend that using general tax funds to finance Social Security would destroy the program's insurance concept.

In recommending that Social Security benefits be allowed to lag behind the government's inflation yardstick, the Consumer Price Index, the commission suggested that they be tied instead to the average increase in wages. To make this idea more palatable, the panel suggested that when inflation fell below 5 percent, beneficiaries be given a "retroactive catch-up" to compensate for the loss they sustained when inflation was higher. That proposal has drawn fire from retiree organizations, as have several of the panel's other recommendations.

The less-than-enthusiastic reception for the latest proposed solutions to Social Security's problems should come as no surprise since they are so similar to others that have fared no better. But Congress cannot delay much longer the task of choosing from the options available a combination of measures to safeguard the long-range solvency of the program. It has been estimated that, by the year 2000, there will be only two workers paying into the Social Security system for every person drawing benefits from it. The present ratio is three workers per beneficiary. Add to that the prospective drain on the system's trust funds by inflation and recession, and it becomes obvious that, however unpopular they may be, new steps must be taken to insure the long-range soundness of the program. If Congress does its job, there will be no more easy votes on Social Security.

THE COMMERCIAL APPEAL
Memphis, Tenn., March 15, 1981

PROSPECTS FOR the financial soundness of the Social Security system are as gloomy as they've ever been, but a congressional commission has recommended one change, at least, that is overdue — a change in the annual cost-of-living raises for retirees.

Those raises are tied directly to the Consumer Price Index, which has been criticized widely as being an inaccurate economic indicator. It's a particularly poor guide to actual living costs of the elderly. The index includes, for instance, the cost of new housing, which has risen sharply in recent years. But not many Americans, let alone older Americans, buy a house every year. Few of the elderly even have mortgage payments.

When Congress enacted the cost-of-living escalator, it assumed that wage increases would keep ahead of the CPI as they had in the past and that Social Security payroll taxes would continue to be more than adequate to meet annual benefits. But surges in world oil prices and other inflationary factors have riddled that assumptions. Last year retirees received a 14.3-percent increase in benefits, at a cost of $16.8 billion. The average pay raise for workers was 9.5 per cent.

BECAUSE OF the CPI's inaccuracy and because the economic predictions upon which the escalator was based have proven false, it's only logical that an adjustment be made. In addition, Congress needs to find a way quickly to save the Social Security trust funds from going broke.

The National Commission on Social Security, which was authorized by Congress in 1977, issued a report Thursday in which it said the trust funds would be insolvent by the end of 1983 if the funding structure isn't changed.

Regarding the CPI issue, the commission recommended that the government compile a special index for the elderly. This index would reflect the fact that working Americans have expenses the elderly don't share. It would also help to eliminate another inconsistency in the program. Payroll-tax increases, which finance benefits, are indexed to average pay raises. The benefits, themselves, are indexed to the CPI, which has grown faster than wages.

The commission also recommended that general revenues be used to shore up the trust funds, that federal, state and local government employes be included in the program by next year to increase revenues, that a 2.5-per-cent surtax be levied on individual income taxes next year to help finance the Medicare part of the trust funds and that retirement eligibility be extended from age 65 to age 68, starting 20 years from now.

What happens, though, when government employes retire and begin claiming benefits? When will withholdings such as the surtax stop? How much of general revenues can be committed without undermining efforts to balance the overall budget or draining funds from other necessary public services? The commission wasn't very reassuring.

It said Social Security's financial troubles have their roots in "deep-seated and serious" economic problems — inflation, unemployment and low productivity. Unless these problems are solved, the commission said, Social Security will require new funds "above the level which the public would support. At that point there will be no way, short of major reductions in benefits, for the system to pay its way."

EVEN IF THE problems do subside, however, there's another potential, long-term funding crisis in the retirement of the baby-boom generation born between 1945 and 1960.

In 1950, the benefits of each person drawing Social Security were paid for by 14 workers. Last year the worker-beneficiary ratio was slightly more than 3-1. By the year 2030 the ratio is expected to drop to 2-1. How great a pay-roll tax would be necessary to finance benefits under those circumstances? One estimate is that the tax could be as high as 20 per cent of wages. Michael Boskin, an economics professor at Stanford University, says that, in such a crisis, "a sharp polarization of society on the basis of age will be almost unavoidable."

The proposed changes in the system, especially the cost-of-living recommendation, would help stave off insolvency by 1984. But the need of Social Security reform would seem to reach far beyond that date.

Schweiker Proposes Merging Funds; Reagan's Revised 1982 Budget

As the Reagan administration completed its transition into office and began to consider the problems of the Social Security system, many trial balloons were raised about the steps to be taken. One of these was the suggestion by Health and Human Services Secretary Richard Schweiker that the Medicare and disability trust funds be merged with the dwindling trust fund for old age and survivors' benefits. This would temporarily bail out the retirement portion of the program, Schweiker argued, and give the Administration time to ponder more lasting solutions to the system's problems.

In his revised 1982 budget, submitted to Congress March 10, President Reagan proposed several measures that would reduce the amount paid out by the system in benefits. These included: the elimination of the minimum benefit program as of July 1, 1981, with the benefits lost by the "truly needy" to be replaced by Supplemental Security Income payments; elimination of payments to adult students who were the children of retired, disabled or deceased workers; elimination of the lump sum death benefit of $255 if the deceased had no surviving spouse or children; and the tightening of eligibility requirements for disability benefits to include only those who had worked in employment covered by Social Security for one and a half years out of the three years preceding disability.

The Dallas Morning News
Dallas, Texas, March 17, 1981

IT CAN'T be much longer before the news becomes generally known — that the Social Security system, pronounced in perfect health by President Carter and Congress just four years ago, is about to go deep in the hole again.

The latest reminder came Sunday on ABC's *Issues and Answers*, when Human Services Secretary Richard Schweiker bruited the system's problems and offered some short-term solutions.

What's the matter with Social Security? Basically the retirement portion of the program is once again running out of money, the $227 billion tax increase of 1977 having failed to offset the effects of inflation. The Reagan administration projects a $40 billion deficit in the retirement program by 1986. A more pessimistic Congressional Budget Office thinks $63.5 billion is nearer the mark. Meanwhile the disability and Medicare funds are running surpluses.

So what do we do? For the short run, Schweiker says, we can bail out the retirement program by merging it with the disability and Medicare "for the next three to five years."

Expected opposition notwithstanding, such a suggestion may prove irresistible. Yet one has to hope it doesn't set a bad example. Once you start dipping into other funds, the habit grows and grows.

The hardening conviction within Congress is that the way to bail out the system permanently is to dip into general revenues, thus obviating the need for another onerous increase in the Social Security tax rate. Such a scheme would be absolutely awful.

To begin with, what revenues are the gentlemen talking about? Those that the White House is trying to reduce in order to stanch the hemorrhaging budget? What "compassionate programs" — that is the vogue phrase among those resisting the Reagan cuts — would we cut in order to save Social Security?

A philosophical problem likewise arises: It is that using general revenues would partly convert Social Security into a welfare program. However inadequately financed the present program, benefits at least depend on contributions.

Schweiker may be right: We may have to merge the various trust funds for a few years. From there it will be necessary to undertake genuine and fundamental reform of the system — for the first time ever.

Like it or not, the country will have one day to raise the retirement age and scale down benefits for future beneficiaries. It would help a lot also to whip inflation. Then we will have to find ways of relying less on Social Security and more on private retirement systems and annuities. A formidable challenge. Better to have it out on the table, though, where we can no longer pretend we have it licked, when in fact it isn't licked at all.

SAN JOSE NEWS
San Jose, Calif., March 18, 1981

HEALTH and Human Services Secretary Richard Schweiker wants to buy a little time in which to reform the nearly bankrupt Social Security system by juggling balances among the system's three trust funds. The idea's a good stopgap, but it's no more than that.

Social Security's old-age pension fund is running in the red by anywhere from $40 billion to $63.5 billion, but the Medicare and disability trust funds are piling up healthy surpluses. That's why Schweiker wants to lump all three funds together for three to five years: The surpluses could offset the deficit — for a while.

The idea has merit so long as the Reagan administration and Congress don't mistake stopgap for solution. Social Security's long-term problem is fundamental: Too few persons are paying into the system, and too many are taking too much out of it. It's bound to go broke unless this ratio is reversed.

That's why it's essential that government workers, as well as private sector employees, be brought into Social Security. That's why some benefits, such as payments to college-age survivors of Social Security recipients, should be scaled back or eliminated. That's why the minimum retirement age may have to be advanced to 67 or 68 years. By 1987, Social Security's maximum tax bite on the individual will have increased more than 100 fold, but it still won't produce enough money to avert bankruptcy unless Congress undertakes top-to-bottom reform of the system.

Schweiker's trust fund juggling will buy Congress some reform time — but none to spare. The Congressional Budget Office estimates the Social Security system as a whole could be broke by 1983 if no structural changes are made in it.

THE DAILY OKLAHOMAN
Oklahoma City, Okla., March 17, 1981

THE Social Security system admittedly is in a heap of trouble, but a "temporary" remedy suggested by a member of President Reagan's cabinet is not one of the new administration's better ideas.

Health and Human Services Secretary Richard Schweiker has proposed merging Medicare and disability trust funds, which currently enjoy surpluses, with the ailing trust fund for old age and survivors benefits which experts warn will be exhausted by 1985 or sooner. Schweiker's idea apparently is to buy "two, three, four years" of time while the administration tries to come up with politically acceptable solutions for the system's longer range problems.

This idea smacks of sending good money after bad, and it hardly gets at the underlying reasons for what ails Social Security — proportionately fewer people paying into the system to finance steadily higher payments to a growing number of recipients.

Pending major restructuring of Social Security, revising the indexing formula to put a cap on the amount of automatic benefit increases seems a sounder approach to bolster the diminishing old-age trust fund.

THE CHRISTIAN SCIENCE MONITOR

Boston, Mass., March 20, 1981

Given the political sensitivities of tampering, even slightly, with US social security benefits, it is understandable that the Reagan administration chose to propose only short-term changes in the nation's federal retirement program rather than undertake any major reform. But the inescapable fact remains that if the administration is to get a firm handle on spiraling federal budget outlays it will have to come to terms with the social security issue.

Since its inception back in the mid-1930s, the social security program has become the largest transfer program in the federal budget. Benefit payments alone run well in excess of $118 billion. Roughly 35 million Americans annually receive benefit checks. Significantly, of the $30 billion earmarked for automatic cost-of-living increases in federal programs this year, $18 billion to $20 billion will go to social security payments.

The Reagan team proposes a phasing out of social-security student loans; an elimination of the $122-a-month minimum benefit payment; and weeding out of unqualified disability insurance recipients. Through these changes, Congress could save upwards of $15 billion or more through 1985. These cuts alone suggest the enormous potential for savings possible under a close scrutiny of the social security system.

That system, which has become perhaps the most sacrosanct of all US entitlement programs, faces a broad range of challenges. In immediate terms, despite a hike in contribution levels mandated by Congress, the retirement program trust fund is expected to show a deficit by 1983. Looking farther down the road, the real financial crunch will come after the turn of the century when the ratio of retired persons to workers jumps sharply and current employees will face a massive tax burden to keep the system solvent.

Few economists call for the elimination of the social security system. Rather, at issue is the adequacy of the system's taxing process, benefit levels, and whether social security is now being asked to do "too much." Originally intended only as a supplemental retirement program for workers in commerce and industry, the system was eventually broadened to include disability and medicare programs while coverage has been extended to farm and domestic workers.

In recent years (and in the past few weeks) a number of innovative proposals have been put forth for reforming the system. The time is here for Congress to give them a fair examination; every delay simply imperils the system and hastens the day of reckoning. Thus, one common sense proposal is to change the effective date of the annual social security increase from July 1 to October 1, a step that would save between $4 billion and $5 billion annually over the next five years. Lawmakers should also give serious thought to either revising the formula used to compute benefits (the Consumer Price Index) or pegging benefits at less than 100 percent of the CPI. The fact that the CPI overstates the inflation rate (by giving added weight to home mortgages costs, for instance) has been noted in these pages before.

To mention some other ideas, substantial bipartisan support exists in Congress for basing cost-of-living increases on the prevailing wage rate in the private sector. Mr. Reagan, however, feels bound by his campaign pledge not to change cost-of-living increases. Whether he remains adamant in that position, or for political reasons would prefer that Congress take the lead in initiating the change, is a matter of speculation. In any case, while the idea has some appeal, there is question whether linking benefits to prevailing wages would save money in the long run (despite short-run savings), since historically wages in the US have risen faster than the cost of living. Moreover, if wage levels were to decline social security benefits, assuming they would not be reduced, would again be outpacing the private sector.

In terms of the long-range stability of social security, Congress should weigh raising the retirement age (to 68, perhaps) some time around the year 2000, as recently recommended by a presidential commission. It should also consider establishing "means tests" and taxing benefits above a certain to-tal-earnings level (i.e., private income plus social security benefits), a reform which would protect those on the bottom rungs of society most needing social security. Such a change, in turn, would be more palatable to other social security recipients if the limit on earned income were raised at the same time.

Using general revenues (either in part or whole) for financing the medicare portion of social security is still another reasonable proposal. The fact that medicare payments now come out of a social security health insurance trust fund distorts the purpose of social security and complicates evaluation of the social security system on its own merits.

Finally, a more controversial proposal — recommended recently by the President's Commission on Pension Policy — would establish a minimum universal pension system that would integrate private pensions (which would become mandatory) into a comprehensive system along with social security benefits. The current two-tier system obviously presents great inequities since approximately 30 percent of all retirees subsist entirely on social security benefits, and benefits from private plans vary sharply.

In raising these alternatives we do not argue that any one proposal or combination of proposals will necessarily be the "best solution" for setting right the social security system. Obviously, some will work better than others. But the range of possibilities being offered by an increasing number of economists and tax specialists suggests that lawmakers need not feel constrained in their handling of the issue. It is important to remember that when social security was first put into effect, relatively few American workers looked forward to enjoying several decades or more of retirement. But, with today's increased longevity, two to three decades of retirement is hardly unusual. That means enormous benefit costs.

The nation's legislators must show as much open-mindedness and imagination in meeting the current grave challenge to social security as the framers of the system displayed in 1935.

RAPID CITY JOURNAL—

Rapid City, S.D., April 8, 1981

While there is general agreement that the Social Security program isn't very secure, there is less agreement on what should be done to put the system on a secure financial footing.

For years, the program has been a political hot potato. Few politicians have been willing to face the ire of recipients by trimming benefits. Now, however, they are caught in a crossfire from working people unhappy about the ever-rising payroll tax that finances the program.

As a result, Social Security is being examined with a view toward trimming some of the features that have been added to the program but which have little to do with the original purpose — insuring Americans against destitution in their retirement years.

While long-term changes will take considerable study and debate, four quick fixes have been proposed to remove some of the Christmas tree ornaments attached to the program over the years.

They are:

Eliminating the $122 a month minimum benefit. Originally designed to help the poorly skilled and infrequently employed, chief beneficiaries of this feature now are federal employees who retire early on government pensions and take jobs covered by Social Security. Federal retirees could still participate in the program but their benefits would be based on their contributions while employed in the private sector with no minimum benefit. The truly needy can be taken care of under the Supplemental Security Income (SSI) program.

Eliminating student benefits given to college students simply because one of their parents received Social Security. This is another welfare program targeted for the poor but which now serves the middle class. Because help could come from other student aid programs, little hardship would be caused by not accepting new recipients and reducing existing benefits over four years.

Eliminating the $255 lump sum death benefit. About half of the $200 million in annual payments goes to an insured worker's estate even if there is no bereaved spouse or minor to collect it.

Placing a cap on disability payments and tightening eligibility requirements. Under the current system, it's possible for a recipient to receive more in benefits than their previous wage income. Also, some receive benefits without truly being disabled.

More needs to be done to reduce the huge gap between legislated benefits and legislated taxes to pay those benefits. The four proposals outlined above would save $20 billion over five years and would be a starting point. They would move the Social Security program back toward its basic objectives without doing any real harm to anyone.

THE MILWAUKEE JOURNAL

Milwaukee, Wisc., March 16, 1981

The Reagan administration has a strong case for its proposals to tighten Social Security benefits in several areas. Regrettably, however, the White House is weakening its own position by proposing to loosen the program's purse strings in another area.

The president is basically right in seeking to:

—Cut the minimum retirement benefit.

—Make it harder for people to qualify for disability benefits.

—Phase out the special college benefits now paid to adult students who are survivors of workers once covered by Social Security.

—Eliminate the lump-sum death benefit now paid to the heirs of Social Security beneficiaries.

The minimum benefit goes to persons who work only briefly in jobs covered by Social Security.

Thus, it is subject to double-dipping abuses by retired government employes. Under the proposed change, Supplementary Security Income benefits would augment the income of needy persons in the categories now receiving the Social Security minimum, while double-dippers no longer would find it easy to qualify for their extra dollop.

The present problem with the disability program is that persons only marginally disabled have been able to take advantage of it. That apparently would be remedied.

As for the college benefits, it's undoubtedly nice for a worker to know that his children will be able to go to college if he dies prematurely. However, the financially strained Social Security program shouldn't be expected to bear such a burden. Needy survivors have access to the same college aid that other needy students receive, and the nonneedy can pay their own way.

The $225 lump-sum death payment was once thought of as a funeral allowance. It is too small to be of any real help but large enough to add hundreds of millions of dollars to the government's Social Security costs. Thus, it is one of the least painful places for a budget trim.

So far, so good. But Reagan also insists on redeeming a foolish campaign pledge. He proposed that workers be allowed to draw full retirement benefits at age 65 while remaining fully employed. The cost would be astronomical.

Even now, retirees may earn up to $5,000 in part-time employment without forfeiting any Social Security benefits. For each $2 of wages above $5,000, the retiree forfeits $1 in Social Security benefits. However, Reagan says *nothing* should be forfeited — in effect, that any worker at age 65 could remain on the job and draw full Social Security.

Such fiscal nonsense makes it hard for Reagan's sensible proposals to get the consideration they deserve.

THE WALL STREET JOURNAL

New York, N.Y., April 3, 1981

For years now the Social Security program has been politically sacrosanct; any politician critical of it was risking destruction at the hands of the gray panthers. But times are changing and there now is an offsetting danger, the unhappiness working people feel over the ever-rising payroll tax that finances Social Security. There also is increasing enlightenment about the extent to which the program, during its glory years, was loaded with extra goodies that had little to do with the original purpose of insuring Americans against destitution in their declining days.

As a result, both the administration and Congress are this year looking at Social Security with a view toward genuinely reducing the government's obligations, both in the short and long term. Ideas that in the past have had short shrift have gained new life, such as changing the indexing formula to the lower of wage or price rises, or raising the retirement age for people now entering the work force, or even putting the price mechanism to work to help control Medicare costs. The hope a few years back that Social Security could be spared by transferring some costs to the general budget has gone aglimmering as the general budget itself has soared out of control.

Longer-term changes will require prolonged debate in Congress that would detract from the more immediate needs for budget savings. But the Reagan budget cutters have come up with four quick fixes that would save nearly $3 billion next fiscal year. These changes, currently before the Senate Finance Committee, merely involve removing Christmas tree ornaments Congress has attached to the Social Security program. The targeted programs either overlap income aid available elsewhere or need better administration.

Here are the candidates for cutting:

Minimum Benefits. This law puts a floor of $122 a month on payments to beneficiaries. Although designed as a welfare device to transfer income to the poorly skilled and infrequently employed, it now subsidizes federal employes who have retired early on government pensions to take jobs covered by Social Security. Scrapping

this will end the rip-off by the double-dippers; the truly needy can replace their support, dollar-for-dollar, under the Supplemental Security Income program. Expected savings from scrappage: $1.3 billion in 1982.

Student Benefits. This is another straight welfare program targeted for the poor but now serving the middle class. Last year over $2 billion was handed out to college students simply because one of their parents received Social Security. Since payments could be picked up through other student aid programs, little hardship would be caused by the Reagan proposal to accept no new recipients and reduce existing benefits by 25% annually. Figure a saving of $1 billion in 1982.

Death Benefits. Here's some remarkable waste: This law mandates a $255 lump sum payment to an insured worker's estate—even if there is no bereaved spouse or minor to collect. About half the payments made now go to such estates. Cutting this will save $200 million in 1982.

Disability Benefits. Two problems to be righted here. Under the current system of overlapping benefits, it's possible for recipients to "earn" more than their previous wage income. Also, under the current system, some people have obtained benefits without being truly disabled. The administration has proposed a "megacap" on benefits to prevent the former and stricter eligibility and review to prevent the latter. This should yield about $400 million in savings in 1982.

Longer-term fixes in the Social Security system will, on the whole, provide larger savings. For example, changing the indexing system to tie benefits to either average hourly wages or the CPI, whichever is lower, would yield $4.2 billion in 1982, given present economic assumptions.

But the Reagan proposals are an excellent starting point. Their savings, some $20 billion over five years, are useful and reasonably predictable. They do little real harm to anyone. They would move back toward the basic objectives of Social Security before it was converted to political ends costly to working people. Gray panthers need lose no sleep over any of these changes and the politicians should respond accordingly.

Roanoke Times & World-News

Roanoke, Va., March 17, 1981

The Reagan/Stockman proposed cuts in Social Social benefits are among the mildest correctives to a critical program that shows signs of having gotten out of bounds. Fortunately the average citizen, using his own resoures, can reach a thoughtful, satisfying conclusion on each. These would end the burial and educational benefits and place disability benefits under tighter control. In turn:

● Does every survivor, or next-of-kin, truly need the $255 burial benefit which can be picked up after every funeral of someone covered by Social Security? By relying on his own knowledge and experience, and by a careful study of the obituary pages, the citizen can reach his own conclusion. Many times this extra money, always welcome, is not truly needed. In our opinion, most of the time it is not truly needed. Where it is indisputably needed, the local governments should be called upon to meet their traditional responsibility.

● Should the burdensome Social Security tax be used so that people who have not had a college education help pay for others to obtain such an education? There are some fine people today who have

had a good education because their widowed or disabled parent was astute enough to get help from Social Security. Their parent was wise and they were lucky. Nonetheless, it is unfair and duplicative of expense to mix educational benefits with a retirement program.

● Several studies have shown that those receiving disability benefits receive higher benefits for a longer time than those receiving retirement benefits. That is because they enter the program earlier. Although no one on the outside can be sure of the facts in a disability claim, observation suggests that the definition of "total disability" varies with time, among regions and between individuals. All that David Stockman, budget director, wants are regulations to promote uniformity and discourage abuse.

The government and its people will be lucky if the above changes are enough to maintain for a while the soundness of the Social Security programs. More, we guess, will have to be done eventually. But failure to go along with the above relatively modest proposals suggests a lack of concern not only with the Social Security problem, but also with the menace of inflation.

House Panel Votes to Raise Retirement Age

Raising the eligibility age for full retirement benefits was one of the changes recommended most often by commissions studying the Social Security system. The House Way and Means Subcommittee on Social Security, beginning markup of a plan to revise the system, agreed in April to raise the eligible retirement age from 65 to 68, phasing the change in over ten years beginning in 1990. The right to retire at 62 would be retained, but those who did so would receive substantially reduced benefits. The subcommittee also agreed to fund half of the system's Hospital Insurance Trust Fund (Part A of Medicare) through general revenues. The panel's Democratic chairman, Rep. J.J. Pickle of Texas, said the subcommittee would await details of the imminent Reagan Administration plan to revise the system before completing markup of the bill.

Rocky Mountain News
Denver, Colo., April 15, 1981

THE House subcommittee on Social Security has stepped in where most politicians fear to tread. It has approved a plan to raise the eligibility age for full retirement benefits to 68.

No doubt the subcommittee will be assailed from all sides and the critics will include many colleagues in the Congress.

Cutting back on Social Security benefits is an unpopular and, in the minds of many, a politically dangerous thing to do. The senior citizens' lobby is strong and getting stronger as the average age of Americans advances.

But unless something is done to slow the financial drain, the Social Security system is headed for insolvency.

It is widely conceded that the tax which finances the system cannot be raised much higher. Workers already complain mightily about the bite that the Social Security tax takes from their paychecks.

Nor does there seem to be much sentiment for switching to general tax revenues to finance the system. That would turn Social Security into a welfare program.

The only answer, then, appears to be to keep people working longer, thereby reducing the outflow from the pension fund and increasing the inflow of revenues from the Social Security tax.

The proposal advanced by the House subcommittee actually is a compromise.

While raising from 65 to 68 the age at which a person could receive benefits, it would retain the right to retire at 62. However, the benefits to those who retire at 62 would be sharply reduced — from 80 percent under the present system to 64 percent.

Age 65 would be considered the normal early retirement age, and those who retire then would receive 81 percent of full benefits.

The change would be phased in over 10 years beginning in 1990, which means it would not be fully implemented until the turn of the century.

There's no assurance that the subcommittee's plan or any other along similar lines will be adopted soon. But the subcommittee deserves credit for having the courage to tackle this sensitive issue.

ST. LOUIS POST-DISPATCH
St. Louis, Mo., April 15, 1981

A House subcommittee's recommendation that the Social Security retirement age be raised from 65 to 68 represents a profound social and economic change that is not likely to be well received by either older workers looking toward retirement or employers anxious to make room for new, young employees, who generally are paid less than those they replace.

The idea behind the recommendation is to preclude the financial crisis that faces the Social Security system in the long run, assuming that all the demographic projections are correct. The change, which would be phased in over a 10-year period beginning in 1990, would eventually save $15 billion a year. Savings or tax increases totaling $19 billion will be needed in the '90s or by the turn of the century, according to projections.

Before it is possible to raise the age at which full benefits can be received, however, the subcommittee's recommendation must be approved by its parent committee, Ways and Means, by the full House and the full Senate and signed by the president. Thus, those who do not accept the projections or who believe there are better ways of averting the funding crisis will have ample opportunity to make their views known.

Besides calling for a higher retirement age, the subcommittee endorsed President Reagan's recommendation that the minimum benefit and student benefit be abolished. However, like the Reagan administration, the subcommittee declined to ask for a change in the automatic cost-of-living adjustment, even though it is the major cause of the retirement system's financial problems. In the year beginning July 1, for example, it will add more than $12 billion to Social Security outlays.

The inflation adjustment is by almost unanimous agreement too generous and could be modified without imposing hardship on retirees. Given the enormous layers of increases it automatically adds to the Social Security system year after year, it is imperative that the cost-of-living payments be curtailed.

The Morning News
Wilmington, Del., April 14, 1981

The refrain "ailing Social Security system" is as tiresome as it is true. Unfortunately, just as tiresome and true is Washington's foot-dragging over reforms to this national payout system crucial to the retirement years of most Americans.

Social Security's biggest problem, as one study after another has shown, is an expected shortfall in revenue due to the dilemma of a shrinking work force having to provide for an expanding retiree population. Among other factors adding to that underlying problem are inflation and automatic cost of living increases in the benefits paid out; unemployment and the resulting reduction in Social Security payroll taxes; obligations for education and other benefits foisted onto Social Security during prosperity years and now exerting a drain on the fund.

Just as the causes for Social Security's financial problems have been analyzed time and again, so have some sensible remedies. Except for the regular raising of payroll taxes, however, essentially nothing has been done to cope with the problems, leaving Americans with the unpleasant prospect of ever-escalating taxes to meet the government's obligations under the Social Security system.

Now, thanks to a package of reforms being put together by the House Social Security Subcommittee, there is a glimmer of hope that some meaningful changes will be made. The most important change proposed would advance the age for full retirement benefits from 65 to 68. This change has been recommended by several responsible commissions and would go well with recent congressional action changing the mandatory retirement age from 65 to 70. The House subcommittee recommends that the age change be phased in beginning in 1990. This would give those now in the work force ample time to prepare for the change.

Also included in the committee's reform package is a proposal to eliminate the limit on what a person over 68 can earn without losing Social Security benefits. At present, that limit affects persons up to age 72. There are proposals to reduce the benefits payable to persons choosing early retirement at age 62, and for proportionate reductions in benefits up to the proposed new retirement age of 68.

The committee estimates that once implemented these reforms could save the Social Security system more than $15 billion a year. Remember that implementation would not begin until 1990, thus still leaving a financial problem for the present decade. But patchwork remedies for the short-range will be more acceptable once steps have been taken to assure the long-range security of the Social Security system. The House Ways and Means Committee must act next on these proposals — the sooner the better.

THE SACRAMENTO BEE
Sacramento, Calif., April 11, 1981

The House Subcommittee on Social Security recently voted — with some trepidation, no doubt — to raise from 65 to 68 the age at which a person can retire with full benefits. It represented the first important benefits cut ever voted in the program's 45-year history. More importantly, it represented Congress' willingness for the first time to suggest unpopular but necessary measures to keep this program solvent.

Although the Social Security tax rate jumped from 6.13 percent to 6.65 percent last January, with more increases scheduled for 1982, 1985 and 1986, the system still stands on the brink of bankruptcy. Raising the retirement age has been recommended by several groups, including one of President Reagan's task forces and a President's Commission on Pension Policy, as one way of addressing the system's long-term problems.

The proposal, designed to save $15 billion a year, would not affect anyone now on the rolls or retiring in the next 10 years. The new retirement age would be phased in over 10 years, perhaps longer, starting in 1990. Congress already has moved to encourage additional work by those over 65 by prohibiting forced retirement before the age of 70. Workers, moreover, generally are healthier, and many jobs are less strenuous today for 65- and 68-year-olds than in the past.

Demographics represent the most compelling argument for increasing the eligibility age. The baby-boom generation begins turning 65 in 2010, increasing from 11 percent to 23 percent the number of people in that age bracket. If the present retirement age continued, the system would have only two contributors for each beneficiary, and contributions would have to increase 50 percent to make up the difference. Changing the retirement age to 68 would increase that ratio to 4 to 1.

The change in the retirement age, by itself, can't solve the system's problems, but it's encouraging because it represents the first attempt to face those problems realistically and the first indication that Congress will be willing to consider other measures, some of which may well turn out to be even more unpopular. Among them:

● A tax on Social Security benefits that would treat them like any other private pension income — which is also taxable. While the average tax increase would be about $350, the double exemptions the elderly already receive would mean retirees with little or no income other than Social Security would pay nothing. The additional federal tax collections would be about $3.7 billion annually.

● Changing the method used to calculate cost-of-living increases for current retirees which are now pegged to the Consumer Price Index. The benefit hikes could be indexed instead to the average annual increase in prices or wages, whichever is lower. This could save an estimated $4 billion in 1982.

However distasteful these and other proposals seem, they certainly would not break faith with persons participating in Social Security as opponents contend. Indeed, if such measures are not implemented — and soon — the program will collapse. That would be a devastating breach of the public's faith, not only in the Social Security system, but in the leadership that allowed it to fail.

THE DAILY OKLAHOMAN
Oklahoma City, Okla., April 13, 1981

FOR the first time in Social Security's 45-year history, a congressional subcommittee has voted for a major change in the old age and survivors benefit program, the original basic function of the system.

And as expected, the move has drawn a critical and apprehensive response from those who exhibit a knee-jerk reaction to any suggestions for change, despite growing public awareness that Social Security is in deep financial trouble.

The measure approved by the House Ways and Means Committee's Social Security Subcommittee would boost the age at which full retirement benefits are paid from 65 to 68 — but not all at once. The change would be phased in over a 10-year period beginning in 1990.

Thus it would not affect those already receiving Social Security checks or those 10 years or less away from retirement.

Coupled with the higher age requirement is a provision that should prove popular with just about everybody: the limitation on what a beneficiary could earn without a corresponding loss of benefits would be removed entirely for those over 68, instead of age 72. Currently, a person on Social Security must forfeit one dollar of benefits for each two dollars earned over $5,500 a year.

The most controversial portion of the bill would further reduce benefits for those who elect to retire early. Persons could still retire at age 62 — which upwards of 70 percent are electing to do now — but their benefits would be cut by 36 percent instead of 20 percent as now. Those who chose to retire at 65 would receive 81 percent of full benefits.

Of the countless commissions, both governmental and private, that have studied the problems of Social Security over the years, increasing the age at which full benefits are paid has been one of the recurring consensus recommendations. It recognizes the increasing longevity of the population, for one thing. For another, it would contribute substantially to solving the short-term drain on the old age and survivors' trust fund which, if nothing is done, will go broke by 1983.

Other commonly proposed remedies for the system's short-term crisis include elimination of the minimum $122 monthly benefit for those with brief coverage; separation of Medicare from Social Security because its benefits are unrelated to earnings; revamping the spouse's benefit; and revising the formula for inflation adjustment, which many studies have criticized as excessive.

Even if all of these reforms were adopted tomorrow, however, the longer-term weakness of Social Security would not be addressed. That underlying problem stems mainly from demographics: the ratio of those paying into the system to those drawing benefits is steadily diminishing as the birth rate slows and the population ages.

Nothing much is likely to happen to this latest subcommittee initiative until the Reagan administration unveils its Social Security proposals in about a month. But no matter what Congress does to relieve the short-term crunch, nobody has yet devised a permanent rescue operation that does not envision either a reduction in basic benefits or higher taxes — or both. The patchwork being proposed for now does not come to grips with the major restructuring of Social Security which nearly all authorities agree is necessary to avert eventual collapse of the system.

President Proposes Revision of System

Outlining the Reagan Administration proposal to revise the Social Security system in a news briefing May 12, Health and Human Services Secretary Richard Schweiker said it would keep the system "from going broke, protect the basic benefit structure and reduce the tax burden of American workers." Saying that the retirement fund would run out of money in 1982 under its current set-up, the Secretary said: "The crisis is inescapable. It is here. It is now. It is serious. And it must be faced."

The Reagan proposal would reduce monthly payments for those retiring at age 62 to 55% of full benefits (compared with 80% under current law), with the rate rising proportionally as the age of 65 was neared. Those who retired at the age of 65 would be eligible, as before, for full benefits; contrary to the current system, however, there would be no reduction in benefits for those who continued to work after age 65. (Until 1983, recipients between the ages of 65 and 72 who earned more than $5,500 per year forfeited half their benefits.) Under the Reagan plan, this retirement earnings limit would be phased out by 1986.

The President's plan also called for a three-month delay in the annual cost-of-living allowance scheduled for July, 1982. This was the only measure that would immediately affect the 36 million beneficiaries currently receiving Social Security. Other elements of the Reagan plan would: eliminate "windfall" benefits for retirees who had spent most of their working life in a job not covered by Social Security, but qualified for benefits under current formulas; revise the formula used to determine a recipient's initial benefit; and tighten up disability requirements. The Administration estimated that the proposed cutbacks would save $46 billion over five years, and held out the promise of a reduction in Social Security payroll tax rates a year or two after the cutbacks were enacted.

Rocky Mountain News

Denver, Colo., May 13, 1981

PRESIDENT Reagan has added his weighty influence to an overdue move to reform the Social Security system.

The combination of White House and congressional concern may finally get the program on a more stable financial basis.

Congress has tinkered with Social Security for years — adding benefits and then trying to offset them with increased taxes — until the system has become an unbalanced hodgepodge.

At least one of the Reagan administration's recommendations may not sit well on Capitol Hill because it would reduce benefits for future retirees. Beginning in 1987, instead of receiving an average of 41 percent of their working take home pay, retirees would receive a pension amounting to 38 percent.

That's a major structural change that may be necessary to keep the Social Security program solvent, but it is one certain to arouse opposition in many quarters.

Another thrust of Reagan's plan is to encourage people to work longer and thereby stay off Social Security's benefit rolls longer. He would do this by sharply reducing benefits for those who take early retirement at 62 instead of at the normal retirement age of 65.

Those retiring at 62 are entitled to 80 percent of the payment they would get if they waited until 65. Reagan proposes to cut that payment to 55 percent.

The president also would eliminate "double dippers." These are people who work most of their lives in jobs exempt from Social Security coverage, such as government workers who collect pensions from a separate plan, and then work just long enough in "covered" jobs to collect another dollop from Social Security.

Among other changes, the president recommended removal of the lid on outside earnings for retirees. Social Security beneficiaries below the age of 72 now are penalized if they earn more than $5,500 a year; they lose $1 of Social Security money for every $2 of earned income. The aim of Reagan's recommendation is to encourage older people to continue working and paying Social Security taxes as long as they are able.

A major reform that Reagan didn't recommend, but which ought to be made, is to change the way cost-of-living increases are calculated for retirees. However, the Senate already is tackling that problem and has suggested changes that would slow down the rate of increase.

Obviously, something has to be done to keep the system solvent. Between them, White House and Congress ought to be able to come up with an acceptable package.

THE  SUN

Baltimore, Md., May 18, 1981

History might well record that President Reagan's early popularity crested last Tuesday and then started a slow decline toward reality. In a contentious democracy, this is not surprising. It is downright unnatural for an American president to enjoy a positive job-approval rating from three quarters of his fellow citizens, especially if he is an ideological president intent on a redirection of government policy.

What started undercutting the president's popularity was his forced march toward sharp cuts in Social Security benefits as Congress nervously contemplated the deficits embedded in his budget. Mr. Reagan would have preferred to put off this bullet biting, but his numbers would not let him. Faced with deficits causing many of his followers to wince and the markets to go into a tailspin, the president had to try to make his call for 10 percent tax rate cuts acceptable. He chose greater-than-expected cuts in Social Security benefits.

The reaction is now building. An ABC-Washington Post poll shows the president's overall approval rating down from 73 percent to 67 percent, the voters opposed to benefit cuts by 49 percent to 33 percent and a widely held suspicion (39 percent) that he is breaking campaign promises. The president, in short, is taking on the old folks—millions of citizens who vote, defend their interests and, until now, have rated him highly.

Social Security recipients may be the first of his constituents to be offended, but they won't be the last. As Congress enacts spending cuts, many middle-class voters (not just the poor) will be affected by changes now only dimly perceived. And while the president's tax cuts will be welcomed, especially as individuals contemplate their paychecks, the president will remain hostage to inflation and interest rates.

Congress does not believe the low inflation forecasts in the Reagan budget; House Democrats who went along with his popular budget resolution may now start fighting. Nor are many business leaders convinced that Mr. Reagan's untried "supply-side" theories will work out as planned. It was their worry about deficits in fiscal 1982 that brought on the hurried move to reduce Social Security benefits.

The president is on the mark in seeking to reverse the nation's inflation psychology, and the policies that cause it. Some Social Security benefits are rising faster than the Consumer Price Index and need to be cut back. Retirement age calculations need to be brought in line with longer life expectancy.

But the whole Reagan approach lacks balance—and fairness. Social welfare cuts have to be assessed in light of the impact they will have on individuals and state and local governments. The soaring defense budget still needs some pruning and prioritizing. The much-touted Kemp-Roth tax plan needs substantial modification: perhaps only a 5 percent cut in tax rates for next year and 10 percent for the year after.

Mr. Reagan's popularity inevitably will have to decline to more normal levels as he makes hard choices. But to sustain his rapport with the American people, he must make sure this decline is for the right reasons.

the Charleston Gazette

Charleston, W. Va., May 18, 1981

PRESIDENT Reagan has proposed some drastic changes in an effort to meet the Social Security funding crisis. We do not rise to contest them, but suggest that some of his proposed steps need not be taken if one of them is sharply expanded. We think it possible to attack the problem without reneging on what persons approaching old age regard as a contract.

Reagan wants to make retirement at age 62 less attractive by drastically lowering benefits paid at that age. He would eliminate the minimum benefit and cut back sharply on benefits for children and widows. He would tighten eligibility for disability. He would delay the payment of cost of living increases. He would retire workers who are sick to pay the Social Security tax.

The finding of the American Association of Retired Persons is that most retirements at 62 are unofficial disability retirements by persons who at an earlier age were unwilling to face the hassle of medical documentation of their ills. If benefits at 62 are sharply lowered, it is likely that additional thousands will apply for disability benefits before they are 65 and accept whatever hassle is involved. In this case, even revised eligibility rules will not do much to keep down disability retirements.

We support without question Reagan's proposition that it is not a function of Social Security to send children to college, but reducing payments to widows and/or children would send many to public welfare agencies. Eliminating the minimum payment would do so beyond doubt.

We think the best approach is modification of cost-of-living increases. Most workers have no such benefit, and we doubt that there would be a general uprising if twice-a-year Social Security adjustments were reduced even to one every two years. This we believe, would be the approach most acceptable to the nation's elderly citizens.

We suggest, too, that the adjustment be based not on the cost of living index but on the average wage, which lags behind. Under the present practice, workers periodically provide Social Security pensioners more than they, themselves, receive.

THE DAILY HERALD

Biloxi, Miss., May 20, 1981

President Ronald Reagan's plan to overhaul Social Security merits a higher mark for audacity than for fairness. We suspect that the citizen response it is generating will mean what eventually evolves from Congress will be significantly different from what the president proposed.

Since 1977, when Congress last tinkered with the Social Security system, it has been widely known that the system remained in financial trouble, that additional changes would be necessary. Congress has preferred to defer making those changes until it no longer had the option of waiting.

The option to wait is now expiring and the new president, his healthy voter mandate in hand, last week revealed his system to slash $46.4 billion in benefits over the next five years. His plan includes some sound recommendations and some not so sound; it omitted some ideas it should have included.

The Reagan plan, for instance, would reduce the $122 minimum benefit, aid to college students and the $255 lump sum death benefit. Why should Social Security guarantee a minimum $122 monthly benefit to a worker whose covered earnings entitle him to only $60 per month? That sort of generosity is what has gotten Social Security in the mess it's now in. The lump sum death benefit falls in a similar category; most Americans already have burial insurance, which is what the $255 is supposed to provide.

One area where the Reagan proposals seem sound is applying more stringent requirements for disability insurance. Workers will have to work for 7½, instead of five, of the past 10 years, to qualify and only medical factors will be weighed to determine disability. At present, a worker's age, education and job experience are also considered.

The most ambitious cuts the president wants will penalize early retirees the heaviest and these cuts will undoubtedly have the hardest going through Congress. The $126 per month average penalty is too much and comes too rapidly. The president would have it begin next year and that schedule will disrupt the career plans of too many workers who have been depending on the Social Security system to provide them, at age 62, 80 percent of their full benefits and not the 55 percent the Reagan plan calls for.

This group of workers has a grievance that will roar in their Congressmen's ears.

The president missed an opportunity, we believe, to expand the system by gradually bringing into it newly hired federal workers. He obviously fears trying to mandate immediate inclusion of federal workers not now covered, but since he was so bold in his other proposals, he should not have been timid about mandating coverage for newly hired federal employes.

Nor should he have held fast to continuing to peg cost-of-living increases to beneficiaries to the Consumer Price Index. The CPI includes such items as the cost of housing and many economists believe it is not a true reflection of the inflation rate, especially the effective rate relevant to Social Security beneficiaries.

Congressional heads were already awhirl with the Reagan budget and the Reagan tax cuts when the Reagan Social Security proposals dropped on them. Before they have time to study these proposals, we suspect, they'll be deluged with reactions from their constituencies. Those reactions, perhaps more than fiscal reasoning, will be instrumental in deciding what changes will actually be made in the troubled Social Security system.

CHARLESTON EVENING POST

Charleston, S.C., May 21, 1981

Last week, the Reagan administration created a firestorm in Congress with its proposals to cut Social Security benefits in order to put the program back on an even financial keel. House Speaker "Tip O'Neill" branded them "despicable" and promised to "fight them all the way." Democratic Rep. James Shannon recalled the president had promised to leave Social Security as part of a "safety net" for the needy, and shouted: "He has gone too far. It's time we stood up." Another Democrat complained it would be "bordering on the unethical" to cut pensions for those about to retire while Sen. Byrd termed the cuts "precipitous, harsh and very unfair."

The controversial proposals would cut benefits 10 percent by 1986, include added penalties for those who retire before age 65 and tighten eligibility for disability checks. The administration and the Congress most likely will reach some compromise, probably one that will delay implementation. But unless some drastic action is taken, an inescapable crisis for Social Security waits around the corner. Some facts:

— Social Security costs go up more than $2.5 million every day.

— The $15.4 billion cost-of-lving increase planned for next month is more than the whole program cost 20 years ago.

— At the current rate, money to finance the Old Age and Survivors' Insurance benefits will run out next year and the long range deficit is calculated in the trillions of dollars.

— Until 1949, the maximum annual Social Security tax was $30. It is now $1,975.

— Over the years there has been a major change in the population mix, leaving fewer and fewer workers to pay the benefits to more and more retirees.

The issues will be hotly debated in Congress and ultimately resolved, but the debate will not end. The alternatives, it seems to us, are these: cut benefits, increase taxes, or see the system go bankrupt.

The Knickerbocker News

Albany, N.Y., May 18, 1981

Our national economic doctor, Ronald Reagan, has decided on the diagnosis and prescribed his medicine for the illness riddling our Social Security system.

It will make a few individuals sicker (including, from the bellows of agony already ringing in the air, individuals in Congress); it will certainly help keep the ailing patient alive for a while; but will the cure be complete? Probably not without more surgery.

President Reagan has proposed a three-month delay in next year's Social Security cost-of-living increase — an administration trial balloon suggesting the delay might be this year was rapidly and unequivocally shot down — as well as a tightening of requirements for disability pensions and several other similar, equally minor, changes. They're minor, that is, unless it's *you* who finds himself cut out. The president's biggest and most controversial proposal, though, and the one that pinches the most people, is a sharp reduction in the amount of Social Security paid to those who retire early, at age 62 instead of 65.

Most people do quit the rat race early. Last year, a full million of the 1.6 million Americans retiring on Social Security were under 65. And until now, those retiring early would get 80 percent of their full monthly allotment. Mr. Reagan would reduce that to 55 percent; it works out to $126 a month less for the average worker, a punishing penalty that would undoubtedly discourage many early retirements.

Which, after all, is the goal here. If fewer people retire, less must be paid out and the Social Security system has a chance to get back on its financial feet.

It's pleasantly reassuring to think about this in the abstract — fewer people retiring, less money paid out. The problem comes when we begin looking at individuals. The 60- and 61-year-olds who have worked their entire lives and had planned on a few years of leisure while their health was still good enough to enjoy it; most of the rest of us, who now must, almost certainly, grit our teeth and work until age 65 before considering retire-

ment, though the standard to now has been 62; the border-line disabled, who would be cut out of Social Security by Mr. Reagan's plan, but who will find it difficult to support themselves. By this one, personal standard, Mr. Reagan's plan is certainly not "fair" to most Americans.

But there are other considerations. First of all, Social Security, when it was devised so many years ago, was clearly and without doubt *not* supposed to support a generation of retired Americans. In announcing the revolutionary concept, President Franklin Delano Roosevelt emphasized Social Security would be there to assist retirees, and shouldn't be confused with a national pension plan.

For too many years now, we have leaned too heavily on Social Security in our old age, and sloughed off the old-fashioned ways of financing retirement — savings, for instance. How long has it been since someone has told you he or she was "saving for his old age"? It used to be a common, smile-producing axiom.

So, we have gotten soft and dependent on government for sustenance in our dotage. But Social Security is not a "savings account," by any means — for one thing, there are no "savings." As soon as the money from this week's paycheck goes into Social Security, it is paid out in next month's Social Security checks. And, while those about to retire have indeed paid into the system for decades, the money they can logically expect to receive back far, far outdistances the amount they put in over the years.

So Mr. Reagan's reforms will hurt some individuals in the short run, individuals who have — mistakenly or not — been depending too heavily on the Social Security in their future. But we mustn't let our very real sympathy for the few cloud our judgment, and the facts are crystalline: Without reform, the Social Security system will collapse, bankrupt, from the weight of its load.

It seems to us a question of inconvenience, disappointment and disgruntlement now, or a major disaster later. By all means, we must avert the disaster.

Albany, N.Y., May 19, 1981

Ronald Reagan has proposed some Social Security belt-tightening that already has half people in this country restless and muttering into their Ovaltine. But we don't think he's gone far enough.

Mr. Reagan would, among other things, make it much more difficult to retire early by cutting sharply back on early Social Security payments. The outcry is coming from those who had planned on an early retirement and who feel themselves unjustly deprived.

But we would go even farther. As we concluded in a recent series of editorials on retirement and Social Security, we believe the retirement age should be gradually raised to 68. Americans are living longer; their productive years have stretched well into their seventh decade. Democrats in Congress have proposed this particular step; a study of the Social Security system done by a presidential commission seconds the notion. According to projections we've seen, this action by itself would be almost enough to ensure financial viability for Social Security into the foreseeable future.

We would also suggest Mr. Reagan consider defying the gray-power lobby by re-working the formula under

which Social Security increases are tied in to the cost of living index. The way it's done now artificially inflates the cost-of-living raises granted those on Social Security and a fairer system could readily be devised.

We would also like to see federal employees, who now enjoy their own, separate Social Security-like benefit plan, join the rest of us under the leaky umbrella. If federal workers were brought into the system, their dollars would help it over the next few rocky years, until the long-range changes could have an effect. The day when federal workers were compensated by better-than-average benefits for poor salaries has passed. A separate system costs us, the taxpayers, more to administer and support. We see no sense in continuing the practice; Mr. Reagan, however, under heavy pressure from the politically astute, active government workers, who form an effective lobby and voting bloc, is likely to disagree.

But if he could beat his way through this dense woods, we're sure these changes would make sure Social Security can survive so that not only our parents, but ourselves and our children and their children will have a cushion — but not total support — in our old age

ALBUQUERQUE JOURNAL

Albuquerque, N.M., May 17, 1981

President Reagan is proposing to export his politics of austerity to future generations with his Social Security belt tightenings, but given the alternatives his approach is perhaps the best.

His changes would seem to be aimed hardest at those Americans who by choice or force of circumstance will retire between ages 62 and 64, after next Jan. 1.

Reagan's wide-ranging set of changes will, he says, keep the massive retirement fund from going broke under the brunt of "baby boom" retirees coming into the program after the turn of the century.

The simple truth is that the trust funds underlying the Social Security system are emptying faster than workers' taxes — already at alltime high levels — are replenishing them.

Reagan proposes to cure the problem by stemming the outflow, rather than increasing the inflow.

But the funds' outflow is only another way of defining the inflow into the pockets of Social Security recipients.

Reagan seeks to minimize the impact of his changes on current recipients. A few-months delay in implementing cost of living increases for 1982 would be the primary impact proposed.

But for those born after 1920, Social Security's formulas in the Reagan proposal would mean retirement stipends based on smaller percentages of income, than under the present formulas.

The early retirement penalty proposed would lower a 62-year-old's benefit from 80 percent of full Social Security to only 55 percent. In addition, the percentage for calculating benefits for full-term 65-year-old retirees would also be altered downward.

The alternative is Social Security's coffers running dry, no benefits for anybody.

The Reagan administration would do well to assure, however, that the Social Security formula tinkering doesn't tear further holes in the vaunted "safety net" for the truly poor, in the Reagan austerity program.

The abrupt change in the early retirement penalty has great potential for working individual hardships on those too close to retirement to change their long-term financial planning. Perhaps the early retirement penalty would better be phased in over five or ten years.

In addition, the paring or elimination of "social welfare" programs, such as survivors allowance to minor children, should be done only where it can be shown that nobody is totally cut adrift from needed aid.

As noted, Reagan's proposal would minimize the impact of his changes on current recipients. In addition to being those least able to alter their financial planning, this group is also the one most organized politically.

Few Americans not close to and actively planning for retirement have a clear idea of their entitlements under Social Security.

It is this group — those born after 1920, who would bear the brunt of the Reagan benefit paring.

Richmond Times-Dispatch

Richmond, Va., May 17, 1981

That the Social Security system teeters on the brink of financing disaster is indisputable. Demands on the system are outpacing contributions so rapidly that it will collapse into bankruptcy by the autumn of 1982 if something is not done, and done quickly, to alter the trend.

And that "something" must be more efficacious than Congress' previous timid efforts to rescue the system. Four years ago, it sought to assure the system's solvency for another 50 years by approving a series of increases in the payroll tax that finances it, but they clearly have not worked. Despite these additional burdens on workers and employers alike, the Social Security program has continued to sink into trouble. And over the years, if the system remains unchanged, the problem will worsen, for the number of workers paying into the system will decline as the number of retirees withdrawing from it will increase. At the moment, there are about five workers for every retired American, but, because of the nation's falling birthrate, the ratio will dwindle to three workers for every retiree by the year 2030.

It is on the basis of these dreary facts that President Reagan has proposed measures designed to save the Social Security system, and it is on the basis of these dreary facts that Congress should act. Unfortunately, its tentative reaction to Mr. Reagan's move has reflected the same timidity that has characterized its previous approaches to the Social Security problem. Awed by the voting power of Americans who are already receiving benefits and those who are about to retire, most congressmen cringe at the thought of approving controversial changes that would reduce the flow of money from the system. Clearly, Congress will need courage to face the challenge.

This is not to suggest that it must endorse, in every detail, the president's proposals. They deserve intensive and critical examination. The point is, rather, that Congress cannot substantially strengthen the Social Security program without running the political risk of offending important blocs of voters. Its sense of responsibility for the welfare of future generations of Americans will, we hope, inspire it to take that risk.

Nothing in Mr. Reagan's plan, it is important to stress, would significantly affect the benefits of people who are now on the Social Security rolls. Some of the recommendations that would affect future retirees are clearly commendable and should be easy to justify. In this category are Mr. Reagan's proposal to encourage people to work longer, and thus pay into the system longer, by raising the ceiling on the amount a retiree could earn without losing any of his Social Security benefits; his proposal to counter the impact of "double dipping," which describes the practice of people who retire on federal pensions and work long enough in private industry to qualify also for Social Security benefits, a practice that places a heavy drain on that system.

Mr. Reagan's recommendations for increasing the penalties for early retirement and for revising the procedure for determining eligibility for disability benefits are more debatable, but the president has made a strong case for each of them. It seems especially strange that the present disability standards include not only medical factors but the individual's education and work experience as well.

But there are certain constructive possibilities for changing the Social Security system that Mr. Reagan did not recommend. Some of its financial problems stem from the formula used to calculate cost-of-living increases for Social Security benefit recipients. That formula, which includes some factors irrelevant to the financial needs of retired people (such as the cost of buying a home), exaggerates their cost-of-living needs and thus inflates Social Security costs. The formula obviously should be changed. Portrayed during the presidential campaign as an ogre determined to destroy the Social Security system, Mr. Reagan made certain promises designed to emphasize his support for it; and one of those promises was not to tamper with the cost-of-living formula. But Congress is under the restraint of no such pledge and should change it. Still another constructive move would be to include federal employees, including congressional workers, in the Social Security system. Their payments into the program would strengthen it, and, after all, if the system is good enough for workers in the private sector, it should be good enough for employees of the federal government that administers it.

As Congress approaches the Social Security problem, it should heed the words of Richard S. Schweiker, secretary of health and human services:

"The crisis is inescapable. It is here. It is now. It is serious. And it must be faced."

Failure to face the crisis now would lead to far more horrendous problems in the future. President Reagan recognizes this, and so should Congress.

Post-Tribune
Gary, Ind., May 17, 1981

President Reagan's prescription designed to put the Social Security system back on a sounder financial base is going to anger some people, actually be unfair to some.

That would be true of any system designed to accomplish that purpose.

Yet those most likely to be inconvenienced — even penalized to a degree — need to bear in mind that they along with millions of present and potential future Social Security benefit recipients could be hurt much worse unless some fiscal corrections are made, and quickly.

For details of the trouble in which the system finds itself, and why, we refer you to an Associated Press review of the problems appearing on Page 1 of this section. The central point is that unless remedial steps are taken soon, bankruptcy could result in shattered dreams for millions of Americans.

The basic trouble is, of course, that contrary to wise insurance practice, the system started out paying its beneficiaries out of current revenue instead of a carefully built, actuarily sound reserve fund. That wasn't a simple case of governmental stupidity. It was in part a recognition of the immediate needs of so many of the elderly in the depth of the depression when the Social Security system became public policy. That has been complicated, of course, by age group changes that weren't clearly foreseen at the time and that haven't been recognized with sufficient lead time since.

As a result, the Reagan administration has recommended several changes. One would considerably reduce the percentage of full benefits a person could get on retiring at 62 instead of waiting until 65, and that could force some wrenching lifestyle alterations on a great number now anticipating early retirement in the next few years. Another would delay next year's built-in "cost of living" raise for those now on Social Security from July of 1982 until October, a change that would cost the average beneficiary $100 and some considerably more. That cost will be painful for those already hurt by inflation, but alternative answers could be much more painful.

Congress could make other changes in addition to — or in lieu of — those suggested by the White House, including gradually advancing the age of eligibility for full benefits from 65 to 66. Such potentials need to be weighed carefully in committee, but the country cannot afford a long delay.

There are those who advocate junking the whole current system and substituting a method of private insurance for retirement backed by employer cooperation. Actuarily, that would probably be more sound. The trouble is, however, that unless Social Security contributions are in the form of a tax we all have to pay, too many would refuse — or delay too long — the need to plan for their own retirement.

Social Security has its faults, but those who remember the situation of many of the aged in the 1930s know it has been a vast improvement. What's required now is adjusting that improvement to fiscal reality, and the Reagan administration deserves credit for taking a more necessary than popular step in that direction.

The Honolulu Advertiser
Honolulu Ha., May 17, 1981

There must be change in the Social Security system, either in taxes or in benefits. Otherwise, the trust fund upon which monthly checks are drawn for 35 million retired, disabled or widowed Americans would go dry next year.

The Reagan administration has outlined one set of proposals to meet the problem, and others have been offered or are being discussed in Congress.

BRIEFLY, the Reagan changes would:
- Cut back benefits for those taking early retirement at 62, from 80 percent to 55 percent of full pensions. The change would take effect Jan. 1 and affect workers who turn 62 next year or after.
- Change the formula for calculating a retiree's initial benefits, scaling them down in the period from 1982 to 1987 from the present 41 percent of pre-retirement earnings to about 38 percent. This would not affect present retirees.
- Delay the cost-of-living increase in benefits for three months in 1982, from July 1 to Oct. 1, and make it effective that date in later years. That would let the increases coincide in the future with the start of the new fiscal year.
- Collect Social Security taxes on the first six months of sick pay, all of which is now exempt.
- Impose tougher standards for collecting disability insurance payments.
- Reduce the "windfall" for retired state or local government employees who collect a pension and then work again to qualify for Social Security benefits.
- Gradually scale down and then eliminate the penalty for a retired person who keeps on earning while receiving Social Security checks. The present limit of $5,500 in "free" earnings would go to $10,000 in 1983, then go up $5,000 a year until reaching $20,000 in 1985, with limits disappearing entirely in 1986.
- Reduce Social Security tax rates from the increasing amounts now scheduled in future years.

In addition, the Senate Budget Committee has approved a measure to change the formula for cost-of-living increases in Social Security checks. Instead of the Consumer Price Index, used now, it would key them either to that or to the average increase in wages, whichever was the lower.

EVERY ONE of the proposals is certain to come under fire from one group or another, but the bitterest criticism thus far has been directed at the plan to cut benefits for early retirees.

"The most blatant flaw in the proposal is its punitive treatment of future retirees," Bradley Schiller, professor of economics and public administration at The American University in Washington, writes in an article on the front page of this section.

"The proposal amounts to a whopping 30 percent benefit cut for those who will retire between ages 62 and 65. ... That does not mean a 30 percent cut merely for three years, but for the rest of their lives.

"The accumulated loss to an average worker retiring at 62 would amount to $23,000 in today's dollars.

"The inequity of all this is striking. Nobody else is being asked to take a financial cut of this scope in the name of fiscal austerity. Why should those retiring next year get far smaller benefits than those retiring this year? Both groups worked just as long and paid roughly the same payroll taxes.

"Indeed, future retirees will have paid much higher taxes than today's retirees because of continually rising Social Security tax rates."

ALTHOUGH IT, TOO, is drawing some criticism, the Senate committee's proposed change in computing cost-of-living increases has much to recommend it.

Since the increases were tied to the Consumer Price Index nine years ago, it has become apparent that the CPI overstates the effects of inflation. The result has been a gradual relative gain in benefits to retirees at the expense of workers paying higher and higher Social Security taxes.

The shift to the "average wage" base could be expected to end that.

Interestingly, the projected savings from that proposal are greater than those from the slash in early-retirement benefits. They are estimated at $26 billion over a five-year period, as against $17.9 billion.

The scaling down of initial benefits to the average of 38 percent of pre-retirement income has a similar historic justification in that the lower figure was the norm before benefits were skewed by the Consumer Price Index. Nevertheless, an element of inequity would remain because payments to current retirees would continue to move upward from the somewhat higher starting point.

WHATEVER ELSE is said, the president has displayed rare political courage in coming to grips with Social Security reform. The growing crisis in its financing has been apparent for years, and yet the obvious unpopularity of helpful changes has kept both the White House and the Congress from facing up to them.

Now that step has been taken, and the debate — which is likely to resemble a barroom brawl — is opening.

Out of it, a workable, reasonable program should emerge.

It must. The minimum living standards of millions of Americans, now and in the future, are at stake.

Pittsburgh Post-Gazette

Pittsburgh, Pa., May 16, 1981

Budgetary pressure for Social Security reform was left pent up this week inside a House and Senate conference-committee agreement to a $695.4 billion ceiling on federal spending for Fiscal Year 1982. That situation exists because there is a $4.5 billion difference between the Senate and House assumptions for Social Security spending in 1982. And that discrepancy seems certain to force the issue of Social Security reform when Congress attempts in the weeks ahead to fit federal programs under the spending ceiling.

Anticipating the inevitable pressure for Social Security reform generated by the Senate Budget Committee's assumed reduction in cost-of-living payments to public pensioners, the Reagan administration hastily unveiled its own plan to avoid eventual bankruptcy in the Social Security trust funds Tuesday, only two days before the joint committee hammered out the budget agreement.

Still, no solution is indicated in the budget agreement negotiated this week. And before a choice is made between reforms assumed by the Senate version of the budget and those changes proposed by the administration, Congress can anticipate a strenuous debate that will be certain to draw maximum public attention.

Actually, a modest reform of Social Security is assumed by both houses in the version of the budget awaiting Congress' ratification next week. About $2.5 billion will be dropped from anticipated FY 1982 Social Security spending as a result of a package of lesser reforms that includes elimination of the $122 minimum monthly Social Security payment, which has been going even to those recipients who are entitled to less according to standard calculations. Budget committees for both houses also agreed to phase out benefits for college-student survivors. And a lump-sum death benefit will no longer be paid when there is no immediate family survivor to a deceased beneficiary. By most calculations, however, those savings account at best for no more than a third of the adjustments needed to stabilize the nation's all-inclusive pension program.

Beyond those alterations, the House has shown little enthusiasm for a larger version of the unpopular reform. So the debate seems likely to come to a head over two different approaches — one suggested by the Senate and the other by the administration.

Following the version assumed — but not actually legislated — in the Senate's 1982 budget, reform would concentrate on a scaling down of cost-of-living raises for pensioners under Social Security, veterans, railroad and other federal retirement programs. That reform would be achieved by allowing Congress to base the cost-of-living adjustment on the average national increase in wages (rather than prices) whenever it is lower. That reform was originally advertised with savings of some $6 billion but has since been scaled down to the $4.5 billion assumed in the Senate budget.

The Senate approach would reduce long-term costs. But longer-lasting savings could be achieved from structural reforms in the program that have been recommended by the administration. Those reforms would reduce the benefit paid upon early retirement to 55 percent (from the present 80 percent) of the pension due at age 65. Over the long run, that particular reform would certainly have the effect of discouraging early retirements. This year, however, it might hasten early retirements, since the limit would not go into effect before next January.

The administration also proposes to abolish benefits paid to children of workers who retire before age 65, alter the formula for determining initial benefits to retirees, and delay payment of cost-of-living increases from July until October. Further, the administration would control the costly double-dipping that occurs when pensioners under independent federal retirement programs also draw Social Security. Yet while trimming benefit programs, Mr. Reagan would also allow Social Security pensioners latitude for supplementing incomes by abolishing the present limit on outside earnings.

After a quick study, some congressional budget experts believe that the Reagan reforms might yield less than the $9 billion in savings promised by the administration. Nevertheless, Mr. Reagan's plan does take a more varied approach. And in offering a longer list of reforms, the administration has provided a broader forum for a crucial debate.

San Francisco Chronicle

San Francisco, Calif., May 15, 1981

SOMETHING HAD TO BE DONE to save the Social Security fund from insolvency in the symbolically fateful year of 1984, and it looks as though it will be done. With David Broder and other analysts, we give President Reagan full credit for courage in responding to this necessity.

Either those Social Security beneficiaries of the present or those of the future are going to have to give up some part of their prospects if the whole old-age insurance system is not to go down the tubes.

President Reagan's program, announced the other day, sets out to save the Social Security fund from going broke while preserving intact retirement benefits for those now getting them. Yet at the same time it holds out a future promise of reduced Social Security taxes for the younger workers of the country — and their employers — upon whom the burden of providing these benefits falls. It is, as Broder writes, "carefully crafted," but the plan nevertheless has caused an uproar.

CRITICS FIND IT easy enough to home in on specific proposals with the charge that the president is ripping his famous "safety net" to shreds and creating a "calamity, a tragedy and a catastrophe" for the nation's old folks.

True it is that since Franklin D. Roosevelt started up the old age and survivors insurance program in the middle '30's, presidents and other politicians have never dared to do what Reagan has done: urge Congress to cut back benefits. Reagan, however, is not in fact reducing the expectations of the 36 million persons presently in the over-65 category of Social Security beneficiaries; they will receive cost-of-living increases of 11 percent on July 1, and next year's increase will come to them on the same consumer-price-index basis (we think unwisely), but it will be three months delayed.

WHAT REAGAN DOES intend to cut are the expectations of those in other categories:

● Disability pay beneficiaries, so as to relate "disability insurance more closely to a worker's earnings history and medical condition;"

● Double-dippers in other retirement funds;

● Most particularly, those retiring at age 62 would be cut from the present level of 80 percent of full benefits to 55 percent.

● A proposal working in distinct favor of retirees would phase out the earnings test that now reduces Social Security benefits one may receive.

The administration may find itself up against an organized gray-haired chorus of denunciation for its plan to rescue the Social Security fund, but the wiser element of retirement-age Americans, not to mention those younger who are paying for it, are bound, we think, to approve of this bullet-biting approach.

The TENNESSEAN
Nashville, Tenn., May 14, 1981

IN proposing major benefit reductions for future Social Security recipients and other changes, President Ronald Reagan is going to find that he has a political tiger by the tail that he will have difficulty in trying to cage.

Mr. Reagan's proposed changes, unveiled Tuesday, would reduce from 80% to 55% the share of full retirement benefits received by workers retiring before age 65. It would change from July 1 to October 1 the date on which cost-of-living increases take effect. It would tax the first six months of employee sick pay and change the computation formula to bring about a 3% cut over the next six years for a worker entering retirement.

There is a small carrot to go with the stick. The "earnings test" for recipients over 65, under which benefits are reduced $1 for every $2 earned above $5,500, would be phased out over a three-year period, and a cut in Social Security taxes beginning in 1985.

Since about 70% of workers covered by Social Security accept reduced benefits and retire before age 65, it is clear that millions will feel the pinch of the reduced benefits, especially those who have little or no choice but to take early retirement,

either because of prolonged illness or lack of job opportunity.

The Reagan administration is painting early retirement as a luxury the system can no longer afford, but those who have paid into the system for years with the anticipation of at least having the safety net of early retirement are going to be very concerned about it.

Mr. Reagan has repeatedly promised that he would not reduce benefits for those already on the Social Security rolls. He was on the defensive about that in both the 1976 and 1980 campaigns. So that is why he opposed a Senate resolution of last week which would have changed the formula for calculating cost-of-living increases in a fairly modest way.

The Senate was, in effect, offering him a favor by taking the initiative. But his judgment that such an action would have been a repudiation of his promise not to reduce benefits for those already on the rolls as well as raising a mammoth howl of protest from the millions now on those rolls undoubtedly caused him to aim at future recipients.

Their outcry may not be as loud immediately, but the action, if approved, is not going to redound to the credit of this Republican administration.

THE BLADE
Toledo, Ohio, May 16. 1981

EVEN the economy-minded Reagan administration has shied away from the idea of making trims in the Social Security program. But as the trust fund sinks deeper into a financial quagmire, President Reagan has wisely decided to act.

For the most part, his proposals to scale down the benefits would not affect current recipients of benefits, and most of the cutbacks are not new. What is novel is the forthrightness with which the White House is addressing this politically tender topic.

The biggest change would be the increased penalty for retiring before age 65. At present one can retire at 62 and receive 80 per cent of benefits. Mr. Reagan's proposal would cut that to 55 per cent and make similar cuts for spouses' allowances. On the other side of the ledger, though, administration officials held out the hope that the increasingly onerous Social Security taxes might be reduced somewhat for the 114 million persons paying into the system and that all present earnings restrictions on Social Security recipients over 65 would be phased out by 1986.

Those now receiving benefits would be affected only in one major respect. The 1982 cost-of-living adjustment — but not the one for this year — would be delayed three months, from July to October. This would cost the average pensioner very little, but would save the Social Security trust fund billions of

dollars over the long haul. This is a rather small price to pay if it guarantees that the Social Security trust fund will not become insolvent within a few years.

To be equitable the Administration should also seek similar delays in federal employees' pension cost-of-living adjustments — as well as reduction of their twice-a-year increase to one per year.

In line with these proposals the Senate already has accepted a recommendation by its budget committee that benefit increases ought to be based on either the Consumer Price Index or the national average increase in wages, whichever is lower. The CPI tends to exaggerate the actual impact of inflation because of excessive reliance on housing costs and other outlays that are seldom incurred.

The Senate action and the Reagan administration's proposals represent tacit acknowledgement that politically unpopular changes in Social Security are unavoidable and that equitable changes can be made without cutting deeply into the present level of payments.

The Social Security system is in danger of insolvency largely because politicians have been adorning the program with excessive benefit increases, usually enacted during congressional election years. But if these ill-advised tactics cause the system to become insolvent, the political fallout for incumbents might be a good deal worse.

FORT WORTH STAR-TELEGRAM
Fort Worth, Texas, May 16, 1981

Tampering with the Social Security program can be politically explosive, and the Reagan administration has demonstrated a great deal of courage in recommending some drastic changes in the retirement system and in seeking quick action on the proposed changes in order to stave off bankruptcy.

Public reaction to the administration's proposals — particularly from retired persons or those soon to join that group — has been overwhelmingly unfavorable, which, while understandable, is unfortunate. Because it has been general knowledge for some time that if something isn't done soon to shore up the system's sagging financial structure, the fund established to furnish assistance to retired people will run out of money, possibly by next summer.

Social Security became an issue during last autumn's presidential election, with then-President Jimmy Carter charging that his opponent, Ronald Reagan, would abolish the program. Reagan denied it, and the proposals he unveiled to Congress this week would, instead, tend to alleviate some of the financial shortfall, at least for the time being, and strengthen the system's fiduciary position.

The key feature in the Reagan proposal calls for a significant reduction in Social Security benefits for workers who take early retirement.

Currently, workers can retire at 62 and still draw 80 percent of the benefits they would receive if they waited until 65 to quit working. Under the Reagan plan, the benefits for retiring at 62 would be cut to 55 percent, providing a pursuasive incentive for people to stay on the job three years longer.

Administration officials say adoption of this segment of the Reagan plan would save $17.6 billion during the next five years alone.

Benefits for those currently retired will not be reduced under the Reagan plan. Originally, it called for a $4.5 billion saving next year by asking the nation's 36 million Social Security beneficiaries to forfeit their cost-of-living increase for three months. But that idea was shelved shortly thereafter, and Health and Human Services Secretary Richard Schweiker promised that the issue "will not rear its ugly head again."

The administration proposal calls for additional savings by trimming benefits to spouses, taxing sick pay for the first six months of an employee's illness, eliminating benefits to dependent children of early retirees, eliminating "windfall" benefits for retired federal workers who also collect Social Security benefits and tightening worker disability assistance requirements.

Some of the savings would be offset by a plan to lower the Social Security tax rates on 114 million workers currently paying into the system, but overall, the Reagan plan, if adopted, could go a long way toward bailing the system out of its immediate financial difficulties.

However, with Americans' life-expectancy figures ever on the increase, it is almost inevitable that eventually the retirement age will have to be shifted from 65 to a higher figure. Sixty-eight is the most frequently mentioned age under programs introduced in the Congress.

But until that is accomplished, the Reagan plan offers the best short-term advantage for a program that is in deep trouble.

THE LOUISVILLE TIMES
Louisville, Ky., May 13, 1981

President Reagan has painted himself into a corner on Social Security, as his rescue proposals for the sacred, but financially beleaguered retirement program make clear.

Mr. Reagan has promised not to meddle with the cost of living adjustments that retirees receive annually to compensate them for inflation, a position that he doesn't want to retreat from.

As the U.S. Senate has recognized, however, a change in the way these increases are calculated would be a fair and an effective way of shoring up the Social Security system in the short term.

In spite of his pledge, even Mr. Reagan is calling for a three-month delay in the increase due in July 1982, at a cost of $4.5 billion to older Americans.

The Senate decided last week to break the link between the cost-of-living increases and the Consumer Price Index. After July 1, under the bill, adjustments would be based on the previous year's average wage increase if wages went up less than prices.

With the economy in its present state, retirees would get somewhat smaller increases than they do now. That's because, as many economists agree, the CPI exaggerates the rate of inflation. The Senate's plan would therefore save the system, and those working people who contribute to it, $8 billion a year.

The President has rejected the idea, for the usual reasons. No politician is eager to face the wrath of 31 million Americans who now get Social Security checks. Mr. Reagan is also reluctant to stir up a controversy that could divert attention from his economic plan.

No sooner had the Senate acted, therefore, than the President rushed forward with his plan, in the hope of nipping the congressional initiative. Although Congress has turned to putty in Mr. Reagan's hands, it should remain firm on this important economic issue.

Some parts of the Reagan plan are valuable, notably the limit on double-dipping by ex-bureaucrats who make minimal contributions to Social Security.

But Congress must be extremely cautious of the proposal to allow beneficiaries to earn as much income as they want without losing benefits. The limit, now $5,500 for persons under 72, would be phased out by 1986.

That would mean billions in benefits could go to workers who receive full salaries. This would conflict with the original purpose of the system, which was to replace lost earnings. By rewarding older persons for working longer, moreover, this change would make it even harder for younger workers to advance.

With the Old Age and Survivors trust fund a year from bankruptcy, Congress must act promptly. The Senate action is an excellent place to start.

The Kansas City Times
Kansas City, Mo., May 20, 1981

That the Reagan administration Social Security proposals do not apply to retirees now receiving monthly checks must be emphasized again in order to allay spreading fears of the public. Even suggesting changes of such magnitude for those now dependent on the system would be cruel and unjust, to say nothing of impossible to enact just from a political standpoint.

In the wake of opposition following last week's release of the president's ideas, it must also be stressed they are just that. Executive proposals are not written in stone but offered as starting points for discussion. At the same time, Congress will have its say on this matter, as it always does on presidential proposals, weakening, strengthening or substituting its own program for the original. Until that usually lengthy process runs its course, the Social Security system will remain as it is. And the administration may be seeing the first gathering of stormy clouds.

In the large package which includes tightened eligibility provisions for disability and survivor benefits, one area that must be worked on is the major feature of the proposal, a reduction from 80 percent to 55 percent from full benefits for those who retire at 62. Making it effective in January, as the president has suggested, would impose an impossible hardship on persons now on the brink of retirement. People plan retirement budgets carefully years in advance of taking leave of the work force. Hasty action on such a basic underpinning of retirement income is indeed changing rules in the middle of the game, a move Congress will hardly make. If Congress accepts this change — a big if — it should consider phasing it in after a reasonable period of time, either gradually reducing benefits, changing the age at which they are available or both.

Already some congressional leaders are expressing reservations about the proposals, particularly the timing surprise. At the least, there will be compromise. Sen. Robert Dole, chairman of the Senate Finance Committee, predicts little will be done soon on the early retirement matter. "Those people who are going to turn 62 in the next few years don't have very much to worry about," Dole told the country Sunday. Someday we may look back and see that as the beginning of the slowdown for the Reagan Juggernaut.

Another consideration is that of the 70 percent of Americans who retire before age 65, a third of them do so because poor health prevents them from working, according to unpublished Labor Department statistics. Unable to qualify for disability benefits now and more unlikely to do so under the proposed tighter rules, this group would be whisked quickly into poverty. They must be protected, which the administration's flat cut at the chronological age does not do.

No matter how unpopular it may be, no matter how politically dangerous, revamping of the Social Security system is needed if it is to remain solvent and a reliable institution to cushion the workforce against poverty when wages stop. The president is right in forcing the issue. That doesn't mean the country must or will swallow his package as it is.

YOU COULD ALL DRAW STRAWS...

SOCIAL SECURITY

THE OVERCROWDED LIFEBOAT

The Seattle Times

Seattle, Wash., May 17, 1981

THE Reagan administration's decision to back away from a suggested deferral of living-cost increases due Social Security retirees was prudent in both administrative and political terms.

A lot more discussion and study is in order before any dramatic changes are made in the Social Security program. And any move toward precipitous cuts in benefits could have sowed destructive political land mines under Mr. Reagan's popularity. (Some political experts are puzzled at the timing of raising Social Security issues at this point, since the President's budget and tax proposals need more support in Congress.)

The decision against attempted deferral of the benefit increases due July 1 does not diminish, of course, the need for some kind of additional measures to safeguard the financial integrity of the Social Security system.

Earlier last week, the administration unveiled a long-range plan for saving some $53 billion by phasing in certain benefit changes through 1985. These included disincentives for early retirement and less generous benefits for future retirees.

Many on Capitol Hill, including this state's Senator Henry M. Jackson, believe the government never will be able to bring inflation under genuine control unless restraint is practiced in granting higher pension benefits both to Social Security and military retirees based on shifts in the cost-of-living index.

Almost any major changes in the present setup will require heavy measures of political courage. A spokesman for Mr. Reagan acknowledges that the President is prepared to abandon his campaign promise that Social Security benefits would never be cut. He will do so "reluctantly" and "sorrowfully," an aide said, "because the trust fund is going broke."

Nonetheless, less painful (and more equitable) options remain available in the search for ways to stabilize the trust fund and even out the onerous (and still rising) Social Security taxes paid by employers and employees.

Among the alternatives: Confining Social Security to its original purpose as a retirement system and shifting its health and disability obligations to the general treasury.

The Charlotte Observer

Charlotte, N.C., May 15, 1981

After ignoring some sound proposals already before Congress for restraining the escalation of Social Security benefits, the Reagan administration has hastily offered a Social Security reform plan of its own. It's encouraging that the administration is, in the inelegant phrase of Health and Human Services Secretary Richard Schweiker, "trying to keep the old lady from having no check at all." But there are better ways to address the problem.

The administration's plan, aimed at saving more than $46 billion over the next five years, would cut deeply into benefits for people who retire at age 62. It also would cut benefits for future retirees and eliminate benefits for children of early retirees. It would stop Social Security benefits to "double-dippers" who receive federal pensions but also qualify for Social Security because they spent part of their careers in the private sector. It would delay annual cost-of-living adjustments from July to October, beginning next year — or maybe this year.

Alternative proposals already suggested by Sen. Ernest Hollings of South Carolina and others have several advantages over the administration's plan.

Instead of cutting benefits below the level future retirees have been counting on, Sen. Hollings advocates changing the method of determining cost-of-living adjustments for Social Security recipients and people drawing federal pensions. The Consumer Price Index, which is the basis for those adjustments now, includes mortage interest and real estate costs and perhaps other factors that have little impact on the cost of living for most retired people.

There also are proposals to bring federal employees under Social Security, which would substantially increase income to the Social Security fund. That would be a fairer solution to the "double dipping" problem than denying government retirees the Social Security benefits they earned while employed in the private sector.

And instead of cutting early retirement benefits — a betrayal of trust for workers who had planned to retire at 62 in the next few years — it would be better to gradually increase the retirement age, as some members of Congress already have suggested.

Mr. Reagan's aides might have saved some time and trouble by embracing those congressional proposals instead of dreaming up their own.

TULSA WORLD

Tulsa, Okla., May 13, 1981

UNTIL last Tuesday, the budget cuts proposed by the Reagan Administration mostly affected the "other guy" — welfare recipients, Government employees and special interest groups of a hundred kinds

But on Tuesday, the White House hit John Q. Public with the hardest and perhaps the most necessary fiscal reform proposal of all — a cutback in future Social Security benefits.

This is politically tough because it touches nearly everyone, even though the cuts are projected in the future. (No immediate cuts for present beneficiaries are proposed, although future increases will be affected.)

It is necessary because Social Security and other previously "untouchable" income security programs account for well over half of Federal expenditures. No truly dramatic fiscal reform can be accomplished without changes in this huge slice of the Federal tax-and-spending pie.

The details, of course, will be subject to debate and amendment. But in general, the Administration has proposed saving a lot of money with a minimum of hardship for future beneficiaries.

For example, reducing benefits for early retirement (at age 62 instead of 65) will save $17 billion between 1882 and 1986. Postponing the annual cost-of-living increase from July to October will save $6.3 billion by 1986. Tightening up rules for disability assistance will save $10 billion.

The changes will permit a slowdown in future Social Security tax increases that officials say could mean a lifetime saving of as much as $33,000 for a young person now entering the work force. But there is a dark side, too.

It means that Americans born in the 1920s, 30s, 40s and 50s — who have been paying for generous benefits for today's retired citizens — will have a less generous retirement program for themselves. For example, an average worker retiring in 1987 at age 62 under present law would collect $575 a month; under the Reagan program, payment would be $380.

But it is a price that will have to be paid — either in much higher Social Security taxes or in reduced benefits. And Americans are in no mood for vast new tax payments.

Harsh reality has finally caught up with the Social Security program.

HOUSTON CHRONICLE

Houston, Texas, May 17, 1981

President Reagan has grasped the nettle of Social Security funding. It had to be done; that doesn't mean it won't hurt.

The Social Security program requires attention to avoid financial trouble that would be disastrous to all who depend on it. Several different plans are under consideration in both the House and the Senate. Some only call for short-term adjustments, such as changing the cost-of-living formula that automatically raises Social Security benefits.

The Reagan administration proposal, called "a plan to save Social Security," addresses problems that will be faced well past year 2000. The administration in seeking a long-term solution is acting in the best interests of all those who participate in the Social Security program.

No proposal for changes in Social Security could possibly escape criticism. Some were finding fault with parts of Reagan's plan within minutes after it was disclosed, saying it violated a social contract with the elderly. The administration proposal has several positive aspects, however. While it would delay for three months the cost-of-living increase next year, it does not reduce the cost-of-living formula as some other plans would. While it would penalize those who retire before age 65, it does not increase the age for retirement with full benefits. And it does not tap general revenues for Social Security purposes but instead holds promise of a future reduction in Social Security taxes.

The administration's Social Security proposals will be subjected to examination in congressional hearings along with the other programs that have been put forth. No single plan — including this one — could be expected to make its way through Congress without change. A bipartisan approach might even be achieved. A long-term solution would be best. As Rep. J.J. Pickle, D-Texas, chairman of the House Social Security subcommittee, said, to do nothing would be the worst possible option.

AKRON BEACON JOURNAL
Akron, Ohio, May 15, 1981

FOR SEVERAL years there has been much talk about major reform of the Social Security system in order to assure its long-term stability. Now, apparently, there is to be action, and it is none too soon.

The Reagan administration has proposed, among other things, sharp cuts in Social Security benefits for men and women who retire before age 65 and delaying for three months the annual cost-of-living increase.

Whether the three-month delay would be from July to October of 1981 or 1982 is now being debated. "The sooner the better" would seem to be a good principle to follow, whatever the steps taken to reform and strengthen the system. In any case, these two changes alone would save at least $23.9 billion by 1986.

Other revisions are proposed, most of them politically palatable and generally sensible. Just which of the Reagan proposals — or others being considered in the House and Senate — may be adopted is uncertain. What does appear certain is that pressure from the White House and realization in the Congress that time is running out will result in action.

The alternative is a bankrupt Social Security system possibly by 1982, and not later than 1983. That must not be allowed to happen.

The 70-year-old President's plan to cut benefits for those who retire at 62 from 80 percent to 55 percent of full entitlement may be the easiest to sell to the Congress. The House Subcommittee on Social Security, headed by J. J. Pickle, D-Tex., already had proposed raising the retirement age for full benefits from 65 to 68.

In the Senate, Ernest Hollings, D-S. C., has proposed that the Consumer Price Index be discarded or modified as the basis on which to figure annual increases in Social Security benefits.

Sen. Hollings would use an index based on real dollar increases in wages rather than on inflated prices, and there are economic experts who agree that the present formula is not a proper one. Last July it resulted in a 14 percent increase in benefits.

The Bureau of Labor Statistics has now announced that the CPI will bring an 11 percent increase beginning in July.

Both figures are inflationary and, when built into the Social Security system, simply aggravate inflation and the problems of the system.

The incentives the administration has built into the proposals to continue working until 65 are important and reasonable.

Currently, 70 percent of Social Security pensioners retire early. In 1948, 50 percent of all men over 65 were in the labor force; today only 20 percent are. Meanwhile life expectancy has increased.

Together these two factors have lengthened the average period from retirement to death by four to five years — and put an additional strain on the dwindling Old Age and Survivors Insurance trust fund.

Other important changes recommended by the administration would abolish the limit on how much retirees can earn without losing Social Security benefits and would eliminate windfall benefits for retired federal workers who also get Social Security.

The dual-pension problem could be eliminated by bringing everyone into the Social Security system and phasing out separate federal programs for government employees, including the Congress.

President Reagan's proposals are at least a necessary first step in the right direction.

This is the first time in the system's 46-year history that a president has made recommendations for major reforms in the program. Changes made in the Carter administration — to raise the tax rates and earnings base on which the tax is collected and to shift some disability funds into the old-age fund — simply delayed the day of reckoning.

That day has now come. The President obviously knows it. The Congress knows it.

Together they must work out a plan that guarantees workers who retire in the decades ahead the Social Security protection they helped to pay for.

President Reagan does not want to change the formula for figuring increases in benefits for those over 65. He proposes instead a one-time, three-month delay in raising benefits.

That would provide quick, temporary relief for the system. But it would not solve the long-term problems.

Besides, there is room for adjusting the index on which annual increases in benefits are figured without being unfair to retirees, and the Congress ought to consider all the possibilities.

The Providence Journal
Providence, R.I., May 13, 1981

Since at least 1976, urgent warnings have been heard that the federal Social Security program is headed down the road to fiscal disaster. Fearful of alienating the 36 million elderly Americans who collect Social Security — $140 billion next year, 20 percent of the federal budget — neither Congress nor successive administrations have dared to address the problem squarely.

Now, warned that the retirement fund may go bankrupt by next year (and one forecast that all three trust funds may be in deficit by 1983,) there is a belated stirring alongside the Potomac.

Last week, the full Senate voted 49 to 42 to cut $7.9 billion in benefits next year. That vote constituted a non-binding recommendation to tax-writing committees that cost-of-living increases should be based either on average wage increases or the Consumer Price Index, whichever is lower.

President Reagan, reversing a campaign promise not to touch Social Security, followed suit yesterday with his own set of recommendations. The White House proposed the following package: Cut benefits to workers who elect to retire at age 62 to 55 percent of full entitlement, rather than the current 80 percent; postpone the next cost-of-living increase from July 1, 1982 to October 1 (saving $4.5 billion); lower the payroll tax on workers paying into the system; and phase out the limit on earnings for pensioners who work.

Earlier on, Mr. Reagan had asked Congress to cut certain Social Security benefits, including aid to college students 18 to 21 years old, the $122-a-month minimum benefit, the $255 lump-sum death benefit, and to tighten restrictions on disability payments.

Any of the money-saving recommendations would be useful. But even if all were passed, it should be recognized by all Americans that they are stopgaps. They do not constitute the thorough overhaul the Social Security system absolutely must have if it is to continue beyond the next two or three decades as a self-supporting system.

The need for a basic restructuring of the system is as simple as it is inevitable, based on demographic facts long known and clearly understood. The products of the postwar baby-boom, working adults today, have produced far smaller families. As the baby-boom generation crests into a wave of retirees 20 or 30 years down the road, fewer workers will have to support a much larger number of pensioners. One study projects a crushing $600 billion to one trillion dollar deficit if no changes are made.

Useful as Mr. Reagan's recommendations are, they simply do not go far enough. One clearly equitable and desirable change, which he has opposed, is the Senate-approved proposal to rework the formula tying Social Security increases to the Consumer Price Index. As it stands, the annual increases outpace inflation, giving retirees an unjustifiable leg up at the expense of millions of workers.

Also not included in the Reagan formula are such possibilities as gradually raising the retirement age to 68, separating Medicare from Social Security to be funded through some other means, and including civil service workers in the Social Security system.

For the moment, it is heartening that both Congress and the Reagan administration have at least been galvanized into some forward motion on Social Security reform. But halfway measures cannot in the long run cope with the inexorable mathematics of actuarial realities. The sooner that fact is recognized and dealt with, the better for us all.

Senate Rejects Reagan Plan in Unanimous Vote

The Senate May 20 unanimously adopted a resolution rejecting key elements of President Reagan's proposed cuts in Social Security benefits. The 96-0 vote reflected strong opposition to reducing the benefits of early retirees, and to cutting benefits more than many deemed necessary to make the program solvent. (A report released by the House Select Committee on Aging May 20 estimated that the Reagan benefit cuts would save more than twice the amount of money required to keep Social Security financially sound for the next 75 years.) The nonbinding resolution, sponsored by Senate Finance Committee Chairman Robert Dole, said that Congress would not "precipitously and unfairly penalize early retirees." A similar expression of opposition, approved the same day by the House Democratic Caucus, called the planned reduction of benefits for workers nearing retirement age an "unconscionable breach of faith" with that generation.

The Administration immediately signaled its willingness to negotiate. President Reagan, in a letter to congressional leaders, said the Administration was not "wedded to any single solution," and that he was committed to only three basic principles: to "preserve the integrity of the Social Security trust fund and the basic benefit structure," to "hold down the tax burden on workers who support Social Security" and to "eliminate all abuses in the system that can rob the elderly of their rightful legacy."

Chicago Tribune
Chicago, Ill., May 27, 1981

The world's greatest deliberative body, by a vote of 96 to 0, has thundered its disapproval of President Reagan's proposed cuts in Social Security expenditures. The unanimity is no surprise, since the distinguished solons didn't have to agree on a plan of their own to keep the system from going belly-up next year. Last Wednesday's vote provides proof, if any were needed, that a Republican-controlled Senate can be just as foolish as a Democratic one.

Voting for this resolution, we might note, required no great courage. It objected only to any change that would "unfairly and precipitously penalize early retirees" and any "reductions which exceed those necessary to achieve a financially sound system." Who could disparage such fine sentiments?

The administration plan, as we have noted, has its share of flaws, and there are parts of it that shouldn't be enacted. But the President deserves credit for braving grave political dangers in order to try to keep Social Security in business. His early retirement cuts, at least, make good

sense. They would save Social Security about $17 billion by 1986 besides producing new revenues for the general treasury. Since early retirement benefits were not permitted until 1961, this change can't be construed as a violation of Social Security's original pledge. It is hardly unfair to discourage workers from leaving the labor force before the basic retirement age. The pressure for early retirement (at government expense) has come largely from labor unions eager to increase their influence by tightening the labor market. To reverse this trend now is "precipitous" only in the sense that hurrying to throw a drowning man a rope is "precipitous." The action is hasty because it has to be.

Some of the President's cuts are more questionable, and others deserve prompt rejection. The administration, however, has offered a badly-needed change from the "tax and tax, spend and spend, elect and elect" philosophy that has led Social Security into its current predicament. Whatever its flaws, this plan is better than nothing—and nothing is what the Senate offered on Wednesday.

The Wichita
Eagle-Beacon
Wichita, Kans., May 22, 1981

The Senate's unanimous rejection of the Reagan administration's proposal to discourage early retirements doesn't mean it's a bad idea. It may, in fact, be a good and sensible way to slow the outflow of Social Security funds. But the brake must be applied much more deliberately.

The Reagan administration wanted to start next year in cutting benefits for those who retire at 62. After next January, the plan would have given them only 55 percent of the normal retirement benefit rate, instead of the present 80 percent.

So large a cutback, applied so soon, would be unfair to those who had been preparing for early retirement in the next year or so, and there was immediate and widespread public protest. Even many who had no intention so soon or so early were alarmed by the Reagan

administration's haste to implement drastic changes.

Sen. Bob Dole, R-Kan., who heads the Senate Finance Committee, read the public mood correctly and took the correct action in sponsoring the resolution which told the administration to slow down.

The Social Security system's financial future is extremely shaky, and with improved health care, the number of Americans of Social-Security-collecting age will be increasing for many decades. To help keep the system solvent, millions of low-income Americans already are paying more in Social Security taxes than they are in income taxes.

Encouraging later retirements can help ease the burden, but it must be done gradually, with plenty of advance warning.

The Des Moines Register
Des Moines, Iowa, May 25, 1981

The Senate handed President Reagan a rebuke when it voted 96 to 0 to condemn two of the main features of his plan to cut Social Security benefits.

First, the Senate resolved that "Congress shall not precipitously and unfairly reduce early retirees' benefits...." This was a reference to Reagan's proposal to cut Social Security benefits for workers who retire at age 62 from 80 percent of the age-65 figure to 55 percent.

That proposal would have pulled the rug from under thousands of workers now in their late 50s and early 60s who have planned to use the early-retirement option.

Second, the resolution said that Congress will not support cuts in Social Security "which exceed those necessary to achieve a financially sound system...." According to a study by the House Select Committee on Aging, Reagan's proposed cuts would reduce benefits by 23 percent over the next 75 years — twice as much as needed to overcome Social Security's financial problems, according to the Reagan administration's own estimates.

As Chairman Claude Pepper (Dem., Fla.) of the Committee on Aging charged, this suggests that Reagan hopes to use the Social Security cuts not only to keep the system solvent but to help balance the budget and reduce the size of the federal government.

The Senate's criticism is justified, but the resolution should not be misunderstood. Social Security faces serious financial problems in the years just ahead and in the next century. Congress must face these financial problems, preferably this year.

Some benefits must be reduced if the system is to be kept in sound condition. The Senate and Chairman J.J. Pickle (Dem., Tex.) of the House Social Security Subcommittee are on record in favor of cuts.

Pickle wants to raise the age at which workers can retire with full benefits from 65 to 68, beginning in 1990. The Senate recently voted to modify the formula for adjusting Social Security benefits for inflation.

Such cuts are preferable to those proposed by Reagan because they would not have such a disruptive effect on people planning to retire in the near future.

It was easy for the Senate to attack Reagan's proposals. It will be much harder for Congress to make the changes that will be needed to put Social Security back on a sound financial footing.

THE MILWAUKEE JOURNAL
Milwaukee, Wisc., May 22, 1981

So now what? The US Senate has risen thunderously to strike down President Reagan's flawed plan for keeping the Social Security system solvent. However, the threat of bankruptcy remains. Pension checks must be backed with cash, not oratory.

Mistake us not. The Reagan plan was unfair. It would have yanked the rug from under prospective early retirees, sharply cutting benefits without decent warning. The plan also was unwise. It would have removed the limit on outside earnings by Social Security recipients after age 65 — a step dubious in principle and rash in its fiscal implications.

Hence, the Senate had cause for rebellion. Yet, we gag a bit when some senators who have obliged Reagan's request to slash food-stamp benefits for poor families are moved to outrage by Reagan's proposal to tamper with benefits for Social Security recipients — many of whom are truly needy but many others of whom are truly well-off.

The discrepancy in behavior is explained at least in part by a political fact: Social Security beneficiaries are drawn chiefly from the powerful middle class, not America's largely impotent underclass.

In any event, the need to deal with Social Security's financial and structural problems is undeniably urgent. The challenges — both short term and long — are severe. They inevitably entail raising taxes or reducing benefits or some combination of the two. None of the choices is painless.

Reagan bravely but clumsily sought to address Social Security's deep ills. Congress has some other prescriptions in mind. What's required now is the suspension of self-righteous rhetoric and the construction of a sensible bipartisan solution.

The Chattanooga Times
Chattanooga, Tenn., May 27, 1981

In the wake of an uproar from Congress over its plans to revise drastically the Social Security system, the Reagan administration has let it be known it is open to compromise on the issue. The most interesting aspect of this controversy, however, is President Reagan's exercise in tightrope-walking over the issue of reductions in benefits. Caught between a campaign promise opposing reductions and the real need to restructure the retirement fund to maintain its solvency, Mr. Reagan seems to be relying on semantics, thus obscuring his commitment to the latter goal.

The president, for instance, opposed a Senate action to reduce future cost-of-living increases by linking them to the more realistic wage growth index. The change, a reasonable one in our view, would save the retirement fund $7.9 billion in Social Security payments next year. But Mr. Reagan objected that that amounted to a reduction in benefits. A few days later, however, he proposed delaying until October an increase scheduled for July. The proposal was nothing more than a trial balloon, and it was promptly disavowed in the face of protests by congressmen and constituents. But both proposals are alike in one respect: neither amounted to taking away something the elderly had in hand. If delaying an increase, as Mr. Reagan suggested,

was not a reduction in benefits, then neither was the Senate's plan to scale down future increases.

The same cannot be said, however, of the Senate Finance Committee's approval of the White House proposal to increase the cost to the elderly of the Medicare insurance program. The action, if approved by both houses of Congress, would require Social Security retirees to pay nearly $200 million more in premiums to protect their Medicare insurance for medical and drug bills. Additionally, the committee also raised the deductible, which means elderly patients will have to pay a larger share of hospital bills out of their own pockets. That change is expected to save Social Security more than $120 million next year.

There is no disputing the fact that saving the Social Security system will require substantial — and painful — changes. But Mr. Reagan is trying to have things both ways. For understandable political reasons, he wants to keep a campaign pledge not to reduce Social Security benefits, while at the same time getting credit for "saving" the system. In fact, however, he is opposing a measure — changing the cost-of-living adjustment formula — that would help the system the most, and supporting proposals that would reduce retirees' net benefits because of the proposed Medicare changes.

The Evening Bulletin
Philadelphia, Pa., May 22, 1981

President Reagan's plan to chop Social Security benefits got its first test in the Senate this week. It flunked dismally. But that doesn't mean that the whole plan is as dismal as a 96-0 vote would have you believe.

The vote attacked Reagan's proposal on two fronts:

☐ His plan to penalize pre-65 retirement by cutting benefits from 80 percent of full scale to 55 percent.

☐ The size of the proposed cuts which the Senate concluded are more than needed to insure solvency.

Repudiation of the early-retirement penalty shows that the senators are more attuned to Washington's most potent lobby — the elderly — than to logic.

These days, 70 percent of workers are quitting and drawing benefits before age 65. Company failures, ill health and other unavoidable factors contribute to that huge number of early retirements. But many walk away from jobs because they can afford to.

On the second point — overcutting benefits — we think the Senate may be a lot closer to the mark. Rep. Claude Pepper's House Select Committee on Aging just issued a study of the Reagan proposals. It contends that they would cut benefits by 23 percent over the next 75 years, whereas only an 11 percent reduction is needed to keep the system

out of the red. It's now up to the Reagan people to refute that claim or cut their own cuts.

Social Security began in 1935 as a supplement to people's private pensions or retirement lay-aways. Since then, Congress has added wives and children, the disabled and their wives and children, early retirement and automatic cost-of-living increases. There is some social justice to all those add-ons, but the extra load is sinking the ship.

In addition to the early-retirement proposal:

☐ Having disability decided on a medical basis, rather than advanced education or limited work experience, is closer to the original idea of disability.

☐ The plan to reduce "double-dipping" by government retirees who get fat civil-service pensions is on target.

Reagan's plan to scale down the basis for computing future benefits over the next five years seems drastic. The net effect will be to cut the average benefit from 42 percent of pre-retirement pay to 38 percent by 1986, with little prospect of pensions filling the gap. That's going to spell hardship for a lot of retiring people. Reagan promised not to alter the cost-of-living formula, but that looks like another way to do the same thing.

THE ANN ARBOR NEWS

Ann Arbor, Mich., May 22, 1981

SOCIAL SECURITY benefits are being so righteously defended by Congress this week that anyone who had lost track of the calendar might think this is an election year.

The stage has been set simultaneously in the Senate and House for bidding for votes back home by resuming the game of adding *new* Social Security benefits and costs. This creates colorful political drama, but doesn't restore solvency to the basic Social Security program, meaning its old age trust fund.

The Republican-controlled Senate followed a Democratic lead by voting 96-0 for a declaration that "Congress shall not precipitously and unfairly penalize early retirees."

The wording of this first flat-out Senate rebuff to President Reagan is by Senate Democratic leaders. The House Committee on Aging, headed by Rep. Claude Pepper, D-Fla., has provided what looks like detailed support for the Senate's sweeping condemnation of President Reagan's proposals for cutting social costs. According to Rep. Pepper, the President's proposals for discouraging early retirements and cutting some benefit costs would have entirely evil effects. Pepper lists these as:

A loss of $100 in 1982 for each current receiver of Social Security benefits if cost of living increases are delayed; phased-in cuts of 10 percent off benefits now scheduled for 18.1 million persons aged 56 through 61 who can be expected to retire during the next five years; loss of one-third of the "promised benefits" expected in the coming five years by more than seven million who have taken early retirements; removal of about four million current benefit receivers, including students, from Social Security rolls.

All of this, Pepper calculates, adds up to reductions in Social Security benefits more than twice the amount — $18 billion — that needs to be saved to prevent the system from going broke next year.

There is no reason to question the accuracy of his calculations. The apparently wide gap between proposed and needed savings means that Secretary of Health and Human Services Richard S. Schweiker, who prepared Reagan's Social Security plan, is trying to create a negotiating situation.

WHEN REAGAN was governor of California, he made quite sweeping declarations of intentions to cut welfare and education spending. Eventually, he showed willingness and ability to bargain with state legislators. Each side got something.

The Senate and Rep. Pepper ought to take that record as a cue for making counterproposals on Social Security, specifying alternate ways of cutting costs.

So far, the best Congress is offering, in response to the Reagan/Schweiker proposals, is a bland promise to "carefully study all options in order to find the most equitable solution to ensuring the fiscal integrity of the system."

There's a vaguely implied acknowledgement in those words that something must be done, in terms of cutting some benefits and/or earmarking some income tax revenue for Social Security. This political posturing is not good enough, not when everyone understands that the number of Americans eligible for old age Social Security benefits will continue growing in the next few decades.

THE LINCOLN STAR

Lincoln, Neb., May 21, 1981

The proposal to trim down the Social Security system appears to be President Reagan's biggest political blunder thus far — akin to former President Carter's water project hit list that was floated in April 1977, only months after Carter was sworn into office. The hit list itself and the way he presented it to Congress, without prior consultation with leaders, soured Carter's relations with Capitol Hill and led to an estrangement between the two branches that lasted throughout his term.

Reagan's proposing his Social Security plan likely will not lead to the same negative end as Carter's lamentable hit list fiasco, but there are similarities.

Reagan's plan, featuring a penalty for early retirement, more stringent disability requirements, an over-all reduction down the road of benefit increases and a rollback in payroll tax increases, apparently was prepared, like Carter's, without much congressional or constituent input. Although administration sources now say the proposal was just a trial balloon, one among a number of ideas launched only to attract comment, there is more reason to believe it was seriously meant to fly.

Reagan's Social Security plan, like Carter's water project hit list, offends a well-organized constituency that fights back. There are no bigger or more sacred cows in Washington than Social Security and the pork barrel system — unless it is the defense budget.

Reagan has run into the buzz saw of the older American lobby just as Carter ran into a swarm of killer bees agitated by pork barrel defenders.

Another parallel, the most important one, is that the proposals of both presidents are and were mostly sound from a conceptual standpoint. Reagan wants to save money and correct structural wrongs his advisers see as leading Social Security into bankruptcy; Carter wanted to reform federal water policy and cut out waste and save money by eliminating or reducing a number of expensive boondoggles.

Reagan's plan is said to be "two steps away from death row." Although Reagan has a more solid popularity base than Carter had, both in Congress and among the people, and although this initiative probably will not lead to a permanent estrangement between president and Congress, it nonetheless has proved Reagan human in the political sense. Indeed, you can't win 'em all. Opposition to it has united Democrats who have been in disarray, and congressional leaders of both parties say that some parts of it may be implemented, but only over time.

There is need for reform of Social Security, of course, just as there was and is need for reform of water policy and for an end to waste in public works appropriations. But Reagan, as Carter, is finding out that it is devilishly hard work taking the sacred cows to slaughter.

THE BILLINGS GAZETTE

Billings, Mont., June 1, 1981

The temporary setback the Reagan administration received when the Republican-controlled Senate turned down one of the planks in his Social Security reform platform is not likely to more than mildly alter his goals.

Popular as President Ronald Reagan may be today with his captivating smile and down-to-earth solutions for what's wrong with America, the U.S. Senate has a way of its own.

The Republican majority chose the proposed cut in early retirement benefits under Social Security as a place to take a stand, to show its independence of the White House

Added to that, there is not much doubt that many senators, new and old, highly resent the dogmatic, almost dictatorial approach that David Stockman, director of the budget, has taken since his appointment.

The overwhelming rejection of the Social Security cut for early retirees was a Senate signal to the White House that it would have its say in deciding what measures will be taken to assure solvency of the system.

It was a popular point at which to make a show of force. It doesn't mean that the Republican majority is going to rebel at Reagan's goals. Indeed not. The Senate Republicans are letting the president know they are not a band of sheep.

President Reagan understands this. His record as California governor shows he can roll with a punch and make a quick recovery. He's already demonstrated that as president in his willingness to talk over the promised tax cuts and proposals on Social Security changes.

No doubt changes are going to be made in the Social Security system. When they are, the Congress will make sure it shares whatever political rewards are to come from public recognition of the accomplishment.

Newsday

Long Island, N.Y., May 25, 1981

When a president is rebuked by his own party's leaders in Congress, that's trouble.

But it happened to President Reagan when Sen. Robert Dole (R-Kan.) made it clear that the Senate would oppose the Republican administration's Social Security reforms, as the Democratic House has done.

We can't say we blame Dole; Reagan's hastily prepared proposals demanded far too much sacrifice from soon-to-retire Americans. Making Social Security solvent will be hard enough politically without spreading the burden unequally.

But having made their point to the White House and the electorate, Dole and his Republican colleagues who control the Senate have given themselves an obligation: to come up with the essential changes that will enable the Social Security system to survive an expected cash shortfall next year and an even more far-reaching crisis when the baby-boom generation of the '50s becomes the retirement-boom generation of the 21st Century.

Congress has come up with some good ideas, such as moderating cost-of-living increases for present Social Security recipients and phasing in changes in retirement age over years rather than months. Paying for Medicare out of general revenue would help, too. But up to now it has seemed unlikely that Congress would make such hard choices unless the White House took the lead.

Now the White House has tried, and Congress has rejected its plan. That means Congress must take the lead itself. To do so may make some constituents unhappy, but holding Social Security together now will be a lot easier than putting it back together later.

The Times-Picayune
The States-Item

New Orleans, La., May 25, 1981

The gloating of Senate Democrats over the adverse public reaction to President Reagan's Social Security proposals should not obscure the fact that the system is in deep financial trouble and that some reductions in benefits to most, if not all, categories of recipients appear inevitable if the system is to avoid bankruptcy within the next few years.

The basic problem is that despite steady increases in withholdings from workers' salaries, and matching amounts contributed by employers, the system is paying out more in benefits to retirees and others than it is taking in.

Largely responsible for the growing Social Security deficit is the fact that the system has been expanded far beyond its original purpose of providing a basic retirement income for the nation's workers. Gradually it has been used to pay for medical care and provide benefits for dependents, the disabled and even college students. At the same time, Congress has voted generous increases to retirees, including raises indexed to the cost of living — that is, to inflation — and made early retirement at age 62 increasingly attractive to millions of workers. All these factors have combined to overload the system.

As a result, the Social Security fund ran a deficit of $3.5 billion last year and is projected to register a deficit of $6.3 billion this year. Unless Congress cuts benefits or provides additional money the Social Security system will be bankrupt by 1985, reports the national magazine, U.S. News & World Report.

Some members of Congress have advocated using General Fund revenues to make up the Social Security deficit, but this would simply shift the burden of the drain to other government programs. The Social Security system should be reformed to make it the self-supporting system it was intended to be and once was.

Politically, the problem is to make the reforms equitable so large groups of present beneficiaries as well as workers paying more and more into the system do not feel cheated. Mr. Reagan's plan seems to have encountered the strongest reaction from workers approaching the early retirement age of 62 suddenly faced with the prospect of seeing their benefits cut from 20 percent less than the maximum received for retirement at 65 to 45 percent less, and from current beneficiaries, for whom one cost-of-living raise was to be deferred for a quarter.

If the Social Security fund is to be rescued from bankruptcy — in other words, if there is to be a Social Security fund — it appears inevitable that some combination of raising the retirement age, reducing the rate of benefit increases and tightening eligibility requirements for the disabled and others will have to be approved by Congress.

It will take political courage, but any pretense that such reforms are not absolutely necessary misleads those currently dependent on Social Security as well as those who are basing their plans for retirement on it.

THE CHRISTIAN SCIENCE MONITOR
Boston, Mass., May 22, 1981

It is all very well for the Democrats to stomp up and down gleefully and make political hay of President Reagan's "stumble" over social security reform. But, it ought to be asked, where have *they* been for the last twenty years? And what do *they* propose doing about an old-age security system that is adding dangerously to inflation and fast going broke? Mr. Reagan's proposed plan can perhaps be criticized in certain of its aspects. But there is no faulting his courage in taking on a nasty problem and addressing it forthrightly.

Not a little political hypocrisy is at work here — among the public as well as the legislators. Democrats were far less vociferous when it came to the President's budget cuts. The reason is plain: their constituents were signalling they wanted to give the Reagan economic program a chance. The poor — the most affected by the cuts — had no political power to make their opposition felt. Now, however, the pocketbooks of all Americans, including the vast middle class, are touched and the voice of outrage is heard across the land. The lawmakers in Washington, Republicans as well as Democrats, hear that voice loud and clear and — surprise? — have acted accordingly in dealing Mr. Reagan's plan a solid rebuff.

The most controversial element of the Reagan approach is to reduce benefits for those retiring before age 65. This indeed would seem to put a hardship on those older workers planning for retirement in the immediate years ahead. But to call this, as the congressional resolution does, an "unconscionable breach of faith" with those who have been contributing to social security their whole lives is hardly a valid argument against the plan or some revised version of it. The plain truth is, the whole system is a "breach of faith" with its original aim — to provide supplemental benefits to retirees' savings and private pensions. It has since become the sole source of funds for many retired Americans — a trend not resisted by the now-so-indignant legislators — and rising benefits have contributed to its financial crisis.

There are basically three ways out of this dilemma: raise payroll taxes, increase the age of retirement, or reduce benefits — or combine these elements in some way. Obviously reform cannot be totally painless although it can strive to be as fair as possible. The Democrats themselves are aware of this. It should not go unnoticed that the chairman of the House social security subcommittee — Rep. J. J. Pickle of Texas — would propose raising the age at which full social security benefits are paid from 65 to 68. Is it imaginable the general public would like that any better? Yet something has to give or the tax burden on young workers will become intolerable.

The question now is whether Congress will follow through on its promise of a bipartisan effort to find solutions — and long-term rather than stop-gap solutions. Many proposals ought to weigh in the debate:

Social security benefits could be taxed, a move which would work to the benefit of low-income retirees. The Consumer Price Index, by which the cost-of-living adjustments are determined and which now overstates the impact of inflation on the elderly, could be revised. The whole program could be gradually shifted to a bona fide insurance system.

Whatever the formula of reform, the goal is a stable, solvent — and equitable — retirement system. Elderly Americans should be assured that they can count on reasonable benefits following a lifetime of work, and the American people as a whole should be willing to support a progressive program that is compassionate toward those least able to care for themselves in old age. This goal cannot be achieved without some sacrifice, however — and the politicians do the people a disservice by not confronting them with the facts.

The Virginian-Pilot

Norfolk, Va., May 23, 1981

Talk about a tough issue. Try Social Security.

No sooner had Ronald Reagan proposed benefit cuts than he was rebuked 96 to 0 by his Republican-controlled Senate.

Representative Olympia Snowe, R-Maine, wondered "if the White House switchboard has been ringing like the phone in my district office." House Speaker Tip O'-Neill called the president "stonehearted."

Who's surprised by the fuss? Social Security is our most precious social program. It's part of the fabric of American life.

And with good reason. Its beneficiaries have worked all their lives. They have paid into the system and they expect something back.

Unfortunately, the system is about $50 billion short for the next five years. That's bad news for workers, retirees, and younger folks who, when they become older folks, would like to see something left.

Mr. Reagan proposed that one

who retired at age 62 receive not 80 percent of his benefits but only 55 percent. That abruptly switched signals on people who had been saving and planning for years under the present ground rules.

The United States Senate voted to index future cost-of-living hikes to a measure that more accurately stated the true rate of inflation. That proposal was more even-handed. That proposal would still permit beneficiaries—as it should—substantial future cost-of-living increases. But Mr. Reagan felt it broke with campaign pledges.

A House of Representatives subcommittee, meanwhile, proposed raising the retirement age for full benefits from 65 to 68 at some future date. That disadvantages those who for reasons of health and workplace pressure have to retire earlier.

So there are three plans. And nobody likes anybody else's. But, as Tidewater Congressman Robert Daniel says, the country has "got to do something. If there were a politically palatable solu-

tion, it would have passed already."

There are some things not to do. We must not merge the Social Security system with the federal employe pension fund, which Mr. Daniel rightly terms a relatively independent and self-sustaining system.

We must not increase payroll taxes. Working families are already paying to the limit.

And we must be wary of the temptation to infuse the system with general revenues. For where would the infusion stop? And where would federal deficits and printed money ever end? And would the tiny remaining incentive for fiscal discipline in Congress disappear? No one—young, old, or middle-aged—needs what could become a recipe for 20 percent inflation.

If the Social Security issue degenerates into partisan or generational warfare, nothing will be accomplished. Leaders in Washington must devise some bipartisan plan that will strengthen the system's main purpose of assisting the elderly and address its main problem of future solvency.

The San Diego Union

San Diego, Calif., May 25, 1981

Rep. Claude Pepper, chairman of the House Committee on Aging, is complaining that the Social Security reforms proposed by President Reagan would break promises which the government has made to the American people.

He is absolutely right. But whose promises were they? It was the Congress of the United States — of which Mr. Pepper has been a member for most of the last 40 years — that turned Social Security into a system that now faces collapse.

This was obscured in the fireworks display that greeted Mr. Reagan's proposals on Capitol Hill last week. If there was any doubt that Social Security is one of the most politically sensitive issues in Congress, now we know for sure. The record shows that in a congressman's book, it is politically permissible only to make Social Security bigger and better — never to make it something less for the sake of keeping it financially sound.

The book of promises goes back to 1935, when Social Security first promised a modest supplementary retirement benefit to working people at age 65 in re-

turn for an equally modest payroll tax described as a "contribution" to an "insurance" fund. In 1939 the promise was extended to dependents and survivors. In 1954 the system began paying benefits for permanent disability. In 1965 medical care was added. And bigger benefits were promised. The average benefit today is twice what it would have been if the original benefit amounts had been increased only to reflect inflation.

The economic and demographic miscalculations which have undermined the future viability of the Social Security system are now familiar enough. What Mr. Reagan is telling Congress is that another temporary bailout — like delaying a cost-of-living benefit increase for three months next year, which Congress appears ready to approve — is not what the system needs. It needs a significant revision in the accumulation of promises it now represents.

As the rockets went off on Capitol Hill, especially over his proposal to reduce benefits for people who retire early, Mr. Reagan sent word that his list of reforms is open to negotiation. Noting the

volume of the Democratic voices in opposition, he called for a bipartisan effort to save the system — "a constructive debate, and then an honest legislative response."

The key word is honest — a package of reforms that levels with the American people about what they can reasonably expect from a Social Security system entering an era when the number of retired beneficiaries will be pulling inexorably ahead of the number of active workers whose earnings must support it.

Mr. Reagan has laid his ideas on the table. Some of them displease many Americans whose future hopes are pegged to the present promises of Social Security, and their feelings have found a ready sounding board in Congress. Now that we know such reforms would be unpopular, we need to hear what the critics would do instead.

They do not deny that the Reagan reforms would put the system in the black and keep it there into the next century. What better ideas do they have to overcome the ruinous $156 billion deficit otherwise in prospect for the retirement fund? That's what everyone is waiting to hear.

THE INDIANAPOLIS STAR
Indianapolis, Ind., May 24, 1981

THE reaction was loud, swift and widespread. From the youngest Republican senator to Democratic octogenarian Rep. Claude Pepper the answer was a clear "No" to the Reagan proposed cut in Social Security benefits for early retirees.

As we said in an editorial last Sunday, the administration's plan of cutting benefits significantly next Jan. 1 was too abrupt and would have played havoc with the carefully laid retirement plans of many Americans.

But what of the several sensible changes advocated by the Reagan administration? Will the storm of protest over the swift cutbacks for early retirees force their shelving too? If so, that would be a disaster. The Social Security program is in need of overhaul. Congress in its ardor to slap down one unfair change must not shy away from rational reforms.

The administration's proposals to have the cost of living adjustment delayed by three months next year and also to consider a standard other than the Consumer Price Index for that adjustment make sense. So does the suggestion for using a slightly different formula for calculating benefit payments. Nor is there anything wrong with making changes in early retirees' benefits as long as those changes are phased in over several years, so as to give everyone a fair chance to plan for the future.

There are also other reforms, in particular a gradual change in the age for drawing full benefits from 65 to 68, or perhaps even 70, that must be considered. The House Social Security committee has already made good progress on this issue.

The Congress' swift rebuff to the president was justified. But the Social Security system's need for changes to assure fiscal soundness is real. No one expects Congress to be as quick about putting a sensible reform package together as it was in rejecting the cutback. But there is every reason to call on our legislators in Washington to put such a package together during this session of Congress. To delay beyond that would be to fail their constituents.

The Hartford Courant
Hartford, Conn., May 27, 1981

The Reagan administration would rather forget about the massive cutbacks in Social Security benefits it proposed two weeks ago.

As other presidents learned from experience, there is no way to reduce benefits for the elderly without provoking a strong, emotional response. President Reagan advocated major changes and the fallout has been predictably heavy.

The need for reform is not disputed. Social Security's main trust fund has been running deficits since 1975 and could exhaust its reserves in about 18 months. What doomed the Reagan proposals was the bluntness and arrogance of their authors. They pushed their federal budget blueprint on the assumption that people really were in favor of increasing defense expenditures and reducing social services. Having succeeded beyond original expectations, they turned to Social Security.

Would people planning to retire before age 65 be satisfied with getting 55 percent of their Social Security benefits instead of the present 80 percent?

Should benefits for children and widows be curtailed?

Should eligibility be tightened for persons who retire early for reasons of health?

The Reagan administration answered these questions with a big Yes. Moreover, some of the major changes would be effective in January, a timetable that could disrupt retirement plans for millions of people.

A better sense of caution would have made the administration recommend phasing in these and other changes over several years, not months.

For instance, the plan to discourage early retirement, and a House subcommittee proposal to raise the retirement age from 65 to 68 are sensible over the long run in a country which has virtually done away with mandatory retirement.

The plan to delay the cost-of-living increases from July to October, beginning in 1982, also deserves serious consideration — but only with another change. Automatic increases in benefits should be tied to changes in average wages in a given year, not to changes in the Consumer Price Index, as is presently done.

Most working people have to live within the limits of wage increases, rather than changes in inflation rates. That seems a reasonable way to calculate cost-of-living increases for Social Security recipients. And it could save the trust fund several billion dollars a year.

The most practical way to help pay for Social Security, however, is the one Mr. Reagan has resisted and some members of Congress have advocated: to tap general tax revenues for some of the benefits that never were intended to be part of Social Security.

Medicare is one such benefit, as is the minimum payment of $122 a month for people too poor to have even qualified for Social Security during their working years.

There is no good in pretending that Social Security is entirely a government pension plan in which today's workers are paying for tomorrow's retirement. They are not. Today's contributions only pay for today's retirees.

Social Security is part insurance, part welfare and part nationalized health care. Using general tax revenues to finance some of these programs is not a radical idea.

Democrat Chronicle
Rochester, N.Y., June 3, 1981

PRESIDENT Reagan is completely right when he says the Social Security system needs help.

Thirty years ago, 14 workers paid into Social Security for each retiree who drew benefits from it. That ratio is now 3.3 to 1 and it will drop further, into the next century, as people live longer and as the post-World War II "Baby Boom" population bubble grows older.

And, of course, politicians would rather put off solving a sticky problem that is apt to reap much more blame than credit for reformers.

Then why not more support for President Reagan's attempt to reform Social Security, in which he called for widespread reductions in benefits? Because those reforms were crafted precipitously and without enough concern for those people already making their retirement plans.

Mr. Reagan had promised not to cut benefits to current recipients, and he had promised to hold down the tax burden on workers who support Social Security. Foreclosure of those options left few others available aside from directing action toward future retirees.

But it's one thing to change the rules for those retiring in the year 2000 or beyond; it's quite another to change them for those retiring next January.

So the net result of the administration's proposal was to stir up a hornets' nest and shake public confidence in a Social Security system whose main foundation rests on confidence — confidence that the dollars paid in earnest into the system today will be available as promised 40 years hence.

THE SOCIAL Security system is a covenant between workers and the government, and the president's team was wrong to threaten that covenant.

Yet reform of Social Security mustn't lose its headway as a result. Congressional Democrats can capitalize on the administration's political blunder, and the public can benefit; this is an opportunity and a challenge to them to suggest a better plan.

Such a plan should take a long look at divorcing Medicare from its sole dependence upon Social Security revenues, underpinning Medicare with general revenue funds if necessary.

Also, federal employees should be integrated into the Social Security system.

Finally, the present "retirement test" to determine eligibility for Social Security benefits should be kept intact, and not eliminated or liberalized as suggested (at various times) by the president.

These are some of the areas reformers should be looking at. But the challenge is to make reforms that will keep Social Security solvent *without* pulling the rug out from under those who have planned their working lives upon promised rules and benefits, and who are soon to collect on those promises.

COLA Change Voted by Senate, Defeated by House Panel

Just before the Reagan Administration proposals for revision of the Social Security system were unveiled in May, 1981, the Senate gave its vote of approval to a much-debated method of cutting benefits. By a vote of 49 to 42, the Senate approved a resolution to base the cost-of-living increases for Social Security recipients on the national average increase in wages, rather than on the consumer price index. (The average wage rise in recent years had been much lower than the increases in the price index.) The measure would save an estimated $7.9 billion in fiscal 1982. The Senate had swung back and forth on the issue, defeating the same resolution a month earlier by a vote of 86 to 12.

In November, the House Ways and Means Committee rejected a plan by the chairman of its Social Security Subcommittee, Rep. J. J. Pickle, that included a revision of the annual cost-of-living formula identical to the Senate plan. Pickle's proposal would also have gradually increased the retirement age to 66, and cut payments to new beneficiaries by revising the initial benefit formula.

St. Louis Globe-Democrat
St. Louis, Mo., May 12, 1981

Congratulations are in order for members of the U.S. Senate who voted to tie the Social Security cost-of-living increase in the coming year to average wage increases rather than the Consumer Price Index, which has consistently overstated the cost-of-living increases.

When the government began making the cost-of-living adjustments for Social Security and other government programs, the idea was to make sure that these benefits were raised enough so that none of the buying power of those receiving the benefits would be eroded. But it never was the intention to give recipients cost-of-living payments that actually exceeded the overall inflation rate · by a significant margin.

Thus tying Social Security benefits to the increases in the wage base will mean a saving of about $8 billion in fiscal 1982. As expected, some critics of the Senate move are attempting to make political hay from the change in the cost-of-living formula. Sen. Daniel P. Moynihan wasted no time in charging that the Senate majority had broken a contract with the older people on Social Security.

This is nonsense. There never was a contract to overcompensate retirees for the effects of inflation. This too-high Consumer Price Index has been used for so long simply because politicians in Washington haven't had the courage until now to use a formula that comes closer to reflecting the true inflation rate.

THE CHRISTIAN SCIENCE MONITOR
Boston, Mass., May 11, 1981

If anyone still doubts that a major reordering of political and social priorities is underway in the US — as reflected in the Reagan administration's impressive budget victory last week — what is happening to the social security system should more than bring the message home. Congress and the administration are now on the verge of devising ways to trim back the huge outlays under that system and other federal retirement programs.

The recent recommendation by the Senate to trim $7.9 billion in social security benefits next year is believed to be the first time since the mid-1930s that a branch of Congress has gone on record favoring deep cuts in the system, which has become the most widely backed of all federal transfer programs. Today it acounts for something like 20 percent of total federal outlays. During fiscal year 1982 alone the social security system is scheduled to disburse $140 billion to 36 million Americans.

The need for reform is urgent. And while many older Americans will be concerned about the direction of reform, they should understand that without changes the system itself may collapse. The true danger for Americans is not that reforms will be made, but that they may be short-range or cosmetic in nature rather than thorough and far-reaching. It must be better understood by the public that the restructuring of the system is necessitated by present and future economic conditions, and that intelligent reform will work in the best interests of all citizens. Failure to find solutions will only put off the day of reckoning for persons receiving benefits as well as the proportionately shrinking work force funding the system.

The problem is essentially mathematical. Fewer and fewer workers in the decades ahead will be funding a system for more and more retired persons, and the system, based on the current formula used to calculate payments – the Consumer Price Index (CPI) – will too often be paying out benefits that actually outpace the inflation rate. There already is concern that one of the three social security trust funds may go bankrupt next year; some analysts see even the other funds eventually doing the same thing.

What is intriguing in the emerging congressional reexamination of social security is the role of the administration. During the presidential election, Mr. Reagan promised that he would not fundamentally alter social security as part of his economic recovery plan. Retirement benefits, he said, were to be part of those "safety net" programs left untouched by federal budget officials. And Mr. Reagan has indicated that he would not seek reform or scrapping of the CPI.

Last week's 49 to 42 Senate vote, however, raises a question about whether the administration may in fact be covertly signaling its support of changes in the system. The Senate vote is a nonbinding recommendation to congressional tax-writing committees that, starting July 1, cost-of-living increases should be based either on average wage increases or on the CPI – whichever is lower. The Senate would also delay payment of increases from July 1 to Oct. 1 starting in calendar year 1982.

The administration has yet to propose its plan. But a press spokesman has said that $8 billion in cuts will have to come out of such federal benefits areas as social security disability payments; supplemental security income; veterans', military, and civil-service retirement programs; and the railroad retirement system.

US retirement programs must be preserved. But that means they must be put on a sound financial basis.

The Star-Ledger
Newark, N.J., May 12, 1981

Although it may have been overshadowed by the House approval of the Reagan economic plan, the Senate finally faced up, in a firm, assertive manner, to a politically sensitive issue — a reasonable moderation of cost-of-living increases for Social Security recipients and federal pensioners.

In a surprise action — reversing its own previous position — the Senate recommended a $7.9 billion reduction in outlays for these higher benefits.

Under the proposal recommended by the Senate Budget Committee, future hikes would be determined by either the Consumer Price Index or the national average increase in wages, taking the lower figure. The price index no longer would be the sole determinant triggering rises in benefits.

* * *

There has been rising — and understandable — criticism of the index formulation because it does not accurately reflect actual rises in living costs. It is critically flawed by distortions (such factors as rarely recurring home purchases, abnormally high interest rates, et al) that project unrealistically high inflation levels.

The result has been overly generous rises that have severely strained Social Security resources, a regressive problem that has been privately acknowledged by the legislative and executive branches. However, remedial reforms have been resisted because of political concern over repercussions by the powerful bloc of the elderly.

* * *

This long overdue revision of the indexing formula faces an uncertain fate without strong backing by the Reagan White House. The President has shied away from cutting cost-of-living increases even though he is aware of the need for this action to avert bankrupting the Social Security Trust Fund.

It is difficult to rationalize this position by an Administration staunchly committed to Draconian curtailments in other social programs, a selective fiscal ambivalence that the President should be hard put to justify.

San Francisco Chronicle
San Francisco, Calif., May 12, 1981

SOCIAL SECURITY benefits, for the first time in memory, are on their way to being reduced in their impact on the federal budget. Last week the Senate finally addressed the issue of the Consumer Price Index, long the subject of complaints that it unrealistically reflects the actual cost of living, particularly for the elderly. On a close vote senators agreed to replace it by an index based on the national average increase in wages. This would save nearly $8 billion for fiscal 1982. It will not, however, deprive present Social Security recipients of an increase of 11.2 percent in their benefits due July 1. The CPI index has already guaranteed them this substantial boost.

Social Security outlays are now running over $150 billion and heading fast toward insolvency. The need for still other substantial curtailments besides the indexing reform must, we believe, be faced, probably by upping the age of eligibility for full benefits to 68.

The Birmingham News

Birmingham, Ala., November 9, 1981

When it comes to rescuing Social Security, Democrats in Congress are cowardly lions. They roar a lot, but they flee at the first sign of being counted among those who would restore the system to health.

Under pressure from top Democratic leaders, the House Ways and Means Committee rejected a proposal to raise the regular retirement age of Social Security beneficiaries and change the way cost-of-living increases are calculated.

Behind the rejection are Democratic hopes that inevitable changes in Social Security benefits can be hung around the necks of President Reagan and congressional Republicans and that Democrats can profit politically by so doing.

Left as main issues for House-Senate conferees are whether to reduce the minimum Social Security benefit for persons also receiving government pensions or who are living overseas and how to rob Peter to pay Paul.

TULSA WORLD

Tulsa, Okla., November 6, 1981

CONGRESSIONAL Democrats, with the agreement of many Republicans, have decided to follow Scarlet O'Hara's philosophy when confronted with perplexing problems: Worry about them tomorrow.

No better example can be found than the way they have decided to ignore the troubles of the Social Security system. A head-on attack on the actuarial woes of the system is required if the system is to be sound in the future.

As it now stands, the system could be bankrupt in a couple of years, depending on the economy.

But tampering with Social Security is political dynamite and Congressional elections are but a year away. Congressmen shutter to think of running for re-election at the very time that cost-of-living raises for Social Security recipients were being lowered or that millions of folks learned their retirement had been delayed from age 65 to 68.

Thus the House Wage and Means Committee decided the only safe thing to do was to squelch such proposals and consider instead shuffling money from the various trust funds of Social Security to be able to ride past next year's election.

"It's a disgrace the way we have turned tail and run on Social Security," said Rep. Barber Conable, R-N. Y., who with Democrat J. J. Pickle of Texas has been trying to change the system to ensure its solvency.

He's right, of course, and Congressmen will find, like Scarlet, that tomorrow does come and with it the same old problems that were avoided yesterday.

Meanwhile, its rob-Peter-to-pay-Paul time for Social Security, so Congress can get about the important business of getting re-elected.

The Salt Lake Tribune

Salt Lake City, Utah, November 6, 1981

If the Social Security system is (or ever was) in as bad shape as President Reagan and others in high places said, the chances seem good that it will remain in that sad shape for some time yet.

Judging by Congress' lack of eagerness to address the supposed danger of the system going broke, either the lawmakers are plain remiss in their duty to millions of Americans or the need for remedial action is not, and never was, all that urgent.

Of the two options, the latter is probably nearer the truth. One has to assume that there is still ample time to perform whatever tinkering is necessary. The collective wisdom of the national legislature may not be overwhelming but it is sufficient to realize that Social Security cannot be allowed to falter.

The same Congress that over the years has loaded benefit upon benefit on the Social Security wagon surely won't turn its politically sensitive back on some 36 million retirees now.

If that reading of the situation is correct, there is nothing to worry about. And never mind that the House Ways and Means Committee this week defeated an attempt to deal with the system's long-term financing problem and also decided to abandon the attempt to draft a solution for its alleged short-run funds shortage.

In the good old days when the lawmakers were sweetening the Social Security pie about every other year, the sugar was always stirred in prior to an election. Now that congressional action regarding Social Security is more likely to involve tightening up or even taking away, the system's needs are not likely to get significant attention until after the next nationwide election in November, 1982.

If we are not mistaken, 1982 is the year the retirement trust fund was supposed to run dry. Your friendly representatives in Congress apparently know that it won't. That's some comfort, but not much.

The Boston Globe

Boston, Mass., November 11, 1981

Sooner or later Congress will have to pass a Social Security package more or less like that rejected last Wednesday by the House Ways and Means Committee. Better sooner than later, for the integrity of the system and for the retirement planning benefit of millions of workers still on the job.

The Ways and Means Committee vote rejected an amendment to a Senate bill that would have trimmed future increases in benefits by linking them to wage increases rather than changes in the Consumer Price Index. More important, it would have raised the retirement age by stages to age 68 by the end of the century.

These modifications in the system are necessary to cope with a bulge in the working population that will reach retirement age in that period. The work force thereafter will decline quite signficantly, just as the number of births has declined steadily for the past 20 years.

The importance of passing such legislation, sponsored in this case by Rep. J. J. Pickle (D-Tex.), chairman of the subcommittee on Social Security, is that it will help prevent nasty surprises for future retirees. If they know now that they will have to work an additional year, two or three, they will be psychologically prepared for the fact when the time comes.

Surprises are the bane of any retirement system. The legislation now passing through Congress has had to undo one such surprise, President Reagan's elimination of the minimum $122-a-month benefit, unwisely enacted by Congress last July in its rush to a summer recess.

The Pickle amendment unfortunately got involved in matters that are partially extraneous. President Reagan has established, but not yet named members to a special commission to study the structure of Social Security. Legislators like Pickle doubt seriously whether the commission will discover anything not already well known to those familiar with Social Security issues and argue that the commission will merely delay necessary changes in the system.

In fairness, at least some of the committee members who voted against the Pickle amendment did so on the grounds that it was flawed in various ways and that a better approach can be found. The fact remains that they did not generate legislative alternatives to those offered by Pickle.

It is unquestionably true that the Pickle amendment did not by itself go far enough with some issues. The health insurance portion of Social Security distributes benefits on the basis of medical need rather than on any basis connected with earnings of beneficiaries, as are retirement and survivor benefits. Health insurance should be supported at least in part by general revenues rather than payroll taxes.

Congress cannot hope to escape from the problem by putting it off. Furthermore, Congress does the public no favors by postponing shifts in the system. It merely guarantees that future retirees will have a more difficult time planning and that all surprises will be unpleasant ones. The elderly do not need that.

THE LINCOLN STAR

Lincoln, Neb., November 6, 1981

There can be hardly anything but apprehension in the wake of a House Ways and Means Committee rejection of a proposal to change Social Security for the sake of the program's fiscal integrity. And it is baffling, to say the least, to watch Washington's inability to take a realistic approach to this matter.

The plan rejected in the House committee would have raised the age for full retirement benefits under Social Security from age 65 to age 66, hardly a massive or crippling change. Also, the proposal would have slowed cost-of-living increases after 1983 by using a measuring stick other than the present cost-of-living report. A bonus would have been provided for those who postpone retirement to age 67 or 68.

None of those is a sweeping change, none of them would affect the benefits of current retirees and none of them could have worked a very great hardship on anyone in the future. All of them were defeated in the face of growing evidence that the program is headed for financial disaster within the current decade.

We do not believe that the program should be changed in any manner that would reduce current benefits or that the intent of the program should be seriously impaired for future retirees but it is ridiculous for the country to go along year after year doing nothing in the face of pending difficulties. It is ridiculous for our elected representatives to refuse to look seriously at this program, much less to consider any changes, at all.

Such a head-in-the-sand position can be based only in political cowardness. The approach in Congress is bedded in the belief that when disaster strikes, the problem will then be met.

We think that is largely true. We do not believe the government would ever let the Social Security program default or go completely broke. But it is quite possible that the program could be in such financial straits as to make radical surgery necessary, while a minor operation could well avert that pending doom.

One of the House backers of the proposed changes, Republican Rep. Barber Conable of New York, remarked that "it's a disgrace the way we've turned tail and run on Social Security." The tail-turning is purely political, with too few public officials willing to take the heat that changes would engender. They are unwilling to run the risk of possible voter reaction against them. Such an attitude may serve their personal security today but it does nothing for the benefit of future Social Security recipients who could find the program badly shattered.

THE INDIANAPOLIS NEWS

Indianapolis, Ind., November 10, 1981

Social Security continues to face the same old problems, and Congress continues to avoid applying any new solutions to them.

House and Senate conferees have been reduced once again to considering a short-term measure to tide the system through its immediate funding crisis. The House Ways and Means Committee guaranteed this when its members recently rejected two measures: The first to raise the retirement age of beneficiaries and the second to change the way cost-of-living increases are calculated.

Congress has been rife with much ado about what turned out to be nothing this session toward reforming Social Security. Proposals, such as the one to eliminate the minimum benefit, have had more lives than a cat and then inevitably have died. In the process, however, Congress and the President have managed needlessly to scare and worry countless individuals who do, or are expecting to, rely upon Social Security in their retirement.

Democrats defend a Maginot line against any reductions in Social Security benefits; consequently, this Congress is unlikely to approve any in the near future. That won't make the problem go away. Social Security's pension and disability funds are predicted to have no reserves by late 1982. New figures indicate that because of larger-than-expected hospital costs, the Medicare fund will be in financial trouble sooner than expected.

Right now, however, Congress is likely to approve nothing more than permitting the system to borrow from its solvent funds to bail out those running dry. As a solution, that proposal is attractive only in comparison to the notion of borrowing funds from general tax revenues.

Clearly, because inevitably it will involve discussion of curbing benefits, the issue is a political hand grenade. It has to be solved, not tossed around.

Just as clearly that is going to take a bipartisan effort. No one party on its own has the political courage to talk about cutting Social Security benefits. The past year's talk without action serves no constructive purpose.

THE DENVER POST

Denver, Colo., November 7, 1981

MILLIONS OF Americans inched closer to financial insecurity Wednesday when the House Ways and Means Committee refused to reform the U.S. Social Security System. Pressured by House Speaker Tip O'Neill, the Democratic majority voted to continue the present "Ponzi scheme" which buys political popularity at the risk of ultimate bankruptcy.

A Ponzi scheme is a sort of chain-letter. A swindler named Ponzi once borrowed money and secretly used the borrowed capital itself to pay the lenders extravagant dividends. The purpose was to lure still more victims. Eventually Ponzi skipped town, leaving a few early investors with windfall gains and a massive number of destitute latecomers. The theory has lived on in such ploys as Glenn W. Turner's "Dare to be Great" pyramid sales scheme — and Social Security.

Of course, Social Security doesn't share Ponzi's dastardly *motive*. It was born with the noble goal of providing a financial floor under older Americans. But the method of financing *is* similar to Ponzi's — and subject to the same mathematical laws that eventually undermine all chain letters.

Political demagogues pretend the system is like a private pension plan, with retirees drawing benefits from trusts established from their contributions. That isn't true. People pay in, all right, but that money isn't invested. Except for a relatively small reserve, it is paid out as fast as it comes in. Lately, outflow has been faster than income.

In 1938, an entire generation began to draw Social Security despite having paid in little or nothing. Each generation after that intial one has paid taxes to support the retirees ahead of it — counting on those born still later to keep the chain intact. That system worked well enough in the beginning because average life expectancy was about nine years less than today. At the start, there were about nine workers for every retiree, a light burden.

Today, longer life expectancies and lower birth rates have dropped the ratio of active workers to retirees to 4-1. When the post-World War II "baby boom" reaches retirement age around the year 2010, there will only be *two* workers for each retiree. Then, the present system must either tax the next generation mercilessly — or go belly up. Even today, the Social Security tax is stiff — higher than income tax for many — and programmed to go higher.

There is a simple way to stave off Social Security bankruptcy — raise the retirement age to 68.

Because the underlying problem is long-term, that change could be phased in gradually so that people nearing retirement now don't have to upset long-laid plans. Raising the age for full benefits increases the number of active workers paying in while reducing the amount of benefits paid out. It also ensures that retirees can receive a decent sum.

Americans aren't "washed up" at 65 — they're not only living longer, those extra years are healthier as well. That fact was recognized recently when Congress outlawed mandatory retirement at age 65. It's time to extend the same realism to Social Security.

The plan defeated Wednesday was a bipartisan effort drafted by Social Security subcommittee chairman J.J. Pickle, D-Texas, and senior Republican Barber Conable, R-N.Y. It would have ensured the system's future solvency in a number of ways, including raising the basic retirement age. On O'Neill's orders, the plan was killed on a largely party-line vote of 18-14.

But, while Democrats may relish posing in the next election as the champion of Social Security benefits, the fact is that O'Neill's tactic undermined the financial security of every working American. Even those people drawing on the system now must wonder whether they can live out their days before the Ponzi scheme collapses under their feet.

Annual Trustees' Report Forecasts Insolvency by 1982

The annual report by the trsutees of the Social Security Administration in 1981 once again warned that the system faced financial collapse. The trustees—the Secretaries of the Departments of Health and Human Services, Labor and the Treasury—stated that without congressional action the retirement fund "will be unable to make benefit payments on time beginning in the latter half of 1982." This grim repetition of the system's funding problems promised to intensify the political battle already raging in Congress, as Democrats and Republicans alternately accused each other of ignoring the crisis and attempting to undercut support for the elderly.

Herald News

Fall River, Mass., July 27, 1981

House Speaker O'Neill has once again assailed President Reagan in terms of the administration's Social Security proposals. The Speaker claims that the Social Security system is not as badly off as the President believes. Perhaps he is right. In the dense area of government financing it is almost impossible for the public to know what the facts are.

This is part of the trouble. It is not that the public mistrusts either the President or the Speaker. They are both honest men. But it simply does not know whose figures to believe, or whose view is correct.

In terms of government this happens all the time. All spring successive statements indicated Boston was on the verge of bankruptcy. Then, without much, if any, explanation, it was learned that the city had funds that could be used to stave off financial collapse. The public was pleased, but mystified. The next time Boston is in a fiscal crisis, it will be wary about crediting the prophets of doom.

The same thing applies to the confusion over Social Security.

The system is far too important to far too many people for confusion about its condition to be tolerated for long. The first order of business is to find out precisely how serious its plight may be. That will not be as easy as it seems. Otherwise the present disagreement between the President and the Speaker of the House would not arise.

Easy or not, it must be done, and the public must be told precisely what the facts are. The people dependent on Social Security must know where they stand.

The current controversy has partisan implications. So much is obvious. But it also has vital implications for millions of Americans, who have a right to clear cut explanations about the system whose solvency they have relied on all their working lives.

The News and Courier

Charleston, S.C., July 8, 1981

The visible result, so far, of Ronald Reagan's warnings of trouble ahead for Social Security is a sharp drop in presidential popularity. People seem to be confusing the messenger with the message. They are taking it out on Mr. Reagan for bringing bad news. A suprising number have jumped to the wrong conclusion that the president has it in for them when he says what they need to know: Social Security system is going bankrupt.

Congress has not been helpful in clarifying the presidential message. Republicans have stood back from it. Democrats have scoffed at it.

It's about time both sides dropped the foolishness. Congress created the situation in which Social Security is said to be spending a dollar for every 90 cents it takes in. It should be doing what it has to do to end it. It doesn't have all the time in the world . The trust fund for the principal Social Security program that provides retirement and survivors benefits is scheduled to run out of money soon.

Much can be done by both parties in Congress to help voters understand more clearly the nature of the Social Security problem and wean them, if possible, from the urge to cut off the head of the messenger who brings bad news. Republicans have a way to go in creating the atmosphere of crisis which ought to prevail in connection with this issue — of all issues. Democrats need to make it a bipartisan effort.

Mr. Reagan's ideas for restoring solvency by trimming benefits — not wiping them out, as some hysterical people claim — and reducing program eligibility offer the easiest way out of difficulty. If people don't like his ideas then perhaps they will want to raise taxes or tap general revenues. Either way, they had better get moving. A time bomb is ticking in the Social Security system.

THE ATLANTA CONSTITUTION

Atlanta, Ga., July 7, 1981

The headline says, "Social Security Called In Danger Of Going Broke." That is both true and not true.

First, rest assured that Social Security is not going to go "broke" in the strict sense. There is, for sure, a shortfall of hundreds of billions of dollars rapidly developing between the current benefits already promised to retirees and persons nearing retirement, and the funds available to Social Security to pay those benefits. But, if the need should develop, the federal government would fund the benefits in some shape or fashion, probably from general taxes, until the Social Security program can be put on a financially sound basis.

Second, obtaining that financially sound basis will take years, even decades. Social Security cannot continue to operate forever under its current system. Warnings about Social Security difficulties have been made for years now, but real debate about the changes has begun only recently; the current Congress may well begin making the needed changes.

More than likely, the first major changes will be raising the retirement age and changing the cost-of-living adjustments. The retirement age, the age when one can receive full benefits, will probably be phased in over a considerable period of years from the current 65 to 68. In conjunction with this, the early retirement age will probably be increased from the current 62 to 64 or 65.

The cost-of-living adjustments have been controversial for years now. Under current regulations, Social Security retirement benefits are boosted annually a percentage equal to the increase in the Consumer Price Index. This year, benefits went up 11.2 percent; last year, 14.3 percent. These increases add many billions of dollars to Social Security benefits. The idea for the adjustments is to keep retirees up with inflation. But the fact is that some elements in the Consumer Price Index are greatly overweighted in terms of their effects on most retired persons. For example, the cost of housing and home loans make up some 40 percent of the CPI; how many retired persons do you know who are buying new homes and paying current mortgage interest rates? A special CPI will likely be developed for determining Social Security benefit adjustments.

Other changes will probably be made in Social Security over the coming years, both in how the system is financed and how it pays benefits. Social Security can be made a financially secure system without placing an unduly heavy tax burden on workers. There are various reasons why Social Security went wrong, but the prime thing to be understood now is that the "promises" will be kept; a perfect example of this is how quickly Congress earlier this year killed the Reagan administration's proposal of severely reducing the benefits paid to those persons currently choosing early retirement. The second prime thing to understand is that Social Security must be corrected, or in a few more decades, the entire financial wherewithal of the United States could not support it.

THE SACRAMENTO BEE

Sacramento, Calif., July 9, 1981

Yet another study on Social Security, this one a Cabinet-level report, warns that the system faces financial collapse, possibly next year, unless Congress does something. The warning is no longer new. We hear it repeatedly, watch television commentators ask whether retirees will get their checks next month, or wonder what life would be like without Social Security. The problem is, of course, serious, but predictions that the Social Security sky is falling only creates fears without shedding light on the problem or its possible solutions. The latest report by the secretaries of Labor, Treasury, and Health and Human Services added new information, not encouraging, and reiterated the possible solutions, none of them easy.

The report's pessimistic new wrinkle is that borrowing from the system's disability and Medicare funds — which have surpluses and thus are frequently mentioned as a source for making the retirement program solvent — won't work, at least not for long. Congress might buy some time through interfund borrowing, perhaps four years under adverse economic conditions, or perhaps enough to get us through the '80s under better conditions. But even these funds face long-range problems of their own due to soaring health care costs and the growing numbers of elderly people.

Besides interfund borrowing, the only alternatives for saving the system without actually cutting benefits are using general funds or raising Social Security payroll taxes. Neither approach has much political support. As for reducing benefits, the Reagan administration's proposal for such reductions for those who retire at age 62 (from the present 80 percent of full benefits to only 55 percent) ran into a storm of opposition from the Congress and the public. A less draconian proposal by Rep. J.J. Pickle, D-Texas, to increase the retirement age from 65 to 68 and to use a portion of the Medicare funds for the troubled pension fund met with mixed reaction.

But if the system is to avert bankruptcy, it will have to undergo fundamental changes in financing and disbursements. Congress will have little choice but to enact some combination of those proposals which have drawn vehement opposition. Unfortunately, there is no agreement on Capitol Hill, no national consensus, except on the fact that Social Security is in trouble.

Which is why Senate subcommittee hearings this week on the problem could be pivotal. The hearings are intended to determine the seriousness of the situation and to create a climate of bipartisan cooperation on a solution. Congress, busy with tax legislation, isn't likely to take up Social Security this year. And with the matter postponed until 1982, an election year, chances of adopting a bill containing politically unpopular provisions will require strong bipartisan support. If Congress fails to achieve that cooperation and fails to act soon, then there may indeed be reason to heed worried voices wondering about next month's Social Security check.

THE WALL STREET JOURNAL

New York, N.Y., July 13, 1981

The Reagan administration's timing on its Social Security plan has been the only misstep in an otherwise impressive economic policy performance. This spring—amid a growing consensus that *something* had to be done to head off the fast approaching crisis—the House and the Senate trotted out some modest and generally sensible proposals. Then came the Reagan plan, which also contained some modest and sensible cuts and changes.

Well. Just like the third person on a match, the Reagan plan drew all the heavy fire. So heavy, in fact, that some foxhole companions panicked: The Senate passed a sense of the Senate resolution condemning the plan by a vote of 96 to 0.

Now, two months later, things are unchanged. Members of Congress returning from July 4 picnics back home report that the voters are still outraged by the Reagan plan and the Social Security system still lurches toward disaster. Indeed, fresh proof was offered last week by the trustees who said, simply, that without help OASI "will be unable to make benefit payments on time beginning in the latter half of 1982." That means next year.

Perhaps it's time, then, to take another, cooler look at the Reagan plan. As we opined this spring, one of the most attractive ways to get the system back on its financial feet would be to encourage people to stay in the work force longer. And we don't mean that your 87-year-old grandma has to go out and wheel an ice cream cart around town; we mean the group who now takes "early" retirement at age 62 instead of waiting for "normal" retirement at age 65.

That is exactly the group targeted by the Reagan plan. Under the current system, people can opt for retirement as early as 62 and receive 80% of their full benefits; the rate rises from 80% as retirement age increases. The administration plan would cut that rate to 55% at age 62 but leave unchanged the achievement of 100% of full benefits at age 65. (This is in contrast to the House plan which would move normal, full retirement up from age 65 to age 68.)

Having people stay in the work force three years longer makes good sense. The retirement age of 65 was set when Social Security was created in 1936. Now people live longer and in better health. Life expectancy runs about 80 years and studies show that only 10% of early retirees cite bad health as the reason. (We could, of course, point out that our own President is 70 years old and in great shape.)

Having people stay in the work force three years longer also makes good economic sense: More payroll taxes will be paid and fewer benefits will be drawn. And there is reason to believe that removing the financial incentive to retire early will be effective. After all, the financial incentives have certainly worked the other way: Paying benefits to pre-65 retirees began 30 years ago—that also marked the beginning of the trend toward earlier retirement. For example, in 1957, only 16% of those eligible were receiving benefits by age 64; in 1976, that number had leaped to over 61%. It's now even higher.

Ending the financial incentives to early retirement is a good provision of a good overall plan to restore Social Security to good health. The Reagan plan deserves a second chance.

Houston Chronicle

Houston, Texas, July 9, 1981

The hearing on Social Security being held by a Senate subcommittee is producing sounds reminiscent of tom-toms. Just as a tribe might pound drums while working up to an unpleasant task such as war, congressmen are beating on tables at hearings as they get prepared to either cut Social Security payments or increase taxes, or both.

The facts being brought out at the hearing are no surprise at all. For months now, statisticians have been pointing out that the Social Security changes made in 1977 are not protecting the system from financial difficulty. The combination of inflation, early retirements, longer lives and fewer workers means the funds available will not cover promised benefits. The figures can't really be argued with.

The three Cabinet officers who issued the Social Security System's annual report spoke of urgent needs, financial crisis and even the possibility of going broke. Some Democrats declared the Republicans were exaggerating the situation to help balance the federal budget. That only amounts to some people beating the drums louder than others. It doesn't change the figures one whit.

We admire the approach being taken by Rep. J.J. Pickle, D-Austin. Rep. Pickle in 1979 became chairman of the House Ways and Means Committee's subcommittee on Social Security. He knew it was not likely to be a post that would win him popularity, but he sharpened his knowledge about the system and has been carefully stating the need for changes for many months now.

"The immediate, imperative problem that is upon us is to keep Social Security solvent," Rep. Pickle declares. He has several options and says almost any one is acceptable except the one of doing nothing, which would mean the monthly checks would stop. Sooner or later, the rest of Congress is going to have to stop beating the drums and join Rep. Pickle in facing the facts.

The Providence Journal

Providence, R.I., July 9, 1981

The national Social Security system, warns its trustees, may go bankrupt as early as 1982. Despite that scary report, elderly Americans ought not panic. Congress won't let it happen.

This prediction has nothing to do with actuarial data, and everything to do with politics. No congressman wants to face up to 35 million angry retired American voters. Witness the Senate's 96-to-zero vote earlier this year against President Reagan's proposal to cut back early retirement benefits from 80 percent to 55 percent for those who elect to retire at age 62 instead of 65.

But Congress has turned its back to reality for the last time. With the Social Security fund about to run out of money next year, it can do only one of two things — either cut benefits or find new sources of revenue. It has already demonstrated its spine in regards to the first option. That leaves it looking for new income.

The most obvious source for new revenues, higher payroll taxes, has already been preempted. Last January the tax went up to 6.65 percent, for employers as well as workers, on the first $29,700 earned. That was the first increment in a schedule that will raise the tax to 7.65 percent of a rising base figure over the next decade.

There are a baker's dozen of other options. The least politically traumatic, and therefore most promising, include: Folding the thousands of government civil servants, who now have their separate pension fund, into the Social Security

system; revising the annual cost-of-living adjustment (COLA) downward, either to a more conservative version of the Consumer Price Index, or to the average COLA gained by working Americans; and taxing Social Security benefits for upper-income recipients.

A strong case can be made for separating the Disability Insurance, Survivors' Benefit and Medicare programs from the Social Security system and handling them on their own merits. But as they are funded separately, they are a neutral factor in the pension fund figures. (Medicare's Hospital Insurance fund, incidentally, is in potentially worse trouble than the Social Security fund, posing yet another major problem for Congress.)

Two other options should be, but for political reasons probably won't be adopted. One is President Reagan's proposal to discourage early retirement by sharply cutting back the benefits. As noted above, the Senate unanimously buried that one earlier this year, giving Mr. Reagan his first defeat in Congress.

The other justifiable change, probably too hot for Congress to handle, is raising the retirement age to 68. Americans are living longer and enjoying better health today than they were forty years ago when the retirement age was arbitrarily set at 65. There is no reason why the span of productive working years should not be correspondingly lengthened — no reason, that is, other than the frustration of millions of middle-aged Americans who are looking forward to packing it in at age 65.

The Charlotte Observer

Charlotte, N.C., July 8, 1981

It should have come as no surprise to anyone when trustees of the Social Security system announced Monday that the retirement trust fund will be bankrupt by the end of next year unless it can start bringing in more money or paying out less. The trustees issued the stark warning on the eve of Senate hearings on the president's Social Security reform proposals, hoping to inject a sense of urgency into those deliberations. Clearly, a sense of urgency is appropriate.

The administration's proposals drew bipartisan fire when they were announced about two months ago, and Social Security Commissioner John Svahn says the administration is willing to negotiate on some points. But he said the administration won't bend in its opposition to tapping general revenues to bail out the retirement fund. It shouldn't.

There is room for debate over various proposals to save the system, but two possibilities ought to be ruled out at the start: going into the general fund, and raising Social Security taxes again. Either move would undermine efforts to hold down federal spending and stimulate the economy through tax relief.

While the administration is right

about what *shouldn't* be done, some of its proposals are unnecessarily harsh. For example, it would cut benefits to early retirees sharply and abruptly. A better plan would be to phase in a higher retirement age schedule.

And there are some promising proposals the administration isn't backing. One is to revise the basis of adjusting benefits for inflation, perhaps by establishing a separate inflation index for that purpose. The Consumer Price Index is too heavily weighted by new housing costs and other items that have little impact on most retired people. Congress also ought to give serious consideration to bringing federal employees, who have a separate retirement plan, into the Social Security system — a move that would add substantially to revenues.

All those proposals fall far short of real structural reform, of course. The immediate need is for change that will get the system past the current crisis. But an administration elected with a mandate for large-scale change ought to take a fresh look at the structure and purpose of the system.

An internal study might trigger partisan controversy, but Mr. Reagan could minimize that possibility by appointing a bipartisan commission to study the system and its future.

THE INDIANAPOLIS STAR

Indianapolis, Ind., July 28, 1981

Thirty years ago Sen. Robert A. Taft and others were warning that the Social Security was unsound and headed for bankruptcy.

Instead of stabilizing the system, liberals in Congress kept extending it to cover more and more classes of beneficiaries, creating and adding new and growing welfare functions to the program.

This increased drain made Social Security even more unsound and hastened the day of its impending bankruptcy.

No doubt it would have been better if Congress, not only in drawing up the Social Security Act of 1935, but in subsequent legislation, had the so-called Old Age and Survivors Insurance element of the program separate from all other phases.

This would have facilitated better public scrutiny of the OASI program and its financing and weaknesses. It also might have helped, to some extent, to depoliticize the OASI program, which is the hottest political volcano in Social Security and one of the hottest in U.S. politics.

Instead, at the outset, various welfare features were woven into Social Security and at intervals from then on many others were added while benefits were immensely increased. The day of reckoning drew closer.

Now in mid-1981 we are informed by the three Cabinet officers who are its trustees that Social Security's retirement fund will go broke by the end of next year and that the related Medicare program may collapse within the decade unless taxes are raised or benefits cut.

No matter how officials juggle the retirement fund and the Medicare and disability funds, the day approaches when more money will come out than is going in.

One way to postpone the day of reckoning is to cut benefits. Another is to raise taxes.

Either way will be painful. A combination of the two would be painful. But the alternative is bankruptcy. That would be both painful and calamitous.

Reagan administration preliminary proposals for saving Social Security are not Holy Writ. The door was left open to alternatives by the Cabinet officers who compiled the report, Health and Human Services Secretary Richard Schweiker, Labor Secretary Ray Donovan and Treasury Secretary Donald T. Regan.

At the same time, any alternatives cannot stray too far from the pattern and substance of those general proposals.

The approaching debacle has been a long time in the making. Reckless, vote-snaring politicians turned the Social Security system into a gargantuan horn of plenty and spread the delusion that there could be no end to the benefits.

It wasn't true. At last, the country may have a President with the will to tackle the mess inherited from generations of lawmakers who proved themselves to be little more than confidence artists. But only time will tell how Mr. Reagan can handle this painful but inevitable issue.

The San Diego Union

San Diego, Calif., July 9, 1981

Congress has brought the Social Security system to the edge of bankruptcy by promising more than the system could deliver. Now Congress must find a way to keep solvent this fund that is the basic retirement support of millions of Americans.

This week, the Social Security system's trustees warned in their annual report that the Old Age and Survivors Trust Fund will run out of money by the end of next year. Even combining the trust fund with the Medicare and disability funds, which are still solvent, will not head off bankruptcy for long, unless the national economy improves phenomenally. Although the trustees may exaggerate the problem, as Sen. Daniel P. Moynihan, D-N.Y., charges, the trust funds are undeniably in trouble.

We've had other warnings about Social Security solvency, but this one seems to confirm the worst. Still, it's unlikely that Congress will allow the Social Security system to go broke. Aside from the shattering consequences of bankruptcy, the 35 million beneficiaries of the pension fund are a voting block too strong to ignore.

Thus, Congress has three choices: It can raise Social Security taxes again, reduce benefits, or give the pension fund a transfusion of tax money from general funds. Payroll taxes went up sharply this year and will rise again in 1982. Therefore, unpopular as it will be, a reduction in benefits is more likely than another tax increase.

Congress will be tempted, of course, to bail out the system with an infusion of general fund money — a course that will only lead to increasing deficits and bigger bailouts in the future unless necessary reforms are made.

One relatively simple reform should have been in place long before now, and that is abolishing the annual adjustment of benefits to the Consumer Price Index. Many economists believe this yardstick of inflation runs ahead of actual price increases and itself is inflationary.

Similarly, Congress ought to resurrect the Reagan administration's proposals that came under such bitter partisan attack earlier this year. The administration prudently wants to reduce benefits for those who retire before 65, tighten eligibility for disability benefits, and introduce phased cuts in future retirement and survivors pensions. These steps would not only give Social Security the quick relief it needs, but would help solve the long-term financial problems, as well.

Basically, the Social Security system suffers from the excessive expectations of Americans who have been told by their political leaders that the federal system would keep them in middle-class comfort in their old age. In fact, Social Security was established as a supplement to private savings, rather than a total support for the elderly.

As Social Security is reorganized along sound lines, it will become less burdensome to the economy. Congress, therefore, should lose no time in encouraging a return to the plan's original concept of supplementing individual thrift and reliance on private pension plans.

The Reagan administration has provided a means to do this by proposing that the favored tax treatment now accorded some workers for Individual Retirement Accounts (IRA) be extended to all workers. The administration would increase the maximum contributions from workers with no private pension plans from the present $1,500 to $2,000 a year tax-free. Workers with pension plans could contribute $1,000 a year tax-free to an IRA.

The immediate financial problems of Social Security require a reduction of benefits the system cannot afford to pay. The long-term problems should be met by thrift incentives and the encouragement by Congress of private pension plans to reduce the dependence of most Americans upon a system that was only intended to be a safety net.

The Burlington Free Press

Burlington, Vt., July 8, 1981

Without major changes in the nation's Social Security system, the old age and retirement trust fund will go broke by late 1982, unable to meet its commitments to the elderly, according to three of President Reagan's cabinet officers who serve as the system's trustees.

They have predicted, too, that the Medicare program could be in trouble in a decade unless taxes are increased or benefits slashed.

The trustees' comments in their annual report paint a dismal picture for millions of recipients of Social Security and those who are nearing retirement. Unless something is done to correct the ailments of the system, those who expected to derive benefits from it could be forced to continue working beyond conventional retirement age.

When Social Security came into being in 1935, it was designed to provide supplemental benefits to the elderly. It was not a pension program. President Franklin D. Roosevelt, its architect, saw it as a means of helping elderly who were living on the verge of starvation during the Depression. Through contributions from employers and employees, a trust fund to provide money to meet the minimal needs of the aged was to be built up by the government.

Since that time, however, Social Security has been expanded to cover other programs that were not included in the original legislation. And the government has borrowed from the trust fund from time to time and has never repaid its debt.

Medicare and the disability fund have been created to share the contributions made by workers and their employers. Medicare amounts to a national health insurance program for the aged.

The disability fund covers those workers whose careers are cut short by disease or injury. Neither program properly belongs in the Social Security system. As welfare programs, they should be funded by general revenues. Congress must consider a proposal to sever them from the system.

Federal employees are covered by a separate retirement system that is supported by the public's tax dollars. In many cases, retired federal employees take jobs in the private sector and work until they can qualify for Social Security benefits. Congress must take steps to stop the practice and put federal employees under the umbrella of Social Security, even though congressmen are beneficiaries of the retirement system. It is patently inequitable to ask employees in the private sector of the economy to contribute money to the federal retirement program.

If those fundamental changes are made in the Social Security system as soon as possible, it is likely that the trust fund's solvency will be restored and the government will be able to meet the commitments it has made to the nation's elderly for some years to come.

NEW YORK POST

New York, N.Y., July 8, 1981

When the Reagan Administration's plans for drastic cuts in the Social Security system were rejected by a stunning 96-0 Senate vote, the message seemed to be that the President had invaded an impregnable political sanctuary, and had been given a rough lesson in "political realism."

But the issue would not go away. It has been abruptly revived by the annual report of the Social Security Board of Trustees warning that the massive program faces the real peril of bankruptcy. Even under the most optimistic projections, the report declares, the system will "barely get through the early 1980s."

There is no mystery about the causes of the approaching crisis. Large increases in the number of early retirements have not been matched by growth in the work force. As a result, total payments to beneficiaries increasingly exceed the contributions of those still at work, and their employers.

Meanwhile, the generous cost-of-living provisions continually increase the payouts and, indeed, the 36 million Americans who receive Social Security checks have just received a further 11.2 rise that will deplete the fund by an additional $15.4 billion in the coming 12 months.

It requires no mathematical genius to work out that ways must be found either to increase contributions to the fund or to decrease benefits — or, most plausibly, both. Obviously provisions that discourage early retirement represent one elementary recourse.

There is no wholly painless formula. The intolerable alternative is to let things drift in deference to immediate political pressure. No change in the structure now contemplated could conceivably come close to creating the human and national disaster that collapse of the system would trigger.

"Social Security can regain permanent solvency if it does not become a political grenade, being lobbed back and forth for exploitive purposes," Sen. William Armstrong (R-Col.), chairman of the Social Security subcommittee, said as his panel began hearings yesterday.

It will be hard for many politicians to accept the spirit of that statement. But they will poorly serve their constituents if they try to deny or minimize the reality of the crisis.

ST. LOUIS POST-DISPATCH

St. Louis, Mo., July 8, 1981

The annual report of the trustees of the Social Security Administration will undoubtedly be used by the Reagan administration to reinforce its contention that Social Security benefits must be curtailed, but in fact there are other, far less onerous solutions to the impending funding crisis. That the system faces a funding crisis toward the end of next year, as the trustees warned, is undeniable. Its precise dimensions are unclear, but they are indicated by the fact that last year's expenditures of $145 billion exceeded revenues by some $4 billion and that this year the difference will be even greater.

It does not follow, however, that the problem requires the significant benefit cuts proposed earlier by President Reagan and implicitly endorsed by the trustees, who are the secretaries of the departments of Health and Human Services, Labor and Treasury.

Underlying the alarming predictions of a bankrupt Social Security system are the twin evils of inflation and unemployment. The former causes outlays to go up — beginning July 1, for example, $15 billion was added to expenditures for the coming year by the automatic cost-of-living adjustment — and the latter causes receipts to go down — people who are not working do not pay the payroll tax. If both inflation and unemployment were to drop sharply over the next 12 months, the crisis would largely evaporate. No one, however, expects such a happy development.

But if economic conditions are not likely to improve sufficiently to solve Social Security's funding problem, neither are things apt to be so dismal as to require the cutbacks proposed by Mr. Reagan. That depends, of course, on which of the administration's economic projections one chooses to rely on. For purposes of estimating revenues and expenditures for the 1982 fiscal year and arriving at a federal deficit, the Reagan administration made some optimistic assumptions about economic growth and interest rate. But, reporter Jon Sawyer of the Post-Dispatch's Washington bureau reported the other day, the economic forecast used to justify the cuts in Social Security outlays was a good deal gloomier. It turned out, Mr. Sawyer disclosed, that the White House officials who prepared the package of Social Security cuts altered the projections supplied them by a private economic consulting firm.

As a result, the cuts Mr. Reagan proposed are well in excess of what will be needed. Indeed, they are so much so as to permit a cut in the Social Security tax in a few years, even by the administration's pessimistic projections. Whatever case can be made for reducing the payroll tax, it surely cannot rest on an impending funding crisis that requires sharp cutbacks in benefits for the disabled, for those who would retire early and for all retirees of the future. In fact, however, that is precisely what the White House has done.

Some alleviation of next year's projected crisis was contained in the budget measure that Congress approved at the end of June. It abolished the minimum benefit and payments to survivors who are attending college. Additional steps that could be taken include a modification of the cost-of-living formula; shifting money from the trust funds that enjoy a surplus to those that are running low, which Congress permitted last year; using general revenue funds to finance Medicare, or a portion of it, or using them to augment payroll tax collections when unemployment exceeds a certain level, and increasing the Social Security tax.

The point is that, contrary to the impression given in the trustees' report and encouraged by the White House, the sky is not falling on the Social Security system. Its funding problems are real enough, to be sure, but they are susceptible to a solution that stops short of the retrenchment favored by the administration.

Detroit Free Press

Detroit, Mich., July 8, 1981

SINCE WE'VE known for a while that Social Security is in trouble, the latest sepulchral report from the system's trustees — three members of President Reagan's cabinet — isn't exactly news. The gloomy reiteration of Social Security's problems is more likely designed to push Congress into accepting the president's proposals for a drastic slash in benefits and eligibility as the only way to rescue the system. But is it?

There are actually two separate issues facing Social Security. The first is the short-term problem, caused in great part by the sluggish economy: in the current recession, payroll taxes are not bringing in enough revenue to cover the outgo. The second is the long-range one: around the turn of the century, when the baby boom generation begins to retire, the number of persons drawing benefits will grow faster than the number of active workers paying into the system. At that point, unless changes have been introduced, the system will require a prohibitive level of taxation to support itself, or else go broke.

The trustees' report is more gloomy than the private studies on which it is based, but Social Security Commissioner John Svahn says the trustees are putting the problem in the worst possible light on purpose, in order to motivate Congress to prepare for the "worst case."

What this translates into is a program to cut deeply into the income of the elderly — especially the low-income elderly — in the 1980s with the excuse that it is necessary in order to solve a problem that will emerge 25 years hence. Some economists have speculated that the administration has a balder motive: that Mr. Reagan is simply trying to wring some $40-$80 billion in savings out of Social Security in order to bring the rest of his budget into the appearance of balance.

Social Security is in financial trouble, and it does require some changes and reforms. But as a raft of analysts have pointed out, the short-term problem can be solved in a number of ways. It is only the Old Age and Survivors' Insurance portion of the fund that faces immediate depletion. OASI could be kept afloat by a temporary transfer from the disability or other trust funds, or even from general revenues, while Congress works out the answer to the longer-term problem.

That answer might well include a gradual phasing in of a later retirement age, or an adjustment of the benefit formula — but the key word would be gradual. What the administration proposes is an abrupt change that would fall most heavily on those expecting to retire within the next two to five years, on low-income workers and the marginally employed who are not covered by other pension plans.

For millions of Americans who are nearing retirement after a lifetime of earning average or below-average wages, Social Security has held out the only promise of stability, security and self-reliance in their old age. Unless Congress has the will to decree otherwise, it is a promise that Ronald Reagan seems determined to break.

The Star-Ledger

Newark, N.J., July 10, 1981

How secure is Social Security?

A Reagan Administration report paints a grim picture. The trust fund which finances retirement payments will not be able to pay benefits next year, says Social Security Commissioner Jack Svahn, adding: "That's not a prediction, that's a certainty."

Cut benefits or hike taxes, the report warns, or the program will not survive.

Neither alternative is popular, and no one seriously believes there is any chance whatever that any elected or appointed official would permit the Social Security program to spend itself into oblivion.

But a small band of Senate Democrats, led by New York's articulate Daniel Patrick Moynihan, insists that the program is in better financial shape than the Reagan Administration portrays it. At a Senate subcommittee hearing, Mr. Moynihan said he doesn't believe a $100 billion cut in benefits is needed to save the program.

Joining in the opposition, Sen. Bill Bradley of New Jersey accused the White House of keeping two sets of books "by predicting a low-inflation, high-growth economy in its tax-reduction lobbying campaign and by forecasting a high-inflation low-growth economy in its assessment of Social Security's ills."

Even the Administration critics, however, agree that the program is racing headlong into serious financial problems just ahead, a unanimity that exposes Sen. Moynihan's glib characterization of the Reagan cutback proposals as "political terrorism" for what it is: Demogoguery for constituent consumption.

* * *

Sooner or later, the Democrats will have to produce a solution of their own. It probably will include such cost-saving changes as a gradual rise in the retirement age (now 65) at which full benefits are paid, and some adjustment in the cost-of-living formula intended to keep inflation from destroying the purchasing power of the monthly Social Security check.

As the hearings proceed, it would be well to remind Sen. Moynihan and his colleagues that President Reagan is not responsible for compromising the financial integrity of the program. Social Security is in fiscal trouble because an excessively generous Congress, currying votes in a shameful, undisguised manner, tacked on programs and ratcheted up benefit payments to irresponsible levels.

Social Security was never intended to be the sole support of retirees, but merely a supplement to savings and pension plans. By their oratory, promises and reckless changes to the system, Congress altered the public's perception of the program and raised expectations too high. Now that the balloon is about to burst, let's not forget who inflated it to the breaking point.

The Miami Herald

Miami, Fla., July 11, 1981

THE CAMEL, it is said, is a creature designed by a committee. So is the Social Security system. It was designed by the same committee that designed the straws that broke the camel's back.

Now that design committee — its name is Congress — must either remove some straws or put props beneath the camel. If it does not, the Old Age Survivors Insurance (OASI) trust fund, which pays retirement benefits to 36 million Americans, will be bankrupt within 18 months.

Congress could stave off that monumental disaster by borrowing from Social Security's other two trust funds, which pay disability and Medicare benefits. That shell game would last only a few years, however. Then those funds would be broke, too.

On Monday, the Secretaries of Labor, Treasury, and Health and Human Services, who are the Social Security system's trustees, formally reported their gloomy news to Congress. There are only two solutions, the trustees said: cut benefits, or raise taxes.

On Tuesday, a Senate committee began hearings on the Social Security crisis. The hearings immediately turned partisan. Democrats accused President Reagan of using invalid projections to justify his recent recommendations to raise the retirement age to 68 from 65, whack benefits to early retirees, and exclude some current recipients altogether.

The President's recommendations stirred a political firestorm, and he hastily retreated. He shouldn't have. His projections may be pessimistic in some particulars, but their general thrust is beyond dispute.

Mr. Reagan is not to blame for the system's endemic problems. Nor are the elderly who receive the benefits that created the problems, except insofar as they have demanded more and more from an OASI fund that can give no more without going broke.

The fault rests almost entirely with Congress. Successive Congresses have perverted the Social Security system's original concept of actuarial soundness into one of actuarial madness. Theoretically, the OASI fund should hold and invest the payments a worker makes when young until he retires. Then he should receive a pension paid from his own contributions, his employers', and the interest earned on both.

Congress is a body of politicians, not actuaries, however. Over the years, Congress has voted escalating Social Security benefits to be paid from a fund that it knew could not long sustain them. Soon it must rectify its profligacy, whatever the political consequences, or bring upon the nation's retirees social consequences of infinitely greater — indeed intolerable — gravity.

Instead of flaying President Reagan, let Congress turn to the urgent task of redesigning the Social Security camel and removing or lightening the straws that are breaking its back.

The Dispatch

Columbus, Ohio, July 9, 1981

IT IS TOO BAD that politicians, being politicians, are squeezing the maximum amount of publicity from the Social Security shortfall during current hearings before the U.S. Senate.

And it is doubtful the congressmen wringing their hands realize they are scaring the dickens out of Social Security recipients and also those soon to become eligible.

Statements such as the system will be bankrupt, completely bankrupt or effectively bankrupt in a year or two are frightening to those who have financed the program with a lifetime of toil.

The Congress has the figures which show no longer can the system be rescued by a series of temporary dikes.

Social Security recipients should rest assured the system will not be abandoned. If it were, the deserving elderly gentry would rebel at the ballot box and there would be more replacements in the Congress and administration than there are on the baseball fields today.

The goal of Congress should be to restore soundness — the integrity — of the Social Security system as soon as practical.

Today 115 million Americans pay Social Security taxes. About 35 million receive benefits from the old-age and disability funds and another 25 million participate in the Medicare program.

The Reagan administration says it is willing to compromise in pursuit of a bipartisan solution. Of course, the major problem is that the ranks of the elderly retired have been increasing out of proportion to the wage earners funding the system.

The public is aware there is no magic wand solution and that the two words around which a solution will evolve are benefits and taxes.

Increasing the eligible age for full benefits, penalizing those who retire early and reducing overall benefits will be considered. It is conceded that Social Security taxes are at a back-breaking level.

Social Security reform means different things to different people. The system never was designed to permit one to live at the same level of subsistence as when working. It is supplemental to a private pension program.

The system won't die but the frequent financial shortfalls ought to be corrected for the peace of mind of the recipients.

Minimum Benefit Fight Threatens Budget Reconciliation in Congress

Although the Reagan Administration had relaxed its position on Social Security reform considerably since May, the issue flared up again in July as Senate and House conferees struggled to reach an agreement on the President's tax-cut bill for 1982. One of the provisions of the bill would eliminate the $122-a-month minimum benefit by March, 1982, a step the Administration insisted was necessary to avert bankruptcy. Democrats, calling the talk of bankruptcy alarmist, scrambled to restore minimum benefits.

The House July 21 approved a non-binding resolution calling on budget conferees to strike the minimum benefits measure from the reconciliation bill; in the Senate, a more substantive effort to save minimum benefits was tabled the same day. When the issue threatened to keep the budget reconciliation bill from reaching the floor, it was decided to allow separate votes on the conference report and on a bill to restore the minimum benefits that it would eliminate. On July 31, the House passed the bill to restore minimum benefits by a vote of 404 to 20. The bill was sent to the Senate, where action was postponed until after the summer recess. (The budget reconciliation bill was cleared by the conferees July 23, and by the full Congress Aug. 4.)

SYRACUSE HERALD-JOURNAL
Syracuse, N.Y., August 7, 1981

About canceling payment of $122 a month to those 65 years and older who haven't paid enough into Social Security to qualify for a pension.

And about which we've heard so much how the administration and Congress are forcing recipients to live on crusts of bread …

Consider this:

Some 300,000 of the 3 million recipients of the $122 monthly payment will find their income is reduced appreciably once the minimum is eliminated.

As for others, President Reagan again stated:

"What we want to do is get rid of those people for whom it, the minimum payment, is not a necessity, and then take care of those other people in some way that does not raid the Social Security fund."

He suggested providing for them under the supplemental Social Security program; i.e., through direct payments from general taxes, not from the special payroll taxes levied on employees and their employers.

With this transfer of cost, the Social Security system would save up to $750 million of the annual billion-dollar cost.

That's worth doing.

Chicago Tribune
Chicago, Ill., August 11, 1981

Is President Reagan backing down from his vow to abolish the minimum Social Security benefit? No one knows for sure. In an interview published Wednesday in the Washington Star, Mr. Reagan said he was willing to restore the payment for poor retirees.

But the Office of Management and Budget, which first proposed the reduction, says it doesn't know what the President meant. The Department of Health and Human Services likewise pleads ignorance. Social Security Commissioner John Svahn says Mr. Reagan neant only that poor beneficiaries will get compensating payments from Supplemental Security Insurance, the system's welfare program. And the House subcommittee on Social Security, which opposed the cut, says it's heard nothing from the White House.

Mr. Reagan's waffling makes no sense, political or budgetary. He just won a bitter fight to eliminate the $153-per-month payment, which goes to workers who have paid as little as $1,450 into the trust fund. Despite two fierce House denunciations, expressed in non-binding resolutions, House-Senate conferees went along with the White House. So why should the President compromise now, after he's gotten what he wanted?

The case against the minimum benefit is as strong now as ever. Originally a $10-per-month payment for retirees who had worked irregularly or at low-paying jobs, it has grown into a handsome windfall for some 800,000 affluent retirees, most of them double-dipping federal pensioners. Only about one-sixth of minimum beneficiaries are poor, and this group would be eligible for payments from SSI adequate to offset the entire loss. Scrapping the payment would save $1.3 billion next year.

The only plausible argument against abolition is that many poor old people will refuse to apply for SSI, which carries the stigma of welfare. Some nuns whose orders have paid their Social Security taxes are also forbidden to accept welfare. But the truth is that the minimum benefit itself is welfare. From the beginning, it was based on the principle that retirees deserved a certain level of income even though they hadn't earned it. It does no one any good to pretend that the minimum benefit is earned.

The President was right about this issue from the start. He shouldn't surrender now that he's won.

The Cincinnati Post
Cincinnati, Ohio, August 8, 1981

To hear Democratic politicians tell it, President Reagan is Scrooge incarnate, the meanest man ever in the White House, because he got Congress to end the minimum Social Security benefit of $122 a month.

The Democrats are onto an emotional, vote-getting issue that they mean to ride for all it's worth. This may be good politics and, in fact, there's only one thing wrong with their accusation of Reagan. It isn't true.

A look at the $122 benefit is in order. It goes to 2.7 million recipients who haven't paid enough Social Security taxes to qualify for that amount, usually because they paid in for a short time.

Now if the $122 were a recipient's only income, nobody with a heart or a head would want to cut it. But it goes to, among others, millionaires and well-off people, and in their case it's an unearned windfall.

Among those enjoying the minimum are 450,000 federal retirees who receive separate generous pensions. They managed to latch onto the minimum by moonlighting or working a few years after retirement.

An unknown number of state and municipal workers with their own pensions also collect the unearned minimum. In all, about 800,000 recipients have other pensions or spouses who work or receive pensions. This group has an average income of $20,000 and hardly needs to be subsidized by Social Security.

Admittedly, there are elderly people who would suffer real need if their benefits dropped below $122 a month. But they would become eligible for Supplemental Security Income, food stamps and Medicaid, a benefit package worth more than $10,000 a year to a retired couple.

It's also true that some recipients would fall through the federal "safety net" and really have to try to live on less than $122. But Reagan proposes to change the law and keep the former minimum for this small group.

If those who did not earn the minimum benefit and do not need it because of other income are paid only what they did earn, the hard-pressed Social Security system will save $7 billion over the next five years.

That would be sound government practice and not Scrooge-like cheapness, despite what the Democrats would have us believe about Reagan.

The Des Moines Register

Des Moines, Iowa, July 30, 1981

The cavalier manner in which Congress has agreed to abolish the minimum Social Security benefit of $122 a month suggests that Congress doesn't take seriously its responsibility to the nation's retired workers.

If this decision is not altered before it takes effect next March, several hundred thousand elderly Americans would have to accept a cut in their already meager standard of living. Most of those who would feel the brunt of this cut are over 70.

Currently, a worker who has worked long enough to qualify for Social Security benefits receives a check for at least $122 a month, regardless of how little he or she paid in Social Security taxes. The Reagan administration is upset that some 400,000 former government workers took advantage of the program by working just long enough in non-government jobs to qualify for the minimum benefit. These 400,000 already get government pensions and other income that average $900 a month. To many of them, $122 a month from Social Security is just icing on the retirement cake.

At the other extreme are hundreds of thousands of elderly Americans who worked for years in poorly paid jobs, or who put in years at work before the Social Security tax was collected. The minimum benefit allows many of these retired workers to get by without applying for welfare.

Those workers who rely on the minimum benefit to stay off welfare should not be treated the same as those to whom the benefit is a bonus. Yet Congress has made no distinctions in voting to abolish the minimum benefit. This meat-ax approach to Social Security reform would hurt most those who least deserve to get hurt, while many "double dippers" would suffer little.

Some 3.1 million Americans are eligible for the minimum benefit. Of these, 1.2 million would not be affected by the decision to eliminate the benefit. Roughly 1 million of these people have or had spouses who qualified for Social Security benefits above the minimum; another 200,000 would qualify for a check of around $122 a month based on their own employment history.

The Social Security checks of the other 1.9 million would be cut by an average of about $60 a month by the decision to abolish the minimum benefit. Some of the people in this group are government workers already drawing sizable pensions; they wouldn't feel much of a pinch. Another 500,000 already receive Supplemental Security Income benefits in addition to Social Security because they are poor. These 500,000 would get additional SSI benefits to offset the cut in their Social Security check.

Still another 580,000 elderly Americans would be eligible to apply for SSI benefits because their incomes are so low. The Reagan administration estimates that only one out of four of these people — or some 145,000 — would apply for SSI. The remaining 435,000 would not apply, largely because many old people consider SSI to be "welfare" — and many older Americans are too proud to apply for welfare.

This leaves several hundred thousand who are poor by most standards but who would not quite qualify for SSI. One reason is that to be eligible for SSI, a person must have an extremely low income and few assets. These guidelines have not been adjusted upward since 1972, even though inflation has raised the cost of living since then. They should be adjusted.

The Reagan administration argues that eliminating the minimum benefit would save more than $1 billion a year. Some of this would be offset by increased SSI payments. The savings would be drastically reduced if all the old people who were eligible for SSI applied for it. The administration is counting on these people to accept a cut in their income, rather than accept "welfare."

This is a cruel way to run the Social Security system. It would have been better to make changes to eliminate the potential for abuse of the minimum benefit, while continuing to protect the hundreds of thousands of elderly Americans who rely on this monthly check to provide the bare essentials. Congress needs to correct this problem.

THE BLADE

Toledo, Ohio, August 9, 1981

IT is understandable that the Democrats are desperately fishing around for an issue on which to rail at the league-leading Reagan administration. But the more they argue that the Administration is heartlessly trying to cut Social Security payments to the poor, the more it becomes apparent that they have no alternative to offer.

Revenue for the system is not increasing as quickly as necessary. A shrinking working population base is forced to shoulder the burden of more and more retirees every year. Despite the approval of a tax increase several years ago, one of the system's trust funds continues to slip toward insolvency.

The Reagan administration has proposed cutting out the minimum, $122-a-month benefit paid to 3 million persons. Although Congress appears reluctant to approve this measure, it would save $7 billion annually.

Contrary to appearances, the cutback would not push most of the recipients into poverty. A fair number of those now receiving the minimum payment are retired government workers who entered the private sector and thus benefit from two public pension plans. Others have other sources of income to supplement the minimum payment.

As a sweetener to the 200,000 persons who would be hurt severely by the change, Mr. Reagan recently said that they should be made eligible for welfare. His approach toward preserving the Social Security system for future Americans is hardly as cold-hearted as the Democrats make it out to be.

The Democrats' remedy, however, is to snipe at the problem without offering anything in the way of a plan that would restore solvency. This reflects in part the political minefields that surround this issue. Republicans are just as cautious about suggesting reforms that hit their constituents in the wallet. But Mr. Reagan has forthrightly offered remedies for this problem, unpopular thought they may be to a large segment of the population. To their discredit, the Democrats have not done the same. Their performance hardly marks them as the party of ideas or of courage.

St. Petersburg Times

St. Petersburg, Fla., August 4, 1981

Who are the old folks who will receive smaller Social Security checks because of the Reagan Administration's dropping of the $122 minimum benefit?

The best answer to that question is that nobody knows.

One answer came last week from Claire Thompson, operations officer for the Pinellas office of the Social Security Administration. "When you stop and really look at who's in this category, the people who will lose cash are the non-needy."

We wonder.

THE ADMINISTRATION estimates that 3.1-million elderly will be affected. It expects to pay out $1.3-billion *less* in the 1982 fiscal year from the Social Security trust funds and it expects to pay only $300-million *more* in Supplemental Security Income (SSI) payments. That's a net loss for retired Americans of $1-billion a year.

Little is known about the retirees who will get less, according to the staff of the Senate's Special Committee on Aging (of which Florida's Lawton Chiles is a member). Of the 3.1-million retirees affected, 500,000 are receiving SSI payments already. SSI will make up the Social Security loss so they still will get $264.70 a month. However, 500,000 elderly persons are now eligible for SSI but consider it welfare and refuse to apply out of pride. In any case, only the most destitute qualify for SSI. Any old person with over $1,500 in liquid assets is not eligible for SSI.

Another 360,000 retirees affected by the killing of the Social Security minimum are federal retirees who also earned Social Security benefits. They are taking advantage of a quirk in the system that neither Congress nor the Administration will remedy. Perhaps some of them do not deserve Social Security benefits, but the federal retirees are a small percentage of the total.

Another 200,000 are old folks whose Social Security credits put them very close to the $122 minimum. Their checks will be smaller, but only slightly so.

That accounts for 1,060,000 of the 3,100,000 retirees, but that's it. Nobody knows anything about the others. "Social Security just doesn't have any information on them," a committee staffer said Monday. "We're interested in how old they are and what they've paid in, not their assets."

The committee staff is quick to point out that even these figures are provided by the Administration, which wants to minimize the effects. The committee has not conducted any independent analysis.

The Administration estimates that 200,000 to 300,000 old persons will receive substantially less because the minimum payment will be dropped.

Another guess is that many of them live in rural America.

SO IT IS NOT necessarily true, as Thompson said, that "the needy elderly will not suffer." Some will suffer if they are too proud to apply for welfare. Some will suffer if they have $2,000 in a bank account to pay for their burial expenses. Perhaps most of the suffering will be in the less visible, rural sections of America.

It is suffering, just the same, and it is worse because those suffering are old folks who deserve better from their fellow Americans, particularly their President.

The Charlotte Observer

Charlotte, N.C., July 28, 1981

Sometimes the legislative process works the way it's supposed to. That appears to be happening in the case of Social Security. The compromise plan now emerging in Congress would avoid the threatened bankruptcy of the system in the short run and keep it solvent into the next century, based on reasonable assumptions about the future.

Whether or not it was a deliberate strategy, the rather drastic proposals by the Reagan administration in the spring seem to have had the beneficial effect of spurring Congress into action.

Democrats in Congress, after a certain amount of demagoguery in response to the excesses of the Reagan plan, now acknowledge the urgency of the situation and have offered some proposals of their own which, although not altogether painless, would minimize the impact on those already nearing or past retirement age. The administration has accepted some of those modifications, putting a reasonable set of reforms within reach.

Both sides have agreed to allow the retirement fund to borrow from Medicare and disability funds to avoid running out of money in the next few years. Both sides apparently have agreed to eliminate, at least for future recipients, the minimum monthly benefit that goes to retirees whose payments into the Social Security system are so small that they otherwise wouldn't get any benefit.

The minimum benefit issue is a particularly good example of the process working as it should.

The Republicans argued that recipients of that benefit include a lot of well-to-do people who simply don't need the extra $122 a month. They noted that those who genuinely need the money could obtain additional welfare support if their Social Security checks were cut off.

House Democratic leader Jim Wright of Texas responded by accusing the administration of trying to salvage the Social Security system at the expense of "the poorest and oldest and the most politically defenseless."

Since each argument was correct as far as it went, a reasonable compromise would be to agree to eliminate the minimum for those who don't need it but preserve it or replace it with some other form of assistance for current recipients who do need it. Congress seems to be moving toward such a compromise.

The plan now taking shape probably will gradually increase the retirement age, change the basis for the annual cost-of-living adjustment of benefits, and reduce the percentage of benefits available to those who choose early retirement.

While such a plan falls short of the kind of wholesale reform some people advocate — converting Social Security into a true system of individual trust funds, for example — it deals responsibly with the immediate problems of the system.

And it avoids the extremes that initially marked both sides of the debate: the Republican proposals that would abruptly terminate all minimum benefits and force people nearing early retirement to change their plans; and the Democrats' unfortunate inclination to dip into the general fund to make up for Social Security shortfalls.

ST. LOUIS POST-DISPATCH

St. Louis, Mo., July 28, 1981

Congress is expected to ratify this week the decision of one of its conference committees to abolish the minimum Social Security benefit, which would save about $1 billion annually. The minimum benefit is $122 a month and is intended for those retired persons whose earnings were so low during their working years that they would receive a mere pittance if their benefit was computed in the regular way. About 3 million of the 35 million Social Security recipients receive the minimum benefit.

What has made it a candidate for abolition is the discovery that it is a windfall for many, perhaps the overwhelming majority, of those who receive it. Some people who receive federal pensions and some housewives whose husbands have an ample income work just long enough to qualify for it. If they knew they were going to receive the small sum that their earnings and work time would entitle them to in the absence of the minimum, critics say, they would not bother to take jobs. They also say that those for whom the minimum benefit was actually intended could be transferred to the Supplemental Security Income program, providing welfare for the elderly, blind or disabled poor who are outside the Social Security system.

If so, then of course the minimum benefit ought to be eliminated. The problem is that the move is being made primarily on the basis of a General Accounting Office study. This is not to say that the GAO is unreliable — on the contrary, its studies have identified scores upon scores of potential savings through the years — but that such a change is ordinarily undertaken only after a congressional committee has thoroughly examined it.

Under the conference committee agreement, the minimum benefit is not to be terminated until next March, which gives Congress time to make absolutely sure its decision was the correct one.

The Star-Ledger

Newark, N.J., July 28, 1981

Congressional negotiators, working to resolve differences between the House and Senate over $37 billion in budget cuts, agreed to eliminate the minimum on Social Security payments.

Agreement was reached only two days after the House had given thundering approval (405-13) to a nonbinding Democratic resolution expressing opposition to any shrinkage in benefits to persons who are receiving monthly checks. The rapid turnabout by House conferees exposes the resolution for what it was: A politically motivated grandstand play.

The minimum benefit, currently $122 monthly, originally was adopted by Congress as a way of saving the Social Security system from bogging down in the costly process of mailing out large volumes of tiny checks. In practice, however, the minimum has become a financial disaster for the federal government and a windfall for many Americans who contributed briefly to the Social Security fund.

Cost-conscious Reagan Administration officials point out that some three million persons receive the minimum, but as many as half of these are federal workers or military personnel who take jobs in the private sector after retirement and qualify for Social Security benefits. Because of the minimum, they receive monthly checks for sums that greatly exceed what they are entitled to on the basis of their payments into the fund.

Other recipients of the minimum are mostly low wage earners, or people whose jobs were not covered by Social Security during many of the years they worked. These people are, in President Reagan's phrase, "the truly needy," and they will be hurt by the removal of the minimum unless the White House is correct in its prediction that their loss in benefits will be made up by welfare. There are some borderline cases, perhaps 300,000, who will be pinched by the cutback.

Under the conference agreement, the reduced payments would show up in checks mailed March 3. Persons affected by the change ought to be given as much advance notice as possible so those who are eligible can arrange for supplemental income and cushion the impact of smaller Social Security payments.

Eliminating the minimum will save the government hundreds of millions of dollars annually and terminate the free ride which the "double-dippers" have been enjoying. If the truly needy are kept from harm by the Administration's social safety net, almost everyone should benefit from the change.

Reagan Reverses Stance on Minimum Benefits, COLA Delay

In a televised address to the nation Sept. 24, 1981, President Reagan abandoned his plan for a three-month delay in cost-of-living adjustments (COLAs) to Social Security recipients. "Our feet were never embedded in concrete on this proposal," he said. In addition, Reagan asked Congress to restore the minimum Social Security benefit to lower-income beneficiaries. He also proposed establishment of a joint task force with Congress to review options available for the restoration of fiscal integrity to the system. The bulk of the speech was an appeal for additional budget cuts; Republican congressional leaders had reportedly warned the President Sept. 21 that his entire package faced defeat over the Social Security issue.

The day of the speech, the Senate Finance Committee agreed to allow the retirement fund to borrow from the disability and Medicare funds, and to restore the minimum benefit for all current recipients except those who lived outside the U.S. or received government pensions of more than $300 a month.

ST. LOUIS POST-DISPATCH
St. Louis, Mo., September 21, 1981

Some modification in the automatic cost-of-living formula for Social Security recipients is probably warranted, but the three-month deferral in the payment that President Reagan has proposed is not justified because it is being sought for the wrong reason. Mr. Reagan is not seeking to safeguard the integrity of the Social Security trust fund, which would be a defensible reason for the retrenchment, but to avoid telling the Pentagon that its spending increase will not be as large as originally authorized.

The $2.8 billion that would be saved next year by postponing the effective date of the cost-of-living increase from July 1 to Oct. 1 would not be spent on the military; that would be illegal. But the unspent money would show up in the budget ledgers as an offset to the military and other spending that is pushing general fund expenditures beyond general fund tax receipts, which is to say, into a deficit.

Why, though, should the elderly, disabled, widows and orphans help pay for the deficit spending of the generals and the pork barrel crowd and others? Only the imperative to avoid a funding crisis for the Social Security system or to avoid an increase in the Social Security payroll tax could justify a cutback in their cost-of-living payments.

The 1982 budget threatens to run a deficit of at least $60 billion, instead of the $42.5 billion forecast a few months ago by the White House, because of excessive increases in military spending, extraordinarily high interest rates and an unnecessarily large income tax cut. It would be politically impossible to undo the latter and interest rates are not, strictly speaking, under the control of the White House. Nonmilitary spending has already been cut by $35 billion. That leaves the military. If it cannot be expected to absorb the entire $16 billion in additional retrenchments the president seeks, it could surely sacrifice more than $2 billion of its spending increase. In any case, Social Security ought to be off limits.

The Cleveland Press
Cleveland, Ohio, September 22, 1981

President Reagan is making a mistake in trying to defer cost-of-living increases in Social Security and other pension programs to cut next year's budget deficit.

Whether or not the move can be justified on economic or moral grounds, the saving would be a setback to pensioners already struggling against inflation.

It also would open the president to another and even more fierce round of accusations that he is trying to balance the budget on the backs of the poor and defenseless.

What makes the pension deferral plan seem even more inappropriate is the pitifully small reduction the White House proposes in the defense budget.

Social Security recipients would have to forego about $2.9 billion. Delayed increases in federal civilian, military, railroad and veteran pensions and in food stamps and black lung benefits would add another $3 billion.

By contrast, the defense budget would be trimmed only $2 billion in fiscal 1982, a reduction of about 1%. Surely more than that can be sliced from the $222 billion military budget without damaging the nation's defenses.

And what's wrong with reviving the president's earlier recommendation to increase "user charges" to boat and airplane owners and other individuals and firms that benefit from special government services? The $2 billion the White House estimated this would raise in fiscal 1982 would nearly offset the loss Social Security recipients would suffer under the latest budget-cutting plan.

Rockford Register Star
Rockford, Ill., September 18, 1981

There may be some who were reassured by President Reagan's mid-week pledge that he has "no plans to propose additional cuts" in Social Security benefits in order to balance the 1982 federal budget. We were not.

It's not that we do not believe the president will try to live up to his pledges. Rather, it's that the wording of this pledge is misleading.

The key word is "additional."

A 14-point Reagan proposal, made last spring, is stalled in Congress right now, but is very much alive and could be revived without breaking the president's pledge.

For that matter, the president already has made it clear that he will push for one major 1982 reduction in Social Security benefits — a three-month delay in making cost-of-living adjustments. This will cost Social Security recipients between $2.8 billion and $4 billion in 1982, depending on when the change is made.

It has been estimated that the entire 14-point program still pending would reduce benefits by $82 billion from 1982 to 1986 and would reduce 1982 benefits by up to $8 billion.

Thus the president could, without breaking his pledge, reduce Social Security benefits by $4 billion to $8 billion during the fiscal year starting next month. This in comparison with the token $2 billion the president has set as the absolute limit on 1982 reductions in the planned record INCREASES in military spending.

In addition to the delay in cost-of-living adjustments, the pending program would, among other things, penalize early retirement and reduce the size of minimum benefits.

It also must be noted that the president's Social Security pledge involves only fiscal 1982, where spending cuts of only about $17 billion are needed to meet Reagan's budget deficit goals. Another $75 billion must be cut during fiscal 1983 and 1984 to reach his balanced budget goal. He has made no promises to protect Social Security when the time comes to make these $75 billion in cuts.

Because of the political dangers involved, it may be that the president will elect not to reduce any Social Security benefits. And, for the same political reasons, it may be that Congress would not allow any cuts. But there is nothing in the pledge made by the president last Tuesday which would prevent major and almost immediate reductions in Social Security payments — reductions made basically so he can protect the massive in increases in dollars he has promised the generals and the admirals.

OKLAHOMA CITY TIMES
Oklahoma City, Okla., September 22, 1981

PRESIDENT Reagan's reported decision to press for a three-month postponement of scheduled cost-of-living increases for Social Security recipients has stirred a predictable outcry of congressional opposition.

Democratic leaders pledge to fight the president tooth and nail on this issue, and there is no denying the political hazards involved in tampering with any of the income maintenance and entitlement programs.

What's been overlooked in the shuffle, however, is how much additional Social Security tax withholding is already legislated and scheduled to go into effect through the remainder of this decade.

For all the contributors to Social Security, as distinguished from recipients, another tax increase is coming Jan. 1. The rate on employees and employers will rise from 6.65 to 6.7 percent, and the wage base will go up $2,400 to $32,100.

That will mean a maximum bite of $2,151, an increase of $176 from this year. And until Congress bites the bullet on structural Social Security revision, the outlook is for more of the same — indefinitely.

"WHEN I WAS YOUR AGE.....!"

ARKANSAS DEMOCRAT
Little Rock, Ark., September 19, 1981

Ronald Reagan has checked Social Security reform to the Democrats for now, spoiling the double political game they've been playing with the issue – which is one of accusing him of unconcern for the elderly as well as a plot to balance the budget on their retirement checks.

Mr. Reagan does propose to delay the SS cost-of-living increase by three months this year – and Democrats are making the most of that. But he says that he'll ask for no cuts, least of all with a view toward budget balance. That spikes the Democratic tattle about his using SS reform to raise money for budget balance – and it also leaves up to the Democrats any proposals for making sure pension checks keep flowing.

Since they have already made it clear that they have no stomach for real reform, we'll probably see the quick fix that Sen. David Pryor proposes – borrowing from the sounder two of the three SS funds to keep the old age and survivor fund healthy.

Maybe it's just as well for now for all hands to fight shy of full reform. Mr. Reagan does intend to dip into the other less explosive yet highly sensitive entitlement programs – food stamps, welfare, Medicare, unemployment compensation and veterans pensions – for the cuts needed to assure budget balance. Though the Democrats will fight that, too, they won't have anything like the political accompaniment that the "gray panthers" would furnish them if Social Security were the target. Leaving it out helps keep the battle lines clear.

The Burlington Free Press
Burlington, Vt., September 21, 1981

President Reagan should either fish or cut bait in making proposals to reduce the budget for Social Security.

Last Tuesday, the president said he had no plans to propose new cuts in Social Security and would not balance the federal budget "at

Editorials

the expense of those dependent" on the program. After a meeting between the president and Republican congressional leaders at which he was urged to consider cutting entitlement programs, David R. Gergen, chief White House spokesman, said, "The president announced that he has no plans to propose additional cuts in Social Security programs beyond those he has already submitted to the Congress. This announcement is intended to dampen and end any speculation that the president is examining further cuts in Social Security ... as a means of balancing the budget."

But the next day the White House said Reagan was resurrecting a plan to delay for three months the cost-of-living raises for Social Security recipients, a move he proposed last spring. Under the plan, the annual cost-of-living increase in monthly Social Security benefits would be deferred from July 1, 1982 until Oct. 1, 1982. It is estimated that the move would save $2.8 billion next year.

It appeared that the same congressional leaders who had suggested the cuts in entitlement programs met with David A. Stockman, Reagan's budget director, Wednesday night to be briefed on the new budget-cutting proposals.

The president's indecision must have sobering effects on millions of elderly who are receiving Social Security benefits. More than that, they must be deeply disturbed by an administration that has not taken a consistent and coherent position on the issue.

If Reagan was convinced that cuts must be made in Social Security to balance the federal budget, he should have been candid about his intentions and explained his grounds for reducing benefits to recipients.

Waffling on the issue only creates doubts in the minds of the nation's elderly.

The president should understand that he has an obligation to warn those senior citizens who will be deeply hurt by the reductions that they will be required to make the same sacrifices as other Americans under his economic program.

That would be a consummate act of political courage.

Herald News
Fall River, Mass., September 23, 1981

Republican congressional leaders, including Senator Howard Baker, have told the President they fear he risks defeat if he tries to push through his latest cutback proposals. They are especially dubious about the prospects for getting his plan to postpone cost of living increases in Social Security benefits approved by the House.

The skepticism the GOP leaders feel about the President's new proposals reflects the public's uncertainty about whether the administration's economic package will work.

The President himself last weekend pointed out that it is absurd to say his plan won't work when it hasn't been tried yet. He reminded the public that it does not go into effect until the start of the federal government's fiscal year, which is October 1.

The point is well-taken, but to be fair to the skeptics, it is the administration's poor guess about the dimensions of the federal deficit that has triggered their loss of confidence.

Had the administration's guess been more nearly accurate, the second round of cutbacks the President is seeking would not have been needed. While it is true that his program does not really go into effect until the beginning of next month, the budgetary cutbacks he is now seeking are based on the size of the anticipated deficit, and it is already clear that the administration's estimate was billions short of what that deficit will really be.

One bad guess does not invalidate the President's economic program as a whole, but it does create an atmosphere in which the administration's predictions will not be accepted on faith as they were last spring.

The difference in feeling on Capitol Hill is what prompted the GOP leaders to warn the President that pushing for more cutbacks now entails a risk of defeat.

THE BLADE

Toledo, Ohio, October 5, 1981

IT is somewhat misleading to suggest that federal officials have turned their backs entirely on Social Security's short and long-term financial woes. Nevertheless, these problems have slipped in recent weeks toward the bottom of the list of pressing national issues.

Last week President Reagan, in a move that reflected public fallout from a variety of attempts to trim costs, said he was agreeing to restore the $122-a-month ·minimum benefit. To cover any short-term deficits in one of the Social Security trust funds, Mr. Reagan pledged to transfer money from another fund if necessary. He also promised to create a bipartisan committee to review the system's problems.

Millions of older Americans have spoken out loudly on this issue, and both Mr. Reagan and Congress have been listening. With congressional elections due next year, politicians are likely to steer away from any changes that might provoke voter wrath.

The two choices that most of them are avoiding like the plague are simple enough: cut benefits (a step Mr. Reagan proposed earlier this year but which ran afoul of congressional and public opposition) or raise taxes. Within those approaches are a host of long-overdue specific remedies, including changing the excessive formulas used to calculate cost-of-living increases. But neither public officials nor recipients apparently are ready to accept sweeping changes.

The President made a timely political gesture by reaffirming his commitment to the millions of Americans who depend heavily on Social Security. But Mr. Reagan, Congress, and the public are someday going to face a day of reckoning when drastic modifications cannot be avoided. That day has been put off again, but it cannot be held in abeyance forever.

NEW YORK POST

New York, N.Y., September 28, 1981

House Speaker Tip O'Neill concedes that President Reagan's proposal for a bipartisan task force to "review all the options" for keeping the Social Security system solvent is an offer he cannot refuse.

But O'Neill's response hardly provides assurance that creation of such a committee — five appointed by O'Neill and five by Republican Senate Leader Howard Baker — will "remove Social Security once and for all from politics." Nor is the President likely to hold any large illusions on that point.

The real question is whether, in the long run, the politics of responsibility will prevail over short-term gamesmanship.

As Mr. Reagan quickly learned when his initial proposals were shot down in the Senate, probably no domestic issue is more subject to demagogic exploitation than this one. For millions of Americans who have invested in the Social Security system and relied on it as safeguard for their latter years, any prospect of change creates deep anxiety — even if they themselves are not immediately affected by the revision.

But that is only part of the story. The other part is that the Social Security explosion of the last decade has created the specter of a major national crisis. The retirement fund can calamitously vanish within the next 10 years if there are no increases in revenue or reductions in benefits.

That is the appalling danger to which the President has sought to alert Congress and the country. It is a danger that must haunt Democrats and Republicans alike.

The President has now reiterated that "our feet are not embedded in concrete" with respect to his original recommendations. In effect he has again challenged his critics to present alternative remedies. But he rightly insists that the gathering storm cannot be averted by pretense that the thick clouds portend only a brief springtime shower.

That is the case he has once again taken to the people. Mr. O'Neill's apparent acceptance of a bipartisan task force is at least tacit recognition that the case is beginning to be heard and understood.

THE ☼ SUN

Baltimore, Md., September 27, 1981

President Reagan, as expected, has been forced to retreat on his plans for revamping the Social Security system. The president had wanted to delay a cost-of-living increase scheduled for July and then to push forward with a proposal to raise the retirement age from 65 to 68. But with strong warnings from Republican leaders that the moves probably would not survive in Congress, Mr. Reagan made it plain in his speech Thursday night that he has backed off.

The president had hoped to achieve two ends. He would have gotten off the ground with the reforms he has pledged to make in the ailing Social Security program and he would have made a giant step forward in his efforts to balance the budget. A delay in the cost of living raise, to cite administration projections, would have shaved $5 billion from the 1982 federal budget.

There is no reason to believe the president is going to abandon his hopes for basic reforms in the the Social Security system. Indeed, he should not. Hardly anyone doubts that the fund is in deep trouble and needs shoring up if it is to meet future obligations. In fact, one of the biggest fears haunting Americans has been the fear of a total collapse of the system.

But while Mr. Reagan's action likely is more a concession to prevailing political conditions than a change of heart on the issue, it is nonetheless another hopeful sign that the "big scare" approach to the Social Security problem might be giving way to a sane search for solutions.

In recent weeks, there have been other indications that the aura of doomsday is receding and solid efforts to rescue the program are on the rise. Perhaps the strongest such signal came from Senator William L. Armstrong, R-Colo., and Representative J.J. Pickle, D-Tex., a few days before Mr. Reagan reversed his direction.

The two chair respectively the Senate and House committees charged with overseeing the future of Social Security; they also will figure prominently in any future reforms. Both insisted this week that a bipartisan solution will be found to rescue the system.

They predicted that it is only a matter of time before political leaders recognize that the "best thing to do is to do the right thing." The point is one we hope will be domininant when the Social Security task force which the president called for in his Thursday night speech begins its work.

The Oregonian

Portland, Ore., September 26, 1981

President Reagan didn't bite the bullet on Social Security reform; he bit his lip. The president's reversal on minimum benefits and his proposals to borrow from disability and hospital funds and to set up a joint administration-congressional task force to work out a non-partisan solution to Social Security funding by 1983 sounded more like vintage Carter than varietal Reagan.

As he called on the Congress to restore the minimum Social Security benefit of $122 a month for some 2 million people in an address to the nation, the Senate Finance Committee, headed by Sen. Bob Dole, R-Kan., had already voted unanimously in the afternoon to take the action and the House had passed a restoration bill.

It was significant that Dole, after hearing the president's speech, in which Reagan called for $16 billion in cuts above the $35 billion trimmed from the budget earlier, predicted the defense budget would have to be cut back more than president's proposed $2 billion trimming that mostly slows weapon procurements.

The president still is resolved to balance the budget by 1984, but the game plan is being drastically changed, proving that even political euphoria (following last summer's budget and tax victories) must give way to the power of numbers.

In recognizing that his proposed $2.9 billion cut in Social Security had no chance, not even in the Republican-controlled Senate, the president faced reality, but he is still in the awkward position of trying to seem to move forward on the issue while actually retreating. His proposed non-partisan task force that would review ways to reform Social Security would not remove the matter from politics. Whatever the recommendations, they would have to be enacted by a politically sensitive Congress that has ducked most of the options that have been discussed for years.

Some fresh options do exist. Sen. Daniel Patrick Moynihan, D-N.Y., has proposed financing Social Security's long-range shortages by restoring the heavy tax reductions the oil industry received this year. Having been given deregulation that permits it to charge as much as the traffic will bear, the oil industry does not need tax breaks in order to encourage investment.

The Senate Finance Committee has moved to cover a loophole in the minimum Social Security law by voting to take $1 from the Social Security checks for every dollar paid out over $300 by those with government pensions.

But this is a tiny trickle of reform, hardly matching Reagan's original proposals that would have reduced benefits by $82 billion in five years. The committee also approved the president's new endorsements to shift funds between programs. It passed other, earlier presidential proposals requiring payroll deductions for the first six months of an employee's illness and limiting maximum benefits for disabled workers. These are logical moves, but they pay only for the $5.3 billion cost of the minimum benefit that is being restored.

Unless the president is willing to exercise leadership in pushing a long-term program for Social Security reform, there is not much hope that Congress, faced with elections every two years, will do much more than keep the political wolves from the door by patching up the system each time it threatens to bleed red ink.

Richmond Times-Dispatch

Richmond, Va., September 30, 1981

Reagan has proposed to study the program could help immensely by impartially compiling evidence to justify changes in the system and by recommending, again impartially, ways to strengthen it.

For help, the commission could draw on the results of studies that have been made by other interested groups, including the National Federation of Independent Business and the American Institute of Certified Public Accountants. A major recommendation of both of these groups is that the social transfer — or welfare — aspects of the Social Security program be shifted to the general fund. Under this proposal, only those people who worked and paid into the Social Security insurance fund would receive retirement benefits from it — and the benefits would be in proportion to the workers' contributions. The minimum monthly benefit would be abolished, and needy people who now rely on that money would receive payments from the federal government's general funds instead.

"Participants in an insurance program should pay only for what they receive and receive only what they paid for," says the NFIB. "Transfers should be funded by universal taxes."

One of the principal speakers at a recent NFIB seminar on Social Security was octogenarian Frank Bane of Alexandria, a former Virginia welfare commissioner who served as the first executive director of the National Social Security Board, and it was he who most succinctly identified the cause of the Social Security system's problems.

"As soon as we established the Social Security program," he said, "people started talking about increasing benefits."

Now the system is reeling under the impact of all of those increases, and Congress needs to act quickly and responsibly to relieve the pressure. Else the program will collapse.

Called to the bedside of a hemorrhaging patient in dire need of major surgery, the doctors have decided to prescribe transfusions and ignore the cause of the bleeding. This will not cure the patient, of course, but it will delay the need for more radical treatment for a while.

The patient is the Social Security system and the doctors are the Senate and the House of Representatives. They know, as surely as they know that 1982 is a major congressional election year, that the system is in serious financial trouble. They know that money is flowing out of it faster than it is flowing into it from normal revenue sources, and they know why. Yet they lack the courage to take the action that would be required to restore the system to financial health; and because of their timidity, President Reagan has been forced to abandon, temporarily at least, his remedies for the program's ailments.

A principal reason that it is in trouble is that while it was conceived as an insurance program it is now doubling as a welfare system. Benefits are going not only to retirees who worked and paid into the system — and whose employers paid into it — but also to people who contributed little or nothing at all to the insurance fund. Whether they have earned it or not, all Social Security recipients are assured a minimum monthly payment that totals $182 when cost-of-living allowances are included.

At the rate it is dispensing benefits, the Old-Age and Survivors Insurance fund, the major Social Security program, will run out of money by next fall if nothing is done to ease the financial pressure on it. Increasing payroll taxes to pump additional revenue into the fund is not a viable option, given the fact that such taxes have been increased by 840 percent since 1962 and probably have reached the limit that the American public is willing to endure. Public reaction to the proposed elimination of the minimum benefit is causing Congress to reconsider that remedy; and it quakes at the thought of making other changes in formulas and benefits that might incur the wrath of retired voters or voters who are about to retire. So it is likely that, for the moment, Congress will simply give the OASI fund transfusions by lending it money from other Social Security funds.

Eventually, however, the financial problems that plague the Social Security program will have to be faced and dealt with realistically if the system is to serve future generations of Americans effectively. Only Congress has authority to develop solutions, but the special commission that President

The Pittsburgh Press

Pittsburgh, Pa.,
September 27, 1981

By backing away from his highly controversial Social Security proposals, President Reagan has refocused attention on his main target: getting the federal budget into closer balance.

This doesn't mean that adjustments in Social Security can be put off indefinitely. But the quick fix he proposed in his Thursday night address is about all that can be expected from Congress this year on this volatile issue.

This would involve inter-fund transfers among the various Social Security accounts to keep them all temporarily solvent.

Meanwhile, Mr. Reagan wisely recommended a bipartisan approach toward solving the long-term problems facing Social Security.

It is now up to Democratic House Speaker Thomas "Tip" O'Neill to join wholeheartedly with the president and the Senate Republican majority leader in setting up a blue-ribbon committee to recommend permanent reforms to get the Social Security program on a secure financial footing.

* * *

In pursuit of his main target — holding the 1982 budget deficit to about $43 billion — the president proposed $13 billion worth of additional spending cuts and $3 billion in minor tax increases.

The major reduction would come from an across-the-board cut of 12 percent in appropriations for most government functions other than defense.

The president also would save some money by delaying cost-of-living increases in various federal pension programs, except for Social Security. Further reductions would be made in food stamps and certain other "entitlement" programs.

* * *

The main quarrel with the president's package is the relatively small reduction he proposes in defense appropriations — only $2 billion in fiscal 1982.

It could be that Mr. Reagan is playing this card close to his vest because he expects Congress to lop off a few billion more on its own.

But even that would still leave the military with far more money than it received this year and probably with more than it could wisely spend next year.

* * *

Actually, the important thing is not whether the package comes out of Congress precisely as Mr. Reagan presented it.

What's important is that Congress not lose sight of the goal of a balanced budget in 1984.

Wavering from that course could have economic consequences far more serious than today's grumbling.

The Morning News

Wilmington, Del., September 28, 1981

On Social Security, President Reagan staged a gracious but unfortunate cave-in in his television address to the American people.

First, the president took pains to outline the reforms he had proposed earlier; with a slight tone of bitterness he noted that they would not fly. However, what he failed to point out in his review was his administration's monumental error in proposing instantaneous changes without phase-in periods.

For example, the suggested lowering of benefits for early retirees would have been implemented the first of next year; that was not enough notice to enable those contemplating early retirement to adjust their plans rationally. Similarly, the cuts in minimum benefits were to be sprung on an unexpecting public.

The other flaw that the president carefully avoided mentioning is that his assurance that his plan would make possible a reduction in Social Security taxes by the mid-'80s deserved no more credibility than former President Carter's assurance that the enactment of higher Social Security taxes would keep the system solvent into the next century. We now know that in spite of the higher taxes the system's old-age fund is threatened by a deficit by the end of 1982. So much for reforms in Social Security that are supposed to take care of us for the next 20 years or more.

The Reagan reforms, in short, were ill-conceived and sprung on the American people with insensitive abruptness. Not surprisingly, they got exactly nowhere.

The president recognized that in Thursday night's television address and did an about-face. He dumped his reform program. He put the burden of proposing a fresh set of reforms on a bipartisan congressional committee, yet to be appointed. And, most alarmingly, he advocated that to carry the Social Security system through the next few years, money be borrowed from the Medicare and disability components of the system and allocated to the old age benefits component. Such borrowing may make it possible to squeak by until the end of this decade.

Does that mean that any serious effort at reform may be put off until then? Does that mean that the total Social Security system will be in a state of financial crisis by 1990 instead of having just one of its components in deep trouble as is the case now?

By caving in so completely to the political reality of congressional reluctance to make downward adjustments in Social Security benefits the president is taking the politically easy, do-nothing road on this issue. That may be the only way that he can for the moment shore up support for other aspects of his national program, such as the escalation of spending on armaments or the painful cuts in food stamps and revenue sharing.

But this short-range maneuver does nothing to assure the close to 200 million Americans who hope to be benefiting from Social Security in the future that they will indeed be able to get anything out of the system when their turn comes, say in the year 2000 or beyond. For those folks, the safety net would look a lot safer if the president could have had the foresight to back some of the well thought out reforms put together in a package by the House committee headed by Rep. J. J. Pickle.

That package includes a gradual phase-in of raising the retirement age to 68 by the year 2000 — an overdue recognition of the changes in longevity. It also contains reductions in benefits for early retirees; these would also be phased in instead of implemented instantaneously as Mr. Reagan had proposed. Limits on what persons over 68 may earn without losing benefits would be done away with in the Pickle committee's proposal. And there would be changes in the way cost of living adjustments are calculated.

The reforms worked out by Rep. Pickle's committee are closely in line with those recommended by nonpolitical experts in the field. But that has not helped to make them palatable. Mr. Pickle is, of course, a Democrat and the House is Democrat-dominated. Republican Reagan could hardly be expected to buy their package.

What's more, the nation's 36 million elderly and disabled persons have been so put on edge by the abrupt and deep cuts proposed by the Reagan administration, that they are going to use every bit of their substantial political muscle to fight any reform. These older persons, and those very close to retirement, have been scared silly about the imminent bankruptcy of the Social Security fund and by the threat of cutbacks. They will have to be persuaded that their benefits are not in jeopardy before their confidence and support can be gained for any kind of rational reform.

The president, with his poorly conceived plan of this spring and his total reversal last Thursday night, has delayed the enactment of any kind of rational program by several years. We are all the worse off because of that unfortunate turn of events.

Nevada State Journal

Reno, Nev., September 30, 1981

Of all the battles President Reagan must face in the coming three years, Social Security reform may well be the most difficult. Twice Reagan has charged up the steep hill of change and twice he has been forced to turn around and charge right back down again.

No one can deny that in both instances, his retreat was not only politically astute but absolutely necessary for preservation of administrative life and limb. And yet if Reagan cannot somehow find a way to successfully storm the barricade and bring the American people with him, the system will collapse — and millions of dreams with it.

The facts are absolutely clear. The system is not paying for itself, and will go bankrupt if something is not done. The reasons for this are also absolutely clear: (1) all sorts of costly fringe benefits have been added to a program originally conceived of only as a retirement aid; (2) thanks to medicine, people are living longer and drawing more money out of Social Security than its originators ever thought possible; and (3) pension checks are tied to rampant inflation, which is helping to bleed the fund dry. On top of this, the ratio of workers to retirees has shifted drastically, from 42 workers for each retiree in 1945 to 3.2 to one now. By the early 21st century, when the baby-boom generation retires, the ratio may have deteriorated to an intolerable two to one. This increasingly crushing financial burden on the work force almost guarantees a taxpayer revolt somewhere down the road.

Therefore Reagan, Congress and the American people must find a way to prevent both the revolt and the collapse of Social Security. To do this, changes will have to be made in the system and its benefits.

In his Sept. 24 speech to the nation, when the president admitted defeat once more, he backed off from cuts in Social Security as a means of reducing the federal deficit and recommended restoring the minimum benefits taken away during earlier budget cutting. This sounds like an out-and-out defeat. But it was not quite a defeat — and therein lies a grain of hope.

On one hand, Reagan merely bowed to the inevitable. The Senate Finance Committee voted Thursday to restore most of the Social Security minimum benefits, and rapid passage of the restoration is expected in both houses. So in recommending this, Reagan was in fact recognizing a fait accompli. The Senate Finance Committee also voted to permit the retirement fund to borrow from the richer disability fund in order to keep the retirement fund afloat through 1982 — and Reagan in effect went along with this, too.

Yet at the same time, the administrative-congressional decision to borrow is a positive step. Indeed, it is one of the steps necessary to straighten out Social Security. But even more important was Reagan's reaching out to the Congress for a joint solution. In asking House Speaker Tip O'Neill and Senate Majority Leader Howard Baker to join him in appointing a Social Security task force, Reagan has moved the issue toward a bi-partisan, non-political approach. And this is what should be done; despite early House Democratic claims that the major responsibility lies with the president, the fact is that the responsibility lies equally with the administration and the Congress. And the less political this difficult issue can be made, the better the odds are that something positive can be achieved — and that it can be achieved before chaos sets in.

Time is especially important. Some congressmen believe that reallocating taxes among the disability and retirement funds and Medicare can keep Social Security solvent through the 80s, but this is wishful and dangerous thinking. Every year that we wait makes the task more difficult and the necessary changes more painful and difficult. The hard decisions must be made now, not in 1990. And Congress must join this current president, now, in good faith and good will to get the job done.

The Courier-Journal

Louisville, Ky., September 26, 1981

THE SHIP is foundering, the storm grows worse and the crew looks mutinous. The Captain coolly surveys the scene, makes a few mental calculations and then proclaims boldly: "Keep bailing, men. I'm setting up a bipartisan commission to study the situation."

So it went Thursday night as President Reagan announced his plan for saving Social Security system from imminent bankruptcy. The first step is one that even Mr. Reagan admits is only a stopgap: borrowing from diminishing Medicare and disability fund surpluses to keep the system's main retirement and survivors' fund solvent, at least through next year. Meanwhile, the President and congressional leaders will appoint a commission to recommend long-term reforms.

Tossing political hot potatoes into the laps of study commissions is a venerable Washington tradition, of course, and sometimes the commissions even come up with good ideas. But the good ideas all too often remain on the shelf — until the next commission, studying the same problem, dusts off the old reports and tries again.

With Social Security, the situation is too urgent to permit the luxury of such repeated exercises. Interfund borrowing may get the system safely past 1982, but more must be done. Mr. Reagan's proposals of last May, which he has now abandoned, were at least a start, whatever their flaws.

The President's original plan would have scrapped the $122-a-month minimum benefit, sharply lowered benefits for those who retire before age 65 and delayed next July's cost-of-living increase for three months. Though Mr. Reagan gave these proposals a respectful burial Thursday night, some or all of them could be disinterred by the new study commission.

More likely, however, the commission will want to take a hard look at the central problem of Social Security: the recent explosion of benefits, fueled by inflation indexing, and the much slower growth of the wages of the men and women who foot the bill.

Political risks changing?

The disparity is striking. Between 1970 and 1980, average retirement and survivors' benefits grew 55 percent in constant (non-inflated) dollars. In the same decade, average weekly wages of private-sector workers rose less than 2 percent, again in constant dollars. To make matters worse, the ratio of workers to retirees has been shrinking. Today there are just over three workers paying into Social Security for every person receiving benefits. Three decades ago, the ratio was 16 to 1. When the baby-boom generation begins retiring early in the next century, the ratio will drop to about 2 to 1.

Until now, Congress has operated on the assumption that it is politically safer to raise Social Security payroll taxes than to slow the growth of benefits, much less to cut them. But as the huge, multi-stage tax increase adopted in 1977 continues to load a bigger and bigger burden on workers, that assumption could crumble. The awful

truth is starting to dawn on today's young workers: unless things change, they will pay far more than previous generations into the system — and will retire just about the time when cuts in benefits will have become unavoidable.

So the posturing in Washington about "fairness" and "keeping our promises" must be kept in perspective. There's also the question of fairness to those who are supporting the system today. Whatever recommendations the study commission comes up with, Congress is going to have to displease someone. There simply is no painless way out of the mess Congress made when it got so generous with other people's money in the 1970s.

San Francisco Chronicle

San Francisco, Calif., October 15, 1981

THE DEMOCRATIC leadership in Congress has now accepted, with slight modification, President Reagan's proposal for a study commission to recommend changes that will insure the future solvency of the Social Security system. Under that proposal, there are to be seven Republican, seven Democratic members and one independent member of the group and they are to make their final report by next April 15.

This is all well and good. The commission may involve itself in many complexities concerning eligibility rules for various Social Security programs, but its basic concern will be narrow indeed; the system does not take in enough money to meet its future obligations. Benefits must either be modified, restrained or cut, or income of the system must be increased by additional taxes. It is that simple.

But putting the problem in its most simple form does not deal with the tough political reality of enacting reform in a matter which involves the basic economic interest, if not sustenance itself, of some 40 million people. And it is here that the commission may perform a valuable national service if it delivers a united and bipartisan recommendation, one that can find sufficient support on both sides of the House and Senate to win enactment.

IT IS UNFORTUNATE that the past history of such special commissions does not encourage optimism that this one will be effective. Ad hoc committees and commissions are typically created when politicians want to sidestep or evade issues and not when they want to confront them. Recommendations are often delivered merely to shelves. This commission's recommendations will be of such importance, however, that this must not be the ultimate result.

The Senate has now acted to allow the Old Age and Survivors' Trust Fund, the most important of three funds, to borrow from the other funds, which are in more robust condition. This is a short-term remedy and should not lull anyone into believing that a long-term one has been found.

There will be great temptation in Congress to delay a decision which is bound to be painful. That decision, however, must be made before the elections next year lest the Social Security system be damaged still further.

The Times-Picayune
The States-Item

New Orleans, La., October 15, 1981

With the acceptance by the Democratic House leadership of President Reagan's proposal of a bipartisan task force to evaluate the needs of Social Security, this vexing national concern could — and certainly should — be removed from politics once and for all.

The proposed composition of the task force has the potential to ensure an objective study of the troubled retirement system and produce a consensus on recommendations for congressional action.

Five of the 15-member study group will be named by the administration, with no more than three to be Republicans. Three are to be named by Thomas P. "Tip" O'Neill, Democratic speaker of the House, and three by Senate Majority Leader Howard Baker. Robert Byrd, the Democratic leader of the Senate, and Robert Michel, leader of House Republicans, each are to name two.

The formula calls for six of the 10 to be named by the four congressional leaders to be from outside government. There have been reports that one of those to be named by President Reagan will be a political independent, thereby ensuring that the study group will include seven Republicans, seven Democrats and an independent.

This mix — particularly its inclusion of outside experts — should be able to provide Congress and the American people with a clear understanding of the options available for future Social Security financing.

Already there has been general bipartisan agreement on the need to make long-term changes in the system, although disagreement between key members of Congress and the administration over the means aborted the president's original efforts to improve the system's solvency.

Because of political pressure, both sides have agreed to restore the $122-a-month minimum benefit to all but 400,000 of the 3 million individuals who now receive it and to shift money among the three Social Security funds as a stop-gap "solution" to the financial problem.

Speaker O'Neill's insistence that the task force report be issued before next year's congressional elections leaves open the possibility that the issue once again could become a political football. Members of Congress of both parties should resist any such temptation. The bipartisan task force lays the foundation for a resolution of a serious national problem, and members of both parties should use it to help educate the public about the options available for remedial legislation.

Senate Restores Minimum Benefit, Approves Interfund Borrowing

The Senate Oct. 15 unanimously approved a measure designed to maintain the solvency of the Social Security system through the 1980's. The 1981 bill, passed by a vote of 95 to 0, would restore the $122-a-month minimum benefit for approximately 2.7 million of the 3 million people currently receiving it, but left most future retirees eligible only for their earned benefit, even if that were less than $122. To avert a funding shortage in the retirement system, the bill directed that OASI should get a slightly larger share of the payroll tax that also financed Medicare and disability benefits, and allowed the three trust funds to borrow from one another should any one of them reach a dangerously low level.

Opinions differed over how long the measure would tide over the financially strapped system. Sen. Daniel Patrick Moynihan of New York, speaking for the Democrats, called the bill a "gracious retreat" by Republicans and said the reallocation would be enough to bolster the old age fund at least through the 1980's. Senate Finance Committee Chairman Bob Dole of Kansas disagreed, calling the bill a "cosmetic approach" and stating that under certain economic conditions the system might still be insolvent by 1984.

The San Diego Union

San Diego, Calif., October 20, 1981

The Senate voted 95-0 last week to restore the minimum Social Security benefit which it had voted to take away only two months ago. The 1981 battle for Social Security reform has ended with both Congress and the Reagan administration in full retreat.

At least for now. The shortage of money in the retirement fund will be relieved by borrowing from surpluses in the Medicare and disability funds. We are told this will put off the Social Security "crisis" for another few years, although we have heard that before.

With all the public backing President Reagan brought to his battle to cut the federal budget he was unable to prevail with the Social Security reforms which were originally part of his package. The experience of the last few months has reaffirmed two simple truths about Social Security:

First, there are any number of ways to save the system from the financial debacle that lies ahead — by reducing future benefits, by advancing the retirement age, by changing the formula for calculating cost of living increases, by tapping the general fund to cover costs not met by the payroll tax.

Second, there is no political consensus of sufficient strength to make any of these options acceptable to Congress.

The conclusion is that the Social Security problem is not so much a financial one as a political one, but that only begs the question. Perhaps it has been a mistake all along to assume that Social Security can be overhauled in a politically acceptable way to make it financially sound. Perhaps the system needs to be dismantled and rebuilt along entirely different lines.

One of the more interesting recent studies of the problem takes that direction, and it may offer a clue to the President and Congress. Dr. Michael Boskin of Stanford University, in a study commissioned by the National Federation of Independent Business, traces much of the trouble with Social Security to the fact that it is trying to be both a "pension" and a "welfare" program at the same time.

Dr. Boskin would separate these two aspects of Social Security. The payroll tax would be used to finance a "retirement annuity" for covered workers, with its benefits based actuarially on what they had paid in. Social Security itself would assume no responsibility for keeping a retired person's income above a specified level. Those who could not live on their earned annuity would become clients of a separate welfare program financed from general revenues.

This offers one way to keep Social Security from being drained in the future by benefit obligations that exceed the amount which covered workers are paying into the system. The minimum benefit is a classic example of "welfare" getting mixed up with Social Security. Those drawing the minimum benefit, usually people who have worked only intermittently or part-time, are getting a return on their Social Security dollars six times greater than that received by full-time workers.

Before the administration and Congress take another run at reforming Social Security, they should consider the possibility that the program as it is now designed is beyond reform. That is a radical notion, to be sure, but it may be the beginning of wisdom in dealing with this perplexing problem.

THE ATLANTA CONSTITUTION
Atlanta, Ga., October 19, 1981

The Reagan adminstration, along with the Senate and House, has moved to restore the minimum Social Security payment that they voted this summer to eliminate. But don't believe they were moved by the "goodness of their hearts" to restore the minimum. They were moved by politics.

And voters shouldn't forget the original vote, come next election day. That first vote showed the true colors of those who supported it. President Reagan and his Republican administration were willing to take money from the poor elderly in order to boost the Pentagon budget.

The minimum benefit went to about 3 million Americans. Some of these (about 400,000 persons) were former government employees who had retired with a government pension, but then worked long enough in a civilian job to qualify for Social Security too. But the vast majority of those receiving the minimum benefit were elderly men and women — many of them poorly educated — who had worked all their lives in low-paying jobs, or in jobs that were not covered by Social Security for many years. The result was that the Social Security minimum was their major — and often only — source of income in their old age.

The minimum was only $122 a month. But President Reagan and his supporters pushed for its elimination, and won Senate and House votes last summer to do so. But then, those folks in Washington began hearing from the folks at home.

President Reagan and Congress had, in effect, found one person out of four "guilty", but voted to "execute" them all. Last week, however, both the Senate and House, at Reagan's urging, voted overwhelmingly to restore the minimum. The two bills differ some — the House said return the minimum to all previously receiving it, the Senate said to eliminate federal pensioners making over $300 a month and recipients living overseas — but it's for sure that the poor elderly persons who depend on the Social Security minimum to put food in their tummies will get it back.

The "sinners" may have reformed. But their transgression is not to be forgotten.

The Dallas Morning News

Dallas, Texas, October 19, 1981

IF you've been wondering why Wall Street has not been convinced that Washington cost-cutting is for real or for long, you can quickly find the reason by looking at the Minimum Benefit Waltz. As performed by Congress.

It's a simple dance — one step forward, one step back — but it is dangerous. That's because it is danced atop a runaway Social Security system, accelerating toward disaster, with no one at the controls. Bankruptcy looms ahead, but Congress just dances faster. Just as Wall Streeters expected.

The minimum benefits program of Social Security was originally set up as welfare support for those whose wages had been too low or jobs too few to qualify them for adequate earned Social Security benefits. Since it was passed, though, Congress has added several other aid programs that can provide the truly needy elderly a much higher level of support than the $122 a month given by minimum benefit.

When you hear and read all those sad stories about poor old Uncle Max, who has been a friend to man and dog for 70 years and really needs that $122, you aren't hearing all the story. You aren't hearing the reason, if any, kindly old Uncle Max isn't drawing SSI, food stamps, Medicare or aid from other programs that were designed to replace and improve on the minimum benefit.

He could be, for example, one of the 450,000 double-dippers who are retired from the federal government. These folks, receiving federal pension checks averaging $16,000 a year, have been smart enough to get in enough quarters of private sector work to qualify for the minimum benefit, thereby qualifying for an unearned extra payment meant for the very poor.

Or he might be one of the 300,000 getting the unearned benefits despite the fact that they have spouses still employed, drawing an average $21,000 a year at their jobs.

The vast majority of the people now drawing unearned benefits under the minimum benefit program either are not poor or could draw higher benefits from other programs.

That's why, when Reagan tried to get this outdated and expensive welfare appendage cut from the regular Social Security system, Congress at first went along with him.

The facts clearly showed that this is a program that is not needed and that runs counter to the earned-benefits principle on which Social Security was founded.

But then came the political pressure from the Social Security lobby, from the elderly who didn't understand the issue, from the liberals in Congress and the media.

And so, both the House and the Senate bolted for the exits. Both reversed earlier votes. Reagan, bowing to the inevitable, backed off. Now the minimum benefit will go right on handing out checks to double-dippers and others who are far better off than millions of the workers whose SS payments support them.

Washington, after a brief try at getting Social Security under control before it is too late, has now panicked and gone back to its political dancing.

On Wall Street, no one is surprised. They may be cynical there, but they have taken a realistic measurement of Washington willpower.

The TENNESSEAN

Nashville, Tenn., October 21, 1981

THE Republican Senate followed the Democratic House last week and voted to restore the only major Social Security benefit that President Reagan was able to get Congress to cut during the summer.

That was the restoration of the minimum benefit of $122 a month, which, it was argued, had become a windfall for millions of recipients who didn't really need it. Accordingly, President Reagan recommended abolishing the minimum, claiming it would save as much as $1 billion.

The idea was to transfer those for whom the benefit was intended to the Supplementary Security Income, a welfare program for impoverished elderly, disabled and blind persons.

Repeal of the minimum caused such a furor that the House passed a countervailing bill restoring the minimum, having discovered that well-to-do persons and retired federal employees were not exploiting the program to the extent that it had been argued. Too, those transferred to SSI would have ended up with an even smaller benefit than the $122 or forfeited some services to which they were entitled.

So, a decision made in haste and without proper information as to what it would do in practical terms has now been undone, and is it only right that the minimum benefit should be restored.

BUFFALO EVENING NEWS

Buffalo, N.Y., October 29, 1981

The Senate has adopted a reasonable compromise on the controversial issue of minimum retirement benefits paid by Social Security. But it patched only a Band-Aid across the financial woes that underlie the entire national pension program.

The $122 minimum monthly benefit, which Congress had voted to abolish shortly at the behest of President Reagan last summer, goes to people who have not earned enough to entitle them to regular Social Security benefits.

Ending the program so quickly had rightly aroused sharp complaints, and the Senate has now voted, as has the House, to continue the program for most people who currently receive this benefit. Except for members of certain religious orders, however, no one who retires in the future would be eligible for the minimum payment. This preserves the program for most of those now under it, but calls a halt for all but a few in the future.

Given the more gradual phaseout, this would not be unfair. Many who now receive the minimum benefit are not poor but receive other kinds of pensions. Still others who receive the minimum have substantial assets or income from other sources, according to the nonpartisan Congressional Budget Office. Moreover, those who are truly needy would be entitled to Supplemental Security Income, a shift that would transfer their financial support from Social Security to general revenue funding.

The Senate also authorized the transfer of funds among Social Security's three big reserves as a means of preventing a cash shortage late next year, as some experts have forecast. "For the moment, Social Security is safe," said Sen. Daniel Moynihan, D-New York.

But it is truly safe only if the economy does not deteriorate sharply in the year ahead, something that would cut into payroll-tax revenues. Moreover, inter-fund money transfers don't provide long-term answers to a huge national program that has slipped in recent years toward the margins of insolvency.

Third White House Conference on Aging Focuses on Social Security

Social Security was uppermost in the minds of the 2,300 delegates who attended the third White House Conference on Aging Nov. 30–Dec. 3. One of the major resolutions passed was one declaring opposition to the use of general tax revenues to pay for Social Security benefits, a position with which President Reagan concurred. Many of the other resolutions ran counter to Reagan's policies, however. The conference called for continuing a high level of federal aid to older people and opposed any reductions in current Social Security benefit levels. Establishment of a national health insurance system that would cover home health services for the elderly was advocated, as was federal aid for dental work and mental health services.

Some of the 600 resolutions adopted were overlapping or even contradictory, at least in part because of a ruling by Health and Human Services Secretary Richard Schweiker that the resolutions prepared by each of the 14 working committees had to be approved or disapproved on a single vote at the conference's final session. This voting procedure caused a good deal of dissension, as did the appointment of some 400 delegates to the conference by the Reagan Administration only several weeks before it began. Critics contended that the administration was attempting to pack the key panels on Social Security and health care with supporters to prevent criticism of Reagan's policies.

President Reagan himself put in an appearance at the conference Dec. 1 and made a speech in which he lamented having been "portrayed as somehow an enemy of my own generation." Saying that "many who rely on Social Security for their livelihood have been needlessly and cruelly frightened" by his political opponents, Reagan said he would keep his 1980 campaign pledge to "restore the integrity of Social Security and do so without penalty to those dependent on that program." "What we can't afford," he continued later, "is supporting, as disabled, people who are not disabled or educating from Social Security funds young people from families of affluence and wealth."

ST. LOUIS POST-DISPATCH
St. Louis, Mo., November 30, 1981

The third decennial White House Conference on Aging begins today. The first one, in 1961, is credited with starting the drive for Medicare. The second, in 1971, led to the federal ban on most mandatory retirement before the age of 70. The new one is expected to produce a political ruckus.

It should, of course, be far more important than that. Persons over the age of 65 now constitute nearly 12 percent of the population; in 50 years they will account for one of every five Americans. They have growing problems as the government struggles to maintain Social Security, Medicare and Medicaid, and inflation hurts all of those who exist on fixed incomes. But they also constitute a growing political force.

The issues confronting this new conference arise between the increasing problems of the elderly and their increasing political power. The larger number of older persons will mean new strains on Social Security and other federal programs which the Reagan administration has at one time or another proposed to cut back. But the administration evidently does not want the conference to become a focus of criticism.

Last month, about half the 1,800 original conference delegates were subjected to a telephone survey supposedly made in behalf of the White House conference. They were asked what they thought of President Reagan's performance. Eventually it was acknowledged that the survey was financed by the Republican Party, with the name list provided by Health and Human Services Secretary Schweiker. He said the poll was intended to see what concerned senior citizens. He did not say why that concerned the GOP.

Then the Department of Health and Human Services decided to add 400 new delegates to the 1,800 chosen earlier, mostly by governors and congressmen. The original group consisted of professionals and volunteers in programs for the elderly. The additions, in the words of *The Wall Street Journal*, "seem to have been chosen mainly on the basis of loyalty to President Reagan."

Finally, after the administration replaced the conference's executive director, the conference's advisory committee adopted new rules restricting debate and limiting voting to a single final report incorporating recommendations of all 14 conference committees. The head of the committee couldn't "imagine 2,000 delegates being able to conduct proper debate." Critics, including some Republican delegates, thought the purpose was to stifle debate.

It might be considered a minor miracle if this conference managed to produce concrete ideas, but Jack Ossofsky of the National Council on Aging notes that "older people are 'younger' than ever before" because of better health and higher levels of education, and they are as interested in better job opportunities as anyone else, especially in working without severe losses from Social Security, in pursuing assistance for more care in the home for the "elderly elderly," and above all, in keeping Social Security on an adequate basis. After all, that was what the federal government promised them decades ago.

President Reagan himself might provide inspiration for the conference; he was elected president at an age when many older persons are supposed to retire from the public scene. But the nation's senior citizens no longer need to retire so soon, and in the White House Conference they may well demonstrate that they are not ready to retire at all from their share of national life.

Herald News
Fall River, Mass., November 24, 1981

Next week the White House Conference on Aging will bring together representatives of most of the nation's organizations for the elderly. The conference, sponsored by the President, will be directed by Health and Human Services Richard Schweiker, and will consider economic and social problems created by the steadily increasing number of elderly persons.

There can be no real doubt that the President of the United States, who is himself over 70, is sensitive to the difficulties many senior citizens have in making ends meet in this period of inflation.

He himself has certainly demonstrated to the nation and the world how to attack successfully the problems of aging. Not even serious gunshot wounds slowed down his customary vigor for long.

Yet, simply by accident, the President is being forced to come to grips with the fiscal crisis in the Social Security System. The crisis has been building for some time. President Carter brought it to the attention of Congress, but it is President Reagan who is being forced to tackle it, because some means of handling it must be found before 1984.

His initial proposals for changes in the system aroused such a storm of protest that he dropped them, and nothing to resolve the crisis has been done since. Congress has been considering various plans to make the system at least temporarily solvent, but has taken no action.

There is no question that the future of Social Security will be discussed at the Conference on Aging, as it should be. This, it seems, would be an admirable opportunity for the President to appear as the spokesman for this sizeable and growing segment of the population, and explain to the delegates the various options the government can consider to make Social Security truly secure.

Certainly the conference should give the President a chance to display to its best advantage his remarkable abilities as a conciliator to a group whose age span and basic interests are parallel to his own.

The Charlotte Observer
Charlotte, N.C., December 1, 1981

If ever there were a president who could be admired and supported by America's burgeoning older population, it's Ronald Reagan — the oldest man ever elected president of the United States, a politician whose vigor ought to tell Americans how wrong is the thoughtless notion that those past "retirement age" have little to contribute to the nation.

The president ought to be making friends and political allies at this week's White House Conference on Aging. Instead, the administration has angered onlookers and delegates alike by manipulating voting rules and even the delegate list at the once-a-decade conference so as to minimize the admittedly real danger that the conference might become a forum for criticizing Mr. Reagan's budget-cutting proposals.

Are the president and his advisers afraid of honest debate? Why not let delegates speak their mind on budget cuts and the president's proposals for dealing with the runaway Social Security system? Among the more than 2,200 delegates — most chosen by governors and Congress — there are surely enough sensible, pragmatic people that a useful public debate could be conducted about the Social Security system's real problems. The debate is needed to help push the question back into the public view and encourage Congress and the administration to deal with it rather than dance around it.

Two previous conferences on aging produced recommendations for landmark legislation — including Medicare, a higher mandatory retirement age, and nutrition programs for the elderly — and raised the nation's conscience about ageism, an attitude among the young as deadly as sexism and racism because of the unrealistic limits it sets on the abilities of valuable citizens.

The 1980s have been dubbed "the decade of the elderly," as the nation begins to confront problems inherent in a nation with a growing proportion of older citizens. People over 65, now 11% of the population, will constitute more than 20% in about 50 years. These older people have different problems and concerns, and their growing political strength will influence public policy.

As Rep. Claude Pepper, the 81-year-old Florida Democrat who spoke during Monday's opening session, told the delegates, the conference "couldn't be more timely."

"As America grows older," he said, "we require nothing less than a re-thinking of attitudes. You can build a strategy this week, not only for coping with aging problems, but also for taking advantage of the promise inherent in the world's growing elderly population."

There is something badly wrong with the apparent attitude of Mr. Reagan's advisers, who want to stifle such a vital debate. The president ought to reject such small-minded politics and appear at the conference to encourage a robust discussion on such issues as Social Security, encouraging more people to work past retirement age and the enormous projected increases in the nation's health care and nursing home costs because of the growing numbers of older Americans.

DESERET NEWS
Salt Lake City, Utah, November 27, 1981

Today, one of every seven Americans is 60 years old or older. But when today's pre-schoolers turn 60, one of every four may be that age or older.

Those are some of the prospects the White House Conference on Aging will have to deal with Nov. 30-Dec. 3 in Washington, D.C. The conference will bring together citizens from across the nation to help formulate a proposed national policy on aging.

The 1981 conference is the fourth time a national forum on aging has been held in Washington since 1950, although the first was not formally called a White House Conference. Others were held in 1961 and 1971.

Some aspects of the aging of the nation's population already have been thoroughly reviewed in national forum. The most conspicuous is the effect on the Social Security system of fewer younger workers supporting more older retirees. That is only one of the social programs to feel the impact of longer life expectancy for Americans.

The White House Conference must deal with such vexing problems as these: How can we enhance those extra years of life to make them more rewarding? How can we tap the skills and experience of the growing elderly population? What role should government play in dealing with these vital issues? And in areas where a government role is appropriate, should it be at the local, state, or federal level?

Increasingly, some of those decisions will come at the ballot box as more and more citizens join the ranks of the elderly. Older Americans have become the fastest-growing segment of the population. Lower death rates and longer life expectancy have increased the number of people aged 60 or over four times as fast as those under 60 since 1900. In that year, only 4.9 million Americans were 60 or over, and life expectancy at birth was 47. Today, there are 34 million older Americans, and average life expectancy is 73.

Not only are there more older Americans, but an increasing number of them are women. Thus, many of the problems of the elderly are problems of women. With their increasing numbers, older women could become a potentially powerful political group.

The "graying of America," then, could well see an injection of political activism concerning retirement income and other issues.

The Union Leader
Manchester, N.H., December 1, 1981

It appears that the White House Conference on Aging may accomplish little other than to give President Reagan's political foes one more opportunity to play politics at his expense. Indeed, one wonders whether such conferences aren't fatally flawed in the first place. By their very nature they are political.

But we do hope that the New Hampshire delegation succeeds in its goal to have the national conference go on record in support of removing the earnings limitation on Social Security and establishing tax incentives to encourage industry to retain older workers.

The Granite State delegates probably will get a receptive ear from the President on both counts.

The problem is that there is no indication that these common sense proposals will be given a more friendly reception in this Congress than they have in others.

The politicians seem ever willing to "give" the nation's elderly citizens anything —except the opportunity to live out their remaining years with the dignity that derives from the knowledge that society still views them as productive citizens.

Portland Press Herald
Portland, Maine, December 1, 1981

There are disturbing signs that the national White House Conference on Aging has called 2,266 delegates to Washington to orchestrate support for President Reagan from the elderly, not to hear what they have to say.

No one expects such conferences to be free of political pressure. But the proper direction for that pressure is from the grass roots up, not from the administration down.

For weeks, the Reagan administration has been fretting that the conference on aging could become a national forum for taking harsh aim at some recent federal budget cuts.

To find out what delegates were thinking, the Republican National Committee commissioned an indirect poll. Then the administration named 200 delegates of its own.

Now delegates have been directed to wrap up their policy agenda for more than 25 million elderly people with a single final vote, casting only one vote for or against the recommendations of 14 separate policy committees.

No wonder many delegates have complained. The administration's rules make it possible for 7 percent of the delegates—the majority on a single committee—to set policy the remaining 93 percent cannot alter.

That may be shrewd politics, but it's heavy-handed democracy. And it's out of place at a time when there are more elderly people than ever before. Currently there is one person over 65 years of age for every two American citizens under the age of 15.

The changing balance in population requires balance in public policy as well. Older Americans deserve a free, unrestrained voice in how that balance is struck.

THE COMMERCIAL APPEAL
Memphis, Tenn., November 29, 1981

WHITE HOUSE conferences usually come and go without leaving a mark on the political landscape. Not so the conference on aging.

Twice before this once-a-decade meeting has influenced federal policy toward the nation's elderly. The 1961 conference is credited with sparking Medicare, while the federal ban on most mandatory retirement before age 70 came after the '71 session.

THIS YEAR'S conference has no specific agenda, but the 2,200 delegates gathered in Washington this week do have specific concerns. Mostly, they want the Reagan revolution to confront a demographic revolution — the aging of America — and all that it implies.

Older Americans declared themselves early on in this year's battle of the budget. When the administration proposed cuts in Social Security last spring, the outcry was such that the President drew back the suggestions and even retreated from his stand against the minimum benefit payment, which Congress had approved.

The policies and politics involved, however, won't be confined to this year or this White House. Our nation is growing older, and the problems that involves will only escalate until they are dealt with reasonably and maturely.

Citizens over 65 now comprise more than 11 per cent of the U.S. population. Fifty years from now they will make up one-fifth. Yet already about 28 per cent of all federal spending goes to finance programs for people in this age group, with biggest increases coming in the cost of medical care.

The conferees are aware of these trends, and so are federal officials. They know that to tread on such sensitive issues is to walk into a political minefield. For not only do older Americans constitute a potentially powerful political force, but younger people also are mobilized behind their cause. As a recent Louis Harris poll indicated, Americans of all ages support keeping Social Security benefits at current levels even if it means a tax increase.

Faced with that united a front, where do Washington and the nation go?

Why not ask the White House Conference on Aging?

CONFERENCE CRITICS already have charged that behind-the-lines maneuvering may affect the meeting's outcome. One fight involves the number of last-minute delegates asked by the administration; another revolves around rules for the conference, which some fear could mute dissent, while still another goes back several months to a Republican Party poll of conferees whose participation is supposed to be nonpartisan.

The graying of America involves problems too large to let the conference on aging turn on such small political hassles. The session should not become one more White House conference where political ideologs posture and prattle on. An aging nation stands to learn from the delegates, from people most affected by federal aging policies. Why not allow them this chance to advise the rest of us?

The Honolulu Advertiser
Honolulu, Ha., December 2, 1981

Senior citizens are often thought of as a "minority group," and in a way they are. Those over 65 make up slightly more than 11 percent of the population.

But there is one big difference: We are all aging (and in that sense future members of the group). The concerns of seniors will soon enough be felt by younger Americans.

(Two articles on the opposite page reflect some of those concerns.)

Indeed, Congressional Quarterly reports that in 50 years those over 65 will constitute more than 20 percent of the population—one out of every five Americans.

THIS GIVES A special sense of urgency to the third decennial White House Conference on Aging now taking place in Washington. As Americans turn gray in greater numbers, the Reagan administration's budget cutting ax appears to be getting closer to programs that the elderly have come to rely on.

Some participants are concerned the administration wants to conference to rubber-stamp Reaganomics. They point to some 400 extra delegates invited by the White House, and conference rules which force them to accept proposals in an all-or-nothing fashion.

But beyond procedural disputes, delegates also have longer-term concerns. The most pressing is the future of the Social Security system.

In an attempt at "reform," the Reagan administration last May made some early recommendations which proposed cutting back benefits. The storm of criticism which greeted the move led to the quick withdrawal of the proposal. As a compromise, President Reagan earlier this fall proposed a task force to look into shoring up Social Security.

It was that task force which Reagan referred to yesterday when he told conference participants: "The charge of the task force will be to work with the Congress and the president, not only to propose realistic, long-term reforms to put Social Security back on a sound financial footing, but also to forge a working, bipartisan consensus so that the necessary reforms will be passed into law."

THE TWO PAST aging conferences were instrumental in getting important legislation. The 1961 meeting led to formation of the Medicare program, and anti-age discrimination and "older American" legislation came out of the 1971 conference.

This conference could make its mark by offering proposals to help strengthen the Social Security program. If they do, and if those proposals work, the 1981 meeting may be looked back on as being one of the most successful in protecting the well-being of all Americans as they grow older.

The Washington Post
Washington, D.C., December 1, 1981

FOLLOWING THE FASHION in such get-togethers, the White House Conference on Aging began yesterday in the midst of a blow-up over agenda, delegates and procedures. It would hardly be a White House Conference without the predictable tussling, but there are real issues here too.

Last year, through almost 200 separate programs, the elderly claimed about one-fourth of the federal budget. Next year, despite large cuts in most domestic spending, that share will rise to 30 percent, or more than $7,500 for each person over age 65.

By most measures, federal aid for the aged has been a great success. Twenty years ago, over a third of the elderly were poor. Now, thanks primarily to Social Security cash benefits, less than 15 percent are counted as poor, even when the value of medical, food and housing benefits is left out of the count. Generally rising living standards, more adequate government benefits and modern medical science have brought a longer and fuller life to most older people. The great majority of the aged own their own homes—usually outright or with low-rate mortgages—and most can afford to live independently. In recent years, moreover, indexing of Social Security benefits—the major source of income for over 60 percent of the aged—has provided better inflation protection for the old than most wage earners have had.

Inflation, however, has not been without its costs to the elderly. Few private pensions are adjusted for rising prices. The aged are also heavily represented among the depositors in savings and loan accounts and the holders of long-term bonds. They received negative returns, after adjusting for inflation, on their investments to the great benefit of those generally non-elderly people who bought cars and houses over the last decade. Losses of this kind are a special source of anxiety for the old who have little chance to recoup when the economy improves.

Overshadowing all these immediate difficulties, however, is the growing concern that the consensus that has supported vast increases in public spending for the old may begin to break down. The proportion of people who are old—especially those who are very old—will continue to grow over the next 30 years and accelerate sharply thereafter. You can quibble over the numbers somewhat, but it is an almost inescapable conclusion that, by the second quarter of the next century, maintaining the present structure of retirement and medical benefits will claim about a quarter of workers' earnings.

This wouldn't leave room for many other public benefits—such as education and health care for children. It used to be that the interests of the old and young were frequently pitted against each other in families forced to choose between, say, an operation for mother and college for the kids. An expanding view of public responsibility has made those agonizing choices less frequent. It's worth some thought as to whether there are not some compromises to be made now—perhaps in a gradual postponement of the retirement age or an expanded role for private pensions and savings—that can avoid a replay of that inter-generational competition in the public policy choices faced by the next generation.

The Star-Ledger

Newark, N.J., December 12, 1981

If nothing else, the White House Conference on Aging proved that nothing is dearer to the hearts of the nation's 25 million elderly than Social Security.

President Reagan, in an unscheduled appearance before the delegates, struck the right chord when he pledged he would never betray the millions of older Americans who are presently receiving benefits under the depression-born program.

An astute politician, Mr. Reagan is not likely to forget the applause which followed that pledge of non-betrayal.

Before the four-day conference ended, the 2,200 delegates officially approved 600 resolutions, almost all of them concerned with economics — a ban on mandatory retirement at 70, expansion of Medicare coverage, increased supplemental security income (SSI) for the needy, bigger rent supplements, greater tax relief for the elderly, among others.

But feisty Rep. Claude Pepper (D-Fla.), the 81-year-old chairman of the House Select Committee on Aging, was on target when he observed: "The single biggest accomplishment of this conference is a strong reaffirmation of their support for Social Security."

Mr. Pepper and Reagan Administration representatives worked together for hours to hammer out a resolution adopted by the conference's Social Security Committee. The resolution opposes cuts for current beneficiaries and endorses "fiscally reasonable" attempts to prevent cuts in the future.

Benefits, however, are rising faster than contributions from employers and workers, a fiscally irresponsible condition that cannot be allowed to go unchecked. Even the increased contributions scheduled to go into effect with the new year won't solve the problem.

A presidential commission, soon to be activated, seems to be the best way to develop a bipartisan blueprint to bring benefit schedules into line with employer-employe contributions to the Social Security system. Unless Republicans and Democrats rise above party, Social Security financing will remain a political potato too hot to handle.

In the meantime, the work of the conference will be embodied in a report to Congress and the Administration and can be expected to influence policy on the aging for the decade ahead.

THE MILWAUKEE JOURNAL

Milwaukee, Wisc., December 6, 1981

If there is to be any hope of finding remedies for Social Security's long-term problems, politicians must learn to talk straight. They cannot keep practicing the sort of verbal gamesmanship that President Reagan demonstrated the other day at the White House Conference on Aging.

Decrying how political demagogy had frightened the elderly, the president vowed that he "will not betray those entitled to Social Security benefits." He also talked of working for a bipartisan consensus "so that the necessary reforms will be passed into law." What is he really saying? It is hard to divine.

We surely endorse the idea of a bipartisan approach. It is the only way politicians will ever make the long-term adjustments necessary to keep the Social Security system solvent and affordable; neither party is going to take the heat all by itself.

However, the president can't build bipartisanship by flailing at unnamed "demagogs." In reality, the only major scare that Social Security proponents have had this year is one that emanated from the White House. It was the administration's proposal to sharply curtail early retirement benefits, reduce the benefits of future retirees, eliminate the $122 minimum benefit and delay the 1982 cost-of-living increase.

The proposal was crude and inequitable, but the administration deserved some credit for at least daring to tackle an unpopular assignment. The credit had to be forfeited later when Reagan totally repudiated the proposal. His withdrawal from the fray has left the cause of Social Security reform without the important help that his leadership could provide.

Instead of adding to the confusion, Reagan should be acquainting the public with the sorts of changes that the Social Security system will need. In our opinion, the government should, among other things, gradually raise the normal retirement age by a year or two; make early retirement a relatively less attractive option; require government workers to enroll in the Social Security system; phase out the minimum benefit, and base cost-of-living increases on a formula less generous than the overstated Consumer Price Index.

Most of the changes could be relatively modest, but changes are essential. The president and Congress should start facing that fact — forthrightly.

ARKANSAS DEMOCRAT

Little Rock, Ark., December 3, 1981

The White House Conference on Aging, now convened in Washington, isn't the kind of gathering that goes with deep budget cuts in social programs. It presents foes and critics of Reaganomics with the perfect opportunity to denounce the president for punishing yet another group — the elderly.

A number of delegates are making the most of the Democratic charge that the president lumps the elderly in with the welfarists as targets for cuts in their meager standard of living. If anything has damaged Mr. Reagan with this constituency it's that — and though he wasn't scheduled to appear, he couldn't afford not to. So in a surprise appearance before "my own generation" Tuesday he spoke to the chief fear of the delegates and the chief political charge of the Democrats — that he plans to cut Social Security.

He took the offensive, denouncing the "political demagogery" and "lies" about his intentions as having needlessly and cruelly frightened the elderly — and repeated what he has said all along: that putting Social Security on a sound financial basis is the one certain way of making sure that the elderly do get their pensions.

The Democrats know that. Both parties must sooner or later enact the reforms that will save the system. In his address, the President said he would soon name his promised taskforce to work at a bi-partisan solution. Meanwhile, the conference's most important committee — the committee on Economic Well Being — has voted overwhelmingly to oppose any cuts in present Social Security payments, but refuses to give the same backing to future retirees and has also voted against dipping into general revenues to support the system.

Since these votes supports the president's own views, there were cries of committee-packing and complaints that Mr. Reagan wants to be able to claim that the conference backs his positions.

As for committee-packing, most of the delegates on the committee were not White House-named. They were chosen by governors and members of Congress. And as for using general revenues for Social Security, nobody seriously suggests that as the solution to the Social Security crisis.

However, Mr. Reagan's appearance didn't still the muttering of those who feel he is out to get the elderly. And the Democratic demagogery will continue. There's nothing he can do, moreover, to prevent the explosion of demands for new programs for the elderly being heard in the conference committees.

Recommending new programs has been the conference's function over the years, and it's loaded with them this time — one being a demand for national health insurance, which Mr. Reagan isn't about to support as a government program.

That brings up another sore point with many of the delegates. They won't get a separate vote on each committee proposal but will have to accept or reject all committee recommendations as a package. That's an administration rule — applied in the declared interest of time-saving but certainly open to criticism. But the size of the big vote will determine whether there's majority backing for the bulk of the proposals coming out of the 14 committees — and, meanwhile, Mr. Reagan has been wise indeed to grasp the nettle, show up and declare himself on the subject of Social Security. Staying away would have been ruinous.

The News and Courier
Charleston, S.C., December 3, 1981

When he made a surprise appearance before the White House Conference on Aging, President Ronald Reagan vented his frustration as being "portrayed as somehow an enemy of my own generation" for his efforts to bail the Social Security system out of its current fiscal crisis.

"We will not betray those entitled to Social Security benefits," he promised the assembled group, "and we will, indeed we must, put Social Security on a sound financial base."

He's right. The Social Security system is a fiscal shambles. Daily, the fund pays out much more than it collects — about $2.5 million more. At the current expenditure rate, money to finance the Old Age and Survivors' Insurance benefits will run out in the next few months and the long range deficit is calculated in the trillions of dollars.

The cause of the problem is simple arithmetic. There has been a major change in the population mix, leaving fewer and fewer workers to pay the benefits to more and more retirees who are living longer and longer.

Some Democrats would have you believe the solution is to use the revenues from the general fund to bail out Social Security. All that would accomplish is to add to the existing oppressive income tax burden. Borrowing from other pockets within the system merely depletes them while postponing the inevitable crash.

Congress already has rejected once an administration proposal that would cut benefits by 10 percent, include added penalties for those who would retire before age 65 and tighten eligibility for disability checks. We would go further and recommend phasing in a delay on minimal Social Security payments to age 65 and maximums to age 68.

The Social Security system needs major legislative surgery — and soon! The alternative is to see the system go bankrupt.

The Knickerbocker News
Albany, N.Y., December 3, 1981

Two of the nation's most powerful constituencies — the working class and the elderly — have finally gotten through to Governor Reagan. Yes, Governor Reagan, for in strategy, style and substance, the statements he made in Washington Tuesday seemed more appropriate for the recent chief executive of California. It is a welcome sign.

When Mr. Reagan was running California, he showed a capacity for the pragmatic, a willingness to reach a political accommodation. The zealot on the campaign trail became the mediator in office.

Now Mr. Reagan is showing the same approaches to troubles with the nation's fired air controllers and the elderly who depend on Social Security benefits.

In an apparent attempt to ease strained relations with organized labor, Mr. Reagan has raised the possibility that fired controllers might be eligible for federal jobs, though not in airport towers. The president won wide public support for his stern handling of the illegal air strike; he deserves the same support for his efforts to temper justice with mercy, principle with peacemaking.

Mr. Reagan has also taken a conciliatory approach on Social Security, telling the White House Conference on Aging that his administration will not "betray those entitled to Social Security benefits, and we will, indeed we must, put Social Security on a sound financial basis."

Mr. Reagan made a campaign issue of putting Social Security's house in order, but cutting entitlements was presumed to be the means toward this end. Now a special panel will study the whole system, although finding the even-handed solution that Mr. Reagan seeks won't be easy. Only last August, congressional experts were saying that Social Security could make it into the next decade by simply transferring money from the health trust fund into the retirement fund. By late October that hope had vanished. New estimates showed that even in a robust economy, the combined fund reserves won't be enough to cover payments by 1985.

Congress, of course, could raise the Social Security tax or take monies from the general revenues and put them into the trust fund. But neither option is likely to appeal to Mr. Reagan, who wants to stick by his tax cuts and, at the same time, avoid widening the federal deficit. This leaves the unattractive third choice of returning to an idea he espoused and later abandoned — postponing some cost-of-living increases.

Behind the conciliation, there still lie hard choices.

The State
Columbia, S.C., December 3, 1981

A LARGE group of Americans in Washington end a conference today on a subject that is or will be dear to the hearts of all of us — aging.

Their meeting, the White House Conference on Aging, has dealt with the broad implications of the aging of America — "the graying of America," as some are fond of calling it.

It is an enormous problem, and it will become greater in a very few years with an aged population that is growing rapidly. Those over 65, now just over 11 percent of the population, in 50 years will comprise more than 20 percent — one out of every five Americans.

And the fastest growing category among the aged is going to be the "old-old" — persons who are in their 80s or older. That will be a result of better health care and of improved socioeconomic conditions.

A study by *Congressional Quarterly,* a Washington-based reporting service, predicts some of the profound consequences which are likely:

— There will be severe strains on Social Security as well as private pension programs with more people spending more years — even decades — in retirement.

— There will be incredible increases in demands for health care and nursing home care that will escalate the costs of Medicare and Medicaid programs.

— And the elderly will become a powerful influence politically, at the polls as well as in the legislative halls, because of their large numbers.

This week's conference was the third White House Conference on Aging, the first being held in 1961 and the second in 1971. Its purpose was to bring together diverse interests in the subject to make some policy recommendations for the Administration's guidance.

With that objective in mind, and the present unsteady Social Security system which everyone is concerned about, the Administration was reported to have been apprehensive about criticism of its Social Security policies. In his speech at the conference, the 70-year-old President denied he is "an enemy of my own generation," but said Social Security has to be put on a "sound financial base." Indeed, it must, if the nation is not to betray its elderly.

Some Democrats on Capitol Hill allege that the White House has sought to control the outcome of the conference so as to avoid the kind of criticism which could be parlayed into next year's political races.

Thus, the conference is important for another reason, for what it might mean for the aged. The political stakes in 1982 congressional elections are high. The Democrats will be strengthened in their attacks on Mr. Reagan's Social Security proposals by any substantial criticism of his policies from this conference. And the Republican White House would be better off politically if its policies had the approval of the nation's elderly.

The politics of this conference aside, the nation must develop its long-range policies to deal with the great oncoming problems of its elderly.

Roanoke Times & World-News

Roanoke, Va., December 11, 1981

IF PASSING resolutions could solve the problems, then Americans could take considerable comfort from the recent White House Conference on Aging. The conference (in one vote for the entire list) passed more than 600.

And despite charges that the Reagan administration had sought to manipulate the outcome, most of the final recommendations appeared to enjoy support from administration friends and foes at the conference. That's probably because most of the recommendations, taken by themselves, are unexceptionable.

Social Security benefits should be adjusted to reflect cost-of-living increases twice a year instead of once, the conference said, and the outside earnings test that limits benefits for working older people should be abolished. Various old-age assistance programs should be expanded. Medicare and Medicaid should be extended to include an advance-payment system and to cover home health care and services. National health insurance should be established for long-term care of older people who are not completely self-sufficient but who do not require institutionalization.

The problem is that such goals, worthy as they may be, conflict with others equally worthy. At the same time it called for expanded social programs for the elderly, the conference said anti-inflation economic policies and a balanced federal budget should be top priorities. At the same time it called for increased Social Security benefits, the conference said the system should not be funded from general revenues.

Passing a resolution that two plus two equals three is easy work. The impossible part is making two plus two equal three in actual practice. Many of the conference's recommendations appear so mutually exclusive that, if adopted by Congress, they would simply wipe out each other's intended effect.

This is not to say the affair was useless. Earlier conferences on aging, in 1961 and 1971, led to such far-reaching programs as Medicare and private-pension regulation. Some of the proposals this year — not requiring people to retire solely because they reach age 70, enabling older homeowners to convert the equity in their homes to income without having to move out, handing out stiffer penalties for crimes against the elderly — may find their way into law.

Nevertheless, the news media were probably right in focusing on the political disputatiousness of the conference rather than its formal recommendations. There was no way for conference participants to resolve the basic policy dilemma about aging that faces America in the decades ahead: how to finance medical care and retirement benefits for a growing elderly population, yet not overburden a shrinking population of active workers.

On that, the political disputation has only just begun.

THE BLADE

Toledo, Ohio, December 14, 1981

FEW surprises came out of the recent White House Conference on Aging, especially as the delegates voted their pocketbooks on the question of preserving the Social Security system.

As expected, they endorsed preservation of present benefits and displayed little interest in any kind of bullet-biting measures that might enhance the system's long-term fiscal integrity.

Keeping benefits at reasonable levels for most recipients is desirable, of course. But sooner or later Congress is going to have to decide whether to increase sharply the payroll taxes that sustain the system, restrict benefits, or limit eligibility. The longer it delays — and the longer Americans somehow expect the system to magically bail itself out — the more severe those cuts will have to be.

Not everyone on Capitol Hill, however, is arguing his own self-interest on the issue of federal pension systems. Hastings Keith, a former congressman, and John Macy, Jr., who headed the Civil Service Commission in the 1960s, are waging a lonely struggle to impose tough, corrective rules on retirement systems. In particular they are supporting universal coverage — requiring all Americans to contribute to Social Security rather than to other governmental pension systems. As former government employees, the two would suffer as a result of such a change.

The White House conference did provide a forum for groups concerned about problems facing the elderly, but as with most such gatherings the recommendations will quickly be forgotten.

The Boston Herald American

Boston, Mass., December 6, 1981

As might have been expected, the White House Conference on Aging concluded in a controversy that illuminated the basic disagreement between the Reagan administration and the politically potent and highly organized senior citizens' lobby.

The conference adopted a mix of resolutions, some of which were contradictory, and mostly opposed what the seniors' lobby regards as unwarranted tampering with Social Security and other federal programs benefiting the elderly.

The hotly debated resolutions themselves were overshadowed by a controversy over whether the administration had stacked the conference by appointing key committee members.

Led by feisty, 81-year-old Rep. Claude Pepper, D-Fla., chairman of the House Select Committee on Aging, the senior citizens' lobby bored in on the administration's plan to bring entitlement programs for the elderly under budgetary control. This opposition is understandable enough. But the welfare of senior citizens is inseparable from the economic welfare of the nation as a whole, and the Social Security System is on the brink of insolvency.

Mr. Reagan has made several unsuccessful attempts to control the Social Security hemorrhage. Earlier this year, Capitol Hill resoundingly rebuffed his proposal to reduce benefits for those who elected early retirement.

The powerful senior citizens' lobby, which had a big hand in shielding Social Security from reform, remains oblivious to the dangers of maintaining the status quo.

The nation has an obligation to care for its senior citizens, and President Reagan has pledged to meet this obligation. Seniors cannot, however, completely escape the pain required to arrest inflation — the chief threat to their security — and to resolve the nation's budgetary crisis.

SYRACUSE HERALD-JOURNAL

Syracuse, N.Y., December 14, 1981

Ronald Reagan left the governor's office in California with a reputation for pragmatism. If he couldn't get a full loaf, he settled for half.

It's no surprise, consequently, that he disowned past attempts to fiddle with Social Security in addressing the recent White House Conference on Aging.

Said Reagan the president:

This administraion will not "betray those entitled to Social Security benefits, and we will, indeed we must, put Social Security on a sound financial basis."

Last August, he thought postponing cost-of-living increases dictated by inflation would fix the system. Rebuffs in the Congress taught him, apparently, that he is dealing with a powerful pressure group.

Now, a special panel is assigned the job of studying the entire system.

That's the usual route of political retreat. Still, there's no reason to doubt that the panel can find a solution, acceptable to the administration and its constituency.

FORT WORTH STAR-TELEGRAM
Fort Worth, Texas,
December 8, 1981

The third White House Conference on Aging to be held since 1961 concluded optimistically last week, despite hassles about procedures and charges that the Reagan administration had stacked the key committees.

The optimism perhaps comes from the delegates feeling that they got a chance to say something about the many things that concern the elderly of this country. The conference has no explicit power to resolve issues, but it has very strong power at the ballot box. The administration and Congress are sure to take what was done at the four-day conference very seriously.

In that respect, the meeting was worth the time and funds that were put into it. For the problems usually associated with growing old — retirement income, medical care, boredom, housing, companionship, employment and many others — will increase as the percentage of the population over 65 years of age increases. At present, 11.1 percent of the U.S. population is 65 and over. That percentage is expected to increase to 20.4 by 2030.

Who will support those elderly citizens? As the percentage of aged citizens grows, the percentage of those of working age shrinks. That means that a smaller percentage of workers will be supporting a larger percentage of elderly persons. And the Social Security and Medicaid programs already are in trouble.

And a good portion of those older citizens will be women. Older women outnumber older men by 50 percent and that percentage is expected to increase. The birth rate has been dropping and that means that there will be fewer children to care for the growing number of elderly, most of them women living alone.

Not all the problems facing the elderly are major. The conference also recommended the permitting of pets in public housing so that the elderly can have some companionship.

And there were many more issues addressed by The White House conference. In spite of the bickering about politics, the resolutions expressed concerns that politicians are not going to be able to ignore. Theirs will be no easy task. They will have to face the dilemma of not overtaxing the workers while trying to provide more for the retired.

Government does have a responsibility to its citizens who have served it well and now seek some return on their contributions. The question is: how much can it afford?

CHICAGO Sun-Times
Chicago, Ill., December 5, 1981

The White House Conference on Aging has ended four days of backbiting and parliamentary maneuvering by passing a confusing mishmash of contradictory resolutions.

One section of its report, for example, calls for using general revenue funds for Social Security, while another section says using general revenue funds would "jeopardize the fiscal integrity" of Social Security.

Other recommendations, such as national health insurance, aren't likely to be heeded by the Reagan administration, which would rather not have held the conference, but was forced to by the 1978 Older Americans Act.

In a clumsy effort to stifle dissent, the administration stacked important committees with its sympathizers. The 2,200 delegates weren't allowed to discuss or amend committee recommendations from the floor.

The most that can be said for the $6 million fiasco is that it was no worse than the last conference—on the family—which turned into a series of shouting matches and walkouts over abortion and homosexuality.

Other conferences—on small business and libraries—were quickly forgotten after making predictable requests for more federal aid.

True, the 1961 aging conference started the drive for Medicare, but we wonder if it would have if a Reagan, rather than a John F. Kennedy, had been president.

White House conferences merely formalize—at taxpayers' expense—the normal lobbying process. And they give presidents a chance to turn the demands of interest groups to their own political purposes.

Then, why have them? We can't think of a good reason.

Houston Chronicle
Houston, Texas, December 7, 1981

There was no doubt about what the delegates to the White House Conference on Aging had on their minds: benefits.

And there was no doubt among the delegates on one more thing: benefits should not be cut.

The recommendations of the conference are all nice, but it would be disparaging the wisdom of those in attendance to say that all the recommendations fit the test of reality.

Social Security, for instance, is an integral part of our society now, but to. say that it should be maintained forever with no changes in the existing benefit structure doesn't fit the facts.

Social Security payments have changed in the past, and will change in the future as society and governments change. To freeze it in place would be to endanger its future.

Benefits, and the political maneuvering, attracted the most attention at the conference. But there was another side. The delegates also were interested in an end to discrimination on the basis of age. They called for freedom of choice in housing, work and lifestyle.

Perhaps the most significant development was the very vigor with which the conference was conducted. The lesson to be drawn is that no society can afford to waste such experience and enthusiasm.

AKRON BEACON JOURNAL
Akron, Ohio, December 5, 1981

DESPITE the political infighting that accompanied the White House Conference on Aging, the meetings concluded Thursday serve a useful purpose.

The problems of aging — security, health, crime, housing, the economy — need to be studied not only by the elderly but by the young and middle-aged, and particularly by all in the Congress. After all, people over 65 now account for 11 percent of the population, and by 2030 will account for 20 percent.

Statistics from the Census Bureau and the Social Security Administration show that the elderly now are doing relatively well; federal policies have helped most of them avoid grinding poverty. Even so, as the delegates indicated, they are worried about their security benefits and health programs.

And if they are worried now, then the Congress should be doubly worried for the future, faced as it is with maintaining the solvency of a Social Security system that is rapidly approaching insolvency while the number of Americans dependent upon it is increasing rapidly.

Because of infighting and inflexible voting rules, the conference reached conflicting conclusions: for instance, that the Congress should bolster the Social Security fund if necessary from general revenue funds, but also that the use of general revenues would jeopardize the fiscal integrity of Social Security.

The business of the conference was also clouded by allegations that the Reagan administration attempted to dominate committee leadership in order to lend support to administration positions on Social Security reform, health care and the economy. Copies of letters and papers circulated by Republican state officials supported some of the charges.

In the end, whatever subterfuge or efforts to manipulate the conference existed proved ineffective. The final report was basically a reflection of the views of the delegates. And just to make doubly sure, the recommendations will be submitted again to the delegates for a vote by mail.

Regardless of the vote or attempts to influence it, the conference has reminded the Congress that the elderly have important concerns and needs — and that their votes count, too.

Funding Bill Clears Congress: Bipartisan Panel Named

Legislation to shore up the old age and survivors' trust fund and retain the minimum Social Security benefit was passed by Congress Dec. 16 and signed into law by President Reagan Dec. 29. In its final form, worked out by Senate and House conferees after a month-long impasse, the bill permitted OASI to borrow from the system's healthier disability fund and Medicare fund, but only from Jan. 1, 1982 until the end of that year. The bill also authorized continuation of the minimum monthly benefit to current recipients and those who became eligible before the beginning of 1982. To fund the partial restoration of the minimum benefit, Congress for the first time taxed sick pay, making the first six months' worth taxable.

The formation of a 15-member bipartisan task force to seek a more lasting solution to the Social Security system's financial problems was announced Dec. 16. President Reagan named five members of the panel. The other 10 members were named by House Speaker Tip O'Neill, House Minority Leader Robert Michel and Senate Majority Leader Howard Baker. The chairman of the panel, appointed by Reagan, was Alan Greenspan, former chairman of the Council of Economic Advisers in the Ford Administration.

The Dispatch

Columbus, Ohio, December 22, 1981

PRESIDENT REAGAN announced Sept. 24 that a committee would be named to seek financial reforms for the troubled Social Security system. The 15-member body has now been appointed — almost three months later.

We hope the committee moves with more alacrity to solve the dilemma. It has a year to make its recommendations.

If the committee takes the full year, it will be rapidly approaching a time when all three Social Security trust funds will be bordering on bankruptcy.

Economist Arthur Greenspan, who served the Ford administration as chairman of the Council of Economic Advisers, will chair this new, important committee in which Reagan is placing so much faith.

The president named five members as did Senate Majority Leader Howard Baker and House Speaker Thomas P. O'Neill. This selection procedure should assure a bipartisan consensus.

Reagan's charge to the committee is to set forth recommendations containing realistic, long-range solutions.

Before recessing for the holidays, Congress enacted legislation to allow interfund borrowing within the Social Security system. This is strictly a short-term answer since even Medicare will be out of money by 1984.

Patchwork is not the answer in light of the fact that the Social Security trust funds today are spending $12,300 per minute more than they are taking in.

It is time the task force became operational so the president can get on with fulfilling his commitment to restore the fiscal soundness of the Social Security system.

THE RICHMOND NEWS LEADER

Richmond, Va., December 30, 1981

In a display of its customary political courage in dealing with a program that benefits 35 million Americans, Congress confronted the many problems afflicting the Social Security program... and blinked. It hastily took a tuck here and stitched a dart there and happily postponed the time of reckoning — preferably to a non-election year — before going home.

As a result, 3 million Americans will have their minimum benefits restored, and 5,000 applicants who would have qualified for the minimum payments since Congress abolished the floor now will be able to draw the minimum. Except for members of some religious orders who have taken vows of poverty, no new applicants will receive minimum payments after January 1. Congress lifted the exemption on payment of Social Security taxes on the first six months of sick pay to finance most of the $6.1 billion the restored benefit will cost during the next five years.

This was strictly a political decision. A good number of those drawing minimum benefits also draw handsome pensions from the military or from the federal government. Yet Congress flatly refused to reduce the minimum benefits for those with other pensions of $300 a month or more, so the door to the double-dippers and triple-dippers remains open.

And what of the major financial problems that afflict Social Security? It is no secret that the fund paying retirement benefits faces imminent bankruptcy unless Congress makes some drastic adjustments in the program. Why, the answer to that is simple: The funds financing disability and Medicare payments are in danger of bankruptcy further down the road, so Congress will permit the retirement fund to draw from the disability and Medicare funds to hasten their financial depletion. Congress will get around to dealing with the program's multiple problems in, oh, say,1983. Next year, 1982, is an election year, and nobody wants to tinker with Social Security when votes are up for grabs.

Meanwhile, there will be another task force — following in the footsteps of 1,392½ similar task forces — to study Social Security and come up with proposals for bailing the thing out. The difference in this task force, it is said, is that it is truly a bipartisan effort which will put itself above political games to make some tough proposals. Anyone who believes that sees the Headless Horseman every midnight of the full moon. No task force is needed to outline the program's problems: Social Security is over-promised, to the tune of more than $4 trillion in unfunded liabilities. It is over-generous, to the extent of providing hefty cost-of-living increases and benefits that seldom bear any relationship to contributions. It is under-funded, despite the biggest peacetime tax increase in history — an increase that was supposed to end the program's financial problems in 1977, forever.

So what will the task force say that is any different from the proposals advanced by dozens of previous task forces and experts? Not much. The choices are clear: Payroll taxes must be increased to an astonomical level, benefits must be decreased, retirement age must be postponed — we've heard it all, with various refinements. So has Congress, but the appeal of the new task force is that it won't say anything for a while, giving Congress additional time to procrasticate before it has to make unpopular choices. Just think: If Congress can delay long enough by juggling funds until the entire program goes down the tubes, it won't have to make any choices at all.

CHARLESTON EVENING POST
Charleston, S.C., December 17, 1981

House and Senate conferees trying to iron out differences on Social Security legislation did a smart thing the other day, something that should have been done long ago. They agreed to permit borrowing among the system's three trust funds. The idea is to keep the retirement fund afloat with money borrowed from the hospital and disability insurance funds. The conferees did not stop there. They wrote a provision limiting the interfund borrowing to 1982. The intent of the limitation is to prod Congress into taking meaningful action — not just some stopgap measures — before January, 1983, to rescue the Social Security system from the brink of bankruptcy.

Authorizing interfund borrowing should buy enough time next year to enable Congress to correct the imbalance of payments that has put the retirement fund in such deep trouble. Benefit scales have to be revised so what is paid out does not exceed what is paid in. The ratio of workers supporting the fund to retirees drawing benefits is out of kilter because all sight has been lost of the original intent of the Social Security program.

Congressional approval Wednesday of the conferees' agreement is encouraging. If rescue is to be effected, however, more members of Congress are going to have to screw up their courage and do some things likely to be politically unpopular.

If anyone in Congress or out doubts that time is running out on the Social Security retirement fund, he need only consider what the program administrator told a House subcommittee last week. Discussing a plan to update Social Security's aging computer system, John Svahn said his agency has lost 20 percent of its computer programming staff in the last year and has been unable to recruit replacements for 700 vacancies that now exist. "It's difficult," Mr. Svahn said, "to get people to come into a program that looks like it's close to collapsing."

If anything can, that kind of perception should move those dreaming of retirement to light fires under their congressmen and senators.

The Honolulu Advertiser
Honolulu, Ha., December 28, 1981

Congress clearly did the right thing with its interim steps this year on Social Security.

Its final actions included passage of a bill to restore the $122-a-month minimum benefit that both houses earlier in the year voted to abolish at the request of President Reagan.

In reversing themselves on this matter, both Congress and Reagan were admitting it was a mistake to take even such a modest minimum away from up to to 3 million people who had come to depend on it. even if they had not contributed enough to the system to qualify for regular Social Security benefits.

BUT THAT was the easy part, and it should serve to remind everyone that the difficult task of reforming Social Security lies ahead, specifically after next year's elections.

The bill Congress passed in its final days also allows borrowing among the three main Social Security funds (old age security, disability and Medicare) until January 1, 1983. That is a quick-fix measure to help make sure the system keeps going financially until the reforms are made.

In a sense, the furor over the minimum benefits this year showed how difficult it will be to make cuts or major changes. For, if there were howls against reducing benefits to those who technically didn't earn them, what will there be if and when efforts are made to trim those of people who feel they did earn them?

Reagan got a taste of that when pressure forced him to abandon a controversial plan to defer cost-of-living increases scheduled for 36 million Social Security recipients next July.

TO GAIN perspective—and to take some of the heat—Reagan and the leaders of the Democratic House and Republican Senate have named a 15-member commission to draft long-term reforms aimed at putting Social Security back on a sound financial footing. It is headed by economist Alan Greenspan, chairman of the Council of Economic Advisers under President Ford.

Notably the reporting deadline is the end of 1982, some two months after the November congressional elections. That should help remove the issue as a major political factor although senior citizen groups will make sure it gets some attention.

The previously reported economic plight of the Social Security system itself is important enough, but the issue is compounded by other matters. As Greenspan noted: "We have got a large number of problems which relate not only to the issue of Social Security benefits but to private pension fund systems, to private savings and a number of questions which did not really surface prior to 1979, a period of major inflation and interest rate changes."

BY MID-1983, it is hoped, the national economy should have improved enough to change some of those factors and make economic decisions easier in Washington. But even with that, Social Security remains one of the tough and probably painful decisions facing the nation this decade.

It can be delayed, but it can't be avoided.

Lincoln Journal
Lincoln, Neb., December 16, 1981

And so Congress and President Reagan have made good on reversing a humdinger of a judgmental error before it imposed a frightful political penalty. Like the implacable opposition of 3 million voters.

There will be no break, after all, in the $122-a-month minimum Social Security benefit going to 3 million Americans.

Termination of benefits had been scheduled in March of 1982 under Reagan-sponsored legislation which was thoughtlessly, blindly passed by Congress earlier this year.

Once the full import of that ghastly political mistake, of a Social Security benefit cut to some of the poorest beneficiaries, was drilled into their minds, Reagan and the Congress promised to undo the mischief before Christmas. And that they've now accomplished.

The bill has a couple of interesting wrinkles.

After Jan. 1, all new applicants for the minimum benefit are to be refused. They're out of luck. The line on program expansion has been unmistakably slashed across the landscape.

Therefore, as present minimum beneficiaries die, the number of elderly in the program — costing $6.1 billion a year — relentlessly will shrink.

Another thing the act does is permit the Social Security system's three trust funds to borrow from each other. This is an arrangement the Reagan administration resisted earlier in the year.

The transfer authority is only to the end of 1982, however. That guarantees another brawl about the time of the 1982 congressional election — if not in a post-election lame-duck session.

There is no small truth to the complaint of Colorado Sen. William Armstrong, a Lincoln Northeast High School graduate. Armstrong says Congress is simply temporizing with the great financial problem of the Social Security system, which is money going out faster than money coming in.

Another hard truth is that some scaling of Social Security benefits is almost certain when Congress does confront the issue which Republican Armstrong stresses. The American public needs to condition itself to that eventuality.

TULSA WORLD
Tulsa, Okla., December 18, 1981

PRESIDENT Reagan has formed a bi-partisan commission and charged it to develop long-term solutions to Social Security financing problems.

"For too long, too many people dependent on Social Security have been cruelly frightened by individuals seeking political gain through demagoguery and outright falsehood. This must stop. The future of Social Security is much too important to be used as a political football."

With those words, inarguably true, the President appointed Alan Greenspan, a conservative economist and chairman of the Council of Economic Advisers in the Ford Administration, to chair the committee.

Reagan appointed four other members and Senate Majority Leader Howard Baker and House Speaker Tip O'Neill named five each. All three men crossed party lines in naming their members, giving the commission a truly bi-partisan makeup.

Even those members of Congress who have been making political hay by accusing Reagan of trying to torpedo Social Security know that something must be done to change the system if it is to remain fiscally sound.

Basically, the system has to be changed to reflect the aging of the population, meaning that retirement ages will probably have to be raised in the future.

It is the hope of Reagan, presumably with the concurrence of Baker and O'Neill, that the commission will agree on a plan that will command the support of Congress.

Let's hope that comes about.

The Chattanooga Times

Chattanooga, Tenn., December 24, 1981

Just before Congress adjourned last week, it gave nearly three million Americans a Christmas present of sorts by retaining the $122 minimum Social Security benefit for current recipients. At the same time, it decreed that persons retiring after Jan. 1, 1982, will receive only the amount to which their contributions to the system entitle them; in many cases, that could be much less than $122. Combined with other economies, that change will improve the Social Security system's fiscal health, but not much. Sooner or later, preferably sooner, Congress must do more to ensure the system's viability.

President Reagan's suggestion to eliminate the minimum benefit was short-lived. The House protested vigorously, the Senate condemned the cut 95-0, and shortly thereafter Mr. Reagan himself backed off the idea. That at least made sure that the poorest Social Security retirees would not have to supplement their meager check with public assistance.

In voting to alter the minimum assitance provisions, Congress wisely allowed the retirement fund to borrow temporarily from other Social Security trust funds to prevent it from going broke before the end of next year. Nevertheless, Social Security's long-term health is anything but assured, even with the tax increases that become effective on Jan. 1, 1982, and thereafter. The need for additional reforms is obvious, yet Congress is not expected to push for those reforms until after the 1982 elections, a delay that emphasizes the political considerations present in any dealing with Social Security.

The Democrats are not free of blame in this matter but they clearly have gotten a bad rap from Republicans, particularly Mr. Reagan, in two areas. Republicans roundly criticized the Democratic-dominated Congress and former President Carter for approving Social Security reforms in 1977; the legislation was denounced then as the "biggest tax increase in history." So the president's recent charge that Democrats have done nothing to ensure Social Security's solvency is wrong. Congress believed that tne legislation establishing periodic increases in the tax rate and wage base through 1990 would keep the system fiscally sound. That expectation has been undermined, however, by inflation, unemployment and the soaring cost of Medicare.

On Jan. 1, the Social Security tax for employees and employers will increase slightly from 6.65 to 6.7 percent, computed on a wage base of $32,400 (a substantial increase over the present $29,700). This means that employees who paid the maximum $1,975.05 in 1981 will pay about $195 more in 1982. Altogether, the revised rate structure will produce about $4.8 billion for the retirement, Medicare and disability trust funds. But there's a kicker: Fiscal experts agree that even that gigantic sum is insufficient to rescue a system whose outgo has exceeded its income since 1975.

The picture is further complicated by the fact that Americans' increased longevity has drastically reduced the ratio of retirees to workers: whereas in the past there were as many as six contributors to the system for every recipient, today there are only about half as many. Clearly, Congress will have to enact more comprehensive reforms — soon — if the system's fiscal integrity is to be preserved.

What reforms? Several reasonable ones have been suggested; among them: gradually raising the retirement age from 65 to 68, smaller cost-of-living increases, or shifting Medicare from the Social Security system to the general fund. Unless these or other reforms are approved, the system could go bankrupt — with severe consequences for the more than 36 million retirees. The president and Congress evidently believe it is safer to play politics by delaying consideration of such fundamental reforms. But the anger of retirees upset over such reasonable change will be small potatoes compared to the outpouring of wrath from working and retired Americans if Congress and the White House imperil the entire system with such dilly-dallying.

HOUSTON CHRONICLE
Houston, Texas,
December 27, 1981

Social Security proved to be 1981's hot potato in Washington. President Reagan had some ideas on how to change the system to make it more fiscally sound, but had to back away from his own suggestions. Congress approved elimination of minimum benefits, but had to restore them. Congressional committees did the very least they could on Social Security financing, putting off the hard decisions.

There is no mystery why Social Security is such a hot political issue — a lot of people who vote are involved, either as contributors or recipients. Some recent figures illustrate the degree of that involvement.

A study has found that 24 percent of households paying Social Security taxes in 1979 paid more in Social Security than in personal income taxes. If it is assumed the worker indirectly pays for his employer's contribution too, 51 percent of taxpaying households paid more to the retirement system than to the Internal Revenue Service.

Another study found that Social Security represents the only income for 25 percent of the the nation's elderly households and provides at least half of the income for two-thirds of them.

With Social Security's payroll bite rivaling that of the IRS, and with two-thirds of the elderly households heavily dependent upon Social Security checks, it's no wonder both the president and Congress kept juggling the issue from hand to hand.

Trustees Cite Economic Recession in 1982 Report

In their 1982 annual report to Congress, submitted April 1, the three trustees of the Social Security system warned that the system would not be able to pay benefits by July of the following year. They warned that Social Security's short-term outlook was "significantly worse" because of the economic recession. "A series of economic downturns more severe than anticipated have led to the current financial crisis," wrote Treasury Secretary Donald Regan, Labor Secretary Raymond Donovan and Health and Human Services Secretary Richard Schweiker. For the seventh straight year, the trustees said, the old age and survivors' trust fund and the disability fund had paid out more than they had received. By the end of 1981, the two funds had dwindled to $24.5 billion, equal to about two months' payments.

In 1981, Congress had temporarily authorized the old age fund to borrow from the disability fund through the end of 1982, to cover financial needs through mid-1983. The trustees said that unless the legislation were renewed, the old age fund would run out of money. If the economy improved, they added, "the three combined trust funds would just be able to pay benefits on time through the 1980's, but there is no margin of safety to provide for even slightly less favorable economic conditions." The trustees' projections were based on economic assumptions more pessimistic than those officially adopted by the Reagan Administration.

AKRON BEACON JOURNAL
Akron, Ohio, April 7, 1982

THERE IS no doubt that the Social Security system is in trouble. How could it not be, with rising unemployment reducing payments into the trust funds, and inflation and an aging population increasing payments out of them?

But there is a doubt, growing year by year, that the Congress, whose members are not dependent upon Social Security benefits for retirement income, will find the courage to take steps necessary to restore stability.

There are ways to accomplish that; but the corrections or changes require political courage.

Almost as soon as Congress passed the biggest tax hike in its history in 1977 — all to bolster Social Security — warnings began again that the Old Age and Survivors Insurance and Disability Insurance trust funds would be exhausted before the end of the century. The reckoning date has been steadily moved up. Last week, trustees said that without a tax increase or benefit cuts, the retirement fund could run out of money by July 1983, and the Medicare fund between 1986 and 1991.

Democrats and Republicans may argue about when but not whether the system will go broke. They agree that there are serious financial problems, but neither party wants to take the political risk of cutting or delaying benefits or of expanding the Social Security base. When President Reagan suggested cuts last fall, protests were so loud that he retreated, and the Congress took the easy way out: It restored the minimum benefit President Reagan had cut and approved borrowing from the disability and Medicare funds to shore up the retirement fund. That is a delaying tactic that jeopardizes all three funds.

Solutions to strengthen the system do exist. Some options:

● Eliminating the minimum benefit of $122 a month that is paid even to retirees whose earnings or periods of employment under Social Security did not qualify them for that much.

● Including Congress and other government workers, the military — everyone — under Social Security. This would eliminate double- and triple-dippers, those who qualify for more than one public pension.

● Using a different, more realistic base to calculate annual cost-of-living increases in benefits. Last year the increase was 11.2 percent, or more than an added $1 billion monthly.

● Taxing Social Security benefits. Those retirees who depend solely on such benefits would have little or no tax liability. Those for whom Social Security benefits are only part of their total income should face the same tax liability that many other public retirees, like teachers, face.

● Changing the age at which retirement benefits are available.

These are only some possibilities. Congress could choose to go on borrowing from one fund to rescue another and, when all three are bankrupt, use the general fund to support Social Security. The fact that the annual federal deficit is expected to pass the $100 billion mark in 1983 and the national debt has already reached $1 trillion should dispose of that idea.

Perhaps the best option would be for Congress to put its members under Social Security. Then they might get serious about solving financial problems in a system in which they would have a stake.

The Houston Pos
Houston, Texas, April 15, 1982

The 1982 annual report of the Social Security System Board of Trustees underscores the urgent need to solve the giant pension program's short-term financial problems and to protect its long-term solvency. The report warns that the largest of the system's three trust funds — the Old Age and Survivors Insurance fund — is spending more than it is taking in and will run short of cash by next July if steps are not taken to shore it up. Obviously, Congress isn't going to let it go broke.

The trustees made a similar prediction about the fund last year, warning that it would be depleted by late 1982 unless action was taken to keep it solvent. Congress responded by approving a temporary interfund lending arrangement that allowed OASI to borrow from the Medicare and disability trust funds. But that is not likely to work well again. Continued dipping into the other funds would only weaken them. The Social Security trustees expect the Medicare trust fund to remain stable until the end of the decade, barring further heavy borrowing from it. But the fund is then expected to face its own fiscal crunch.

We are fast running out of quick, easy fixes for Social Security. More substantive, lasting remedies are needed. The most promising prospective source for those solutions is the National Commission on Social Security Reform, which will report its findings and recommendations by the end of the year. The 15-member bipartisan panel was formed by President Reagan to study the pension program's problems and help shape a consensus on how to solve them. Five members of the commission were named by Democratic leaders.

The president gave the commission freedom to consider all options, even those with which he disagrees, such as using general revenue funds to transfuse the Social Security trust funds. The panel faces one of the toughest assignments ever given a government advisory body. Not that it is the first commission to wrestle with Social Security's problems. Few federal programs have been subject to such intense scrutiny. But, as the trustees' annual report makes clear, the system's troubles are becoming increasingly difficult to cope with.

The search for solutions is complicated by politics, the vagaries of the economy and public skepticism about the future of Social Security. The current OASI difficulties, for instance, have been aggravated by the recession. Unemployment has reduced the payroll tax collections that provide revenue for Social Security. And though inflation has abated somewhat, it is still high enough to force cost-of-living increases in beneficiaries' pension checks.

Raising the payroll tax would put more money in the system's trust funds. But Congress boosted the tax only a few years ago in a move that was supposed to solve Social Security's funding difficulties well into the future. The lawmakers will be wary of voting another sharp increase soon. And if raising payroll taxes is politically sensitive, cutting benefits is dynamite, as the president found when he made suggestions along that line. It was then that he created the reform commission.

The first priority is to keep the system fiscally sound until, according to Social Security actuaries, it begins to accumulate a surplus, which is expected to last until early in the 21st century. Next, attention must be given to the system's long-range problems. These are expected to develop after 2025, when the post-World War II baby boom generation begins to retire, increasing the ratio of pensioners to workers contributing to the system.

Congress and the administration will want to give the most careful consideration to the forthcoming recommendations of the Social Security Reform Commission. But in the final analysis, they will be responsible for deciding how to restore the ailing system to fiscal health. That must be done, however politically unpalatable the job may be.

The Oregonian
Portland, Ore., April 4, 1982

The short-term outlook for Social Security is for an even worse condition, thanks to the recession and high unemployment, than its loudest critics believed a few months ago.

President Reagan only Wednesday said he won't support a reduction in benefits to help his deficit. While his feet stand in concrete, Social Security's books are being washed in a bath of red ink. The trustees of the fund — three members of President Reagan's Cabinet — said in a report that the short-term outlook for Social Security is significantly worse than a year ago.

For the seventh straight year, the combined old-age and survivors and disability funds paid out more than they took in. While these funds were losing money, the Medicare fund rose by $5 billion, putting the combined system in the black by $3.1 billion. Congress allowed transfers among funds in 1980.

The future of the red-ink funds promises more red ink. Medicare can't be depended upon to continue to erase their deficits. If the funds were depleted, Social Security would have to get general fund money in order to mail out monthly checks. The current prediction is that all funds combined will be unable to meet their obligations by the end of 1983.

President Reagan, in rolling back from a proposed cut in benefits, is not about to change his mind in an election year, nor is the Congress expected to do anything. Everybody is waiting on a report from a commission that is studying the problem, hoping for a soft political answer — a miracle.

The president and the Congress are counting on an end to the recession later this year to save their hides by stopping the bleeding. But unless reforms are undertaken this year, there is an excellent chance the system will have to tap the general budget, further increasing the soaring deficit that is fueling high interest rates.

THE CHRISTIAN SCIENCE MONITOR
Boston, Mass., April 5, 1982

Guess what's back in the news again, if you haven't already heard. The short-term stability of social security, according to the system's board of trustees in their annual report last week, is "significantly worse" than was estimated last year. Unless Congress and the White House take some action the retirement trust fund will be out of money by the summer of 1983.

Still, as social security commissioner John Svahn is reported to have said: "No one who's receiving social security benefits needs to worry about losing those benefits." That possibility, says Mr. Svahn, "isn't going to happen." And why not? Probably, one can assume, because presidents and lawmakers must eventually face the electorate.

It needs to also be recalled that the social security "problem" is not merely financial in nature. It is a political problem. Unfortunately, Congress and the administration have tidily put off any resolution until after this year's congressional election, when a special 15-member commission issues its report. The commission will obviously have to make some tough recommendations.

The American people overwhelmingly wish to save their social security system. Since that is the case would it not behoove Congress and the White House to truly depoliticize the issue, reach the broadest possible consensus, and then forthrightly go about the task of putting the social security house in order?

Detroit Free Press
Detroit, Mich., April 4, 1982

THE ANNUAL report of the trustees of the Social Security system is gloomier than ever, forecasting bankruptcy of the system by 1983. The gloom is compounded by the difficulty of dealing with Social Security's problems in an election year and over the opposition of the president, who has been reluctant to tamper with Social Security since his own proposals for change were howled down last year.

Last year Congress kept the system afloat by letting it borrow from the disability and Medicare trust funds, but the borrowing authority runs out Dec. 31. Even if it is extended, the disability and Medicare trust funds themselves will be drained by 1984. And with nine percent unemployment, Social Security is collecting less money from payroll taxes, at the same time the automatic cost-of-living factor forces the system to pay out higher benefits.

Much of the budget debate has centered on the president's refusal to cut his defense budget, but the administration has been equally reluctant to tackle the problem of how to trim rapidly escalating entitlement programs — with the stunning exception, of course, of food stamps. But it is unlikely that Social Security can be bailed out, or the federal deficit trimmed, without some changes, such as modifying or uncoupling the link between Social Security benefits and the inflation rate. Indexing, which began as a humane and automatic way to help the elderly keep up with rising costs, has become a big engine in driving up the inflation rate. Even with the recent changes in the way the Consumer Price Index is figured, there is a good argument that the CPI overstates the impact of inflation on retired persons.

The Medicare fund is in temporarily good shape, but eventually the escalation in health-care costs — not just for the elderly, but for all of us — is going to have to be confronted as well. The president's solution is to encourage competition in the health-care industry. But it is probably true that without more active intervention by the federal government, the costs will continue to zoom. There are too many pressures on health-care providers — the threat of malpractice suits, the patients' expectations, the enormous costs of space-age medical equipment — to expect them voluntarily to shoulder the burden of cost containment.

All of this is by way of pointing out that large budget questions are still being skirted by both Congress and the president. The deficit cannot be handled without looking at entitlement programs and health-care costs. The Social Security fund will not be back on a sound basis until the general economy rebounds and the unemployed go back to work.

Whatever solution is devised for Social Security, it will require special consideration for the elderly poor, who will be most hurt by any increase in health-care costs or cutbacks in the cost-of-living adjustments. Chances are Congress will grasp at a short-term answer for next year, perhaps borrowing from the other trust funds or the Treasury. That will not eliminate the need to confront the longer-range problems of the system — and the link between what ails Social Security, the federal budget and the economy at large.

CHARLESTON EVENING POST
Charleston, S.C., April 5, 1982

The report by Social Security trustees that the system won't be able to pay regular retirees' and survivors' benefits by mid-1983 unless corrective action is taken soon confirms previous assessments of the stability of the funds involved.

At this moment it is an exaggeration to say the retirement fund is bankrupt. It is no exaggeration to say the fund's short-term status has worsened significantly as a consequence of economic downturns. It is no exaggeration to say, as the trustees have just said, that congressional action to avert the deepening crisis is imperative "in the very near future."

Yet there are no signs either the administration or the Congress will step in immediately to bolster the system. The trustees themselves made no recommendation, pending a special commission report on Social Security reform, due in December. And because the obvious relief measures are either higher payroll taxes or decreased benefits, Congress does not appear eager to jump into a politically sensitive issue in this election year. Indications are, in fact, that Congress will put off doing anything until after November, then let a lame-duck Congress take up the matter of propping up the failing Social Security funds.

That is a cowardly approach. It is hardly the approach that millions of constituents, worried about how their financial future, are likely to endorse. People who have spent their working lives paying into a retirement fund now deemed shakier than ever ought not tolerate congressional delays in fixing what is wrong.

DESERET NEWS

Salt Lake City, Utah,
April 5, 1982

Only three years ago, Congress bolstered the Social Security System with its biggest tax boost in history: a $227 billion increase spread over 10 years. That was supposed to put the system on a sound financial basis through at least 1989.

But this week Social Security's trustees reported that because of the economic downturn, the system may be unable to pay benefits on time by July, 1983, unless something is done.

That's a worst-case prognosis, but nevertheless must be taken into account in adjusting the program to fit today's economic conditions. The three trustees of the Social Security System — the secretaries of Labor, Treasury, and Health and Human Services — say that an economic upturn would permit the system to pay benefits on time through the 1980s, as planned — but "just barely." There is "no margin of safety to provide for even slightly less favorable economic conditions," the trustees warn.

So even with an improvement in the present economic outlook, Social Security would just be getting by. That's an unhealthy condition that needs more attention from Congress.

Last year congressmen approved a stopgap measure to allow the three systems — disability, old-age, and Medicare — to borrow from each other. That alone is not sufficient to guarantee the viability of the three funds. Even if inter-fund borrowing authority is extended for the disability and old-age funds, both would be unable to pay benefits on time in the last half of 1983.

The Reagan administration already has moved to limit some Social Security college benefits to minor children of deceased Social Security beneficiaries. While that may appear harsh to some, it must be viewed in this light: Congress so increased benefits in the Social Security system, particularly in the late 1960s and early '70s, that they were far out of line with the economy as a whole. One of those benefits was a guaranteed Social Security income for college-age minor children of deceased beneficiaries. If the system is to survive, then, some of those benefits will have to be cut back.

Congress has two choices: It must either cut benefits, or increase payroll and other taxes to support Social Security. It cannot let a system go broke because of its own past largesse.

The Times-Picayune
The States-Item

New Orleans, La., April 3, 1982

The trustees of the Social Security system have again reminded Congress and the Reagan administration that time is running short for reforming the troubled financial system upon which millions of the nation's retired workers and others depend.

In their annual report to Congress, the trustees warned that the system will be unable to pay retirees' and survivors' benefits on time, starting in July 1983, unless Congress makes basic changes in the system in the near future.

Despite benefit cuts made last year in the system, its "short-range financial status is significantly worse than was estimated last year" because of the recession, the trustees reported.

Last year, Congress, with the eventual approval of the administration, adopted a stopgap measure enabling the Old Age and Survivors Insurance Trust Fund to meet its obligations thorough 1982 by borrowing from the better-off disability and hospital funds. After the issue became hopelessly embroiled in politics, President Reagan, with bipartisan congressional approval, appointed a special Commission on Social Security Reform to study the system's problems and recommend specific reforms. The commission's report is expected by the end of the year.

Congressional action on the issue is highly unlikely before the November elections or before the commission issues its recommendations. Even so, John A. Svahn, Social Security commissioner, says the timing for congressional enactment of Social Security reforms is "pretty good." Borrowing from the other two funds to bolster the sagging old-age fund, beginning in October, would give Congress "several months to act and shore up the system," said Mr. Savahn.

Returning long-term solvency to the Social Security system is going to require some very hard choices by Congress and the administration. But there are few tasks of higher priority before the nation. For that reason, it is essential that the effort be devoid of partisan politics.

Dole Urges Special Session of Congress

The Social Security issue had become more and more of a political morass in 1982, as the congressional elections approached and the problems of the system escalated under poor economic conditions. Most congressmen were content to leave the complex issue in the hands of the bipartisan committee, created in 1981, which was due to present its conclusions by December. Kansas Republican Sen. Robert Dole, however, who was not up for election in 1982, pressed in early September for a special lame duck session of Congress to deal with Social Security reform. Dole, the chairman of the Senate Finance Committee, argued that the period after the November elections and before the start of budget battles in 1983 would be the perfect time to tackle the problem. "There is a real window of opportunity between Thanksgiving and Christmas," said Dole, adding: "Even politicians aren't too political in that period."

San Francisco Chronicle

San Francisco, Calif., September 3, 1982

SENATOR ROBERT Dole, the Kansas Republican, has urged President Reagan and congressional leaders to call a special post-election session of Congress on Social Security to assure the system's solvency. The chairman of the Senate Finance Committee and author of the recent tax increase bill says there are convincing financial, administrative and political reasons for moving quickly on the matter.

He is right about the pressing nature of the problem. And he is also correct in acknowledging that nothing can be done before the seasonal political winds subside and the ballots are counted in November.

That was pretty much the lesson of last May when GOP leaders had to withdraw their budget resolution proposing three-year savings of $40 billion in Social Security, to be achieved either through reduction in benefits, or an increase in taxes. This was simply too volatile a proposal for its time. Moderate Republicans felt the issue would be so thoroughly exploited by Democrats that it had to be shelved.

DOLE'S CALL for a special session has been supported by the chairman of the National Committee on Social Security Reform, Alan Greenspan, who says "the sooner the issue can be addressed the better." The commission was appointed by Reagan to report after the election on recommendations for assuring the system's financial stability.

In his letters to Reagan and congressional leaders, Dole noted that authority for interfund borrowing among three Social Security funds to finance retirement benefits expires in December. He said the retirement fund will be "unable to continue meeting its benefit obligations by July of 1983."

And while there is disagreement over how significant Social Security deficits are, Dole said, most agree on a number of points: That the system "faces insolvency in the near future" and implementing changes will require "adequate lead-time for an already-overburdened Social Security computer."

So some action clearly must be taken at the first appropriate political moment.

Rocky-Mountain News

Denver, Colo., August 31, 1982

SEN. Robert Dole's proposal for a special session of Congress to deal with Social Security is a good one.

Dole, chairman of the Senate Finance Committee, would have Congress come back for a late November-early December session.

There is no ideal time, of course, to grapple with so controversial a subject. But the period after the November elections and before the new Congress convenes would be about as non-political as could be found.

Moreover, the congressional leadership and the president could agree that the special session would be confined to fixing the Social Security system. If anything needs concentrated effort, it is this.

Dole was at least half right on another suggestion — that Social Security's financial problems might be solved through a combination of payroll tax increases and lowered benefits for future retirees.

We hope he isn't seriously considering an increase in the payroll tax. The tax already is so high on employees and employers that it's becoming a drag on the economy, and it is scheduled to go even higher over the next five years.

Many workers now pay more Social Security taxes than federal income taxes. The tax on employers is taking a growing slice of income that could be used for business expansion.

Dole is right, though, about the need to curb benefits for future retirees. That could be done through raising the retirement age and revising cost-of-living adjustments so that annual increases in benefits don't outrun the real rate of inflation.

Bringing all workers into the Social Security system also would improve its financial base. Federal government workers are exempt, as are employees of some state and local governments that chose not to join the system.

Whatever the solution for solving the program's problems, it is essential that Congress find it soon. A special session late this year could head off a financial crisis that could hit the program as early as next spring.

The Boston Herald American

Boston, Mass., September 8, 1982

Two political parties, like two heads, can be better than one.

That is the idea Sen. Robert Dole of Kansas had in mind when he proposed that Democrats and Republicans join forces to save the Social Security program. And the time to join those forces, in Dole's opinion, is in a political off-season, such as between November's election day and Christmas, when the winds of controversy are not blowing as violently as they are at other times.

Social Security is in trouble. Its financial foundation has been crumbling for some time. The program must be saved. It must be saved not only for the 35 million Americans now receiving benefits, but for millions in the future who will find it as a necessary source of support in their advancing years.

The best hope according to Sen. Dole is a bi-partisan coalition, and proper timing. The attractiveness of the period picked by the senator is increased by the fact that a 15-member National Commission on Social Security Reform will have made its report by that time.

Dole put it this way in a letter to House Speaker Tip O'Neill and Senate Majority Leader Baker: "As I see it, there is a real window of opportunity for positive action after the election and before the 98th Congress convenes. Political pressures would be at a minimum."

Robert E. Thompson, chief of the Washington Bureau of The Hearst Newspapers, said this about the Dole proposal to save Social Security:

"There is no better time to seek to resolve the matter than in a post-election session.

"If Congress and the White House, three months before an election, can put together a bi-partisan coalition to pass a tax increase, they certainly should be able, nearly two years before the next election, to form a coalition to save Social Security."

Chicago Tribune

Chicago, Ill., September 16, 1982

Can there be anyone left in Washington who doesn't appreciate the need to do something about the Social Security system? It has been insolvent for the last decade—the result of overgenerous benefit increases, which have drastically raised costs, and of a stagnant economy, which has reduced revenues. The trust fund will run out of money sometime next year unless something is done. Yet so far Congress and the President have done nothing.

The excuse is politics. You can't expect the politicians to do anything about such an explosive issue in an election year, says the prevailing wisdom. That doesn't explain why Congress rebuffed Mr. Reagan when he proposed some spending cuts last year, a full 18 months before the off-year elections. But it does give force to the argument for a special postelection session of Congress to confront the Social Security crisis.

That recommendation originally came from the Democratic side of the aisle, courtesy of Sen. Ernest Hollings of South Carolina. It has since been seconded by Senate Finance Committee chairman Robert Dole, a Kansas Republican. Their thinking is that only with the 1982 elections over, and the 1984 elections 24 months away, will Congress and the President be able to overcome the pressure to placate beneficiaries—who include one in every six Americans.

Unfortunately President Reagan says he won't decide whether to request a special session until he's seen the report of his advisory commission on Social Security—not due until after Nov. 2. But the commission's suggestions, whatever they are, won't make action any less urgent.

Given the lamentable stalling on this issue—the impending bankruptcy has been expected since 1979—this proposal is probably the only hope for statesmanlike action. A certain amount of demagoguery is inevitable even in a postelection session, but the incentives for it will be less than at any other time.

And there will a strong incentive for leaders on both sides, and in the White House, to keep the debate as calm as possible. The inescapable fact is that by next summer, barring legislative correction, the Social Security Administration will not be able to send out its monthly checks. It will be politically much worse for our elected officials—all of them—to slap together a desperate patchwork solution at the last minute than to do what needs to be done this year. That's something both Tip O'Neill and Ronald Reagan should think about.

THE DAILY OKLAHOMAN

Oklahoma City, Okla., September 7, 1982

IT'S rather a narrow "window of opportunity" that Sen. Robert Dole, R-Kan., sees in calling for a special lame-duck congressional session to deal with Social Security after the November elections.

Whether even a lame-duck Congress dealing exclusively with Social Security could pick its way through this political minefield in the limited time available is highly problematical.

Calling Social Security's financial bind "the most pressing issue yet unresolved by Congress and the administration," the chairman of the Senate Finance Committee says "there is a real window of opportunity" for dealing with the problem after the November elections and before the 98th Congress convenes in January.

It's true, as Dole says, that "political pressures would be at a minimum" at that time, since a lame-duck session would include members of Congress who chose not to seek re-election and those defeated in November.

But the initial White House reaction was understandably cautious. "Let's wait and see," said deputy press secretary Larry Speakes. Twice within the last two years, Congress has refused to consider proposals by the Reagan administration to put the troubled Social Security system on a steady course by slowing the growth of benefits.

It was to remove the issue from election-year politics that the administration handed it over to a bipartisan 15-member presidential commission with instructions to report its recommendations before the end of the year.

The president would have to await the commission's report before calling a special session to act on its recommendations. These are expected to include proposed changes in the formula for cost-of-living adjustments and a gradual increase in the retirement age from the current 65 to 68 in light of the fact that people are living longer productive lives.

Dole has mentioned both of these possibilities and has suggested also that a solution might include advancing the date of payroll tax increased now scheduled to take effect in later years.

In this politically sensitive realm, opposition is bound to occur no matter what is proposed. But time is running out on the ailing retirement trust fund, which is functioning now on borrowings from the still-solvent funds supporting health insurance (Medicare) and disability payments.

Dole notes that legislation to re-authorize such borrowings will have to be enacted before June. Otherwise the nearly depleted retirement fund would be unable to meet its obligations by next July. The skyrocketing costs of health care are placing the Medicare fund itself in jeopardy, and Congress must deal with the onrushing insolvency of the entire system.

Whether it can do so in less than two months is highly questionable, particularly in view of its past timidity when confronted with this prickly subject.

Newsday

Long Island, N.Y., September 2, 1982

Every time Congress or the Reagan administration has tried to assure the solvency of the Social Security trust fund, it has run into trouble.

Early in his term, the President underestimated the effect of a proposal to end the minimum Social Security benefit, which is paid to people who haven't worked enough to qualify for regular benefits. That turned the issue into a political football, and the game is still going on.

Since then, while Washington has done only minor tinkering, the trust fund has grown so thin that it could run out of money for monthly checks by next July.

That needn't be cause for alarm: The immediate problems can be patched over if they're addressed soon. The system's long-term difficulties are stickier — although there's still enough time to remedy them without great inconvenience to future retirees. All providing, however, that the administration and the Democrats in Congress agree to treat the issue as something more than an opportunity to make points with the voters.

Earlier this year, President Reagan appointed a nonpolitical commission to seek ways of keeping the trust fund afloat. Now Sen. Robert Dole and Rep. Dan Rostenkowski, who chair the committees that over-see revenue measures, are suggesting that Congress meet in a lame-duck session this fall to deal with the Social Security's ills.

"I don't know any time that's less political than right after an election," Dole said.

Americans are right to be cautious about lame-duck sessions; some legislators attending them have already been voted out of office and are no longer adequately accountable.

But Dole's argument for this session has merit. The Social Security issue has been so politicized that it needs to be dealt with in the least politically charged setting possible. And the solutions have been put off so long, there's little time left to get at them.

The Virginian-Pilot

Norfolk, Va., August 31, 1982

Social Security may be America's last taboo. Every time someone talks about reforming it, Claude Pepper erupts with angry jeremiads and Dan Rather spins tales of old people forced to choose between eating dog food or freezing to death. Nothing gets done.

That may change, however, because it has become clear that the system is bleeding America dry. It grows more rapidly than inflation, gobbles up nearly as much income as the income tax, and threatens to prevent future generations of Americans from enjoying the fruits of their labors. Moreover, it will go bankrupt sometime next summer if it isn't revised. This gruesome reality has led Sen. Robert Dole to suggest that Congress convene after the November elections to work on nothing but Social Security reform.

That is a splendid idea. Congress never has come out and admitted that Americans spend too much money on Social Security or that the program threatens the nation's fiscal integrity. Such a statement — implied by the mere existence of an emergency session — would represent an important first step toward rescuing Social Security before it squashes the working man.

One cannot hope for more than a small morsel of progress, even if Congress goes along with Senator Dole, because the Claude Peppers and Dan Rathers still have clout. But tiny steps are better than none at all.

The danger is that Senate Republicans might trade important parts of the president's original budget — defense spending, for example, or the indexing that begins in 1985 — for relatively insubstantial concessions from the Democrats, such as pushing back cost-of-living adjustments by a month or two. A similar thing happened with Senator Dole's tax bill, and the Kansas Republican already has hinted that he might court Democrats by including new "loophole closings" in a Social Security compromise.

Still, no one should be scared away from taking a look at Social Security for fear of what might happen. For unless Congress acts soon to staunch the hemmorhaging of the entitlements system, America's economy will be too sick for Reaganomics or any other kind of -nomics to cure.

The San Diego Union

San Diego, Calif., November 3, 1982

With the election finally behind us, we can hope that our political leaders can now return to a rational discussion of the Social Security problem. Since the campaigns started early this year, those involved in politics have: 1. tried to avoid the subject, 2. blundered by talking about solutions, or 3. exploited it in a way that carried demagoguery to new heights.

Social Security is in deep trouble. November benefit checks for the elderly were covered with borrowed money. The retirement fund is expected to need $11 billion in loans from the disability and Medicare funds to cover its obligations during the balance of the current fiscal year.

Not only is the system in trouble, but there is no way of solving its problems without stepping on political toes. That explains why Sen. Robert Dole sees the coming lame-duck session of Congress as a rare window of opportunity to come to grips with the issue of Social Security reform.

The National Commission on Social Security Reform is scheduled to meet next week to take final action on what promises to be a controversial report summing up its year-long study. Alan Greenspan, the chairman, offers little comfort about what it will contain. The President and Congress, he says, may have to settle for the "least worst" of the options for putting the system on a sound financial footing.

But what is least worst may depend on one's point of view. The option of raising payroll taxes would not please President Reagan, who is trying to keep taxes down for the sake of economic growth. Nor, would it please younger workers paying into a system that promises only a distant and dubious return.

Advancing the age for eligibility for retirement benefits, or phasing out the early retirement option, would irritate those workers now nearing 62 or 65. Tinkering with the automatic cost-of-living increases in future benefits would be resisted by those now retired and accustomed to seeing their checks rise with the consumer price index.

Finally, the option of forcing employees of federal, state, and local government to meld their now-separate pension systems with Social Security would be perceived by them as a threat to their potential retirement income.

With all those political considerations, Sen. Dole thinks the best hope for action lies in putting Social Security on the agenda of the rump session of the 97th Congress convening at the end of this month. Some members will be retiring at the end of the year, thus free of re-election considerations, while the rest will not have to face elections again for two to six years.

That the lame-duck session would confront the issue is only a long-shot possibility. Its agenda already is crowded with major appropriations bills hanging over from the pre-election session. The familiar Social Security "crisis" may be greeting the 98th Congress when it convenes in January.

Whether it is an expiring Congress or a new one that finally tackles Social Security reform, there is precious little time to spend in debating the options offered by the Greenspan commission. Somewhere among the "least worst" choices is a formula that is workable and fair. The President and Congress must find it before Social Security falls under the approaching shadow of the 1984 elections and we are back where we started.

The Wichita
Eagle-Beacon

Wichita, Kans., September 2, 1982

The proposal by Sen. Bob Dole, R-Kan., calling for a lame duck session of Congress devoted to Social Security reform is a good one. Almost everybody in Congress agrees the Social Security system is dangerously close to bankruptcy, but almost nobody up for re-election this November — as all members of the House of Representatives who want to keep their jobs are — wants to rock the political boat now.

Though this doesn't say much for members' commitment to principle, the reality is that members will feel more free to speak and vote on the basis of what they know is true, without fear of immediate political consequences, after the fall elections. Even outgoing members — those who have just been defeated or did not run again — may welcome the chance to deal with a problem that has plagued previous sessions of Congress, but which always has eluded solution.

What to do about Social Security's financial crisis needs to be worked out as objectively as possible in a nonpartisan atmosphere. A lame duck session should have about as much potential for freedom from normal partisan pressures as any session of Congress could have.

As 5th District Rep. Bob Whittaker, R-Kan., suggested Wednesday in a breakfast appearance sponsored by the Wichita Area Chamber of Commerce, Social Security's fiscal problems have grown out of good intentions and bad actuarial planning. As life expectancy rates have increased over the years, benefit payout projections that once looked quite fundable now represent an enormous potential problem. The question almost has shifted from being one of "if" the money runs out to "when."

While retirees whose economic survival depends on the regular arrival of their Social Security checks cannot be suddenly cut off or their benefits reduced — nor would anyone want them to be — there must be gradual readjustment of the whole program.

Mr. Whittaker pointed out that some young Americans, whose Social Security taxes must help support today's elderly, already are paying higher Social Security taxes than income taxes. Yet, unless something is done quickly, their own future retirement benefits may be in jeopardy.

Mr. Whittaker thinks Mr. Dole's proposal makes sense. So do we.

ARGUS-LEADER

Sioux Falls, S.D., September 10, 1982

President Ronald Reagan should accept the advice of Senate Finance Committee Chairman Robert Dole and call a special post-election session of Congress to solve Social Security's financial problems.

Present estimates are that the system will no longer be self-supporting by next summer. Such problems are better solved before they occur than afterwards.

Dole suggested that one compromise might include moving up the date of payroll tax increases that are now set to take effect in later years, and reducing the growth of benefits, not cutting present benefits. That's a logical approach.

Both Reagan and Congress would have done better to address the problem during the last year and a half instead of delaying it. After creating an uproar last year about some modifications in Social Security, Reagan backed off.

He appointed a bipartisan National Commission on Social Security Reform to study the agency's funding problems. The commission's report should be ready for action after the November election by a lame-duck session. Dole believes that such a session can effectively deal with the political problems inherent in making changes.

Basically, Social Security needs some minor adjustments before next July to keep it solvent. Generally, these can be accomplished with changes over a long period that won't seriously affect individuals whose retirement is forthcoming within a few years.

Any major changes, such as extending Social Security to nonprofit institutions and federal employees, would require a strong recommendation from the commission and determination by congressional leaders to reach a long-term solution now instead of delaying it.

Social Security's problems are typical of other federal entitlement programs in which Congress and the administration have no control over increasing costs without taking legislative action.

Congress on Aug. 18 approved a three-year $13.3 billion package of spending cuts. The bill cut in half the annual cost-of-living adjustment for federal retirees under age 62 over the next three years. Adjustments will be made every 13 months instead of every 12 months. These changes are expected to save $3.3 billion in all.

"Double-dipping" by military retirees who collect both military and civil service pension benefits was eliminated. Technical changes were made in computing pay of government workers and retirees. These moves are expected to save the government about $4.1 billion over three years.

Social Security should not be exempt from the kind of fiscal restraint shown by Congress in its actions affecting retirees.

A lame duck session of Congress would have a big advantage in dealing with the Social Security problem. As Dole says, there is no time less political than right after an election.

Detroit Free Press

Detroit, Mich., September 7, 1982

SEN. ROBERT Dole's proposal to deal with Social Security reform in the "window of opportunity" between the November election and the end of the year is one that the president would be wise to accept.

The need to restructure parts of the Social Security system is exceeded only by the political difficulties of doing so. There will never be a better time to confront the issue than in those few weeks when a lame-duck session will be free of the pressures of an election campaign or the distractions of the organizing of a new Congress.

Despite the system's looming deficits, the mere suggestion of changes in Social Security brings down a hailstorm of protest, mostly from retirees and older workers. No one in Washington seriously proposes reducing benefits, only a slowdown in the rate at which benefits will increase in the future. Most of the long-term reform proposals would be phased in gradually, with little or no perceptible impact on persons now receiving or about to receive benefits. Such subtleties are lost on an angry and sometimes fearful constituency, however, and it is doubtful there will ever be a more propitious time to attack the problem.

Coincidentally, Sen. Dole's request for a special session was made the same day the Congressional Budget Office released its latest projection, showing a $155 billion deficit in the 1983 federal budget even *after* last month's $99 billion tax increase. Except for defense spending (which also needs pruning), Social Security and similar entitlement programs are the only areas left in the budget where the rate of spending can be slowed with significant effect.

The president, understandably, may not want to rattle Republican candidates by talking about Social Security before Nov. 9. But if he does not embrace Sen. Dole's proposal and call the Congress back to work immediately after the election, Mr. Reagan may be chucking the last good chance for dealing with Social Security in any rational manner right out that window of opportunity — and slamming it shut for some time to come.

Retirement Fund Borrows From Disability and Medicare

The financial predicament of Social Security's retirement fund became painfully apparent in November when OASI was forced to borrow nearly $600 million from the hospital and disability insurance funds. The loan, the first required since the establishment of the system, was necessary to cover November benefit checks. Treasury officials warned that the borrowing could total as much as $1 billion, and that later loans were also expected. (Another $3.44 billion was in fact borrowed from the hospital insurance fund to cover December benefit checks, and Administration officials said at the end of December that a total of $13 billion would have to be borrowed to carry the retirement fund through the first six months of 1983.)

THE RICHMOND NEWS LEADER

Richmond, Va., November 2, 1982

For the first time in its history, the Social Security retirement program is in the red. After Social Security checks went out for October, only about $1.5 billion remained in the retirement program's reserve. So money had to be borrowed from the disability and Medicare reserves to back the checks mailed this month.

The need to borrow money from other Social Security funds must be a sobering rebuke to those who have insisted there is no need to worry about erosion of the retirement program's reserves. Every time the program has faced financial problems, Congress has slapped another Band-Aid on it, blithely reassuring everyone that lasting solutions had been found. Who can forget President Jimmy Carter's assertion in 1977 that one of the biggest tax increases in history would solve Social Security's problems well beyond the year 2000? Here we are, only five years later, and Social Security is down to its last billion or so.

Early this year — in an attempt to defuse Social Security as a political issue in an election year — President Reagan appointed a bipartisan commission to study the problem and issue some recommendations. Even so, many candidates have been unable to resist the temptation of using Social Security as a campaign issue. They have played on the fears and insecurities of the retired, who simply seek reassurance that any changes in the program will affect only future retirees. Those drawing retirement benefits do not need to hear demagogic statements such as the one by Dick Davis, who in effect said younger workers can go to Hell if they balk at paying higher Social Security taxes. Retirees know, even if Dick Davis does not, that Social Security is an intergenerational pact whose stability depends on the goodwill of its younger supporters. And young workers vote, too.

Although the special commission has delayed its recommendations until after the election, the commission reportedly is leaning toward proposing that scheduled increases in the payroll tax be accelerated. That would bring an almost immediate 2 per cent increase in the payroll tax rate, from the current 13.4 per cent total levied on workers and employers — to 15.3 per cent. If, after several months of deliberation, that is the most innovative idea the commission can propose, it could have saved its time. The Social Security tax, of course, is a tax on employment. In a time of high unemployment, the government shouldn't be creating fresh disincentives to hiring and job creation, as the Reagan administration acknowledges in opposing any payroll tax increase at this time. And remember: Jimmy Carter promised that his $227 billion, ten-year payroll tax increase would bail out Social Security for at least three decades.

An increase in the payroll tax would slap yet another Band-Aid on Social Security, without addressing any of the real problems afflicting the program. A combination of several steps would go far toward matching projected revenues to expected outlays. A phased-in increase in the retirement age from 65 to 68 by century's end, taxation of the share of benefits attributable to employers' payroll taxes, changes in the means of fixing cost-of-living increases, merger of Social Security with other federal retirement programs — the commission has before it any number of possible alternatives to payroll increases. Yet Social Security — as a program with a vocal, largely middle-class constituency — is so politically volatile that Congress always opts for short-term fixes over long-term solutions.

So the talk of an accelerated increase in payroll taxes persists, although Democrats and Republicans, Liberals and conservatives, all know that such an increase would merely postpone the hard decisions that must be made about Social Security. Meanwhile, the commission's report is expected to be released after a three-day meeting in mid-month. If this commission's efforts are to be worth more than the long-forgotten efforts of numerous similar commissions, it will avoid relying on the tempting snake oil remedy of a payroll tax increase. Rather, it will offer more credible proposals for saving Social Security. In 1977, Congress socked it to workers and their employers; this time around, more equitable solutions can be found to reduce the expected costs of future benefits.

ALBUQUERQUE JOURNAL

Albuquerque, N.M., November 10, 1982

Not too long ago, some politicians would cry "Lies!" if someone said Social Security would go broke soon unless the system was overhauled. You don't hear too many politicians issuing such denials today.

The best evidence that adjustment is needed took place when officials announced the Social Security old-age trust fund had to borrow from a smaller fund to meet November obligations. It was the first time interfund borrowing has been necessary.

The problem has been the same all along: the Social Security system spends far more money than it takes in — about $17,000 more per minute, in fact. The inevitable has finally happened: the once-bulging supplementary retirement fund is on the brink of default.

Solving the problem has been hindered by political wrangling and campaign rhetoric. But with the election over, the federal government has a golden opportunity to act. It must do so or more borrowing will be needed to meet December obligations. And farther down the road, officials know the two smaller funds also will run out of funds — unless something is done.

President Reagan, whose initial attempt to overhaul Social Security was bitterly opposed by many Americans, has called for a special congressional session where the problem may be addressed. Fearing ouster at the polls, most people in Congress have refused to do what needs doing. Now they're going to have to swallow hard — or betray millions of Americans who paid into the system counting on payments after retirement.

The politicians in Congress are awaiting a report from Reagan's special Social Security study commission. Expected tomorrow, the report will focus on options for overhauling Social Security. The task is to study the detailed analyses and choose the option that will enable Social Security to fulfill its objectives.

Part of the financial problem facing Social Security is that politicians saddled the system with extra obligations. When Congress acted, the system had the money to pay for the extras. Now it does not. Once intended to provide a supplement to the retirement funds saved by workers, the fund now provides many retired persons with almost all their income. Worse, it has been asked to provide money to more and more categories of recipients. Now millions of non-retired Americans receive money from the fund originally intended to help the nation's retired people. It is possible that some benefits being paid now to non-retirees will be either cut back or moved out of the fund entirely.

But clearly an overhaul is needed quickly. The interfund borrowing only dramatizes the point. The politicians may fear reprisals at the polls if they vote for cuts, as they must, but the system faces a much worse crisis if Congress does not take action.

The Des Moines Register

Des Moines, Iowa, October 20, 1982

Early next month, the Social Security trust fund that pays old-age and survivor benefits to more than 30 million Americans will borrow money from one of the two other Social Security trust funds. Otherwise the November checks could not be mailed on time.

This kind of borrowing will enable the old-age fund to get by until next June. But, as an article elsewhere on this page points out, unless Congress takes further action, the old-age fund won't have sufficient reserves to mail out the checks on time next July. Beyond then, the National Commission on Social Security Reform has estimated that the old-age and disability trust funds will need an additional $60 billion to remain solvent through the next five years.

This shortfall is a direct result of recent economic problems. Social Security benefits have been raised to keep pace with high rates of inflation, even as high unemployment has limited the revenues raised by the payroll tax levied on workers' wages.

Urgent as the short-term crisis is, it is dwarfed by Social Security's long-term problems. Simply put, Social Security does not have a workable plan for paying out all the benefits it has promised to members of the huge baby-boom generation — workers now in their 20s and 30s. Experts warn that the long-term deficit could exceed $1 trillion unless changes are made.

These problems were not discovered yesterday. It long has been evident that changes would be needed to put Social Security on a more secure financial footing, but recent efforts to make such changes have been engulfed in political demagoguery.

We hope that the Social Security commission's forthcoming report will persuade Congress and the president finally to take more responsible steps toward solving the system's financial problems. The starting point should be a national debate on reform proposals, a debate designed to promote a needed bipartisan consensus. Several points already seem clear:

● The long-term problem needs attention now, both because it will be easier to resolve now than later, and because younger workers need to be convinced that they have a stake in Social Security that justifies the continued drain of payroll taxes. A recent ABC News/Washington Post survey found that 69 percent of Americans aged 18 to 44 don't believe that Social Security will exist by the time they retire.

● The short-term crisis could be postponed by extending the authority that allows the old-age fund to borrow from the two other funds, but proposals for borrowing from general tax revenues make little sense when federal budget deficits are running in excess of $100 billion annually.

● In recent years, Social Security benefits have tended to rise faster than the wages of the workers who support the system. That hardly seems fair. It would be more reasonable to keep increases in Social Security benefits in line with increases in average wages rather than with the rise in prices.

● There are limits on how high payroll taxes should be raised to support the system, and a good case can be made that those limits have been almost reached. The tax burden will become crushing if reductions are not made in the benefits promised to members of the baby-boom generation. Probably the least painful, most equitable way would be to gradually raise from 65 to 68 the age for retirement with full benefits.

Right now, the most important step to be taken is for Congress to put partisan and election-year politicking aside and get serious about tackling the problem.

Wisconsin ⚖ State Journal

Madison, Wisc., October 25, 1982

Too many members of Congress for too many years have pledged undying support for the principle and benefits of Social Security, ignoring its massive problems in favor of votes.

As a consequence, they've socked employers and employees with escalating taxes and, still, the system continues to live beyond its means.

It has reached the point where the heaviest tax for millions is not the federal income tax, not the property tax, not the sales tax — but the Social Security levy.

For the first time, Social Security officials plan to let the old-age trust fund borrow money to pay benefits in November, when 34.6 million payments for old-age, survivor and disability benefits will total $13.3 billion.

The plan is to borrow up to $2 billion from Social Security's disability or health-insurance (Medicare) funds. Without borrowing, the old-age fund would not have enough money to cover its $11.9-billion portion of November payments.

The current crunch exists because monthly benefits have been exceeding revenues from the payroll tax for months upon months, leaving the old-age fund with a chronic deficit.

President Reagan had the guts to recommend reform in his first year in office, seeing it as essential to *guaranteeing* lasting benefits for the elderly, the disabled, the unwell.

The Reagan proposal had good and bad elemenents, but it was a workable vehicle for debate. Although it honestly faced the deteriorating situation, Democrats led the way in shooting down the proposal.

Thankfully, the Reagan initiative forced Congress to appoint a bipartisan National Commission on Social Security Reform. It won't report until November, so leery congressional candidates won't have to deal with the tender subject before the Nov. 2 election.

Nevertheless, voters should beware of candidates who swear they shall never scale back benefits. If they don't, it will mean that much more money will have to be extracted from taxpayers to support Social Security — one way or another.

The candidate who is a true friend of Social Security will discuss problems and options with constituents of all ages, with an eye on retaining a workable and, yes, indispensable program.

THE DAILY HERALD

Biloxi, Miss., November 9, 1982

If you are one of the people who has been doubting that the Social Security System is really in trouble, you may banish your doubt. The Treasury Department last week announced it had to borrow about $1 billion from the Disability Insurance Trust Fund so that the Old-Age and Survivors Insurance Trust Fund could make the November pension payments.

This is the first interfund loan since the Social Security Act of 1935. It tells everyone, unmistakeably, that Social Security's troubles are real and they are serious. They can no longer be viewed as "political utterings" or as "estimates" or "predictions" of coming money shortages. The money shortage is here and now.

The pension fund this month had on hand fewer dollars than it needed to pay the November benefits.

When Congress was debating whether or not to authorize Social Security borrowing among its different funds, this newspaper editorialized in favor of authorizing the borrowing. It seems illogical to have one or two funds with a surplus while another fund runs short of money needed to fulfill Social Security's prime mission.

Congress agreed and authorized the borrowing.

The borrowing itself can be viewed as one more step toward bankruptcy. Everyone knows Congress won't let Social Security go bankrupt; to contemplate such a disaster would be to foment rebellion.

What everyone doesn't know is what Congress will do to prevent the bankruptcy. Borrowing among funds is only a temporary measure, not even equivalent to a band-aid on a' cancer. Borrowing only alleviates this month's money shortage; it begins to create a similar problem in the fund from which the money was borrowed. Borrowing itself becomes a problem when interest must be paid and when repayment comes due.

What happened last week was not a one-time procedure; it was only the first. The Treasury Department said the Old Age and Survivors Insurance Trust Fund will need to borrow between $7 billion and $11 billion between now and next June 30. The bulk of that money may be borrowed next month since the Congressional authorization expires at the end of December.

Congress could extend the authorization during its lame duck session. Congress could follow Sen. Robert Dole's suggestion that the lame duck session set a special agenda to deal with Social Security's problems, though that prospect now appears dim.

The Salt Lake Tribune
Salt Lake City, Utah, November 1, 1982

Candidates are tiptoeing through the minefield of Social Security reform, fearing any misstep on the emotional issue will blast their chances of election. But it will have to be faced boldly when Congress reconvenes and any step taken to shore up the dwindling funds is bound to be unpopular with a large portion of the electorate.

Prompt action is needed. The retirement fund will borrow from disability and Medicare funds to cover next month's payments to retirees. If such borrowing is allowed by Congress to continue, all three trust funds will run short of money to meet commitments by the end of 1983. To keep all three funds healthy for the next five years, a $50 to $60 million gap must be closed.

President Reagan is strongly opposed to further increases in the payroll tax. And that should be a last resort. The tax is already slated to rise from 13.4 percent, split between workers and employers, to 15.3 percent in 1990. This adds to the non-wage portion of worker compensation that has been climbing faster than wages and makes employers reluctant to hire more workers.

Without a hike in the payroll tax, few other options remain. And to cover the huge shortfall, they will have to include a sharing of the burden by retirees. The National Commission on Social Security Reform will make its recommendations in a month.

The emotional uproar that greeted President Reagan's earlier Social Security proposals made it clear the public won't stand for major modification of benefits to the retired or those near retirement.

Other short-term solutions have been proposed. Bringing new government employees into the Social Security system and making all retirees pay income tax on half of their benefits are two steps worthy of consideration. But they wouldn't nearly fill the gap. For the major savings needed, limiting of cost-of-living increases in the future for all retirees seems the likely alternative, regardless of the storm it will create.

Inflation is down and retirees have been better shielded against inflation the past few years than the average worker or taxpayer. With many workers facing unemployment, and businesses struggling for survival, limiting benefit increases to retirees seems more equitable than further large increases in the payroll tax.

The Miami Herald
Miami, Fla., November 6, 1982

TODAY, for the first time in its 47-year history, the Social Security pension fund will borrow money — about $1 billion. The loan is necessary to fund the December checks for 31 million retirees and dependents of deceased workers. It will come from the Disability Insurance Trust Fund of the Social Security system.

The relative solvency of the disability fund compared to the retirement fund demonstrates the changing demographic trends that have helped render Social Security's basic financial assumptions obsolete. Many more workers now maintain their health until retirement and into advanced age. And automatic cost-of-living increases in pension checks long ago wrecked any pretense of actuarial soundness in the retirement program.

Retirees and those anticipating retirement soon are understandably upset, some to the point of panic, at the specter of Social Security "going broke" and not sending out the checks that are the sole lifeline for millions of Americans. News of the borrowing, which could affect both Medicare and disability funds and may reach as high as $11 billion by next June, adds an unbearable level of anxiety.

The Administration and Congress should recognize that fear and the fiscal realities that have caused it. Instead of hiding from the issues, as they did during the campaign season, both major parties and both policy-making branches of the Government should address the problem now, in the brief hiatus before the next round of electioneering begins.

Next week, the President's bipartisan National Commission on Social Security Reform is scheduled to meet to work on its final recommendations. That report is due on Nov. 15 or, at the latest, before Congress comes back for a lame-duck session beginning on Nov. 29. Senate Finance Committee Chairman Robert Dole wants Congress to take up the special commission's report at that session.

Congress certainly should. There never will be a good time for timid politicians to address such loaded questions as raising the retirement age, slowing the increase of benefits, increasing payroll taxes, reducing the tax-exempt nature of the pension, bringing Federal employes into the system, and applying a financial-need criterion for unearned benefits. Any time large numbers of voters are made to give up anything is a bad time for politicians.

But something must give, and soon, on Social Security. Now, with the long-awaited threat of borrowing finally a reality, the necessity for reform is beyond dispute. A better time is not likely to occur.

The Evening Gazette
Worcester, Mass., October 19, 1982

The news that the Social Security Administration is in deep trouble comes at an awkward time — three weeks before the election.

If those nice blue checks are to be mailed next month to the 36 million people who are expecting them, the Old Age and Survivors Insurance fund will have to borrow up to $2 billion from the health and disability funds.

The crisis has arrived sooner than expected; as recently as August, the actuaries were saying that the retirement fund had enough reserves to last until next July.

This is the result of 30 years of deceit and politics. Congress has told the American people so often that Social Security is an "insurance" program, that millions believe it. But it isn't; it has been a giveaway program with no solid financial base. It now costs $209 billion a year — one-quarter the total federal budget. Just the retirement part will be in the red by at least $20 billion this year, and by three times that amount next year, if nothing is done.

President Reagan, after his modest efforts at reform were shot down by a Congress in panic, appointed a blue-ribbon bipartisan commission to come up with overhaul recommendations. But it looks as if the commission is going to recommend still another tax hike — the worst possible solution.

Workers now pay 6.7 percent payroll tax, which is scheduled to jump to 7.65 percent in three steps by 1990. The payroll tax is matched by the employer, but some economists say that is misleading. Actually, they claim, the whole 13.4 percent is coming out of the workers's paychecks, in that the company otherwise would be able to pay the equivalent in wage increases.

The proper way to straighten out Social Security is to reorganize it so it can be set up on a sound basis. The medical and welfare functions should be separated from the Social Security Administration and put elsewhere. Future benefits should be cut back, and people now working should be encouraged to plan for more of their own retirement income, through IRAs and the like. Later retirement should be encouraged. Annual cost of living raises should be set on a more realistic basis. A last-ditch proposal is to tax Social Security retirement income for those retirees who make enough to get into the taxable brackets.

Finally, federal workers, including members of Congress, should be brought into Social Security. It might change congressional attitudes remarkably if the members had to depend in their old age on the system they habitually treat so cavalierly.

The crunch that has hit the Social Security retirement will be a blessing in disguise if it leads Congress to show some intestinal fortitude and make real reforms. But the chances of that are only 50-50, at best.

BUFFALO EVENING NEWS

Buffalo, N.Y., November 8, 1982

Social Security, the massive pension program that helps to support millions of retired Americans, reaches a distressing benchmark this month. For the first time since the first checks went out in 1940, Social Security must borrow to cover the cost of retirement benefits.

For 42 years, month in and month out, the combination of reserves stored in the old-age trust fund, plus temporary interfund transfers and revenues pouring in from payroll taxes paid by American workers, has provided enough money to finance benefits. No longer.

The unhappy truth is that the reserve fund that has tided finances over fallow periods in the past has been drawn down and is now virtually empty. We are confident that Congress won't allow any lapse in monthly benefit checks, and there are ways to remedy the sorry condition. But the need to borrow underscores the urgency of the situation, and exposes the reality that benefit costs are outstripping Social Security payroll taxes.

Contrary to popular view, Social Security does not deduct money from workers' paychecks and tuck it away in some government fund to be repaid to those same workers when they retire. Benefits are financed largely out of payments deducted from present workers, making Social Security a straight pay-as-you-go transfer of money from younger Americans to older Americans, except for some tapping of reserve funds.

Moreover, the number of workers helping to support each beneficiary is dropping — and will continue to drop in the years ahead because of falling birth rates. With benefits escalating because of inflation and with the recession leaving more workers unemployed, the pinch has inexorably tightened on Social Security finances.

There is no shortage of possible ideas to correct either the short-term or long-range problems afflicting Social Security. What has been lacking is a clear consensus in Washington on what to do and a determination to act. That, in turn, reflects the fact that there is no easy or wholly painless way to keep Social Security solvent. Either future benefits must be moderated or taxes increased, or some combination of the two must be adopted. Whatever solution is chosen is bound to displease some constituents and create political risks.

But now the campaign is over, and the National Commission on Social Security Reform, a presidential advisory panel, is expected to submit its recommendations in a few weeks. Then it will be up to Congress to adopt a responsible plan to protect the benefits of present and future retirees.

THE SACRAMENTO BEE

Sacramento, Calif., October 26, 1982

For the first time, next month the government will have to borrow to make Social Security payments. It will borrow only from itself — the Social Security old age trust fund will borrow either from the disability or the Medicare fund or both — and will pay interest as the law provides, no great disaster. But it is still a clear warning that the problems of the Social Security system, which Congress has been assiduously avoiding, cannot be avoided any longer.

The solutions necessarily involve some combination of reductions in benefits and increases in taxes: If there is less of one, then there has to be more of the other. Among the proposals: adjustment of the cost-of-living formula under which most beneficiaries have been receiving increases greater than the increases in living costs to which most retired people have been exposed in recent years; a gradual shift toward later retirement, possibly combined with reductions in benefits for those who choose to retire early; extension of benefits and Social Security obligations to federal workers and other public employees now exempt from the system, and further increases in Social Security taxes.

The President's Commission on Social Security Reform, headed by Alan Greenspan, a conservative economist who was President Ford's chief economic adviser, appears to be considering all those remedies, even though the administration still insists it will not accept any further increases in Social Security taxes.

None of the remedies is pleasant, but unless the current problems of the system continue unattended, they are not likely to be so severe as to justify the sort of avoidance in which Congress — indeed, nearly all politicians — have been engaged. It's to be hoped that after next month's election, when the commission is expected to make its recommendations, Congress will be in a somewhat more responsible frame of mind and less likely to engage in the kind of political grandstanding to which this issue so easily lends itself.

The fact that, when Congress returns, the system will be paying its benefits with borrowed money ought to be an additional sobering influence on a matter that is long overdue for sober discussion and resolution. Borrowed money, borrowed time.

Minneapolis Star and Tribune

Minneapolis, Minn., October 30, 1982

Next week 32 million Social Security pensioners will be able to cash their checks as usual — but only because some money to back them has been borrowed from the trust funds for health and disability benefits. The same will be true every month through next June. After that, unless the rules change, money will have to come from other sources to prevent each month's old-age checks from being delayed or reduced.

Social Security's long-predicted cash crunch is here. And partly because short-term solutions have been evaded, larger long-term problems are becoming more severe. There is no assurance now that Social Security can meet its bills when today's young workers start to retire. Congress should act on both issues this year. And it should not look for easy ways out.

One bad idea is to continue borrowing from the other trust funds until they run into red ink too. The respite would last only into 1984, when the crunch would get worse. Another misguided notion is to start paying pensions from general revenue as well as from the Social Security wage tax. The result would be an end to pay-as-you-go discipline, plus big new boosts to federal deficits. Equally mistaken are thoughts of hiking the payroll tax — already headed above 15 percent in 1990. The wage tax falls heavily on young low-income workers and on labor-intensive businesses. Neither group would welcome being penalized to help Congress avoid reform.

These easy-out approaches assume that if Social Security benefits are touched, the elderly will take political revenge. The assumption is insulting. It paints the elderly as a greedy class beyond the reach of rational discussion and beyond concern about their grandchildren's prospects. It implies that the young are too foolish to understand —

though polls show otherwise — that a lack of reform now will undermine Social Security for their own old age. Such cynicism blocks responsible solutions to Social Security problems.

One ingredient of reform is a gradual increase in retirement ages. With lengthening life expectancy can come a small increase in work expectancy too; and changes can be scheduled to give ample time for retirement planning. Another sensible way to cut future pension costs is to alter the formula for cost-of-living adjustments. Workers and pensioners should get roughly equal protection against inflation. In recent years people on Social Security have received much more.

The Social Security system needs more income as well as less expense. Coverage of civil servants would help; it would also reduce the resentment that many people feel toward government employees' (including congressmen's) separate pension programs. There is good reason as well to make half of each Social Security pension subject to income tax, earmarking the revenue for the old-age trust fund. The pensions are tax-free now because they are treated like welfare for the poor. But many elderly get Social Security payments in addition to other income. If the total reaches a taxable bracket, it should be taxed; the poor would not be penalized.

Social Security works by wage earners sharing their incomes with retired people. Such a system can be balanced, fair, and stable if voters understand its limits as well as its benefits. The system now is out of balance and poorly understood. There is no shortage of sound ideas to make it self-sustaining and reliable again. There is a shortage of political will to be frank with the public and to tackle the job. The president and Congress should make up that lack — soon.

The Detroit News

Detroit, Mich., October 25, 1982

The Social Security Administration's need to borrow $1 billion to cover its November payments has elicited the customary cries for reform.

Like you, we've heard it all before — as have the politicians who, especially during an election year, regard the subject as the herpes of American politics (i.e., under the circumstances, keeping one's distance is superior to a close encounter).

True, President Reagan appointed a bipartisan commission that is considering several solutions for saving the system before it, and its devoted recipients, go broke. The commission, of course, is scheduled to make its recommendations *after* Nov. 2.

Actually, there aren't many alternatives. Congress can either increase payroll taxes or it can change the benefit structure to reduce the program's cost. Or it can do both.

Alternatives like those have a paralyzing effect on elected officials, and for good reason.

President Reagan is still licking his wounds from last year when he tangled with the senior citizen lobby by suggesting several reforms, including cutbacks in disability payments, increased penalties for early retirement, a 10 percent reduction in benefits for all retirees, and a three-month delay in cost-of-living increments.

The Democrats, to nobody's surprise, charged that the president was trying to rob older Americans of their rightful benefits. The Democrats, of course, were longer on umbrage than on useful suggestions.

As a result, whenever he speaks to seniors, Mr. Reagan prefaces his remarks with assurances that their Social Security payments are guaranteed by the sacred honor of the Republican Party. At the same time, he's telling workers that his administration is opposed to Social Security tax increases.

Wonderful.

Meantime, up there on the Hill, Tip O'Neill has been braying so loudly about the administration's alleged antipathy toward the "golden-agers" that the Democratic funding alternative is often overlooked. It is, of course, to keep borrowing from Social Security's disability and Medicare funds.

But won't this short-term solution simply postpone the day of reckoning and eventually bankrupt the entire system?

Sure. But the Democrats aren't concerned about long-range economic consequences when they can, they think, earn immediate political dividends by advancing demagogic policies.

People, however, aren't dumb. They know it was the Democrats' fly-now, pay-later philosophy that put the Social Security system — and the whole nation — behind the eight ball in the first place.

That's apparent even to many who have long manned the "progressive" barricades.

Michael Kinsley, former New Republic magazine staffer and seeker of social justice, is currently struggling to save Harper's magazine from extinction. His October editorial laments the "grandfather-clause" ethic that "exempts people from some change in the rules simply because they got there first." He sees Social Security reform as inevitable, but he warns that those who "got there first" aren't about to acquiesce.

Mr. Kinsley insists that the issue is not whether benefits will be reduced — but when, and by how much. He suggests that Congress do something soon by making minor program adjustments to ease the transition period, adding:

"Asking present retirees, who are getting far more out of the system than they put in, to share the burden of adjustment is also fairer to future retirees, who are putting in far more than they will ever get out."

A good idea.

For a while it appeared that the president's commission might be moving in just that direction by recommending the system's benefit formula be linked to labor costs — to free the Social Security Trust Fund from fluctuations in the national economy. This way, benefits could be connected to current economic conditions rather than to outdated calculations that have been overtaken by events.

But this solution, which surfaced in August, crash dived when the seniors were told

it was another administration attempt to cast them adrift.

As Mr. Kinsley ruefully concludes: "Any suggestion that today's benefits be reduced in any way — or even that they not increase faster than the average worker's wages — sets off the Claude Pepper Tabernacle Choir singing 'Shoot if you must this old gray head!' and the suggester soon slinks away abashed."

But we would ask retirees to understand that the payroll-tax burden on today's workers (the retirees' sons and daughters, after all) are already cruelly high. We would ask them to participate in a national compromise on a problem that poses a serious threat not only to the integrity of the Social Security system, but to the social fabric.

Working people and their families ask their elders to brace the politicians with a show of reasonableness. After all, it's not as if, like the Eskimos of old, granny was to be abandoned in the tundra.

DAYTON DAILY NEWS

Dayton, Ohio, October 28, 1982

October, 1982, is a date to remember. It's the last month that Social Security took in more money than it gave out. Unless major revisions are made, only borrowing will allow the system to meet future payrolls.

Thanks to 1981 legislation, it can borrow immediately from two solvent trust funds — Medicare and Disability. But those are not so flush as to pick up the difference for long.

What Social Security needs is a fast money infusion. As politically unpopular as it might be, that means increasing Social Security taxes, a drop in the amount paid out, or a combination of the two.

The most obvious money saver is to cut the cost-of-living allowance from the Consumer Price Index and tie it instead to a more accurate inflation reading, such as the average annual increase in prices or wages.

And the Social Security base could be enlarged by requiring the 3 million federal civilian workers, the 4.8 million state and local employees and the million non-profit agency employees to start paying full time. Eighty percent of them eventually draw benefits from Social Security, anyway. Full participation would stop the time-honored practice of Federal employees retiring early so they can work to qualify for Social Security and thus double-dip at the federal till.

And maybe it's time to tax the Social Security pensions of the upper middle and high income bracket retirees.

All these options will be considered when the president's National Commission on Social Security Reform holds a brainstorming session Nov. 11-13.

The recommendations the committee makes must be given serious consideration on their merits, not on the fact that everyone prefers the plus times of the good old days. These are new times. The growing number of retirees and the decreasing number of employed workers paying into the system are forcing us to make some tough, unpopular decisions if we want to see Social Security solvent into the next century.

Panel Outlines Problems; Seeks Reagan, O'Neill Involvement

The bipartisan National Commission on Social Security Reform, meeting Nov. 11-13, defined the scope of the crisis facing the system. During a three-day session in Alexandria, Va., the panel agreed that between $150 billion and $200 billion should be raised between 1983 and 1989 to alleviate the system's short-term funding problems, and warned that deficits could rise as high as $1.6 trillion over the next 73 years. The commission was unable to reach a concensus on a specific plan to solve the financial problems, although there appeared to be general agreement that future federal workers should be required to participate. Suggestions that President Reagan and House Speaker Tip O'Neill become involved came from all sides, including the commission's chairman, conservative economist Alan Greenspan. Republican commission member Sen. William Armstrong commented: "It would be foolish for us to forge ahead now without finding out what is acceptable to the President and the Speaker." Reagan and O'Neill ruled out any intervention, each saying they had "no plans" to meet with the other on the issue. The commission received White House permission to delay its final report, originally scheduled for Dec. 10, until mid-January, 1983.

The Charlotte Observer
Charlotte, N.C., December 14, 1982

The Social Security reform commission has done most of what it was appointed to do. It has taken the volatile issue out of the political arena for a while and studied and set forth the various options for preventing the bankruptcy of the system, which is already relying on interfund borrowing to keep monthly checks flowing.

Now the commission — scheduled to hold its final meeting on Friday — is waiting for some signal from President Reagan and congressional leaders before making a specific recommendation. What that means, of course, is that the issue has moved back into the political arena, as it eventually had to, for that is where the decisions must be made.

Alan Greenspan, chairman of the commission, said Sunday the panel tentatively favors a combination of higher Social Security taxes and lower cost-of-living benefit increases to keep the system solvent. Apparently commission members feel the only remaining issue is how that combination should be weighted: How much of the shortfall should be made up by taxes, and how much by slowing the growth of benefits?

We wish the commission would recommend a formula weighted toward slowing the growth of benefits, keeping new taxes to a minimum. In fact, we believe federal employees — now covered by a different retirement fund and not required to participate in Social Security — should be brought into the program as a way to eliminate or at least hold down any increase in Social Security taxes.

The Social Security tax is, in effect, an income tax of the most regressive type. It applies at the same rate to everyone, regardless of the level of income, up to a point, and then beyond a certain level of income it ceases to apply. A relatively low-paid employee pays a higher percentage of his income in Social Security tax than does a high-salaried person.

Adding to that regressive tax burden at a time of recession would run counter to efforts to stimulate economic recovery and would weight most heavily on those who can least afford to pay more. With inflation down, cost-of-living increases in Social Security benefits can be significantly reduced without putting an unfair burden on recipients.

Once a plan to deal with the short-range problem of Social Security solvency is enacted, we hope the administration or Congress will move on to a study of the long-range future of the system. Although today's Social Security recipients have paid into the system, the amounts they are receiving far exceed what they put in. It has become a sort of welfare system in which today's workers pay ever increasing rates to provide checks for today's beneficiaries.

It ought to be possible to phase out that system, in a manner that doesn't short-change anyone, and replace it with a system in which retirees draw out what they have put in, plus the interest it has earned —with other methods of assistance for the disabled and other retirees who, for whatever reasons, have not had the opportunity to contribute fully.

The Houston Post
Houston, Texas, December 16, 1982

The refusal of President Reagan and House Speaker Thomas P. O'Neill to heed pleas by the National Commission on Social Security Reform to help break the deadlock over ways to solve the giant pension system's problems emphasizes the political volatility of the issue. The commission chairman, Alan Greenspan, and two key members, Sens. Robert Dole, R-Kan., and William Armstrong, R-Colo., appealed to the president and O'Neill to become involved or send a signal that they will support a series of firm recommendations. Otherwise, the 15-member bipartisan panel has indicated it will probably offer a list of options to cure Social Security's ills without making specific proposals.

All the options are likely to sound familiar — increase Social Security payroll taxes, cut the program's benefits, raise the retirement age, use general revenue to help finance the program, etc. They are familiar because they have been proposed before in one form or another by a series of commissions and committees that have studied Social Security's problems over the years. So, why doesn't the present commission take the bit in its teeth and select from the list of options a package that, in its best judgment, will cure the pension program's fiscal ills?

The panel understands that the measures needed to rescue Social Security from the threat of insolvency must be made at the political level. The commission itself, though it was named by the president, Democrat O'Neill and Republican congressional leaders, is not a policy-making body. It is serving in a bipartisan advisory capacity. As Greenspan explained, it has gone as far as it can go without guidance from the next level of government — the one that created it and the one empowered to act on its advice.

Though it has been unable to reach a consensus on ways to solve Social Security's problems, the commission has performed a useful service by persuading all but the most dedicated optimists that the program's deficiencies are real and in urgent need of repair. The panel has agreed that the huge government-administered pension system will need an extra $150 to $200 billion by the end of this decade and that its deficit over the next 75 years will amount to 1.8 percent of the nation's taxable payroll.

Those figures spell serious trouble for the program in both the short and the long terms unless steps are taken to put it back on a sound foundation. But the decisions on those steps must be made through the political process. Our elected representatives, aware that Social Security reform is probably the hottest political potato they will be called upon to handle, have shied away from making those hard decisions. They have, instead, treated the symptoms of the system's ills. Congress, for example, has approved temporary interfund borrowing so that Social Security's deficit-threatened Old Age and Survivors Insurance trust fund could borrow from the other two trust funds, Medicare and disability insurance. But that is only a stopgap device that could hasten the insolvency of the lending funds.

The whipsaw effects of inflation and recession, coupled with past failures to adequately fund Social Security, have contributed to the system's present plight. But the program also suffers from the distortion of its original purpose. When it was established in 1937, Social Security was intended as a floor on which individuals could build their retirement nest egg. It was not meant to be a complete retirement program. Yet, today a majority of the 31 million retirees receiving Social Security benefits depend on the payments for more than half of their retirement income. The reform commission should be encouraged to address the system's problems with firm recommendations, not merely a list of options. It will take a measure of political courage to put Social Security back on a sound fiscal base. But that is the price that must be paid for the neglect and abuse of the system in years past.

THE INDIANAPOLIS NEWS
Indianapolis, Ind., December 20, 1982

If anyone is under the illusion that the National Commission on Social Security Reform has come to grips with the problems facing Social Security — guess again.

At best the Commission has defined the system's short-term financial problems and offered various patchwork proposals to keep Social Security afloat for about a decade. The options are not new: accelerating payroll deduction increases, delaying Cost of Living Allowance increases to recipients or readjusting the COLA formula, raising the retirement age, requiring universal participation in the Social Security program and the like.

A recent report by The Mercer Bulletin, however, concludes that while the problem has been defined reasonably well over the next seven years, the Commission has "missed the mark completely over the longer term from 1990 onward."

The mammoth financial problems facing Social Security are expected to hit after the turn of the century when the post-war baby boom generation begins reaching retirement age.

According to The Mercer Bulletin, the Commission also dealt with only a limited aspect of the Social Security system — old age and retirement benefits. It ignored funding problems facing the Hospital Insurance and Supplementary Medical Insurance aspects of the system where large deficits are projected.

"If the total Social Security problem is too large for the Commission to tackle and it wants to handle only one fourth of the deficit," the Bulletin says, "that is understandable. But, we should hope that the Commission will tell the public clearly that it is trying to resolve only one fourth of the Social Security deficit and that the other three fourths ... is going to be left for another time."

Its report also warns that the Commission may have used overly optimistic projections on fertility rates as a basis for its conclusions and failed to come to grips with basic structural problems evolving from a changing social and economic environment.

Part of the Commission's problem appears to stem from its deliberate bipartisan posture. The Commission is obviously taking the Social Security problem one step at a time and attempting to win political consensus every step of the way — walking on eggs. Unfortunately, Social Security is a highly partisan issue along political, economic, generational and philosophical lines and it is unlikely that any proposals dealing with the system's real long-term problems will achieve broad support.

The Commission has drawn attention to the plight of Social Security and that has generated a healthy debate about what to do. To that end the Commission has performed a worthwhile mission. But, ultimately, the real solutions are going to have to emerge from heated debate in Congress — partisan give and take — and the decisions are going to be political.

The Salt Lake Tribune
Salt Lake City, Utah, December 21, 1982

Regardless of what it eventually recommends, the president's bipartisan commission on Social Security reform is a success.

It accomplished what it was set up to do: keep the Social Security controversy out of the 1982 election campaign.

Beyond that, the commission under chairmanship of Alan Greenspan, who headed the Council of Economic Advisors under President Ford, has reached agreement on the probable deficit the retirement system faces in the short run. At last report, it could not arrive at a consensus on how to overcome the deficit of several hundred billion dollars in this decade.

The fact that a panel of 15 experienced and intelligent individuals could not reach agreement after months of supposedly studying the system's problem would be profoundly disappointing if it were not for the virtual certainty that the commission's belated findings, even if unanimous, will be picked apart, amended, diluted, misrepresented and generally disregarded by the new Congress which must write the necessary rescue legislation.

Blue ribbon commissions, even those assigned subjects of the utmost importance, seldom see their work enacted into law in anything like the form it is served to the lawmakers. Many such commission reports don't win even lip service recognition from Congress although, as in the case of the Greenspan panel, members of the legislative branch hold many of the seats.

What must be done to "save" Social Security is widely known. But the salvation entails the difficult options of raising taxes or cutting benefits or some combination of the two. There is only so much money going into the system and only so much can come out. To break even, income and outgo must be brought into balance and kept that way. Few politicians have the stamina to stand on that obvious proposition. Neither, it seems, does a solid majority of the Greenspan commission.

At some point the rising pressure to meet the Social Security challenge before the checks stop clearing will force the cowards and the connivers to face the reality that Social Security can be toyed with no longer, that an impatient citizenry is fed up with the posturing and demagoguery. That time is almost at hand.

Rocky Mountain News
Denver, Colo., December 21, 1982

AS Sen. William Armstrong explains it, the National Commission on Social Security was a success, despite appearances to the contrary. Forget for a moment, the Colorado senator argues, that the commission was kept at arm's length by both President Reagan and House Speaker Thomas P. "Tip" O'Neill and therefore failed to devise specific recommendations. For the first time, a group representing virtually the entire political spectrum agreed that a severe problem exists and that action is required — soon.

The senator has a point.

Less than two years ago, when Reagan first suggested that Social Security was careening toward disaster and that adjustments in the system might have to be made, so great was the outcry that within days he reversed directions. Why, Reagan suddenly insisted, changes weren't even being contemplated. Meanwhile, the demagogues were having their day, pumping up fear in the elderly for the very existence of Social Security and equating *any* change with callousness.

Lately, though, the scare rhetoric has a softer edge to it. Reality, not to mention reason, is catching up with even the most obtuse member of Congress. No longer is the argument about whether something should be done, but exactly what. And it is this new consensus that the commission, on which Armstrong served, helped crystallize.

To be sure, the lack of cooperation from the president and the House speaker frustrated commissioners — and with reason. Without some guidance about what would be politically acceptable, they were unwilling to suggest a blueprint for putting Social Security on a sound and enduring financial basis. Previous "solutions" proposed without prior bipartisan approval had suffered a rough fate, and commissioners were reluctant to risk another such setback. They decided to let Congress devise the specifics; they would merely lay out the options.

Armstrong is among those who believe that the differences between Democratic commissioners, who generally favored higher Social Security taxes, and Republicans, who were more inclined to reduce the rate at which benefits grow, weren't insuperable. That, too, is good news.

The bad news is that the problems the commission pinpointed remain: an estimated $150 billion to $200 billion shortfall in revenue for this decade alone, and a long-term deficit of 1.8 percent of payroll, or about $1.6 trillion. In addition, if Congress is going to act at all before the 1984 elections, it will probably have to be in the next six months. That's a tight timetable for such a sensitive issue, but perhaps the mood for reform is finally right.

THE [image] SUN

Baltimore, Md., December 24, 1982

President Reagan and House Speaker Thomas P. O'Neill, Jr., missed a chance this month to put the Social Security commission on a fast track toward bipartisan agreement. They rejected an appeal by commission leaders for guidance on resolving the deadlock. But Mr. Reagan has given the panel an additional 15 days, until mid-January, to make recommendations. Whether or not the panel succeeds, the two men have an obligation to take the lead in finding an acceptable solution to the retirement-fund dilemma.

The National Commission on Social Security Reform already has performed a useful function. It has defined the problem—a $200 billion short-fall through 1989—and laid out dozens of potential approaches to solving it. Before the commission's report on the shortfall, there were some liberal Democrats who would not even admit to a problem. But that can be chalked up mostly to partisan politics prior to an election.

The panel also seemed to be closing in on a mixture of the higher taxes that liberal Democrats prefer and lower benefits that conservative Republicans would like. Economist Alan Greenspan, chairman of the Social Security study panel, says there has been some tentative agreement on accelerating scheduled payroll tax hikes and delaying cost-of-living increases to recipients. That is a good beginning for a compromise.

One idea we find attractive is a plan to tax benefits and return the money to the troubled old-age trust fund. This might net $15 billion next year. Because the income tax is progressive, it would fall most heavily on well-to-do retirees without hurting low-income recipients. The idea has been rejected in the past as unsuitable for an insurance program, but Social Security has never been an annuity. Current wage-earners fund benefits to retirees, and recipients traditionally have gotten back many times what they put in. Besides, Social Security was set up to bring dignity and sufficient income to America's elderly. Well-off recipients already have both.

There is no shortage of ideas from which a reasonable package of reforms could be devised. What is lacking is a strong public commitment by Messrs. Reagan and O'Neill to a compromise. So far, neither man has inspired confidence on this issue. The president put the matter in the hands of a commission all year after an abortive attempt to make deep benefit cuts. The speaker spent the year making it an emotional election issue.

There no longer is any excuse for either man to stay in the background. The new Congress will have only a few months to find an answer before the system is in serious trouble again.

THE BLADE

Toledo, Ohio, December 20, 1982

MEMBERS of the presidential commission on Social Security have been dragging their feet on proposed remedies for the problems of the nation's biggest social insurance system, and their tactics reflect little credit upon them.

The Social Security reform issue has been so politicized that it now takes a courageous politician, indeed, to get out in front on it. Still, the elements for a compromise between Republicans who generally favor holding down increases in benefits and Democrats who would make up the difference through taxation are there.

It has been suggested, for example, that scheduled tax increases be speeded up somewhat, that increases in Social Security payments be scaled to wage increases rather than the cost of living, and that a one-time delay of three months in raising benefits be enacted. Slightly bolder advocates of reform also suggest that the earnings test for recipients be ended and that the combined income from Social Security benefits and other sources be taxed at the $20,000 level or higher.

Finally, mandatory coverage could be extended to all government employees, at least those starting in the future or with less than five years of service. The federal civil service, for example, has both advantages and disadvantages, but there is no reason to continue such an elaborate dual governmental pension system, particularly when the taxpayers are paying most of the cost, as is the case with federal pensions. (It also has been suggested that the federal civil service pension could be a means of supplementing Social Security retirement allotments in the same way that company pensions do in private industry.

The point is that it would not require drastic changes in Social Security to make the system sound until the end of this century or even longer. News stories suggest that the commission members are waiting for an agreement between President Reagan and House Speaker Thomas O'Neill on this issue.

That would be a long wait if statements from the White House and Congress are any indication. An administration spokesman and Speaker O'Neill both have stated publicly that the commission should be expected to draft concrete proposals. The panel should make its own recommendations and let the chips fall where they may.

The American public seems absolutely convinced that Social Security is necessary as the basis for a financially secure old age. There could well be a lot of political credit for anyone, in or out of Congress, willing to become the architects of a plan to put the system on a sound financial footing for the next half century or even longer.

The panel is showing no leadership by cravenly marking time until the President and the House Speaker come to some kind of agreement. It is, after all, up to the commission to come up with solutions to the problem, not to shilly-shally.

DESERET NEWS

Salt Lake City, Utah, December 23-24, 1982

After almost a year of deliberation, a presidential panel has finally agreed on the extent of the problem facing the Social Security system — a shortage of up to $200 billion through this decade.

But that's just about the limit of the panel's consensus.

This week the study group sought — and received from the White House — an extension of its December 31 deadline for submitting recommendations on how to bail out the beleaguered Social Security system.

The new deadline of January 15 falls only 16 days before President Reagan is to deliver his budget message to Congress, which will have to approve any repair work on Social Security.

The reason for the delay on the part of the panel is unsettling. The 15-member commission, dominated by Republicans, is split along partisan lines on how to meet Social Security's financial crunch.

If a commission of experts cannot set aside its political differences for the good of the nation, how much chance do Congress and the White House have of rising above partisanship on this sensitive issue?

The challenge facing the commission and the nation's leaders comes down to a simple but stark choice between increasing Social Security taxes or trimming benefits — or a combination of the two.

There's still time for the presidential panel to produce the consensus agreement that is needed if political bickering is to be contained.

But if the commission can't or won't agree on a set of specific recommendations for reforming Social Security, the panel should at least outline the options and try to rank them in order of what seems most workable and most agreeable.

Richmond Times-Dispatch

Richmond, Va., December 17, 1982

It was a commendable plan: Since Social Security reform is an extremely sensitive issue on which politicians are reluctant to act, establish a commission to assume responsibility for recommending controversial but necessary changes. But even commendable plans can fail, and this one, it appears, has turned out to be simply another exercise in buck-passing.

President Reagan proposed the commission last year after some of his suggestions for strengthening the Social Security program, which is sinking steadily and rapidly into deep financial trouble, created a political firestorm on Capitol Hill. It was his intention that the bipartisan commission would objectively consider the program's problems and suggest improvements for Congress to consider during its lame-duck session, now moving to a close.

Unfortunately, the commission has smashed into the same sort of political stone wall that has immobilized the president and Congress. Democratic and Republican members of the panel are at odds on major reform proposals, and they are now saying that agreement is impossible unless Mr. Reagan and House Democratic Leader Thomas P. O'Neill Jr. forge a compromise. Commission Chairman Alan Greenspan has cancelled a meeting the panel had scheduled for today. So the buck that the president and Congress had passed to the commission has been returned to them.

It has been a disgusting display of irresponsibility, especially by Congress. Everybody knows that the Social Security system faces a financial crisis, but the political leaders who control it lack the courage to make the changes necessary to produce enduring solutions to its problems.

Traditionally, Congress' response to the Social Security system's financial needs has been to increase payroll taxes. Since 1949, a study by the American Council of Life Insurance has shown, average Social Security taxes have increased almost 5,000 percent.

Obviously, such a "remedy" cannot be pursued forever. Fair and sound long-range solutions will entail changes in Social Security benefits. But Congress cringes at the thought of making substantial changes, lest it be punished for depriving workers of their just rewards. Is it possible that the rights of retirees are being exaggerated? Consider these facts:

● During the past three years, Social Security benefits went up by 40 percent while average wages rose by only 30 percent. Social Security increases have been tied to increases in the Consumer Price Index, which overstates the rate of inflation.

● Present retirees are not merely receiving, typically, benefits equal to the amount of money they paid into the system. They are receiving more. A worker who paid the maximum amount of Social Security taxes, who retired in 1981 at age 65 and who has a 65-year-old spouse is receiving a total of $14,138 a year in benefits. The total that any person could have paid into the system from 1937, when the Social Security program began, to 1981 is $14,766. *So in one year, this worker receives almost as much as he contributed in payroll taxes during his entire career.*

But assuming that the federal government is obligated to retirees and those workers who are about to retire to maintain the present level of benefits, there are ways Congress could strengthen the system without breaking faith with these people. Here are some:

● It could stop using the Consumer Price Index as the guide for benefit increases. It would be fairer and financially more responsible to limit increases in benefits to average wage increases.

● Congress could raise the normal retirement age from 65 to 68, effective, say, 10 years from now. After all, life expectancy has increased since the Social Security retirement age was established. The insurance council says that 40 years ago, a 65-year-old person could expect to live 12.8 years. Today, a person that age can expect to live 16.6 years.

● If Social Security coverage is to continue to be mandatory for workers in private industry, it should be mandatory for all other workers too. Now, civilian employees of the federal government, including members of Congress and their staffs, do not participate in the Social Security program. Participation is voluntary for employees of state and local governments and non-profit organizations. Bringing these workers into the program would augment its financial base.

None of these changes would imperil the "rights" of present retirees. Since both political parties believe that a strong Social Security program is in the national interest, they should put partisan politics aside and give these and other constructive recommendations prompt and thorough consideration. This constant buck-passing on Social Security reform is costing the American people too many bucks.

CHARLESTON EVENING POST

Charleston, S.C., December 27, 1982

President Reagan says he is leaving it to the National Commission on Social Security Reform to take the initiative in developing a rescue plan for the system's failing retirement fund. And he has given the commission 15 more days to do the job. The commission, for its part, has been saying it can't shape bipartisan recommendations without guidance from the president and from House Speaker Thomas P. O'Neill. Speaker O'Neill says Mr. Reagan has not said anything to him about Social Security in months, and besides, the commission was supposed to come up with recommendations and didn't. A White House spokesman said the ball's in the commission's court.

Given the seriousness of the Social Security situation, it is not an encouraging picture. It is not an inspiring picture. President Reagan has a point, of course, when he says that the commission has available the expertise to develop a plan to bring the retirement fund safely back from the brink of bankruptcy. It has become painfully clear, however, that the commission does not have the leadership it needs to accomplish its mission — Chairman Greenspan and congressional members notwithstanding.

Mr. Reagan can say that he is not afraid to tackle Social Security problems. Tip O'Neill can say he will be glad to go over to the White House anytime the president calls. But that is not the way it looks. It looks as though the president and the House speaker have withdrawn from the arena. It looks as though the reform commission wants to avoid any heat. It looks as though there is a leadership vacuum when millions of Americans are depending on elected officials in high places to do something to keep their dreams from turning into nightmares.

The Des Moines Register

Des Moines, Iowa, December 17, 1982

It's bad news that President Reagan and Speaker of the House Thomas P. O'Neill Jr. (Dem., Mass.) won't cooperate on finding a solution to Social Security's financial problems. Both made it clear on Monday that they have "no plans" to confer on Social Security.

The bipartisan National Commission on Social Security Reform apparently has reached a stalemate. Chairman Alan Greenspan and other members have strongly suggested that it will take political leadership from the top to resolve the impasse. That means Reagan and O'Neill.

Their involvement is so important because the barrier to solving Social Security's problems is essentially political. The commission already has agreed that Social Security will need $150 billion to $200 billion — to be raised through tax increases or benefit reductions or both — to make it through the next seven years.

The commission has been told by experts that there are various ways to fill the deficit, among them:

● Revise the system for protecting Social Security recipients from inflation, pegging it to wage levels rather than price indexes.

● Move up payroll-tax increases scheduled between now and 1990.

● Tax Social Security benefits, but in such a way that people entirely dependent on Social Security would not be taxed.

A package combining these elements would hardly wreak major damage on the basic structure of the Social Security system. However, even these relatively modest reforms could be political dynamite.

The best way — perhaps the only way — to overcome the logjam is to create a bipartisan package of remedies for Social Security's problems. Only with bipartisan leadership will a majority in Congress be likely to agree on the painful actions needed to save Social Security.

It is essential that the leadership in creating such a bipartisan agreement come from the top. Those two stubborn men, Reagan and O'Neill, must drop their opposition to working together on this issue. Without their cooperation, the stalemate could be prolonged to the point that seriously disruptive emergency action would be required.

SOCIAL SECURITY ACTION TEAM

"THE UPSHOT IS: I'M APPOINTING ANOTHER PANEL TO STUDY THE FINDINGS OF THIS PANEL, WHICH WAS STUDYING THE FINDINGS OF MY FIRST PANEL..."

Wisconsin State Journal

Madison, Wisc., December 17, 1982

The National Commission of Social Security Reform was the handiest alibi members of Congress had when asked prior to the November election what they would do to fix the troubled Social Security system.

They could shrug and say they were waiting for the report of the national commission, conveniently scheduled for release *after* the election.

It turns out that report may say simply that the commission can define the problem but can't agree on what to do about it. So what's new? The only thing new is the fact that Congress no longer can duck.

The commission has agreed on one thing — there will be a Social Security deficit of $150 billion to $200 billion through 1990 if nothing is done. It says this will mean raising taxes, lowering benefits, finding new sources of revenue or a combination of these options. Again, what's new?

The commission has made one tentative recommendation: to extend compulsory coverage for new federal workers and employees of non-profit organizations.

Plaintively, commission members say there isn't much point to making recommendations unless President Reagan and House Speaker Thomas P. O'Neill Jr. get together on a package.

That's ridiculous.

The only reason for the commission was that Reagan and O'Neill & Co. couldn't agree.

Reagan can say, rightfully, that he made his proposal in mid-1981. It was shot down by Congress. Democrats used it to try to shoot down the president politically. The Democrats were immune from specific criticism because they hadn't formulated a specific cure.

You can bet Reagan isn't going to offer himself as a target again, while O'Neill continues to seek protective coloration.

• That puts the heat on Rep. Dan Rostenkowski, D-Ill., chairman of the House Ways and Means Committee, where Social Security legislation will originate.

Rostenkowski isn't known as an heroic leader on this or any other subject, but says he will hold hearings in February.

"We're going to have to produce a package, because we have to . . . it's that simple," said a Rostenkowski aide.

Now to hear Rostenkowski say that — and produce.

St. Louis Globe-Democrat

St. Louis, Mo., December 3, 1982

Social Security is in the final overtime — and time is running out fast on vitally important decisions that will have to be faced in the first half of 1983.

If past performance is any indication of what the future has in store during the next six months, heaven help the more than 100 million Americans in the program. That total includes the 36 million already drawing monthly benefits and double that number who still are working and paying increased taxes to the system in the hope that benefits also will be available when they retire.

Congress has refused time and again to effectively address the grave problems besetting Social Security. Capitol Hill is not alone in the procrastination. The foot dragging, even in the present precarious state, is continuing on all sides to this very moment.

The White House is silent as President Reagan is wary that he will once again be devoured on the issue by the Democrat demagogues. The National Commission on Social Security Reform, whose members were selected by Reagan and House Speaker Thomas P. "Tip" O'Neill Jr., D-Mass., was to have completed its work in December but instead requested a 30-day extension to conduct further deliberations. The president demurred and allowed the body only until Jan. 15 to come up with some recommendations.

A year ago, Congress skirted the real issue of insufficient revenues from payroll taxes and took the cowardly way out by permitting interfund borrowing which expires on this last day of 1982. Even the transferring of these funds leaves a lot to be desired. The Social Security system didn't appear to know what it was doing dealing in the short term. It borrowed a total of $17.5 billion — about $3 billion more than it had planned originally — and $13.5 billion of the total sum is being transferred on the last day of the year.

The $3 billion miscalculation is an inexcusable error of more than 17 percent. It's possible top administrators don't have a firm grasp of what is going on in the system. People counting on the program now and in the future should hope the officials are much sharper than they appear to be. Perhaps, the administrators are cognizant of congressional ineptitude and are playing it safe by adding a few extra billions to buoy the system a while longer if Congress should follow its usual lackadaisical pace and miss the mid-year deadline.

Social Security is in dire straits indeed. If Congress fails to act on the matter, the system will not have sufficient funds to cover all of the benefit checks for the month of July. In some liberal quarters, the possibility of renewing the interfund lending authority has been brought up. That would be another congressional copout to avoid the hard decisions that have to be made if the system is to survive.

Borrowing for Social Security benefit checks is no better than the deficit spending that abounds in the rest of the federal budget. That reckless approach has pushed the current national debt to $1.175 trillion.

A similar disaster cannot befall Social Security. It's not a matter of peanuts: An astounding $1 trillion will be paid out to the program's recipients in the next four years! With that massive price tag, all sides will have to share the additional burden equitably for there is no simple, totally painless solution.

The national commission has identified more than 80 options for restructuring Social Security financing to achieve both short-and long-term solvency. The tools are there. The question is whether Congress has the courage to change its usual course and do right by this important issue for a change.

THE LOUISVILLE TIMES
Louisville, Ky., December 16, 1982

After a year-long study, the National Commission on Social Security Reform has agreed that the system has a money problem. There is also a fragile consensus on the depth of that problem. Since the commission was formed last Dec. 16 because it was evident the Social Security System was going broke, its conclusions do little to advance the debate.

That was probably inevitable. The President appointed the commission — as presidents will do — in order to put a hot political problem on the back burner during an election year. Mr. Reagan's mandate to the bipartisan, 15-member panel called for it:
el2
✔ To "propose realistic, long-term reforms to put Social Security back on a sound financial footing";

✔ To "forge a working bipartisan consensus so that the necessary reforms will be passed into law."

Both goals ran up against political reality: No bipartisan consensus is possible without some agreement between Mr. Reagan and House Speaker Tip O'Neill. Neither has signalled his willingness to do so, and both have suggested that the panel still has a duty to recommend reforms for the system.

But its chairman, Alan Greenspan, is threatening to cancel tomorrow's final meeting of the panel unless top aides of Mr. Reagan and Speaker O'Neill indicate they have agreed on reform measures. He concedes defeat too easily.

The commission must at least make an attempt to exercise its responsibility before it expires on Dec. 31. There is no shortage of possible steps — some interim, some of a long-term nature — that have been thoroughly studied. At the least, the commission should debate some and take a vote on them.

These could include a modification of the annual cost-of-living adjustment that is tied to the Consumer Price Index. The growth of Social Security payments could be curtailed if the annual adjustment were tied to the increase in wages, rather than prices. Less attractive, but a favorite of the panel's Democrats, is an acceleration in scheduled payroll tax increases.

Certainly the panel should be able to recommend that coverage of federal and non-profit workers be phased into Social Security to help broaden its base. Subjecting benefits to taxation should provide no hardship if the income tax system remains progressive.

There is no paucity of solutions for the system's ills. There is a paucity of the political courage necessary to enact them. If a bipartisan study panel lacks that courage, how can it ever expect the Congress and the White House to screw theirs to the sticking post?

THE CHRISTIAN SCIENCE MONITOR
Boston, Mass., December 14, 1982

It would require the highest act of charity for the American public to put the best face on the work of the 15-member presidential commission on social security. Granted, after almost a year of deliberation the commission has managed to agree on the extent of the problem facing the beleaguered system — a financial shortfall of between $150 billion and $200 billion through the 1980s. Yet, despite time, study, and the airing of countless reform proposals, the commission seems unable to come up with a consensus agreement that could keep the issue from exploding into a political free-for-all in Congress next year.

If even a commission of experts cannot set aside its political differences for the good of the nation, how can the nation's elected officials be expected to do so? Can the American public help but become slightly cynical when the chairman of the presidential commission, economist Alan Greenspan, and Senate Finance Committee Chairman Robert Dole, have to go on national television (as they did this past weekend), and urge President Reagan and House Speaker O'Neill to work out a compromise between themselves so that the commission can then reach agreement by the day of its final meeting later this week?

The point is that there is still time for the commission to produce a consensus agreement that can avoid the political bickering that seems likely if no such compromise is struck. Indeed, the broad outlines of a consensus seem already evident from the commission's own work:

● Cutting back some future benefits. Such logical steps might well be along the lines of the consensus plan sought by commission member Alexander Trowbridge of the National Association of Manufacturers. He would seek a permanent three-month delay in the month that cost-of-living increases are granted — from July to October; also, he would link future benefit increases to wage increases, with an offset for productivity gains.

● Speeding up tax increases for social security already written into law. It is instructive that Mr. Trowbridge, as a businessman, would not be averse to a modest increase in payroll taxes as part of a compromise.

● Requiring federal workers to join the system.

● Gradually extending the standard retirement year for future beneficiaries. The age is now set at 65.

The commission has rightly estimated that the system's financial plight is serious. But that plight can hardly be looked upon as grave, in the sense that some newspaper and magazine headlines have observed of late, and some politicians eager for publicity would aver. Reforms will be required. But they need not be draconian for recipients or add up to a gutting of the system.

The members of the social security commission have had a unique opportunity to serve the American public. How much better it would be for all if they could take the few days left at their disposal, put aside partisan differences, and carry out the mandate given them. To do less would be not only disheartening but inexcusable.

THE COMMERCIAL APPEAL
Memphis, Tenn., December 14, 1982

IT HAS BEEN evident for some time that the problems of the Social Security system are going to be solved only if everybody is willing to give something as well as to demand something.

Those who think the solution lies in cutting benefits must be willing also to accept some increase in Social Security taxes or at least a speed-up in the increases which already are scheduled.

Those who want to include federal government workers in the program must also be willing to accept a different formula for determining the annual cost-of-living adjustments. The combinations are many. Nobody is going to win everything. There are too many factions, too many special interests and political constituencies involved in this thing to expect a clear victory by anyone.

So Alan Greenspan and his presidential commission colleagues are entirely right when they say they cannot issue a report recommending changes in the program unless they are given some assurances by the two political leaders who really count — President Reagan and Speaker Thomas P. 'Tip' O'Neill — that what they recommend will have a reasonable chance of passage by Congress.

Is that a cop-out by the commission? Not really. It was charged with finding out what the Social Security system needs to keep it solvent. Knowing what the top political leaders are willing to accept and how much they are willing to give is a real part of that answer.

THE COMMISSION could report its multiple findings without conclusions or recommendations. But that wouldn't carry much weight. Or it could report conclusions and recommendations only to find them unacceptable in part to all sides.

Either way, the report would be useless and the problems would remain. And the monthly pension funds could run out next year unless Congress in desperation approved dipping into general revenues to make up the shortfall without making any corrections.

The commission has defined the size of the problem as seen now, and it has come to reasonable agreement on the many possible ways the problem could be relieved. Given the diversity of the membership of that commission, it would be unreasonable for anyone to expect it to do more than it has.

The commission is putting the monkey right where it belongs by turning to those two political leaders. If they fail to respond, they will be blamed for the mess that will result.

SYRACUSE HERALD-JOURNAL
Syracuse, N.Y., December 8, 1982

The long-awaited and much-anticipated report from the task force studying the Social Security mess now shapes up to be a mish-mash of evasive double-talk.

Sen. Robert Dole is chairman of the Senate Finance Committee and a member of the president's special commission which has been mandated to study the situation and report back before the end of the year. Yesterday, he as much as said the group will do nothing but re-list the options instead of coming up with solutions unless there is "some guidance from the president and Tip O'Neill (House speaker) before the commission holds its last session."

Can you imagine the president, still shell-shocked from the lumps he took after his remarks last year about Social Security, sticking his neck out again just to pull a namby-pamby commission out of a hole?

The options have been fed to us so many times, we can't swallow them again. This group was supposed to give answers.

"It will take a package in which the president has to accept some things he doesn't want to give, and in which Tip O'Neill has to do likewise. Therefore, now is the time for the president and the speaker to weigh in with the commission and tell us."

That's double-talk for, "This is a cop-out. Let's toss the whole thing back to the Congress."

Bipartisan Panel Unveils Compromise Reform Package

The National Commission on Social Security Reform agreed on a compromise plan to return the Social Security system to solvency only hours before its midnight deadline on Jan. 15. The package of proposals would produce an estimated $169 billion revenue gain for the system from 1983 to 1989 through a mixture of tax increases, benefit-growth reductions, and coverage for new federal workers and employees of nonprofit organizations. Under the commission's plan, state and local governments would also be prohibited from withdrawing from the system. The panel's report strongly recommended that Congress "not alter the fundamental structure of the Social Security program or undermine its fundamental principles," but proposed that the system be handled by an independent agency rather than by the Health and Human Services Department.

Major provisions of the package called for: a six-month delay in the July, 1983 COLA, and the use of January instead of July dates for subsequent COLA payments; taxation, for the first time, of half the retirement and disability benefits for those whose annual incomes were $20,000 or more ($25,000 for married couples); moving up the scheduled 1985 payroll tax to 1984 and a portion of the 1990 tax hike to 1988; and eliminating "windfall" benefits for those who became eligible to retire after 1983.

The fragile, last-minute compromise was opposed by three members of the commission. Two of them—Rep. Bill Archer and Sen. William Armstrong—objected to the proposed payroll tax hikes. Differences over the system's long-term problems remained unresolved; nine of the 15 members, all Republicans, favored a gradual increase in the retirement age, while the Democratic members preferred to raise payroll taxes if necessary. Particularly adamant in his opposition to raising the eligibility age was House Rules Committee Chairman Claude Pepper, whose strategic post in Congress and influence with the elderly community made his support almost essential for the plan's passage. Although congressional leaders and the White House expressed optimism that the package would be approved by Congress, groups that felt that they would be adversely affected by the reform, including federal employee unions, immediately began mobilizing to defeat it.

The Orlando Sentinel

Orlando, Fla., February 9, 1983

Rep. Bill Archer is right, of course. The widely acclaimed, bipartisan fix proposed for Social Security is not a cure-all. Far from it.

Even so, the proposal must be passed if the nation's largest retirement plan is to avoid another emergency loan — probably dipping into general revenues this time — so it can continue sending out checks after May. If there were ever any doubts, the verbal exchanges of the past few days should have confirmed that the package is a delicate compromise that has to be addressed in its present form.

In other words, to tinker with it is almost certain to kill it.

Rep. Archer, a Republican from Texas, was on the Greenspan Commission, which produced the rescue plan. He now fears that many people believe it is a cure-all. The truth is, in 75 years, the rescue plan can raise only two-thirds of the system's $1.6 trillion long-term liability.

Eventually, greater changes must be made if Social Security is to survive. The chore now is to buy time.

One change that must come eventually is to raise the retirement age from 65. Florida's Rep. Claude Pepper, now chairman of the Rules Committee, and House Speaker Tip O'Neill vow to sink the rescue effort if that proposal is pushed now.

At present, the greatest danger facing the reform package lies in the camps of federal workers and government retirees, not from the mass of workers who will pay more in Social Security taxes to keep the program afloat. Their fear is that if federal workers are brought under Social Security's umbrella, their Civil Service retirement program may be threatened.

The Greenspan compromise recommends that all new federal employees be brought into Social Security, starting next year. The Civil Service program is one of the world's most liberal pension systems and, as you might expect, federal workers are fighting tooth and nail against any perceived threat to it.

Many experts warn that unless this rescue is successful, Social Security will die. The nation won't let that happen, but other temporary cures aren't very attractive.

The best long-term options are either to revise it to a sound — though not so remunerative — system or fold it into a new national retirement program. Such a program, gathering *all* American workers into a mandatory private pension plan, has been proposed.

For now, though, the problem is to resolve the short-term concerns about Social Security. Don't tinker with the compromise plan.

The Washington Post

Washington, D.C., January 17, 1983

THE SOCIAL SECURITY plan that emerges from the Greenspan Commission's long labors is a decent and reasonable compromise. It deserves the support that it has received from both President Reagan and Speaker O'Neill. The sooner it is enacted into law, the better.

It is as close to absolute fairness as any Social Security revision can ever be. The very term "fairness" has to be handled with some caution here, for in a pension system every minor detail and subsection, simply because it exists, quickly becomes the accustomed way of doing things and, therefore, by a familiar habit of mind the definition of what's fair. From that, it is only a short step to the accusation that any departure from present practice is necessarily unfair. But is it? The opponents of this compromise might ask themselves whether it would be fairer to Social Security beneficiaries, present and future, to wage a long campaign of political attrition in pursuit of ideological purity while the system's reserves get closer and closer over the coming year to exhaustion.

The really crucial step in the forcing of this compromise was Alan Greenspan's achievement in eliciting an agreement among the commission's diverse membership that the Social Security system was indeed running out of money. Once the Democrats had accepted that truth, the debate got much narrower and more productive. And once the Democrats had come that far, the White House was aware it could not let the negotiations fail without unpleasant consequences to itself. One of those consequences would surely have been to poison the atmosphere in which the president's budget goes to Congress later this month. That, fortunately, can now be avoided—if the compromise holds.

The most important innovation proposed here is to tax half the benefits going to people with substantial other income. There has never been a real reason, in concept, why Social Security benefits should not be subject to income tax. It's just that things have never been done that way. But why—for a couple with more than $25,000 a year from other sources—is it unfair to tax Social Security income like any other income? Similarly, there is nothing inherently wrong in postponing cost-of-living adjustments. The benefits overcompensated for inflation in the 1970s. A modest adjustment downward now—not a reduction in the benefit, but in the rate at which it rises—is not inequitable.

Several members of the commission, on its right wing, refuse to accept the compromise on grounds that it requires tax increases. But the only other possibility is a much more drastic erosion of benefits. If one thing is obvious in the current American politics, it is that a very large majority of American voters do not want their Social Security system to be brought into balance solely at the expense of the benefits. Most voters seem to want to see the basic structure of benefits preserved, even if it requires increased taxes. That attitude, incidentally, seems increasingly to apply to more parts of the federal budget than Social Security alone.

The Seattle Times

Seattle, Wash., February 4, 1983

ALAN Greenspan, the economist who headed the Social Security reform commission, gave a tart little lecture to the key House Ways and Means Committee the other day. Committee members would be well advised to accept his every word as scripture.

Some committee members talk about tinkering with the carefully crafted compromise worked out by the commission. We hope such talk is nothing more than political posturing.

Because, as Greenspan warned the committee, if Congress fails to enact a Social Security rescue bill, it would send a "terrible signal" to financial markets — a verification of their view that the federal budget is out of control.

The only sure way to avoid failure on Social Security reform is to adopt the commission's compromise, which has been accepted — albeit with considerable nose-holding — by the Reagan administration and leading congressional Democrats.

Ways and Means members tempted to change the bipartisan formula should consider the consequences of yet another congressional failure to rescue Social Security. Greenspan wasn't kidding.

The Birmingham News

Birmingham, Ala., February 6, 1983

Congress should get cracking with the rescue plan for the Social Security system recommended by the bipartisan commission. The plan is by no means the best one for putting Social Security on a sound financial basis, but it's probably the only one floated which has a chance for approval.

Speedy action is important, for the longer it is debated, the larger the opportunities for deforming it and the harder it will be to develop a consensus. Speed is also important to put to rest the worries of those now receiving benefits and those about to retire. The crisis in financing has hung like the sword of Damoclese over the heads of those who depend on it for a livelihood and health care.

Urgency is also desirable to remove the crisis atmosphere surrounding discussions of possibilities for the system. Only when that crisis atmosphere is removed can government officials begin to think and talk intelligently about long-term changes which will stand the test of time.

Few of those acquainted with the system and its financing believe the changes proposed by the commission will suffice more than for a few years. One hopes that the present crisis will have served, at least, to convince responsible members of Congress that something of a more permanent nature must be devised.

Literally scores of options to the present system are available. But first, the philosophy that stands behind the way the system is constructed and how it actually works needs revising. For years, it has been touted as a retirement insurance system, as an earned annuity. Or course, it is not. It is more like a chain letter, with the last persons to come in left holding an empty bag.

If it is to be an obligatory or forced retirement system, funded solely by taxing workers' income, then only workers who have paid into it over a lifetime should be eligible for full retirement benefits. In that case, a welfare program for those who are ineligible should be created and provided for by tax monies from the general fund.

In discussions, actuarial tables should be examined to see if age 65 is a proper age for healthy Americans to retire automatically. When Social Security w is created by Congress in the '30s, life expectancy for both males and females was considerably lower than at present. The thinking then, when unemployment was still very high, was to create a system that would open up jobs by enticing those 65 and over to retire.

Raising the early retirement age to 65 and the regular age to 67 or 68 makes good sense, both from the standpoint of worker productivity and from a concern for the wishes of workers covered by the system. Forced retirement for a healthy, productive worker. still interested in his job, is a dubious reward for those who gave unstintingly to their jobs.

The system should never be tied to inflation rates or any other variable to make increased benefits automatic. Increases should be made only after conscious decisions by members of Congress and only if increases are matched by additional income for the system. That requirement would keep Congress honest as regards vote-buying, it would work to dampen inflationary trends and keep the system sound.

The money paid into the Social Security fund should be invested as are funds in private retirement systems. Interest or dividends from these investments will be available to pay for costs of administering the system, cover unforseen outlays the system could incur in future years or paid out as additional benefits for retirees.

Another question that is critical for the future is whether the system is expected to provide total income for retirees. When the present system was established, it was seen as only a supplement to workers' savings or to private pensions established by workers or by their employers. But over the years, that concept has been replaced by the notion that Social Security is the main source of retirement income.

This is important, for if Social Security is to provide the total or main source of retirement income, workers will be required to pay a lot more into the fund than they presently do, inflation or no inflation. The system can no longer depend on unlimited expansion of the economy to provide the added dollars needed each year.

A viable retirement system can be developed; it can be equitable and it can receive the support of a majority of Americans; but it cannot be done in a crisis atmosphere or when Congress is seen to use it as an incomes transfer device or as a devious means of acquiring unearned political power.

One hopes these considerations are not lost entirely on those now involved in the attempt to rescue the system from insolvency.

Maine Sunday Telegram

Portland, Maine, January 30, 1983

☐ No one is overjoyed with the recommendations of a Social Security reform commission. That's obvious. Nevertheless, the proposal stands as the only viable way of rescuing the national retirement system from bankruptcy.

That stark realization—that Social Security could go belly-up without swift action to save it—was enough to unite such usual political adversaries as President Reagan and House Speaker Thomas "Tip" O'Neill Jr. in support of the plan. And it should be more than enough to persuade Congress to approve the package.

It won't be easy for members of Congress to resist the opposition of powerful special-interest groups, including the elderly and federal employees. But they must find the courage to do so.

There is, quite frankly, no practical alternative to the commission plan to keep the system solvent over the remainder of this century. If Congress rejects the commission plan, no consensus is likely to be developed for any alternative.

In short, Congress is faced with a take-it-or-leave situation. Efforts to tamper with the compromise package will almost certainly destroy the fragile bipartisan coalition which developed it.

Obviously, no one really likes all the pieces of the package. The elderly oppose the proposed six-month freeze on cost-of-living hikes as well as the provision to tax half the benefits received by recipients with incomes of more than $20,000 a year.

Federal employees don't like the requirement that new federal workers join the system. Workers and their employers don't like the idea of making increased payments into the system. Some workers at non-profit institutions object to being forced into the system. And the list goes on.

But what's the alternative to the commission plan? Only one that we can see. A bankrupt Social Security system.

"OK, BOYS, HEERE WE GO! ACT NONCHALANT! SMILE... WAVE TO THE PEOPLE!"

THE MILWAUKEE JOURNAL
Milwaukee, Wisc., January 17, 1983

The National Commission on Social Security Reform has put together a rather impressive plan for dealing with the retirement program's severe financial problems.

It isn't everything that we have recommended, and probably isn't everything that anyone wanted. But it probably is as reasonable a package as anybody can expect, given the need to accommodate disparate political and economic needs. After all, the commission was a bipartisan group, and it had to come up with a solution that would satisfy President Reagan on one side of the scale and House Speaker Thomas O'Neill on the other.

In the process of raising needed funds, several of the plan's provisions introduce a new element of fairness. For instance, retired persons with substantial income would be required to pay income tax on half of their Social Security benefits, and the self-employed would have to pay Social Security taxes comparable to employer-employe contributions. They now pay substantially less.

The plan also would move toward the important goal of making Social Security universal. Federal employes and the employes of nonprofit organizations would have to join as of Jan. 1, 1984. We think participation should be compulsory also for state and local government employes. Though the commission did not suggest that all such groups be required to join the system, at least it said those now in the system shouldn't be allowed to withdraw.

Ideally, the commission should have gone farther than it did in curbing the growth of the basic benefit. Overly generous increases in benefits, based on the unrealistic Consumer Price Index, have given many retired persons an unfair advantage over working taxpayers. Still, the commission didn't entirely ignore that problem. It suggested that cost-of-living raises be delayed in a way that would save the retirement fund some $40 billion in the next six years.

The commission also called for acceleration of Social Security taxes by $40 billion in the same period. We find that regrettable, but recognize that it probably is necessary under the circumstances.

On the whole, the package deserves passage. It will not solve all of the Social Security program's problems in the long run and may not be entirely sufficient for the short run. Still, it will help greatly.

Understandably, some politicians are fearful of losing popular support if they support the plan. The political shock can be held to a minimum, however, if all political factions brace themselves and dive into the cold water together. The bipartisan recommendations make that possible.

THE ARIZONA REPUBLIC
Phoenix, Ariz., January 30, 1983

IMPERFECT as the package of Social Security reforms proposed by President Reagan's commission to study the system unquestionably is, Congress should approve it.

Otherwise, the system will go broke at midnight June 30, and 36 million beneficiaries will not receive their promised checks in July unless Congress authorizes payment from the Treasury.

If the checks don't go out, that would cause untold misery.

If the Treasury pays the benefits, the effect on the federal deficit would be nightmarish.

Both the president and House Speaker Thomas P. O'Neill have approved the reforms. So have Senate Majority Leader Howard Baker and Chairman Bob Dole of the Senate Finance Committee.

But that does not ensure them of being enacted into law. The path to enactment is strewn with mines.

The House Ways and Means Committee is certain to draw up a bill incorporating the proposed changes in the Social Security Act.

But it's not at all certain that Chairman Claude Pepper of the Rules Comittee will permit the bill to reach the floor with no amendments permitted.

If Pepper doesn't, there will be chaos.

In the Senate, the problem is the possibility of a filibuster.

Some of the more conservative Republicans oppose the package because it provides for increasing taxes.

The proposed changes will keep the Social Security solvent only until about the year 2000, when the baby boom generation comes of retirement age.

After that, no amount of tinkering will be able to save the system from collapse or the economy from disaster.

Thus, the proposed changes merely would give Congress a breathing spell in which to carry out a complete overhaul.

A growing number of economists believe Social Security should be scrapped altogether and replaced with another system.

But first things first.

The immediate problem is keeping the system from going bust at midnight June 30.

Arkansas Gazette.

Little Rock, Ark., January 18, 1983

The best news out of Washington in recent weeks was the announcement Saturday that the President, the Speaker of the House and the majority leader of the Senate had joined a special presidential commission in approving a program to keep the Social Security system "solvent" through 1990. Cutting the costs of Social Security and raising its revenues are the third-ranking priority in coping with the federal deficits now afflicting the country.

Cutting the exorbitant Defense budget is first, and restoring some revenues lost in the tax cutting orgy of 1981 is second, in the priorities, but the uncontrolled cost of Social Security is the third urgent element in restoring fiscal responsibility. The government's deficit this year is moving toward $185 billion, which is intolerable. Defense and Social Security take well over half the federal outlay.

All parties made concessions in the compromise on Social Security. The program is clearly acceptable even if none of the participants is entirely satisfied. It is a combination of diverse elements, all of them working either to save money or to raise it. Payroll taxes for Social Security would be increased — that is, increases already scheduled would be moved up on the timetable. Meantime, the next (July 1) cost-of-living increase in Social Security checks would be delayed for six months, giving the Social Security fund some immediate respite. Social Security recipients in middle and upper incomes would pay tax on their Social Security income. New employees of the federal government and employes of non-profit organizations would be required to join the Social Security system, broadening the tax base. Self-employed persons under Social Security would be required to pay at the full rate, rather than at three-quarters.

These are major measures and, if enacted, they will give major relief to Social Security financing. Instant opposition is already registered in some of the quarters where special interests are affronted, these including, notably, Social Security recipients who concede nothing toward cost control and the lobby of federal employes. It will be a hard fight to pass the program, and amendments must be treated with extreme caution but the array of leaders announcing support is nonetheless impressive, at least suggesting that partisan bickering and conniving can, in fact, cease at the water's edge.

Reno Gazette-Journal

Reno, Nev., January 25, 1983

In the world, they say, nothing is perfect. And in the world of Social Security, nothing is even close to perfect.

So the compromise agreement on how to save Social Security is far from faultless. In fact, almost everyone can find something wrong with it, and some are finding almost everything wrong with it.

The poor old thing is an ungainly oddball, born of an unhappy mating of liberals and conservatives. It is the product of a group of officials who don't want to do anything, but know they must do something. It is jerrybuilt, hammered together with bent nails and odd-sized boards. It looks like it could collapse at any minute.

The creature wobbles awkwardly onto the stage, apologizing to right and left, and squats center platform, begging our approval.

It opens its crooked mouth and squawks: "I'm all you got, baby. Do you love me?"

Well, no, frankly. Not even the parents can love this orphan child. And yet, it is very truly all we got, and we had better embrace it.

It is remarkable, in fact, that the warring and timid factions of Washington have been able to agree on even this much of a solution to Social Security's impending bankruptcy. Traditional liberals look fondly at all the ornaments tacked onto the program's once lean frame, and wish they could add more. Traditional conservatives want to rip the ornamanents off. Some even want to disenfranchise those wastrels who have the nerve to retire at 65. Keep them out of Social Security until they're 70 — or older, they say. That will teach them.

That is one of the changes that was jettisoned by the bi-partisan National Commission on Social Security Reform. Thank God for that. If people contribute all their lives to this system, they should at least have some opportunity to receive some of the benefits.

So what do we have as our solution? The payroll tax for Social Security will go up faster than originally planned. Some increases scheduled for 1985 and 1990 will be brought in early, but workers will get an offsetting tax credit for 1984. The cost-of-living increase scheduled for July will be delayed six months, but extra benefits will be given to needy elderly.

Coverage will be expanded to new federal employees and all employees of non-profit groups. State and local government employees now in the system will not be permitted to get out (but those not in the system can remain out if they wish).

Wealthier retirees will find half of their Social Security paycheck taxed. The Treasury will reimburse the Social Security fund for military retirement credits. And if Social Security reserves fall below 20 percent of annual payments, retirees will get the lower of the rise in the Consumer Price Index or the average nationwide increase in wages.

What does the proposal fail to do? Perhaps its most grievous failure is to shore off some of the accretions added to Social Security over the years, accretions having nothing to do with retirement. The system needs a thorough overhaul, but Washington lacks the courage to do the job.

The compromise also fails to raise all the money needed for the next 75 years. The changes proposed will raise only two-thirds of that money, so further adjustments will be needed early in the next century.

On the other hand, for the first time the Treasury will become at least minimally involved in Social Security. And this might be the wave of the future. As the number of retired persons grows and the number of workers decreases, general revenue might have to be used to pay retirement checks.

Taxes will go up, but not drastically. A worker earning $20,000 a year will pay $43.20 more a year through 1989. The six-month delay in benefit increases will not hurt the retired that much, especially now that inflation has slowed.

Taxing of benefits does seem unfair. Even though retired people earning more than $20,000 a year are fairly well off, they paid into the system like everyone else and they should get equal benefits.

So this solution isn't the best in the world, but it's not the worst, either.

We don't love ya, baby, but we'll take you. Why? Because nothing better is likely to come along.

Detroit Free Press

Detroit, Mich., January 27, 1983

WHATEVER the inequities and fallacies in President Reagan's tax and budget programs, they will not be mended by torpedoing the tenuous compromise on Social Security, which is exactly what the Democrats in Congress now seem to be contemplating.

Democratic leaders are urging that any delay in the cost-of-living increase for Social Security recipients be tied to a reduction in the scheduled July tax cut, but what they are most likely to get is a stalemate on both questions.

The need to do something about the Social Security deficits is critical. And it is difficult enough to reach consensus on reforming Social Security, without tying reform to the fate of other controversial issues.

Mr. Reagan's tax program has indeed provided inordinate benefits for the wealthy. But it is unlikely that the Democrats can successfully use Social Security reform as a club to make him change it. The attempt to tie Social Security reform to other items on the Democratic agenda, no matter how worthy, is to risk destroying the bipartisan compromise necessary to achieve any solution on Social Security at all. In trying it, the Democratic leadership is flirting with demagoguery again.

ALBUQUERQUE JOURNAL

Albuquerque, N.M., January 19, 1983

Much detailed analysis is needed before Americans can be sure the president's special Social Security commission actually helped put the system on sound footing. But at first blush it appears the system *could* be more solvent than it is now if the recommendations are accepted by Congress.

One troubling aspect of the Social Security fiscal problem, though, remained unattended by the commission, Congress or the White House. That is the growth in number of eligible recipients who would never have qualified for Social Security's retirement supplement when the system began five decades ago. Those beneficiaries receive a growing sum of money from workers currently paying into the system.

As most Americans know, the Social Security system pays much more money to its 36 million benefit recipients than it has taken in from workers. The rise in unemployment has only made the problem worse. The system has been borrowing from its smaller, still solvent sibling funds just to make monthly payments.

Reform has been especially difficult for politicians who feared defeat at the polls by angry voters. Reagan's 1981 effort was quickly mauled by those who understood neither the proposed reform nor the gravity of the problem faced by the system. Members of Congress did more poorly than Reagan — they didn't even propose any reform.

Finally, a bipartisan commission of 15 persons was convened to look at the problems and offer solutions. Of that number, only three voted against the compromise package just announced and backed by Reagan and House Speaker Tip O'Neill.

Essentially the compromise plan, if passed by Congress, will speed up planned worker tax increases, force some government workers to join, prohibit those eligible to quit the system from doing so, postpone the payment of cost-of-living adjustments to recipients, and tax the benefits of middle- and upper-income Social Security recipients. For the first time, general revenues from the Treasury would be available to meet obligations if the higher worker taxes still failed to pay all benefits — an ominous thought. All of these measures are designed either to raise revenue or postpone spending.

In theory, those steps are supposed to keep the system in the black for the next 50 years. But early press coverage of the compromise has obligingly included this disclaimer: "barring severe economic conditions." Further, the commission did not recommend steps needed to eradicate about one-third the long-term Social Security debt.

Social Security's structural problem, as even the commission noted quietly, is that "When Social Security began, only retirement benefits were paid to workers. Today, there are about 21 general types of benefits provided under Social Security."

This clearly is not the same system begun by Congress during the Depression. Politicians anxious to give constituents something for nothing found dozens of "eligibility" categories into which they put millions of people. Over the years the cost of those new categories finally caught up with the system. The commission's solution was not to tighten eligibility, which is a must, but to speed up tax increases and force other workers — facing their own pension crises — to join Social Security.

This problem, hardly ever noted by members of Congress, lurks behind the veneer of solubility given to Social Security by the commission. That the commission didn't focus on the problem much probably helps explain the sighs of relief coming from the White House and Capitol Hill. But by glossing over it this time, the commission, Congress and Reagan have only pushed it off on the next generation. Let's just hope that next generation has more fortitude than this one.

The State

Columbia, S.C., January 19, 1983

THE SOCIAL Security Reform Commission's long-awaited proposals to save the retirement system are disappointing in some ways, but the key points stand an excellent chance of approval and should go far in restoring the system's credibility.

Although the complex compromise falls short in some respects, it is surprisingly constructive and is palatable enough to win the nod both of President Reagan and of Democratic House Speaker Tip O'Neill.

That the rescue proposals were gutsy can be seen by the opposition it has already generated. As one observer commented, they offer something for everyone to dislike. That was expected since semidrastic measures wi'' be needed to save the system. The program, of course, must be saved. It would be disgraceful to break the faith and fail to provide the basic benefits that retirees and those near retirement feel they have been promised.

But the retirees, too, will pay a one-time price, a modest one considering what is involved in finding the $167 billion needed to bail out the system over seven years. Instead of reaping a cost-of-living hike in July, the 36 million beneficiaries will have to wait until next January for the estimated 5 percent benefit increase.

Also, 4 million retirees and other Social Security recipients with adjusted gross incomes over $20,000 for individuals and $25,000 for couples (not counting their Social Security) would have to pay income tax on half their benefits starting in 1984.

The 116 million taxpayers and their employers would also pay heavily. They would pay higher payroll taxes in 1984. The current rate of 6.7 percent, not scheduled to rise until 1985, will increase to 7 percent next Jan. 1, with workers getting a one-time, refundable income tax credit for 1984 to offset the extra payroll tax.

In addition, the 6.5 million self-employed, who now pay a 9.35 percent tax, will have to pay the combined employer-employee rate of 14 percent starting in 1984.

The plan would bring all federal workers hired in 1984 or later into the system, as well as the remaining 15 percent of non-profit organizations that are not now covered.

Defections from the system by state and local governments would also be banned when the bailout package is enacted.

Lobbies for the elderly are already opposing the reforms despite the support of Rep. Claude Pepper, the 82-year-old Floridian who serves on the commission.

A majority of the commission wants to insert in the final report an increase in the retirement age from 65 to 66. This is a good proposal. Sixty-five may have been appropriate when the system was created in 1935, but with longer life expectancy today, it would be relatively painless to up the age gradually. This change alone could wipe out one-third of the system's long-range deficit that would still remain after new taxes and reduced benefits.

Perhaps the most damaging blow to the system in the long run would be the speedup and increase of taxes. This tax diverts money that could be used to expand the economy, create jobs and provide a base of support for Social Security in the years ahead.

Nevertheless, considering the emotional nature of Social Security and the political climate, no more could have been expected from the reform commission. Its report will certainly be a positive step in reassuring the elderly and maintaining confidence in the system.

WORCESTER TELEGRAM.

Worcester, Mass., February 5, 1983

We hate to say it, but U.S. Rep. Claude Pepper is becoming a walking advertisement for mandatory retirement.

Pepper, 81, turns the old folks on by chanting "Hands off Social Security." He never tells them that hands off would mean collapse of the system within six months. He has managed to demagogue the issue to the point where a lot of the elderly think that anyone trying to save the system is out to take something away from them.

Pepper was at it again the other day. When Rep. J.J. Pickle came out in favor of gradually raising the retirement age over the next 20 years, Pepper roared his opposition. When Pickle pointed out that something had to be done by the year 2000 to keep the system solvent, Pepper declaimed that he was against cutting any benefits "now or ever after."

That may play well in St. Pete, but it does nothing to close the multi-billion-dollar gap between income and outgo that will remain even after the new Social Security bailout plan is in place.

Instead of being the best friend of the old folks and their Social Security benefits, as he claims, Pepper has become an albatross around their necks. He is writing a prescription for disaster.

ST. LOUIS POST-DISPATCH

St. Louis, Mo., January 19, 1983

All things considered, the National Commission on Social Security Reform has managed to produce as fair, balanced and reasonable a set of recommendations as could possibly have been hoped for. The commission found an answer to the Social Security's funding problem without altering the basic benefit structure, as President Reagan had originally wanted to do, and without raising the system's payroll taxes onerously, as many feared it might do.

Instead, it imposed a small sacrifice on Social Security recipients by asking them to defer their cost-of-living increase by six months and on taxpayers by asking them to pay higher rates sooner than they otherwise would have. And, in a significant departure from the past, the commission recommended that some general revenue funds be earmarked for the Social Security account.

The commission's call for postponing Social Security's cost-of-living increase will, happily, be made more tolerable by the fact that the inflation rate has dropped drastically in the past two years. That means that the purchasing power of Social Security benefits has remained pretty well intact and that the increase beneficiaries would forgo would be small. Nor should advancing the tax increases be very burdensome. The increase scheduled for 1985 — from the present level of 6.7 percent to 7 percent — would go into effect in 1984. The tax increases already scheduled for 1985 and 1986 would be left in place and the 1990 tax increase, to 7.65 percent for both employers and employees, would be moved to 1988.

The tax changes would produce $40 billion in additional revenues through the end of this decade; a like amount would be saved by shifting the cost-of-living increase payment from July 1 to Jan. 1.

The 15-member, bipartisan commission also recommended that half of Social Security benefits be subject to the income tax when a recipient's income from other sources exceeded $20,000 ($25,000 for married couples) and that the Social Security system be compensated for the value of future benefits that will be paid to military personnel who were not required to pay the Social Security tax. The two actions would constitute, for the first time in the system's history, a direct infusion of general revenue dollars into the Social Security trust fund — $18 billion for military personnel and $30 billion in income taxes paid by retirees on their public pensions.

That could turn out to have been an unfortunate precedent, but under the circumstances it is a chance worth taking. And the commission minimized the risk by devising the general revenue transfer in a way that would insulate it from the customary appropriation process and thus prevent it from becoming a target for opportunists every year.

Together with other revisions — compelling new employees of the federal government to participate in Social Security, prohibiting employees of state governments and nonprofit institutions from withdrawing, increasing the tax on the self-employed, for example — the changes are expected to produce new revenues and achieve savings amounting to about $169 billion through the end of the decade. The commission wisely decided against looking beyond the '80s, though many of the correctives it recommended for the immediate future would help minimize problems in the 1990s and after.

Because the commission's recommendations are a compromise, they necessarily contain features that of themselves are objectionable. But considered in the context of the entire package of recommendations, they are essential components of a solution that Congress can live with.

St. Louis, Mo., February 14, 1983

Eight Republicans on the National Commission on Social Security Reform have recommended raising the normal retirement age from 65 to 66 in the early part of the next century, and the idea seems to have caught hold, so much so in fact that it is on the verge of being regarded as conventional wisdom. Congress, however, ought to stay away from the proposal, surely for now and perhaps indefinitely.

First, it is not part of the package of short-term correctives agreed to by the commission. The commission's package envisioned changes that would produce $168 billion in revenue growth or cost savings through the 1980s. The recommendation for delaying the normal retirement age — by raising it one month a year beginning in 2003 — was put forward in a separate opinion by the eight Republicans, who were looking ahead at what is thought to be Social Security's long-range problem, expected to develop in the first part of the 21st century.

Accordingly, House Speaker Thomas P. O'Neill is right in saying that in opposing the delayed retirement age he is not jeopardizing the commission's package of recommendations. Furthermore, it shouldn't be part of the Social Security debate at this time; injecting it now would only make agreement on the short-range remedies more difficult.

·Secondly, Americans ought to know that the only ways to raise the regular retirement age and save the Social Security system money — the presumed objective of the recommendation — would be to penalize those who retire early with smaller benefits or to raise the early retirement age, now 62. Prof. Merton C. Bernstein of Washington University, who was a consultant to the Social Security Commission, has pointed out that 65 percent of those who retire do so before the normal age of 65. Ill health or unemployment are most often the reasons.

But if we raise the retirement age, can we also assure workers the better health and the continued employment that would make working to 63 or 64 more feasible than it is today? And even if we could, do we want to make early retirement less attractive?

Social Security's long-range funding problem can't be treated as a simple taxes and expenditure equation. It has to be analyzed in the context of employment trends, health conditions and the social situation. In short, there are humanitarian considerations that the proponents of later retirement apparently have not addressed. In any case, it won't be necessary to do so for another 10 or 15 years.

The Burlington Free Press

Burlington, Vt., January 18, 1983

Among the panaceas for the ailments of the Social Security system, the National Commission on Social Security Reform has recommended doses of higher payroll taxes, delayed cost-of-living increases for recipients, inclusion of federal workers in the program and taxation of the benefits of those with incomes from other sources.

What is alarming about the plan to tax benefits is that it would penalize those people who have made provisions for receiving additional income when they retire. The commission's proposal calls for taxing half the Social Security benefits of single persons with incomes of $20,000 and over and married people with incomes of $25,000 and over, excluding Social Security. It would deprive people who have invested in the nation's business and industry or deposited their money in banks of the benefits they are entitled to under the program. And it would be patently unfair to a class of people for no other reason than that they have been thrifty. If they are taxed, they will be paying a tax on a tax, since they already paid withholding taxes on earnings that were subject to Social Security taxes during their working lives.

Such a tax would abolish the incentive for other people to put aside additional money for their retirement through investments and savings while they are in the work force. At the same time, it could mean that the national economy would be deprived of an important stimulus, since investors provide the dollars for business and industrial development and savers' money is put back into circulation through the medium of housing, automobile and appliance loans by banks. Faced with the possibility of paying taxes on Social Security benefits if their incomes exceeded arbitrary limits, many people who might be considering those alternatives might well drop their plans and decide to depend solely on Social Security as a source of income during their retirement.

Taxing Social Security benefits, no matter how high income from other sources might be, appears to be another instance of the government giving with one hand and taking away with the other.

Congress should reject the step as a means of remedying the ailments of the Social Security system.

The Knickerbocker News

Albany, N.Y., January 26, 1983

As compromises go, it's hard to fault the complex bailout advanced by the National Commission on Social Security Reform. After months of debate and study, it has recommended a combination of revenue-raising measures and curtailments in benefits that will amount to $169 billion and keep the system solvent for the immediate future.

Because it is a compromise, the sacrifice is spread over many fronts. Federal workers now covered under a separate pension system, for example, will have to join Social Security, and state and local governments will lose their right to withdraw from the system, as they have been doing in record numbers recently. Not suprisingly, their representatives are protesting these recommendations, but they should not be allowed to prevail. Bringing more workers under the system while preventing others from deserting is vital to halting a serious drain on the system's funds.

Other proposals are equally sensible: the commission would delay next January's cost-of-living adjustment until July; raise the self-employment rate from 9.35 percent to 13.4 percent, the current sum now shared equally by employer and employee, and increase the payroll tax rate from 6.7 percent to 7 percent in 1984 and 7.65 percent by 1990.

Nor do all of the recommendations require sacrifice. Some benefits, such as those paid to widows and widowers and divorced persons, would rise. Moreover, the delayed retirement benefit for those aged 65 to 70 would rise from 3 percent to 8 percent a year.

In sum, a sound plan for the present. But on a broader issue, the commission offers neither compromise nor direction. As Peter Grannis notes in a memorandum from the Heritage Foundation, "True reform of Social Security cannot begin until Americans and their Congress recognize the problem for what it really is: part insurance and part welfare."

To its credit, the commission did attempt to address the welfare issue by introducing, for the first time, a means test. It would subject to federal tax half the Social Security benefits paid to individuals who have $20,000 in other income, or $25,000 for couples — on the principle that they are well off enough to afford it.

Even so, it's only a modest approach to a major controversy over whether Social Security can afford to pay the added welfare benefits that politicians have assigned it in recent years as a sure way of attracting votes. Critics complain these benefits have pushed the system bankruptcy and would be more appropriately paid for out of general revenues. They are right, notwithstanding the other side of this debate — that even as an insurance program, Social Security pays out in benefits to a worker far more than it takes in through payroll taxes. To proponents of this side of the argument, Social Security is really welfare for all since nearly every worker will receive more from the government than he could purchase through his payroll taxes alone.

Such an argument, while understandable, misses the point: If Social Security must pay out more to workers who pay into it, how does it follow that it will be better equipped to do so if it must also pay purely welfare benefits, for which no comparable tax has been assessed? The commission doesn't answer this question. But as Mr. Grannis notes, Congress must — and soon.

THE KANSAS CITY STAR

Kansas City, Mo., February 9, 1983

The National Commission on Social Security Reform has given us neither any surprises nor radical proposals for change. If the "product" of the bipartisan group retains bipartisan support in Congress and from the administration, it is expected to stave off short-term deficits, the kind that forced borrowing to pay current benefits.

The major recommendations are somewhat like a house. How well one works to shore up the system presupposes others are in place. All are unpopular with one group or another, but saving one constituency pain by eliminating that objectionable section will reduce the effectiveness of the rest of the structure. To be improvements rather than merely destructive, amendments would have to accomplish the same objective as items replaced.

As predicted, the commission's compromise has combined changes in the law that nick workers and cut benefits. They include speeding up payroll tax increases scheduled through 1990, making the self-employment Old-Age and Suvivors Disability Insurance tax rate comparable to the employer-employee rate and mandatory Social Security coverage for all new federal employees and all workers of non-profit organizations. Those three items would add an estimated $78 billion annually to the system. On the other side, the commission proposed taxing 50 percent of benefits for recipients earning more than $20,000 ($25,000 for joint returns) and delaying the July 1983 cost-of-living increases for six months, then setting a January date for all future COLAs. The savings would be about $70 billion. Of the commission's 10 major recommendations, these are the ones that involve the largest sums of money and are the most controversial. The rest, as well as suggestions from commission minority reports that include gradually raising the retirement age, and outside plans will be disassembled and re-shaped, praised and condemned before Congress does what it must before adjourning.

Even most of its harshest critics agree that many reasons exist for preserving and strengthening the Social Security system. For all its problems, we haven't devised a better way to keep most of the elderly out of poverty. And to look at it from a cynical perspective, no politician dares to approve gutting or abolishing Social Security. He or she couldn't get three votes to be local garbage collector after such a performance. It's not the most noble motive. But it is a persuasive one.

DESERET NEWS

Salt Lake City, Utah, January 18, 1983

A $169 billion plan to rescue the Social Security system from financial distress has been clearly labeled as a "compromise" package, and like all compromises, it has something to anger almost everybody.

Objections already have been voiced this week by organizations for the elderly, for small businesses, and for government workers.

Social Security is such a sacred cow that any attempt to tinker with the system is regarded by most politicians as akin to playing with a sensitive bomb that could blow up in one's face.

For that reason, getting the plan through Congress is going to be difficult because the temptation to play politics will be overwhelming. Yet unless both sides approach it on a bipartisan basis, the whole rescue plan is likely to fall apart.

The tendency to shoot from the hip for political gain was clearly evident in the past election when President Reagan's declaration of the obvious — that something would have to be done about Social Security — was immediately translated in Democratic campaigns as a GOP "threat" to the retirement program.

Both President Reagan and House Speaker Thomas P. O'Neill Jr. have endorsed the plan, although neither appears enthusiastic and the necessary commitment to push the legislation to successful passage may be lacking.

However, 82-year-old Rep. Claude Pepper, D-Fla., a vigorous spokesman for the elderly, is backing the program, although some special-interest organizations for retired persons are trying to change his stand.

Under the proposals unveiled this past week by the National Commission of Social Security Reform, scheduled Social Security tax increases for 1985 will be moved to 1984 and a 1990 increase will become effective in 1988 instead. A scheduled cost-of-living increase next July will be delayed until Jan. 1, 1984.

Other moves that already have come under fire include taxing the Social Security benefits of persons whose other income tops $20,000 a year; a ban on state and local government employees dropping out of the program, and inclusion of new federal workers under Social Security.

All of these things together won't put Social Security on a sound actuarial basis, but they will close an estimated two-thirds of the revenue gap in the current pension program.

Congress must move quickly to pass the proposals if they are to pass at all. Delays, amendments and efforts to hang back and reap political hay by making the other party carry the burden will only unravel the whole plan, according to legislative leaders.

It will be a significant test of Congress — to see if that body can deal with a vital problem, make tough choices, and ask citizens to make sacrifices, or whether our elected representatives will be paralyzed by politics.

THE SUN

Baltimore, Md., January 17, 1983

The National Commission on Social Security Reform has at last come up with a $169 billion bipartisan blueprint to keep the system solvent and politically viable for the rest of this decade. Now the burden shifts to Congress, which must act this spring if the issue is not to be engulfed in 1984 electioneering that would coincide with a projected financing crisis in the retirement system.

It took months of hard study and acerbic bargaining for the commission to come up with a plan acceptable to President Reagan, House Speaker Thomas P. O'Neill and four-fifths of its membership. In the end, as commission chairman Alan Greenspan put it, 12 of his 15 colleagues "swallowed very hard and accepted individual notions that we personally did not actually support." Whether Congress can swallow hard too, despite the opposition of powerful special-interest groups, will be a severe test of its ability to serve the needs of the American people as a whole.

Under the Greenspan Commission proposal, payroll taxes on wage-earners would be accelerated to produce $40 billion for the Social Security system. Beneficiaries would have to wait from July until next January for their next cost-of-living increase, thus reducing system payouts $40 billion. The Social Security benefits for retired persons in comfortable income brackets would be taxed, raising $30 billion. New federal workers and employees of non-profit organizations would be brought into the system, a boost of $24 billion. Further withdrawals from the system by state and local government workers would be halted, an estimated savings of $3 billion. The self-employed would have to pay as much in Social Security taxes as employers and employees combined.

To enumerate these proposals is to see how widely and fairly the Greenspan Commission attempts to spread the pain. Although it did not advocate immediate action to stop the drain caused by high cost-of-living benefit adjustments, it called for a change in 1983 to make these adjustments reflect either the wage or the cost-of-living index, whichever is lower. Although it dropped the administration proposal to increase the penalty for retiring at age 62 instead of 65, it did offer incentives for persons to continue working until 68.

The Greenspan Commission's achievement is a triumph for bipartisanship. If the likes of old antagonists Ronald Reagan and Tip O'Neill can agree, then Congress ought to agree as well. The time for exhaustive study is over. The issues and the options are only too well known. This is a moment for action. It will not soon come again.

Lincoln Journal

Lincoln, Neb., January 17, 1983

The best element of the Social Security bailout "compromise" approved Saturday is its bipartisan wrapping. What is the point of designing Utopia if one is unable to bring it into reality? In politics, that ordinarily means victory, either at the ballot box or in the legislative chamber.

After gaining the approval of both President Reagan and House Speaker Thomas P. O'Neill Jr., the package of proposed system changes was opposed by only three of the 15 members of the presidential study commission on Social Security — and all three of them represent especially conservative thinking, Republican and Democrat.

The bipartisan agreement is vital. That is so because the revision will be severely tested in its forthcoming passage through congressional fire. Interest groups almost immediately declared their opposition. But if President Reagan, Sen. Robert Dole and Rep. Barber Conable Jr. can hold Republicans in line and Speaker O'Neill and Rep. Claude Pepper, with some help from AFL-CIO President Layne Kirkland, are able to discipline Democrats, the emergency legislation can be passed.

And passed it ought to be. This inevitable "compromise" may not have all the features of the most comprehensive rescue program outlined in this space several times, but it has many of them. That would include:

• Beginning the taxation of Social Security for middle and upper-income retirees.

• Phasing federal and non-profit institutional employees into the Social Security system.

• A one-time six-month delay in the annual cost-of-living adjustment in retirement benefits.

• Prohibiting future withdrawals from the system by state and local government workers.

• Reimbursing Social Security trust funds from general tax revenue for credits due military retirees.

• Eliminate "windfall" benefits now available to double-dippers — retired federal civilian or military workers who qualified for federal pension benefits before becoming members of the Social Security system.

The most serious omission in this list is the failure to change the Social Security indexing formula. By now we assumed most Americans have realized it's crazy to grant annual benefit increases based on changes in prices, rather than changes in wages — because it is payroll-taxed wages which must maintain the core fiscal health of the system. One can hope that the agreement for falling back on average national wage changes for indexing rather than the Consumer Price Index when Social Security reserves fall below 20 percent of annual need is but a good directional start.

The second shortcoming was the decision not to advance gradually the age of retirement benefits qualification by a couple of years.

Because the trust fund is in such sad financial shape at the moment — due essentially to the nation's depressed economy and high unemployment; no jobs means no payrolls to tax — we'll have to accept the bad taste of accelerated payroll tax increases. Employer as well as employee. All compromises have a downside, though, and this item fills that prescription.

It, as well as the implicit reaffirmation that Social Security is a national income redistribution/maintenance program rather than a pure pension scheme, is probably the reason the principled conservatives on the commission could not support the compromise — and will likely oppose the whole business in the months ahead.

If it's this or nothing, then better this. The good clearly outweighs the bad.

Fort Worth Star-Telegram

Fort Worth, Texas, January 19, 1983

The word that best describes endorsements of the compromise recommendations reached by the Social Security reform commission is "reluctant."

The word that best describes the initial criticism of the recommendations is "expected."

There is no way to save the Social Security system that would please everyone. Admitting that, the commission members agreed to measures which they, individually, did not support. President Reagan supports the compromise despite inclusion of tax speed-ups which he doesn't like. Congressional Democrats like Tip O'Neill support the compromise despite similar reservations.

Not perfect, it may be the best that can be had under the circumstances. It addresses the immediate problems and begins to look ahead toward the long-range fix. It spreads the cost among retirees and those paying into the system.

But, as expected, there are those who already oppose the salvage plan.

Government workers, and more particularly the Postal Workers Union, don't want to be included in Social Security. Retired persons don't like the delay in cost-of-living increases. Many employers don't like the speeded-up Social Security tax increases.

Those areas of opposition will be expressed soon in committee hearings as Congress moves to begin work on the subject.

Those in opposition will get their day in court.

But the system must be saved. Government is the art of the possible, and to their credit, both the president and the leaders of Congress have arrived at a plan which is at least workable.

Not perfect. There is a delay until 1988 and some eqivocation in the pegging of cost-of-living increases to wages rather than prices, but that is more a long-term than short-term finger in the dike. But what has been reached is possible, and probably passable, in this Congress.

It is something, if Congress holds the line against the special interest critics whose oxen are gored, that the president can sign.

In the prescription are bitter pills for everyone. But as Commission Chairman Alan Greenspan said of the body's compromise, we must all "swallow hard" for the common good.

Los Angeles Times

Los Angeles, Calif., January 18, 1983

In a display of political maturity that is all too rare these days, a national commission has produced a fair and workable plan to rescue the Social Security system from bankruptcy. Congress should accept the proposals, with gratitude and relief.

The country may never know what backstage heroics on the part of its chairman, Alan Greenspan, Sen. Robert Dole (R-Kan.) and other key participants snatched the diverse and divided National Commission on Social Security Reform from its seemingly hopeless deadlock of a week ago to its sudden agreement over the weekend.

However it came about, the compromise has the support of President Reagan and Rep. Claude Pepper (D-Fla.), chairman of the Select Committee on Aging. Just a week ago, Reagan was trying to put distance between himself and the commission. Pepper, the feisty 82-year-old lawmaker who sat on the commission as a champion of Social Security, is the one member whose vote was crucial to an agreement.

Given such testimonials, Congress should simply accept the commission findings as the best way to save Social Security and write the recommendations into law with a minimum of fuss and debate.

Some of the arguments being mounted against the proposals might have merit if the nation had unlimited resources to carry the financially troubled national pension system through this decade. The resources are not there. The Social Security system must pay its own way. The commission's proposals will make that possible.

The commission plan will go too far for some and not far enough for others but, as Greenspan warned over the weekend, plucking at the loose strings could cause the whole package to come unraveled and leave Congress with no plan at all and Social Security with debts that it could not meet.

Under the commission proposal, a combination of changes in benefits and taxes would add $169 billion to Social Security funds by 1990. The commission's first finding, published some weeks ago, was that the system would fall short of meeting its commitments during the rest of the decade by $150 billion to $200 billion unless adjustments are made.

The main elements of the commission plan include a six-month delay of cost-of-living increases due in July of this year, and a tax on half the benefits paid to higher-income pensioners. Social Security taxes would rise from the present 6.7% of taxable income to 7.65% by 1990. The nation's self-employed would pay 14% of their taxable incomes into the system, compared with a present 9.5%, and newly hired federal workers and employees of non-profit organizations such as hospitals would be drawn into Social Security. Federal workers are now excluded from the system, and non-profit employees have a choice between joining and not.

The American Assn. of Retired Persons plans to fight the six-month freeze on benefit increases and the imposition of taxes on any part of benefits. A union representing 750,000 federal workers plans to resist being pulled into Social Security. Small business groups balk at higher taxes for the self-employed.

If all these groups have their way, there will be nothing left of the commission plan. If any one group gets what it wants, Congress can scarcely turn down the others. It is a classic instance in which well enough is best left alone.

Very few compromises produce perfect solutions. We would have preferred, for example, to see all local government employees covered by Social Security. The commission would lock in only those who have not yet voted themselves out or, as in the case of Los Angeles County, been pulled out by their governments.

The formula that links cost-of-living increases in benefits to the consumer price index could be changed at once so that benefits might grow more slowly. The commission settled for a trigger to change the formula later if Social Security reserves do not grow fast enough.

The commission passed up a proposal to extend the age at which Americans become eligible for full retirement benefits from the present 65 to 66 or 67. But time alone may take that decision out of politics. Declining birthrates and a consequent decline in the number of young people available for work may force employers to make it attractive for older workers to stay on.

But the commission's job was not to produce a report that would make everyone happy. Its job was to save the system from further damage from recession by showing how its books could be balanced without hurting the 36 million retired Americans who depend on its checks every month.

It has done that job well. It is now up to Congress to show the same political maturity in implementing the proposals that the commission showed in shaping them.

DAYTON DAILY NEWS

Dayton, Ohio, January 20, 1983

Republican and Democratic leaders are going to have to circle the wagons and squeeze them tight because the lobbyists are swarming down off the ridges in full war cry against the Social Security reforms.

The president's bipartisan commission came up with a compromise. President Reagan was smart enough to give a little and take a little in order to get the backing of Democratic leaders in Congress.

The Republicans want the problem solved because they don't want the Democrats beating them over the head with the Social Security issue in the 1984 election. The Democrats want the system repaired because they are its loudest cheerleaders and if something isn't done they could be cheering a dead team.

Now the proposed repairs are being targeted by the lobbyists.

Small businesses don't like the accelerated payroll tax deductions. Nobody else likes that either, but it would be foolish to tap the general treasury for Social Security payments.

The associations representing retired folks don't like the idea of freezing the cost-of-living increase next July or taxing retirees in any benefits they might get once their non-benefit earnings top $20,000. Yet that tax is quite fair because it taps only the better off.

As for the cost-of-living benefits, they should have been keyed immediately to the rise in the average wage. (Under the proposed plan, the cost-of-living increases will be modified only when Social Security reserves fall below 20 percent of the system's annual payments.)

And federal workers are going to protest the proposal that they be required to participate in the system.

President Reagan seems ready to take full credit for the compromise plan if Congress approves it. He deserves the credit. He may have handled the question more gingerly than one handles a hot potato, but he did handle it. The result should build more confidence in the system, barring a ravenous depression that would pull a plug out from the whole scheme and about every other retirement scheme around.

The Wichita

Eagle-Beacon

Wichita, Kans., February 4, 1983

After nearly three-and-a-half decades of service in Congress, spending 14 years in the Senate before moving to the House, Rep. Claude Pepper, D-Fla., is one of the more remarkable people in government. Over the years, he has established himself, among other things, as the foremost voice for the nation's elderly. Mr. Pepper, now 82, still plays that role, though he relinquished the chairmanship of the House committee on aging recently to become chairman of the more powerful House Rules Committee.

But it seems a little sad that such a respected figure now is threatening to block needed Social Security reform legislation in order to protect the potential retirement benefits of Americans who cannot possibly qualify for them for another three-and-a-quarter decades. "If you put one item in there cutting benefits I cannot support this bill," he warned 69-year-old Chairman J.J. Pickle of the House Social Security subcommittee, a fellow Democrat, from Texas.

The specific benefit Mr. Pepper was trying to protect was the right to retire at age 65. The committee's largely Republican majority has proposed retirement age be raised in 2015 — 32 years from now — to 66, and that it be indexed thereafter to longevity tables. Since many Americans already are trying to work to age 70, a one-year difference that far down the line for workers who are now about 33 seems hardly worth niggling over.

Considering the financial state of the Social Security system, it's essential it be stabilized as quickly as possible. Mr. Pepper, who should be trying to assure that it will continue to be able to care for the elderly as long as possible, should be helping reform legislation along instead of threatening to scuttle it.

RAPID CITY *JOURNAL*

Rapid City, S.D., February 11, 1983

In the face of testimony that the Social Security rescue plan Congress is considering won't be enough to cure the system's problems, a provision to gradually, but slowly, raise the retirement age should be included.

That won't be easy. Both House Speaker Tip O'Neill and Rep. Claude Pepper, the 82-year old advocate of benefits and programs for the elderly, have announced their opposition to raising the retirement age.

Although a majority of the bi-partisan commission on Social Security reform favored raising the retirement age to 66 by the year 2015, that feature was not part of the package finally submitted to Congress.

When Social Security was established nearly a half-century ago, life expectancy in the United States was less than 55 years. Allowing participants in the program to receive benefits at 65 appeared fiscally sound because those workers who did live long enough to collect benefits weren't expected to live as long as they now do.

There's nothing magic about age 65 being the right retirement age. Some people younger than that are unable to continue working. Many more are well able to go on working. The slow rate of increase in the qualifying age for Social Security benefits would have little effect on most individuals but in the aggregate it could contribute to the financial salvation of the program.

Pepper says if any cut in benefits is put into Social Security legislation he will not support the package. It is hard to conceive that an increase from 65 to 66 over the next 30 years is a real "cut' in benefits, particularly when the package under consideration contains a provision to tax Social Security benefits of recipients with incomes above certain levels. That really represents a reduction in benefits which those people expected to receive at retirement and, in effect, adds another income transfer aspect to the system.

The fate of the Social Security reform package, which has been described as a collection of politically unacceptable provisions designed to prevent Congress from doing nothing to put the system on a solid footing, rests on the equal and opposite pressures from interest groups who don't like parts of the package. If action is taken to satisfy one of those groups, the compromise package will fall apart.

However, a gradual increase in the retirement age should be politically acceptable. Because it could be a major factor in addressing the third of the projected deficit the compromise package doesn't cover, Congress should override the objections of O'Neill and Pepper and make it part of Social Security reform legislation.

OKLAHOMA CITY TIMES

Oklahoma City, Okla., February 9, 1983

PROSPECTS for anything more than a temporary Band-Aid on the gaping wound in the Social Security system appear even more remote, now that House Speaker Tip O'Neill has weighed in with his personal views on the problem.

The speaker has come out strongly in opposition to any move to raise the age at which Social Security recipients may retire with full benefits. In so doing, O'Neill tacitly admitted his Democratic colleagues in the House of Representatives are unwilling to assume the political risk attendant upon any major structural reforms in the ailing system.

Here is what he said at a press briefing this week: "We think it's basically wrong to increase the age. We (Democrats) would have a problem with that one, and I am personally opposed to it."

With O'Neill now on record firmly against raising the retirement age — and with octogenarian House Rules Committee Chairman Claude Pepper, D-Fla., having previously taken a similar stand — it would appear the higher age option will not receive any serious consideration in the House.

Foreclosing this option increases the likelihood that Democrats in the House will press for higher tax withholding as their preferred "solution" to Social Security's rapidly depleting retirement trust fund.

Accelerating higher payroll taxes already scheduled later in the decade is one of the key recommendations of the bipartisan commission named by President Reagan to recommend options for solving Social Security's short-term fiscal crunch. But the commission also warned that Social Security will need about $1.6 trillion over the next 75 years to ensure the system's solvency.

That staggering amount would have to come from higher taxes, revised benefits, or a combination of both.

Virtually every study of Social Security in recent years has pointed to the need to raise the retirement age to reflect increased longevity of the population. Most of the proposals suggest gradually phasing in the change — raising it from the current 65 to 66, a month at a time, between the years 2003 and 2015.

It's hard to fathom the opposition of doctrinaire liberals like O'Neill and Pepper to this plan, especially since it wouldn't affect the bulk of workers now paying into the system. It makes a good deal of economic and political sense.

Each year of congressional failure to face the basic demographic facts of life affecting Social Security means an increasingly dismal outlook for young persons entering the labor force. All they can look forward to is tax increases ad infinitum to pay benefits to a segment of the population that is growing disproportionately faster than the number of workers paying taxes into the system.

This declining ratio of workers to recipients, which is expected to diminish to about two to one by the year 2000, is the crux of Social Security's long-term problem. The O'Neills and Peppers of Congress are doing the country a profound disservice by their refusal to face the facts.

TULSA WORLD

Tulsa, Okla., February 4, 1983

THE fate of the compromise plan approved by a bipartisan commission appointed to reform the Social Security system is said to hang on the approval of one man in the House of Representatives: 82-year-old Claude Pepper of Florida.

If so, the plan is in trouble. Pepper is taking advantage of his age and his role as protector of the elderly.

The commission approved an approach that would increase payroll taxes, delay for six months July's cost of living increase for retirees and tax benefits of middle and upper-income retirees to wipe out about two-thirds of the system's anticipated long-term shortfall.

But it couldn't agree on how to close the gap on the rest of the expected deficit. Republicans on the commission wanted to do it by extending the retirement age one year by 2015, but Democrats wanted to do it by increasing the payroll tax in the next century.

Now we have the spectacle of an 82-year-old man claiming to represent the interests of the elderly nearly 35 years into the future. He vows to drop his support of the compromise if the retirement age is raised by one year.

Rep. J. J. Pickle, D-Tex., told Pepper that raising the retirement age is "an absolutely inevitable development in the history of our country."

He's right, of course. Simple comparison of longevity tables of 1935 and 1983 make that abundantly clear.

The House will be making a big mistake if it lets Pepper dictate on Social Security simply because he is 82 years old and a big hit with today's retirees. After all, the group he claims to be protecting in 2015 is just now starting to work and thanks to Pepper's intransigence on changes in benefits will soon start paying huge increases in Social Security taxes.

A little less Pepper please.

THE SAGINAW NEWS

Saginaw, Mich., February 7, 1983

The gasps of disbelief — and relief — could hardly be suppressed when Florida's Rep. Claude Pepper consented to the Social Security rescue plan now before Congress.

This champion of more and more for the aged had actually agreed to less: A six-month benefit freeze and a partial tax on wealthy retirees' benefits.

Even Pepper, it seemed, understood that without reforms by May, there might be no checks in July.

They gasped too soon. Pepper is threatening to scuttle the whole package if Congress dares to secure Social Security for at least the next 75 instead of just 20 years. As chairman of the House Rules Committee, he could do it, too.

What made Pepper hot? It's a proposal to raise the retirement age to 66 — not now, not next year, but over a 12-year period starting in 2003.

That's a cut in benefits, stormed Pepper. "My honor is committed not to cut Social Security benefits."

Honor is not always the same as good sense.

When he rails against reforms due in 2015, Pepper, 82, presumes to speak not for his fellow older Americans, but for people pondering whether they, too, will draw benefits 30 and 40 years from now.

He presumes too much. He ponders too little.

Three years after Pepper came to Congress, average American life expectancy was 62.9 years. In 1979, it was 73.8. People who reached 65 could expect to live for 16 more years.

In 1940, a retiree was supported by 159 active workers. In 1980, the ratio was 3 to 1. By 2030, it will be down to 2 to 1. Without changes, Social Security taxes could take up to a fifth of each worker's income. Pepper wouldn't have to worry about that. But millions of other Americans would.

The plan Pepper went along with would handle two-thirds of the projected shortfall. The proposal to delay retirement slightly is a bid to take care of the other third.

Texas Rep. J.J. Pickle, at 70 no kid himself, tried to explain the facts of future life to Pepper, that raising the retirement age is "an absolutely inevitable development in the history of our country."

Pepper replied that "I don't make any distinction between the present and the future."

For the sake of that future, he should quit living in the innocent past of belief that Social Security would always be there, no matter what.

Pickle and Pepper — a combination to relish — themselves are living commentary on this issue. The Texan shows that turning 66, or 70, is no barrier to continued contribution to society. Pepper is an argument for drawing the line somewhere — for Congress, anyway.

THE COMMERCIAL APPEAL
Memphis, Tenn., February 8, 1983

AS CONGRESS begins consideration of the rescue package that the National Commission on Social Security put together, organizations representing millions of federal government employes and retired federal workers are mounting a campaign to avoid being taken into that system.

That opposition began even before the commission submitted its final report.

Unfortunately, it continues even though the commission took note of those objections.

Much of that opposition still is based on the belief that everyone now drawing a federal pension would be put into the Social Security system with drastically reduced benefits.

That is not true.

The proposal clearly states that only new federal employes would be wrapped into Social Security's blanket.

Rep. Dan Rostenkowski (D-Ill.), chairman of the House Ways and Means Committee, says his committee and the full House "will adopt legislation in this regard similar to that recommended by" the reform commission and that "some progress has been made to reconcile these systems."

Rep. William Ford (D-Mich.), chairman of the House Post Office and Civil Service Committee, says that if some form of Social Security coverage is enacted, his committee "will act expeditiously and responsibly to guarantee that federal employes covered by Social Security will also earn retirement benefits under the Civil Service Retirement System, and that benefits for current employes under the CSRS will be maintained."

SO IT APPEARS the conversion will begin. But many federal workers still will argue it should not have been done.

Should federal civil service employes be given special pension consideration?

Civil service was instituted to eliminate the spoils system. It provided for selection of the best qualified workers for every job, and because it offered them lifetime protection against dismissal, pay scales could be somewhat less than what workers in private business could get.

Pensions were provided at a time when most workers in private enterprises did not have them.

Federal pension benefits have been kept well ahead of those in most private plans. Federal employes with 30 years service can retire at 55.

Other workers usually cannot retire with full benefits until their 60s.

Future benefits in the federal system have been linked to the cost of living, originally with increases coming twice a year.

Most private plans have no such escalators.

The civil service plan bases retirement income on the three highest consecutive years of pay, with a minimum pension 80 per cent of actual salary, well above most private plans.

Those federal benefits are well above what Social Security provides, too.

That's why the federal workers are concerned. And because so many retired federal workers vote, Congress will turn handsprings if necessary to protect them.

BUT ARE those special considerations for civil service workers still justified? The argument that they are not as well paid as workers in private enterprise no longer holds.

Federal workers demanded and were given "comparability" — pay equal to that in private industry so they wouldn't be lured away from federal jobs.

They still have greater security than most private sector workers. And when they retire they can take second jobs without having their new income reduce their pension benefits.

It is natural for them to want to protect what they have, and neither the commission nor Congress has proposed taking away any of it.

But there is a growing feeling that new civil service workers should have comparability in pensions as well as in pay.

It makes sense. Congress should provide it.

BUFFALO EVENING NEWS
Buffalo, N.Y., February 3, 1983

Two influential Democratic leaders in Congress, Sen. Robert Byrd and Rep. James Wright, have now fortunately withdrawn from any effort to link together in a single law reforms to the Social Security system and changes in the scheduled midyear cut in personal income tax rates.

These dissimilar issues should be dealt with separately, on their own merits, and not mixed together.

What Sen. Byrd and Rep. Wright had initially suggested was really a quid pro quo: in return for their support on the proposed compromise to shore up sagging Social Security finances, they would try to exact a delay in the income tax cut for upper-income families.

Rightly and promptly turning thumbs down on this mischievious tactical maneuver, House Speaker Thomas (Tip) O'Neill, also a Democrat, stressed that the Social Security package, when it comes to a vote, must be considered as a "separate and distinct piece of legislation." And Sen. Daniel P. Moynihan, a Democratic member of the bipartisan National Commission on Social Security, emphasized that "to reopen the negotiations at this time couldn't be done. It's a bipartisan agreement, and has to stand on its own."

Few topics that come before Congress radiate with such fervent political vibrations as Social Security, the national pension program that has sunk into financial distress and now cannot pay its own benefits out of current payroll revenues. The problem hasn't been to conceive ideas that could solve the financial troubles, for there were abundant options. Rather, the difficulty has been to fashion a blend of ideas that would win the majority support among conflicting factions of Congress necessary to write a compromise into law.

The contribution of the National Commission on Social Security was to identify what appears to be that elusive compromise. Its recommendations, including a six-month delay of a cost-of-living increase in benefits and an acceleration of already-approved payroll tax boosts, gained the support of such diverse leaders as Democrat O'Neill and Republican President Reagan.

Far from a faultless answer, it nonetheless offers an acceptable solution in facing up to the perils of Social Security financing through 1990.

But the plan still must survive the rigors of debate and decision in Congress. Thus, leaders such as Speaker O'Neill, the president and others sensibly want to keep irrelevant, dissimilar issues like income-tax rates out of the debate on Social Security, and to minimize the risks of tampering with the commission compromise so painstakingly put together. "If this thing begins to come apart in small ways," Rep. Barber Conable, Republican member of the commission, warned, "it is likely to come apart totally, and the result is likely to be disastrous — in a legislative sense, in a fiscal sense and in a political sense."

His is a pertinent word of caution that those who want to make changes in the recommended package, unless they have the support of an equally broad majority consensus, should ponder with utmost care.

House Passes Bill Modeled on Commission Plan

The House March 9 approved a bill, by a vote of 282 to 148, that closely paralleled the proposals of the National Commission on Social Security Reform. The bill also addressed the long-range problems of the system that the commission had left unresolved, attaching an amendment to raise the retirement age. (The system's long-range deficit was estimated at $1.8 trillion over the next 75 years.) Debate over this issue was the major source of controversy in the House, with conservatives favoring an increase in the retirement age and liberals favoring a future increase in payroll taxes. In the end, the members of the House voted, by a margin of 228 to 202, to approve an amendment by Rep. J.J. Pickle to raise the retirement age very gradually from 65 to 67 by the year 2027. An opposing amendment by Rep. Claude Pepper to increase the payroll taxes again in the year 2010 was defeated by a 296 to 132 vote. When the measure was rejected, House Speaker Tip O'Neill, who had supported the tax increase, commented: "History is being written on this floor...In America, each generation has always paid for the generation that has gone before them."

Included in the Pickle amendment was a provision that would cut the benefits of those who retired at age 62 from the current 80% of full benefits to 70% in 2027. Other provisions of the House bill required inclusion of members of Congress under the system, increased payroll taxes for the self-employed, extended emergency jobless benefits, increased Supplementary Security Income benefits and made significant alterations in the way the government reimbursed hospitals under Medicare.

St. Petersburg Times

St. Petersburg, Fla., March 13, 1983

When Congress passed the Social Security Act in 1935, the great fear and threat to the pride of many older Americans was that they would end up in the county poor house. Fewer than 15 percent of U.S. workers were covered by any retirement plan. Because it has quieted those fears, Social Security is one of America's greatest achievements.

The future of this achievement ultimately depends upon the resolve of the American people, as reflected in Congress, to protect it. Supporters of Social Security can take pride and satisfaction in the speedy and responsible action of the U.S. House of Representatives this past week to do exactly that. If the Senate follows its schedule, it will act this week and then it will deserve to share the compliments with the House.

IT NEVER IS easy to make the necessary adjustments in Social Security. When the program is opened for review, a strange contest ensues between supporters of Social Security and its strong but politically intimidated opponents. This time the process was advanced by a presidential commission, which hammered out a moderate compromise that balanced slightly reduced benefits against small tax increases.

The House enacted the commission's program with one exception. It added a provision to increase gradually the retirement age from 65 to 67 between the years 2003 and 2027.

The Senate Finance Committee departed even further from the commission's recommendations. It would increase the normal retirement age to 66 over 15 years beginning in 2000, reduce benefits by 5 percent beginning in 2000 and phase out during 1990-1994 the earnings limit on persons receiving Social Security pensions.

The later retirement and the reduced benefits in the future are not constructive changes. They aggravate divisions between the young and the old. They create two classes of Social Security contributors, those eligible for retirement at age 65 and those who must wait until 66 or 67. It is significant that the major impact of the House proposal would fall upon persons 23 or younger, not a single one of whom voted for it, or could have voted at all since the Constitution limits membership in the House to persons over 25.

The move to amend the Social Security contract for the young carries the taint of taking it out on the unrepresented. If this unwise change is written into the law, we would expect that generation of Americans to demand a full share of benefits by the time they are in their 50s, when Congress will be much less likely to ignore them.

IT'S TRUE that 65 was arbitrarily chosen as the retirement age. But it has worked out remarkably well on the consideration that should count most when people decide when to retire — the health of the worker. Early retirement at age 62 is not a choice taken by dropouts; more than half of those who retire early do so for health reasons.

We urge Florida's Sens. Lawton Chiles and Paula Hawkins to oppose all efforts to increase the retirement age and to reduce benefits in the year 2000. They should stand firmly in support of the recommendations of the commission.

Among the world's 22 wealthiest nations, the United States ranked 16th in social spending before President Reagan's deep cuts in many of the programs. West Germany and the Netherlands spend twice as much of their Gross National Product on pensions for the elderly as the United States. France spends one-and-a-half times as much.

In 1983, Social Security has rid Americans of the fear of the poor house. But our country has not been overly generous with its elderly and this moderate program to reinforce the program won't change that.

The Cincinnati Post

Cincinnati, Ohio, March 11, 1983

After the House voted 282 to 148 Wednesday to "rescue" the nation's retirement system, largely by raising taxes, Speaker Tip O'Neill proudly said, "Because of this bill Social Security is secure for the next 25 or 30 years."

Have you heard such a promise before? Yes. In December 1977, when President Carter signed the biggest payroll tax increase in history and said his action guaranteed "that from 1980 to 2030 the Social Security system will be sound."

Everybody knows what happened. With near-criminal negligence Congress kept benefits tied to the faulty Consumer Price Index, which overstates inflation. Due to economic mismanagement, prices climbed, benefits rose even more and the "sound" trust funds showed huge deficits.

Here we go again. Last night the Senate Finance Committee approved a measure similar to the House bill which will not untie benefits from the CPI before 1988. That leaves time for inflation to return and tear holes in the system. Worse yet, of the $165 billion extra needed to run Social Security for the rest of this decade, about 75 percent will come from new taxes.

When higher payroll taxes on workers, employers and the self-employed kick in next January, the results may well be slower economic growth and higher joblessness. That is a terrible risk the politicians are forcing the nation to run just as it recovers from recession.

If such a bleak situation develops, Social Security's revenue, which after all is based on wages, will fall below anticipations. And there will be new horror stories about the trust funds going broke and perhaps another presidential commission to recommend even higher payroll taxes.

In spite of intense federal employee lobbying, the measure also mandates that all federal employees hired after Jan. 1, 1984, join Social Security. Conservatives are pleased that the bill will raise the retirement age for full benefits to 66 by the year 2000 and 67 by 2027. They argue that as life expectancy rises, people should be willing to work longer.

There's another way to look at it: Persons 40 or younger will have to work an extra year for full benefits, persons 23 or younger two extra years. All because lawmakers lack the courage to tailor benefits to revenues.

The Miami Herald

Miami, Fla., March 13, 1983

CLAUDE Pepper best characterized the Social Security-rescue bill when he commented, "This bill gives us all something to complain about." Indeed it does. That is the nature of compromise, and compromise is the nature of this bill, which passed the House and comes before the Senate next week.

In Candide's best of all possible worlds, Congress would offer true reform. It would end the pyramid-game financing scheme in which current workers' money is poured out in Social Security checks for current retirees. Real reform would substitute an actuarially sound, annuity-type program in which each worker's contribution is invested and returned to him later with no swelling of benefits through taxes on younger workers.

Unfortunately, such a switch would create an astronomical unfunded liability. How else to take care of all the current retirees, in addition to those now employed, whose money was paid out instead of being invested on their behalf? In an era of $200 billion annual deficits, Congress understandably could not accept such a burden even though the final result would be an independent Social Security system.

So the House accepted the compromise offered by the President's National Commission on Social Security Reform. Both current recipients and current contributors would have to give up something. New Federal workers and elected officials would be drawn in. And a small step toward actuarial soundness would occur through a gradual raising of the retirement age to 66 for those born in 1943 and to 67 for those born after 1959.

Today's workers and their employers each would be taxed an additional 0.3 per cent of wages up to the maximum, now $35,700. That's a top increase of $107 each for 1984, which would be offset by an income-tax credit for that year. Current workers in their early 40s also would sacrifice from two months to two years off the date at which they could retire with full benefits.

That delay is equitable because the nation's average life expectancy at birth, which was 59.7 years in 1930, had grown to 73.8 in 1980 and likely will increase as much again before 2027. The average man who turned 20 in 1940 was expected to live only 3.5 years past the retirement age of 65. The man who turned 20 in 1977 now is projected to enjoy 13 years of post-65 retirement.

Current recipients reaped a windfall from inflation-driven cost-of-living increases in recent years. They would yield some of that advantage through a six-month delay in the inflation-adjustment that was due in July of this year. If inflation produces a similar distortion after 1987, the new cost-of-living hikes would be pegged to average wage increases instead of prices.

These and the other elements of the compromise rescue package are welcome and deserve prompt approval from the Senate to end the immediate crisis. Congress then should seize the opportunity to develop a long-range *genuine* reform that separates Social Security's insurance aspects from its welfare functions.

It might take several generations to phase in such a program, but the goal of an impregnable, independent, and depoliticized Social Security system would be well worth the sustained effort.

The Hartford Courant

Hartford, Conn., March 11, 1983

There is no painless way to ensure the financial stability of the Social Security system. Its continued integrity depends upon political consensus born of mutual suffering.

That's why the compromise bail-out plan drafted by a bipartisan commission earlier this year sought to inflict as little pain as possible on each of the elements in the Social Security equation.

The House of Representatives prudently upheld the spirit of that compromise Wednesday in approving a bill that proponents hope will meet the revenue needs of Social Security for the next two to three decades while delaying more dramatic restructuring of the system to a later time.

The House bill follows commission recommendations to increase payroll taxes for both employees and employers; require new federal employees and workers in non-profit institutions to join the system; postpone cost-of-living benefit increases for six months this year to save money; and subject to taxation a portion of benefits received by higher-income recipients.

In a far more controversial move, the House by a narrow margin amended the plan to push the retirement age to 66 in 2009 and 67 in 2027. Opponents of the amendment — including all members of Connecticut's House delegation except Stewart B. McKinney, 4th District Republican — say raising the retirement age will fall unfairly on blue-collar and low-income workers who are least able to continue working in advancing years.

But the contrary arguments — that the nation will need more older workers in the 21st century, and that Americans are not only living longer lives, but healthier ones — are compelling.

Pressure to restore the retirement age to 65 is promised as the Senate takes up the bill, but it should be resisted.

The most obvious alternative to the reasonable, phased increase in retirement age is an even bigger hike in payroll taxes or a claim on general revenues. That will make those who pay carry a much heavier burden under the bail-out plan than those who receive, and that disparity could lead to an unraveling of the political consensus needed to keep the system going.

Although it's bitter medicine, some reduction in benefits along with tax increases is necessary.

THE ATLANTA CONSTITUTION

Atlanta, Ga., March 14, 1983

They said it couldn't be done, but the U.S. House not only has adopted the politically difficult recommendations of a presidential commission for resecuring Social Security. It went the commission one better.

With solid bipartisan support — in fact, only the fringes of each party dissented from the basic plan — the House has shored up the short-term funding for the Social Security system and has begun the process of slowly raising the eligibility age after the year 2000. Even the commission, whose members had no personal political stake in the recommendations, had been unable to confront that necessary longe-term decision.

The House accepted the recommendations that are intended to steady Social Security through the rest of this century. A cost-of-living increase scheduled for this sumer will be put off six months. The payroll taxes that fund the system will be increased through the end of this decade.

In addition, new federal employees will be enrolled in the system for the first time to broaden its base, and Social Security benefits will become taxable for single retirees with incomes of $25,000 a year and retired couples with $32,000 incomes.

The House accepted a committee amendment, pushed by Georgia Rep. Wyche Fowler, that for the first time will require members of Congress and other federal officials to contribute to the system.

All of this was solid work, and it was further strengthened by the decision of the House to raise the Social Security retirement age to 66 by 2009 and to 67 by 2027. In addition, after 2000, persons who retire at 62 will receive benefits at 70 percent of the full level, rather than the current 80 percent.

The steady increase in the ratio of retirees to working-age population makes those changes necessary, and lengthening life-expectancy makes them just.

The House has set a model for Senate action in its management of the complex and touchy Social Security issues. Its hearings were swift and germane; floor action was deft and responsible.

Events and trends have a way of slipping away from even the best efforts of lawmakers to anticipate them, and it is probably a good bet that further adjustments in Social Security will be necessary within the time frame anticipated by the House legislation. But the approach Congress is taking is unquestionably square with the current information and can relieve retirees of the anxieties many have had that the Social Security system might come tumbling down around them. It will not.

THE DENVER POST
Denver, Colo., March 11, 1983

THE U.S. House of Representatives, showing rare political courage, took a giant step Wednesday toward saving the Social Security system by adopting the package proposed by a bi-partisan reform commission.

That package will not cut present benefits by a single penny. But it does put some limits on the future growth of benefits. Coupled with several tax increases and the inclusion of new federal workers in the system, the package was expected to generate $165 billion in savings or new revenue in seven years.

That solves a short-term crunch. But Social Security's most serious problem is long-term, and there, by the estimates of its own authors, the bipartisan package only covered about two-thirds of the expected shortfall. That raised the chilling specter that the reform would save the system for everybody except those who will pay most of its cost — the "baby boom" generation born after World War II.

Cynics doubted that the House would have the courage to solve so long-term a problem on an issue that generates such immediate political pressure. But led by Rep. J. J. Pickle, D-Texas, it did. Pickle, backed by 152 Republicans and 76 Democrats, succeeded in raising the age for normal retirement gradually to 67 in the next century. Recipients can still retire early, as young as age 62, but will receive benefits that are proportionately lower.

That change is expected to cover the remaining long-term deficit. "Baby boomers" will have to work longer to qualify for full benefits. But they can plan now in confidence that the system they will support all their lives will still be solvent when they need it.

This newspaper has long urged raising the retirement age to 68 gradually by 1995. The Pickle plan does less and does it later. But, combined with other parts of the package, it is an acceptable compromise. It's fairer to the "baby boom" than it looks. While that generation may work a year or two longer than their forebears, it is also likely to have more years in retirement, due to longer life expectancies.

Republicans Ken Kramer and Hank Brown, the only Colorado representatives to support Pickle, deserve praise for their courage. Sen. Bill Armstrong, a member of the original bipartisan commission, also deserves credit for focusing attention on the failings of the original bail-out package.

But now that the retirement age issue has been addressed, Armstrong would be wise to back the House package as the Senate takes up the bill. It contains tax increases which everybody hates — but the total good far outweighs the bad. Further political controversy is much more likely to worsen the package than to improve it.

'Whew! For a while there I thought we were going to come up empty'

Los Angeles Times
Los Angeles, Calif., March 10, 1983

Congress has moved the Social Security system closer to a safe harbor where it should be protected from the riptides of demography and economics for at least a decade.

Perhaps the most remarkable aspect of Wednesday's decisive House vote to change the system was that as recently as three months ago even the architects of the reform plan had no real confidence that they could get it through Congress.

Now the plan to pull the system out of the red with a combination of higher payroll taxes, a slower rate of growth in benefits and other major changes is on its way to the Senate, where the sailing should be as smooth as it was in the House.

The closest that the plan came to trouble was on a choice between raising the age at which full retirement benefits take effect to 67 years or raising payroll taxes in the 21st Century. The House chose the higher age.

Nearly all working Americans will give up something under the plan in order to keep the country's oldest and most successful social program alive. Any other proposal so riddled with some degree of sacrifice for so many people would certainly have bogged down somewhere in Congress' minefield of checks, balances and niggling amendments. But so thorough is the acceptance of this plan that Sen. Robert Dole (R-Kan.) expects to move an almost identical bill out of his Finance Committee and onto the Senate floor today.

Politically, success depended on moving the reforms through Congress with virtually no changes in the recommendations of the reform commission that, in the end, had the support of every political leader in Washington from President Reagan on down.

The tactic succeeded, although a number of well-organized interest groups made heroic efforts to tear off parts of the proposal that were offensive to them. Associations representing the elderly tried to avoid a six-month postponement of the next scheduled cost-of-living increase in benefits. Federal employees blanketed Washington radio and television stations with paid advertisements insisting that Congress reject a proposal to include new federal employees in Social Security. The lobbying efforts failed.

The package as it left the House will increase Social Security revenue by $165.3 billion by 1990. Payroll taxes will go up in stages to 6.2% of income by the end of the decade. Benefits will grow less rapidly than the cost of living. Couples whose retirement income, counting half their Social Security benefits, is $32,000 a year will pay taxes on benefits—a first for the system.

What makes the relative ease with which the reforms are moving toward law so surprising is that most elements of the package have been rejected, item by item, by Congress in recent years. Senators voted in 1981, 98 to 0, against taxing any part of Social Security benefits. Five years ago, Congress voted not to include federal workers in Social Security.

The turnabout came in two closely related steps. First, economist Alan Greenspan persuaded the very diverse membership of his reform commission to agree that, unless something was done, the Social Security system would run a deficit of $150 billion to $200 billion by the end of the decade. That put an end to arguments about whether the system really was in desperate difficulty.

With that settled, the commission then agreed that Social Security was an integral and indispensable part of American society, a symbol of its social conscience and its resolve to ease the burdens of old age and disability. It rejected, implicitly, the notion that the system could or should be made voluntary or otherwise weakened.

At that point, it became clear that in politics desperation concentrates the mind every bit as wonderfully as the prospect of hanging, and all Americans, young and old, can be grateful for that.

The Seattle Times

Seattle, Wash., March 13, 1983

THE U.S. House of Representatives has met its first-priority responsibility of the year by passing the Social Security bailout bill.

The rescue mission was accomplished by a satisfying 282-148 bipartisan vote. Keeping in mind the many years that Congress has ducked its responsibility to save America's basic retirement system from catastrophe, Speaker Thomas (Tip) O'Neill was not overstating the matter when he called it "landmark legislation." ·

Considering the controversy that has surrounded every major facet of the compromise measure put together by the Social Security Reform Commission, it is remarkable that when the bill reached the floor, there was extensive debate on only one issue — raising the retirement age in two steps from 65 to 67 by the year 2027.

After a bitter scrap in which that change was approved, 228-202, even Rep. Claude Pepper, D-Fla., who had led the anti-change forces, voted for final passage because, he said, otherwise "there would be chaos in Washington."

Rep. Claude Pepper

Pepper is dead right. A failure to hold the compromise package together would produce chaos, with every affected special-interest group renewing its assault.

The Senate and the White House should act promptly to complete the rescue operation.

ARGUS-LEADER

Sioux Falls, S.D., March 12, 1983

The U.S. House has shown its ability to act forthrightly by approving 282-148 a bipartisan program to bail out Social Security.

The measure conforms generally to the outline recommended by the National Commission on Social Security Reform, with one major exception. The House approved raising the retirement age to 67 in the next century. That is essential to help guarantee Social Security's funding for an era in which Americans are living longer and the working force will decline in proportion to those in retirement status.

Everyone shares part of the burden of making Social Security solvent. This July's cost-of-living increase will be delayed for six months. Payroll tax increases will be accelerated. The levy will go up on the self-employed. Affluent retirees will pay income tax on half their benefits.

Sharing the cost involves other important changes. New federal workers, starting in 1984 will have to join the system. So will President Reagan, his cabinet, top appointees and all employees of non-profit organizations. No state and local governments will be able to defect from Social Security once the measure is signed into law.

The measure is a compromise — and an excellent one. As Rep. Dan Rostenkowski, D-Ill., said the changes "are all unpopular. Voted separately, not one of these provisions would survive. But together

the sacrifice they demand is fairly spread. Together, the system is changed."

One of the more interesting facets of Congress' search for a solution was the controversy over raising the retirement age from 65 to 67. The reform commission couldn't convince its panel members to make the change.

However, Rep. J.J. Pickle, D-Texas, who probably knows more about the Social Security system than any other lawmaker, was convinced it had to be done to save the system. His amendment prevailed and Rep. Claude Pepper, D-Fla., 82-year-old champion of the aged, lost his fight to keep the retirement age at 65.

However, the retirement age question is not settled yet; the Senate Finance Committee approved raising it to 66. Another Senate change would reduce benefits for new retirees by 5 percent in the next century.

It will be up to the Senate next week to be as forthright as the House in handling the legislation. Compromise by a conference committee will be essential so Congress can send a completed measure to President Ronald Reagan sometime this month or early in April.

Enactment should prevent Social Security from running out of money later this year and end the political wars of the last two years over how to save the system.

Houston Chronicle

Houston, Texas, March 13, 1983

As the Social Security reform package was being debated, one member of the U.S. House after another stood up to criticize it. But when the final vote came, the package passed.

There were no cheers of celebration, just sighs of relief. Those who voted for the bill hope it will meet their expectations despite its flaws. Those who opposed it suspect it is just setting the stage for more trouble in the future.

The compromise as pieced together by a presidential commission was altered only slightly. Rep. J.J. Pickle, D-Austin, an authority on Social Security's financial matters, succeeded in getting the bill amended to raise the retirement age, now 65 for full benefits,

in increments beginning in 2003 until it reaches 66 in 2009 and 67 in 2027. That was a change supported by Rep. Bill Archer of Houston, also an expert on Social Security. Archer is very concerned, however, about the tax increases the measure imposes and he fears that Congress is taking another Band-Aid approach.

The Senate will debate the measure this week. The Senate undoubtedly will stick close to the House bill, but if there are necessary changes, this is the time to make them. Six years ago, a bill was passed that was labeled a solution to Social Security financing. No one wants another Social Security crisis six years from now.

Rockford Register Star

Rockford, Ill., March 14, 1983

No longer can all Social Security system problems be solved only by bigger tax increases piled upon big tax increases, a fact recognized last week by members of the U.S. House. It was the most promising vote yet on the critical Social Security issue.

Instead of putting all the burden on taxpayers, these congressmen voted overwhelmingly to split the cost of Social Security reform among all segments of our society.

Producing the fairest and most equitable Social Security rescue plan yet offered, the House voted to:

- Increase tax rates.
- Slow the growth in benefits.
- Force future federal employees into the system.
- Impose a partial tax on benefits paid to more affluent Americans.
- Gradually increase both the retirement age and the penalty paid by those who retire early.

This House-approved version closely follows recommendations made, after a year of debate, by the 15-member National Commission on Social Security Reform. But it improves upon those recommendations by including the changes in retirement ages.

With the steep rise in life expectancy in recent years, this is a crucial change. It also will be almost painless. Those now 40 years old, still a quarter century away from retirement, will be the first to feel this change. They will collect full benefits at age 66, instead of the traditional 65. Those now 23, more than a half century from retirement, will have to wait until age 67 to retire with full benefits.

Rep. Claude Pepper, D-Fla., and House Speaker Tip O'Neill, D-Mass., fought the change in retirement age, seeking instead even larger tax increases. But they lost the key House votes when congressmen agreed instead with Rep. J.J. Pickle, D-Texas, who argued: "We can't keep on raising taxes."

Of course we can't. No one segment of the public can be asked to bear all the burden of solving massive problems. Nor can any segment be excused from sharing the burden.

This House bill isn't perfect. Few bills are. It leaves some problems unsolved. Most major bills do. But imperfections involving secondary issues are no excuse to voting against the bill, as did Rep. Lynn Martin, R-Rockford. There will be plenty of time to clean up the secondary issues after the main problem is solved.

House members showed unusual political courage in passing this bill, since it will not satisfy any of the special interest pressure groups involved in the Social Security debate. All that remains is for the Senate and the president to show the same courage.

THE SUN

Baltimore, Md., March 14, 1983

The House showed courage and common sense when it voted to raise the Social Security retirement age to 67. It was a hard, unpopular step to take, but 228 members (including Marylanders Beverly Bryon and Marjorie Holt) saw the necessity and the logic. It is necessary because of the pressing financial problems of the Social Security system and logical because Americans live longer and healthier lives now than we did when the system began nearly 50 years ago. In another 50 years, the actuaries expect the typical 65-year-old to have a life expectancy of 17 years compared to 14.5 years today.

As with virtually any change from the status quo, this one provoked strong opposition. But the fact is that many of those voicing the opposition will never be affected by the change. Many will be affected so slightly that they will hardly notice the difference. Under the proposal approved by the House, it would take 44 years to complete the transition to later retirement. That is enough time for today's 23-year-olds to get used to the idea.

The Democratic-controlled House was probably the toughest hurdle for the later-retirement proposal, although it had been advocated for at least two years by chamber's leading expert on the system, Representative J. J. Pickle of Texas. The Republican Senate should have little trouble going along, even if some senators balk at various proposals in the rescue package.

Three members of the Maryland delegation voted in favor of the entire package — Representative Roy Dyson, Clarence Long and Barbara Mikulski. They should be applauded. For Mr. Dyson, it meant accepting a hotly debated proposal to include federal workers in Social Security despite the opposition of many constituents who also happen to be federal workers. He realized that once the bill reached the House floor, it was a take-it-or-leave-it deal. And, as Ms. Mikulski told a group of her constituents in South Baltimore, "The question you have to ask yourself is, 'If we voted the bill down, what would we get in its place?' "

The answer, as we see it, is an even bigger headache in July when the system would run out of money once again.

AKRON BEACON JOURNAL

Akron, Ohio, March 13, 1983

SOCIAL SECURITY is too much a part of the American fabric to let this national pension system be crippled by decay and inattention.

That was the motivating force behind the wise votes in the House of Representatives to reform and save Social Security rather than to let the system drift into disaster.

And, without action, disaster lay ahead.

The reforms are necessary. They represent compromise in the best sense of that word. They also will mean some pain for some people, but not nearly so much as the alternative. That was to do nothing, wait for collapse, and invite a national catastrophe of the first order.

The fact that the campaign to repair Social Security is now well under way, has proceeded without any major hitch through the House, and appears certain to receive similar approval in the Senate is a credit to President Reagan, Speaker Tip O'Neill, and many others in Washington.

Indeed, repair of Social Security — a repair being carried out without undue harm to any segment of the society — may well be one of the most lasting domestic achievements of the Reagan administration and of this House speaker's tenure.

There has been much argument over the details of the reforms, originally pieced together in a complex package by a special bipartisan presidential commission.

Spokesmen for groups representing those on Social Security argued against a feature of the legislation that will delay a scheduled cost-of-living benefit from this July 1 until January.

Leaders of federal government employee unions opposed a feature that will bring all future government employees under Social Security.

And 82-year-old Rep. Claude Pepper, the Florida Democrat and the eloquent spokesman for senior citizens, opposed one feature added by the House — raising the eligibility age beginning in the year 2000 from 65 to 67, with the full effect of that taking place in the year 2027.

In the end, each argument by some interested group or party against a specific detail of the rescue plan fell apart because of the importance of the overall goal.

Those who led this successful effort realized that dealing with a system as complex and as widespread as Social Security meant from the start that virtually no segment of the society could escape some effect of the rescue plan if the rescue of Social Security was to be achieved at all.

The system did not get into trouble overnight. Those still alive who were in on its founding under Franklin D. Roosevelt remember all too well that it was never intended then to be all that it later became. Over the years, Congress and presidents added to its benefits bit by bit, and bit by bit brought on the contemporary crisis.

Many of the additions were justified, and have led to a more humane and economically sound society. But few in positions of leadership totalled up the bills along the way or worried unduly about how Social Security would support itself in the future. Until recently.

Now the rescue plan is in progress, and should pass the Senate without great difficulty. More alterations may be needed later, but at least Social Security will be made whole for the years immediately ahead.

No one need worry that it will become bankrupt in this century, or that the checks will stop.

It is a good rescue plan, well crafted, balanced and fair overall. Recognizing the reluctance of Rep. Pepper over some details, it is accurate to use his own words to declare that what the Congress and the President are enacting should, indeed, "preserve this great institution."

WORCESTER TELEGRAM.

Worcester, Mass., March 13, 1983

The Social Security bailout package, approved by the House and on its way to the Senate, contains disappointments for various groups.

Working Americans won't like the big boost in Social Security taxes next January. Hospitals won't like the new tough rules on Medicaid. Retirees won't like the elimination of their July cost-of-living increase. Younger workers won't like the idea of having to wait until 66 to retire. Federal workers won't like the mandatory inclusion of all future federal employees into Social Security. Self-employed persons won't like paying the full employer-employee tax instead of just part of it.

But those who should be angriest of all are the prudent people who have saved over the years for their own retirement. If a single individual has been frugal enough to provide himself with private retirement income of more than $26,000 (including Social Security) or if a retired couple has set itself up with the princely sum of more than $28,000 a year (including Social Security), the punishment will be severe.

If their retirement income exceeds those levels, one-half of their Social Security income will be subject to the federal income tax, at whatever their bracket demands. If they stay under those levels, it won't be touched.

As Mr. Micawber might have put it: "Retirement income $25,999 — bliss; retirement income $26,001 — misery." Or, to put it another way: "Retirement income $25,999 — federal tax, $3,100; retirement income $26,001 — federal tax, $4,380."

This is an outrage. It turns the Reagan economic philosophy upside down. Instead of encouraging personal savings, this Social Security "reform" will discourage them. Instead of giving people incentive to plan for their retirements, it will penalize those who do so. Instead of treating people fairly, it will draw a sharp line between levels of retirement income. It will encourage outrageous kinds of finagling. A retired couple will be pushed from a marginal tax rate of 28 percent to a marginal tax rate of 50 percent if it adds one dollar to its retirement income of $27,999.

It is particularly outrageous for the Reagan administration to be a party to this scheme, which flouts everything that Reagan is supposed to stand for.

Will the Senate allow it to stand? Does anyone in Washington know what's going on? Who is going to stop the thievery?

BUFFALO EVENING NEWS

Buffalo, N.Y., March 13. 1983

Apart from the House decision to raise to 67 the age at which Americans would be eligible for full benefits in the next century, we have few reservations about the impressive reforms for Social Security approved by a large bipartisan majority on Capitol Hill.

Anyone who has even casually followed developments is aware that this huge retirement program, begun in 1935 and now helping support 36 million beneficiaries, is beset by dangerously shaky finances.

Despite rapid and recent increases in payroll taxes, Social Security can't meet even its current obligations without resort to temporary borrowing devices. There are no painless solutions to this problem, but the alternative of doing nothing would bring chaos and bankruptcy.

The House-passed package generally adheres to the recommendations of a bipartisan presidential commission that wisely concluded that neither the beneficiaries nor the workers now financing the program should bear the entire burden of shoring up its finances.

The approved plan would accelerate some already scheduled payroll tax increases, extend coverage to new federal workers, tax a portion of the benefits of higher-income retirees and delay for six months this year's cost-of-living increase in benefits. In all, these measures would raise an extra $165 billion by 1990.

Confronting the long-term problems, the House voted to gradually raise the age for full Social Security benefits from 65 to 66 by the year 2009 and to 67 by 2027. There would also be reduced benefits for those choosing to retire early.

These changes are designed to ease pressures for much higher payroll taxes in the future when comparatively fewer workers will be supporting larger numbers of retirees. However, while a case can be made for such action in view of lengthened life spans, we believe it would be more compassionate and equitable to maintain 65 as the age when Americans can stop working and qualify for full benefits.

If financial realities demand some adjustment in the retirement age, the Senate, which must still act on the issue, should explore a compromise that would raise the retirement age only to 66.

Whatever the differences on the age issue, they must not be allowed to imperil enactment of the responsible overall reform package endorsed by a decisive House majority.

During the debate, Rep. Barber Conable, R-Alexander, and an influential legislator in this area of public policy, said the "issue is whether Social Security can be reformed ... or if the only answer to crisis is to raise its cost to the taxpayers." The enlightened House response is that it can be so reformed.

The Times-Picayune
The States-Item

New Orleans, La., March 14, 1983

With all hands determined not to rock the boat, members of the House and Senate are moving swiftly to approve the compromise plan to keep the Social Security system solvent. The basis for the rare spirit of bipartisanship is an acute awareness of all members of Congress that the plan before them is the best that can be achieved at this time. At the same time, there is almost unanimous sentiment among students of the Social Security problem that the plan is not the ultimate solution, that additional changes undoubtedly will have to be made in future years.

The plan approved by the House tracks very closely the proposals recommended by the National Commission on Social Security Reform. It would increase payroll taxes, take all new federal employees into the system, postpone cost-of-living benefit increases for six months and make some income, other than that from Social Security, received by higher-income retirees subject to the federal income tax. The plan also would gradually increase the retirement age to 66 by the year 2009 and to 67 by 2027.

A similar version passed swiftly by the Senate Finance Committee would raise the retirement age to 66 in 2015. The bill also differs in some other respects from the House measure.

For instance, it would cut benefits to new retirees by 5 percent in the next century; the House bill does not contain such a cut. The Senate bill would change the benefit checks of Social Security retirees from 42 percent of the final wage to 40 percent.

In addition, the Senate committee, acting on an amendment offered by Louisiana's Sen. Russell B. Long, voted to allow a cut in cost-of-living increases as a last resort to keep the system solvent during emergencies.

A key change in the bills in both houses would tax some of the benefits received by persons whose taxable income outside Social Security exceeds $25,000 for an individual or $32,000 for a married couple filing jointly. At the same time, the Senate measure would phase out, over five years beginning in 1990, restrictions on how much retirees ages 65 through 69 can earn without losing benefits.

Differences in House and Senate versions will have to be ironed out by a conference committee, but the prospects are excellent that the compromise plan will be enacted by the end of the month. Because it is a compromise, the plan inevitably spreads the burden of salvaging Social Security over most, if not all, involved, including workers who will not be retiring until the next century.

Final Reforms Passed by Congress

A Social Security reform bill hammered out by Senate and House conferees was cleared by Congress March 25 and sent to the White House for signature. The final plan, adopted in the House by a 243 to 102 vote and in the Senate by a margin of 58 to 14, would raise approximately $165 billion over the next seven years. The House-Senate conference committee, in working out the final version of the bill, eliminated several amendments that had been approved by the Senate. One Senate amendment would have delayed extension of Social Security coverage to new federal workers until a supplemental civil service retirement system could be established; another would have increased the retirement age to 66 by 2015, and reduced initial benefits by 5% after the turn of the century.

The final version of the bill would, as of Jan. 1, 1984:

—Extend Social Security coverage to all new federal employees and employees of non-profit organizations.

—Prohibit state and local governments from withdrawing from the system.

—Accelerate already scheduled payroll tax increases through the 1980's, raising the tax rate from 6.7% of payroll for both employers and employees to 7.65% in 1990.

—Delay the annual July COLA until January, beginning with the July 1983 payment.

—Increase taxes for self-employed persons by 33%, and offset the increase somewhat with a tax credit.

—Impose a tax on the benefits of those individuals whose adjusted gross income, plus half of their Social Security benefits, exceeded $25,000 ($32,000 for a married couple).

—Allow the three trust funds to borrow funds from one another through 1987.

—Raise the retirement age gradually to 67 by the year 2027.

—Decrease the penalty placed on retirees with outside earnings, and increase the bonus given those who delay retirement past the age of 65.

—Reduce "windfall" benefits.

—Change the investment procedures of the trust funds in an effort to achieve higher income.

Other minor provisions were included to help widowed, divorced and disabled women, to prevent the payment of benefits to deceased individuals, and to lessen the use of phony Social Security cards.

President Reagan hailed passage of the bill as an event that lifted "a dark cloud" from the Social Security program. Opinions differed widely over whether the bill's provisions would be sufficient to cope with the strain on the system that would occur when the so-called "baby boom" generation retired. In a talk with high school students later March 25, Reagan suggested the possibility of another look at the basic structure of the system. "I'm not sure that we shouldn't take a long-term look at the structure of Social Security," the President said, to see "what's going to happen to you when you get out on the job market."

The reform bill was signed into law April 20 in a ceremony before a large audience on the south lawn of the White House. President Reagan thanked the Democratic leaders in Congress for putting aside their "dark suspicions" in order to work out a bipartisan compromise, and said the bill "demonstrates for all time our nation's ironclad commitment to Social Security." House Speaker Tip O'Neill, who was standing nearby, concurred: "It shows, as the President said, the system does work," he said.

The Washington Post

Washington, D.C., March 27, 1983

WITHIN THE LIMITS of what can be known about the future, it seems safe to say that the reform measure passed by Congress will put the Social Security retirement system on a sound financial basis for many years to come. That Congress should have agreed to any reform measure at all is remarkable. Only a few months ago bitter partisan wrangling seemed likely to block any action except a stopgap measure needed to keep Social Security checks flowing. That the measure that emerged should be—as it is—an essentially sound and reasonable compromise is near miraculous.

There are many heroes in the fight to rescue Social Security. Some who spring to mind include those members of the bipartisan Social Security commission—notably chairman Alan Greenspan, former Social Security commissioner Robert Ball, Sens. Daniel P. Moynihan and Robert Dole and Rep. Barber Conable—who refused to give up trying for a compromise when, early this year, the commission seemed hopelessly deadlocked.

In the House, Ways and Means Committee Chairman Dan Rostenkowski got things off to a good start by urging his colleagues to forswear the campaign bickering over Social Security, and begin working to restore public confidence in the system. With strong support from its leadership and from Social Security subcommittee chairman J. J. Pickle, the House quickly produced and passed a bill that not only adopted the commission's major recommendations, but actually went beyond them to solve Social Security's long-run as well as short-run problems.

Sen. Dole's Finance Committee followed suit with a measure that differed in certain respects from the House version, but achieved essentially the same results. At this point, however, we run out of heroes. The bad guys who set off the chaos on the Senate floor came from both parties. Their shenanigans jeopardized the fate of the most important piece of legislation likely to be considered by this Congress.

Thanks to strong Republican leadership in the Senate and the stalwart behavior of the House conferees, the Senate floor fights over interest and dividend withholding and Social Security coverage of government workers came out all right in the end. But, with a few notable exceptions, Senate Democrats—several of whom aspire to still higher office—managed on some key votes to do severe damage to the Senate's reputation for responsible behavior.

It will be an enormous relief to everyone involved —the administration, Congress and the public—to have Social Security off the political agenda. It would be comforting, but unrealistic, to think that Social Security could now be put on automatic pilot, its problems solved for all time. The future is simply too complicated for that to be likely. Still, much has been accomplished. The country has reaffirmed its support for its most important social program. Many myths about that program have been dispelled. And the political system has demonstrated that, when pressed hard enough, it can compel tough decisions and sustain them.

Pittsburgh Post-Gazette
Pittsburgh, Pa., May 26, 1983

The Social Security rescue legislation now on President Reagan's desk wasn't printed in blood, but it might have been for the pain it caused the congressmen who voted for it.

Sensible, balanced and necessary as the legislation was, its enactment lay at the end of a political minefield. Republicans and Democrats in Congress were able to cross it only by linking hands — to make sure they wouldn't stab each other in the back — and standing on the shoulders of an independent commission. It was that bipartisan group, responding to offstage promptings from President Reagan and House Speaker Tip O'Neill, that crafted a compromise proposal that was more politically palatable than the sum of its parts.

The rest was relatively easy going for the $165-billion rescue package. Republicans who didn't like its accelerated payroll taxes or its first-time levy on affluent recipients' benefits endorsed the plan anyway because it also temporarily froze cost-of-living increases for Social Security pensioners. Democrats viewed the two components of the plan from the opposite vantage point, but also lent their support. A last-minute Senate amendment that threatened to unravel the compromise agreement, a proposal by Sen. Russell Long of Louisiana to postpone the inclusion of federal workers in Social Security, wisely was deleted by a House-Senate conference committee.

Finally, in one area, Congress, emboldened perhaps by the commission's example, added its own bit of statesmanship to the rescue plan by voting to increase the age for full retirement benefits from 65 to 67 — albeit in gradual fashion, over 44 years.

As with many ordeals, now that the Social Security crisis is resolved, congressmen in both parties may want to forget quickly how close they came to a poisonous confrontation over the issue. That would deprive the experience of some of its instructional value.

At various times in the last few years, both parties have attempted to paint themselves as friends of the elderly and the other side as malignantly indifferent to the needs of that increasingly powerful constituency.

Instead of canceling each other out, these charges and counter-charges combined to create a near-hysteria among Social Security recipients that could have doomed even the moderate rescue initiative now on President Reagan's desk. That should be a lesson for both parties the next time they are tempted to capitalize on a politically "sexy" issue.

Detroit Free Press
Detroit, Mich., March 28, 1983

THE SOCIAL Security reform package that passed Congress last week relies heavily on hope and taxes, but it is better than might have been expected, given the hypocrisy and timidity that marked the debate of the past two years.

If you overlook the substantial drag that increased payroll taxes will be on job creation and personal income, the reforms don't bite anybody too badly, too soon. The postponement of the next cost-of-living increase is not entirely painless, but given the rate at which Social Security benefits have outpaced wages over the past decade, it is not entirely unfair, either. The partial tax on benefits for higher-income recipients merely recognizes that current retirees receive far more in Social Security benefits than they and their employers ever put into the system.

The gradual raising of the retirement age to 67 in the next century reflects the increased longevity of Americans and the need the country will have to keep more older workers on the job. Bringing new federal workers into the system eliminates the unfairness of the double-dipping that many federal retirees enjoy and also broadens the collection base.

The question is whether Congress, in trying not to hurt anybody too much, did enough to heal the system. Sen. William Armstrong, R-Colo., one of the most conservative members of the president's Social Security study commission, believes Congress could be wrestling with Social Security deficits again as soon as 1984 or 1985.

The compromise was indeed based on some optimistic assumptions. Congress did not go as far in raising the retirement age or revising the COLA formula as many experts recommended. It rejected Sen. Russell Long's "fail-safe" mechanism to reduce COLA if the trust funds start to run dry again. It has barely begun to deal with some other issues that affect Social Security, including the health care costs that are draining Medicaid.

But the pressures to enact greater structural reforms were at least counterbalanced by the pressures to do nothing at all. The Social Security bill passed in the face of opposition from the gray lobby, the federal workers and a variety of incorrigible optimists. That it may be imperfect is less surprising than that it was enacted at all. If the House and Senate conferees guessed wrong, the system may need more work and need it much sooner than the country will want to hear about. For the time being, though, this latest patch ought to stick.

The Star-Ledger
Newark, N.J., March 28, 1983

The U.S. Senate almost blew the delicately balanced compromise package that had been stitched together to save the Social Security system by attempting to kill a key provision. Fortunately, the House stood firm against the destructive excision.

What had made the bailout legislation palatable was the carefully conceived bipartisan agreement that everyone would share the burden of restoring actuarial soundness to the endangered program. Persons presently receiving benefit checks would have to wait for cost-of-living increases, young Americans would have to work longer to reach retirement age, employers and employes would have to pay higher Social Security taxes, and some recipients with higher independent incomes would have to pay taxes on their Social Security benefits.

To round out the $165 billion rescue plan, the legislation called for bringing into the system all new federal employes, their tax contributions being essential to ensure adequate funding for the program.

In the House-approved version of the bill, the agreement to include new civil servants was honored. The Senate, however, caved in to an amendment by Sen. Russell Long (D-La.) that would have delayed coverage for these federal workers—and their payments—until Congress establishes a supplementary pension plan for them.

The move was a sham and a shame, because if Congress wants to consider a supplementary retirement arrangement for these new workers, it is free to do so. Nothing in the Social Security rescue bill precludes such action. That is an independent issue, to be settled on its merits.

The Senate, which over the years has been viewed as the more dependable, more responsible body of the bicameral Congress, defiled its reputation by attempting to give unnecessary special treatment to this one group when everyone else is being asked to sacrifice.

Fortunately, the House came to the rescue and saved the Senate from its misdirected generosity. In the critical showdown, when differences between the House and Senate measures had to be ironed out in conference, the House insisted on keeping the original plan to enroll new federal workers in the Social Security program. Supplemental benefits can always be debated later, and approved retroactively, if that is the eventual decision of Congress.

In another difference, the Senate had voted to raise the retirement age to 66 and reduce benefits by 5 per cent for those retiring after the year 2000. Again, the House conferees opposed any change in the benefits formula and insisted on a gradually rising retirement age, to reach 67 in the year 2027.

The bailout package will make no one happy. It demands that virtually all Americans assume some of the pain of saving a system from threatened bankruptcy, and that, in the final analysis, is its saving grace.

Arkansas Gazette.

Little Rock, Ark., March 28, 1983

Social Security has been rescued by Congress, again, and this time there are some real reforms in the legislation. Critics say that the new act isn't comprehensive but, no matter, it will do well enough until the next crisis comes along, a few years down the road.

Major new provisions:

— New federal employes will now have to come into the Social Security system, broadening the system's tax base. A joint conference committee restored this reform, quickly, after the Senate adopted an amendment by Senator Russell Long of Louisiana sabotaging it. In the future, workers in the federal establishment will come under the same basic rules of retirement applying to the rest of us.

— This year's cost-of-living increase for Social Security recipients will be postponed until next January 1, saving billions of dollars in fiscal 1983 and fiscal 1984 for the Social Security fund.

— Payroll taxes will be increased on a stepped-up timetable, to bring in scheduled revenues sooner. In addition, recipients with high incomes will pay taxes on their Social Security benefits.

— In the long range, the retirement age will be increased to 67, but not until the next century. The actuarial outlook will be brighter in this fashion although no one will be affected any time soon.

Anyway, another Social Security crisis is resolved. The action in Congress reminds us that the government can act decisively when it has to, especially when Congress and the President are in accord. On this issue the outcome was never really in doubt, whatever the cries of panic, because the very good faith of the Republic is vested in the Social Security system.

THE BISMARCK TRIBUNE

Bismarck, N.D., March 31, 1983

It's sometimes difficult to maintain faith in our government representatives — particularly those at the federal level and especially those in Congress.

But then, just when it seems they've all gone bonkers, a majority of them will come along and do something that seemed impossible just a few short months ago.

Such is the case with House and Senate action on Social Security, and 243 representatives and 58 senators deserve a tip of the hat for approving a bailout plan that is both reasonable and equitable. (Rep. Byron Dorgan, D-N.D., Sen. Mark Andrews, R-N.D., and Sen. Quentin Burdick, D-N.D., all voted for the measure.)

The bill, which is expected to be signed by President Reagan the week of April 10, represents a compromise that could be called remarkable. The compromise, which will pinch just about everybody — the working person who pays into the system now, the retiree who receives benefits now, and even future federal workers who will be forced into the system — was struck quickly and with a minimum of political bickering.

At this point, we should add a note of caution. We should recognize that the bill probably is not perfect, that it probably will not solve all of the present and future problems in Social Security funding. But one can seriously question whether a perfect bill can be drafted by mere mortals. Social and economic forecasts are not perfect, certainly, and without being able to look into the future with absolute confidence, we would be asking the impossible if we demanded a perfect bailout bill.

Oh, some people, such as Sen. Russell B. Long, D-La., thought they had an answer in a "fail-safe" provision that would have automatically reduced cost-of-living increases if Social Security trust funds dipped below a certain level.

Sen. William L. Armstrong, R-Colo., a backer of the "fail-safe" provision, said that without the "fail-safe" measure, "You can't be sure we won't be back in 1985 and 1986 patching up Social Security again."

Long's proposal was defeated, however, and properly so.

Such a provision would have been unfair; for, it would have placed an undue burden on recipients only.

Without the "fail-safe" measure, we are then left with the compromise version of the bailout.

Rep. Barber B. Conable Jr., R-N.Y., who served on the reform commission that came up with the basis for the bill, said all that needed to be said during brief debate in the House the other day:

"It may not be a work of art, but it is artful work ... It will do what it was supposed to do: It will save the nation's basic social insurance system from imminent disaster."

Amen.

The Dallas Morning News

Dallas, Texas, March 26, 1983

Social Security pulled into the Capitol Hill Repair Shop, gears stripped, radiator gushing, rear end wobbling, fuel line clogged. The men in the pin-striped overalls pumped in 10 gallons of gas, readjusted the carburetor and presented the bill — $164.3 billion.

For less blatant instances of consumer fraud whole enterprises have been closed down by the authorities.

The Social Security rescue plan agreed to by both houses of Congress, and sure to be signed by the President, is supposed to solve all the tormented system's financial problems. So, come to think of it, was the last plan, way back there in 1977.

Social Security's basic need is for basic overhaul. But overhaul, as doleful experience has showed, can be risky. The serious reformer commonly gets accused of despising old people. His logical riposte is that he loves old people — so much so that he wants Social Security to stay on sound financial footing. But this gets hard to explain clearly. Far easier to give over the heavy work of reform and just make minor adjustments.

The present adjustments, weighed against the reforms actually needed, are minor all right. Payroll tax increases are speeded up; one cost-of-living increase is postponed; general revenues are tapped; the retirement age is raised slightly in the next century; new federal employees are herded into the system; and taxes are levied — for the first time — on benefits, specifically the benefits of bloated plutocrats earning more than $25,000 — $32,000 on a joint return.

What Congress should have done was reduce benefit growth (per-capita monthly benefits in the last four years have increased *50 percent*) while decoupling Social Security's two functions, welfare and retirement. Welfare should be funded from general revenues, retirement from contributions made solely for that purpose.

But the National Commission on Social Security Reform — whose recommendations formed the mold into which Congress poured its legislative batter — instead ducked reform. A quick fix was the best it could suggest.

Tax increases, which will dampen economic growth, make up more than three-fourths of the Social Security package. How ironic, since economic growth — more people working and paying into the system — would go far toward easing the system's problems.

Small businessmen and diligent savers are Congress' main victims. A second irony: They happen also to be the nation's economic backbone.

No, the congressional repair shop hasn't seen the last of Social Security. Or can't we tell by the grinding of gears as it drives slowly away?

St. Louis Globe-Democrat
St. Louis, Mo., March 26-27, 1983

Those now receiving Social Security benefits should breathe easier now that Congress has finally finished action on the second "rescue package" for the system in a little over 5 years.

Employers, the self-employed and wage earners may not be so enthralled when they begin to feel the effects of some of the changes.

The final version is fairly close to the patchwork assembled by a presidential commission. The only major structural changes are the provisions which will raise the retirement age to 66 and 67 in two stages — to 66 in 2009 and 67 in 2027. Raising the retirement age is justified by the fact that the longevity of Americans is constantly on the rise.

Among the hardest hit will be the self-employed. Their Social Security tax, now three-fourths of the combined employer-employee tax, will rise to 100 percent of the combined tax. Thus it will be 13.4 percent this year and rise to 14 percent on Jan.1, 1984. To partially offset this higher tax, the self-employed will be permitted a tax credit of 2.7 percent in 1984, with this credit dropping to 2.3 percent in 1985 and to 2 percent from 1986 to 1989.

Employers and employees will see their Social Security tax rise to 7.05 percent in 1984, and to 7.51 percent in 1988 before reaching 7.65 percent in 1990. The tax base, now $35,700, will rise automatically with the average national wage.

New federal employees and employees of not-for-profit organizations also will be required to join the system.

Rather than seek to revise the cost-of-living formula so that it would more accurately reflect the true rate of inflation, Congress accepted the idea of postponing cost-of-living benefits scheduled for July 1 to next Jan.1. Retirees won't like this but the fact that inflation was absolutely zero in the first quarter indicates they would not have received a very large COLA increase on July 1 anyway.

Another change will tax benefits for the first time. Benefits to be taxed are those which, including half of the Social Security benefits, exceed $25,000 for single taxpayers and $32,000 for married taxpayers filing jointly. Those attempting to justify discriminating against persons earning above these amounts, call it "taxing the rich." This is more liberal thinking — that people who earn more should be penalized for their enterprise.

There is no overriding philosophy in these changes. They are all arbitrary and aimed at holding together a system which is fundamentally flawed. Most of the welfare-type provisions remain. The system is neither a legitimate pension nor insurance. It is a politically-rigged hodgepodge.

Those still working would be well advised to put away as much money as possible each year in Individual Retirement Accounts. Even though members of Congress are claiming they have restored the solvency of the Social Security system for the next 75 years, it should be recalled that this is what they said when they "reformed" the system in 1977.

THE RICHMOND NEWS LEADER
Richmond, Va., March 28, 1983

The more things change, the more they remain the same:

March 27, 1977 — "The Carter administration is readying a plan to shore up the ailing Social Security system and make sure it survives its so-called short-term financing problem over the next 10 years." (*The Washington Post*)

November 5, 1977 — "The Senate voted yesterday to raise Social Security taxes for 100 million American workers .... After three days of debate, the Senate passed a bill to put Social Security on a sound financial basis for the next 75 years." (From wire dispatches)

December 14, 1977 — "House and Senate conferees reached agreement last Friday on a payroll tax increase that would bring in $227 billion over the next decade to shore up the Social Security trust fund. But they broke up in disagreement over a nongermane Senate amendment...." (From wire dispatches)

December 15, 1977 — "House-Senate conferees agreed yesterday on the biggest peacetime tax increase in history — more than $200 billion over the next decade to replenish the sagging Social Security trust funds.... The higher taxes, to be paid equally by workers and employers, would more than triple the payroll payment by highest salaried workers by 1987." (From wire dispatches)

February 24, 1983 — "A $165 billion Social Security rescue measure cleared its first House hurdle yesterday [in the Social Security subcommittee].... The subcommittee...tentatively approved many of the proposals made last month by the National Commission on Social Security Reform .... Social Security actuaries say the rescue plan will yield almost $165 billion in new taxes and savings over seven years." (From wire dispatches)

March 10, 1983 — "The House of Representatives gave final approval last night to a rescue plan designed to restore Social Security to financial stability.... [The plan] would provide $165.3 billion in additional revenue, mainly through expanded payroll taxes, to the system through the end of the decade." (From wire dispatches)

March 24, 1983 — "The Senate, with bipartisan support, approved a plan last night designed to assure the solvency of Social Security for the next 75 years." (From wire dispatches)

February 22, 1983 — "The Social Security Administration said it will face a somewhat wider deficit during the next 75 years than the one estimated by the panel President Reagan appointed to recommend ways to solve the system's financial problems." (*The Wall Street Journal*)

Stay tuned.

Chicago Tribune
Chicago, Ill., March 29, 1983

Most congressional measures intended to solve Social Security's problems end up being profiles in cowardice. But the bill passed last week by Congress showed that even on an issue of such extreme political sensitivity, the legislators can rise to statesmanship.

Faced with a deficit that promised to bankrupt the trust fund within months, Congress and the President had fobbed the problem off on an advisory committee. In another rare display—an advisory committee actually coming up with serious answers to hard problems—it formulated a delicate compromise consisting of some tax increases and some benefit reductions. The package was constructed so skillfully that it was able to attract the support of politicians as far apart as President Reagan and Rep. Claude Pepper.

Congress, however, was under intense pressure to alter that compromise. Federal employees opposed being required to pay Social Security taxes. Conservative groups objected to speeding up the tax increases already scheduled between now and 1990. Lobby groups for the elderly fought the six-month delay in this year's cost-of-living adjustment. Though both the Senate and the House wavered, in the end they resisted all this pressure.

For that alone, the legislators deserve praise. But they went further still. The compromise package dealt only with the short-run problem—how to keep the trust fund from going bust this year. It ignored the threat of a huge explosion in expenditures and taxes in the next century, when the Baby Boom generation retires to be supported by a shrinking workforce. Rep. Daniel Rostenkowski of Chicago had noted that oversight, and had called for a gradual increase in the retirement age. Apparently he won the argument. The conference committee voted to raise it to 66 by the year 2009 and 67 by 2027, while agreeing to remove penalties for those people who continue working into their 70s. And the House and Senate ratified the change.

This time, at least, the members recognized that the politics of interest group pressure was not the answer—in fact, it was the problem. So, seeing what plainly had to be done, they drew themselves up, scorned the political risks and did it. After years of being damned for timidity on Social Security, our representatives have earned themselves high praise.

The Kansas City Times

Kansas City, Mo., March 28, 1983

Now that Congress has finished its work on the Social Security package, Americans at least will be spared daily bulletins on impending crisis.

Battle-scarred from too many political debates and assurances that this or that change will perfect the system unto the next generation, the public will view any such claims for this fix with distrust. Given the uncertainties inherent in parts of the formula — inflation and longevity are two examples — designing a foolproof system is nearly impossible. And politicians have consistently avoided making structural changes that would enhance the system's stability.

Two major changes, among the most controversial that threatened to unravel the package, were finally accepted by the conference committee. Including new federal workers and raising the retirement age to 67 in the next century provide another source of revenue and should decrease outlays.

With the National Commission on Social Security Reform doing so much advance-guard yeoman labor and bartering, getting congressional agreement was relatively smooth and probably happened more quickly than the public expected. The changes, however, have opponents. They hurt wage earners; they hurt retirees. They will draw blood from some people; to others, they will merely be irritants. But compromise is the strength of the package, the easiest path to raising the Social Security trust fund out of its deficit condition without a frantic uprising from one of the groups that had to be affected by any type of "rescue."

The bill, undramatic as it is, affirms that elderly citizens will not be abandoned. A growing aversion to government-supported social service has not terminally infected this nation's concern for the old.

All participants in the Social Security system can be grateful that Congress wrapped up the bill before it immerses itself in next year's budget battle. If spending on retirees' benefits got tangled with fights over funding various domestic programs, the water would be muddied beyond hope.

CHARLESTON EVENING POST

Charleston, S.C., March 28, 1983

Working people and retirees understandably might feel relieved that Congress has passed legislation aimed at rescuing the Social Security program from the brink of bankruptcy. They should not, however, feel any obligation to applaud Congress for a job well done.

What House and Senate finally have gotten around to doing could have been done, and should have been done, several years ago. Nobody needed a crystal ball to predict that the Social Security retirement fund was headed for big trouble. Nobody needs special insight to recognize that the reason the rescue mission was so long getting under way and the reason the rescue was necessary in the first place are one and the same: politics.

It is true that the population profile and the workforce profile have changed substantially since the Social Security program began in the 1930s. The worker-beneficiary ratio is different. Fewer people are paying into the system, more are drawing out. The trouble started, though, when Congress turned Social Security into a political toy chest by extending benefits way beyond what the founders ever had in mind.

Perversion of the system for political purposes is what put Social Security in jeopardy. Political considerations — the fear of incurring the anger of some voters drawing unearned benefits — delayed decisions and revisions required to restore the program to financial stability.

The remedies worked out to correct some of the consequences of irresponsible stewardship now are getting the headlines. Cost-of-living increases will have to be delayed. Payroll taxes will have to be increased. Federal employees will have to be dragooned into the program. Income taxes will take bigger bites of benefits. Acute problems, they say, dictate radical solutions.

If past congressional actions which made Social Security a political football can be described as brazen, then the reaction of millions of people who have paid billions of dollars into Social Security's retirement fund can fairly be described as surprisingly benign. The politicians did what they did because the people putting up the money didn't jump up and down and shout their objections. From now on retirees, employers and employees better keep a close watch and make their wishes known in unmistakable ways if they want to look forward to any real security.

TULSA WORLD

Tulsa, Okla., March 27, 1983

CONGRESS HAS passed and President Reagan is prepared to sign a bill that rescues Social Security from the brink of financial disaster. With luck, it will ensure stability in the retirement and survivors' benefit program well into the next century.

For members of a divided Congress with few important or lasting accomplishments, the Social Security reform will surely be remembered as "their finest hour." It will also go down as one of the major accomplishments of the Reagan Administration. Oddly enough, it is a compromise that is far from satisfactory to either liberal Democrats or Reagan Republicans. But it gets the job done. It keeps the system solvent without any drastic loss of benefits for any substantial group of Americans or without the exorbitant tax increases that would have been required under the existing rules.

Liberals would have solved the problem by simply pouring in more money with no change in the inflationary benefit formulas. Some conservatives would have made up the shortage by massive and painful cuts in benefits. The final product was finely balanced between the two extremes.

It increases worker contributions gradually from 6.7 percent of earnings next year to 7.65 percent in 1990.

No present benefits are cut, but some future increases are delayed. The age for collecting full retirement benefits will be raised from 65 to 67 early in the next century. Early retirement will still be optional, but the penalty will be increased.

Federal employees from the President down will be forced to join the system. State and local government workers now in the program will no longer be allowed to opt out. But those not now in the system may remain out if they choose.

Few Americans will consider the new program a perfect plan.

Federal employees, with some justification, are unhappy at being forced to contribute to another system when they have their own satisfactory retirement programs.

Workers planning on early retirement will not be happy. Many workers, too young to look ahead to the time when they will need Social Security benefits, will complain about the substantial increases in taxes.

But the over-all program is a masterful blend of sensible cutbacks in expenses and reasonable increases in tax revenues.

It is a model of how a complicated controversy is supposed to be settled in a representative democracy. Everyone has been heard. Everyone's interest has been considered. Concessions have been made on all sides.

It shows what can be done when politicians decide to act as statesmen and make a serious effort to solve a serious problem.

Part IV: Medicare and Disability

In addition to the trust fund that pays retirement benefits, there are two other funds financed by the Social Security payroll tax. These are the disability insurance (DI) and hospital insurance (HI) trust funds. Disability benefits are usually paid to disabled workers less than 65 years old and their families; some discussion of the program is included here because the problems of one Social Security trust fund impinge on the other two, especially since interfund borrowing was authorized in 1981. Hospital insurance, though financed through the payroll tax, is a branch of the Medicare program. Being subject to the distinct problems involved in health care, it is most often treated as an issue separate from the "Social Security system," commonly used to refer to the retirement and disability programs alone.

Spawned by the first White House Conference on Aging in 1961, the federal health program called Medicare was enacted in 1965. It consists of two parts: Part A, or hospital insurance, and Part B, or Supplemental Medical Insurance. All recipients of Social Security retirement or disability benefits are automatically entitled to Part A of Medicare without premium payments, and anyone over 65—or otherwise entitled to Part A benefits—may elect Part B, which is financed through general revenues and premiums paid by beneficiaries. Nearly all beneficiaries of Part A, which covers hospital stays and certain related services, also enroll in Part B, which covers physicians' services. Benefits of both parts are available irrespective of financial need. Beneficiaries must, however, pay part of the cost of medical services under both Parts A and B, in the form of deductibles and coinsurance.

Medicare costs, which have increased at an average annual rate of almost 19% since 1972, have risen much more sharply than medical prices in general. The differential is due primarily to the rapid growth of the beneficiary population, which reached 17 million in 1982. Roughly three-quarters of Medicare spending for the elderly is for inpatient hospital care, with the remaining quarter spent on physicians' services. Soaring hospital costs have thus been a major factor in Medicare's funding problems. Legislative efforts to control hospital costs have failed, and most proposals for controlling the costs of Medicare have concentrated on increasing coinsurance and deductibles, or the cost to the beneficiary. Apart from the financial problems of Medicare, it has been criticized for not covering services of prime importance to the elderly: prescription drugs, long-term nursing home care and non-skilled nursing care.

Special Health Care Problems Posed by Elderly Patients

Due primarily to medical advances, the elderly are not only living longer but remaining healthy longer. The rapidly growing segment of the population aged 65 years or over consumed nearly 30% of total health expenditures in 1980, and 50% of federal health care costs. Yet their special needs—including long-term care and services as opposed to acute health care—have remained largely unfulfilled; only a tiny percentage of doctors specialize in geriatrics.

One problem highlighted in recent years has been the tendency for the public and medical profession alike to regard mental fuzziness in the elderly as the onset of senility, when it would not be so interpreted in a younger patient. Often, these symptoms may result from chronic depression, loneliness or reactions to a battery of drugs prescribed for different ailments. Another tendency has been for government mental health programs to concentrate on the under-65 patients; a study by the U.S. Commission on Civil Rights issued in 1978 reported that patients over 65 were "seriously underrepresented" in government-funded health care centers, although their need for such services was greater than that of any other age group.

The Oregonian
Portland, Ore., July 26, 1980

Man has difficulty accepting that, like dogs, cats and all other animals, he has a finite life span, determined, not in the stars, but in the cells and genes.

A study reported in the New England Journal of Medicine finds that the average human life span will peak sometime in the next century at age 85.6 years, but that while the length of the average life cannot be further increased, old age will have a higher quality — more free of painful and crippling diseases in the final years due to improved technology.

This does not mean that some lucky few will not continue to live beyond 100 years. But although the average American lives at the present time to be 73 years old, the numbers of those living beyond 100 has not been increased by the miracles of modern medicine and health care. When the maximum medical care is applied, more people will simply wear out, their cells unable to regenerate and keep the minimum body processes ticking in reasonably good order, the article said.

If 85.6 years turns out to be the top limit of the average life and not the biblical prediction of three score and 10 (70 years), then mankind will have to reconsider applying expensive, high medical technology on the aged in an effort to beat the unbeatable — nature's natural life span, said Dr. James F. Fries, author of the medical journal article. He suggests this in supporting the belief that life spans of average human beings will peak out no matter what new discoveries in medicine are obtained.

This is putting unacceptable limits on the human mind, declaring it is incapable of defeating the aging process. That this secret will be difficult to unravel, but will ultimately yield itself, we have no doubt

Human beings need not collapse all at once, like the "marvelous one-hoss shay," but will some day find themselves looking at the 85.6 limitation the way we now smile back on that mythical human barrier — the four-minute mile.

THE SAGINAW NEWS
Saginaw, Mich., July 26, 1978

It's not to pick a fight with the nation's physicians to say it doesn't hurt them to be reminded a lot of older persons they write off as senility cases aren't.

In fact it's worth taking note of when specialists on aging claim 10 to 20 percent of the nation's elders — some cooped up in nursing homes — are not suffering irrevsible dementia.

Dementia is the fancy word used in medical circles for signs always associated with aging, progressive loss of memory and brain function. Senility is the common phrase we all use.

At a meeting of the National Institutes of Health in Bethesda, Md., leading specialists on aging read it out for the nation's physicians on this common "illness."

They ticked off a bedsheet list of often unspotted — but very often treatable physical ailments — that lead to the faulty conclusion: "this patient is senile and there's not much we can do."

They run the range of everything from heart disease, strokes, infections, anemia, nerve diseases, kidney and liver failure to reactions from medicines, faulty diets and sometimes plain, old-fashioned alcoholism or something equally as serious, mental depression.

All of these are treatable and many times reversible symptoms of what are all too commonly diagnosed as advanced signs of senility.

The tragic aspect of such diagnostic oversight often means remaining years in nursing homes or even mental hospitals.

It sort of reminds us of the well-worn story of the elderly gent who went to his physician complaining of an aching leg and was told it was just a sign of his age.

"But, doc, he replied, "the other leg is just as old and how come it doesn't hurt?"

The seminar at NHI in Bethesda was no joke. It would be nice if a lot of doctors got its message.

The Idaho STATESMAN
Boise, Idaho, October 17, 1982

It's rather frightening to hear doctors discuss, as they did in a recent Statesman article, the ethical question of whether we ought to cut medical costs by refusing to provide intensive — and expensive — care to newborns or the elderly.

Surely there are less drastic steps than that to curtail our country's soaring medical costs, which amounted to something like $1,200 for every American last year. One cannot think otherwise when one hears stories of doctors who defraud the federal Medicare program by ordering unnecessary tests, or the recent account of how manufacturers and hospitals inflate the cost of a $900 pacemaker to $7,500 or more by the time it gets to the patient.

Ironically, part of the reason such abuses occur is that the United States has tried to provide medical care for everyone. Our good intentions have resulted in systematic waste. Too often, under both private insurance plans and government programs for the needy, health care is provided on a cost-plus basis. There's no reason for a hospital or doctor to cut costs.

Numerous proposals have been made to try to change that situation. Most recently, the Reagan administration has proposed that states adopt a new Medicare payment system to encourage hospitals to hold costs down.

Under the Reagan plan, hospitals would be paid a fixed fee based on a patient's diagnosis and a statistical analysis of past experience with such cases.

In California, the Legislature already has taken similar action concerning the Medi-Cal program. A new law designed to introduce competition into the health-care system empowers a state health-care czar to negotiate fixed-price contracts with doctors and hospitals. It also encourages private insurance carriers to do the same thing.

It is too soon to tell whether these ideas are the be-all and end-all of medical-cost containment, but they seem to be on the right track. They make a lot more sense than letting babies or old people die in order to save money.

The Washington Star

Washington, D.C., January 14, 1978

Whatever it is that makes "discrimination" scramble so many people's thought processes, it's still doing it. This time, the subject is bias against the old, and the follies cluster around the Civil Rights Commission's study of age discrimination in federal social programs.

The commission's 15-month inquiry, which produced a 112-page report, is to be the basis for new HEW regulations implementing the 1975 congressional ban on "unreasonable" discrimination because of age. Predictably, it unearthed plenty of what it was looking for. The report faults major national projects dealing with jobs, health care and education for unequal treatment of the over-65s.

To begin with, the report charges that people over 65 are "seriously underrepresented" as recipients of mental health services. Although they have more mental health problems than any other age group, the old are often bypassed to treat the young, on the grounds that investing limited funds in them promises a better return.

The commission found the justification perhaps more outrageous than the fact.

Is it? Not if there's an element of pragmatism in your philosophy.

Obviously fewer years of life are at stake in the mental health of the aged. Furthermore, doctors are generally agreed that they have comparatively few successes with emotional disturbances of the later years. If money and professional skill were unlimited, it would be worth it to deal with them. Since they are not, a degree of selection is called for. It doesn't mean going over the brink with Jeremy Bentham to decide it might be sound public policy to put more of the money where more of the hope is.

Besides, it may be relevant to note that a very hefty investment — roughly a quarter of the federal budget — is already set aside to pay for Medicare, Social Security and other programs specifically benefitting the old. Among the commission's recommendations, those having to do with jobs, which might lessen the tax burdens of these, are much more defensible.

The commission report recommends raising the compulsory retirement age on federally funded projects from 65 to 70, which could do quite a bit for the mental health problems of the elderly as well as holding down the public expense of geriatric services. There are costs linked with the benefits, of course — fewer new jobs for the young, and slower promotions — but the benefits include enlarging the national stockpile of seasoned competence.

As for those to whom that translates as keeping deadwood around five years longer, there's a glimmer of truth to be conceded, but only a glimmer. Between unions and civil service practices, most jobholders are overprotected in today's American labor force. But it can also be argued that a 69-year-old drone who can't be fired does no more harm than one who's 30.

Hold the congratulations though. The vice chairman of the Civil Rights Commission, Stephen Horn, is on hand with another example of the way the idea of discrimination can skew thinking about individual entitlements and the public good.

Mr. Horn likes just about everything in the bias report except that it advocates raising the retirement age for university professors along with other workers. They're mostly white males, he notes, and letting them stay at their desks and blackboards another five years would "perpetuate the ethnic, racial and sexual complexion of American higher education for still another generation."

In his eagerness to get one set of category ratios right, he's ready to forget another. Having the right number of blacks, Chicanos and women on the faculty matters more than having the right number of old people.

And, as for the notion that in the exercise of intellect above all else, maturity has value, well, the discrimination hunters aren't very discriminating.

The Louisville Times

Louisville, Ky., February 22, 1983

Ever wonder why it is that Ronald Reagan, at 72, is bursting with good health while your next-door neighbor, at 62, is plagued by illness or financial troubles — or both? Most of us shrug off the disparity as one of life's mysteries.

At a seminar sponsored by the Southern Newspaper Publishers Association Foundation last week, 25 reporters and editors met at the University of Kentucky to ponder issues related to "Our Aging Population." Appropriately, the conference was held at the new Sanders-Brown Building, UK's headquarters for research on aging.

Old people loom large in the future of America. Thus, not only the needs and problems of our older citizens, but also the nature of the aging process, demand more attention. Demographics provide the most sobering indicator of all: By 2000, largely because of the post-World War II baby boom, one-half the American people will be 50 or over.

Sources of the gerontological boom are no mystery. Advances in medicine, housing and diet have increased average life expectancy. Federal medical and social programs cushion the economic blow of old age.

Medicare, Social Security, nursing home conditions and retirement are all key elements in providing for an aging population, and all seem in some way wanting. Quick fixes may be politically palatable in 1983, but many of those who are making them are unlikely to be around to witness the fruits.

The unusually comfortable status many older Americans enjoy today could be deceptive for those who plan future policies. Dr. Loren Baumhover, director of the Center for Aging at the University of Alabama, suggested that up to 85 per cent of those over 65 live "fairly well, prosperous and successful lives, free of debilitating illness."

However, their material well-being is in part due to the fact that four-fifths of the population today is under 65. That group provides the revenue to fund federal old-age programs. Even with that large source to tap for money, Medicare is heading for calamity by 1988, and the prospects for Social Security, despite a reform package now under consideration, are shaky at best.

In a time when older people are much more numerous, the medical care dilemma in particular will loom larger. The aged, now just 19 per cent of the population, use a disproportionate share of health-care services, explained Dr. Zhaven Khachaturian, chief of the National Institute on Aging's physiology of aging branch. An internist, for example, spends 60 per cent of his time on 40 per cent of his patients.

Translate the graying of America into dollars, and the disparity is even more pronounced. In 1975, $35 billion was spent on all health care in America. By 2000, $81 billion in 1983 dollars will be spent for nursing home care *alone*, Dr. Khachaturian said.

Over the next 20 years, effective planning of medical resources and, particularly, hospitals and nursing homes is essential. That lesson should have been learned in the 1950s and 1960s, when public schools and universities were excessively expanded to make room for the baby boom generation. The Rand Corporation recently predicted that by 1990 — just eight years from now — the nation will need up to 10,000 geriatric specialists to care for the older population. Currently, there is no board certification for gerontology — and, according to *The New York Times*, only 720 physicians identify their specialty as geriatrics.

In short, planning is essential if aged Americans are to expect their final years to be as rich as those of, for example, the man chopping wood in the photo. Unfortunately, problems are too often ignored until they are upon us. As Mr. Reagan has remarkably demonstrated, citizens older than 65 can lead extraordinarily rewarding lives. However, delay in facing the demands of an aging nation may condemn many to long, but not particularly comfortable, declining years.

Government Vouchers in Lieu of Medicare Insurance Weighed

One of the early ideas advanced by the Reagan administration to deal with escalating Medicare costs involved a voucher system intended to introduce competition by private insurers. As advanced by the Department of Health and Human Services, the proposal would give Medicare recipients the option of receiving government vouchers with which to purchase their own health insurance, rather than using Medicare. (The amount of the vouchers in one year would be approximately equal to the average amount received by each Medicare beneficiary over a one-year period.) Proponents of the plan argued that the demand for health insurance created by this new market of voucher holders would be an incentive for insurance companies to offer special benefits for the elderly, such as catastrophic health insurance, and that the resultant competition between private insurers would drive down both the cost of insurance and of medical care. Such a system, they said, could reverse the current tendency for Medicare to pay hospitals whatever they charged for treating acute illnesses of the elderly, while contributing little to prevention treatment, care in nursing homes, and other specialized services. Critics countered that the system would have little effect upon the fees charged by doctors or hospitals, since private insurers might have as little influence over the cost of the care provided as had Medicare itself. In addition, opponents feared that the system might result in inferior medical care for the elderly.

BUFFALO EVENING NEWS
Buffalo, N.Y., August 23, 1981

The Reagan administration displays a constructive flair for innovation with its current studies of a program under which persons eligible for Medicare, mostly the elderly but also those who get disability benefits, could receive vouchers to pay for their own preferred kind of health insurance protection.

An official of the Department of Health and Human Resources emphasized that no final decisions have been made, but conceded that this idea is under review.

And why not? The American system of delivering and paying for health care is not yet so effective that it can rest on its laurels.

There is little incentive for patients today, for example, to help hold down the costs of services provided by physicians, hospitals and other health-care providers. Most persons are covered either by private or government insurance programs, and these third parties act as financial middlemen between patient and hospital.

In recent years, with the system losing competitive disciplines, costs have soared. In June, according to the consumer price index, medical-care expenses rose 10.1 percent over the past year. That was an improvement over some recent periods but it still surged ahead of the overall price index. Moreover, who hasn't heard Medicare patients complain of awkward forms and complicated procedures?

The administration idea under examination would allow persons eligible for Medicare to choose a voucher, perhaps worth an average of roughly $1,700, and buy the protection they wanted from plans offered by private sources, such as Blue Cross-Blue Shield, hospitals, physicians' groups or other non-government program sponsors.

A lot here depends on details, which are not yet known. But such a plan could conceivably widen the choices open to individuals and stimulate competition among private groups in devising new forms of coverage and exerting added pressures to hold down health-care costs. We have long supported the idea of a catastrophic national health insurance program, something Congress has never approved and the Reagan administration opposes. Yet with a voucher plan, private insurers might be able to include this kind of coverage, which would protect lifetime savings from huge bills brought on by prolonged and severe illness.

The actual feasibility and worth of a voucher plan would require scrupulous study. Also, Washington would have to make sure that acceptable programs met minimum standards to safeguard both the individuals covered and the Social Security payroll deductions financing the vouchers. But if carefully constructed, there would seem to be nothing inherently amiss about a voucher program. At the very least, the idea should be given open-minded exploration as a possible means of ensuring better health protection for the elderly at less cost.

The Washington Post
Washington, D.C., December 17, 1981

HEALTH AND Human Services Secretary Richard S. Schweiker hopes to enlist the consumer in the battle to control the rising costs of medical care. After several months of study and consultation with specialists and interested groups, HHS has sent to the Cabinet a set of proposals to encourage more careful use of medical services.

At the core of the proposals is the common-sense idea that when people have all or most of their medical bills covered by insurance, they aren't very worried by the cost of what they buy. As a result doctors may prescribe unneeded services, and all health care providers may raise their prices more than if they had to consider the possibility of scaring customers away. To curb this "overconsumption" of health care, HHS would put more of the cost of routine health care on the public and private health insurance consumer, while increasing coverage for prolonged, high-cost treatment.

Since most working-age people obtain their health insurance through their employers, the proposals would use tax credits to encourage companies to offer their workers a choice of health plans. There would be a ceiling on business tax deductions for contributions to health plans so that companies would have a stronger financial incentive to offer plans with more limited coverage or better cost control. Workers choosing less expensive plans would also get tax-free rebates. All plans, however, would have to provide full coverage for very high medical expenses.

The Medicare program for the elderly and disabled would be redesigned to shift more of the cost of short hospital stays to patients while increasing protection against catastrophic expenses. A "voucher" option would reimburse persons choosing a private plan instead of Medicare—but the plan would have to provide equal or better coverage.

These are not revolutionary proposals. Their details have been carefully chosen, and they respond to most of the criticisms leveled against earlier versions. The Medicare voucher, for example, provides necessary assurance that the elderly will not be exposed to the risk of less adequate coverage. It also recognizes that most private insurers won't be able to provide lower-cost coverage than the inexpensively administered Medicare program. However, the voucher plan may encourage older people to enroll in efficient prepaid group health organizations, and it may also encourage private insurers to improve the often redundant and overpriced Medicare add-on packages that many older people buy.

The most controversial proposal—and the only one for which large budget savings are claimed—is making patients pay more of the cost of short-term hospital stays. This loss, however, is partially compensated by the new full coverage of longer stays. Protection against devastating medical expenses—while it is not without potential for abuse by health providers—will be welcomed by the elderly.

The idea of using consumer choice to help control the medical market is a sensible one—as far as it goes. Americans, no doubt, consume somewhat more medical care than makes good sense. A lot of that, however, is the fault not of the patient but of the doctors and hospitals who in large measure control his treatment. HHS has still to consider what direct pressures may be needed to make the providers of health care worry about health costs as well as about their patients.

THE DAILY OKLAHOMAN
Oklahoma City, Okla., August 17, 1981

UNTIL its details are worked out and its advantages — if any — are clarified, it's hard to believe the proposal to substitute a voucher system for the present Medicare program is going to get off the ground.

The Reagan administration is said to be weighing a plan under which Medicare's 29 million beneficiaries would be eligible to drop out of the program and instead receive government vouchers to buy health insurance or enroll in group health plans.

Advocates say competition by insurance companies and health plans for shares of the voucher market would lead them to offer extra benefits, such as catastrophic health insurance, and to pressure hospitals and other medical care providers to hold down costs.

A task force from the Department of Health and Human Services is studying ways of restructuring the health care industry to introduce more competition and eliminate the "reasonable cost reimbursement" system now used by most private insurers as well as the government.

Critics of the voucher proposal say its real purpose may be simply to curb the government's costs even if that means a reduction in services. Medicare's rapidly rising costs are cited in some circles as a fatal drawback to President Reagan's proposals to keep the Social Security system solvent while still limiting future increases in the payroll tax.

As long as the proposed change remained optional, most elderly beneficiaries almost predictably would choose to leave well enough alone.

Arkansas Gazette.
Little Rock, Ark., August 16, 1981

Now comes the news that the Reagan administration is tinkering around with Medicare in what may become a major overhaul of the nation's 16-year-old system of paying for health care of 29 million Americans over 65. A special task force, says a spokesman, is working on several options for changes to be presented to Health and Human Services Secretary Richard Schweiker.

It is possible at the moment to examine only the one option that has been revealed as being under study by the task force, and it raises grave questions about what may lie ahead for elderly Americans. This option would provide the elderly with the option of using government vouchers to buy private health insurance.

The general aim of the array of options is to enact President Reagan's ideological conviction that by introducing competition into the health care field the costs of the system can be lowered. A scheme of vouchers, it seems clear enough, likely would have exactly the opposite effect.

David Stockman, the budget director, is among those who argue that competition among insurance firms for shares of the potential $48 billion-a-year voucher market would lead to plans offering extra benefits, such as catastrophic health insurance, and force hospitals and other medical providers to hold down costs. Such an argument ignores the reality. Vouchers would introduce a third party — the private insuror — prominently into the Medicare payment scheme. Private insurors are not charitable organizations and thus would require a certain margin of profit on their own that the health care system does not now have to absorb entirely with the Medicare system.

Without including a system of cost controls imposed upon the whole of the health care field, a government resort to vouchers would be no more effective than current practices that allow providers to perform whatever services they wish, without justifying them to anyone. Indeed, one of the arguments of the private health insurance industry, which already covers most Americans not in government Medicare or Medicaid programs, is that they cannot force providers to lower their charges.

Vouchers also would invite development of a two-tiered system of paying for health care of the elderly, one system for those choosing to continue with the present system and the other for those receiving vouchers. But in neither category would effective cost controls be included.

Vouchers might help address the need for more competition among insurance companies but they would do almost nothing to introduce competition among providers in the health care system — where competition is most needed. An insurance company, for example, might tell a physician it will pay $10 for a particular service, but the physician may insist upon charging $15 and will hold the patient directly responsible for the additional $5 payment. This common occurrence is not likely to change with vouchers in the absence of cost controls.

Medicare is a noble idea beset by some obvious problems, most of which are not of its own making. These problems of abuses can be treated adequately through diligence, without a system of vouchers, which itself could easily become a system of welfare for the private health insurance industry.

FORT WORTH STAR-TELEGRAM
Fort Worth, Texas, August 17, 1981

News that the Reagan administration is considering a drastic restructuring of Medicare should be welcomed by a society concerned over repeated instances of waste, extravagance and, occasionally, fraud in the program.

And the plan apparently favored within the Department of Health and Human Services, whereby Medicare beneficiaries would be able to supplant current coverage with private health insurance paid for with government vouchers, makes a great deal of sense.

At the heart of the voucher plan — apparently just one of several options being pondered — is the administration's insistence that the private sector can handle the problem of financing medical care for the elderly better and cheaper than the government can.

As explained by Dr. Robert Rubin, assistant secretary of HHS, the plan would give Medicare recipients the option of remaining in the existing program — under which the government directly reimburses doctors and hospitals for "reasonable charges" incurred by a covered patient — or switching to the voucher system.

Those who chose to switch would receive a government voucher — $1,700 is the generally accepted figure, arrived at by dividing the 29 million current Medicare beneficiaries into the program's $48 billion annual price tag — to be used for purchasing private health insurance or enrolling in group health plans.

Advocates of the voucher system say the incentive of sharing in the $48 billion Medicare pie would ensure participation by private insurance companies and that the private firms, in turn, would exert pressure on hospitals and other medical care services to hold down costs.

Critics contend that medical care for the elderly would suffer under such a program, but that is a danger that could be avoided if the government provides some strict ground rules for participation by the firms that supply the insurance coverage.

The advantages to such a program are obvious. Although some manner of bureaucracy would be necessary for distribution of the vouchers, a lot of the red tape currently involved in the massive Medicare system would be stripped away, leading to sizable savings.

And, relying on the competitive forces inherent in the free market could go a long way toward reducing the waste and fraud that has plagued Medicare almost since its inception.

Unchecked Abuse Revealed in Doctor's Testimony to Congress

The extent of the potential for abuse in the system of Medicare reimbursement was illustrated in December 1981 by a doctor who testified before the Senate Aging and Finance Committees. Dr. Richard Kones, who had pleaded guilty to a 67-count fraud indictment, related how he had collected at least $500,000 in fraudulent claims over a three-year period. "The system is extremely easy to evade," he said, adding that the false claims he had submitted were "so outrageous that they begged discovery." Kones' exploits included fake personal disability claims and the theft of a $36,000 Medicare check from a Houston, Texas hospital, but most of the money he received came simply from medical claims for services that he had never performed. The testimony sparked calls for increased vigilance in the processing of Medicare claims by the Health and Human Services Department.

The Cleveland Press

Cleveland, Ohio, December 15, 1981

In a federal program as vast as Medicare — $44.5 billion in fiscal 1981 — there must inevitably be some abuses.

But $6.3 billion to $7.4 billion? That's what the most recent study by the staff of the Senate Committee on Aging estimated as the "minimum" loss of tax dollars to cheating and waste in Medicare.

More than human error or bureaucratic inertia are involved when one physician could submit claims for more than $1.5 million in phony services, netting himself $500,000.

Dr. Richard Kones, who has lost his license and is facing a 67-count fraud indictment, told a Senate hearing the other day that he got patients to sign blank Medicare forms on which he inserted photocopies of medical services he never performed.

"In my psychopathology," he said, "I wanted to be discovered. I deliberately made my forms so outrageous that they begged for discovery. I was astonished when some of these forms were paid."

The Department of Health and Human Services never did catch Kones. Postal inspectors got him for mail fraud.

How many more cautious, nonpsychopathic people are defrauding Medicare?

Nobody knows. The chances of being caught are extremely low, and the chances of prosecution even lower.

In 1980, the office of inspector general for HHS referred 41 cases of suspected fraud involving doctors, nursing homes, medical laboratories and others to the Justice Department.

Justice dropped 31 of the cases because they were either too old (more than two years), involved too little money, there was not enough evidence or they lacked "jury appeal." It obtained convictions in only five of the other cases.

At a time when the Reagan administration is urging government inspectors general to go after fraud, waste and abuse like "junkyard dogs," HHS has fewer field investigators than New York State.

Medicare not only needs more dogs, but dogs with teeth.

This will cost money. But the recovery of fraudulent claims, and the prevention of others, would more than repay the effort.

The Houston Post

Houston, Texas, December 19, 1981

The tragedy of fraud in Medicare or welfare is that people in need are punished by federal cutbacks while the big-time crooks have skimmed off large amounts of money at the top. Dr. Richard Kones, a heart specialist who practiced in New York until 1979 before coming to Houston and who is licensed to practice in 10 states, is a startling example. Kones collected at least $500,000 from $1.5 million in claims for medical services never performed. He received $1,000 a month for 19 months by forging claims showing him to be disabled. He defrauded Social Security and stole a $36,000 Medicare check from a Houston hospital.

All this he found easy, despite the fact that in 1974 he had been convicted of Medicare fraud and that more recently he had been convicted in Connecticut of Medicaid fraud and in Westchester County, N.Y., for submitting fraudulent disability claims to his own insurance carrier.

This is puzzling. Any small shop in Houston can have a computer on which it checks charge cards to be sure they are valid before handing over merchandise. How, in this age of the computer, is it possible for a man to move from fraud to fraud, state to state, conviction to conviction, only to move blithely on to other frauds?

Kones may have been telling the unmitigated truth when he said, "My psychopathology led me to want discovery. So I deliberately made my forms so outrageous that they begged discovery." But his testimony before the Senate Finance and Aging committees sounded more like pathological bragging. "The system is extremely easy to evade," he said. Kones appeared before the committee in the custody of two postal inspectors. Having pleaded guilty to 67 counts of an indictment and other charges, he awaits sentencing. But one wonders: If he served only 30 days of his 1974 five-year sentence, how long before he will be on his way to new triumphs in ripping off the public?

It is the public who pays for the Koneses of our society. Because of chicanery like his, Medicare and Medicaid costs have climbed so high that the system that has meant so much to poor and elderly Americans may not survive. Because of frauds like Kones, insurance rates for medical care are climbing out of reach of retired or middle-income Americans. Richard Kusserow, inspector general at the Department of Health and Human Services, says that "for those who desire, an open invitation to violate the programs for their own benefit has existed." That invitation must be withdrawn, that door slammed shut.

The Dispatch

Columbus, Ohio, December 14, 1981

SENATE TESTIMONY given recently indicates that money can be saved in the Medicare program by tightening the safeguards against abuse.

A physician told a committee hearing how he had bilked the system of more than $500,000 by filing false claims. "The system is extremely easy to evade," he said. "The forms I sent in were absolutely outrageous."

The testimony comes at a time when the Reagan administration and Congress are looking for ways to cut spending and avoid huge budget deficits. Preventing fraud is the best way to save taxpayer funds and the lawmakers should do whatever they can to stop the illegal drain of money from the budget.

Legitimate Medicare claims should not suffer because of bogus ones, but they will if fraud is allowed to continue.

The San Diego Union

San Diego, Calif., December 14, 1981

Members of two Senate committees sat through an eye-opening course the other day on how to bilk the Medicare and Medicaid programs.

The instructor, Dr. Richard Kones, knew whereof he spoke. The New York physician admits to having defrauded the government of at least $500,000 by filing phony Medicare and Medicaid claims.

While awaiting sentencing for his conviction on 67 counts of fraud, Dr. Kones decided to perform a public service by telling all on Capitol Hill.

"In my psychopathology, I wanted to be discovered," he said. "I deliberately made my forms so outrageous that they begged for discovery. I was astonished when some of these forms were paid."

Dr. Kones evidently grew bolder as he realized just how easy it was to obtain public funds under false pretenses from the somnolent Health and Human Services (HHS) bureaucracy. He even drew total disability payments while playing tennis twice a week. The paper shufflers at HHS accepted his fictitious heart attack claim without any attempt at verification.

Incredibly, Medicare and Medicaid inspectors haven't yet bothered to question Dr. Kones to determine how his larceny went undetected for years. Thanks to his appearance on Capitol Hill, that oversight at least may now be corrected.

The point of all this is that while Dr. Kones is no doubt a particularly flagrant example of those defrauding Medicare and Medicaid, he is certainly not alone.

A 1978 study showed that fraud and waste were siphoning off as much as $7.4 billion each year from Health and Human Services Department programs, including Medicare and Medicaid.

Whatever the Democrats in Congress say, it's apparent that there are still plenty of targets for President Reagan's budget cutters, and for the inspectors general he has appointed.

They might start by taking another look at Medicare and Medicaid.

Roanoke Times & World-News

Roanoke, Va., December 14, 1981

IT WAS white-collar — and surgical robe — crime of the highest order: A cardiologist and author of several books recently admitted to a congressional committee that in a three-year period he had submitted over $1.5 million in false medical claims, from which he received at least $500,000.

For heart specialist Richard Kones, it wasn't just a case of using the vast system of private and public health insurers for private gain, but of testing it to see how far he could go: "I was completely grandiose in my behavior ... The totals on my forms were outrageous ... My psychopathology led me to want discovery."

Dr. Kones is not your average thief. His case history is filled with intricate schemes, faked personal disability and, in one case, outright theft of a $36,000 Medicare check from a hospital. This combination of professional, crook and daredevil, with perhaps a bit of child tossed in, is not likely one that will crop up often. As he said, in classic understatement, he is "not representative of the medical profession on the whole." But if, as he told the committee, no one, even "with considerable effort, could have made it more obvious," we have to wonder how many others — physicians and administrators alike — are ripping off such a vulnerable system in smaller ways.

The Reagan administration's emphasis has been on fraud at the lower end — the welfare cheaters who squeeze dollars out of the system through false claims. That adds up; but much of the publicity since the administration came in has concerned leakage at the upper end, which takes millions out at a crack. The lack of computer "communication" that allowed Social Security checks to be sent to thousands of dead people has been the worst example.

The health-care delivery system is a sieve, and it goes beyond embarrassment that a physician with an admitted psychopathological problem could show how large the holes in it are.

Hospital Cost Control Plan Proposed

Richard Schweiker, the Secretary of Health and Human Services, announced in October, 1982 that he was recommending a new Medicare payment system under which the government would pay hospitals a flat fee for different types of medical care. The proposed payment scheme would replace the current arrangement, under which hospitals were reimbursed for a portion of the total cost of treating elderly and disabled patients covered by Medicare. As described by Schweiker, the "prospective payment" plan would establish 467 illnesses or combinations of medical problems, known as "diagnosis related groups" (DRGs), to be used in determining the payments hospitals would get. The standard reimbursement level for heart attack treatment, for instance, might be set at $3,100. Such a plan, Schweiker said, would give hospitals "a positive incentive to control costs, because they know in advance how much they will be paid for treating a particular patient." If the care administered cost less than the standard reimbursement, the hospital would be able to retain the surplus.

THE LINCOLN STAR
Lincoln, Neb., December 30, 1982

Whether Congress or Health and Human Services Secretary Richard S. Schweiker is responsible, the plan to contain Medicare costs is little more than a hoax. At best, it is a plan to curtail the cost of the program for the government.

On orders from Congress to prepare something to curtail runaway hospital costs, Schweiker's department has come up with the "novel" notion of fixed fees for some 467 diagnoses or illnesses. Now, any 10-year-old knows that if Uncle Sam says in advance he is going to pay less, he will save money but he will have no impact at all on overall health care costs.

Is the federal government really so naive as to believe that it can wave its magic price wand and halt the rising cost of health care? Apparently.

Schweiker says that the plan "will help restrain health cost inflation and help preserve the best quality health care for all Americans."

Nonsense, absolute nonsense. The federal government can pay in peanuts for hospital care for the elderly but the hospital is still going to charge and get the money it wants for its services. It may not get it out of Medicare, but it will get it out of other patients or out of supplementary Medicare coverage.

In its story on this subject, the Associated Press gratuitously offered the observation that hospitals now are paid according to the bills they submit. That may not be quite as nonsensical, but it is, at best, a gross over-simplification.

Hospitals are now paid under Medicare on a cost reimbursable basis. Hospitals must do business, of course, on a cost operational basis. In other words, Medicare pays what it thinks the hospital should charge and the hospital must operate on the basis of what its actual costs are. The two things can be miles apart.

Neither Congress nor the Reagan administration have any idea of curtailing hospital costs. What they are and will continue to do is to reduce the amount paid by the federal government for health care.

And what that means is that non-Medicare and non-Medicaid patients will end up paying more. What the answer to rising medical care costs is or if there is any answer, we do not know, but citizens ought to know that all the government is doing is shifting its costs to private paying patients.

ST. LOUIS POST-DISPATCH
St. Louis, Mo., January 1, 1983

In yet an another effort to control hospital costs, the Department of Health and Human Services, acting under a congressional directive, has proposed what is known as prospective payments to hospitals for treatment of Medicare patients. Under the plan, hospitals would be paid a predetermined sum for each Medicare patient, based on the category of treatment. For example, if HHS finds that the average cost of treating someone with illness A is $1,700 that is how much it would pay, though one hospital's costs might be $1,500 and another's $1,900.

HHS Secretary Richard Schweiker estimated that prospective payments would save as much as 5 percent a year in Medicare hospital outlays, which in this fiscal year are expected to amount to $38 billion. The proposal is not without its shortcomings, but it is promising nevertheless, especially because it places the burden of cost control on the hospitals instead of the patients.

Heretofore the Reagan administration and the hospital industry's friends in Congress have tended to favor cutting costs by making sick people pay more. The last genuine effort to compel hospitals to control their costs was initiated by the Carter administration in 1979, but the industry fended it off, promising to make voluntary cost containment work. Since then hospital costs have been rising at a rate of about 15 percent a year.

Critics of the prospective payment scheme argue that it would induce hospitals to scrimp on care or to shift more costs to non-Medicare patients. But if the payment formula is realistic and allowance is made for the higher cost of care at teaching hospitals and for other unusual circumstances, it could be an effective way to put a rein on runaway hospital charges. When an industry has an inflation rate three times that of the economy generally, it presents a prima facie case for excessive patient charges and wasteful practices.

Sunday News Journal
Wilmington, Del., December 30, 1982

IF YOU'VE HEARD it once in 1982, you've heard it a hundred times: Medical costs, particularly hospital costs, are out of sight. In the year that ends tomorrow, fees charged by hospitals rose 14 percent, almost triple the national inflation rate. (In Delaware, hospital costs rose by a little less.)

Everyone — providers of medical care as well as those who pay for that care — is worried over this cost problem. Among the most concerned are the folks in Washington, because close to $80 billion of the federal budget goes for health-care related expenditures, with the largest chunk ($56 billion) going to Medicare. So as part of the effort to contain the federal budget with its projected deficit, the Reagan administration is determined to curb outlays for health care, and especially the big-ticket item, Medicare. Over the next three years, Medicare outlays are supposed to be trimmed by $13 billion — that's quite a challenge.

Several steps have already been taken toward that goal: Medicare coverage for some diagnostic procedures has been reduced; a patient's initial payment for hospitalization jumps this Saturday from $260 to $304, thus reducing the Medicare obligation. And this fall, Medicare payments to hospitals are supposed to be standardized nationally according to the diagnosed illness for which the patient is hospitalized. For instance, if a Medicare patient is hospitalized for cataract surgery, the fee the government pays to the hospital will be the same nationwide with, however, some adjustments for local labor conditions.

The plan is to set prospective fees for 467 different diagnoses; that is slightly more categories than the state of New Jersey has been using with reasonable success in setting rates for its hospitals statewide. In New Jersey, however, the fees apply to all patients (whether federal or private insurance pays for them). So as the federal government embarks on setting fees for only one category of patients, there is concern that if Medicare payments fall short, the uncovered costs will simply be worked into the overhead and added to the fees charged to all other patients.

There is also the worry that Washington's prospective, fixed rate payment schedule may create a two-class medical care system of government patients and private patients. That would not be acceptable.

The need to find ways to economize on medical care, as with most other things in life, is real. But let the economizing fall evenly on all — as it does, for instance, with the intent of Delaware doctors not to raise their fees during the first three months of 1983 — rather than affect only the elderly as is the case with changes in Medicare.

The Star-Ledger

Newark, N.J., December 18, 1982

The federal budget continues to soar out of control, despite President Reagan's much-publicized efforts to cut spending. The reasons for this are many and complex, but one of the major problems is that a large area of federal spending continues to advance. This is the money made available for the so-called entitlements, the federal programs long established by statute, such as Social Security, Medicare and Medicaid.

These programs are considered to be political dynamite and politicians are reluctant to make even the slightest alterations in the formula. The cost has been enormous. Social Security payments are tied to the Consumer Price Index and the medical payments, while not affixed to any cost-of-living yardstick, have been rising even faster than the inflation rate.

Richard Schweiker, the secretary of health and human services, states that Medicare pays hospital bills for 26 million elderly and three million disabled Americans. The cost of the program was $50 billion in fiscal year 1982 and has been increasing 15 per cent a year. It is expected to approach $100 billion in 1987.

Against this background, Mr. Schweicker has proposed a drastic alteration in the method by which payments are figured. The secretary would have the government pay all hospitals the same amount, fixed in advance, for treating each patient with a similar diagnosis.

This would be a sharp departure from the method that prevails now, in which there is no formula and the government routinely pays all bills submitted by hospitals that are considered reasonable.

The change proposed by Mr. Schweicker bears considerable resemblance to a pilot program that has been in effect in New Jersey and several other states for two years. The reaction to it in New Jersey medical circles has varied sharply, with strong proponents and antagonists, but a plausible case has been argued for its cost efficiency.

Secretary Schweiker makes a strong argument for this change of methods. He said it would not only limit the government's cost but would provide hospitals with incentive to hold costs down, because they would be paid a flat amount, whatever their own actual costs. He said it also would end the huge discrepancies between treatment at different hospitals for identical ailments.

Mr. Schweicker's proposal faces tough sledding in Congress. There is enormous fear among the lawmakers of making any alteration in the formula for funding any payments to the elderly. And there is sure to be opposition from some of the less progressive members of the health care industry who think the system is just fine as it is now.

However, there appears to be a serious flaw in the Schweicker plan. The cost of medical care varies sharply in different sections of the country. To impose a flat national rate for treatment favors those areas in which costs are lower, such as the Southeast, and is detrimental to the higher cost areas, such as the East and West Coasts.

Nevertheless, the effort to halt spiraling medical costs has to start somewhere. Mr. Schweicker's proposal affords, at the very least, a reasonable base from which reforms can be made. It ought to get serious consideration in Congress.

A related proposal by Mr. Schweicker and others in the Administration has less to recommend it. To raise revenues, he would tax as personal income the contributions employes receive from their employers in the form of health insurance fees. This would place the tax burden squarely on the back of the worker. If the Administration wants to increase taxes, there are better ways of doing it.

TULSA WORLD

Tulsa, Okla., November 1, 1982

HOSPITAL costs have risen dramatically over the past 20 years, and the cost of Medicare, the federal insurance program for elderly and disabled persons, has skyrocketed as well. Much of the problem, of course, has been runaway inflation. But Medicare costs, in particular, are also a result of an official attitude that money is no object.

For years, the federal government has been delivering this message to doctors and hospitals across the country: Take care of these patients and keep them in the hospital as long as you see fit and we'll reimburse you on a per diem basis.

That message has had a simple effect on the medical profession — there has been little incentive to contain medical costs.

But Medicare hospital costs have risen an average of 19 percent over the past three years. The federal government now spends $50 billion annually on the program and that figure is expected to double by 1987.

It's time for some changes.

Health and Human Service Secretary Richard Schweiker has proposed that instead of getting a blank check, hospitals would be reimbursed only a flat fee by Medicare. Thus, a set amount might be announced for an appendectomy. The hospital would receive that amount for providing the service. If a hospital could do the work for less than the flat fee, it would keep the difference.

The object is to encourage hospitals to be economical, rather than extravagant. That is not an unreasonable goal.

FORT WORTH STAR-TELEGRAM

Fort Worth, Texas, January 1, 1983

Last summer, Congress told Health and Human Services Secretary Richard Schweiker to devise a system for bringing the spiraling costs of the nation's Medicare program under control.

Last week, Schweiker handed Congress his response, a 220-page report outlining ways to accomplish that goal. The portion of the report that has been made public indicates that the Schweiker proposal is a sound, well-reasoned approach for bringing order and responsibility to the program's financial structure.

The key to the Schweiker plan is fixed hospital fees. Instead of the government paying whatever a hospital chooses to charge for treatment of patients covered under the program, Medicare is devising a prospective payment method that would set fees in advance for 467 diagnoses.

Fees would be adjusted to take into account local labor costs but otherwise would be the same for all hospitals, which would have to accept the set rates. They could not negotiate higher ones and could not charge patients for costs beyond the deductible (based on an average one-day stay) or other fees authorized by existing laws.

The savings potential of such a change can be put in perspective by studying the variance in payments under the current system. Medicare records show that some hospitals charge $1,500 to treat heart attack patients while others charge $9,000 with no apparent difference in quality of treatment.

The need for economy measures in the Medicare program is obvious. After rising 19 percent annually from 1979 to 1981, hospital room-and-board fees rose by almost 14 percent in 1982. That is nearly triple the general inflation rate. Medicare, which covers 29 million elderly and/or disabled Americans, accounted for 26.6 percent of the $118 billion spent on hospital care in this country in 1981. Figures for 1982 aren't available yet, but they are certain to be as high.

Seventy percent of the program's $56 billion budget is spent on hospitals.

The tax increase passed last August ordered Medicare cuts of $13.3 billion over the next three years. The Schweiker plan is the first step in following that order.

In its upcoming session, Congress should approve that plan or come up with a better one.

RAPID CITY JOURNAL—

Rapid City, S.D., November 29, 1982

While most public-and political attention has been focused on the financial problems of the Social Security system, the Medicare program faces an equally severe crisis.

Created 15 years ago as part of the Great Society program, Medicare is the country's second-costliest domestic program — right behind Social Security.

About 29 million aged and disabled persons, about one-eighth of the population, will receive about $55 million in Medicare benefits this year. Two-thirds of this amount will go to hospitals and one-third to doctors.

Money to pay Medicare bills comes from three sources. Hospital expenditures are funded from 1.3 percent of the current 6.7 percent Social Security tax on employers and employees. Payments to doctors are financed in part by a $12.20 monthly premium paid by beneficiaries. Remaining payments to doctors, about $11 billion last year, are made from general revenues.

The fiscal stability of the program is threatened largely because costs of medical care have been rising at a much faster rate than other consumer costs.

It is estimated that if the economy remains in recession for a while, the hospital-payment financing system could become inadequate as early as 1988. In the more likely case that the economy improves somewhat, the funding shortfall is expected by 1991. But even if the economy rebounds strongly, Medicare won't be able to pay its hospital bills after 1994 or 1995.

Recognition of the problems Medicare faces in the near and long-term future resulted in appointment of a panel charged with proposing solutions.

It's good that the Medicare panel, unlike the bipartisan commission which is studying Social Security reform, has drawn little attention. Working outside the emotion-charged political atmosphere that characterizes the Social Security study, the panel should move quickly to make recommendations to solve Medicare's financing problems in ways that are fair to both Medicare beneficiaries and to taxpayers.

Chicago Tribune

Chicago, Ill., December 1, 1982

The new miracle cure being touted around Washington now for steeply rising, uncontrollably high hospital costs is called "prospective payment." But the term doesn't mean what it sounds like. The concept is unproven and may be hazardous to patients' health. And the argument that "something has to be done" doesn't justify what could be an unhealthy experiment in financing health care.

Congress has ordered the Department of Health and Human Services (HHS) to develop a prospective payment plan for Medicare by the end of this year and will probably begin debating it soon after the new session begins in January. The Reagan administration wants to cut anticipated Medicare spending by $6.3 billion by 1985 and to use changes in Medicare financing as a lever to reform the health care system as a whole. But critics are already taking shots at what the HHS plan is expected to include.

Hospitals now get 35 percent of their funds from Medicare and almost 10 percent from Medicaid. If Congress puts Medicare on a prospective payment basis, there will be strong pressures for health insurance companies and Medicaid to adopt the same system.

The reasoning behind prospective payment schemes goes like this: Currently, insurance companies, Medicare and Medicaid pay hospitals on the basis of the amount of care they give patients; the more care, the more money hospitals get. These financial incentives and other factors have led to an uncontrollable expansion of health care costs—up from $42 billion to $287 billion and from 6 to almost 10 percent of the gross national product since 1965. The federal government's spending for health care rose from $5.5 billion in 1965 to $84 billion last year. Health care costs are increasing at a 13.9 percent rate this year compared to 5 percent for the consumer price index.

Prospective payment plans are intended to change the financial incentives to reward hospitals for cutting back on the care they provide. They are actually a system of fixed fees to reimburse hospitals; if hospitals spend less than the fixed sum, they keep the extra money. Contrary to the present system, the financial incentives are intended to encourage tighter cost controls, fewer unnecessary treatments and less explosive growth of the health care industry.

There is considerable evidence of unnecessary treatment. For example, there is enormous variation in the use of medical facilities for similar illnesses, even within small geographic areas, even by different doctors in the same hospital. Apparent overuse of medical care is most common in areas with a large number of physicians and hospital beds; studies show little or no relation between hospital use and the general level of health in a community.

Three kinds of prospective payment plans are being considered. All are complicated. All require more government regulation and bureaucracy. All are experimental. And all may create some dangers for patients.

The plan that HHS is expected to send Congress would pay hospitals a fixed fee for every Medicare patient, based on his medical diagnosis. Payment for every patient with, for example, pneumonia would be the same, whether he died in 24 hours or went home well in two weeks. Fees would be assigned on the basis of what are called "diagnosis related groups" or DRGs—similar ailments usually requiring about the same amount of hospital resources. New Jersey now uses a payment system with 467 DRGs; it or a similar plan would be incorporated into the national system.

Some modification of fixed DRG fees would probably be made to account for the differences in hospitals and their costs. An inner city teaching hospital, for example, would be allowed bigger payments than a small suburban institution. The Health Care Financing Administration has already worked out an index for individual hospitals based on the types of patients they serve.

But the innate dangers of such a system are apparent. If hospitals overtreat patients now because of existing financial incentives, what is to prevent them from undertreating patients when a prospective payment plan makes it financially advantageous?

The hazards of overtreatment are primarily financial: higher insurance costs and taxes. But the risks of undertreatment are more worrisome: cutting corners too closely could cost lives or shortchange patients who could benefit from expensive treatments they might not be given.

There are other serious objections. A prospective payment plan would add more costly bureaucracy and paperwork to the national health care bill. There is no evidence such a system could reduce rising costs. A similar plan has been used for all hospital patients in New Jersey for three years with uncertain results—data processing problems have been called "staggering" and preliminary surveys show little or no cost effectiveness.

A prospective payment plan could set hospitals and doctors at odds; about 80 percent of hospital charges are attributed to physicians' orders, but pressures of the incentives would be put on hospitals to cut back, not on doctors. Hospitals might be tempted to refuse admission to Medicare patients needing more than average care or to shift some of the costs to other patients and other insurers. It would be easy to drift into a two-tier system of hospital care with the poor and elderly getting second class treatment.

As economist Alan Greenspan put it, prospective payment plans are essentially price controls, with all of their problems and pitfalls.

Medicare Bankruptcy Predicted by 1987

The Department of Health and Human Services reported in July, 1982 that spending for health care in the U.S. had risen to $287 billion in 1981, an increase of $15.1% over the 1980 figure. Of that figure, $118 billion was spent on hospital costs. The steep rise was attributed to inflation, increased "intensity of care," and increases in the size and average age of the population. The costs of Medicare payments, according to the report, had risen 21.5% since 1980; the combined cost of Medicare and Medicaid payments amounted to $76.1 billion.

Sharply increased medical costs, and particularly the soaring costs of hospital care, figured largely in the Medicare report by the Congressional Budget Office (CBO) in February, 1983. The Hospital Insurance (HI) fund, the CBO reported, would run out of funds as early as 1987. By then, it was estimated, hospitalization expenditures would be far outstripping tax revenues to replenish the fund. Even the Administration's new Medicare payment scheme, the CBO said, would not save nearly enough to forestall bankruptcy.

The Providence Journal

Providence, R.I., February 23, 1983

The nation's $50-billion-a-year Medicare program for the elderly is in trouble.

"If you think we face serious deficit problems with the Social Security cash program," said Sen. Bob Dole, R-Kans, the other day, "you're in for a big surprise when you look down the road at Medicare's future. Using the current optimistic assumptions, Medicare could literally go broke sometime toward the end of the decade, perhaps as early as 1987 or 1988."

A study released this week by the Congressional Budget Office (CBO) paints an unsettling picture if nothing is done to change the present system. Clearly, significant measures must be designed in the next year or two that will preserve this almost indispensable program for millions of present and future senior citizens.

What has brought this program almost to its knees? The answer is related to one of the most crucial domestic issues of the day — the skyrocketing cost of hospitalization. While not the only cause of Medicare's difficulties, it outstrips even the aging population, according to the CBO, which predicts that the number of people 65 and over will grow by 2 percent a year between 1982 and 1995.

As part of any long-term solution, said CBO, the federal government will have to address the underlying problem, the rapid inflation of medical costs. "Maintaining solvency through 1995 will require substantial policy changes because the cumulative projected deficit is so large, $300 billion to $400 billion by 1995."

Not only do Social Security and Medicare have a common problem. One exacerbates the other. Late last year two loans totaling $12.4 billion were made to Social Security from the Medicare Trust Fund at an interest rate of 10¾ percent. Whether those loans will be repaid depends on the methods finally adopted to correct deficiencies in the retirement system.

A number of proposals have been offered for patching and mending Medicare. Across-the-board cuts in federal funding have already been made in the current budget, to an extent that some hospitals are complaining of fiscal hardship in serving Medicare patients. Reasonable increases in the present payroll tax of 1.3 percent on employers and employees cannot possibly solve the long-range problem. Neither can increased co-payments by beneficiaries.

Sen. John Heinz, R-Pa, chairman of the Senate Special Committee on the Aging, said a year ago that nearly two-thirds of the elderly have annual incomes below $10,000 and despite Medicare pay 36 percent of their own health care costs.

The prime target should be health care costs in general and hospital costs specifically. The question of federal health planning to control costs calls for close re-examination. Since the administration began cutting back in this area, capital outlays for hospitals and nursing homes in 35 states studied have increased from $4 billion to nearly $11 billion. Marked changes in the system of reimbursing hospitals also seem warranted.

When long-term Social Security financing has been ironed out, clearly Medicare's monumental problems should be given the highest priority. It is obvious now that tinkering won't do. A comprehensive study of national health costs and what to do to bring them under control is essential to prevent calamity befalling the valuable Medicare program and the 26 million elderly Americans whose welfare depends on its continuation.

The News and Courier

Charleston, S.C., March 4, 1983

The cure for the critically ill Social Security fund has been sent to the Congress by the presidential bipartisan commission where it is being "studied" by experts for finishing "touches." But just as economic recovery is, in fact, possible for Social Security, we hear distress calls from the companion Medicare program which, according to a new congressional study, will run out of money in the next four to five years.

If there is a Medicare "crisis" coming in 1987 or 1988, the cure will not be found in the "raise-the-tax-and-lower-the-benefits" prescription for Social Security's retirement fund. The virus affecting Medicare is internal — soaring increases in the costs of medical care which are not only threatening Medicare but all private health insurance programs as well. Other victims of the runaway costs are the poor who turn to federal, state and local governments to provide their health care.

In 1981, while the overall cost of living rose 8.9 percent, hospital costs jumped 17 percent. Last year, inflation dropped to a mere 3.9 percent but hospital bills continued to escalate at a rate of 13.3 percent. Taxes and premiums paid by Medicare clients cannot keep up with cost increases of that magnitude.

Currently, Medicare accounts for 1.3 percent of the 6.7 percent Social Security payroll tax paid by employees and matched by their employers. Plans are to raise the Medicare share to 1.35 percent in 1985 and to 1.45 percent in 1986. Even advancing these increases will not keep Medicare out of the red.

The health care industry is now consuming 15 cents of every tax dollar and will claim 20 cents by 1988. There should not be any talk about raising payroll taxes until there is some serious discussion about containing health care costs. Somehow, the illusion has been created, as a result of the various medical insurance programs, that health care is "free." As a result there are few if any incentives to consider the costs when making treatment decisions.

This open-ended, pay-for-services system that has evolved, simply reimbursing doctors and hospitals for their costs, is no longer affordable. The solution does not lie in the Social Security funding program. The basic responsibility for a cure lies with the doctors and hospital administrators. They have developed the very best medical care in the world. Now they have to make it affordable to the nation.

THE TENNESSEAN
Nashville, Tenn., March 2, 1983

TWO government reports warn that Medicare, which pays medical bills for the nation's elderly, is in about as bad a shape as the system that supplements their retirement.

Unless something is done, Social Security's cumulative deficit could be $200 billion by the end of the decade. Similarly, a new study by the Congressional Budget Office says that Medicare funds will be exhausted by 1987. Medicare's annual report, due in a few weeks, will predict depletion in 1989 and possibly sooner.

In great part, the solution to Medicare's problems lies in repayment of two loans taken out by the Social Security Administration. The old age trust fund borrowed $3.4 billion on Dec. 7 and $9 billion on Dec. 31 from Medicare. Those loans greatly accelerated Medicare's fiscal crisis, and the annual report claims that, unless interest is paid on time, the trust fund will go broke.

Social Security has already skipped one interest payment. And there are fresh doubts that reforms recommended by a national commission will save Social Security. One recommendation was to extend the pension system's borrowing authority until 1987 — an idea that horrifies Medicare's advocates.

Solutions for the pension problem need to be mindful of Medicare's solvency. Social Security should repay its loans in a timely way, and the federal government must manage to augment Medicare revenues and restrain the inflation in health care costs that is also responsible for Medicare's woes.

The Miami Herald
Miami, Fla., February 24, 1983

THE fragile congressional consensus on salvaging Social Security's pension fund had barely been outlined when another grenade dropped last week: Medicare, the health-insurance companion to Social Security, now threatens to post deficits even larger than the pension system's.

That news came in a report from the Congressional Budget Office to the Senate Special Committee on Aging chaired by Sen. John Heinz. It threatens to wreck the Social Security compromise in Congress as well as the peace of mind of elderly Medicare recipients and working taxpayers alike. The pension system already owes the medical fund $12.4 *billion* and has missed its first interest payment on the 10¾ per cent loan. The debt obviously cannot be repaid unless the pension system itself accumulates a surplus.

When it starts to flow in 1987 or 1988, the red ink is expected to spurt from Medicare as blood from a severed artery. By 1995 the elderly health-care deficit is projected to top $400 billion — double this year's record debt for the entire Federal Government.

Such staggering loads simply cannot be endured. No sane standard of humaneness demands that a nation beggar its young and working-age population in order to pay *unlimited* medical bills for its nonworking elderly.

It's no accident that hospital costs rise even when inflation falls. In 1982, hospital-room rates nationally rose 13.3 per cent while inflation rose only 3.9 per cent. The Medicare trough is the primary reason.

Consider the Senate study last year that showed more than 30 per cent of all pacemaker implants to be unnecessary or inappropriate. *Thirty per cent*, at a cost of more than $10,000 each for the device alone.

Consider the sobering fact that nearly one-fourth of all Medicare payments are spent during the final year of terminal illnesses, typically for kidney dialysis and other futile high-technology treatments. Consider the death of Lucille Trunnell, 70, of North Miami Beach. Her final 48 hours of life cost more than $17,000.

Further, imagine how easy it is for doctors and hospitals to keep Medicare patients hospitalized for a few extra days "just in case." Money is no object because Medicare pays. The Government has showed no stomach for demanding that patients be released as soon as possible, receive the minimum treatment needed, and forgo exotic measures that prolong life for only hours or days at exorbitant cost.

If Medicare is to continue its merciful mission of providing needed medical care for the nation's growing pool of retirees, it must demand an end to vendor fraud and the general extravagance that have characterized the program so far.

Senator Heinz correctly asserts that the financial burden should not be shifted to the elderly patients themselves. The alternative will be to excise the parasites — the equipment salesmen, the hospital boosters, the patients who are more bored than ill, and the technocrats who seek to use machines regardless of human or financial costs.

The San Diego Union
San Diego, Calif., February 24, 1983

No sooner has a presidential commission figured out how to bail out the Social Security retirement fund than we hear another distress call. The companion Medicare program, according to a new congressional study, will run out of money by 1987 or 1988.

Announcements of the imminent bankruptcy of Social Security are becoming so familiar that the public will be forgiven some cynicism. Having been told that higher payroll taxes and a delay in benefit increases are necessary to save the retirement system, are we being softened up to receive the same message about Medicare?

It is depressing indeed to realize that all the fuss about Social Security in the last year has dwelled mainly on problems afflicting the pension component of the system. The Medicare and disability components have problems of their own, with different causes and different solutions.

If there is a Medicare "crisis" looming in 1987 or 1988, it will not be treatable by the kind of tax and benefit adjustments recommended as the cure for what ails the retirement fund. The solvency of Medicare is threatened primarily by conditions lying outside the Social Security system itself — by runaway increases in the cost of medical care.

Medical costs are threatening not only Medicare but the viability of many private health insurance plans and the ability of federal, state and local governments to provide health care to the poor.

Hospital costs rose 17 percent in 1981 while the overall cost of living was rising only 8.9 percent. In 1982, the cost of living increased by a mere 3.9 percent while hospital bills were climbing at a rate of 13.3 percent. Payroll taxes and premiums paid by Medicare clients cannot remain at a reasonable level and keep abreast of cost increases of that magnitude.

Medicare now accounts for 1.3 percent of the 6.7 percent Social Security payroll tax paid by employees and matched by their employers. Under present law the Medicare share will rise to 1.35 percent in 1985 and 1.45 percent in 1986. Even accelerating those future increases would not keep Medicare out of the red.

There should be no talk about another increase in payroll taxes until there is more serious talk about cost-containment in the health care industry. It is now claiming 15 cents of every federal tax dollar, and as costs are being projected, it will claim 20 cents of that dollar within five years.

The Reagan administration has proposed reforms in Medicare aimed at making patients, doctors and hospital workers more cost-conscious. As it is, with either government or private insurance creating an illusion that health care is "free," there are too few incentives for all the parties involved to consider cost factors in treatment decisions.

An open-ended, fee-for-service system of medical insurance which simply reimburses doctors and hospitals for their costs is proving to be something the nation cannot afford. The solution to the Medicare problem does not lie with the amount of the Social Security deduction on our payroll stubs. It lies with the health care professions and their institutions. They have figured out how to provide the finest health care in the world, but not how to make it available at a cost the nation can afford.

Wisconsin ⚖ State Journal
Madison, Wisc., February 24, 1983

The latest word from federal officials is that Medicare — the federal health-insurance program for 26 million elderly Americans — will run out of money in 1987 or 1988.

Medicare is an offshoot of the Social Security program, itself due to go broke this July unless Congress acts to adjust benefit payments and Social Security taxes.

What should the federal government do about Medicare? Perhaps its recent action on the Social Security problem provides a model.

Last year, President Reagan appointed the bipartisan Greenspan commission to work out a compromise package on tax and benefit adjustments to keep the old-age benefits program solvent.

The commission waited until the eleventh hour to make its recommendations on the politically touchy problem, but it produced a reasonable package.

The first step is for Congress to approve that package, then a new bipartisan commission should be called to deal both with the long-term problems of Social Security and Medicare, plus related programs.

Those problems were barely addressed by the presidential commission.

Reagan should make the next commission smaller so that it does not become unwieldy, but the Greenspan commission's work set a tone of cooperation. The president should take advantage of that positive mood while it lasts.

Arkansas 🏛 Gazette.
Little Rock, Ark., February 24, 1983

There is more bad news this week for the Social Security system: the Medicare fund will be depleted in four or five years unless rising costs are brought under control in the meantime. The melancholy forecast comes from the Congressional Budget Office.

It is our own thought that Congress should take up the Social Security issues one at a time, or at least let nothing distract the law makers from the urgent task of shoring up the fund for Old Age and Survivors Insurance, which will run out of money this year unless remedies are applied. The President and congressional leaders in both parties have agreed on measures to keep the retirement program solvent. The plan includes postponing for six months the next cost-of-living increase for recipients, moving up the time-table for increases in the payroll tax, and putting federal employes — those hired in the future — under Social Security.

A working consensus has been established for salvaging the OASI, and Congress must not let the consensus be picked apart by amendments advanced for one special interest group or another. The mushrooming costs of Social Security

have to be reduced and the revenue base must be broadened, both to protect the system and to help control the huge federal deficits that are accumulating at every hand.

Some critics of the bipartisan compromise say that it is a short-term remedy, that more measures will have to be taken before the decade is out. The criticism may be valid but a short-term remedy will do until the real thing comes along. The immediate priority is to make the OASI solvent for the time being, and the measures advanced are all sound enough.

As for Medicare, it has loaned the OASI $12 billion and will have to loan more fairly soon, in all likelihood. Congress will need to address the matter of repayment in the next year or two and, beyond that, the direct costs of medical care for the aging must be addressed. The first order of business should be to curb the raging costs of hospital care. The general rate of inflation is down now to 4 or 5 per cent annually, but hospital costs continue to rise 12 or 13 per cent a year. Neither Congress nor the President has been disposed to do anything about this primary problem in the financing of Medicare.

The Morning News
Wilmington, Del., February 23, 1983

FROM THE FRYING pan into the fire. That is the alarming refrain about federal programs for the nation's elderly.

Social Security's imminent bankruptcy preoccupied the government most of last year. Only now, with a reform package making its way through Congress, is there reasonable hope that the trust fund will be financially solvent for the next few years. But no sooner do the retirement benefits seem assured than there is cause for deep concern over Social Security's sibling, the Medicare fund.

The Congressional Budget Office has just completed a study showing that since last year the outlays from the Medicare trust fund have exceeded income. Since the fund had built up a nice cushion, that did not seem too worrisome at first. But the latest study shows that every bit of the cushion will be used up by the end of 1986 (less than four years from now) and by 1990 (17 years from now), the deficit could reach $221 billion.

Clearly, a far-reaching remedy is in order. And the time to start devising the remedy is now. A few days ago, we urged that a national commission on health care issues be appointed (as was suggested by former Du Pont Co. Chairman Irving Shapiro). We urge so once again. That commission must deal with the private and public sector of health insurance, for the two are intricately entwined and depend on each other. For instance, hospitals depend for 35 percent of their patient-care revenue on Medicare; if Medicare could no longer meet its bills, hospitals like St. Francis, Kent General, Wilmington Medical Center and all the rest would be in deep trouble.

A special national commission should be appointed promptly. It would probably need 18 months to do its work. Then additional time would be needed to evaluate the recommendations. So that by 1986, when Medicare is expected to be in the red, the reforms can be in place and the fiscal chaos avoided.

FORT WORTH STAR-TELEGRAM
Fort Worth, Texas, February 23, 1983

Now it's Medicare that is running into financial problems.

For the past year or so, we have been bombarded with warnings that unless major and speedy aid is applied to the Social Security program, it will run completely out of funds by the middle of this year.

But the fact is that the basic Social Security program already is out of money and it has been borrowing heavily from the Medicare fund in order to keep its monthly checks going to the elderly retired. And this action itself is one of the major problems that is threatening the Medicare fund.

Since late 1982, a total of $12.4 billion has been taken from Medicare to rescue the old-age benefits trust fund of the Social Security system. But the real threat to the future of Medicare is not moving funds from one program to another to meet temporary shortages, but the huge acceleration in the price of health care itself.

A new Congressional Budget Office study projects hospital costs for Medicare beneficiaries to increase at an annual rate of 13.2 percent through 1995, while contributions to the fund through Social Security taxes will rise at a rate of only 6.8 percent annually.

Sen. Bob Dole, R-Kan., whose Senate committee has authority over the retirement and health insurance programs, warns that "we face serious deficit problems down the road with Medicare's program." He believes Medicare could literally go broke sometime toward the end of this decade.

A solution to the problem, says Dole, will require outlay reductions "that are much larger than program • ptions currently under discussion, or very substantial increases" in taxes.

The contributions to Medicare are part of the employer-employee taxes for Social Security. About 26 million of the 38 million Social Security recipients receive health care from Medicare.

The Medicare dilemma is but the latest problem to surface concerning the future financing of the Social Security program. It is a problem that must be addressed now by the Congress, because the American people for 50 years now have overwhelmingly supported Social Security as a worthwhile program that is essential for the well-being of our older citizens.

Medicare Payment Plan Passed; More Changes Proposed

The Social Security reform bill passed by Congress in March, 1983 included a revision of the Medicare hospitalization (Part A) cost reimbursement system that had been recommended by the Health and Human Services Department in 1982. (See p. 190.) The prospective payment or "payment by diagnosis" plan would pay hospitals for the treatment of elderly and disabled patients in advance, on the basis of set "prices" for each of 467 diagnosis related groups (DRGs). This policy would for the first time directly link prices paid with services rendered. The Reagan Administration plan was modified in Congress to allow hospitals with special problems to seek more money, and to reflect regional differences in labor costs in the basic DRG rates. A three-year phase-in program was mandated, as was an annual review of the DRG rates. The bill also called for a study on the possibility of extending the prospective payment plan to physicians' charges.

President Reagan, in his fiscal 1984 budget submitted to Congress Jan. 31, proposed additional changes in the Medicare program. The budget called for a one-year freeze on payments for physicians' services provided under the program, and a restructuring of charges to patients for hospitalization. Under the President's plan, Medicare recipients would pay an initial deductible for only two hospitalizations a year, but would also pay a percentage of the deductible for each day he or she remained in the hospital, for up to 60 days; after 60 days, Medicare would pay the entire bill. (Currently, recipients paid a $304 deductible for every hospitalization; the next 59 days of the hospital stay were completely paid for by Medicare, after which the patient paid a percentage of the deductible.) Hospital stays under Medicare averaged 11 days. In essence, Reagan's plan would raise charges for the majority of short-term patients in order to bring them down for the few who required lengthy hospitalization. Another budget proposal called for taxing as employee income some of the health insurance premiums paid by employers.

The Virginian-Pilot

Norfolk, Va., January 30, 1983

A lot of people are experimenting with remedies for soaring medical costs. The most active peddler of nostrums is the federal government, inasmuch as a growing chunk of tax dollars goes for health care provided by Medicare, Medicaid and Veterans Administration and U.S. Public Health Service programs.

Richard Schweiker, the recently resigned secretary of Health and Human Services, handed over his 220-page prescription for whittling costs just before leaving office. The Schweiker proposal would set Medicare-reimbursement ceilings on 467 categories of medical service. If adopted, the plan could produce two unpleasant side effects: (1) Private patients would end up subsidizing losses resulting from the new Medicare reimbursement formulas. (2) Medicare patients would get second-rate medical care.

Meanwhile, Medicare patients in California are going to hospitals that bid low for Medicare business. Some private insurers have begun offering policies that reimburse subscribers for medical services supplied by selected hospitals and physicians for previously agreed-upon fees — Blue Cross and Blue Shield of Virginia are examining that option. Many Americans receive all their medical care from health-maintenance organizations, which provide physician and hospital services.

Health-care costs have been galloping so far ahead of the overall inflation rate that the urge to rein them in is compelling. The general inflation rate slowed to 5 percent last year. But hospitalization costs went up 15 percent. Now President Reagan is trying to restrain the beast.

Mr. Reagan's proposal, the details of which will be disclosed in his budget message on Monday, calls for a tax on health insurance provided by employers and a requirement that the elderly pay a larger share of routine hospital expenses. The administration argues' that these stratagems would reduce demand for medical services, and perhaps they would. Even if they did not, however, they would generate additional tax revenue on the one hand while easing demand for Medicare funds on the other.

The Reagan palliative is more attractive than Mr. Schweiker's. But would it work? Ten percent of the gross national product is allocated for health services. Some health-care experts say that is too little. But corporations, workers, independent purchasers of health insurance and private and public health insurers are struggling under the financial burden. Something has to give. Will it be the quality of health services? The fee-for-service system? Both? Stay tuned.

The Washington Post

Washington, D.C., February 3, 1983

THE ADMINISTRATION'S 1984 health budget proposals proceed from the common-sense observation that when people are not directly confronted with the cost of what they buy, neither they nor the people selling to them have much incentive to worry about whether they get good value for their money. This, of course, is the environment in which, thanks to health insurance, most health care purchases are made. Ultimately the costs of unnecessary and inefficient health care show up in the soaring costs of private health insurance and the ever larger share of the federal budget that goes for Medicare and other health programs.

The administration proposes several measures that would encourage both patients and doctors to be more cost-conscious about their health care decisions. Doctors would face a one-year freeze on Medicare-paid fees. High-cost hospitals would face a lid on Medicare reimbursements for the treatment of specific illnesses. These changes won't be popular with the health industry, but they would provide much-needed pressure for more efficent health care.

Social Security recipients would have to pay more of the cost of shorter-term hospital care and higher premiums for Medicare doctor-bill insurance. But in return they would receive full Medicare coverage for catastrophically expensive long-term hospital stays. This would mean higher out-of-pocket costs for the average recipient, but it would shift coverage toward the sort of cost for which insurance is most suited: expenses that are disastrously high.

The boldest part of the plan would extend these incentives to the far larger number of people covered by private health insurance financed by employers. In recent years, ever more costly and elaborate health insurance plans have been a major reason why fringe benefits have outpaced wage costs. The most generous plans now cover a wide variety of routine expenditures—such as eyeglasses, ordinary dental and medical care and drugs—that workers could easily cover in their household budgets.

Covering such items by insurance is costly for everyone concerned because it encourages people to consume more than they really need and because processing insurance claims is very expensive. But it looks like a good deal—especially to higher tax-bracket employees—because employer-paid health benefits are now tax-free to workers. The administration would discourage this tendency by making workers pay income tax on employer contributions that exceed $2,100 a year for a family and $840 for an individual.

That limit is high enough to allow very complete coverage for the high-cost items for which insurance is suitable. By the same token, it wouldn't affect many workers. The administration estimates that 30 percent of workers with employer-subsidized coverage might be affected, but that—and the associated savings—are probably overstated. If the plan encourages employers to introduce more efficient health insurance plans and use the savings to pay higher wages, few workers will end up paying higher taxes, and many workers will find themselves better off. Stronger measures could easily be justified, but within the limits of the politically possible, this is a good start.

THE MILWAUKEE JOURNAL
Milwaukee, Wisc., February 8, 1983

The Reagan administration is finally beginning to enunciate a strategy for restraining the rapid rise of health-care costs. Although the plan is far from comprehensive, it has some rather promising features.

It is largely based on the belief that patients would request less care (or that doctors would order less) if patients had to bear a bigger share of the expense. Thus, the administration is calling for substantially larger co-payments by Medicare patients, modest but nontheless new co-payments by Medicaid patients and taxation of employer-paid health-insurance premiums above a certain level.

According to a recently reported study by the Rand Corp., the Medicare co-payment requirement would save the government money not just by shifting more of the cost to the patients but also by discouraging hospitalization in borderline cases. The study indicated that 7% fewer people would be admitted to hospitals. The study found no significant reduction of health-care utilization under the proposed Medicaid co-payment, perhaps because it was only nominal — $1 to $2 for each visit to the doctor.

If cost-effectiveness were all that mattered, the case would be rather simple. Co-payments could be jacked up until costs were brought into line. But a decent society must also consider the possibility that undue economic hardship would result or that some patients would be denied essential care.

Medicaid patients are poor. So are some of those on Medicare. Thus, while co-payment can be helpful, it will need to be carefully calibrated to achieve the optimum efficiency without inflicting real hardship. Perhaps a means test will have to be used to determine who makes co-payments and who doesn't.

In order to make deep inroads against the escalation of health-care costs, the government needs to do much more than require co-payments under government programs. It needs to give physicians and hospitals incentives to hold down the cost of care rather than to inflate it. Health maintenance organizations, at least in their model form, provide a logical answer. An HMO agrees to meet the health-care needs of a certain population for a fixed amount per capita or per family. That takes away the traditional, built-in incentive for unnecessary services.

Some observers believe that the administration's plan to tax large health-insurance premiums would stimulate interest in HMOs by causing employers and employes to seek less costly coverage. If so, that would be a point strongly in the plan's favor.

Over all, the administration's proposals are not a bad start toward coping with a vast problem.

The San Diego Union
San Diego, Calif., March 3, 1983

The health legislation just sent to Congress by the Reagan administration may have been inspired, if not written, by a psychologist. It deals with taxes, health insurance, and medical bills, but its underlying purpose is to change the way Americans think about the cost of medical care.

President Reagan is not the first to realize that a big factor driving up the amount spent on medical care in the United States is the something-for-nothing illusion fostered by health insurance, especially government-sponsored programs like Medicare and Medicaid and private plans in which employers pay all or most of the premiums.

The assumption is that when people do not pay directly for care, they visit doctors more often than they need to, spend more days in hospitals than required and undergo more expensive tests and procedures than are necessary. The bills sent to Congress this week take a run at the problem from various angles — all of them bound to generate controversy.

One bill would count employer-paid health insurance premiums as income subject to tax if they exceed $70 a month for individuals or $175 a month for family coverage. While this would raise $2.3 billion in new tax money, it would also have a psychological purpose. By targeting only the most generous health plans, it would encourage workers to opt for less expensive plans that would remain tax exempt.

Other measures would provide Medicare coverage for catastrophic long-term illnesses that now exhaust Medicare benefits, but would also require beneficiaries to pay more for short-term hospital stays. Medicare beneficiaries would get vouchers to buy private coverage if they wanted an alternative to the federal program. The poor who are enrolled in Medicaid programs (Medi-Cal in California) would pay $1 toward a visit to the doctor and $1 a day for hospital care as a reminder that their treatment is not "free."

There is no stampede in Congress to fill these prescriptions. The reaction to the proposed tax on health insurance premiums, a payroll fringe benefit now escaping taxation, has been especially cold. It has the distinction of being opposed by both the U.S. Chamber of Commerce and the AFL-CIO.

But there is no denying that the health insurance system has tended to make both doctors and patients less mindful of the cost of care and rob them of a motivation to hold down the costs. What can be done about this? The administration has offered some reforms that might work, and it is up to the critics to come up with something better.

FORT WORTH STAR-TELEGRAM
Fort Worth, Texas, February 9, 1983

The nation may be approaching a crossroads in its ambivalent attitude toward health care for the masses.

President Reagan's 1984 budget, as sent to Congress, contains recommended changes in Medicare and Medicaid programs, changes designed to cut the federal government's costs.

Federal spending on health care rose from $5.5 billion in 1965, when the broad medical programs were introduced, to $84 billion in 1981. At a time when the government doesn't have enough money to meet its obligations, and when there are cries of alarm about the size of the current and future deficits, federal budgeteers are looking at such programs of social services to see what can be saved.

This week, Charles E. Phelps, an economist with the Rand Corp., forecast that the changes proposed in the budget message would actually save the government more than the $1.2 billion estimated by the administration.

From the standpoint of reducing spending, that is nice to hear.

But it also draws attention to the cost, in human terms, of such a saving.

The Reagan plan would require Medicare beneficiaries to pay a larger percentage of hospitalization costs for the first 15 days of a hospital stay. A patient could have to shoulder as much as $1,500 of hospital expense for an 8-weeks period of hospitalization, compared to approximately $300 now.

As a trade-off, Medicare would pay all costs after the patient was hospitalized 60 days. This catastrophic illness coverage would protect Medicare beneficiaries, most of whom are retired persons, from the thousands of dollars of expense that can accumulate during a severe illness.

The danger is that this would harm the many and benefit the few in order to cut the overall cost of Medicare.

Phelps forecast savings of up to $5 billion because, he figures, fewer elderly persons would be admitted to hospitals.

It is always a good idea to stay out of a hospital if possible, but the administration plan smacks of making it less possible, economically, for many of the elderly to gain needed hospital care.

That is the crossroads we see directly ahead. We must judge whether basic medical and hospital care can be provided for the elderly (many of whom, without sufficient Medicare help, would find it a tragic hardship or, often, an impossibility, to provide adequately for their medical needs) without the provision contributing to national bankruptcy.

Surely it can. The cost in dollars must be ever weighed against the cost in misery, and even in lives, of failure to achieve it.

Newsday
Long Island, N.Y., March 13, 1983

While many household costs have been leveling off or even dropping, one major family expense continues its relentless march upward: Medical costs rose at nearly three times the rate of the overall Consumer Price Index last year and now account for more than 10 per cent of America's gross national product.

Since Congress and the White House still haven't come up with a national health insurance plan that controls costs while assuring all Americans of adequate medical care, the present patchwork system desperately needs some stitching.

President Reagan has sent Congress a package of proposals designed to repair the system by discouraging overuse of medical facilities and holding federal health spending down. The package's chief virtue is that it tackles several different components of the problem at the same time, spreading the burden over various population groups.

The President believes, for example, that extravagant private health insurance plans provided by some companies have led to more frequent and extensive medical care than necessary, helping to drive costs up. His remedy is to tax as income a portion of the cost of the most generous health insurance plans. That would make employees more conscious of the dollar benefits they are getting and raise some money for the Treasury.

Although the plan may not prove especially effective in holding the line on medical costs, there's no reason company-paid health insurance premiums should remain totally exempt from federal income taxes. The proposal deserves congressional approval, if for no other reason than to help narrow the federal deficit.

Reagan also wants to raise substantially the share of hospital bills paid by Medicare patients. But this proposal includes a sweetener: In return for paying more for short hospital stays, Medicare patients would have better financial protection against prolonged illness or injury. That's not an unreasonable trade-off. And the savings could help the Medicare Trust Fund ward off an anticipated revenue shortage in the years ahead.

Reagan also recommends freezing, for a year, the reimbursements that physicians are paid for treating Medicare patients. The idea is to make the doctors share the burden of rising costs. There's an obvious risk that doctors will simply pass costs on to their patients or refuse to treat Medicare patients entirely. Still, the freeze may be worth trying, provided it is carefully assessed after the year is over.

Asking low-income Medicaid patients to pay $1 for each visit to a doctor or hospital emergency room, or for each day they are hospitalized, seems to be a reasonable way to try to hold Medicaid costs down. The idea is not so much to make Medicaid patients help pay for their care as to discourage them from seeking unnecessary medical attention. The danger is that this device will work too well and that poor people will wind up postponing treatment that they really need.

But most poor people can come up with a dollar for something that's important. And the token payment might make it harder for so-called Medicaid mills to stay in business.

The administration's proposals don't add up to the far-reaching reforms that the health-care system really needs. But since a major overhaul will probably have to await better economic times and a new administration, almost any measure designed to hold health-care costs down merits congressional consideration.

The Courier-Journal
Louisville, Ky., February 8, 1983

OBJECTIONS to the Reagan administration's proposals for reform of the nation's health-care system have to be raised reluctantly. Anything that's done will displease many Americans. But the rapid rise of medical costs constitutes a full-blown crisis.

The administration's proposals include (1) sharp cuts in Medicare benefits in return for spending to insure the Medicare-eligible against catastrophic illness; (2) limits on Medicare charges by hospitals; and (3) the taxing of employer-paid health insurance premiums. The first two of these proposals have serious shortcomings. But even without improvements that Congress could supply, such steps could reduce the dangers in the present system.

Those dangers are somewhat disguised, because the anesthetics of private health insurance and government programs have rendered medical care relatively painless financially to so many Americans. But the side-effects threaten to make the economy deathly ill, as well as running government medical programs onto the rocks. Health care, private and public, cost $287 billion last year, almost 10 per cent of the amount spent for *all* goods and services in the United States. That was about $50 billion more than the nation's astronomical defense budget.

Even more ominously, health-care costs rose 11 percent last year, nearly three times the rate of inflation. These costs are reflected in others that hurt the economy. The employer cost of medical services for auto workers and their families is said to add more than $400 to the price of a typical GM car.

Few citizens, presumably, want to return to the pre-insurance days when costs were held down because so few Americans could afford decent health care. But some steps — even some unpleasant ones — must be taken to curb the cost spiral in a system that now has few incentives for economy.

One approach is to give doctors and hospitals profit incentives to hold costs down. That's the basic idea behind health maintenance organizations, which accept specified payments for providing complete health care, and thus have a financial incentive to practice preventive medicine and to push other economies, such as quicker hospital discharges.

Jefferson County's state-sponsored Citicare plan, aimed at providing care for the needy, follows that model. It's encouraging that Kentucky's Department of Human Resources, which already has signed up 90 doctors to participate in Citicare, isn't bound by the vote last week in which the Jefferson County Medical Society rescinded its earlier approval of the plan.

The Reagan administration claims to be encouraging such plans, though it's doubtful that any of its proposals provide sufficient incentive. Meantime, its other cost-cutting ideas have some serious flaws.

For example, the administration would base Medicare payments to hospitals on national averages for specific treatments. This basically good thought has at least a couple of bugs. One is that it could be unfair to smaller or older hospitals, because of their often-higher staffing and maintenance costs per bed, and to teaching hospitals, with their built-in higher costs. The second is that it's likely, if such rates were set only for Medicare, that privately insured patients would wind up paying more — and paying the tab in increased premiums.

Another administration-proposed Medicare reform would have patients paying a greater share of hospitalization costs for up to 60 days, in return for nearly total coverage of any costs after that. That would fill one glaring gap in Medicare, though the proposed reductions have been criticized as a betrayal of citizens who counted on having the present level of benefits after retirement. Betrayal may be too strong a word, but the cutback in short-term hospital care benefits in return for gaining the catastrophic-illness protection would an uneven swap for most patients.

Thus, of the seven million Medicare patients hospitalized each year, only 200,000 stay for the 60 days required to become eligible for the proposed catastrophic insurance. Meantime, a person in the hospital for two weeks would have pay about twice what he does now — $714 versus about $350. Premiums on the supplementary private insurance that most Medicare beneficiaries purchase would rise sharply. So the plan needs careful examination to see how many short-term illness would be converted to crises.

Another Reagan administration proposal, to treat a portion of health-care benefits provided by employers as taxable income, is considerably easier to defend. Again, this is designed to make citizens understand that hospitalization isn't just some magical entitlement paid by the good fairy.

If an employee has to pay taxes on the portion of his medical insurance premiums paid by his employer, he may be even more aware of who is paying for his health care. The tax subsidy in the present arrangement, say some medical economists, has led to some over-generous benefit plans that provide every incentive for higher costs and none for economy.

In addition, the subsidy goes disproportionately to high-income people, who usually have better medical insurance and always gain more from the tax break. The break usually is worth $80 or so to families with a $10,000 to $15,000 income. It's worth eight times that to a $100,000 family.

Despite the flaws, the Reagan administration deserves credit at least for broaching some options. No plan is trouble-free, but the road we're on leads straight over a cliff. We can't be deterred from change by the fact that all the side roads have some chuckholes. But we can take a good look at the map first.

The Dallas Morning News

Dallas, Texas, February 22, 1983

FRANKLY no one should be at all surprised to hear that the Congressional Budget Office is now talking of Medicare's possible bankruptcy before the end of the decade.

The CBO, to be sure, is talking in bookkeeping, rather than in political, terms. Before Congress lets a supremely popular program like Medicare run out of cash, elephants will roost in trees and congressmen will renounce subsidized meals in government restaurants.

But this makes Medicare's situation not a whit less dangerous — or instructive. The reason Medicare's trust fund could be depleted by 1987 or 1988 is instantly recognizable. It's spending more than it's taking in. For one thing the trust fund was forced to give Social Security — the sister fund with problems even more acute — a $12.4 billion transfusion. In the real world (as distinguished from the world of the federal government) this is often called robbing Peter to pay Paul.

Meanwhile medical costs continue to rise faster than any other economic component — three times the national inflation rate last year. In just the last five years, Medicare's costs have risen by an annual average of 19 percent. This is in part because of new technology; in larger part because present government policy leads to inefficient utilization of health care.

Pretty scary stuff. Not that any good purpose is to be served by wholesale pressing of panic buttons. Medicare's problems, like Social Security's, are solvable through corrective surgery. Indeed, the Reagan administration has in hand a set of realistic proposals that deserve Congress' rapt attention.

First, the administration wants to make Medicare customers share more of their own medical costs. Not enough more to hurt anybody — enough, rather, to make people stop and think before utilizing medical care that may not be necessary.

The reason behind unprecedented demand for health care is that, by the federally insured, health care is deemed essentially "free" (like anything else whose cost doesn't come directly out of the consumer's pocket). The administration would address this truth by obliging the beneficiary to pay $28 a day out of his own pocket for the second through 15th day of hospital care and $17.50 a day from the 16th to the 60th day.

A heartless remedy? Then contemplate that after the 60th day, under Reagan's plan, there would be unlimited catastrophic coverage. No one could go broke from paying his hospital bills.

It is not the 2-digit medical bill that terrifies; it is rather the prospect of the 5-digit bill that would wipe out a family's financial future. The Reagan plan would give the greatest protection against the threat that is the most dangerous.

Additionally, hospitals would be told in advance what they could charge for particular kinds of treatment; whatever they saved by less expensive treatments, they could keep. This would not encourage niggardliness: expensive treatment often exists for its own sake, without reference to the patient's needs.

In any case, does the main point come through — that cost-cutting need not mean throwing the elderly sick out onto the sidewalk?

It means no more than entertaining a healthy respect for the health-care dollar, which, contrary to frequent belief, doesn't grow on trees — unless they've got some very peculiar bushes up in Washington, D.C.

THE DAILY OKLAHOMAN

Oklahoma City, Okla., March 7, 1983

CONGRESSIONAL efforts to salvage the financially ailing Social Security system extend to the equally shaky Medicare program, which also is facing onrushing bankruptcy.

Largely because of interfund borrowing to enable Social Security to maintain timely pension payments, the Medicare trust fund suddenly has become seriously anemic. At the end of 1982, it stood at $8.3 billion, down sharply from the $18.7 billion it contained a year earlier.

The Congressional Budget Office warns that if no action is taken, the hospital insurance trust fund will be exhausted sometime in 1987. It says hospital costs attributable to Medicare beneficiaries are expected to rise at an average annual rate of 13.2 percent between now and 1995, much faster than prices generally.

These enormous and routinely increasing health costs could not occur if the recipients in all instances were required to pay the bills out of their own pockets. Only the existence of Medicare and the various privately operated programs that supplement it made possible this growth.

But this third-party financing has brought on a deepening conflict between the health industry's freedom to set its own fees and the insurance system's need for fixed-fee schedules that would enable it to anticipate its costs.

It's with this in mind that the Reagan administration is seeking to establish fixed-fee standards for Medicare's payments toward the hospital bills of 30 million elderly or disabled Americans. Under the proposal now being weighed by Congress, Medicare would pay standard prices for hospital treatment of each of 467 different illnesses or medical conditions, referred to as "diagnosis-related groups."

Each price would reflect the national average cost of hospital care for that condition.

The new system is intended to curb inflation in health care costs by forcing hospitals to keep their Medicare-related expenditures within the fixed limits. Under the plan, hospitals that held their costs below the Medicare standard for a specified service would be allowed to pocket the difference. The present "retrospective" system, under which hospitals are paid after providing services, offers no incentive to curb usage or hold down costs.

But the problems awaiting Medicare are so formidable that it's questionable whether they will yield to such approaches. Costly new medical procedures constantly are being developed, and they inevitably will be used if they represent the difference between life and death.

Coronary-artery-bypass surgery was in its infancy in 1970, but it now has become a fairly commonplace procedure. Health experts estimate Medicare reimbursements for hospital care alone could reach $20,000 per bypass patient this year.

Towering demographic and economic uncertainties also cloud the future of Medicare. The number of persons aged 65 and older is expected to grow by 2 percent a year through 1995. With the permanent disappearance of many jobs in the older smokestack industries, the outlook for employment is murky at best. Congressional economists say that each increase of 1 percent in the unemployment rate reduces the income of the health care trust fund by about $1 billion a year.

These and other intractable problems augur growing pressures for deficit financing of both Medicare and the Social Security retirement program out of general revenues.

THE WALL STREET JOURNAL.
New York, N.Y., March 14, 1983

Hey! What's this little number attached to the Social Security bill steaming through Congress? Gracious! It seems to be about saving Medicare. Funny! The Social Security Reform Commission spent lots of time and money considering that fund's insolvency without once worrying about the Medicare fund. What's up?

What, indeed. It seems the commission buried its head in the sand twice over: first when it considered the Social Security crisis and again when it did not consider the Medicare crisis. Worse, the solution proposed for Social Security will just compound the Medicare problem.

You see, it's all one pot. The money comes in through payroll taxes and is then divided into three funds: retirement, disability and health. But the division isn't as firm as it might be. Last December, Social Security "dipped" (as it's quaintly called) into the Medicare fund for a touch over $12 billion. Social Security promised to pay Medicare interest but, oops, it has already missed the first payment.

What's wrong with this sharing among sisters? Well, aside from the fact that Social Security is probably a deadbeat, the borrowing comes at a time that Medicare needs every dollar itself. Two separate studies, one by the fund's trustees and one by the Congressional Budget Office, suggest the fund could be insolvent by the end of the decade—perhaps by 1987.

Moreover, as part of its solution to the Social Security crisis, the commission proposed—and tne House has agreed—to allow Social Security to continue dipping into Medicare. And dipping is a certainty since the commission's solution leaves a gap of billions of dollars over this decade.

Well, let's say Congress realizes that disaster impendeth and acts to cordon-off the Social Security hand from Medicare's pocket and reduces benefits to restore the fund's solvency. Then how goes it for Medicare?

Still not good. Program costs are estimated to rise at a double-digit pace throughout the decade: That's about twice as fast as revenues will grow and twice as speedy as inflation. Costs increases are propelled by two engines: the rise in people over the age of 65 and the feverish climb in the medical care costs for those people. Now the first motor is beyond the reach of policy makers, but the second demands immediate attention.

And that's why the Reagan administration added a brake on Medicare costs to the Social Security bill. The provision would establish a system of fixed payments for hospital bills of Medicare patients. It would result in savings of about $20 billion by 1988, perhaps enough to avoid a deficit.

But in the end—whether you call it Social Security or Medicare—it's the same problem: The costs for senior citizen entitlements are growing faster than the funding to pay for them. That means that in the end it's the same unpleasant solution: The benefits for some seniors must be reduced.

The Dispatch

Columbus, Ohio, February 8, 1983

THE REAGAN administration has taken the lead in an important, if politically unpopular, effort to rein in rising health costs and to limit their impact on the federal budget.

The important thing is not whether the administration's specific proposals are adopted. They may be the answers to the current problems, or they may not be. That will emerge. What is vital, however, is that Congress and the nation recognize the seriousness of the problems and resolve themselves to act with the administration to solve those problems. They can be ignored only at great national peril.

Medical costs continue to rise at a far faster rate than the overall cost of living. The Bureau of Labor Statistics reports that while the Consumer Price Index rose by 3.9 percent last year, medical costs soared by 11 percent. Comparable figures for 1981 were 8.9 percent and 15.1 percent, respectively. Health care expenditures, as a portion of the Gross National Product, increased from 6 percent in 1965 to 9.8 percent in 1981 — a year in which public and private outlays for health care amounted to $286.6 billion, up from $103.2 billion in 1973.

These increases threaten family budgets just as they threaten the federal budget. The U.S. Department of Health and Human Services (HHS) is expected to pay out $57 billion in Medicare payments in the current fiscal year, and $63 billion in fiscal 1984. As an example of how wildly Medicare costs have grown, when Congress instituted the system in 1965, it estimated that the total annual cost of the program by 1990 would be only $8.8 billion.

Medicare was intended to address the problems of health care costs, but it has, in fact, greatly aggravated them. By removing the medical cost hardship from the patient and making it the responsibility of an impersonal bureaucracy in Washington, Medicare — and its companion, Medicaid — has encouraged higher costs. "Right now," former HHS Secretary Richard Schweiker pointed out recently, "the system lacks any incentive to control costs. We pay whatever the hospitals spend."

The administration has proposed a series of measures to curb medical costs and to reduce federal health expenditures. These measures include:

● Charging Medicare patients part of the hospital bill during each of the first 60 days they are hospitalized. In exchange, the government would pick up the tab for the cost of catastrophic illnesses, those lasting longer than 60 days.

● Collecting higher rates from beneficiaries who buy Medicare insurance to cover doctors' bills, and offering optional Medicare vouchers where beneficiaries could buy health care coverage in the private sector with Medicare dollars.

● Setting a limit on the amount of health insurance that is treated as a tax-free fringe benefit.

● Basing Medicare payments to hospitals on a national average for specific treatments. Instead of paying hospitals whatever the treatments cost, the government would establish fixed payments for 467 categories of hospital treatment. If a hospital could deliver treatment for a cost lower than the fixed amount, it could keep the difference. This would encourage hospitals to work with doctors to control costs.

While we don't particularly advocate any of these measures, we do agree that health care costs are out of control. If voluntary steps are not taken by all parties concerned, then the government will have to impose its own solution.

The other measures proposed by the administration seek to address other problem areas. Their merit can only be determined after rigorous debate.

But they are all steps in the right direction. They recognize that serious problems exist and they propose certain ways to address those problems. Congress, state governments, business and industry and the public have much to gain by resolving the problems — and a great deal to lose by ignoring them. They should all join with the administration in the search for solutions.

Disability Insurance Called Disincentive to Work

The disability insurance (DI) program was established in 1954 to replace a contributing worker's earned income lost in the event of severe or permanent disability. It is financed by its own tax, a percentage of the total payroll tax authorized under the Federal Income Conscription Act (FICA). The rules for qualification are quite strict; the worker must have a physical or mental impairment "of such severity that he is not only unable to do his previous work but cannot, considering his age, education and work experience, engage in any other kind of substantial gainful work which exists in the national economy, regardless of whether such work exists in the immediate area in which he lives." Financially, the DI trust fund has been the healthiest of the three trust funds, despite changes in the law broadening eligibility in 1958 to include the dependents of disabled workers, and in 1960, workers of any age rather than only those 50 years old or over who met the work requirements.

During the 1970's, the number of people on the disability rolls increased dramatically. Various studies showed widespread abuse of the program. The relative generosity of payments, critics charged, was an incentive for those who could in fact work to continue on the rolls. In 1979, legislation was proposed by the Carter Administration that would reduce benefits and increase incentives to return to work.

THE SACRAMENTO BEE
Sacramento, Calif., April 20, 1979

Largely because of the way it was structured, the Social Security disability insurance (SSDI) program has become costlier than it should be and all too often self-defeating. Benefits for many workers are scaled too high, so that a worker who formerly earned $16,000 a year can draw tax-free benefits of $11,000, plus coverage of health-care needs under Medicare after a two-year waiting period. At the same time, the 5 million beneficiaries to whom SSDI pays out $13 billion a year suffer a disincentive against returning to full- or part-time work. If they earn as little as $280 a month, they lose all benefits, including Medicare. Social Security officials believe that's why only 40,000 persons leave the program each year, while nearly a half million more are added.

Legislation proposed by the Carter administration to correct those problems has sailed through the House Ways and Means Committee and certainly merits passage by both houses. In view of the steep increases in Social Security payroll taxes enacted in 1977 to keep the system solvent, it's necessary to make sure such benefits as disability insurance are fairly distributed according to real need. And for the sake of the disabled themselves, it's necessary to remove existing provisions that penalize them if they attempt to return to work but then can't make it.

The major provisions of the legislation would reduce benefits to a lower percentage of a disabled worker's former income; presently, the benefits can run as high as 150 percent for those with families and at least 80 percent for more than a fourth of disabled beneficiaries, with the others falling somewhere in between. Obviously, those non-taxable benefits are better than

many workers can get in a paycheck, considering the costs related to working; at the same time, the health care provided through Medicare is better than they can get through an employer's health insurance. The latter, of course, doesn't cover the disability incurred before employment.

Consequently, the new legislation will extend Medicare benefits for 36 months to those who can or are willing to try to return to work. It also waives the two-year waiting period for Medicare eligibility for persons who return to work for a few years and then are incapacitated again by their disability.

Although the new legislation doesn't provide for vocational rehabilitation under SSDI — an idea proposed before but defeated in Congress — amendments to that end are expected again. Social Security officials and representatives of the disabled contend that unemployability — not incapacity — is the other major reason, next to fear of losing Medicare benefits, why more people don't leave the program for productive jobs. This time around, Congress should therefore make some kind of provision for job-retraining of the disabled. It not only makes good sense for obvious social reasons, but by reducing the number of persons who receive disability insurance for prolonged periods, the job program may in fact make an important difference in maintaining SSDI's solvency. Its trust fund was dangerously depleted during the high unemployment of the '70s. Although it is stable now because of the higher payroll taxes flowing in, the recession many economists are forecasting would dangerously erode it again.

THE ARIZONA REPUBLIC
Phoenix, Ariz., January 11, 1978

THE Social Security bill that Congress passed last year was merely a stopgap, designed to keep the system from going bankrupt. It did not deal with the long-range problem, namely how to cut the system down to size before it devours every wage earner's pocketbook.

When Congress reconvenes this month, the Senate Finance Committee and the House Ways and Means Committee will finally get around to considering one aspect of this problem — Social Security disability pensions.

They are a classic case of how a welfare program that its sponsors sincerely believed was a modest one can grow into a monstrosity.

In the summer of 1956, Congress enacted a bill providing that disabled workers could collect pensions under Social Security when they reached the age of 50, instead of waiting until they were 65.

The sponsor was not a wild-eyed Northern liberal but a deep-dyed Southern conservative, the late Sen. Walter F. George of Georgia.

George estimated that, by 1980, only about 1 million workers would be receiving disability pensions. He figured the annual cost at $860 million, and ventured to guess that it might not even be that much.

This is only 1978, but the number of workers and their dependents receiving disability pensions already tops 4.8 million. The cost has ballooned to about $11.5 billion.

And worse is still to come.

By 1988, the rolls are expected to exceed 7 million, and the cost $33 billion.

One reason is that Congress in 1960 liberalized the program, removing the requirement that a worker be 55 before he could receive a disability pension. Now, in some cases, anyone who has worked in a Social Security-taxed job for as little as six quarter-years, that is, a year and a half, can be eligible for a pension.

The benefits also were liberalized. Today, a young married worker with one child can get as much as $1,051 a month tax-free plus Medicare.

Liberalization of the law is not the only reason for the fantastic growth of the disability pension program, however. Eager-beaver lawyers are another reason. And there are psychological and social reasons, too.

Workers injured on the job more often than not are men with little education and without skills doing manual labor. They can't hope to earn the equivalent of $12,000 a year tax-free plus Medicare by working. So they apply for disability pensions.

And the bureaucrats who pass on the applications are lenient. After all, the money doesn't come from their pockets.

The late Sen. Harry F. Byrd, Sr. of Virginia predicted this would happen, but Congress paid him no mind. Now Congress has a problem on its hands.

THE ▩ SUN

Baltimore, Md., May 30, 1979

The idea of getting as many recipients of Social Security disability benefits as possible back to work is a good one, especially in a time when there is a growing need to control Social Security expenditures. Researchers at the Johns Hopkins University, and elsewhere, point out that chronic disability sometimes becomes an unnecessary way of life created by various societal disincentives to work and incentives not to work. Too many employers, for instance, still hestitate to hire the handicapped. And the disability system itself has some built-in disincentives to returning to work.

A bill recently approved by the House Ways and Means Committee has some laudable features aimed at ending some of these. Under current law, for instance, workers receiving disability benefits who attempt to go back to work face formidable penalties if they fail: loss of Medicare coverage and a long waiting period before they can go back on disability benefits if they find they cannot hold jobs. The House bill would allow workers a trial work period of 12 months—compared to the current 9 months—before they would lose their disability benefits and another 12 months during which they could go back on benefits without having to re-apply and endure a long waiting period. It also would allow them to keep their Medicare coverage for 36 months after they gave up disability benefits.

But some other features of the bill, which are aimed at making disability benefits less attractive, may not be so laudable, especially a provision to place a ceiling on the amount of benefits a disabled worker with a dependent family could receive. This could work a severe hardship on families whose breadwinner is so severely disabled he has no hope of returning to work. Another provision that would harm some disabled people is one that would limit benefits to 80 per cent of a worker's prior average earnings. While this probably is appropriate for workers who held relatively high-paying jobs before becoming disabled, it could cause severe hardships for those whose incomes even before becoming disabled were below the poverty level.

Reducing benefits is attractive to Congress because it would yield immediate returns in reduced Social Security expenditures—an estimated $521 million annually by 1984 from this bill. But eligibility standards for disability benefits already are very strict, and, in the long run, the more positive approach of creating incentives to return to work might yield a larger return than reducing benefits—and be far more humane.

TULSA WORLD

Tulsa, Okla., June 8, 1979

FOR MANY years, disability payments amounted to a relatively small part of the Social Security program. Since 1970, thanks to more liberal rules and a more tolerant attitude toward fraudulent applicants, the disability program has quadrupled to $14 billion a year.

"Some younger people can actually make more money from disability than they earned at work," the Wall Street Journal reports, "and the program lacks incentives for people to return to work."

Snowed under with disability applications, the Social Security Administration now has more Administrative Judges handling these cases than the total number of regular Federal Judges in the entire judicial system. But there is apparently no way to cull all the rip-off artists under present rules.

President Carter has proposed some modest reforms in the disability program along with some reductions in other benefit programs. But his efforts appear doomed to failure.

Congress, ever willing to delay or kill payroll tax increases needed to finance Social Security, is just as determined not to reduce any benefits — no matter how fraudulent or unnecessary.

The Social Security crunch — the difference between benefits and payroll tax revenue — will grow worse as the "Baby Boom" generation begins applying for benefits. There will be a much greater proportion of old people and fewer young workers at that time than ever before. So something has to be done.

Congress' answer so far has been to keep increasing benefits while refusing to increase taxes enough to cover the costs over the long run. If the trend continues, the Social Security program will either be a shambles or it will be financed largely through Government credit. In other words, we will pay for it through inflation.

It isn't an easy problem. Several millions of Americans approaching retirement are counting on benefits that they earned by paying their own share of payroll taxes through the years. But rising SS taxes have become a major burden for some lower income workers. Congress is caught in the squeeze.

Here's a crisis that cries out not only for common sense, but some political courage as well. So far, Congress has come up short on both counts.

Houston Chronicle

Houston, Texas, September 5, 1979

Congressional consideration of any changes in laws pertaining to Social Security is much like trying to maneuver through a very crowded room — you can't help but step on somebody's toes.

Failure to act could endanger the viability of the Social Security trust fund. Automatically allowing for inflation could likewise automatically drain the fund. Increasing the payroll tax and the taxable wage base increases the burden on employer and employee alike. Cutting back on benefits could hurt millions of Americans who need the help.

The Social Security program has been an undeniable success in helping retired and disabled people. There are now about 35 million Americans on the Social Security old-age and disability rolls, and the number is swelling each year. This year there was a 9.9 percent jump in benefits, the largest single cost-of-living increase since automatic increases were written into law in 1972.

There has been a particularly rapid increase in the ranks of those receiving disability insurance benefits under Social Security. Ten years ago the total was 1.3 million; today it has climbed to 2.9 million. Yet the work force covered by the program has increased only about 30 percent during the decade.

A staff report for the Office of Management and Budget is critical of the disability insurance program. The report says many of those on the disabled rolls could return to work but do not because they draw as much from Social Security as they would in wages. Others recover but are continued on the rolls. The report says misuse of the program could reach crisis proportions if something isn't done.

Congress has under consideration legislation that would reduce benefits for the disabled in certain cases and also would provide incentives to those who try to return to work. A coalition of groups representing the aged and disabled is opposing the legislation, primarily on grounds that this might be but the beginning, that other Social Security benefits might be endangered.

With a program so vast, there are bound to be abuses. Some people receive more benefits than they are entitled to, some don't receive their fair share. The payroll taxes are escalating, following the 1977 Social Security revisions, and will have increased $227 billion in the next decade; there is a pinch, but the complaints are muted since most workers know that someday they, too, will depend on Social Security to help them along.

A closer look at the disability insurance program certainly appears to be in order, although any revision of Social Security benefits or taxes can come only after careful consideration, with Congress and the public keeping in mind the many ramifications of any change.

Disability Review Creates Furor; Continued Benefits Voted

In 1980, Congress mandated a three-year accelerated review of the disability insurance program, after reports that as many as 20% to 30% of its 2.7 million recipients were no longer eligible. The mandate called for a tightened schedule of the usual reviews of nonpermanently disabled workers to determine whether or not their impairments continued to preclude them from work. The Reagan Administration implemented Congress' mandate in March, 1981, nine months early; by the end of 1982, some 265,000 individuals had had their benefits stopped.

As the crackdown progressed, congressional offices began to receive reports that thousands of legitimately disabled persons were being told they no longer qualified for benefits; in a few cases, recipients had committed suicide when their benefits were terminated. Critics charged that state review agencies were being overburdened by an overzealous Administration concerned with cutting costs, and were being forced to make decisions without any personal contact with, or adequate medical assessment of, the cases under review. (While approximately 160,000 cases a year were routinely reviewed prior to 1981, the Social Security Administration sent more than 300,000 cases to state agencies for review in that year.)

Approximately two-thirds of those who were thrown off the rolls later had their benefits reinstated by administrative law judges, who were generally the final avenue of appeal in such a case. In the interim, however, many lost their homes and savings, since they were not paid benefits during the lengthy appeals process. In the final hours of the 97th Congress, stopgap legislation was passed to allow those thrown off the rolls to collect benefits while they appealed.

THE BLADE
Toledo, Ohio, September 19, 1982

THE Social Security Administration has wisely backed off a bit from the overzealous manner in which it has been trying to pare ineligible persons from its disability rolls.

The agency has announced that the accelerated process of reviewing eligibility of 2.8 million persons who receive monthly checks will be slowed. Fewer cases are going to be sent to state examiners. When a person's status is first considered and his medical records examined, the recipient will be entitled to a face-to-face interview with federal officials.

An uproar over the speeded-up program began building last year when the Reagan administration announced it would comply with a 1980 law that required doubling the rate at which disability cases were reviewed.

It soon became apparent that Social Security bureaucrats too often were handling the review in an insensitive and arbitrary manner. In the first 16 months 46 per cent of those reviewed lost the right to receive disability checks, and many complained that their medical status had not been thoroughly scrutinized. A later appeals procedure did restore benefits to two-thirds of those who had been cut off earlier, but in those instances the victims were denied disability checks during the months they waited for the appeals to be heard.

The more orderly review procedure now in place should not diminish the value of the law, which requires a review of nonpermanently disabled beneficiaries every three years and permanently disabled persons every five years. Earlier this year Social Security officials said that they may be paying out as much as $4 billion annually to persons who are, in fact, able to work. If the actual amount is anywhere near that, there is a pressing need for the re-examination now under way.

But abrupt and unjustified cutoffs are unfair to many recipients. The more cautious review that now has been ordered may not produce the $4 billion savings sought by the Administration, but it is more just to the millions of Americans who have authentic disabilities and have every reason to receive a helping hand.

THE INDIANAPOLIS STAR
Indianapolis, Ind., October 1, 1981

Early on the Reagan administration pledged to accelerate the effort to weed out ineligibles from the bulging Social Security disability rolls. Repercussions are now being felt in the states, Indiana included.

Between March and August of this year, the Social Security Administration sent randomly selected cases to the states, ordering them to determine whether resident recipients were still unable to work.

Findings were startling — but only to those unaware of the disability scandal that has been brewing for the past five years. For August, the latest month for which statistics are available, 52 percent of Hoosier recipients were found ineligible. The average for the six-month survey period was 40 percent.

Those percentages may well be inflated. Appeal processes could determine that some of those labeled ineligible can prove continuing disability. Even so, preliminary findings hint at the scope of fraud and abuse that begs for exposure.

Seven million Americans and their beneficiaries are drawing temporary S.S. disability, to the tune of about $17 billion annually. Monthly payments average $413 nationwide, compared with $374 for ordinary retired workers.

Disability rolls have multiplied seven times since 1960. A Senate Finance Committee found that by 1976 54.5 workers out of every 1,000 covered by S.S. claimed to be disabled. What intrigued the committee even more was that "recovery rates had declined dramatically." Only half as many workers were recovering from temporary disability as did four years previously.

Acting on the trend, the Carter administration last year passed a law requiring a review at least every three years of all non-permanent disability cases. It is that review, pushed by the present administration, that is now in progress and exposing the widespread abuse President Reagan mentioned in his nationwide address last week.

But temporary disability is only part of a much bigger picture. The New York Times this week reported that nine federal long-term disability programs, including veterans and various worker categories, had 11.38 million beneficiaries in 1978, for a cost of $28.4 billion a year.

All told, an estimated 21 million persons claim disablement benefits. That's roughly 17 percent of all noninstitutionalized adults aged 18 to 64 — in a nation with the most advanced health care system in the world. Behind those incredible figures are not only fraud and deceit but woefully lax law that begs for abuse in a get-all-you-can society.

The Reagan administration has proposed that disability claims be allowed for medical reasons only, without regard to age, education and work experience, factors currently considered. Moreover, claimants must have a prognosis of disability for 24 months, instead of 12, and the waiting period before payment would be extended.

In the light of reports now coming in from the states, the sooner the proposals are enacted, the better.

The Detroit News

Detroit, Mich., November 7, 1982

A breakdown of the Social Security bureaucracy is right now bringing economic hardship, mental anguish, and even death to thousands of citizens most in need of protection: the severely disabled.

In 1980, Congress mandated a periodic review of disability benefit recipients intended to weed out the ineligible. Unfortunately, the Social Security Administration's (SSA) zeal has accelerated the review rate beyond the troubled system's capacity. In 1981, the SSA reviewed 357,000 cases, 197,000 more than in 1980. It planned to boost the caseload for 1982 to 567,000 and still higher for 1983.

Case overloads, delays, confusing standards, and staffing shortages in the SSA and state agencies have resulted in thousands of unjust benefit terminations. Between March 1981 and April 1982, 191,000 cases of the 405,000 reviewed were taken off the disability roles. This is an almost 50 percent termination rate, which is far in excess of the 20 percent projection of ineligibility made by SSA.

It would be fine if these were all freeloaders. But experience shows that half of the terminations are appealed, and two-thirds of those termination decisions are reversed by an administrative law judge. Yet, while appealing their terminations, the disabled and their dependent families are without benefit income and medical coverage for an average of nine to 12 months.

These are not people with large savings to fall back on. For some, the economic and mental stress has led to suicide or further physical deterioration and death.

Between March 1981 and April 1982 alone, at least 36,000 disabled people and their dependents were unfairly denied benefits and reinstated upon appeal. If the current volume of case reviews continues through 1983, the SSA will end up terminating and reinstating at least 200,000 severely disabled.

And this does not take into account those who are not informed enough or well enough to appeal. The mentally disabled are at a particular disadvantage in understanding and fighting termination.

This is the cruelest kind of folly. The ultimate answer is reform of the disability review process, and Sen. Carl Levin, D-Mich., and Sen. William Cohen, R-Maine, have sponsored such a reform bill. But comprehensive reform will not even be considered by Congress until next year. In the meantime, thousands of disabled Americans and their families will suffer without the disability benefits they deserve.

As an emergency measure, Sen. Levin has sponsored a bill to temporarily reduce the number of reviews and to continue benefits through the appeals stage.

Common sense and compassion argue for its swift passage.

DAYTON DAILY NEWS

Dayton, Ohio, December 24, 1982

Basic justice has been returned to the Social Security system. This country's disabled now will be treated as innocent until proven no longer qualified to receive SS and Medicare benefits.

Congress approved the review process in 1980 because of reports that thousands of people were receiving the benefits but no longer meeting qualification for disabled.

But Health and Human Services went after the malingerers with a vengeance. Terminate people first, appeal second. And until the appeal was decided, no money or benefits.

While the plan caught some deadbeats — and the administration is right to do that — it also caught the innocent. Stories poured in about the truly disabled losing their homes or dying unexpectedly because the added stress. Some, faced with no money and no work, chose suicide.

So the lame-duck Congress passed an emergency measure halting the practice. Now those terminated will receive benefits until their cases are heard. If they lose their appeal, they will pay back all interim benefits. And beginning in 1984, review hearings will be face-to-face between recipient and examiner instead of *via* typed reports.

Undoubtedly many of the 2.6 million classified as disabled don't quality for public funds and should be weeded out. But the government is right not to do this at the expense of the truly disabled for whom Social Security is their source of income.

The Salt Lake Tribune

Salt Lake City, Utah, July 22, 1982

Federal tightening of eligibility criteria for Social Security disability applicants and closer scrutiny of those already covered is expected to drop 3,500 Utahns through holes in the safety net for deserving poor promised by the Reagan administration.

This will transfer the financial burden to state and county welfare budgets. The budget-cutting objective of President Reagan's "new federalism" program is thus furthered by regulation rather than, as it should be, by legislation.

Utah agencies were informed that disability determinations being conducted for Social Security are declaring ineligible large numbers of applicants and present recipients. These people, including the chronically mentally ill, handicapped and developmentally disabled, then lose the right to medical help (Medicaid and Medicare) and will no longer receive subsistence payments. Most of these people have no financial means of supporting themselves or access to medical treatment, it was pointed out.

To the budget-cutter in Washington, the number 3,500 is a statistic. In human terms, it's a tragedy. To a person whose survival depends on that meager monthly check and medical assistance when needed, their loss creates panic.

State agencies should, and presumably will, pick up this welfare responsibility abdicated by the federal government, but it will have to do it without any federal reimbursement.

Under Reagan's "new federalism" proposal, about 36 federal programs turned back to the states would "be accompanied by the resources to pay for them."

The proposal has come under heavy fire from some governors and mayors as rhetoric to rationalize serious federal budget-cutting at the expense of states and cities.

Under the proposed swap in the Reagan plan, the states would take over Aid to Families with Dependent Children and the federal government would take over Medicaid routine care. Both programs are now jointly funded by state and federal governments.

The broad concept of Reagan's plan to shift federal programs to state control, along with funds to support them, undoubtedly is viewed favorably in many quarters, particularly in Utah and other western states where federal intrusion on states' rights has been protested for years.

But governors and mayors are well advised to continue their examination of the fine print in the proposal.

Sen. David F. Durenberger, R-Minn., said the proposed realignment of welfare and Medicaid responsibilities is a "doubtful formulation" that could discourage states from paying welfare benefits.

The United States, with a three-trillion-dollar economy, is the most prosperous nation on earth. If it can't afford care for its poor and helpless, its spending priorities are badly out of order.

The News American
Baltimore, Md., December 10, 1982

Better late than never: The people who run the Social Security Administration at last seem to be on the right track in their crackdown on disability recipients. When the effort was launched in October it was as overzealous as it was insensitive, and the results showed it: Many of the people whose benefit checks were eliminated — the man in the iron lung, for example — turned out to have been wronged grievously by their government.

As the result of public outcry the government has, thank heaven, modified the process. Now state officials are required to grant face-to-face interviews to recipients whose cases are being reviewed. This may not eliminate mistakes, but surely it should spare the truly disabled much fear and worry. The new approach has another beneficial aspect. During the interviews, officials are required to take time to explain to clients how they may appeal if they are denied benefits. This too adds a humane touch that was glaringly lacking before.

Obviously the disability rolls should be reviewed constantly. Indeed, only one in 20 persons has been kept on the rolls since the new interviewing process went into effect. The country can ill afford to distribute billions of dollars to people who aren't disabled and don't deserve a check. But it is regrettable that the federal government went about its crackdown with such haste, inefficiency and apparent lack of concern for people's situations. Its heavy-handed, unfeeling approach was outrageous; even though a better system is in place, the fear and confusion left behind will be difficult to overcome.

The State
Columbia, S.C., October 10, 1982

CONGRESS had the right idea when it mandated reviews of people who get benefits from the Social Security disability program. But the way the reviews have been handled has become a nightmare.

Widespread abuse in the program spurred Congress to act in 1980. But it appears now that the reform needs reform. There are signs that the case reviewers have been too harsh. The appeals process is often incredibly slow. And when a beneficiary wins his appeal, legal fees usually devour a good hunk of the money. The effect has been devastating.

The stepped-up reviews trimmed 191,000 persons from the rolls in the 15 months after the reviews began in March 1981. By late July, 2,658 persons had been dropped from the program in South Carolina. A Social Security official said that of 7,392 blind and disabled cases reviewed, 4,149 were kept on the rolls. About 52 percent of those who were dropped asked for reconsideration, and about 10 percent of those were returned to the rolls after a second review. But of those who pressed on to an appeal hearing, about half were reinstated.

Critics claim that at least nine suicides were positively linked to loss of disability benefits. The suicide of an Aiken man was attributed by his friends to his fear of being cut off. Even Social Security officials at local and state levels admit the cut-off has caused major problems.

The long appeal process is one key to the problem. Social Security officials seek assignment of appeal dates within three months after disability checks cease. But lawyers say getting an appeal date usually takes at least a year. And even then, there is no guarantee of what the decision will be, and the entire appeal process may have to be repeated.

It should concern Social Security people that about 50 percent of those who push on to an appeal hearing before an administrative law judge are reinstated. Officials say, however, "that doesn't mean our decision was wrong."

The devastating legal fees have produced lucrative practices for some attorneys. Staff writer Marian Marsh of *The Sumter Daily Item,* who researched the Social Security disability issue, wrote that the going rate for attorney's fees is 25 percent of all back payments. One Charlotte attorney requires $800 up front plus 25 percent of back payments. Attorneys have formed a national organization of Social Security claimant representatives.

U.S. Senator Ernest F. Hollings has vigorously criticized the flaws in the process and promised to work for a bill to correct the problem. He observed that "the states, understaffed and unprepared for the new regulations, are overwhelmed." He is pushing in the Senate a House-drafted measure to continue disability benefits through the administrative law process.

Congress was right in seeking to curb abuse of this federal program. Senator Hollings, although possibly making some political hay, is right in seeking to restore sanity and common sense to the way the process is working.

EVENING EXPRESS
Portland, Maine, December 7, 1982

People who depend on Social Security disability payments deserve a clear set of standards governing who is—or is not—eligible for the benefits.

They don't have it yet. But there could be a measure of progress if a bill proposed by Sen. William S. Cohen and recently approved by the Senate is enacted into law.

Cohen's bill addresses hardships that have arisen under President Reagan's accelerated review of disability cases. In 1980, Congress ordered periodic review of workers receiving disability benefits, starting in January 1982. The Social Security Administration pushed up the timetable, starting the reviews in March 1981. And that, Cohen believes, was before the system was ready.

Across the nation, thousands of disabled people were notified their benefits would be stopped. Yet when they appealed their cases to administrative law judges, two out of every three were reinstated.

Cohen's bill would temper the chaos in that process, allowing disability payments to continue until appeals are decided. That seems both a fair and compassionate thing to do.

In addition, the bill is designed to make the review process more efficient by adjusting the number of required reviews on a state-by-state basis and mandating close attention to the medical records.

Even so, the bill does not confront what Ann DeWitt, head of Disability Determination Services in Augusta, insists must be addressed: the conflict that inevitably arises because bureaucrats and administrative law judges use "two radically different standards" in determining eligibility for disability benefits.

"Our whole system doesn't make any sense to them, and theirs doesn't to us," she says. Unfortunately, it's other people who are caught in the middle.

Cohen's bill helps, but there's more to do.

The Philadelphia Inquirer
Philadelphia, Pa., December 8, 1982

The "horror stories" (as Sen. John Heinz called them) kept coming out. There was the 47-year-old man with heart disease, who, six months after the Social Security Administration declared him no longer eligible for disability benefits because he was fit for work, died of a heart attack.

There was the 45-year-old woman who, about to be advised by the Social Security Administration that she could work even though she had two types of cancer, died of cancer two days before the notice was mailed.

There were several such cases of people who, as Sen. Heinz put it, appeared to have died of the very disabilities which SSA believed were not sufficiently serious to keep them from working. There were other cases of people who committed suicide when their disability benefits were cut off.

Yet these were only the spectacular horror stories. There is another. In its zeal to save money, the SSA has been cutting people off the rolls first, on the basis of evaluations of paper rather than of the people themselves, and then allowing them to appeal — shooting first and asking questions later — and it has been reversed on appeal in two-thirds of the cases.

Meanwhile, the people are without income. That, in most cases, doesn't save money. It simply transfers costs from the federal program to welfare programs at the state level.

The SSA has insisted that its procedures have been in accord with the law, but the results plainly were not the intent of Congress in requiring a review of disability cases.

Now the Senate has passed legislation designed to protect the rights of individuals receiving disability benefits, pending a more comprehensive look at disability in the next session. The bipartisan bill would no longer require a review every three years of every one of the nearly three million cases of "nonpermanent" disabilities. It would continue benefits during appeal until an administrative law judge makes a decision based on a hearing at which the claimant is present.

At the last minute, Sen. Russell B. Long (D., La) tagged on an amendment that would allow benefits to be taken away even though there is no medical evidence of improvement in the claimant's condition. The House Ways and Means Committee ought to remove the Long amendment before sending the bill to the floor, where the House should approve it before adjournment.

The Kansas City Times
Kansas City, Mo., January 1, 1983

A measure of reason has been added to the process for reviewing Social Security disability claims. Besieged by constituents and touched by tragic stories following wrongful cutoffs, the lame-duck Congress ordered that benefits continue while terminated claimants appeal their cases.

Reports that a third of the program's recipients were no longer eligible prompted Congress in 1980 to order a comprehensive review of the disability system. Whether it was flawed procedures, overworked personnel or a too-zealous intent to reduce the rolls to save money, too many terminations were mistakes. About a third of the 265,000 people who have lost their benefits have been reinstated after lengthy appeals. Winning did little to help some, however. Many former recipients lost their homes and savings, and were left with no income and unable to work. A few committed suicide.

A better example of punishing the innocent for the sins of the guilty would be hard to find. Needless to say, dumping recipients until they proved their disabilities — often blocked because of procedures used — was surely contrary to the spirit of the law.

The emergency measure allowing benefits to continue until folks have had their day in court should ease the anxiety in many American homes. It's a good way to start the New Year.

The Washington Post
Washington, D.C., February 6, 1983

CAN AGGRESSIVE management do anything about judges who either won't carry their share of the work or seem to decide cases far too often on a particular side? A pending lawsuit raises this question with respect to the largest adjudicatory system in the Western World—administrative law judges in the Social Security Administration.

Administrative law judges are civil servants who conduct trial-type proceedings over benefits, licenses, rates and fees, labor-management disputes and so forth. They provide an inexpensive alternative to courts. Although not full-fledged judges in the familiar sense, by statute they are given a lot of independence as guards against bias in favor of their agency. About two-thirds of them are in the Social Security Administration conducting hearings and deciding appeals by people whose benefits have been denied or reduced. In fiscal year 1982, 800 of these judges disposed of nearly 300,000 cases, almost all of which involved the emotionally and factually difficult issue of disability.

The statutory test of disability is so tough that people with very severe hardships can still be ineligible for benefits. And after a denial, many request a hearing. Here the administrative law judge is in a bind. There is the danger of pressure from the management to decide cases too quickly and in accord with the agency's fiscal interests rather than the merits. The Association of Administrative Law Judges says that this danger in fact is real: the pressure exists.

Social Security officials have been trying for years to improve the productivity of these judges, some of whom handle almost twice the monthly average of 34 cases, while others handle below 20. (Their legal and clerical staffs average around five people.) And there has been concern that while the "average" administrative law judge decides over half of the cases in favor of the claimant, several judges average over 70 percent in their favor.

These disparities suggest flawed performances by more than a few of these officials. But doing something about it without compromising the rights of the claimants is hard. The pending lawsuit will test whether the measures being pursued by Social Security strike the right balance. At a minimum, however, close scrutiny of the administrative law judges' decisions and reasoning seems a good idea, and some minimum standards of productivity are essential. And when objective evidence—perhaps assessed by other of these judges?—shows a clear problem, management should be free to act through the normal civil service procedures.

Superintending the legality and fairness of the distribution of $170 billion requires attention to productivity and consistency—not just for pocketbook reasons but also because the less arbitrariness there is, the better.

The TENNESSEAN

Nashville, Tenn., February 8, 1983

THE Association of Administrative Law Judges has charged that the Reagan administration has been illegally pressuring some law judges into purging individuals from the Social Security disability rolls.

Administrative law judges decide on appeals from individuals who have been denied Social Security disability benefits or who have been terminated from the program.

In its effort to cut social spending to the bone and reduce the federal budget deficit, the administration seems to use almost any means possible to keep disabled persons from receiving Social Security benefits.

There have been some bizarre stories of people who were unable to work being cut off from their livelihood without adequate study of their conditions. Last May the House Select Committee on Aging held hearings at which it was disclosed that people were being cut off without adequate medical evidence or adequate review and appeal procedures. Rep. Bill Boner, a member of the committee, said the panel found that even a Social Security Administration study showed that 64% of the terminated recipients were being reinstated by the administrative law judges.

Reviews were being made by merely looking at the files, Mr. Boner said, and many recipients being thrown off the rolls were disabled to the point of being institutionalized.

After protests from Congress, the administration ordered new guidelines requiring an interview at the beginning of the termination process so that persons with obvious disabilities would not be denied benefits.

But now, it seems, the administration is exerting influence in another direction to have the disability rolls cut. Some administrative law judges charge that they have been pressured by administrative officials into rejecting appeals and that some judges who rule in favor of disability claimants are subjected to harassment, criticism, "re-education" and possibly punishment by top agency officials.

As Congressman Boner points out, law judges are supposed to remain impartial when considering cases and if they are being pressured as charged "this would be a blatant denial of simple due process." There is a real question, of course, whether an administrative law judge hired by an agency has the independence and freedom to act against the agency's interest in such cases.

Despite its great show of adopting new guidelines to protect claimants, it seems questionable whether the administration is more interested in getting disabled persons off the Social Security rolls than in assuring fair treatment of the unfortunate.

THE PLAIN DEALER

Cleveland, Ohio, January 30, 1983

Injustices have plagued the federal government's process of reviewing recipients of Social Security disability aid since the procedure began nearly two years ago. The intent is to identify and disqualify those persons no longer eligible for aid. The effect, however, is leading to scandal.

Part of the problem has been that many of those knocked off the disability rolls are, in fact, eligible for aid. Numerous recipients whose aid has been terminated have argued, among other things, that case examiners did not give them sufficient time to present medical evidence in their behalf or ignored reports from personal physicians. Most of those who lose their disability income appeal to the Social Security Office of Hearings and Appeals. More than half of those who appeal have won their cases.

Now come disturbing allegations by those administrative law judges who hear the appeals that judges are being illegally pressured by the government to rule against the majority of applicants who come before them.

A suit filed against the government by the Association of Administrative Law Judges charges that judicial performances are deemed unacceptable if more than two-thirds of the rulings favor the claimants. The suit also maintains the judges are being ordered to handle a caseload that does not allow them adequate time to render careful and fair rulings.

It appears as though any concern the government might have about maintaining judicial integrity and impartiality must take a back seat to budgetary considerations. This influences the amount of funds Social Security must dole out, amounting to an underhanded budget cut.

The majority of people receiving disability aid are entitled to the benefits. That's why they were put on the rolls in the first place. It is wrong for the government to stack the deck against aid recipients, not because they are undeserving, but because they are over the quota.

Last year, Congress took an interest in the many problems that already were plaguing the review process. It is set to take action on the matter soon. But Congress now has another area to add to the growing list of complaints — these serious accusations by administrative law judges.

Too many holes exist in this review process. Deserving persons are being harmed. Reform is needed.

Portland Press Herald

Portland, Maine, February 18, 1983

After two years of confusion, Congress will try to set fair, comprehensive standards to determine who is—or is not—eligible for Social Security disability benefits.

For that, Sen. William S. Cohen deserves a major share of the credit. But his job's only begun if Congress is properly to guide the Social Security Administration in administering the $18 billion-a-year program.

The purpose of the program is clear: To provide income for workers who are too disabled to work. Disability benefits are an important part of the social fabric of this country. Yet over the past two years, thousands of recipients have had their benefits abruptly and improperly halted.

What Congress must come up with is a consistent guide to help the SSA distinguish between those who are truly disabled and those who should be supporting themselves. And to do that Congress must establish uniform standards for all who have a voice in disability claims—government workers who process the cases and administrative law judges who rule on cases that are appealed.

As it is, a state claims examiner, going by internal SSA guidelines, may determine a disabled worker is no longer eligible for benefits. The disabled worker can object and appeal. Administrative law judges, applying different rules and standards, can—and often do— reinstate the benefits.

In 1980, a government study projected that a review of the program would show 20 percent of the people receiving benefits were not too disabled to work. Acting on the study, Congress ordered that recipients be periodically reviewed.

But what Congress intended to be a checkrein on improper benefits quickly became a wholesale winnowing that more resembled a purge. Benefits were ended for 45 percent of the people reviewed. Many, of course, appealed the decisions, and two-thirds of them were reinstated. Meanwhile they had lost months of benefit payments.

Investigating the reviews, Cohen found "a disturbing pattern emerged of misinformation, incomplete medical examinations, no personal contact, inadequately documented reviews, conflicting standards, and erroneous decisions." Thirty people, he says, reportedly died of ailments the SSA judged to be no longer disabling.

In response, Cohen and Sen. Carl Levin, D-Mich., last fall convinced Congress to pass stop-gap protection: to continue benefits during any appeal. The temporary law expires in October; Cohen and Levin want a more comprehensive law to take its place. This week, Cohen presented his proposal to the Senate.

Central to it are the development of uniform standards to be applied by claims examiners and administrative law judges alike. The standards include medical improvement in a disabled worker's condition, availability of new and relevant treatment and diagnostic techniques, guidance on evaluating pain, evidence of fraud in obtaining benefits in the first place, or a demonstrated ability to work.

These criteria may change as Cohen's bill is debated, but they give lawmakers a reasonable place to start. No matter what standards ultimately emerge from the Congress, they should be uniformly applied by claims workers and appeals judges.

Beyond that, they should be brought home to the public, both to protect the disabled and to discourage those who would parlay a temporary injury into a permanent income.

Funding for Home Care Sought

Contrary to popular belief, it is estimated that 60% to 80% of the long-term care needs of the elderly, other than nursing home care, are currently provided by friends and family. This is in part because Medicare does not cover long-term care outside the home. Medicare does provide a home health care benefit, but the patient must be in need of "skilled nursing care" in order to qualify. This means that the needs of the great majority of elderly patients are not met under the program; these include care for chronic diseases as well as assistance with simple daily procedures such as bathing or dressing. During the 1970's pressure grew for government funding of home care, and calls were heard to decrease the institutionalization encouraged by federal programs. Nursing homes grew increasingly unpopular because of their high cost and the demoralizing effect they had on many patients. Many states and communities began to offer home services of various kinds; some were partially funded under Medicaid, for which Medicare beneficiaries below the poverty level are eligible, or under a special "social services" grant (Title XX) of the Social Security Act. The resulting array of services, however, with their differing eligibility requirements and coverage, has in many cases been both confusing and expensive. The inclusion of more home care services under Medicare was frequently touted as one possible way of reforming federal reimbursement systems to better meet patients' needs.

The Miami Herald
Miami, Fla., January 9, 1978

GIVEN a choice between health care in their own homes and equally good care in a nursing home, most elderly people probably would opt for the former. That's the human side of a tough question.

Now comes fresh evidence that the economic side is just as firmly in favor of care within the patient's home, except in cases of grave illness or impairment. It convinces us that the entire Federal approach to nursing care should be re-examined.

Investigators have told Congress that in five out of six cases, care is cheaper at home than in an institution. Shifting the emphasis of Federal aid back into nursing care at home could save the taxpayers tens of millions of dollars each year, the General Accounting Office report notes.

As we've pointed out in the past, two-thirds of Florida's $219 million annual bill for Medicaid is spent on institutional services. Of that sum, $78 million goes to nursing homes. Only $657,000 is earmarked for home health services, and much of that usually remains unspent because the present system favors institutions.

Government policy has developed a tendency to prefer dealings with institutions rather than individuals. It's easier to draw up hard-and-fast rules, we suppose, and the paperwork is simpler.

So a growing number of special programs require a welfare client's card as the ticket of admission, which encourages people to sign up for the whole package. Surgery patients choose to spend time in a hospital rather than use the outpatient alternative because it's cheaper — for themselves — that way. And some wind up in nursing homes simply because they can get financial aid there and not at home.

All of this costs money; it is one reason that the Federal tab for Medicaid has swelled from $1.6 billion in 1966 to $17 billion last year. Taxpayers have borne the financial burden for the construction of private nursing homes at a pace that has made health care a hot growth industry dear to the hearts of stock market analysts.

That is irritating enough in an age when government costs are growing like a fiscal weed, but the human side of the question makes things worse. For more money, the people are getting less happiness for the elderly. In adding his "amen" to the GAO report, Florida's Rep. Claude Pepper criticized the "incalculable" cost of "tearing elderly persons from their homes."

Reform is essential in the name of humanity as well as hard common sense. We hope that Congress heeds the GAO findings and concludes that nursing care, like charity, begins at home.

Oregon Journal
Portland, Ore., January 7, 1978

It is odd how long it has taken this society to awaken to the idea that elderly citizens needing some support may often be cared for at home rather than being shipped to various human warehouses.

Several states and many of their communities have been experimenting with assorted programs to furnish the attention needed to let the aged stay in their own homes instead of nursing homes.

Now, finally, the federal government may catch up with the trend. Since the federal government sets many of the rules for the nation's social programs and enforces them with dollars, it is important that it join in the effort.

Congress is being asked to draft the necessary legislation.

Much of the material submitted to Congress to support the concept is based on cold, hard costs. It takes less money in most cases to provide whatever level of help is necessary to maintain the person in the home.

Nursing homes are expensive institutions, but there are considerations other than finances. There is the social one, for instance.

Most people simply would rather live out their lives in their own homes. Even if the family house becomes too hard to handle and must be sold, they usually would rather have a place of their own than a bed in an institution.

A report to Congress indicates that a majority of the residents of nursing homes could continue to live at home with varying degrees of home care provided.

The problem is that, as the impairments of age have made some kind of care necessary for many elders, society has not developed alternatives to the nursing home.

Obviously there are patients who need the thorough care available only in nursing homes. But all of those others could get whatever help is needed to maintain their independence.

For both human and financial considerations, Congress should support the proposal.

The Cleveland Press
Cleveland, Ohio, January 11, 1978

Forty or 50 years ago, when many Americans grew up on farms or in rambling old houses, it was common for grandparents to live under the same roof with their children and grandchildren. Aunts and uncles usually lived down the road apiece.

Times have changed — and not necessarily for the better. Many older Americans now live in nursing homes or mental hospitals because they have no relatives or friends willing or able to look out for them.

The cost — and emotional anguish — of caring for old people this way is staggering. So staggering, in fact, that Congress is considering legislation that would enable many to stay in their own homes.

A bill introduced by Rep. Claude Pepper, D.-Fla., would relax Medicare regulations so skilled helpers could be paid for visiting retirees in their homes to run errands, check on food supplies or perform other chores not requiring a doctor or a nurse.

The bill is broad enough to cover old people who aren't completely "homebound" but need practical assistance to handle the challenges of day-to-day living.

Pepper figures this new emphasis on home care could add as much as $200 million a year to the cost of Medicare, but in the long run it could save much more than that by keeping people in their own homes instead of shunting them into institutions, often at taxpayer expense.

Some studies have indicated that as many as 25 percent of the patients in nursing homes and hospitals could be cared for at home if there were someone willing to look in on them on a regular basis.

That's a statistic we can't afford to ignore in a country in which the number of persons over 65 is expected to rise by nearly 40 percent in the next 22 years.

DESERET NEWS
Salt Lake City, Utah, January 7, 1978

How should America deal with the problems of its senior citizens?

This question is becoming increasingly urgent if for no other reason than the fact that Americans 65 or older are becoming a larger and more vocal part of the population.

As recently as the 1940's, for example, Americans 65 or older constituted only 5% of the total population.

Now, however, senior citizens account for 10% of the population, and their numbers and influence are expected to be even greater by the turn of the century.

To care for the elderly, the federal government ought to spend more money and create more programs for them just as it does for about every other special interest in the country — right?

Wrong.

For many years, this page has insisted that the primary responsibility for caring for the elderly rests with their families rather than with government or anyone else.

This week congressional investigators confirmed that this policy is not just a rigid dogma but is highly practical. That's because taking care of the elderly at home is usually both less expensive and more effective than caring for them in nursing homes or similar facilities.

In five out of every six cases, the General Accounting Office reported, it is less expensive to care for the elderly at home than through the variety of institutions and programs on which the government spends millions of dollars each year.

Then there's the incalculable human cost involved in tearing elderly persons from their homes and their communities. It's not at all uncommon for an older person to go downhill physically and mentally after being placed in an institution.

Sadly, American families aren't always as able to care for aged parents and other relatives as they once were. Families have become more mobile and more loosely knit. No longer is it as common as it once was for Americans to be born, live, and die in one community, with their relatives and neighbors to act as buffers against the crises of life. But that's still no excuse for the neglect that many elderly people suffer from their own families.

With their report on how best to care for the elderly, congressional investigators have emphasized an important but neglected principle:

The proper function of government is to do for the people only those things that need to be done but cannot be done by individuals and families for themselves.

ST. LOUIS POST-DISPATCH
St. Louis, Mo., November 15, 1981

The support President Reagan expressed for expanded coverage of home health care under Medicaid and Medicare at his recent press conference was welcome indeed. Sen. Orrin G. Hatch of Utah has introduced just such a bill, which is now in committee.

Some home care is now covered by Medicaid and Medicare, but much more should be. A report by the Congressional Budget Office says that of up to 2.7 million possible users of expanded home services, only 300,000 to 500,000 are receiving it. Home health care coverage could not only improve the lot of the ailing indigent and elderly but also save the government money. President Reagan used the case of Katie Beckett as an example. The child has been hospitalized for most of her 3½ years, at an expense to the government that has grown to $12,000 a month. She could be cared for at home for much less — $2,000 a month. Medicaid, however, will not cover her home health care, and her parents cannot afford it.

The administration has announced that an exception will be made for Katie Beckett, but her story illustrated the folly of excessive limitation on home health care. Home care is also preferrable because it would enable many elderly citizens to avoid entering a nursing home. Studies have shown that persons who are cared for at home live longer and are more content. A new Missouri law extends home health care to Medicaid patients. A problem, however, is the limited amount of home health care available. Sen. Hatch's bill would also promote the establishment of more of these programs. It's a humane bill and a fiscally sound one.

The Salt Lake Tribune
Salt Lake City, Utah, May 18, 1981

As often as not when one group proposes a solution to a nagging social or political problem another faction is quick to point out why the proposed remedy won't work. Sometimes both sides lose sight of fundamental need for a change.

A case in point is the attempt by a bipartisan body of U.S. senators to reduce what they call the "alarming escalation" of medical costs for the elderly by initiating a six-year experiment in home care as an alternative to expensive hospital and nursing home facilities.

The plan would create a system in which health and social service needs are met at home with the use of federal and state-supported nurses, homemakers, health care specialists and various other types of helpers. Teams of health aides would screen persons seeking to enter institutions for the aged to determine which of them could remain at home if some assistance was provided.

Costs projections indicate that millions of dollars could be saved by such an approach. But then the critics move in and spoil everything.

Opponents of the idea do not deny its cost effectiveness but they maintain that saving money is more apparent than actual. If such home care services were made available, they predict, demand for them would be so great and come from so many people not now seeking help of any kind that the overall cost would be greater than the present level of expensive hospital and nursing home supervision.

Many proponents and the opposition seem to lose sight of the humanitarian aspects of the home care program. Elderly persons entering institutions suffer a variety of costs other than financial. As Sen. Bill Bradley, D-N.J., told The New York Times, "The aged are uprooted from their homes; they are severed from normal contact with their family, friends and community, they experience a serious loss of personal independence and dignity."

When these losses are factored into the cost equation even the feared influx of people not now seeking aid cannot tip the balance against the home care experiment. But more important, an effort toward providing greater access to home supervision should be made because it is the decent thing to do. One short walk through most any facility for the elderly should convince even the most cynical observer that any aged person able to remain at home should have the opportunity to do so.

The Seattle Times
Seattle, Wash., July 15, 1979

THE approaching crisis in overcrowded, understaffed nursing homes, reported the other day, has been predicted for a long time. But nothing much had been done to avert crisis, except talk about it.

The 1979 Legislature managed to deal with some of the problems by providing for higher standards, higher salaries, and better training for employes.

Yet, what has been ignored in the past and continues to be ignored is the inability of existing facilities to keep up with the demand for services.

Nursing homes are designed to serve people of any age who need close, around-the-clock care that cannot be provided at home.

Unfortunately, they also house many elderly citizens who could thrive in a home setting if there were sufficient support services.

Industry executives blame overcrowding on lack of money for expansion. Only 40 per cent of the state's nursing-home residents are private-pay patients. Most of the balance are Medicaid recipients, and the industry argues that reimbursements are too low to cover the cost of care, much less provide money for expansion.

We agree with planners that there is an immediate need for some additional beds. But the degree of expansion should be determined in the context of a broader-based solution to a dilemma that has its roots in social change.

Nursing homes too often in recent history have become homes for people who have nowhere else to go, or places in which to die — without much dignity.

National and local trends triggered by the elderly and disabled point to a strong grassroots movement to keep people in home environments whenever and as long as possible.

Any long- or short-term planning for the future of nursing homes and the people who live in them must include serious consideration of these trends.

A progressive package of care would include more visiting-nurse services, particularly for more remote areas of the state; expansion of food services to ensure nutritious meals, and development of group and boarding homes where elderly and disabled people can share their homes with one another.

Hospice Movement Grows in U.S.

Another alternative to hospital or nursing home treatment that has attracted attention in the past decade is the concept of hospice care for the terminally ill. This system of care, appropriate for those patients with fatal diseases that are not responsive to curative treatment, concentrates on controlling symptoms and allowing patients to maintain as normal a life as possible in the face of impending death. Most such programs incorporate some form of home care services with in-patient facilities, and encourage family members and friends to participate in the patient's care. Many hospice organizers in the U.S. have taken advantage of existing health care systems, using hospital or nursing home facilities, sometimes as part of a cooperative effort to free beds in those facilities for acute-care patients. Such programs have so far been funded through a combination of foundation grants, private donations and federal grants. Advocates of hospice care are pressing for reimbursement under Medicare or other government programs. The chief stumbling block, as with home care, is that hospice services are essentially an "add-on" system that would not directly replace hospital or nursing home care. Its cost-effectiveness would have to be proven over the long term, in ways that might not be immediately apparent.

THE KANSAS CITY STAR

Kansas City, Mo., November 8, 1982

The fear of dying "badly" today is as intense, if not more so, than the fear of death. Life-saving and life-prolonging drugs and machines make possible a frightening dependency and helplessness. Cultural customs and family mobility patterns increase the likelihood that the last days will be spent alone, in an institution.

Many families and patients, dissatisfied with such norms, have turned to an alternative, the hospice. A concept rather than a place, the hospice movement is built on the goal of providing maximum comfort for the patient, physically and mentally, in the home or a homelike environment. A variety of professionals and volunteers may be involved, along with the family and a network of friends and community resources.

It's a relatively young movement in the United States, but the growth indicates its value to the sick and their families. In 1973, there was only one hospice operating in the U.S. Now there are about 750.

Federal officials and lawmakers this year formally recognized their value. Medicare-reimbursed hospice service, for both home care and inpatient care, was extended to eligible persons diagnosed as having a terminal prognosis of six months or less.

Kansas City is fortunate to have a strong base of support for the compassionate and economic concept. It has spread beyond the city's pioneer program, Hospice Care of Mid-America, to the younger Kansas City Hospice, run by a consortium of hospitals, and several other services under private agencies.

Everyone's simplest dream is to make life as good as possible as long as possible. Hospice is helping.

THE ATLANTA CONSTITUTION

Atlanta, Ga., September 9, 1982

Death is, after all, a natural (albeit final) part of living. And for millions it is pointlessly transformed into an artificial ending — an unnatural final act marked by lonely, impersonal, antiseptic rooms; machines working against impossible odds, and a feeling of bitterness and alienation from friends and family at a time when they're needed most.

Almost 70 percent of terminally ill patients in America die in hospitals. Until recently there were few alternatives.

Now, one alternative, called hospices, is spreading quickly. In 1981 there were 440 hospices, up from just 59 in 1978. The hospice approach allows a terminally ill patient to be cared for away from a hospital, perhaps even in his own home, by family and friends under the supervision of a doctor. It focuses on meeting the emotional needs of the dying.

Those dependent on insurance policies or government programs for support in their final days largely have been denied this alternative. In an effort to correct this, the tax bill recently passed by Congress extends the opportunity to Medicare patients.

The bill provides a comprehensive benefit for people expected to live less than six months. Most of the care would be outside hospitals, but there are provisions for limited hospital stays and "respite care" to give a patient's family relief from 24-hours duty.

The provision is both humane and economical. A Congressional Budget Office study showed the program ultimately will pay for itself by substituting for expensive hospital health-care services now provided the terminally ill. Because of this act by Congress, as many as 100,000 more people can now face death with dignity and some control over their final days.

Richmond Times-Dispatch
*Richmond, Va.,
September 9, 1982*

All too often, the American way of death is for families to maintain long vigils at hospitals watching the life slowly, painfully ebb out of a loved one for whom modern medicine offers no cure, only a delay of the inevitable. Such a tragic situation frequently exacts a high price in the patient's dignity, the family's endurance and the insurance company's future premiums.

There is an alternative: The patient is cared for amid the familiar surroundings of home by family members, under the supervision of a physician and with "respite care" by a team of professionals to give the family regular breaks from 24-hour duty. The emphasis is on relief of pain rather than artificial prolongation of life. This humane concept is known as hospice care and it was given a major boost in the tax bill recently passed by Congress.

The measure makes hospice care a Medicare-eligible expense. Participants in the federal program of health care for the elderly, who have a terminal prognosis of six months or less, may opt for a hospice program, in which most care would be at home. Covered would be such services as house calls by physicians and nurses, pain-relieving out-patient drugs, counseling for patient and family members, and even homemaker services.

This broadened Medicare eligibility may enable as many as 100,000 additional Americans to take advantage of hospice care. Isn't it, therefore, a costly new social program the nation can ill afford? Not if it's true, as studies indicate, that the average hospice user will spend thousands of dollars less than if he or she were in a hospital. The Congressional Budget Office figures that during the first five years after enactment, the hospice alternative will save the federal government at least $109 million. The finest rationale, though, is not economic but humanitarian. In the words of Dr. Josefina B. Magno, director of the National Hospice Organization:

"A hospice really provides not only competent care, but it provides a more loving and more compassionate and more appropriate care for the patient at this stage in the illness. The hospice recognizes when illness is no longer curable. A hospice just allows death to come naturally."

The Pittsburgh Press
Pittsburgh, Pa., September 9, 1982

It's difficult to be enthusiastic about any tax-increase bill, but the one passed by Congress this session contains one provision that merits everybody's wholehearted endorsement.

It will permit, beginning in November 1983, the use of Medicare funds to pay for hospice services.

The growing hospice movement is based on the belief that dying patients are better off in their own homes or, if that is not possible, in the homelike atmosphere of a hospice center than they are in hospitals.

Rather than undergo expensive, hopeless and often painful treatment, such patients spend their last days amid family and friends, receiving palliative care from hospice workers under the supervision of a physician. Family members, too, receive help in facing the inevitability of their loved one's death.

A concept imported from Britain, the first hospice in the United States was organized in New Haven, Conn., in 1974. Today there are more than 400 nonprofit hospices throughout the nation, providing care to 12,000 persons a year, chiefly terminal cancer patients.

It is expected that Medicare funding will enable an additional 100,000 elderly persons to choose hospice services. The Congressional Budget Office estimates this will enable Medicare to save $40 million a year by 1986 — when Congress will review the funding provision.

If anything, the figure may be understated. For the care of cancer victims in the last 6 months of life accounts for almost 6 percent of Medicare outlays for aged patients — which is twice the cost of such care for all patients.

In any event, the program can be justified solely by the humanitarian aspects of the hospice system.

Buffalo Evening News
Buffalo, N.Y., September 13, 1982

The hospice movement, a concept imported from Britain in the early 1970s, has gained increasing acceptance as a worthy program to care for terminally ill persons in their homes rather than in hospitals. The growth in the number of hospice organizations, from 59 to more than 400 in the past three years, attests to the preference of many patients for care during their final days in a home surrounding amenable to family counseling and help, under a physician's supervision, in easing physical, mental and emotional strains.

For the first time, hospice care will now be eligible for Medicare benefits under the omnibus tax reform bill adopted by Congress. The provision is expected to add more than 100,000 persons — mainly cancer patients — to the 50,000 now aided by hospice organizations serving the terminally ill. For persons with fewer than six months to live, the coverage will include counseling for the patient and family, pain-relieving drugs and medical supplies.

According to Dr. Josefina Magno, director of the National Hospice Organization, the hospice concept provides not only competent care, but also "a more loving and more compassionate and more appropriate care for the patient at this stage in the illness. The hospice recognizes when illness is no longer curable. A hospice just allows death to come naturally."

The Congressional Budget Office reports that after some initial costs, the hospice benefits can save as much as $48 million by 1986, when the program will be subject to review under the bill.

In advancing the hospice concept at a time when the administration and Congress have had to cut back many social programs, the bill drafters have rightly recognized the importance of humane and compassionate goals in helping patients and families adjust to terminal illness.

DESERET NEWS
Salt Lake City, Utah, September 6-7, 1982

"Death with dignity" is a growing concept on the American scene. The reason is obvious: When death is inevitable, it's much more comforting to face the end in your own home, if possible, surrounded by family and friends.

That idea was markedly advanced recently when Congress approved a bill allowing Medicare to pay for "hospice" services. A hospice essentially is a nursing home for the terminally ill, relying extensively on volunteers. But hospice services also can be extended to the home. Doctors and other professionals are called in when needed.

A study by the Department of Human Services concluded that it now costs the federal government $19,660 in Medicare outlays to care for a terminally-ill cancer patient in the last six months of life. More than 85 percent of Medicare payments for such patients in the last 45 days of life are to underwrite inpatient hospitalizations.

By contrast, hospice services cost less than half as much. More than two-thirds of hospice patients nationally are able to spend their final days in their own homes — cared for by a hospice team of physicians, nurses, social workers, counselors, and volunteers and family members.

Hospices now serve an estimated 50,000 persons, the vast majority cancer patients. That's 10 percent of potential users. With the extension of Medicare to hospices, that number is expected to grow rapidly.

There can be abuses of the hospice act, however, just as there have been abuses of Medicare. Congress must be alert to see that those abuses are held to a minimum. The new law expires on Oct. 1, 1986, so Congress can have a chance to review its success before funding it further.

But all indications are that hospice care for the terminally ill is the wave of the future. As the Washington Post noted earlier this year, "The most important advantage of hospice care is that many patients and families find it a humane and comforting alternative to the high-technology medicine offered by regular hospitals."

Lincoln Journal
Lincoln, Neb., September 26, 1982

Hundreds of Lincolnites know firsthand the humanitarian benefits of the hospice movement now growing in America, thanks to the work of the Hospice of Tabitha.

They have seen death come to relatives and friends, not in the impersonal and sometimes distressing atmosphere of a hospital or nursing institution, but in the comforting surroundings of home, among family members and familiar objects. And they have seen the skilled and compassionate care of the hospice workers supporting not only the dying but those who survive.

Such services should, by the end of next year, be available to tens of thousands more Americans because the federal government has recognized another benefit of the hospice movement — a monetary one.

Advocates of such programs point out that it is often much less costly to care for a dying patient at home than in a hospital or nursing home. Congress agreed, and in the 1982 tax bill is a so far little-noticed provision that will offer some Medicare coverage for hospice services.

There will be start-up costs, but the Congressional Budget Office estimates this new approach can save Medicare as much as $40 million by 1986. Private insurers — and therefore consumers — should realize savings, too, if the insurance industry likewise would adopt a uniformly positive attitude toward hospice care.

This step by government also should foster an even faster expansion of the hospice program in this country. It began in America in 1974, and in five years there were close to 60 active hospice operations. Now the number is about 450, with another 350 under development.

Even with Medicare coverage, not all terminally ill patients — or their families — will regard hospice care at home as a satisfactory alternative to hospitalization. And it obviously is not right for every case.

But as the programs grow and become better known, more Americans will come to see this approach as a humane and dignified alternative for dealing with death, one that can reaffirm the sometimes denied truth that dying is a most natural part — the culmination — of living.

Index